The New Middle Ages

Series Editor
Bonnie Wheeler
English and Medieval Studies
Southern Methodist University
Dallas, TX, USA

The New Middle Ages is a series dedicated to pluridisciplinary studies of medieval cultures, with particular emphasis on recuperating women's history and on feminist and gender analyses. This peer-reviewed series includes both scholarly monographs and essay collections.

More information about this series at
http://www.palgrave.com/gp/series/14239

Eric Knibbs · Jessica A. Boon ·
Erica Gelser
Editors

The End of the World in Medieval Thought and Spirituality

palgrave
macmillan

Editors
Eric Knibbs
Monumenta Germaniae Historica
Munich, Germany

Erica Gelser
Wellesley, MA, USA

Jessica A. Boon
University of North
Carolina—Chapel Hill
Chapel Hill, NC, USA

The New Middle Ages
ISBN 978-3-030-14964-2   ISBN 978-3-030-14965-9   (eBook)
https://doi.org/10.1007/978-3-030-14965-9

Library of Congress Control Number: 2019934460

© The Editor(s) (if applicable) and The Author(s), under exclusive licence to Springer Nature Switzerland AG 2019
This work is subject to copyright. All rights are solely and exclusively licensed by the Publisher, whether the whole or part of the material is concerned, specifically the rights of translation, reprinting, reuse of illustrations, recitation, broadcasting, reproduction on microfilms or in any other physical way, and transmission or information storage and retrieval, electronic adaptation, computer software, or by similar or dissimilar methodology now known or hereafter developed.
The use of general descriptive names, registered names, trademarks, service marks, etc. in this publication does not imply, even in the absence of a specific statement, that such names are exempt from the relevant protective laws and regulations and therefore free for general use.
The publisher, the authors and the editors are safe to assume that the advice and information in this book are believed to be true and accurate at the date of publication. Neither the publisher nor the authors or the editors give a warranty, express or implied, with respect to the material contained herein or for any errors or omissions that may have been made. The publisher remains neutral with regard to jurisdictional claims in published maps and institutional affiliations.

Cover image: Biblioteca Nacional de España

This Palgrave Macmillan imprint is published by the registered company Springer Nature Switzerland AG
The registered company address is: Gewerbestrasse 11, 6330 Cham, Switzerland

Acknowledgements

Our acknowledgments go first and foremost to our advisor and friend, E. Ann Matter. In her career she has been a model mentor for many in the profession, in addition to her own students. Through her early participation in and leadership of such regional and national scholarly groups as the Delaware Valley Medieval Association, the Princeton-Penn Early Christianity group, Consortium for the Teaching of the Middle Ages, and the Society of Medieval Feminist Scholarship, she was a regular source of advice and connections for young scholars and graduate students alike. On University of Pennsylvania's campus, where she spent her entire career, she worked tirelessly in support of tenure-track faculty in many departments across campus, contributed to countless committees, and served as the School of Arts and Sciences Associate Dean and Religious Studies Department Chair. As an advisor, she was extraordinarily generous: not only did she support many dissertation topics beyond her own area of expertise, but facilitated such adventurous work by co-advising with specialists outside the department and even the university. Yet this permission to range widely was paired with thoughtful advice on drafts and the process, as often as such advice was sought. To guide expansive projects without becoming distant and unengaged is a rare gift. Last but not least, her work with undergraduates not only garnered teaching awards, but even led some towards careers in academe.

We would also like to acknowledge the advice and contributions of various of Ann's colleagues and students in the development of this volume. Bonnie Wheeler greeted the prospect of the volume in the Palgrave series with open arms and encouraged us to seek a theme, which J. Melvin identified in a crucial brainstorming session. Ed Peters and Leslie Smith contributed valuable advice along the way, as did Tom Waldman, *beatae memoriae*, whose final illness sadly interrupted his work on an essay for this collection. Carla Locatelli was a source of inspiration to bring this volume together in the first place, a process that all of us have found intensely satisfying as some small contribution toward an advisor who guided us so well.

Contents

1   Introduction   1
    Jessica A. Boon and Eric Knibbs

Part I   Gendering the Apocalypse

2   The Sobered Sibyl: Gender, Apocalypse, and Hair in
    Dio Chrysostom's *Discourse 1* and the *Shepherd of Hermas*   17
    Mary R. D'Angelo

3   The Marian Apocalyptic of a Visionary Preacher:
    The *Conorte* of Juana de la Cruz, 1481–1534   41
    Jessica A. Boon

4   The City Coming Down Out of Heaven (Rev. 21:10):
    Bologna as Jerusalem   69
    Gabriella Zarri

Part II   Apocalyptic Theology and Exegesis

5   Risen to Judgment: What Augustine Saw   93
    Francine Cardman

6	Berengaudus on the Apocalypse Eric Knibbs	135
7	Apocalypticism and Mysticism in Joachim of Fiore's *Expositio in Apocalypsim* Bernard McGinn	163
8	Juan de Horozco y Covarrubias's *Tratado dela verdadera y falsa prophecia* (1588) and the Influence of Medieval Apocalyptic Traditions in Post-Tridentine Spain James F. Melvin	197

Part III The Eschaton in Political, Liturgical, and Literary Contexts

9	The End of the World as They Knew It? Jews, Christians, Samaritans and End-Time Speculation in the Fifth Century Ross S. Kraemer	227
10	End Time at Hand: Innocent III, Joachim of Fiore, and the Fourth Crusade Marcia L. Colish	251
11	The End of a Single World: The Sacrament of Extreme Unction in Scholastic Thought Lesley Smith	281
12	Religious and Amorous "Apocalypses" in John Donne's Metaphysical Imagination Angela Locatelli	315

Bibliography	339
Index	373

List of Contributors

Jessica A. Boon University of North Carolina—Chapel Hill, Chapel Hill, NC, USA

Francine Cardman Boston College, Chestnut Hill, MA, USA

Marcia L. Colish Department of History, Yale University, New Haven, CT, USA

Mary R. D'Angelo University of Notre Dame, Notre Dame, IN, USA

Eric Knibbs Monumenta Germaniae Historica, Munich, Germany

Ross S. Kraemer Brown University, Providence, RI, USA

Angela Locatelli University of Bergamo, Bergamo, Italy

Bernard McGinn University of Chicago, Chicago, IL, USA

James F. Melvin Independent Scholar, Toledo, OH, USA

Lesley Smith Harris Manchester College, University of Oxford, Oxford, UK

Gabriella Zarri University of Florence, Florence, Italy

List of Figures

Chapter 3

Fig. 1 *Last Judgment*. Nicolas Florentino, ca. 1445, Old Cathedral, Salamanca (Photo credit Jessica A. Boon) 53

Chapter 4

Fig. 1 Basilica di Santo Stefano (Basilica of Saint Stephen). Blueprint of the Basilica: 1–3. Chiesa del Crocifisso (Church of the Crucifix); 4. Crypt; 5. Basilica del Sepolcro (Basilica of the Sepulchre); 6. Basilica dei SS. Vitale e Agricola (Basilica of Saints Vitale and Agricola); 7. Cortile di Pilato (Pilate's Courtyard); 8. Il Chiostro (The Cloister); 9–12. Chiesa della Benda e Museo (Church of Mary's Veil and Museum) 72

Fig. 2 Joan Blaeu's Map of Bologna (1640) 76

Fig. 3 Bologna's City Wall: the three circles (https://www.cittametropolitana.bo.it/turismo/Home_Page/Per_turisti/Guide_e_mappe/Bologna_mappa_e_itinerari_turistici) 79

Fig. 4 Location and extent of Bologna's convents at the end of the eighteenth century 82

CHAPTER 1

Introduction

Jessica A. Boon and Eric Knibbs

Fear of the end of time—for all the world or for oneself—is perhaps the most pervasive emotion in human experience. It powers much of religious thought, as the idea of death or concern that the world as we know it will come to a precipitous end has led countless numbers to scour their scriptures, seek counsel from their religious leaders, undertake complex rituals and journeys, meditate on their sins, and change their ways. Within Christian thought, this type of fear is broadly eschatological (Last Things) and more specifically apocalyptic, insofar as commentaries on the book of Revelation, visions of the endtimes, prophecies, and millenarian speculation all provide possible answers to or amelioration of terror induced by plague, war, sickness, accidents, and self-reflection on the sinful nature of humanity.[1] Yet these potential avenues of hope

---

[1] A point central to the collection, Caroline Walker Bynum and Paul Freedman, "Introduction," in *Last Things: Death and the Apocalypse in the Middle Ages*, ed. Caroline Walker Bynum and Paul Freedman (Philadelphia: University of Pennsylvania Press, 2000),

---

J. A. Boon (✉)
University of North Carolina—Chapel Hill, Chapel Hill, NC, USA

E. Knibbs
Monumenta Germaniae Historica, Munich, Germany

© The Author(s) 2019
E. Knibbs et al. (eds.), *The End of the World in Medieval Thought and Spirituality*, The New Middle Ages,
https://doi.org/10.1007/978-3-030-14965-9_1

can sometimes lead to a vicious cycle, when the answers provided by the apocalyptic to eschatological fears are so obscure or threatening as to spark more fear than they relieve.[2]

The apocalypse and the apocalyptic were central to premodern Christian discourse. From biblical exegesis to mysticism, from crusade ideology to Marian beliefs that identify her as the Woman of the Sun, from theology to poetry to art, medieval and early modern devotees regardless of gender, education, and type of religious affiliation (laity, priests, monastics, mendicants, *beatas*) had their daily lives shaped by apocalyptic expectations and eschatological apprehensions. Scholars have long turned to collaborations to try to address the immense range of what is considered a "theological-literary genre"[3] and its impact on beliefs and practices, as no single scholar can address the richness and complexity of contemplation of the endtimes in Christian culture. Beginning with the 1992 volume *The Apocalypse in the Middle Ages* edited by Emmerson and McGinn, interest in the apocalyptic brought together historians of theology, art, literature, and monotheistic religious culture, while the volume *Last Things: Death and the Apocalypse in the Middle Ages* edited by Bynum and Freeman that appeared in the millennial moment of 2000 again united scholars across disciplinary

---

1–18. Briefly put in the book description for a recent Oxford handbook: "Eschatology Is the Study of the Last Things—Death, Judgment, the Afterlife, and the End of the World," in *The Oxford Handbook of Eschatology*, ed. Jerry L. Walls (Oxford: Oxford University Press, 2007), retrieved 28 July 2018, from http://www.oxfordhandbooks.com.libproxy.lib.unc.edu/view/10.1093/oxfordhb/9780195170498.001.0001/oxfordhb-9780195170498. One scholar suggests the distinction between "moral apocalypse" that addresses the fate of the individual believer as opposed to the "political apocalypse" which provides an endtimes scenario for the world. James T. Palmer, *The Apocalypse in the Early Middle Ages* (Cambridge: Cambridge University Press, 2014), 11.

See also the definitions of eschatological and apocalyptic in Bernard McGinn, "Preface to the Paperback Edition," in *Visions of the End: Apocalyptic Traditions in the Middle Ages*, 2nd ed., ed. Bernard McGinn (New York: Columbia University Press, 1998), ix; Michael A. Ryan, "Introduction," in *A Companion to the Premodern Apocalypse*, ed. Michael A. Ryan (Leiden: Brill, 2016), 9.

[2] For emphasis on the optimism and pessimism inherent in all apocalyptic discussion, see Bernard McGinn, "Preface to the Paperback Edition," xvii.

[3] Ian Christopher Levy, "Wycliffites, Franciscan Poverty, and the Apocalypse," *Franciscan Studies* 73 (2015): 296–97, citing Bernard McGinn.

boundaries.[4] In this century, several other major collections have appeared on apocalypticism throughout history that included significant attention to the Middle Ages,[5] but it wasn't until 2016 that another volume was devoted to the full era with contributions from multiple fields, *A Companion to the Premodern Apocalypse* edited by Michael A. Ryan.

It is thus fitting that in this volume dedicated to E. Ann Matter after her retirement, we bring forth a new collection covering many centuries of apocalyptic thought and culture with many different methodological tools, for this reflects Matter's own extraordinary influence and career. Matter's essay "The Apocalypse in Early Medieval Exegesis" in the original *Apocaylpse in the Middle Ages* volume from 1992 remains a classic,[6] but she is equally well-known for her far-ranging work on textual editions of medieval theologians and early modern visionaries, on biblical exegesis, and on analysis of premodern gender and sexuality. Matter's students, colleagues, and professors in America and abroad, in contributing the essays assembled here, assume an expansive approach to the problem of the Apocalypse and of Last Things, in recognition of the diverse themes that have defined Matter's career. They study the Apocalypse and the end of the world as they relate to sacramental

---

[4] Richard K. Emmerson and Bernard McGinn, eds., *The Apocalypse in the Middle Ages* (Ithaca, NY: Cornell University Press, 1992); Bynum and Freedman, *Last Things*. Many scholars have addressed particular topics within their discipline in monographs, far too numerous to list here; recently, a single-author review of the early medieval period has come out, see Palmer, *Apocalypse*.

[5] Bernard J. McGinn, John J. Collins, and Stephen J. Stein, eds., *Encyclopedia of Apocalypticism*, 3 vols. (New York: Continuum Books, 1998), anthologized in one volume as *The Continuum History of Apocalypticism* (New York: Continuum Books, 2003); Karolyn Kinane and Michael A. Ryan, eds., *End of Days: Essays on the Apocalypse from Antiquity to Modernity* (Jefferson, NC: McFarland & Company, 2009). Several Oxford handbooks have also addressed what are often considered overlapping terms: Jerry L. Walls, ed., *Oxford Handbook of Eschatology* (2008); Catherine Wessinger, ed., *Oxford Handbook of Millennialism* (2011); and John J. Collins, ed., *Oxford Handbook of Apocalyptic Literature* (2014).

[6] "The Apocalypse in Early Medieval Exegesis," in *The Apocalypse in the Middle Ages*, ed. Richard K. Emmerson and Bernard McGinn (Ithaca: Cornell University Press, 1992), 38–50. On early medieval apocalypticism, also note E. Ann Matter, "The Pseudo-Alcuinian *De septem sigillis*: An Early Latin Apocalypse Exegesis," *Traditio* 36 (1980): 111–37; ibid., "Exegesis of the Apocalypse in the Early Middle Ages," in *The Year 1000*, ed. Michael Frassetto (New York: Palgrave, 2002), 29–40.

theology, biblical exegesis, apocalyptic prophecy, Marian spirituality, patristic thought, and early Christian and Jewish history. Some of our essays look outwards, to inquire after the interactions of apocalyptic thought with broader political, social, and devotional trends; others shed light on the thought and importance of particularly well-known authors from Augustine to Joachim of Fiore to John Donne or bring lesser-known voices to our attention, such as the visionary Juana de la Cruz (1481–1534) or Juan de Horozco y Covarrubias (1540?–1610).

1   Part I: Gendering the Apocalypse

No edited collection to our knowledge brings gender as a lens to bear on the texts and contexts of the apocalyptic. Although there are monographs that specifically examine medieval women's contribution to and/or consumption of apocalyptic texts and imagery, none of the edited collections listed above thematize gender in medieval apocalyptic (not even in a single essay) or take a female author as their primary topic.[7] Matter would be the first to query this gap, given her contributions as past president of the Society of Medieval Feminist Scholarship and her extensive scholarship and mentoring on issues of gender and sexuality.[8] She is the author of several groundbreaking articles on sexuality and mysticism and a discoverer and editor of women's visionary texts.[9] She frequently

[7] Not even Hildegard of Bingen makes it into any edited volume on apocalyptic thought. Examples of recent work examining gender and the apocalypse can be found in Tamar Herzig, *Savonarola's Women: Visions and Reform in Renaissance Italy* (Chicago: The University of Chicago Press, 2008), whose study was significantly shaped by Matter's guidance (p. xi); and in Renana Bartel, *Gender, Piety, and Production in Fourteenth-Century English Apocalypse Manuscripts* (London: Routledge, 2016). For an example of work on contemporary apocalyptic with attention to gender, see Brenda E. Brasher and Lee Quinby, eds., *Gender and Apocalyptic Desire* (New York: Routledge, 2014).

[8] For example, through collections such as E. Ann Matter and John Wayland Coakley, eds., *Creative Women in Medieval and Early Modern Italy: A Religious and Artistic Renaissance* (Philadelphia: University of Pennsylvania Press, 1994).

[9] Matter, "My Sister, My Spouse: Woman-Identified Women in Medieval Christianity," *Journal of Feminist Studies in Religion* 2.2 (1986): 81–92; anthologized in *Que(e)rying Religion: A Critical Anthology*, ed. Gary David Comstock and Susan E. Henking (New York: Continuum, 1997), 107–15; and *Homosexuality and Religion*, ed. Richard L. Hasbany (New York: Routledge, 2013), 119–32. Ibid., "Discourses of Desire: Sexuality and Christian Women's Visionary Narratives," *Journal of Homosexuality* 18.3 (1989): 119–32. More recently, engaging the history of emotion, she published "Theories of the Passions and the Ecstasies of Late Medieval Religious Women," *Essays in Medieval Studies*

addressed Marian devotion, not only as the culminating discovery of her oft-cited monograph on biblical exegesis, *Voice of My Beloved: The Song of Songs in Western Medieval Christianity*, but also by reaching beyond the medieval to examine contemporary Marian apocalyptic.[10] In Part I of this collection, "Gendering the Apocalypse," three scholars examine apocalyptic rhetoric produced through female figures such as the Sibylls, apocalyptic sermons by a female visionary with an intense Marian devotion, and a heavenly Jerusalem on earth whose contours were marked by convents and Marian imagery.

Mary R. D'Angelo evokes Matter's efforts to revive the memory of female visionaries of the sixteenth and seventeenth with her essay on "The Sobered Sibyl: Gender, Apocalypse and Hair in Dio's *Discourse* 1 and the *Shepherd of Hermas*." Here D'Angelo compares the character and demeanor of the ancient Sibylls to the "fictive female intermediaries" of Dio Chrysostom's *Discourse* 1 and the *Shepherd of Hermas*. The Sibyl of Cumae from Vergil's *Aeneid*, and the Sibyls as imagined in the early empire more broadly, were ancient oracles with unkempt hair who delivered prophecies in moments of possessed fury, while the intermediaries in Dio and Hermas are staid and restrained prophets despite deliberate Sibylline parallels. D'Angelo detects behind the sobered Sibylline characters of Dio and Hermas a new interest in and demand for reason and restraint in prophetesses of the second century, which amounts to a rejection of the Platonic equation of the mantic arts with mania. The shift is intertwined with other historical forces, including renewed secular interest in female probity and restraint in Roman society at the turn of the second century; broader discourses surrounding the New Prophets

---

18.1 (2001): 1–17. In the course of her research in Italy, Matter found and identified the long-lost *Rivilazione* of Lucia Brocadelli in a Pavian library. Critical edition: E. Ann Matter, Armando Maggi, Maiju Lehmijoki-Gardner, and Gabriella Zarri, "Lucia Brocadelli da Narni: Riscoperta di un manoscritto pavese," *Bollettino della Società Pavese di Storia Patria* (2000): 173–99. Translation: Matter, "Seven Revelations," in *Dominican Penitent Women*, ed. Maiju Lehmijoki-Gardner (Mahwah, NJ: Paulist Press, 2005), 212–43.

[10] Matter, *The Voice of My Beloved: The Song of Songs in Western Medieval Christianity* (Philadelphia: University of Pennsylvania Press, 1990). An important article on Song of Songs exegesis by a female mystic came out the same year: "The Song of Songs in the *Exercitia spiritualia* of Gertrude the Great of Helfta," *Laurentianum* 31 (1990): 39–49. For the contemporary, see Ibid., "Apparitions of the Virgin Mary in the Late Twentieth Century: Apocalyptic, Representation, Politics," *Religion* 31 (2001): 125–53.

or Montanists, for whom prophecy involved the displacement of human reason; and the value that Paul placed, in 1 Corinthians, on prophecy spoken with the cooperation of mental faculties, rather than in the absence of them.

In "The Marian Apocalyptic of a Visionary Preacher: The *Conorte* of Juana de la Cruz, 1481-1534," Jessica A. Boon proceeds from Matter's typology of twentieth-century Marian apparitions, especially Matter's identification of a shift towards apocalyptic messages following the Fatima apparitions in the 1920s. Political turmoil and the realignment that Catholic observance experienced after Vatican II inspired this growing apocalyptic focus of worldwide Marian apparitions.[11] Boon finds similar forces in play in Spain around 1500. The early years of the Spanish empire were another era of global crisis and political anxiety, and they too witnessed a new abundance of Marian apparitions and an intensive preoccupation with apocalyptic themes. For her case study, Boon turns to Juana de la Cruz, an abbess of a Clarisan convent near Toledo who channeled the voice of Jesus and who was, like the visionaries Matter has studied, a "living saint."[12] Juana's visions, as set forth in public sermons, came to be assembled in a manuscript known as her *Book of Consolation* (*El libro del conorte*). They include frequent discussions of the endtimes, and they emphasize the agency of the Virgin Mary, who rescues souls from Purgatory and even vanquishes and binds the devil. Boon concludes that this "Marian Apocalyptic" aligned with a broader prophetic and apocalyptic mentality at work in the early Spanish empire. Specifically, Boon shows that Mary in her apocalyptic aspect must have spoken deeply to the Spanish faithful, whose devotion to Mary as *la conquistadora* had grown in strength through the course of the peninsular reconquest and attempts by Castilian political leaders to build an empire in the New World.

In the final essay of Part I, "The City Coming down out of Heaven (Rev. 21:10): Bologna as Jerusalem," Gabriella Zarri explores persistent tendencies to cast the city of Bologna in the mold of the celestial Jerusalem, a framework that she links with the physical construction of

---

[11] Matter, "Apparitions of the Virgin Mary."

[12] On living saints, see Gabriella Zarri, "Living Saints: A Typology of Female Sanctity in the Early Sixteenth Century," in *Women and Religion in Medieval and Renaissance Italy*, ed. Daniel Bornstein and Roberto Rusconi (Chicago: University of Chicago Press, 1996), 219–304.

convents around the city and with Marian imagery. This effort began with the construction of the basilica of Santo Stefano, a monument that legend associates with Saint Petronius, the eighth bishop of Bologna. Petronius is said to have traveled on pilgrimage to the Holy Land and returned with relics for the construction of the church. Santo Stefano accordingly encompasses a complex known as the "seven churches" or *Sancta Jerusalem*, which amounts to a topographic reproduction of the Holy Sepulchre. The importance of Santo Stefano as a pilgrimage site had waned by the later Middle Ages, but its fortunes reversed when the fall of Constantinople severed relations with the East and travel to the real Jerusalem became less feasible for western faithful. Zarri tracks the Renaissance-era resurgence of Santo Stefano, along with the history of Bologna's walls, fortifications, and convents, as a continuous urban history in which the city repeatedly recalls and represents Jerusalem. By way of analogy to "the woman clothed with the sun" (Rev. 12:1), Zarri further traces the history of Marian devotion in Counter-Reformation Bologna, beginning with the column of the Immaculate Conception, the erection of oratories dedicated to the Virgin, and popular devotion to "miraculous images" of the Virgin Mary placed at churches and elsewhere throughout the city. Bologna-as-Jerusalem, Zarri reveals, emerged not as the artifact of any single plan or program, but organically, through the individual histories of its churches, fortifications, religious institutions, and devotional traditions.

2 Part II: Apocalyptic Theology and Exegesis

While a leader in the reconfiguration of the field of the history of Christianity through the lens of gender, Matter also devoted her career to the classic building blocks of medieval studies: the problems of textual criticism, the world of biblical exegesis, and the history of theology. Focused particularly on such early medieval figures as Radbertus and Alcuin, Matter also explored the commentary tradition, the *Glossa Ordinaria*, and the history of education.[13] In Part II of this volume,

---

[13] Among Matter's critical editions, see "*The De partu Virginis*" *of Paschasius Radbertus: Critical Edition and Monographic Study* (Ph.D. Dissertation, Yale University, 1976). Published as *Paschasii Radberti: De Partu Virginis*, Corpus Christianorum Continuatio Mediaevalis 56C (Turnholt: Brepols, 1985). Ibid., with Eric Knibbs, *Alcuini Eboracensis: De fide sanctae Trinitatis et de Incarnatione Christi*, CCCM 249 (Turholt: Brepols, 2012). Among her many essays on Carolingian scholarship, the history of the Bible, and the

"Apocalyptic Theology and Exegesis," four scholars provide careful case studies of theologians and ecclesiastics whose interest in apocalyptic traditions and prophetic texts marked their careers. Spanning early to early modern Christianity, these contributions not only reflect the breadth of Matter's contributions across the premodern, but also her attention to the careful uncovering of manuscript and textual traditions alongside emplacing those texts in their broader intellectual, mystical, and church reform contexts.

Francine Cardman, in "Risen to Judgment: What Augustine Saw," studies Augustine's preaching on judgment, especially the Final Judgment, across his *Sermones ad populum*—his voluminous sermons to his congregation. She finds that Augustine's sermons employ two distinct approaches to the theme of judgment. The first draws on 1 Tim. 6:6–10 and 17–19 to discourage the accumulation of temporal at the expense of eternal wealth, and deploys elaborate financial metaphors to urge his audience to avoid pride and to store up eternal riches in the next life through almsgiving and other good deeds. A second, more strictly eschatological approach discusses the Last Judgment with recourse to Matt. 25:31–47, where Jesus foresees the moment when the Son of Man will come in his glory to separate the sheep from the goats. Cardman traces the evolution of both themes throughout Augustine's career, and ultimately finds an increased emphasis on the Matthaean approach in the final decade of his ministry.

Matter's survey of medieval Latin Apocalypse exegesis provides the point of departure for Eric Knibbs's essay, "Berengaudus on the Apocalypse." Knibbs aims to settle controversies surrounding an enigmatic Apocalypse commentary known as the *Expositio super septem visiones libri Apocalypsi* by a mysterious author known only as Berengaudus. In two letters from 860/862, Lupus of Ferrières

---

Glossa ordinaria, see especially "The *Revelatio Esdrae* in Latin and English Traditions," *Revue bénédictine* 92 (1982): 376–92; "Alcuin's Question-and-Answer Texts," *Rivista di storia della filosofia* 4 (1990): 645–56; "The Bible in the Center: The *Glossa Ordinaria*," in *The Unbounded Community: Conversations Across Times and Disciplines*, ed. Duncan Fisher (Hamden, CT: Garland Publishing, 1996), 33–42; "The Church Fathers and the *Glossa Ordinaria*," in *The Reception of the Church Fathers in the West*, ed. Irena Backus (Leiden: Brill, 1997), 1:83–111; and "Alcuin's Theology," in *Alkuin von York und die geistige Grundlegung Europas*, ed. Ernst Tremp und Karl Schmuki (Sankt-Gallen: Verlag am Klosterhof, 2010), 91–105.

recommended a young Berengaudus to the monastery of Saint-Germain in Auxerre, and so biographical lexica have tended to fold a Berengaudus of Ferrières into the ranks of ninth-century exegetes. Not everyone agrees. The *Expositio* was read widely only after 1100, often in lavish illuminated manuscripts. No copies antedate the eleventh century, and for many art historians especially, the *Expositio* remains a high medieval text. Knibbs confirms other research findings that the *Expositio* possesses an unmistakable affinity to Carolingian-era commentaries, particularly the oeuvre of Haimo of Auxerre. At the same time, Berengaudus uses sources more loosely than was usual for most ninth-century authors, and often departs from Haimonian approaches. Furthermore, on several occasions, tropological meditations drive the excitable commentator to address contemporary abuses in extended, highly informative asides. Together, these suggest that Berengaudus certainly wrote in the early medieval period, but well after the Carolingian era had drawn to a close.

Another, far more famous *Expositio* on the Apocalypse is the subject of Bernard McGinn's "Apocalypticism and Mysticism in Joachim of Fiore's *Expositio in Apocalypsim*," a contribution which does homage to Matter's continuing scholarly engagement with both visionaries and the endtimes. Here, McGinn notes that the ancient traditions of apocalypticism and mysticism, though united in early Christianity, soon went their separate ways. Joachim of Fiore sought to unite these divergent traditions once again, particularly in his *Expositio*. In this commentary, Joachim presented himself as a "new John" with an authority rooted in visionary experience, and he elaborated via his concordist exegetical methods a vision of sacred history as subject to a threefold, Trinitarian structure. The time of the Old Testament for him represented the Father, while the New Testament figured the Son. The political and ecclesiastical turmoil of his age prompted Joachim to suppose that the third age, that of the Holy Spirit, was on its way. McGinn highlights Joachim's vision of the coming third age as one of deeper communal awareness of God, a time when the entire church will be gathered into the form of a contemplative, essentially monastic, community. He further reveals the biblical, liturgical, and affective aspects of Joachim's "communal-ecclesiastical mysticism," which in Joachim's eyes represents the full earthly realization of the spiritual understanding of the Bible, proceeds from the patterns of the liturgical year and monastic worship, and emphasizes both fraternal love and the deep love for Christ that will prevail in the third *status*.

We have seen that major themes of Matter's scholarship include the problem of female visionaries and their relationship to church authorities, as well as the broader history of Catholic female spirituality in the Counter-Reformation. James F. Melvin's essay, "Juan de Horozco y Covarrubias's *Tratado dela verdadera y falsa prophecia* (1588) and the Influence of Medieval Apocalyptic Traditions in Post-Tridentine Spain," touches on all of these matters. Horozco, a Tridentine reformer after the fashion of Carlo Borromeo, wrote the *Tratado* to advise confessors on the discernment of spirits, and scholars have studied the treatise for its discussion of female visionaries and the regulations and interpretations imposed upon them by their male spiritual directors. Melvin draws attention to another, less-studied aspect of the *Tratado*, namely its preoccupation with apocalyptic prophecies and its embrace of medieval traditions relating to the endtimes. Scholars of late medieval and early modern Spain have seen prophecy and apocalyptic thought as a popular, rebellious expression of religiosity, opposed to the agenda of orthodox enforcers and elite church reformers. Horozco, himself a reformer, provides a curious counterpoint to this narrative, for in his *Tratado* he embraces an apocalyptic tone and outlook all while elaborating a standard reformist agenda. Among other things, Horozco deplores various false Joachite prophecies while embracing Joachim of Fiore himself as an orthodox prophet. Elsewhere, and even more remarkably, he embarks upon an extended discussion of the Erythraean Sibyl's ancient pronouncements on the Final Judgment. With this evidence, Melvin finds room to confirm the argument of Bernard McGinn that apocalyptic approaches are "as often designed to maintain the political, social and economic order as to overthrow it."[14]

3 Part III: The Eschaton in Political, Liturgical, and Literary Contexts

The multiple contexts in Part II for examining specific influential church figures lead naturally to Part III, in which four of Matter's colleagues probe the ways in which the apocalyptic is reflected in and shapes political, liturgical, and literary resources. Once again ranging from early

---

[14] Bernard McGinn, *Visions of the End*, 30.

Christianity to the early modern, we find that interreligious interactions have apocalyptic contours, that the papacy embraced apocalyptic ideas as much for political as theological purposes, that scholastic theologians examined the end of time for every individual through careful attention to the sacrament of extreme unction, and that a figure famous for his religious poetry could not avoid apocalyptic overtones.

Rather than theological or ecclesiastical discourses on the end of the world, it is to actual historical events that Ross Kraemer turns in her essay, "The End of the World as They Knew it? Jews, Christians, Samaritans and Endtime Speculation in the Fifth-Century." The fourth and fifth centuries witnessed an array of calamities, from wars to earthquakes and plagues, and these encouraged many to wonder whether the end was coming. The Samaritan, Jewish, and Christian communities of this era also lived in the shadow of a Christian Roman Empire that struggled to impose a new and universal orthodoxy upon its subjects. Kraemer begins with Severus of Minorca's *Letter on the Conversion of the Jews* from 418, which tells of the forced conversion of Minorcan Jews upon the arrival of relics of Stephen protomartyr from the Holy Land. From there she proceeds to an event narrated by Socrates of Constantinople, probably from the 430s, involving another purported mass conversion of Jews on Crete to Christianity associated with the appearance of a Mosaic pretender. A third example comes from the Syriac *Life of Barsauma*, on a contemporaneous uprising in Jerusalem with possible messianic overtones, following the empress Eudocia's grant of permission to Jews to pray at the temple mount. Finally, Kraemer turns to accounts of a late fifth-century Samaritan revolt during the reign of the eastern emperor Zeno, as narrated by Procopius of Caesarea and John Malalas. These diverse instances enable Kraemer to reveal the relationships underlying the eschatological speculations of Jews, Christians, and Samaritans, despite their varying scriptural and religious foundations. The parallels among these events find a historical explanation, in that they represent a response to the same events and unfolded within the related political and ecclesiastical context of a newly Christianized Roman empire.

Marcia Colish broadens McGinn's inquiry into Joachim of Fiore's mysticism by inquiring after the extent of Joachim's political and ecclesiastical impact. In "End Time at Hand: Innocent III, Joachim of Fiore, and the Fourth Crusade," Colish approaches the problem of Joachim's influence on the thought of Pope Innocent III and Innocent's understanding of the eschatological significance of the Fourth Crusade.

After the sack of Constantinople in April of 1204 and the installation of Baldwin of Flanders at the helm of the new Latin Empire, Innocent penned a curious letter to the Latin clergy in Constantinople that cast the unfolding catastrophe of the crusade in positive yet eschatological terms. In this letter, Innocent remarked that the crusaders' conquest opened the way for the reunification of the Greek and Latin churches, as well as the ingathering of the Jews and the Gentiles—all precursors of the Last Days. Scholars have long noted that Innocent built his argument with the help of Joachim's *Expositio* on the Apocalypse, and they have used this early and prominent reception to paint Joachim as an exegete whose thoughts enjoyed mainstream appeal, even in papal circles. Via a careful study of Innocent's ideological production surrounding the Fourth Crusade, Colish shows that Innocent's eschatological conviction was less than total. Rather than a devotee of Joachite exegesis, Innocent was a political actor who deployed Joachim's ideas as a means of goading the Latin clergy in Constantinople to bring the Greek church back into communion with Rome. In later correspondence, Colish shows, Innocent is quick to abandon the ideas he has from Joachim and takes up other rhetorical strategies in accordance with changing circumstances.

In "The End of a Single World: The Sacrament of Extreme Unction in Scholastic Thought," Lesley Smith moves from the strictly apocalyptic to the broader category of eschatology. As her subject, she takes extreme unction and its development alongside the broader elaboration of sacramental theology in the scholastic period from the twelfth through the late thirteenth centuries. After a survey of unction from the earliest centuries of Christianity to the Carolingian era, Smith charts the course of the scholastic debate through the *De sacramentis* of Hugh of St. Victor and the *Sentences* of his near-contemporary, Peter Lombard, followed by the *Summa de sacramentis et anime consiliis* of Peter the Chanter, the *Summa confessorum* of Thomas of Chobham, the *Summa aurea* of William of Auxerre, and the *Summa de sacramentis* of Guy of Orchelles. She concludes with an analysis of two master-pupil pairs from the late thirteenth century, Alexander of Hales and Bonaventure as representatives of Franciscan scholarship, and Albert the Great and Thomas Aquinas for the Dominicans. The problems occupying these scholastic thinkers include the specific function of unction and its role in corporeal healing and the remission of sin; the nature of unction, specifically its material and its essence; its repeatability; its appropriate ministers; the proper moment of its administration, whether at the onset of illness or only just before death; and whether the recipient must request unction or even be aware of its administration. Among other things, Smith notices the greater precision that Aristotelian philosophy lent the discussions of unction through the course of the thirteenth century. As the sacramental theory matured, she shows, scholastic optimism about the possibility of unction working physical cures receded, a development that must reflect not only the growing sophistication of the theorists, but also the simultaneous elaboration of medicine as an academic discipline.

Extending beyond the theological and ecclesiastical, Angela Locatelli takes us to literature, examining "Amorous and Religious 'Apocalypses' in John Donne's Metaphysical Imagination." She surveys apocalyptic themes in literary and aesthetic aspects of Donne's poetry, showing how the theological and religious tradition of apocalypse and eschatology contributed to Donne's approach, not only in his overtly religious poems but also elsewhere in his work. The Apocalypse Locatelli surveys is literary, rather than theological—as defined by John J. Collins, "A genre of revelatory literature with a narrative framework" which "disclos[es] a transcendent reality" with eschatological, salvific, and supernatural aspects.[15] To demonstrate the unity and consistency of Donne's writing on apocalyptic matters, in both secular and religious spheres, Locatelli begins with Donne's sermon XLIII, on Rev. 7:2–3, and explores its thematic connections to Donne's poetry, especially Holy Sonnet VII. From there Locatelli proceeds to detect religious and apocalyptic themes in Donne's secular, amorous poetry, no less than in his religious production. Apocalyptic themes in Donne, present across a wide variety of his works, form a continuity when considered alongside one another, one that extends between two poles—between the naturalistic and scientific outlook of Elizabethan England on the one hand, and an older, traditional, theological view of the world on the other.

***

Taken together, these studies reveal that few aspects of spiritual, theological and intellectual speculation had as far a reach within the history of Christianity as the Apocalypse and Last Things. From biblical exegesis to prophetic enterprises, the end of the world as portrayed in the Bible and delineated in Christian theology is a theme that has inspired hope, fear,

---

[15] John J. Collins, *The Apocalyptic Imagination: An Introduction to Jewish Apocalyptic Literature* (New York: Crossroad, 1984), 5.

and above all voluminous literary and artistic production since Antiquity. As a doctrinal and theological concept central to the Christian tradition, apocalyptic and eschatological thought has intersected with fields as diverse as political thought, literature, popular religious history, patristics, theology, visionary experience, and even urban history. The scholarship of this volume testifies to the wealth of the western apocalyptic tradition no less than the depth, the range, and the significance of E. Ann Matter's scholarship.

PART I

Gendering the Apocalypse

CHAPTER 2

The Sobered Sibyl: Gender, Apocalypse, and Hair in Dio Chrysostom's *Discourse 1* and the *Shepherd of Hermas*

Mary R. D'Angelo

E. Ann Matter's work on contemporary and medieval apocalypticisms, on biblical interpretation especially in the Middle Ages, and on music of the Renaissance and Baroque are justly celebrated, but equally significant has been her contribution to reviving the memory of women political prophets of the sixteenth and seventeenth centuries.[1] These women had

---

[1] See, e.g., E. Ann Matter and Gabriella Zarri, *Una mistica contestata: La vita di Lucia da Narni (1476–1544) tra agiografia e autobiografia* (Rome: Edizioni di storia e letteratura, 2011); Matter, "Lucia Brocadelli: Seven Revelations Introduced and Translated," in *Dominican Penitent Women*, ed. Maiju Lehmijoki-Gardner (Mahwah, NJ: Paulist Press, 2005), 212–43; Matter, "Prophetic Patronage as Repression: Lucia Brocadelli da Narni and Ercole D'Este," in *Christendom and Its Discontents: Exclusion, Persecution and Rebellion, 100–1500*, ed. Scott L. Waugh and Peter D. Diehl (Cambridge, UK: Cambridge University Press, 1996), 168–76; Matter, "The Commentary on the Rule of Clare of Assisi by Maria Domitilla Galluzzi," in *Creative Women in Medieval and Early Modern Italy: A Religious and Artistic Renaissance*, ed. Matter and John Coakley (Philadelphia: University

M. R. D'Angelo (✉)
University of Notre Dame, Notre Dame, IN, USA

© The Author(s) 2019
E. Knibbs et al. (eds.), *The End of the World in Medieval Thought and Spirituality*, The New Middle Ages,
https://doi.org/10.1007/978-3-030-14965-9_2

a long prehistory in the hopes and fears of the ancient world. The most famous of their progenitors may be the Sibyls. Originating as foci of revelation in the Greek world, they became authors first of the Roman oracular books, then of the Jewish and Christian Sibylline Oracles. This essay looks at the fictive female intermediaries in two Greek prose works of the early second century, Dio Chrysostom's *Discourse 1* and the *Shepherd of Hermas*. Each of these women is and is not the Sibyl, and each is shaped by the complexities of gender and prophecy.

A few words of caution: my argument is not that any of the women prophets of later Christianity is dependent on either work. Rather, the mechanism at work is similar to the one Matter describes in "The Personal and the Paradigm." The male authors of the lives of the women saints created a literary and theological pattern that was then available to devout women of subsequent generations to imitate and vary in constructing their own lives and spiritual teaching. Matter points out that Maria Domitilla Galuzzi appropriated such materials, especially the life of Catherine of Siena by Raymond of Capua, and argues that access to her experience can be had only by accepting this choice on her terms.[2] Similarly these two second-century fictions, both written by and largely addressed to men, contributed to the sedimented lore on the theory and practice of prophecy that would travel forward into the world of the medieval women prophets.

A brief summary of the features that the works of Dio and Hermas share suggests a relationship to each other and to the sixth book of the *Aeneid*. Both Dio and Hermas present their readers with a woman who, like the Sibyl, guides the protagonist and the readers through a visionary experience. In both cases, it seems that the woman both is and is not the Sibyl. In both, the narrator meets the woman outside the city, in a setting that is explicitly rustic. In both the rural setting in part expresses an ambivalent relation to the Roman order. Both are sent with a prophetic message conveyed in the narrative. Both offer a choice between virtues

---

of Pennsylvania Press, 1994), 201–11; Matter, "Discourses of Desire: Sexuality and Christian Women's Visionary Narratives," *Journal of Homosexuality* 18 (1989): 119–32.

[2] "The Personal and the Paradigm: The Book of Maria Domitilla Galluzzi," in *The Crannied Wall: Women Religion and the Arts in Early Modern Europe*, ed. Craig A. Monson. Studies in Medieval and Early Modern Civilization (Ann Arbor: University of Michigan Press, 1992), 87–103, at 97–103.

and vices personified as female. In both, the woman's hair attests her prophetic status, yet she is notably free of the fury and *mania* that causes the Sibyl's breast to heave and her locks to come undone in *Aeneid* 6. For Hermas and Dio, the prophet's sobriety is a warrant for rather than a detriment to her prophetic authority.

None of the three works speaks of an "end of the world" portrayed through the sort of cosmic cataclysm that is synonymous with "apocalypse" in the popular mind and that figures more prominently in many of the works discussed in this volume.[3] The darkened suns, falling stars, and cosmic warfare of Mark 13 and Revelation find no substantial echo in these works. But like those early Christian texts, these works announce the end of the present world, the present age of woe, and promise the dawn of a new and better age. The generic disparity of the three works requires acknowledgment: *Aeneid* 6 is a single book of an epic poem, while *Discourse 1* is an epideictic oration with a deliberative purpose, and *Hermas* a Christian apocalypse. Yet the three works show structural and generic similarities that go beyond the central role of a woman prophet. Collaborative research in the Society of Biblical Literature produced a description of apocalypse as genre that fits multiple aspects of *Aeneid* 6 and *Discourse 1* as well as *Hermas*. Adela Yarbro Collins describes it as "a genre of revelatory literature with a narrative framework, in which a revelation is mediated by an otherworldly being to a human recipient, disclosing a transcendent reality that is both temporal, insofar as it envisages eschatological salvation, and spatial, insofar as it involves another, supernatural world." Works of this genre seek "to interpret present earthly circumstances in light of the supernatural world and of the future, and to influence both the understanding and the behavior of the audience by means of divine authority."[4] Virgil and Dio, as well as

---

[3] It plays a significant role in the exegesis of Berengaudus and Joachim of Fiore and later emerges transformed in the poetry of Donne and Sor Juana de la Cruz. See Eric Knibbs, "Berengaudus on the Apocalypse"; Bernard McGinn, "Apocalypticism and Mysticism in Joachim of Fiore's *Expositio in Apocalypsim*"; Marcia L. Colish, "End Time at Hand: Innocent III, Joachim of Fiore and the Third Crusade"; Angela Locatelli, "Amorous and Religious Apocalypses in the sermons and Poetry of John Donne"; and Jessica Boon, "The Marian Apocalyptic of a Visionary Preacher: The *Conorte* of Juana de la Cruz, 1481–1534," all in this volume.

[4] See Adela Yarbro Collins, "Introduction: Early Christian Apocalypses," *Semeia* 36 (1986): 1–11, at 7. The collaboration in research is represented by *Semeia* 14 (1979) and *Semeia* 36.

Hermas, produced narrative texts in which a more-than-human mediator conducts the narrator on an otherworldly journey and interprets what the narrator sees. All three authors offer prophetic messages on the "future" of Rome, messages which are both political and ethical and which promise an end to a world of distress for the suffering just and the beginning of a golden age.

1   THE SIBYL OF CUMAE IN THE EARLY EMPIRE

The Sibyl originated in the world of Greek antiquity. The word at some points appears to be a personal name and at others to refer to a role. Sibyls multiplied and were associated with specific sites, but they seem to have been geographically freer than the Pythia, the female oracle whose home was Delphi. The Erythraean Sibyl appears to have spent some time at Samos and to have wound up at Cumae.[5] The Sibyl was often paired with the Pythia in literary references, but they differed in significant ways. The Sibyl's prophecies were not delivered in response to consultation, but were offered on her own, or rather on divine, initiative, in the form of "discursive pieces of verse addressed to the world in general rather than to any particular enquirer."[6] Unlike the Pythia, she was not consistently identified with Apollo. On the grounds of her association with Samos and her acquisition of the name Herophile, H. W. Parke suggests that she may have originally been a prophet of Hera.[7] Although inspired, she spoke in her own persona, and not with the voice of the god. This feature of her prophecy complicated the ancient theory of prophetic speech, which saw ecstasy as the guarantee of authenticity. Signs of madness were signs of inspiration; the god displaced the prophet's mind. The import of ecstasy as a criterion is evident in Socrates' defense of a lover's *mania* in *Phaedrus* 234E–245B. There he claims that prophecy was once the manic art (*manikē*) and only recently and inappropriately had a tau been added to make it the mantic (*mantikē*) art (244C). Thus true prophecy is the product of *mania*. Socrates cites the Sibyl with the Pythia and the priestesses of Dodona as examples of the madness of inspiration (244A–B). Attribution of madness to the Sibyl may go back

---

[5] H. W. Parke, *Sibyls and Sibylline Prophecy in Classical Antiquity*, ed. B. C. McGing (London: Routledge, 1988), 64–67.

[6] Parke, *Sibyls*, 7.

[7] Parke, *Sibyls*, 9.

as far as Herakleitos (6th–5th c. BCE). Plutarch, the contemporary of Dio and Hermas, cites Herakleitos' observation: "the rough verses from the Sibyl's raving (*mainomenōi*) mouth yet reach across thousands of years" (*Pythian Oracle* 6; *Mor* 145). Thus the Sibyl seems consistently to have prophesied in her own persona yet out of her mind.

In Italy, the Sibyl presided over an oracular cult at Cumae and was the author of the Sibylline Books that held the key to the fate of Rome. Her fame was enhanced by her role in the *Aeneid*, but oracular activity at Cumae was much older than the late republic and early empire. A figure of the distant past in that era, the Sibyl also appeared in the poems of Tibullus, Propertius, and Ovid. Livy referred briefly to her arrival in Italy (1.7.8), and frequently noted recourse to the Sibylline books, often to avert disasters that had struck or been deduced from omens.[8] Writing in Greek, Dionysius of Halicarnassus provides an account of the books' origin and character (*Roman Antiquities* 4.62.1–6) followed by multiple references to their guidance of the early history of Rome. As well as representing her as the prophetic guide to Aeneas, Roman authors treated the Sibyl's great age as proverbial. In the pre-Augustan *Eclogue* 4, Virgil himself takes on a prophetic role to acclaim the arrival of the last age predicted in the "Cumaean song" (the Sibylline Oracles), an age that will produce golden people.[9]

The role of the Sibyl in predicting a change of the ages draws attention to features of *Aeneid* 6 that make it comparable to apocalypses. Harold W. Attridge classed Book Six among Greek and Latin works that display features similar to Jewish and Christian apocalypses. Attridge's list of these features included an epiphany of Apollo, Aeneas' otherworldly journey, the Sibyl as otherworldly guide, the *ex eventu* prophecies of Rome's greatness and of Aeneas' future, scenes of post-mortem judgment, reward, and punishment, a doctrine of metempsychosis, and otherworldly regions.[10] John J. Collins remarks these features as motifs found in Hellenistic and Roman writing that also appear in Jewish and early Christian apocalypses in transformations of the biblical traditions.[11]

---

[8] For example: 3.10.5–7, 4.25.3, 5.13.4–8.

[9] "Ultima Cumaei venit iam carminis aetas;/magnus ab integro saeclorum nascitur ordo" (*Ecl* 4.4–5) and "...surget gens aurea..." (*Ecl.* 4.9).

[10] Harold W. Attridge, "Greek and Latin Apocalypses," *Semeia* 14 (1979): 166.

[11] John J. Collins, *The Apocalyptic Imagination: An Introduction to the Jewish Matrix of Christianity* (New York: Crossroad, 1987), 28.

Aeneid 6 narrates a journey first into a wilderness, then into the underworld. The Sibyl, a priest and prophet whose suprahuman lifespan places her between this world and the other, is the guide and the interpreter for Aeneas' entry into Hades and leads him through the ranks of those dead subject to punishment. When they reach the Elysian Fields, Anchises takes over the interpretive role, showing Aeneas the future of Rome and the role of his progeny (6.703–885). Chief among them is Augustus, whose role it will be to found ages of gold ("aurea condet saecula") and to spread an imperium to the ends of the earth.[12]

Within this structure, the Sibyl (here named Deiphobe, 6.34) functions as a consulting prophet and a priest of Apollo; her madness guarantees the god's presence. Perhaps because she must be sober enough to conduct Aeneas through Hades, her *mania* is manifested primarily in the opening verses of the book, and is especially stressed while she resists the advent of Apollo and submission to the vatic state (6.45–102). Described as raging and raving, the prophet is dread-inspiring, and acts the Bacchant.[13] When Apollo seizes her, she is physically as well as psychically transformed: her expression and color become volatile, her hair comes undone, she pants and heaves, seeming to grow in size and to speak in an immortal voice: "Nor countenance nor color was the same, nor stayed her tresses braided: but her bosom heaves, her heart swells with wild frenzy, and she is taller to behold, nor has her voice a mortal ring."[14] She raves ("bacchatur," 78) through the cave, resisting the god, but prophesying war for Aeneas, to be encountered in Italy, and all too like the one that has driven him here. The cause of strife will again be a "foreign bride" (93–94)—not Helen now, but Lavinia (perhaps Cleopatra, the dux femina of the still recent civil war is also evoked by the phrase). Throughout her prophecy, the Sibyl is driven and goaded by Apollo; when she ceases speaking, it appears that he has dropped the reins and released her (100–102). Her later speeches focus on

---

[12] "Augustus Caesar, divi genus, aurea condet/saecula qui rursus Latio regnata per arva/ Saturna quondam, super et Garamantes et Indos/proferet imperium" (6.791–808).

[13] "Furens": 6.100, 102, 261; "rabida": 6.46, 80, 102; "horrenda": 6.12; "bacchatur": 6.78.

[14] "...non voltus, non color unus,/non comptae mansere comae, sed pectus anhelum,/et rabie fera corda tument, maiorque videri/nec mortale sonans..." (6.47–50). H. R. Fairclough, trans., revised by G. P. Gould, *Virgil*, Loeb Classical Library 63 (Cambridge: Harvard University Press, 1999), 265.

the practicalities of their journey or offer a tour-guide's commentary (but see 261). Thus Virgil's Sibyl is formed by the traditional understanding of inspiration that links the mantic with *mania* laid out by Plato in the *Phaedrus*.

In the Roman context, the Sibyl's association with Apollo, the centuries of her age, her madness, and her hair become increasingly important. At roughly the same time as the *Aeneid*, Tibullus describes the Sibyl as tossing her head, and her flowing hair as she invokes Apollo.[15] Ovid's summary of *Aeneid* 6 also speaks of her as "raging when she has accepted the god" though without mentioning her hair.[16] Ovid's particular interest is in her ten centuries, the great age that is wearing her away to a voice.[17] This debility is also the focus of her brief appearance in Petronius' *Satyricon* (48).[18]

Lucan's *Pharsalia* offers a particularly striking picture of hair as an index of prophetic frenzy. Lucan recounts Appian's consultation of the Delphic oracle, but his Pythia is recast in the mold of the Sibyl, complete with the sounding cavern found at Cumae as the site of her prophecy.[19] So destructive is the effect of inspiration upon the seer that the Pythia desperately resists his efforts to wrest prophecy from her; so significant is her hair that Appius is able to use it to detect the uninspired state in which the reluctant Pythia attempts to fob him off with a lying oracle. When she is first pushed into the sanctuary, her front hair is tightly bound by her fillets and long hair braided with laurel flows down her back; both are undisturbed as she speaks her false prophecy, so that Appius links the calm of the natural world with the composure of her locks in his accusation that she has prophesied falsely. Sure enough, when she submits to the god:

> Frantic she careers about the cave, with her neck under possession; the fillets and garlands of Apollo, dislodged by her bristling hair, she whirls with tossing head through the void spaces of the temple; she scatters the tripods

[15] "haec cecinit uates et te sibi, Phoebe, uocauit,/iactauit fusas et caput ante comas," *Carmina* 2.65–66.
[16] "Deo furibunda accepto," *Metamorphoses* 14.107.
[17] *Metamorphoses* 14.129–54. Also on the age of the Sibyl, see Propertius, *Elegies* 2.24B.33.
[18] Appropriated by T. S. Eliot as the epigraph for *The Wasteland*.
[19] Parke, *Sibyls*, 147.

that impede her random course; she boils over with fierce fire, while enduring the wrath of Phoebus.[20]

Since this is Lucan, Appius' persistence is in vain. Her true prophecy leads to a denouement as violent as the signs of her inspiration.

In the late first century, Statius' celebration of the newly constructed *Via Domitiana* (95 CE) introduces the Sibyl with literary hints before naming her; the road's end is said to be Cumae (actually it went on to Puteoli and Baia). The poet himself becomes a prophet, proclaiming: "I see one white of locks and fillets."[21] Her age and her headdress thus provide clues to her identity. Her madness manifests her inspired state, as she ritually inaugurates and sanctifies the road: "Lo, she rolls her head and in Bacchic frenzy ranging through the new spaces, she completes the road's course."[22] Her prophecy hails Domitian's advent as that of a god, a leader of men and father of gods, who by Jupiter's decree rules "happy lands."[23] For worth he is comparable only to Aeneas; indeed, Domitian would be a more provident ruler of the heavens than their current king (i.e., Zeus; 128–40). Finally she promises that his reign and the new road will outlast the ages of the old Via Appia (162–63).

Taken together, these texts reflect the Sibyl of the Roman imaginary in the early empire, a figure marked by extreme old age and prophetic fury expressed especially in the disarrangement, even derangement, of her hair. This portrait offers a template to Dio and Hermas, with and against which they produce their seers. The prophetic women in their

---

[20] "Bacchatur demens aliena per antrum/Colla ferens, uittasque dei Phoebeaque serta/ Erectis discussa comis per inania templi/Ancipiti ceruice rotat spargitque uaganti/obstantis tripodas magnoque exaestuat igne/iratum te, Phoebe, ferens." *De Bello Civili* 5.169–74. Translation from J. D. Duff, *Lucan: The Civil War* Loeb Classical Library 220 (Cambridge: Harvard University Press, 1928), 251. Unless otherwise noted, translations are mine.

[21] "albam crinibus infulisque cerno," 4.3120.

[22] "en! et colla rotat novisque late/bacchatur spatiis viamque replet," 4.3.121–22.

[23] "Salve dux hominum et parens deorum," 4.3.139; "En hic est deus, hunc iubet beatis/pro se Iuppiter imperare terris," 4.3.128–29. The allusion to gods of whom Domitian is *parens* may both refer to the child who was born in 73, died very young, and was deified shortly after Domitian's accession, and also constitute another prophecy of other children yet unborn. In fact Domitian was the last of his dynasty. See Pat Southern, *Domitian Tragic Tyrant* (London: Routledge, 1997), 28–29.

texts are both modeled on and distanced from the Sibyl of the first-century writers. That Dio and Hermas both write in Greek and these texts are almost all in Latin is not an impediment; Polybius, a freedman of Claudius, had produced a prose translation of the *Aeneid* into Greek in the first half of the first century CE.[24] But it is also likely that both Dio and Hermas had at least some acquaintance with Latin. Further, as Parke points out, traditions about the Sibyl were widely disseminated even before Virgil.[25]

2   Dio's Sylvan Sibyl

Dio Chrysostom was an orator with philosophical interests, a politician and a diplomat, acting as advocate for his native city of Prusa, other cities of the Greek East, and Rome. His work is represented by a collection of eighty orations or discourses (*logoi*) usually cited by number and title. The first four are entitled *Peri Basileia*, a title conventionally translated as "On Kingship." These orations do indeed draw on the long tradition of philosophical advice to monarchs. But *Basileus* was one of the Greek titles used for the emperor, and these four speeches are so carefully attuned to the circumstances of Trajan's first years (98–105 CE) that their import would be better conveyed by "On the Principate" or "On Imperial Rule."[26] In what follows, I leave *basileia* untranslated, capitalizing it where it is personified. *Turannis*, which Dio opposes to *basileia* I translate as tyranny, as it seems to carry the same negative connotations in Dio's four speeches as in English, rather than the earlier neutral sense of rule. These four speeches very tactfully advise Trajan on how to be the ruler he desires to be: a *basileus* and not a *turannos*, that is, a *princeps* modeled on Zeus and not on Domitian, who serves as a shadow antagonist, although he is never mentioned by name. It is clear that Dio draws upon motifs favored in Trajan's propaganda, deploying his art to urge Trajan toward the expectations of the senatorial circle that included Pliny

---

[24] Seneca, *Ad Polybium* 8.2, 11.5.
[25] Parke, *Sibyls*, 147.
[26] Julian Bennett prefers "On Sovereignty." See Bennett, *Trajan Optimus Princeps*, 2nd ed. (Bloomington: Indiana University Press, 2001), 67 and 253, Footnote 39. Two of the eighty are actually the work of Dio's student Favorinus.

and Tacitus.[27] Similar oppositions of *Basileia* and Tyranny (or its deeds) appear in *Discourse 62*, also addressed to Trajan.[28]

Discourse 1 is probably the first of the four, and has been variously dated to 98, 99, and 100 CE.[29] It opens with an encomium of *basileia*, delineating the virtues of the true *basileus* (1–36). Dio follows this by proposing Zeus as the true model for Trajan (37–48). To drive home his exposition of the virtues of the true king or *princeps*, Dio produces a revelation mediated by a prophetic female figure, offering Trajan "a story" (*muthos*), or rather, he corrects himself, "a sacred and salutary message in the form of a myth" (49).[30] Implicit in the story is the reminder that Trajan must make a choice.

The story is set in the time of Dio's exile, which, he observes, providentially allowed him to be untainted by the wrongs done under Domitian (50).[31] Wandering in the Peloponnesus, he became lost in rough and deserted country (52) and found himself in a rustic grove and sanctuary of Herakles. There he met a "woman of Elis or Arcadia" who proffers a story within his story (49). This reference to "Elis or Arcadia" evokes not only the geography of the Peloponnesus but also the idyllic landscapes of Virgil. Dio comments upon the woman's appearance and age: in contrast to Statius' raving and roving Sibyl (as well as the Sibyl of *Aeneid* 6.76–77), she is seated; although she is an elder, she is tall and strong (53), unlike the ancient, shrunken and debilitated Sibyl of Ovid and Petronius.[32] Revealing that she had received mantic and oracular power from the mother of the gods (perhaps Kybele, but possibly Hera),

---

[27] For the common practice of deducing Trajan's propaganda from coins, monuments, and the correspondences between Pliny's *Panegyric* and the four *Discourses Peri Basileias*, see Bennett, *Optimus Princeps*, 63–73.

[28] Pliny also makes this contrast; a particularly Latin version appears in *Panegyric* 45.3: "Scis ut sint diversa natura dominatio et principatus" ("You know that lordliness and principate are by nature opposed").

[29] See Bennett, *Optimus Princeps* 67 and 253, Footnote 41.

[30] For "message" as a translation of *logos*, see especially its use to refer to an oracular pronouncement. Henry George Liddell, Robert Scott, and Henry Stuart Jones et al., *A Greek-English Lexicon*, s.v. *logos* VII.1, citing Plato, *Phaedrus* 275b and *Apology* 20; also its use to mean narrative (s.v. *logos* V).

[31] A less circumspect account of his exile describes Domitian as a hostile *daimon*, contrasting him with his philanthropic successors, Nerva and Trajan, all still unnamed but completely recognizable (*Discourse* 45, 1–3).

[32] *Metamorphoses* 4.30–54, *Satyricon* 48; see above.

she explains that she serves the local herdsmen and farmers with advice on crops and cattle (54).

Promising that Dio will not go away in vain, she provides him with an oracular glimpse of the near future of Rome, foretelling the end of Dio's exile and misery, and that of other human beings, a prophecy fulfilled by the recent death of Domitian (96 CE) and the accession of Trajan in 98 CE (55).[33] To this prediction, she adds a mission. Dio, she promises, will one day meet up with "a man of strength ruling most numerous lands and people."[34] This promise is apparently fulfilled in the very occasion of the speech, as Dio delivers his *Discourse* before Trajan, the very steadfast/mighty man in view.

For that powerful and controlled man, she commits to Dio a story. This story, the moral message of her prophecy, turns out to be a highly elaborated version of the choice of Herakles attributed to Prodicus in Xenophon's *Memorablilia* 2.1.21. Dio has refashioned the anecdote for the circumstances of the new *princeps*. Invoking Herakles is in itself a delicate attention to Trajan, whose early coinage employed the image of Hercules Gaditanus—Hercules coming from Cadiz, as had the Spanish-born Trajan.[35] The two most significant aspects of Dio's reorientation of the trope are the status of Herakles and the terms of the choice. First, Herakles has become a king, while Eurystheus is reduced to his deputy, covering for Herakles as he went about fighting and defending his reign. Indeed, he was *basileus* not only of all Greece, but actually held an *imperium* over the whole world, "from the rising to the setting of the sun" (59–60) and so his rule is a predecessor of Trajan's. Second, the terms of the choice are revised. In Xenophon, Herakles was required to choose between vice and virtue personified as women. Both Cicero (*De Officiis* 1.32) and Philo (*De Sacrificiis* 20–40) produce more philosophical versions of this choice by opposing pleasure (*voluptas, hēdonē*)

---

[33] *Discourse* 45, 4 suggests that a god of a city in Asia Minor had predicted Domitian's assassination; *Discourse* 66, 7 seems to have been written before 96 and to predict the death of Domitian and the end of the Flavian dynasty; see H. L. Crosby, *Dio Chrysostom: Vol. 5*, Loeb Classical Library 385 (Cambridge: Harvard University Press, 1946), 87 and 95, n. 4.

[34] The Greek word I have translated "of strength" implies both might and control; Liddell, Scott and Jones, s.v. *karteros*.

[35] Bennett, *Optimus Princeps*, 72.

rather than vice to virtue.[36] The choice offered to Trajan through Herakles is more starkly revised; it is recast to be the choice as a ruler, and especially a new ruler must make: between *basileia* and tyranny (67–84).

This choice is laid out in an otherworldly journey, narrated and interpreted by the woman seer, but conducted by a male guide. Zeus, his father, committed the young Herakles to Hermes, who led him by a secret road that diverged at a mountain with two peaks (68–69), each surmounted by a female figure seated upon a throne and surrounded by her attendants. The first figure is *Basileia*; around her throne are three female personifications: Justice, Good Order, and Peace; with them is a strong man (*anēr*), without whom it is not right for them to act or even deliberate (75). That these personifications are four evokes the cardinal virtues, but also evades them. Like the female personifications found on the reverse of so many Roman coin issues, *Basileia*'s attendants represent attributes that include both virtues and powers; they are the means and results of good rule. The other mountain peak and throne are occupied by Tyranny, also seated upon a throne, and supported by her attendants, but these are Cruelty, Hubris, Lawlessness, Faction, and Flattery, all female personifications, and all both the drivers and the products of tyranny (82). Herakles, as the story requires, made the right choice, and in the years after, went about the world unseating and destroying tyrants, but supporting true rule and rulers. Since Herakles is Trajan's help and guardian, Trajan will surely follow his example and make the same choice.

In portraying the woman prophet and the female personifications, Dio goes out of his way to reject the picture of the *mania*-driven Sibyl and to place her revelation in the light of sanity: "She said these things not as do the many among the supposedly inspired (*entheōn*) men and women, panting and whirling her head about, and attempting a terrifying glare, but entirely self-controlled and sober."[37] The sobriety of her manner of prophesying is echoed in her physical appearance; she speaks from her seat and her white locks adumbrate her prophetic status, but

---

[36] For Philo's use of the choice of Herakles, see Carlos Levy, "Philo's Ethics," in *The Cambridge Companion to Philo*, ed. Adam Kamesar (Cambridge: Cambridge University Press, 2009), 146–74, at 151.

[37] "...panu egkratōs kai sōfronōs..." (53).

seem controlled (53). The contrast with Statius' Sibyl, whose *mania* rages over Domitian's road, is particularly strong.

Basileia is likewise seated, not in a rustic grove but on a shining throne (70), and she is clothed in white. Her gaze is steady and her expression always the same, welcoming to the good and unbearable to the evil (71). Similarly, her attendants all are decent, stately, and "male-visaged" (73). In contrast, Tyranny's clothing and throne are of variegated substances and colors, the throne is unstable and her expressions are both false and constantly changing; her glance darts everywhere (79–81). Her attendants in no way resemble those of *Basileia*. All aspects of *Basileia* are simple, clear, and reliable; everything about Tyranny is changeable, deceptive, and untrustworthy. Her court very conspicuously lacks the guidance of a male majordomo.

Although Dio has tamed the wild woman prophet who resisted Apollo in the *Aeneid* and raged the length of the Via Domitiana in *Silvae*, he has produced this visionary sobriety not to undermine but to buttress the divine origin of the oracle. Indeed, the woman prophet prefaces her story with strictures on the necessity of divine inspiration, asserting the incomparable superiority of thought and speech that come from the gods and castigating those who pass off messages from their minds as true, without divine inspiration (57–58).

As does *Aeneid* 6, Dio's myth manifests features of apocalypses. That the story is set in Dio's past and in the idealized rustic and remote provinces of Greece bestows on it the aura of a secret, one not merely revealed, but partially fulfilled. It begins with the protagonist wandering in a wilderness, and includes an otherworldly journey, though the journey is that of a new protagonist, Herakles. There are two guides and interpreters—the woman prophet who tells the story, and the divine guide Hermes who leads Herakles to the vision of the two women and interprets for him. The message, both as a retrospective "prophecy" and as an exhortation, is the end of one old world order and the beginning of a new world, both for Dio, who will be able to return from exile, and for Rome, and so for the inhabited world. Most of all, the message is for Trajan in whose power and virtue it lies to make the world new.

3 THE SIBYL/CHURCH IN THE SHEPHERD OF HERMAS

Hermas, unlike the *Aeneid* or *Basileia* 1, is usually classified as an apocalypse, and was one of the texts used in developing the description of the genre.[38] While the text is full of visionary terminology found in Daniel, Revelation and other Jewish and Christian apocalypses, much of the work is devoted to moral instruction. Carolyn Osiek has offered a helpful refinement by characterizing the bulk of its content as apocalyptic parenesis.[39] There is substantial agreement that *Hermas* belongs to the earlier half of the second century, but no consensus on a more precise date. The setting is Rome and its countryside, and is probably indicative of the work's origin.[40] The visionary and ostensible author, Hermas, was apparently a freedperson (1.1.1 [1]). The prophecy opens with a set of five narrative *Visions*. These are followed by twelve revealed commandments, usually called *Mandates*, then ten allegories, called *Similitudes* (or parables).[41] Here too, there is a woman intermediary who is and is not the Sibyl, and who is the major figure in the *Visions*. Like Dio's, Hermas' prophecy puts forward a moral choice presented through female personifications (*Similitude* 9 [78–107]).

The *Visions* warrant the prophetic status of the book; they are secrets bestowed in the past and only now revealed. Their principal intermediary is a woman; as Osiek notes, she is the only fully developed woman revealer among the intermediaries of the Jewish and Christian apocalypses.[42] As in *Aeneid* 6 and Dio, she will give way to a male guide, the shepherd and angel of repentance. Her white hair and age, the book she carries and from which she reads her prophecies, and the location of their encounter outside Rome on the way to the countryside prompt an identification with the Sibyl, presumably the Cumaean Sibyl.[43]

---

[38] See Adela Yarbro Collins, "The Early Christian Apocalypses," *Semeia* 14 (1979): 61–121. She classified it among "apocalypses of cosmic and/or political eschatology with neither historical review nor otherworldly journey" (70, 74–75).

[39] Carolyn Osiek, "The Genre and Function of the Shepherd of Hermas," *Semeia* 36 (1986): 113–21; *The Shepherd of Hermas: A Commentary* (Minneapolis: Fortress Press, 1999), 10–12.

[40] Osiek, *Shepherd*, 18–20.

[41] On issues of integrity and authorship, see Osiek, *Shepherd*, 8–10.

[42] Osiek, *Shepherd*, 16, 58.

[43] On these cues, see also Osiek, *Shepherd*, 58.

When asked by one of her attendants, Hermas confidently makes that identification. The very beautiful youth who interprets this vision at once corrects the seer: she is not the Sibyl but the Church (*Vis* 2.4.1 [8]). In *Similitude* 9.1.1. [78], the angel of repentance further amends this identification: she is the holy Spirit, the Son of God, in the form of the Church. Despite this correction, Hermas' first impression must be of considerable importance to the prophecy. In naming her the Sibyl, he articulates an identity that was suggested to the readers and hearers throughout the first two chapters.[44] Even after he is corrected, he continues to refer to her as the elder woman (*presbytera*; 2.4.2 [8]).

The *Visions* begin when Hermas is journeying into the country.[45] Falling asleep, he is seized by the spirit and carried away through a trackless waste to rough terrain reminiscent of the Campi Flegrei. The other major *Visions* all take place outside the city in rustic settings, the second on a journey a year later (*Vis* 2.1.1 [5]), the third by special appointment with the Lady, at his own farm (*Vis* 3.1.2 [9]), and the fourth also interrupts a journey to the country (*Vis* 4.1.1 [22]), although it seems to take place close to the city. The fifth *Vision*, which introduces the shepherd and angel of repentance who mediates the rest of the revelation, takes place at home and marks a new stage of the revelation. Although Hermas walks in the country again and is again taken to the wilderness, the new revealer takes up residence with him. The most striking of these later journeys is to "Arcadia" in *Similitude* 9, and if Dio's Arcadia seems both geographical and idealized, in Hermas there can be no doubt of its idealized and indeed otherworldly character.

The exurban location of the visions may reflect the ambivalent political situation that is at least part of the great tribulation of the fourth

---

[44] David O'Brien has explored the use of the figure of the Sibyl in the prophecy; he suggests that the author wishes to appeal to Roman converts who held the Sibyl in high esteem, and that the prophecy promotes a theologoumenon about God as creator from nothing that he views as consonant with the theology of *Sibylline Oracles*; "The Cumaen Sibyl as the Revelation-Bearer in the Shepherd of Hermas," *Journal of Early Christian Studies* 5 (1997): 473–96; see especially 485 and 487.

[45] The Greek texts read *eis kōmas*, "to the countryside," at *Vis* 1.1.3 and 2.1.1; among the Latin texts, L² reads *eis koumas*, "to Cumae," at *Vis* 1.1.3 and LL has this reading at *Vis* 2.1.1. This reading has been widely rejected on the basis of the Greek texts and the view that the 130 miles to Cumae make such a journey implausible; so Osiek, *Shepherd*, 43. It is possible that Hermas' identification of the woman as the Sibyl suggested the Latin reading, as no other Sibyls are likely to have been frequenting the countryside of Rome.

vision. This situation is articulated in the first similitude; Hermas (and his "family") live as foreigners in the city, and they are unwanted by its master (*kurios*), whose laws they do not practice. Unlike Dio, Hermas expects no end to this regime; his hope is to be expelled and to return to his true city, and to do that he must treat his livelihood and possessions as temporary, to be cultivated and disbursed with an eye to his future exodus (*Sim* 1.1–10 [50]).

Vision 1 begins with an entirely heavenly manifestation; the heavens open and Hermas is visited by his former owner, Rhoda, who accuses him of a sin of lust against her (1.1.1 [1]). When the heavens close again, he sees a "great white chair of snowy wool." Another woman, white-haired, with shining garments and carrying a book, comes and takes her seat on it (*Vis* 1.2.2 [2]), not unlike a female "ancient of days" (Dan. 7:9). Heavenly in appearance, she does not appear from or in heaven as Rhoda does, and so is at least partly of this world. Her age, her location outside Rome, and her prophetic role inform Hermas that she is the Sibyl. These factors take on new meaning when she is identified with the Church; she is the very first creation (*Vis* 2.4.1 [8]), and herself the spirit of prophecy and the son of God (*Sim* 9.1 [78]), alien to "this city." At the same time, she is the tower of *Vision* 3 (3.3.3 [11]), established in and transcending the cosmos. Further, the forms in which she appears reflect the state of Hermas and his "household," that is, the Christian circles in Rome; she grows younger and more vital as they begin to revive, while her hair remains white, affirming both her ancient origin and her oracular status (*Vis* 3.11–13 [19–21]; 4.2.1–2 [22]). At the end of *Vision* 1, she told Hermas "Act the man" (*andrizou*; *Vis* 1.4.3 [4]); in the second vision, Hermas and the Church are like an old man rejuvenated by an inheritance, who no longer sits but walks, and "acts the man" (*andrizetai*; *Vis* 3.12.2 [20]).[46]

As Dio's *Basileia* is attended by female personifications, in *Hermas* virtues support the Church-tower like caryatids. In *Vision* 3, there are seven. Faith is their origin, and *Enkrateia* (Continence) her daughter, succeeded by Simplicity, Understanding, Innocence, Reverence, and Love. *Enkrateia* is singled out for special attention. She is described as girded and acting the man (*andrizomenē*; 3.8.4 [16]). "Girded" implies

---

[46] On masculinity in *Hermas*, see Stephen Young, "Being a Man: The Pursuit of Manliness in the Shepherd of Hermas," *Journal of Early Christian Studies* 2 (1994): 237–55.

either that her heavy belt holds her tunic above her knees, like that of Artemis or the Amazons, or perhaps that she wears a workman's apron; either way, she is prepared for a journey, and for the heavy work the virgins undertake, and perhaps also to defend the tower, as does Faith, who is similarly dressed.[47]

In *Similitude* 9, in a landscape of Arcadia, Hermas is shown the tower with twelve virgins/girls around it, "in linen tunics beautifully girt about, with their right shoulders bare;" that is, despite their splendid garb and delicate appearance, they are ready for heavy labor, standing manfully (*andreiōs*; *Sim* 9.2.5 [79]). Their task is to ferry stones to the tower, changing them from their disparate colors to white. The list of their names also begins with Faith and *Enkrateia*; next are Power and Patience. These first, "most glorious" four are apparently of particular strength: they support the four corners of the tower's entry porch with the other virgins between them.[48] As with the court of Dio's *Basileia*, the four personifications evoke and revise the cardinal virtues; they are virtues in the literal sense of powers, as are the succeeding eight: Simplicity, Innocence, Purity, Joy, Truth, Understanding, Concord, Love (*Sim* 9.15.2 [92]). They belong to the prophetic world; the Shepherd identifies them as spirits; human beings must wear them/their names in order to become part of the tower (9.15.6 [92]). He also leaves Hermas to their care for a festival in which they "play" or "dance" (*paizein*) with him and pass the night together sleeping on the virgins' linen tunics, but "as a brother, not a husband" (9.11.3-7 [89]). Their "playing" is described in terms of choral dance, and their night out on the mountain is reminiscent of a Bacchic pannychis, but is also its antithesis, characterized by formal dancing, quiet prayer, and innocent sleep.

Opposed to the virgins are twelve very beautiful women dressed in black, with both shoulders bare and their hair loose. They are headed by four who are more powerful: Infidelity, Incontinence, Disobedience, Deceit; they are followed by Grief, Wickedness, License, Bitterness, Lying, Folly, Slander, Hate (9. 15.3 [92]).[49] These women are described

---

[47] Osiek emphasizes that the descriptions cast Faith and *Enkrateia* as defenders of the tower; *Shepherd*, 77-78.

[48] Kirsopp Lake offers a diagram; *Apostolic Fathers: Vol. 2*, Loeb Classical Library 25 (Cambridge: Harvard University Press, 1913), 221, Footnote 1.

[49] The first four are linked by the alpha privative: *Apistia, Akrasia, Apeitheia, Apatē*. These women do not correspond perfectly to the virgins in white.

by Hermas as "wild" or "fierce"; the term (*agriai*) does not indicate mere rusticity, but has a decidedly pejorative connotation in Hermas; it is used of "evil desire" (*Mand* 12.2.2 [44] *bis*), of the commands of the Adversary (*Mand* 12.2.4 [47]), of rapacious ministers who like a vineyard that has gone wild have become useless to the Master (*Sim* 9.26.4 [103] *bis*), and of another "shepherd" who is the angel of punishment (*Sim* 6.2.5 [62]).

As in Dio's myth, the female personifications present a choice. Those who choose to bear the names of the first twelve women put on white, become of one color, and enter God's reign; those who choose the women in black will not do so. As was the case for Dio, the prophecy is one of the judgments for both Rome and the world. For the Christian circles at Rome, and in the cities to which Clement is to write, the message is *metanoia*, with the hope that they can be incorporated into the tower and stand firm in the judgment that will enable the just to receive the promise, while the cosmic terrors that Hermas cannot remember fall upon the gentiles and the apostates (*Vis* 1.3.3–4 [3], 4).

While Hermas makes no explicit rejection of the Sibylline *mania*, his Sibyl/Church is notably serene, composed, and joyous.[50] She delivers her message enthroned or on a couch, reading and interpreting. Acting more like a teacher than an oracle, she calms Hermas' confusion and distress. The elder woman's white hair provides a thread through the visions and the two interpretations of her persona, but changes significantion in Hermas' account and the youth's two explanations. Her age and her seated position in the first vision communicate not only her primordial status as the Church created before all else (*Vis* 2.4.1 [8]) but also the weakness and discouragement of Hermas and his community (*Vis* 3.11.2–4 [19]). When he sees her walking and reading in *Vision* 2, with the hair and flesh of an elder, but a joyous and youthful face, she reflects the ways that Hermas and his "family" have been rejuvenated by the first revelations (2.1.3 [5], 3.12.1 [20]). In *Vision* 3 she is entirely young and beautiful, and seated upon an ivory bench. Covered with a linen cushion, it is the sort used at trials or spectacles (*sumpselion*, a word transliterated from the Latin *subsellium*).[51] There is room for Hermas and apparently others, but he is allowed to sit only on her left, the right being reserved

---

[50] *Hilara*, *Vis* 1.4.3 [4], 3.12.1 [20], 13.1 [21].

[51] For a description of the seat, see P. W. Glare, *Oxford Latin Dictionary* (Oxford: Clarendon, 1982), s. v. *subsellium*.

for the martyrs (*Vis* 3.1.4–9 [9]). This seat, according to the youth, rests on four feet and so is stable; so also those "stones" who repent and are fitted into the tower (*Vis* 3.13.1–4 [21]).

Most striking is her appearance in *Vision* 4.2.1 [22]. Hermas describes her as a virgin, by which he probably means newly marriageable, of perhaps 12–14 years, and as "adorned as coming from the bridal chamber."[52] She is clothed in white to her sandals, with a veil that is worn with a headband (*mitra*) and covers her forehead.[53] Even so Hermas can discern her hair, and so recognize her from the other visions (4.2.1). Her appearance is best understood from her interpretation of the four colors on the head of the monster Hermas had escaped in the preceding vision: Black is for this world, white for the world to come; red for the fire and blood that will destroy this world and gold for those (like Hermas) purified by the fire. As the color of the age to come, the dwelling of God's elect, the whiteness of her garb belongs to the realm of apocalyptic imagery identifying her as the Church of the eschatological future, the bride who with the Spirit says "Come."[54]

Thus the female personifications of the *Shepherd* embody and engender the prophecy; the contrasting virgins and women represent the moral choice the prophecy requires of the hearers, showing what they must serve and what they must avoid (*Mand* 12.1.1–3.1 [44–46]). The manly features of their garb and gait reflect the commands to act the man that aim at the rejuvenation of Hermas and his community. The elder woman, as she is progressively rejuvenated, incarnates the transformation of the Church from this age to the next.

---

[52] The description may be formed in part by the Septuagint version of Ps. 18.6 (19.6 in the Masoretic text and the current numbering of the Psalms).

[53] Osiek compares this description to the outfit of the bride in the Augustan wall painting called the Aldobrandini wedding; the painting lacks only the *mitra*. She rightly rejects attempts to explain the *mitra* by the headgear of the high priest (*Shepherd* 93, Footnote 29); it does suggest ritual garb throughout the Mediterranean, and could be worn by women as well as men.

[54] Osiek rejects the idea that this fourth apparition is the Church as bride of Christ (93), I think rightly. Nothing in the vision evokes the sort of imagery found in Eph 5:23–32 or *2 Clement* 14. She also rejects her identification with the end time, suggesting instead that she is the image of the community transformed by acceptance of the prophetic message. While these interpretations are not mutually exclusive, the content of her interpretation and the fact that this is her last appearance seem to affirm her eschatological status.

4 WHY THIS SOBRIETY?

Dio and Hermas both depict a woman seer of completely sober mien whose white but undisturbed locks provide a guarantee of her elder and prophetic status. Their composure, in contrast to that of Lucan's well-groomed and lying Pythia, is a testimony to their trustworthiness. This transformation appears to reject the long tradition that requires that inspiration be attested by *ekstasis*—by the expulsion and compulsion of the seer's mind by the persona or presence of the inspiring deity.

Were it Hermas alone who chose a sober Sibyl, the change might be explained from the Greek Bible and the emerging Christian tradition. The Septuagint prefers to use the word group *mantis/manteuomai* not for Israelite prophecy, but for foreign seers, false prophecy, and forbidden practices. The contrast is not explicit, but emerges in Deut 18.9–22, which promises prophetic guidance to Israel and is sustained throughout. A few texts associate these terms with *mataios*—empty, profane (e.g., Sir 34.5, Ezek 13.7–9, 19). The New Testament follows this usage; the only use of the word group appears in Acts 16.16, where the slave girl with the "pythic spirit" is said to prophesy (*manteuesthai*). Hermas also uses the word group of a false prophet, comparing those who consult him to the gentiles (*Mand* 11.2.2 and 4 [43]).

As is well known, the later second and early third centuries produced a struggle over prophetic experience. The New Prophets (also called Montanists) embraced the ancient theory of inspiration that insists on the displacement of human reason. They stressed the involuntary nature of inspiration and their surviving oracles include pronouncements in the persona of the deity or the spirit. Tertullian carefully theorized their understanding of prophetic experience, most extensively in his treatise *De Anima* and in his lost *De Ecstasi*.[55] Early Christian writers of the succeeding two centuries disparaged the movement, ridiculing and reviling its members, and in the long run succeeded in putting them to rout and discrediting ecstatic experience as a means of revelation. Both ecstasy and the New Prophecy remained in disrepute until the twentieth century, when interest in the diversity of early Christianity began to take hold.

---

[55] For a careful exposition of his work, see Laura Nasrallah, *An Ecstasy of Folly: Prophecy and Authority in Early Christianity* HTS 32 (Cambridge: Harvard University Press, 2003), 95–154.

But their exclusion was by no means a foregone conclusion. Not all first-century Jews and Christians distinguished the theory and vocabulary of prophecy from the older language of madness and mantic inspiration or rejected it. Philo uses the word group *mant-* quite broadly and is able to claim inspired status for his own interpretations, announcing that his soul is accustomed to be god-seized and to prophesy (*manteuesthai*) "about things which it does not know" (*Cher* 27). Further, he is clearly aware that ancient prophets spoke with the voice and in the person of the deity (*Cher* 49). While he does not always represent *mania* as a good, he explains the best *ekstasis* as that of divine possession and *mania* for prophecy (*Her* 249) and opines that when the divine spirit arrives, the mind is unhoused (*Her* 264–65).[56] Although he does not refer to the Sibyl, he invokes the frenzy of the Bacchic rites as a sign of inspiration.[57] Similarly, the Sibyl who speaks the *Fourth Sibylline Oracle* uses the verb of her own prophetic speech (3) and claims that her prophecy is driven by a divine flail through her mind (18), an image evocative of inspired frenzy.[58] It might be objected that the Sibyl, while a prophet of the true God, is a gentile, and so such terminology and imagery is suitable for her. But the evidence from Philo suggests that at least some Jews could avail themselves of the ancient theory and vocabulary of prophetic possession.

In Paul's struggles to regulate spiritual manifestations without quenching the spirit, he spoke of prophecy as intelligible speech, spoken with, rather than out of, his mind. He argued for its superiority to tongues, or at it least its greater benefit to the other. Although he professed to prefer to speak "one word" with his mind rather than a thousand in a tongue, he still felt the need to thank God that he spoke in tongues (and apparently out of his mind) "more than all the rest of you" (1 Cor 14:18–19). He was willing to boast of a "human being in Christ who fourteen years ago—whether in the body or out of the body, I know not, God knows—was caught up to the third heaven...and heard inutterable utterances which it is not permitted to a human being

---

[56] Philo's treatment of ecstasy in *Who Is the Heir of Divine Things* is extensive and sophisticated; see Nasrallah's analysis of the taxonomy of altered states in Philo in *Ecstasy of Folly*, 36–44.

[57] *Somn* 2.1, *Migr* 35, *Opif* 71, *Her* 69, *Contemp* 12, 85.

[58] On the lash as symbol of frenzy and divine madness, see Walter Burkert, *Ancient Mystery Religions* (Cambridge: Harvard University Press, 1987), 104.

to speak" (2 Cor. 12:1–6). Paul's attempts to assert his authority with the Corinthians, to produce communal order and to promote the common good are not reducible to an argument for rationality rather than enthusiasm. Indeed, he claims "the mind of Christ" for the spiritual to whom have been revealed "what eye has not seen or ear heard" (1 Cor. 2:9–16).[59] At least in the first and early second centuries, then, specifically Jewish or Christian rejection of ecstatic aspects of prophetic experience does not seem to have solidified.

Considering the sobriety of Dio's prophet helps to set the question more explicitly into the political realities of the very late first and early second centuries—that is, the accession of Trajan and the political discourse it inspired. Here again, Pliny's *Panegyric* offers a helpful companion to Dio. Pliny's encomium is formed by contrasting Trajan to those who went before him, especially Domitian, and declaring him incomparable. In particular, Pliny insists that the reign of Domitian displayed his uncontrolled and dissolute character, and that hope for Trajan's principate rested upon his virtues, particularly his moderation and continence. Similarly, Dio begins his praise and instruction of Trajan by a more circumspect contrast between a bad ruler, who "is undisciplined and excessive, filled with mindlessness (*anoias*), pride, arrogance and all sorts of lawlessness" (12–13), and the good ruler Trajan will become. The man whom the elder woman describes to Dio as both strong and restrained is pious toward the gods, disciplined and in control of the passions, always concerned first for the benefit of his subjects, and devotes himself not to pleasure but to toil on their behalf (15–36). The contrast between the raging Sibyl Statius used to celebrate Domitian and the steady seer through whom Dio counsels Trajan echoes this contrast between bad and good ruler, not because Dio was familiar with Statius (though he may have been) but because he responded to the exigencies of Trajan's propaganda. The recent assassination of Domitian and attempted revolt against Nerva made for instability and insecurity; in this context, the serenity and strength of the instructor Dio offers Trajan promise that equal restraint and virtue on his part will ensure the stability of his principate.

While Dio can envisage a *Basileia* whose throne is stable, Hermas is conscious that the lord of "this city" may at any time decree that he

---

[59] See also Nasrallah, *Ecstasy of Folly*, esp. 91–94.

leave, because he does not live by that lord's laws, but by those of his own city. Instability and insecurity in this world are a constant expectation. But the Sibyl/Church who sits on a bench made stable by its four feet (*Vis* 3.13.3 [21]) is also the four-square tower of the *Visions* and *Similitudes*, whose stability comes from the labors of personified virtues, particularly *Enkrateia*.

Ancient Christian disparagement of the New Prophets took particular delight in displaying contempt for and suspicion of the women prophets of the movement. It is worth noting that Paul and Tertullian, both of whom assume the participation of women in prophecy, show considerable anxiety about the female person and especially of female hair.[60] Paul requires that women cover or control their hair when they pray or prophesy, apparently to avoid offending the attendant angels (1 Cor. 11:2–16). If 1 Cor. 14:34–35 is taken to be original to the letter, his ultimate goal is to exclude women from prophetic speech in the community.[61] Tertullian drives home the exigency of veiling both women and virgins, with an oracular dream visited upon one of the women prophets. An angel flogging the bare neck of the unhappy seer sarcastically praises its elegance and invites her to strip further. The flail that drives her inspiration has turned punitive and her angelic mediator has become a voyeur provoked by her indiscretion.[62]

The late first and early second centuries seem to have seen an expanded acknowledgment of women engaged in civic patronage similar to that of the principate of Augustus, and to have invited a

---

[60] See D'Angelo, "Veils, Virgins and the Tongues of Men and Angels: Women's Heads as Sexual Members in Ancient Christianity," in *Off with Her Head! The Denial of Women's Identity in Myth, Religion, and Culture*, ed. Howard Eilberg-Schwarz and Wendy Doniger (Berkeley, CA: University of California Press, 1995), 131–64; reprinted in *Women, Gender, Religion: A Reader*, ed. Elizabeth A. Castelli with assistance from Rosamond C. Rodman (New York: Palgrave, 2001), 389–419; reprinted in Arabic translation as "*Aghteiyat alru'uus, wa al'adhara, wa alsinat alrrijal wa almalaika: ru'uus alnnisaa fi almasihieya almobakira*," in *Gender and Religious Studies*. The Women and Memory Feminist Translation Series, ed. Omaima Abu Bakr (Giza, Egypt: Women and Memory Forum, 2012), 115–43.

[61] Antoinette Clark Wire has made this argument in *Corinthian Women Prophets: A Reconstruction Through Paul's Rhetoric* (Minneapolis: Fortress, 1990).

[62] Note Burkert's discussion of the strikingly similar image from the Villa of the Mysteries at Pompeii; see also D'Angelo, "Veils, Virgins," 151.

corresponding requirement for female probity, restraint, and chastity.[63] While neither Vespasian nor Titus had a consort during his reign and rumors of sexual transgression swirled around the relationship of Domitian and Domitia, both Trajan's wife Pompeia Plotina and sister, Ulpia Marciana, were prominent in his self-presentation. Dio does not mention either of the women, but Pliny makes them exemplars of the emperor's virtue and instruction, especially commenting upon Plotina's unassuming modesty of dress and manner, on her silent progress throughout the city, and on the harmonious and serene relations between the two women (*Pan* 83–84). The women intermediaries of Dio and *Hermas* similarly embody the values of composure, sanctity, and restraint. The Sibyl-Church in particular soothes the anxiety about sexual sin that Hermas manifests in the opening vision (and that he also articulates in *Mandate* 4). She bestows on him the epithet "The Abstinent" (*Enkratēs*; *Vis* 1.1–2.4). That is, the woman intermediaries embody the virtues their revelations enjoin.

Sober Sibyls were not definitive in the project of taming prophecy, especially prophetic women, though they were harbingers of things to come. The New Prophets were yet to make their stand; only after their defeat, ecstatic experience, experience of the spirit, had to be fit into new molds and made amenable to the rational. But divine guidance remained an issue; prophecy required affirmation of its authority, testimony that its revelation came from divine rather than human mind. Like their predecessors of the early Church and Middle Ages, the women prophets of the 16th–17th c., among them Benedetta Carlini, Maria Domitilla Galluzi, and Lucia Brocadelli da Narni, required extraordinary manifestations, visions, and revelations that overwhelmed the seers and were accompanied by levitation and stigmata. Nor were such manifestations a guarantee of universal acceptance; the suspicions that they aroused frequently attracted the attention of the ecclesiastical authorities, including the Inquisition, though they also were received among the pious (and in the case of Lucia Brocadelli, the powerful). Their fictional forebears in Dio and Hermas left to them the exigencies of female virtue, but their serene authority these real women could not share.

[63] Mary Taliaferro Boatwright, "Plancia Magna of Perge: Women's Roles and Status in Roman Asia Minor," in *Women's History and Ancient History*, ed. Sarah B. Pomeroy (Chapel Hill, NC: UNC Press, 1991), 242–78; Shelly Matthews, *First Converts: Rich Pagan Women and the Rhetoric of Mission in Early Christianity and Judaism* (Stanford: Stanford University Press, 2001).

CHAPTER 3

The Marian Apocalyptic of a Visionary Preacher: The *Conorte* of Juana de la Cruz, 1481–1534

Jessica A. Boon

In E. Ann Matter's seminal "Apparitions of the Virgin Mary in the Late Twentieth Century: Apocalyptic, Representation, Politics," she proposes that the typology of Marian apparitions shifted fundamentally following the apocalyptic messages provided at Fatima, Portugal, in the 1920s.[1] Not only was the Catholic world fascinated for decades with the contents of the third "secret" message of Our Lady of Fatima, revealed by the Vatican during the millennium year 2000 to be an apocalyptic vision, but nearly all apparitions since Fatima have had a far more emphatic apocalyptic tone than those that predated it, such as La Salette or Lourdes. Drawing in part on William Christian Jr.'s analysis of Spanish apparitions,

[1] E. Ann Matter, "Apparitions of the Virgin Mary in the Late Twentieth Century: Apocalyptic, Representation, Politics," *Religion* 31 (2001): 125–53.

My gratitude to Sarah J. Bloesch and Ronald E. Surtz for commenting on drafts of this chapter.

J. A. Boon (✉)
University of North Carolina—Chapel Hill, Chapel Hill, NC, USA

© The Author(s) 2019
E. Knibbs et al. (eds.), *The End of the World in Medieval Thought and Spirituality*, The New Middle Ages,
https://doi.org/10.1007/978-3-030-14965-9_3

which were most numerous during the late Middle Ages and after the Spanish Civil War in the 1930s, Matter argues that the apocalyptic quality of contemporary Marian apparitions can be traced to global political troubles, from the Cold War to America's culture wars to the internal Catholic struggle over the ramifications of Vatican II.

In this essay, I examine a case study from another era in which Matter specializes, the late medieval/early modern, a time in which apocalypticism, Marian apparitions, and political anxiety due to global crisis were also rampant. However, this case study focuses on a type of particular interest to Matter throughout her career: a female visionary whose preaching made her one of the 'living saints' found principally in late medieval Italy but also in late medieval Spain.[2] Mother Juana de la Cruz (1481–1534), abbess of a Clarisan convent outside Toledo, spoke publically for thirteen years, putatively channeling Jesus' voice through her raptured body.[3] The audience for Juana's *sermones* included the nuns of her convent, locals who revered her as a saint, and officials of the realm such as Archbishop Cisneros and Emperor Charles V. Her sermons, a liturgical year's worth of which are collected in the manuscript *El libro del conorte* (*The Book of Consolation*, hereafter, *Conorte*), narrate the events that Juana was in the midst of witnessing in heaven, usually the daily feasts celebrated by Jesus, the saints, and the beatified.[4] They

[2] Gabriella Zarri, "Living Saints: A Typology of Female Sanctity in the Early Sixteenth Century," in *Women and Religion in Medieval and Renaissance Italy*, ed. Daniel Bornstein and Roberto Rusconi (Chicago: University of Chicago Press, 1996), 219–304. For analysis of women religious in late medieval Spain, see Ángela Muñoz Fernández, *Beatas y santas neocastellanas: Ambivalencia de la religión y políticas correctoras del poder (ss XIV–XVII)* (Madrid: Comunidad de Madrid, 1994); for a more recent discussion of the living saints phenomenon in the Toledo area, see her "Santidad femenina, controversia judeoconversa y reforma (Sobre las agencias culturales en el reinado de los Reyes Católicos)," in *Modelos culturales y normas sociales al final de la Edad Media*, ed. Patrick Boucheron and Francisco Ruiz Gómez (Cuenca, Spain: Casa de Velázquez, 2009), 387–428, at 387–91, 423.

[3] For discussion of Juana's biographical details, see Ronald E. Surtz, *The Guitar of God: Gender, Power, and Authority in the Visionary World of Mother Juana de la Cruz (1481–1534)* (Philadelphia: University of Pennsylvania Press, 1990), 1–7; for her life and theology, see Jessica A. Boon, "Introduction," in *Mother Juana de la Cruz, 1481–1534: Visionary Sermons*, ed. Jessica A. Boon and Ronald E. Surtz (Toronto; Tempe: Iter Academic Press; Arizona Center for Medieval and Renaissance Studies, 2016), 1–33.

[4] Seventy-two of Juana's sermons were transcribed by fellow nuns in *El libro del conorte* (Madrid, Real Biblioteca del Monasterio, El Escorial J-II-18, early 1520s; a second copy is Archivio Segreto Vaticano, Congregazione Riti, MS 3074). First published in Juana de la Cruz, *El Conhorte: Sermones de una mujer. La Santa Juana (1481–1534)*, ed. Inocente

also include various allegorical pageants enacting important doctrinal or devotional points related to that day's liturgical feast as celebrated on earth. Angela Muñoz Fernández has proposed that Juana's visionary experience was a reimagining of the genre of dream journeys under the rubric of revelatory visionary experience; I would go further in highlighting that the apocalyptic tenor of dream journeys also deeply inflected Juana's visionary experience.[5]

Many of the pageants (*figuras*) in Juana's sermons provide at least one scene related to the end-times, depicting in graphic detail the hellish fate of sinners and of Jews and Muslims who resisted conversion, or the communal Last Judgment when Christ or his cross would render judgment on the souls reunited with their bodies. Some of the scenarios also reference figures from the Book of Revelation, or depict the angels and the Virgin Mary intervening in purgatory. I suggest that Juana's sermons combine apocalyptic genres that scholars often distinguish, yet which were collated together in influential apocalyptic texts published on the peninsula in her era such as Martinez d'Ampiés' *Libro del Antichristo* (Zaragoza, 1496).

Although Juana's sermons are generally classified as mystical visions that she first began publically sharing at the request of her guardian angel, Laruel, the other texts that Juana partially authored—her semiautobiography and a record book from her convent—affirm that throughout her life she received apparitions of the Virgin Mary, who regularly interacted with Juana and performed miracles both for Juana and for others on Juana's behalf.[6] This chapter thus proposes that Juana's blend

García de Andrés, 2 vols. (Madrid: Fundación Universitaria Española, 1999), usually known as *Conorte* (following the manuscript spelling of the title). Six are translated into English in *Mother Juana de la Cruz, 1481–1534: Visionary Sermons*, ed. Jessica A. Boon and Ronald E. Surtz, trans. Ronald E. Surtz and Nora Weinerth (Toronto; Tempe, AZ: Iter Academic Press; Arizona Center for Medieval and Renaissance Studies, 2016).

[5] "Tantas que cabe argumentar la emergencia de un nuevo modelo que transforma la tradición medieval de los viajes y visiones al Más Allá. Cambia el rigistro onírico por el tono oral de la revelación." Ángela Muñoz Fernández, "'Amonestando, alumbrando, y enseñando': Catolicidad e imaginarios del purgatorio en la Castilla bajomedieval," *La corónica* 41.1 (2012): 181–206, at 199.

[6] For Juana's guardian angel, Laruel, see *Libro de la casa*, fol. 20v, 25r. The "semiautobiography" collects miracles starting with her birth, but ends with those concerning the miraculous preservation of her corpse, thus Juana could not have authored the entire work. *Vida y fin de la bienabenturada virgen sancta Juana de la Cruz* (El Escorial, K-III-13,

of apocalyptic genres was also a type of "Marian apocalyptic," in which private Marian apparitions designated the seer as authoritative, yet her publically preached visions of the otherworld disseminated apocalyptic material.[7] Not only do these visions interweave interpretations of apocalyptic symbols with discussions of the fate of individual souls, but Mary herself is presented as an active agent in the otherworld, not simply interceding with Jesus but engaging the devil in battle. I argue that Mary as apocalyptic figure rather than apparitional message-bearer would have resonated strongly with Juana's Iberian audience, as not only had Mary long been a focal point of devotion during reconquest on the peninsula, but Castilian leaders attempting to establish an empire in the New World also frequently justified their endeavors through apocalyptic rhetoric.

1 Juana as Apocalyptic Preacher: Wrestling with Definitions of "Apocalyptic"

In parallel to the dynamics Matter identifies in the twentieth century, many hispanists have highlighted the apocalyptic mentality predominant in post-1492 Castile. Various scholars, including Alain Milhou and Geoffrey Parker, analyze the propaganda campaigns linking King Fernando of Aragon and Emperor Charles V to prophecies concerning the last emperor.[8] Jodi Bilinkoff examines the prophetic visionary

---

mid-1530s, hereafter, *Vida y fin*). A convent record book of devotions and visions attributed to Juana also survives, though in a later hand. *Libro de la casa y monasterio de Nuestra Señora de la Cruz* (Biblioteca Nacional de Madrid, MS 9661, late sixteenth century, hereafter, *Libro de la casa*).

[7] Matter notes that, in discussing the third secret of Fatima, Cardinal Ratzinger terms it a private revelation, in contrast to the first two secrets that were public revelations. Matter, "Apparitions," 131. I am arguing that Juana's private apparitions provided authority for her public apocalyptic sermons. This might provide a different subgenre of the type of "social or corporate apocalyptic mysticism" that McGinn proposes for Joachim in this volume, "Apocalypticism and Mysticism in Joachim of Fiore's *Expositio in Apocalypsim*."

[8] Alain Milhou, *Colón y su mentalidad mesianica en el ambiente franciscanista español* (Valladolid: Casa-Museo de Colón y Seminario Americanista de la Universidad, 1983); and Geoffrey Parker, "Messianic Visions in the Spanish Monarchy, 1516–1598," *Caliope* 8/2 (2002): 5–24. Both kings led crusades against Muslims, an apocalyptic approach to policy in the sense that they believed in the necessity of all converting to Christianity before the end-times could arrive, and because Muhammad was often designated as the Antichrist.

María de Santo Domingo's predictions of Cardinal Cisneros' victory in his campaign in Oran, suggesting that Cisneros may have understood his destiny to be the angelic pope the visionary had prophesized would reform the church.[9] Studies by John Phelan, Alain Milhou, and others consider in great detail the apocalyptic scenarios by which Christopher Columbus and Franciscan missionaries justified the conquest, particularly the identification of the New World as the New Jerusalem and the belief that converting the *indios* would prove one of the last events before the end of the world.[10] John Edwards and Richard Popkin trace a parallel concern in crypto-Jewish texts and Inquisition trials with both the end-times and the advent of a political Messiah. In fact, Popkin terms the entirety of the first half of the sixteenth century in Spain a "millenarian era," in contrast to the second half of the century, a "mystical era."[11]

Even though the first scholar to bring Juana to the attention of hispanists, Ronald E. Surtz, discusses several indications of Juana's understanding of the *Conorte* as itself a book of prophecies whose completion would usher in the end-times, to my knowledge Juana has never been

---

[9] Jodi Bilinkoff, "A Spanish Prophetess and Her Patrons: The Case of María de Santo Domingo," *Sixteenth Century Journal* 23.1 (1992): 21–34, at 31–34; she also discusses King Fernando's support of María on 27–30. There were still more apocalyptic movements during this era. In the early 1520s, the *communero* revolt in part intended to remake society in order to bring about the end-times, while some scholars emphasize the prophetic-apocalyptic approach of those accused of being *alumbrados*. Sara T. Nalle, "The Millennial Moment: Revolution and Radical Religion in Sixteenth-Century Spain," in *Toward the Millennium: Messianic Expectations from the Bible to Waco*, ed. Peter Schäfer and Mark Cohen (Leiden: Brill, 1998), 151–71; José C. Nieto, "The Franciscan *Alumbrados* and the Prophetic-Apocalyptic Tradition," *Sixteenth Century Journal* 8.3 (1977): 3–16.

[10] John Leddy Phelan, *The Millennial Kingdom of the Franciscans in the New World*, 2nd ed., rev. ed. (Berkeley: University of California Press, 1970); Milhou, *Colón y su mentalidad mesiánica*; see also Leonard I. Sweet, "Christopher Columbus and the Millennial Vision of the New World," *The Catholic Historical Review* 72.3 (1986): 369–82; and Melquiades Andrés Martin, "Desde el ideal de la conquista de Jerusalén al de la cristianización de América," *Mar Oceana: Revista del Humanismo Español e Iberoamericano* 9 (2001): 125–38.

[11] Richard H. Popkin, "Jewish Christians and Christian Jews in Spain, 1492 and After," *Judaism* 41.3 (1992): 248–67, at 266; John Edwards, "Elijah and the Inquisition: Messianic Prophecy Among Conversos in Spain, c. 1500," *Nottingham Medieval Studies* 28.1 (1984): 79–94. Note however Melvin's contribution to this volume, "Juan de Horozco y Covarrubias's *Tratado dela verdadera y falsa prophecia* (1588) and the Influence of Medieval Apocalyptic Traditions in Post-Tridentine Spain."

analyzed as one of the apocalyptic voices in early modern Spain.[12] I suggest that the reason for this oversight is a definition of apocalypticism by hispanists that narrows it to its political ramifications without considering the range of content normally labeled apocalyptic in the medieval era. Medieval apocalypticism as a genre in fact covers several categories of texts. The most famous genre, exegesis or prophecy based on the symbolism of the *Revelation*, 2nd Thessalonians, Daniel, and Isaiah that calculated the exact date of the advent of the Antichrist or identified particular political figures as portending the end-times, was popularized in medieval Spain by Arnau de Villanova, John of Rupescissa, and Vincent Ferrer.[13] The second genre of apocalypticism that combines a variety of topics under the rubric "last things," most often through the narrative device of visionary journeys through the otherworld, was featured in popular texts ranging from the *Apocalypse of Paul* to *St. Patrick's Purgatory* to Dante's *Commedia*.[14] This second category, which also

[12] Surtz, *Guitar of God*, 134–36, referencing sermon 72. One scholar describes sermon 65 as "almost apocalyptic" in tone, but does not consider it in relation to medieval apocalyptic texts. Muñoz Fernández, "Amonestando," 198.

[13] For a brief overview of Arnau de Villanova and Vincent Ferrer's predictions, see Bernard McGinn, *AntiChrist: Two Thousand Years of the Human Fascination with Evil* (San Francisco: Harper SanFrancisco, 1994), 78–79, 166–67. For further discussion of Villanova's apocalypticism, see J. Mensa i Valls, "¿Fue Arnau de Vilanova un profeta apocalíptico?" *Bulletin de Philosophie Médiévale* 38.1 (1996): 129–40. Rupescissa circulated in three Castilian manuscripts and various Latin ones for the entirety of the fifteenth century. José Guadalajara, *El Anticristo en la España medieval* (Madrid: Ediciones del Laberinto, S.L., 2004), 89–91; for general discussion, see Leah DeVun, *Prophecy, Alchemy, and the End of Time: John of Rupescissa in the Late Middle Ages* (New York: Columbia University Press, 2009). The premier volume on Ferrer's preaching in Spain, concentrating on his apocalyptic voice, is Pedro M. Cátedra, *Sermón, sociedad y literatura en la Edad Media: San Vicente Ferrer en Castilla (1411–1412)* (Valladolid: Consejería de Cultura y Turismo, 1994).

[14] McGinn discusses two types of Jewish apocalyptic that gave rise to this second Christian genre, one involving journeys to heaven and hell, the other conveying information about the end of history. McGinn, *AntiChrist*, 11. Bynum and Freedman define "last things" as ranging from individual judgment at the hour of death to apocalyptic scenarios. Caroline Walker Bynum and Paul Freedman, "Introduction," in *Last Things: Death and the Apocalypse in the Middle Ages*, ed. Caroline Walker Bynum and Paul Freedman (Philadelphia: University of Pennsylvania Press, 2000), 1–18, at 5. For a similar set of topics within late medieval Spanish apparitions specifically, see William A. Christian, Jr., *Apparitions in Late Medieval and Renaissance Spain* (Princeton, NJ: Princeton University Press, 1981), 4–8.

circulated in medieval Spain, focuses on the judgment of individuals at their death that consigns them to hell, purgatory, or heaven, long before the Last Judgment when souls reunited with their bodies will be delivered to permanent damnation or heavenly glorification.[15] As a result, texts narrating otherworld journeys could be considered as much moral as prophetic or apocalyptic. Yet the terror induced by contemplating the time that would be spent in hell or purgatory between the hour of death and the ultimate Last Judgment did as much to increase apocalyptic apprehension as did interpreting the political events of the day to be the fulfillment of biblical apocalyptic symbolism.[16]

Both of these approaches to the "last things" were popular during the sudden increase in apocalyptic fervor toward the end of the fifteenth century in Italy, and I argue that a similar mix can be found in late medieval Castile, including Juana's sermons.[17] Savonarola's influential sermons that drew on his visions of the end-times inspired a number of visionary women in Florence who recounted similar experiences; while certainly both Savonarola and his followers had strong political voices, it is important to recognize that their visions reimagined popular tropes from *both* categories of apocalyptic texts by providing details concerning

[15] For Castilian versions of *St. Patrick's Purgatory* and the *Vision of Tundal*, see María Eugenia Díaz Tena, "El *Otro mundo* en un milagro mariano del siglo XV," *Peninsula. Revista de Estudios Ibéricos* 2 (2005): 25–43, at 27. An early printed edition survives in the British Library: *La reuelacion de sant Pablo* (Seville: Meynardo Ungut, Stanislau Polono, 1494), BL Ia.52371. For the popularity of Dante in fifteenth-century Castile, see Teresa M. Bargetto-Andrés, ed. *Dante's Divina Comedia: Linguistic Study and Critical Edition of a Fifteenth-Century Translation Attributed to Enrique de Villena* (Newark: Juan de la Cuesta, 2010). For an early printed version, see *La traduccio[n] del Dante de lengua toscana en verso castellano*, trans. Pedro Fernandez del Villegas (Burgos: Fadrique Aleman de Basilea, 1515), at the Palacial Real library in Madrid, I/B/21. For a Castilian-authored duo of apocalyptic letters, see María Teresa Herrera, "Dos cartas apocalípticas en un manuscrito de la Universidad de Salamanca," in *Salamanca y su proyección en el mundo: Estudios históricos en honor de D. Florencio Marcos*, ed. Florencio Marcos Rodríguez and José Antonio Bonilla Hernández (Salamanca: Universidad de Salamanca, 1992), 637–42.

[16] For the distinction between moral and prophetic-apocalyptic readings and the terror induced by them, see José Guadalajara, "La venida del Anticristo: Terror y moralidad en la Edad Media hispánica," *Culturas Populares. Revista Electrónica* 4 (2007): 1–20.

[17] McGinn cites Italy and Germany principally, but of course this is true of Spain post-1492, as my previous paragraph indicates. Bernard McGinn, "Savonarola," in *Apocalyptic Spirituality: Treatises and Letters of Lactantius, Adso of Montier-en-Der, Joachim of Fiore, The Franciscan Spirituals, Savonarola*, ed. Bernard McGinn (New York: Paulist Press, 1979), 183–91, at 186.

the Antichrist while also narrating their own journeys through the otherworld to discover who would be saved, damned, or pass through purgatory.[18]

Other combinations of genres were also available to Juana, such as that found in a 1496 compilation by Martín Martínez d'Ampiés, the *Libro del Antichristo*, which contains four distinct texts.[19] The first and best-known of the texts (and the one from which the compilation takes its name) is a translation of Adso of Montier-en-Der's tenth-century *Libellus de antichristo*, which narrates the life of the Antichrist as a series of inverted parallels to the life of Christ (a particularly impure conception, preaching luxury as a goal, etc.). While some scholars differentiate this type of anti-hagiography concerning Antichrist's life from apocalyptic texts on the end-times, d'Ampiés certainly associated them, as the next text in the compilation is the *Libro del Judicio Postrimero* (*Book of the Last Judgment*) and its descriptions of the fifteen signs preceding the Last Judgment, such as the cross in the sky, the sun turning black, and the bloody moon.[20] This was a popular genre across Europe, often attributed to Saint Jerome, but Ampiés amplifies the discussion considerably based on patristic and medieval sources, with a sprinkling of original elements such as scientific descriptions of astronomical signs like eclipses and shooting stars.[21]

---

[18] See for example Savonarola's vision of the angels presenting stoles and crosses to souls; those who accepted them then survived the pestilence, war, and tribulations that followed. This occurs within the larger context of a journey through the otherworld, the framing of the entire *Compendium*. Girolamo Savonarola, "The Compendium of Revelations," in *Apocalyptic Spirituality: Treatises and Letters of Lactantius, Adso of Montier-en-Der, Joachim of Fiore, The Franciscan Spirituals, Savonarola*, ed. Bernard McGinn (New York: Paulist Press, 1979), 200; the more classical tropes of the journey through the otherworld occur from 241–70. This particular text by Savonarola did not circulate in Castile, though his sermon on *Miserere Mei* did.

[19] Critical (unpublished) edition in Patricia Claire Fagan, *A Critical Edition of Martín Martínez Dampiés's Libro del Antichristo, Zaragoza, 1496* (Ph.D. Dissertation, Boston University, 2001). Citations to Ampiés will give the folio of the 1496 edition and the page number from Fagan's critical edition. For a recent scholarly discussion, see Fernando Gómez Redondo, *Historia de la prosa de los reyes católicos: El umbral del Renacimiento* (Madrid: Ediciones Cátedra, 2012), 1:939–50.

[20] Fagan quotes Emmerson's differentiation of the "life of Antichrist" genre from other types of apocalyptic texts that detail the end days. Fagan, "Libro del Antichristo," *Critical Edition*, 39–40, citing Emmerson, 5–6.

[21] Ibid., fol. 38v, 188–89.

In various of her sermons, Juana raises points found in d'Ampiés' collection. For example, d'Ampiés pairs each of the fifteen signs that will appear before the Last Judgment with a particular vice, ranging from pride to murder to ecclesiastical laxity to the sins of their congregations.[22] Juana provides a parallel in a scenario of hell and purgatory in sermon 51, detailing a pageant put on by the beatified in heaven in which the classic seven vices are each punished on a different day of the week, with pointed critiques of ecclesiastical greed and sloth in particular.[23] This pageant of hell and purgatory is presented during a sermon on the holy cross, whose appearance in the sky is one of the traditional signs of the end-times according to Augustine, Chrysostom, and Amadeus Lausannensis.[24] In another example of d'Ampiés' influence on Juana, d'Ampiés offers an alternative to his Spanish contemporaries' critique of Jews and Muslims, asserting that evil Christians would fare worse at the Last Judgment than Jews or Moors, having knowingly rejected their obligations[25]; tellingly, Juana makes the same claim nearly word for word in her sermon on Epiphany.[26]

In addition to the blending of apocalyptic genres in works on "last things" in late medieval Spain and Italy, another common feature of popular apocalyptic narratives in this era is the role played by angels, who were the primary conveyers of visionary experience in the Book of Revelation (22). For example, Savonarola, his follower Jacopa de

---

[22] Ibid., fol. 44v, 211.

[23] *Conorte* II.51.1164–70. For another discussion combining the evil signs of the devil and criticism of prelates, see ibid., II.65.1343, 1349–52.

[24] Fagan, "Libro del Antichristo," 193 n. 625; fol. 40r, 194.

[25] "Que un mal christiano en el Día del Judicio havrá mayor pena que un moro ni judío ya conocidos por infieles, pues era más a Dios obligado," *Libro del judicio postrimero*, 37r (180). A portion of Ampiés' contemporaries would have agreed with this sentiment, particularly those in the "pro-*converso*" camp of the disputes over the possibility of true conversion from Judaism to Christianity, such as bishop Hernando de Talavera and Alonso de Oropesa. The "anti-*converso*" camp, including Alonso de Espina, would have denigrated both Jews and converts far more than sinful Christians, however. For an overview, see Bruce Rosenstock, *New Men: Conversos, Christian Theology, and Society in Fifteenth-Century Castile* (London: Department of Hispanic Studies, Queen Mary, University of London, 2002). Interestingly, Ampiés expanded the anti-Jewish and anti-Muslim elements in his translation of Adso, so it is also possible that he is not offering an alternative so much as using anti-Jewish and anti-Muslim sentiment to drastically underscore his critique of bad Christians.

[26] *Conorte* I.4.329.

Rondinelli, and Juana de la Cruz all cite their guardian angels as having a role in their prophecies or sermons.[27] Others address angels as a general theme, such as Lucia Brocadelli, whose manuscript was discovered by Matter, or the mid-fifteenth-century Castilian Franciscan reformer Lope de Salazar.[28] In a variation, Vincent Ferrer, the famous preacher traveling in Spain and Italy in the 1410s–1420s, was often called the "apocalyptic angel," as his listeners believed him to be an angel providing apocalyptic warnings.[29]

Juana, although encouraged by an angel in her preaching vocation, is unique among all these Italian and Spanish figures because her visions of the otherworld were not justified by the trope of a journey with a Christian or classical guide, as was typical of the genre.[30] Instead, the narrative device in her sermons is that Jesus is speaking, describing through an enraptured Juana what she was in the midst of witnessing. In other words, Juana does not appear as a character in the sermons, only the heavenly court does: unlike the texts of Dante, Savonarola, Brocadelli, and numerous others, we never hear Juana in dialogue with a guide, angels, Mary, or Jesus. Rather, we are presented with the denizens of the otherworld as they "really" exist for each other, not as a series of examples provided for a journeying visitor. This access to the quotidian afterlife may have been quite effective as apocalyptic rhetoric, as throughout the dialogue and pageants Juana emphasizes how deeply intertwined are the fates of individuals with the fate of the world.

[27] Savonarola, "Compendium," 254. Jacopa de Rondinelli, on of Savonarola's followers, is discussed in Tamar Herzig, *Savonarola's Women: Visions and Reform in Renaissance Italy* (Chicago: University of Chicago Press, 2008), 32–33. For Juana's guardian angel, Laruel, see Footnote 6.

[28] Brocadelli's text was published and translated by Matter in collaboration with Armando Maggi and Maiju Lehmijoki-Gardner. Brocadelli's seven voyages to heaven include multiple interactions with angels. Lucia Brocadelli, "Seven Revelations," in *Dominican Penitent Women*, ed. Maiju Lehmijoki-Gardner (New York: Paulist Press, 2005), 212–43. Recently, a scholar has published a manuscript containing a revelation by an angel to Lope de Salazar in the mid-fifteenth century. Juan Miguel Valero Moreno, "La revelación à Lope de Salazar," *Estudios Humanísticos. Filología* 32 (2010): 105–39.

[29] Laura Ackerman Smoller, *The Saint and the Chopped-Up Baby: The Cult of Vincent Ferrer in Medieval and Early Modern Europe* (Ithaca, NY: Cornell University Press, 2014), 95.

[30] Closer to home than Dante, the thirteenth-century Castilian poet Gonzalo Berceo's last work described Mary as his guide on a journey through the heavens. Gonzalo de Berceo, "Poema de Santa Oria," in *Vida de Santo Domingo de Silos; Poema de Santa Oria*, ed. Aldo Ruffinatto (Madrid: Espasa Calpe, 1992), 179–216.

An example from Juana will serve to give an initial sense of her blending of the two types of apocalyptic material, political and otherworldly. In the midst of a sermon for Pentecost, Juana pauses to justify the possibility of Christian visionary experience in general (and consequently, her own authority to preach). Describing the tongues of fire sent by the Holy Spirit down upon the disciples, she (or rather, Jesus) explains that each disciple received different visions at that moment. Some of the disciples saw Jesus at the right hand of the Father, some saw the Last Judgment, while John saw what he would later write in the Book of Revelation. All also witnessed the particular martyrdom each was fated to endure.[31] The combination of visions granted to the disciples—the contents of the Apocalypse, the individual deaths of the disciples, and the communal fate awaiting souls at the Last Judgment—are the three principal topics interwoven throughout the history of medieval apocalyptic; according to Juana's sermon on Pentecost, then, the Holy Spirit provided fiery apocalyptic visions to *all* the disciples at Pentecost, not just to John. Not only does this passage provide an implicit parallel between the apostles' right to speak based on what they saw and Juana's right to be in leadership based on her visionary experience, but it also situates the apocalyptic material in the last book of the New Testament as one among many types of visionary experience about the end of the world and the fate of souls.[32]

While most scholars have focused on the political impact of late medieval and early modern apocalyptic thinkers based on specific apocalyptic prophecies directed at local Italian and Castilian rulers by visionaries and preachers, I suggest that such a direct connection to politics is not the only marker of a powerful apocalyptic voice. Juana deploys symbolism from the Book of Revelation and medieval predictions concerning the Antichrist in the midst of dramatic scenes of purgatory and the salvation of individuals, all part of festivals put on in heaven for the saints and

---

[31] *Conorte* II.25.826.

[32] I read the following quotation as authorizing Juana's experience of seeing what Jesus used her voice to describe. "And Jesus said: The divine mercy ordained that the disciples would be enraptured in this way, so that they would first see all that they would say and announce to the world. Because no one can be a true witness if s/he does not first see what s/he says and affirms." "Que ordenó la divina clemencia que los discípulos fuesen así arrobados, porque, todo lo que dijesen y anunciasen al mundo, lo hubiesen visto primero. Porque, ninguno puede ser verdadero testigo, si no ve, primero, lo que dice y afirma." *Conorte* II.25.826.

angelic hosts. Thus, her apocalyptic preaching in early sixteenth-century Castile is not only concerned with predicting the end of the world or the triumph of Spanish Christendom, but also provides a vibrant sequence of depictions of the otherworld to teach congregants about the lure of heavenly joys and the terrors of purgatory and hell. Reading Juana's two most traditionally apocalyptic sermons in the next section will give a sense of her integration of several genres of apocalyptic material, in the interests of helping scholars of late medieval and early modern Spain recognize that in this era apocalyptic thinkers regularly connected the political (reading the signs of the end-times) to the personal (questions of individual salvation and the Last Judgment).

2 Sermons on the End-Times

Juana has two sermons in *Conorte* which, by their titles, appear to reflect the focus on prophecies of the end-times and the details of the apocalypse that hispanists argue make the early decades of the sixteenth century a "millennial moment." One of these, sermon 69, is quite straightforwardly a reflection on Revelation 6: during the three days before the Last Judgment, souls will reunite with their bodies while crying and howling, birds will screech, the trees rain blood. The sun will become black like sackcloth, the moon will turn bloody, and stars will rain down. The Last Judgment will follow, which will also take three days because there are so many sinners to condemn.[33] In the midst of this brief exegesis, Juana insists on the salvific effect of devotion to Jesus' wounds, without which no one can be saved; in fact, Jesus even forces the sight of his wounds on sinners during the Last Judgment before condemning them.[34] Juana thus integrates this literal reading of Revelation

---

[33] *Conorte* II.69.1408.

[34] Ibid., 1411. Frescoes of the Last Judgment first commissioned in Spain as early as the thirteenth century depicted Christ showing his wounds at the Last Judgment; the most famous image produced closer to Juana's era is the ceiling fresco in the Cathedral of Salamanca. See Fig. 1. For a discussion of the first such scene in Castile, see Lucía Sánchez Domínguez, "La Gloria de María entre el Cielo y el Infierno. Revisión de la iconografía de la Puerta de la Majestad de la Colegiata de Toro. Fray Juan Gil de Zamora ¿posible autor del programa?" in *La catedral de León en la Edad Media*, ed. Joaquín Yarza Luaces, María Victoria Herráez Ortega, and Gerardo Boto Varela (León: Universidad de León, 2004), 637–48, at 638–39.

Fig. 1 *Last Judgment*. Nicolas Florentino, ca. 1445, Old Cathedral, Salamanca (Photo credit Jessica A. Boon)

6 with the Passion spirituality that became highly popular in Castile in the last quarter of the fifteenth century.[35]

In sermon 66, "which treats some proclamations and signs that our Lord Jesus Christ spoke and explained about the prophecies and signs which will be and appear before the day of the Last Judgment," however, Juana moves beyond direct exegesis to provide an apocalyptic amalgamation that would have been recognizable to a Castilian audience familiar

---

[35] See Muñoz Fernández, "Amonestando," 195 for discussion of this same point in sermon 30. For the late arrival of Passion spirituality to the peninsula, see Cynthia Robinson, *Imagining the Passion in a Multiconfessional Castile: The Virgin, Christ, Devotions, and Images in the Fourteenth and Fifteenth Centuries* (University Park: Pennsylvania State Press, 2013); Pedro M. Cátedra, *Poesía de pasión en la Edad Media: El Cancionero de Pero Gómez de Ferrol* (Salamanca: Seminario de Estudios Medievales y Renacentistas, 2001), 191–297; and Jessica A. Boon, "The Agony of the Virgin: The Swoons and Crucifixion of Mary in Sixteenth Century Castilian Passion Treatises," *Sixteenth Century Journal* 38 (2007): 3–26.

with works like d'Ampiés *Libro del Antichristo*.[36] The first paragraph of sermon 66 includes two types of apocalyptic, for Jesus mentions in the first sentence both the advent of the Antichrist and the signs of the end-times (sun, moon, and stars) described in Luke 21:25 and Revelation 6:12–13 and linked in d'Ampiés' compilation.[37] Yet Juana goes further than d'Ampiés, for she connects the Antichrist and the Last Judgment to questions of individual salvation. She identifies the heaven in which the sun, moon, and stars reside as a symbol for every faithful person: just as the sky is adorned by multiple stars as well as a sun and moon, so every person is adorned by a soul (sun), body (moon), and multiple limbs, forms of intelligence, and powers of the soul (stars), not to mention multiple gifts and treasures given by the Holy Spirit.[38] By reinscribing the Book of Revelation's reference to the sun, moon, and stars as an allegory for the individual, Juana can then reinterpret Revelation 6:12–13 not as a prophecy for the end-times but instead as the scenario that every person must face at death. At death, the soul/sun is covered in sackcloth, i.e., loses its clarity and light from anguish over its sin. The body is represented by the moon covered in blood because the body suffers so much pain at death, a pain felt in all the joints of the body. Juana goes on to describe death as a form of childbirth—bodies are pregnant with souls while alive, dying is the pain of childbirth, sinful souls end up miscarried rather than having new life.[39]

In other words, in sermon 66, Juana interprets the signs from Revelation 6 not as an end of the world scenario but instead as applicable to the individual judgment rendered at the end of every lifetime. It is notable that in early Christianity, some authors, including Augustine, had resisted the "external" reading of apocalyptic passages as a sequence of events that would be experienced by all at a specified future data, but

---

[36] "Que trata de algunas declaraciones y figuras que nuestro Señor Jescristo habló y declaró sobre las profecías y señales que han de ser y aparecer antes del día del Juicio Final." *Conorte* II.66.1359. The editor of the first published edition names the sermon simply "Prophecies and signs that announce the end of the world" ("Profecías y señales que anunciaran el fin del mundo"). Ibid., 1357.

[37] "Hablando el Señor de la venida del Antecristo y de la declaración del Evangelio que dice: *Dijo Jesús a sus discípulos serán señales en el sol y la luna y estrellas, dijo que estas cosas y señales....*" Ibid., 1359.

[38] Ibid., 1360.

[39] Ibid., 1361.

rather interpreted references to apocalyptic symbols of evil as designating the status of every person who dared to sin against God.[40] Early Christian authors had considered these two approaches mutually exclusive; Juana instead combines them.

However, Juana's unique (as far as I know) identification of these astrological signs does not reposition Revelation 6 or any other apocalyptic theme solely in relation to the salvation or loss of particular souls. Instead, she immediately turns to the other aspect of the dual theme she had announced in the first paragraph, presenting an allegorical pageant about the Antichrist performed by the blessed and angels in heaven. Typically, medieval narratives had depicted the Antichrist as either an evil ruler or a false Messiah particularly appealing to the Jews.[41] In fifteenth-century Castile, some popular texts such as the one translated by Ampiés had described the Antichrist as beautiful, therefore difficult to identify as evil (allowing him greater opportunity to tempt sinners). Another Castilian text, however, the *Libro de los grandes hechos* (*Book of Great Events*) attributed to Juan Unay, shows the Antichrist as terrifyingly ugly, poorly dressed, and constantly causing chaos.[42]

In Juana's version, the Antichrist appears as a rich, crowned, yet ugly and bad-tempered king who promises temporal riches, a warning against wealth that Juana intends to fall particularly heavily on greedy prelates and laypersons.[43] Despite the Antichrist's attempts to claim himself as the Messiah,[44] he is so hideous and terrifying that he does not appeal to the Jews, who convert because they find Jesus much preferable as a Messiah.[45] The converts prove to have made a wise choice, as the Antichrist gives those who follow him over to the devil. This detail is particularly interesting, as starting in the thirteenth century, Jews had

---

[40] McGinn, *AntiChrist*, 77–78. For discussion of the theme of last judgment in Augustine, see Cardman's essay, "Risen to Judgment: What Augustine Saw," in this volume.

[41] Ibid., 65.

[42] Guadalajara, *El Anticristo en la España medieval*, 137–38. Unay specifically identifies King Fernando as the last emperor, so this is a distinctly Castilian text. Ibid., 131. For further discussion of both authors, see María Isabel Toro Pascua, "Imagen y función del Anticristo en algunos textos castellanos del siglo XV," Vía *spíritus* 6 (1999): 27–63, at 43–63.

[43] *Conorte* II.66.1364–6.

[44] He is the inverse of Jesus in the sense that Jesus is fully divine, fully human, while the Antichrist is part demon, part man. Ibid., 1370.

[45] Ibid., 1368.

been depicted as natural followers of the Antichrist, an anti-Jewish trope that appeared in the woodcuts in Ampiés' text.[46] According to Juana, however, the Antichrist's ugliness serves to bring about the final conversion of Jews to Christianity, a necessary step before the end-times and one quite familiar to Juana's contemporaries, who interpreted the indigenous peoples of the New World as the lost Jewish tribes whom they could convert to bring about the end-times.[47]

To reinforce the horror produced by the Antichrist, Juana describes him as fighting with John the Evangelist (the presumed author of Revelation), beheading him and ripping his body apart, then fighting figures from the Old Testament, Elijah and Noah.[48] Antichrist ascends to the right hand of the Father, who sends angels to cast him down to hell as they had cast Satan at the beginning of time.[49] After Antichrist's followers repent, John's body is miraculously put back together, a process that greatly improved it, as, among other things, his voice can be heard over league away with the sound of seven voices instead of one.[50] Antichrist's fall and John's miraculous healing are a warning, according to Juana, of the dangers of falling into the darkness of heresy rather than following the light of the church.

Ultimately, in sermon 66, Juana connects the fates of individuals at the moment of entry into the afterlife with the apocalyptic role of the church in providing light to the faithful, by means of an end-times scenario so horrifying that even the Jews would convert. As a contribution to studies of the apocalyptic mentality in post-1492 Castile which scholars have identified primarily in relation to the expansion of empire, I propose that the topic of apocalypticism can (and should) just as easily take us to a consideration of the Last Judgment and the salvation or damnation of souls as to politics, revolution, and conquest. Juana's thinking

---

[46] Debra Higgs Strickland, "Antichrist and the Jews in Medieval Art and Protestant Propaganda," *Studies in Iconography* 32 (2011): 1–50, at 2–8. Dots intended to be the mark of the Antichrist appear on the foreheads of the Jews throughout Ampiés' compilation, as noted by Fagan, "Libro del Antichristo," 30.

[47] Jonathan Boyarin, *The Unconverted Self: Jews, Indians, and the Identity of Christian Europe* (Chicago: University of Chicago Press, 2009), 132–64.

[48] *Conorte* II.66.1370–1.

[49] From Adso on (and thus included in Ampiés' translation), Archangel Michael was understood to be the one who would vanquish the Antichrist. McGinn, *AntiChrist*, 118.

[50] *Conorte* II.66.1371.

in relation to such figures as the Antichrist cannot be separated from her understanding of the fate of individual souls, the role of Satan and demons in damnation, or the Last Judgment.

The rest of this chapter will argue that, like the contemporary trend that Matter identifies after the apparitions at Fatima, the Virgin Mary's role as an apocalyptic figure in medieval Europe generally and medieval Castile specifically was a crucial element of Juana's apocalypticism. Given that Juana's own authority was grounded in large part on her reception of Marian apparitions, personal experience gave her authorizing justification for apocalyptic claims ranging from individual salvation after death to the application of apocalyptic exegesis to contemporary politics.

3 Marian Apocalyptic

While sermon 66 makes the most explicit use of apocalyptic motifs ranging from the Antichrist through quotations of Revelation 6 to the afterlife awaiting individual sinners, an apocalyptic tenor runs throughout *Conorte*. Multiple sermons provide allegorical pageants of heaven, hell, and/or purgatory, at various points referencing the Last Judgment, the battle between Saint Michael and Lucifer, or angelic intervention in purgatory to rescue souls.[51] Rather than analyze every one of Juana's representations of the otherworld, I will concentrate on one sermon that integrates her vision of the "last things" with her Marian devotion. First, however, it is necessary to review the medieval Iberian devotion to the Virgin that held such primacy in the life of Juana and her convent and to examine the variety of medieval texts that rendered Mary an apocalyptic figure in many contexts beyond apparitions.

During the centuries of the Christian reconquest of Iberia from the Muslims, Mary's miraculous interventions into battles, protection of converts, and punishment of "recalcitrant" Jews and Muslims made her a central, if not the primary, figure in Spanish Christianity. Every mosque in conquered regions was repurposed into a shrine to the Virgin, and the popular miracle collections *Cantigas de Santa María* and *Miraglos de Nuestra Señora* emphasized in verse and illustration Mary's active

---

[51] For extensive descriptions of hell and/or purgatory, see sermons 1, 14, 15, 24, 25, 30, 40, 51, 56, 57, 65, 66, and 69. In these sermons, heaven is often an explicit contrast, but given that nearly every sermon recounts the feasts and pageantry occurring in heaven, celestial descriptions abound throughout *Conorte*.

punishment of non-Christians. As Amy Remensnyder's recent work on the influence of medieval Iberian Marian ideals on the conquest of the New World makes clear, Spaniards understood Mary in large part as *la conquistadora*.[52] As far as I am aware, however, no scholar has linked the centrality of Mary in the devotional life of the conquistadors and missionaries to the New World with the prophetic-apocalyptic strand of political thought foundational to their conception of conquest. I suggest that close analysis of Juana lets us do exactly that.

Juana maintained a special relationship with Mary throughout her life, as I have detailed elsewhere, marked by regular direct interactions with the Virgin.[53] Briefly, Juana's convent had originally been established as a *beaterio*, María de la Cruz, after a young girl received six apparitions of the Virgin and had her hand paralyzed into a sign of the cross for a brief period of time. At the beginning of Juana's semiautobiography, she narrates that she was miraculously changed in the womb by God from male to female, in response to Mary's request that someone restore the *beaterio* to its original importance.[54] Throughout her life at María de la Cruz, Juana was a regular recipient of visits from Mary (who appeared herself or spoke through some of the many Marian images throughout the convent), all aiding Juana in her rapid progress toward higher authority in her convent. She would eventually preside over the change in status from *beaterio* to Clarisan convent, and be its abbess until the end of her life except for one year. The other nuns often requested Juana to pass on messages to Mary on their behalf; Juana thus became an intercessor with the holiest of intercessors. Nor was Mary's intervention only on an individual level: both the semiautobiography and the convent record book recount Mary's descent to bless the fields of the convent, providing a feast day not only for the nuns but also for souls in purgatory who were

---

[52] This paragraph summarizes the compelling argument of Amy G. Remensnyder, *La Conquistadora: The Virgin Mary at War and Peace in the Old and New Worlds* (Oxford: Oxford University Press, 2014).

[53] This paragraph draws from Jessica A. Boon, "Mother Juana de la Cruz: Marian Visions and Female Preaching," in *A New Companion to Hispanic Mysticism*, ed. Hilaire Kallendorf (Leiden: Brill, 2010), 127–48, at 138–42, based on episodes found in *Vida y fin*, fols. 1v–12r, and *Libro de la casa*, fols. 40v–52v. For a discussion of convents and Marian devotion in an apocalyptic frame, see the contribution of Zarri, "The City Coming Down Out of Heaven (Rev. 21:10): Bologna as Jerusalem," to this volume.

[54] *Vida y fin*, fol. 2v.

able to attend the festivities and thus be briefly relieved of their sufferings.[55] While the sermons of *Conorte* privilege the figure of Jesus as narrator, it is clear from the semiautobiography and the convent record book that Juana's own devotional life, her authority in the eyes of her fellow nuns, and much of her visionary experience of Jesus (including marrying Jesus after Mary brokered the betrothal) were rooted in a long series of private Marian apparitions and miraculous interventions.[56]

In William Christian Jr.'s famed study of late medieval Spanish apparitions, including the ones that led to the foundation of Juana's *beaterio*, he suggests that most Marian apparitions were tinged with apocalypticism, as Mary usually appeared surrounded by a bright light in accordance her role as the Woman of the Sun in Revelation 12.[57] This point is worth some expansion, given Juana's reception of Marian apparitions: Mary as an apocalyptic symbol or agent had significant precedents in the Middle Ages in both types of apocalyptic texts, i.e., descriptions of otherworld voyages and exegesis of biblical prophecies. An example of the former is a textual tradition found primarily in the Eastern church of the *Apocalypse of Mary* (fifth century), which describes Mary's own voyage through heaven and hell, ending with her sorrow over the damned and her intercession on their behalf.[58] For the latter, the Virgin was also a prominent figure in exegesis of the Book of Revelation, on the Iberian peninsula and elsewhere. As Matter among others has identified, the early medieval Spanish *Beatus* tradition of illustrated commentaries melded the Song of Songs with the Book of Revelation.[59] From the *Beatus* tradition

[55] *Vida y fin*, 112r, and *Libro de la casa*, 35r.

[56] For the wedding between Juana and Jesus, see *Vida y fin*, fols. 26v–27r. An interesting comparison can be found in the late medieval Italian mystic Suor Domenica da Paridisio's assertion that she was able to establish a convent for non-elite women due to the direct monetary contribution of the Virgin Mary. Meghan Callahan, "Suor Domenica da Paradiso as *alter Christus*: Portraits of a Renaissance Mystic," *Sixteenth Century Journal* 43.2 (2012): 323–50, at 327.

[57] Christian, *Apparitions*, 7.

[58] Translated in Emmanouela Grypeou and Juan Pedro Monferrer-Sala, "'A Tour of the Other World': A Contribution to the Textual and Literary Criticism of the 'Six Books Apocalypse of the Virgin'," *Collectanea Christiana Orientalia* 6 (2009): 115–66, at 128–31.

[59] E. Ann Matter, "The Apocalypse in Early Medieval Exegesis," in *The Apocalypse in the Middle Ages*, ed. Richard K. Emmerson and Bernard McGinn (Ithaca, NY: Cornell University Press, 1992), 38–50, at 46. For discussion of the last flowering of the *Beatus* tradition in the high Middle Ages in Castilian Cistercian convents, see John Williams, "Introductory Essay," in *Visions of the End in Medieval Spain: Catalogue of Illustrated Beatus Commentaries on the Apocalypse and Study of the Geneva Beatus*, ed. Therese Martin

onward, iconography of Mary often included the sun, moon, and twelve-star crown even in non-apocalyptic contexts, such as *Books of Hours*.[60] These planetary symbols were likewise central to the Spanish avocation to María de los Angeles (Mary of the Angels) popularized in the late fifteenth century, images that are often difficult to distinguish from the later iconography of the Immaculate Conception standardized on the peninsula in the seventeenth century.[61]

In the later Middle Ages, Marian apocalyptic was also available in sermon form, providing further precedent for considering Juana's sermons as contributing to an apocalyptic genre. Most popular apocalyptic preachers, such as John of Rupescissa, were also devotees of Mary, but often preached on her separately from apocalyptic topics.[62] Savonarola, however, sought a direct audience with the Virgin as the highest goal of his journey through the celestial city; his first description as he finally approaches her is that she was seated on a throne, clothed with the sun and covered with jewels.[63] For that matter, Vincent Ferrer, the premier apocalyptic preacher of the early fifteenth century in southern Europe, opened one of his sermons predicting the imminent birth of Antichrist in Castile with the medieval miracle tale (included in works such as Voragine's *Golden Legend*) in which Mary intercedes with Jesus to delay the apocalypse so that the newly founded mendicant orders could

(Amsterdam: University of Amsterdam Press, 2017), 21–56. It was also Matter's work on the Song of Songs that brought to scholarly attention the high medieval interest in the Song of Songs as a Marian text more broadly, and the integration in Latin texts of Marian readings of the Song of Songs with Marian readings of the Apocalypse more specifically. E. Ann Matter, *The Voice of My Beloved: The Song of Songs in Western Medieval Christianity* (Philadelphia: University of Pennsylvania Press, 1990), 106–11. Matter suggests that both the Book of Revelation and Song of Songs lent themselves especially well to allegorical readings about the status of the Church as institution.

[60] Michael Camille, "Visionary Perception and Images of the Apocalypse in the Later Middle Ages," in *The Apocalypse in the Middle Ages*, ed. Richard K. Emmerson and Bernard McGinn (Ithaca, NY: Cornell University Press, 1992), 276–89, at 280–81.

[61] Rafael García García Mahíques, "Perfiles iconográficos de la mujer del apocalypsis como símbolo mariano (I): *Sicut mulier amicta sole et luna sub pedibus eius*," *Ars Longa* 6 (1995): 187–97, at 189–92. For discussion of the centrality of Spanish painters in the rise of Immaculate Conception iconography, see Suzanne L. Stratton, *The Immaculate Conception in Spanish Art* (Cambridge: Cambridge University Press, 1994).

[62] André Vauchez, *Saints, prophètes, et visionnaires: Pouvoir surnaturel au Moyen Age* (Paris: Albin Michel, 1999), 123.

[63] Savonarola, "Compendium," 256.

convert more souls before the end-times.[64] Based on yet another sermon by Vincent Ferrer, fifteenth-century Castilians developed a unique twist on Mary's direct role in the salvation of souls after their death, a devotion which then spread throughout Europe. In this devotion, Jesus did not just appear to Mary first after his death, a common if apocryphal belief, but indeed he presented to her at that moment the souls he had just rescued from limbo during the Harrowing of Hell.[65] Some authors went even further, suggesting that Mary was a direct intercessor during this episode, not just the recipient of the souls after the fact.

Not surprisingly, given Juana's relationship with Mary, the Virgin is a central figure in Juana's apocalypticism, and indeed she depicts Mary as intervening in purgatory to vie with demons over souls in the afterlife and ultimately even as Satan's conqueror in sermon 57, which is worth examining as a premier example of her Marian apocalyptic.[66] According to the sermon, three days after the feast of Archangel Michael (revered as the vanquisher of Satan in the original fall of the rebel angels), a second battle between angels and devils occurred. This second scene is not prompted by the fallen angels' pride, however, as the first battle had been, but, extraordinarily, as a reaction against Jesus' overwhelmingly possessive

[64] Toro Pascua, "Imagen y función del Anticristo," 27–43.

[65] Jesus was believed to have arrived either at Calvary where she was grieving at the foot of the cross or at her bedroom after she left the tomb, with the souls in tow. James D. Breckenridge, "'Et Prima Vidit': The Iconography of the Appearance of Christ to His Mother," *The Art Bulletin* 39.1 (1957): 9–32.

[66] Ronald E. Surtz and Angela Muñoz Fernández have analyzed Juana's own interventions in the otherworld, as she recounts in her semiautobiography that she began to actively aid orphaned souls by taking physical pain on herself to reduce the pain undergone in purgatory. Juana specifies that she aids souls whose families had died out and cannot pray for them. *Vida y fin*, fols. 99v–102v. These episodes are the focus of Surtz, *Guitar of God*, 37–62; and discussed as part of her analysis of the six sermons on purgatory by Muñoz Fernández, "Amonestando," 181–206. Newman references Juana as an extreme case of the type of purgatorial intervention periodically claimed by medieval women mystics such as Mechthild of Magdeburg and Margery Kempe, who often enumerated the thousands of souls they had saved. Barbara Newman, *From Virile Woman to WomanChrist: Studies in Medieval Religion and Literature* (Philadelphia: University of Pennsylvania Press, 1995), 121–22. This trope was common in late medieval Italy, especially in narratives concerning Catherine of Siena, Stefana Quinzani, and Lucia de Brocadelli. Cordelia Warr, "Performing the Passion: Strategies for Salvation in the Life of Stefana Quinzani (d. 1530)," *Studies in Church History* 45 (2009): 218–27, at 220. On the Iberian peninsula, María Ajofrín (1455?–1489) described being taken through purgatory by an angelic guide. Muñoz Fernández, "Amonestando," 189.

relationship to Mary.[67] The sermon begins with Jesus describing Mary's beauty and physical perfection.

> And Our Lord Jesus Christ said…My beloved [Mary] is the most lovely and completed and perfected [one] in all of heaven.… My beloved is very white and blonde and blushing, and has very beautiful and shapely feet, and very sweet-smelling and resplendent breasts, and a long very white throat, and a red-lipped sweet mouth, and tiny white teeth, and very beautiful and iridescent eyes.[68]

The angels had wanted to have Mary among them to enjoy her beauty on this particular feast day, but Jesus refuses to share Mary with them, wanting to keep her for his own delight. In response, the angels decide to issue a new challenge to the demons by attempting to rescue souls trapped in purgatory,[69] calculating that they would not be able to win a

[67] I discuss this scene in relation to gender fluidity and angelology in "At the Limits of (Trans)Gender," *Journal of Medieval and Early Modern Studies* 48.2 (2018): 261–300, at 276–78.

[68] Jesus is actually speaking to Mary, describing the most beautiful woman he knows and only after several paragraphs making it clear that she is his mother. "Y nuestro Señor Jesucristo dijo….Mi amiga es la más linda y acabada y perfecta que hay en todo el cielo… Mi amiga es muy blanca y rubia y colorada, y tiene los pies muy lindos y entalladas, y tetas muy olorosas y resplandecientes, y la garganta sacada y muy blanca, y la boca muy colorada y dulce, y los dientes menudos y blancos, y los ojos muy hermosos y pintados," *Conorte* II.57.1230–31.

[69] Voragine popularized the belief that angels could intervene in purgatory to alleviate suffering or rescue souls. Philip C. Almond, *The Devil: A New Biography* (Ithaca, NY: Cornell University Press, 2014), 61; see also Muñoz Fernández, "Amonestando," 183. That the belief was known on the peninsula is clear from its appearance in a translation of William of Paris' *Postillas super epistolas et evangelia* by Ambrosio de Montesino in 1512; the "sermon de los finados" references angelic visitation to those trapped in purgatory. The 1535 edition is in the Biblioteca Nacional de Madrid, R/40380: Ambrosio de Montesino, *Epistolas y euangelios por todo el año: Con sus doctrinas y reformas* (Toledo: Juan de Ayala, 1535), 236v–39v. This belief influenced the genre of *artes de bien morir* (*Arts of Good Death*) that first became popular in late fifteenth-century Castile. For example, the first *arte* published on the peninsula alternates in ten of its eleven chapters between describing temptations by devils and counsels of good angels to relieve future pain. "Arte de bien morir," in *Arte de bien morir y Breve confesionario* (Zaragoza, Pablo Hurus: c. 1479–1484), ed. Francisco Gago Jover (Barcelona: Medio Maravedí, 1999), 81–119. I do not draw extensively on this literature in my analysis of Juana, since the first original Castilian *arte de bien morir* did not appear until three years after Juana's death, Alejo Venegas' *Agonía del transito de la muerte*. For discussion of the dissemination of *artes* before 1537, see Ildefonso Adeva Martín, "Los 'artes de bien morir' en España antes del maestro Venegas," *Scripta Theologica* 16.1–2 (1984): 405–15; for a broader discussion of Castilian views of death,

second time without aid and expecting that Jesus would have to release Mary so that she could assist them.[70] This intriguing angelic assumption may refer to a medieval Carmelite belief that Mary descends into purgatory on Saturdays to save souls, a view supposedly ratified by a mythical "Sabbatine bull" issued by Pope John XXII in 1322 and declared heretical in 1617.[71]

An extended scene ensues, in which the angels fly down in sets of four to rescue groups of souls, all the while picking fights with the demons and calling them terrible names.[72] The demons turn to Lucifer to aid them, yet Lucifer is tied down by a gigantic rope, so they spend seven years tearing away his bonds (meanwhile, the angels keep removing souls).[73] Once he is free, we discover that Lucifer is once again the

---

including beliefs concerning who might intercede for them in the afterlife, see Carlos Eire, *From Madrid to Purgatory: The Art and Craft of Dying in Sixteenth-Century Spain* (Cambridge: Cambridge University Press, 1995).

[70] *Conorte* II.57.1232–33.

[71] Joaquín Zambrano González, "Animas benditas del Purgatorio. Culto, cofradías y manifestaciones artísticas en la provincia de Granada," in *El mundo de los difuntos: Culto, cofradías, y tradiciones*, ed. Francisco Javier Campos y Fernández de Sevilla (El Escorial, Spain: R.C.U. Escorial-Mª Cristina, Servicio de Publicaciones, 2014), 2:1075, references the Carmelite belief, but is inaccurate in supposing that it was declared heresy during the Middle Ages. For the dating to 1617, see Joseph Hilgers. "Sabbatine Privilege," in *The Catholic Encyclopedia*, vol. 13 (New York: Robert Appleton Company, 1912), http://www.newadvent.org/cathen/13289b.htm. For the Carmelite order in medieval Iberia, see Jill Rosemary Webster, *Carmel in Medieval Catalonia* (Leiden: Brill, 1999), 74.

[72] *Conorte* II.57.1233. There is an extensive artistic tradition showing angels in general and Archangel Michael in particular as rescuing souls, or weighing them in a balance before choosing which to rescue. For this common scene in eastern medieval Spain, see Paulino Rodríguez Barral, *La justicia del más allá: Iconografía en la Corona de Aragón en la baja Edad Media* (Valencia, Spain: Universitat de València, 2007); for Spain generally, see Barral, "Los lugares penales del más allá. Infierno y purgatorio en el arte medieval hispano," *Studium Medievale. Revista de Cultura Visual - Cultura Escrita* 3 (2010): 1–34.

[73] Revelation 20:13 describes an angel overthrowing Satan (as a dragon) and imprisoning him in a pit. For discussion, see Meredith J. Gill, *Angels and the Order of Heaven in Medieval and Renaissance Italy* (Cambridge: Cambridge University Press, 2014), 219. Scholastic theologians debated the location of Lucifer once vanquished by Michael. While Franciscans such as Bonaventure thought the devil floated free in the air in order to move about and tempt sinners, principal theologians such as Peter Lombard in his *Sentences* proposed that Christ had bound Lucifer deep in hell. Discussed in Almond, *The Devil: A New Biography*, 62–63.

dragon of Revelation 12:7–9 who fights against the angels, yet this time, Michael cannot vanquish him.[74] Viewing the impending catastrophe from heaven, God the Father reprimands Jesus for not sharing Mary with the angels in the first place, as his refusal has reactivated the celestial battle with the fallen angels.[75] Chastened, Jesus finally releases Mary to go to the aid of the angels.[76]

Far more than the object of beauty the angels and Jesus initially fought over, Mary most impressively not only saves the souls the angels had tried to rescue from the devil, but also chains Lucifer up while chanting in a liturgical (or perhaps magical) manner: "In the name of the Father, in the name of the Son, in the name of the Holy Spirit, be tied up, ye chains – may you never more be able to be undone, even if all the demons and all the people of the world desire it, until it be the will of God."[77] Mary has thus averted a terrible catastrophe, i.e., the early advent of the scene foretold in Revelation 20:7, in which after being shut away for a millennium in a bottomless pit, the dragon (or Lucifer) would sally forth.[78] This scene goes beyond the medieval Carmelite understanding of Mary's Saturday interventions on behalf of particular souls to instead laud Mary as having averted the devil's victory nearly brought about by angelic desire and Jesus' selfishness. Likewise, it proposes a far different role for the Virgin than modern apparitions in which Mary predicts the end-times or the medieval miracle tale cited by Vincent Ferrer in which she interceded with Jesus to allow the mendicants time to convert more souls: here Mary is not just depicted with agency but is the

---

[74] *Conorte* II.57.1235–6.

[75] Ibid., 1237.

[76] In the Prado museum, there is a contemporary image of the Virgin saving souls in Purgatory by Pedro Machuca, his 1517 *The Virgin and the Souls of Purgatory*. This scenario becomes a popular one in the seventeenth–eighteenth centuries, see images and discussion in Manuel Trens, *María: Iconografía de la virgen en el arte español* (Madrid: Editorial Plus-Ultra, 1946), 378–84.

[77] "En nombre del Padre, en nombre del Hijo, en nombre del Espíritu Santo sé atada cadena, que nunca más te puedas desatar, aunque todos los demonios y todas las personas del mundo lo quieran, hasta que sea la voluntad de Dios." *Conorte* II.57.1239.

[78] "Satan shall be loosed out of his prison, and shall go forth, and seduce the nations, which are over the four quarters of the earth, Gog, and Magog, and shall gather them together to battle, the number of whom is as the sand of the sea" (Douay-Rheims).

only one with the power to bind the devil.[79] Indeed, she is *la conquistadora*, not just on the Iberian battlefield, but in the afterlife.

Two aspects of Juana's sermon link it strongly to both biblical and medieval traditions concerning the end-times instead of the battle between the fallen and good angels. For one, Mary, once released by Jesus, reaches Purgatory by flying down with angel's wings.[80] This imagery draws cleverly on Marian readings of Revelation 12:13–14, in which Mary as the woman of the sun is able to flee the dragon (who is attacking her son) on wings with which she flies into hiding in the desert.[81] In Juana's sermon, however, rather than fleeing to protect her son, the be-winged Mary leaves behind her (over-protective) son and enters directly into battle with the dragon.

In addition, an apocalyptic reading of the scene should consider the extended description of the dragon at the moment he comes forth out of bondage, for he is described as impossibly ugly, vicious, and bestial.

> And, said the Lord, the body of the great dragon Lucifer is so huge that it has a spine larger than a mountain ridge. And on his body alone he has infinite kinds of faces, all very ugly and terrifying. And as many heads and tails come out of him as he has faces, from all manners of beasts and serpents that there are on the earth, and in all of these heads he has long and sharp tongues and fangs, and with each of these it skewers more than a hundred souls. And the tails are more than ten leagues long and have a great number of eyes, and every one of [the eyes] is larger than a wagon wheel, and from all of them emerge fiery flames of tar. And on each of its heads it has large and sharp horns, and on its tails, claws and mouths and spines and bristles. And all [are] very frightening and repulsive.[82]

---

[79] In comparison, Lope de Salazar's revelation has Mary talking to the devil, but the only weapon she has is her ability to intercede with Jesus to keep the devil tamed. Valero Moreno, "La revelación à Lope de Salazar," 113–15.

[80] *Conorte* II.57.1237. The souls in purgatory confuse her with an angel as a result.

[81] "And when the dragon saw that he was cast unto the earth, he persecuted the woman, who brought forth the man child. And there were given to the woman two wings of a great eagle, that she might fly into the desert unto her place, where she is nourished for a time and times, and half a time, from the face of the serpent." For a discussion of this passage in the apocalypticism of Joachim of Fiore, see McGinn's chapter in this volume, "Apocalypticism and Mysticism in Joachim of Fiore's *Expositio in Apocalypsim*."

[82] "Y, dijo el Señor, es tan grande el cuerpo del gran dragón Lucifer que tiene mayor lomo que los montes. Y, en su cuerpo solo, tiene infinitas maneras de figuras, todas muy feas y espantables. Y, tantas cuantas figuras tiene, tantas cabezas y colas salen de él de todas las maneras de bestias y sierpes que hay en la tierra, y en todas aquellas cabezas tiene lenguas y dientes muy largos y agudos, y en cada uno espeta mas de cien animas. Y las colas

Although the elements of the description are typical of medieval descriptions of Lucifer, the contrast with the enumeration of Mary's exceedingly beautiful features at the beginning of the scene is, I suggest, intentional. While the life of the Antichrist as the exact parodic inverse of Christ's life led those who believed the Antichrist to be ugly to write descriptions in direct contrast to Jesus' physical perfection, here Lucifer is embodied as the inverse of Mary's idealized form.

In other words, the logic of the scene is apocalyptic, but it is Mary, not Christ, who is the primary force that defeats the devil. By these means, Juana interweaves biblical apocalyptic details and medieval developments in apocalyptic spirituality with a scene from the otherworld, showcasing a conquering, beautiful, conjuring Mary as the central salvific figure. Given that the Marian apparitions that Juana received throughout her life were an important source establishing her as leader of her convent, the depiction of the Virgin as not just intercessor but as savior suggests that Mary was as important as Jesus' voice issuing from her body for authorizing Juana's interventions in theology, politics, and apocalyptic rhetoric.

4 Conclusion

Juana de la Cruz, authorized by a sequence of Marian apparitions and serving as the voice of Jesus to convey a range of messages concerning the otherworld and the end-times, is an important figure for analysis of prophecy and politics in the apocalyptic mentality of the early sixteenth century. Mary had been a crucial figure in Spanish ideas of crusade since the early Reconquest, and became ever more integral to Spanish Christianity during the conquest of the New World. In my view, Juana's "Marian apocalyptic" served to reinforce the prophetic-apocalyptic mentality of the early Spanish empire. Juana achieved this not through identifying particular Castilian leaders with various apocalyptic figures, but instead by both linking the apocalyptic to the individual's fate at the hour of death, be it salvation, purgatory, or damnation, and by

---

son de más de diez leguas y tienen muy gran número de ojos. Y cada uno de ellos es mayor que una rueda de carreta, y por todos ellos le salen llamas de fuego de alquitrán. Y en todas las cabezas tiene cuernos muy largos y agudos, y, en las colas, uñas y bocas y púas y cerdas. Y todo muy espantable y hediondo." *Conorte* II.57.1236.

transferring Castilian devotion to the Virgin Mary as *la conquistadora* to the heart of an apocalyptic scenario between the devil and angels. Thus, as E. Ann Matter so rightly points out for the twentieth century, the turn to a Marian apocalyptic authorized by apparitional experience can be deeply enmeshed with urgent political needs at a time of rapid global changes, whether the spread of Communism or the spread of the Spanish empire.

CHAPTER 4

The City Coming Down Out of Heaven (Rev. 21:10): Bologna as Jerusalem

Gabriella Zarri

1 Introduction

Placing itself squarely within the popular medieval topos that described the city as the heavenly Jerusalem, Roman *Bononia* (present-day Bologna) defined itself over time as a holy city, starting with the early construction of Santo Stefano's *Sancta Jerusalem*. The expansion of the city reached its peak in the thirteenth century with the construction of

---

My first meeting with E. Ann Matter took place in Bologna. She found her way to me through a dear friend and an interest in the Italian mystics of the sixteenth and seventeenth centuries. Lucia Brocadelli, the living saint of the Este family, particularly attracted her attention and later became the object of a joint study and other meetings in the city of Bologna. Women, mystics, nuns were the protagonists of conversations and cemented a years-long friendship, with visits to Philadelphia, conferences at the University of Pennsylvania, Leeds, Florence, and also meetings in the city of Bologna. My studies have never concerned exegesis or philological analysis, and insofar as the theme of the Apocalypse lends itself to studies of mystical texts that are familiar to me, I preferred to send Ann a special "postcard" to tell her that I await her still in the city coming down from Heaven.

G. Zarri (✉)
University of Florence, Florence, Italy

© The Author(s) 2019
E. Knibbs et al. (eds.), *The End of the World in Medieval Thought and Spirituality*, The New Middle Ages,
https://doi.org/10.1007/978-3-030-14965-9_4

a third circle of walls that, like the city of the Apocalypse, was sealed with twelve gates. Numerous convents were placed around the walls, far from the noise of the town but protected by the city guards, and stood as bastions in defense of the urban complex. Paintings and sculptures of the Virgin Mary adorned the churches and were also placed in the squares and streets of the urban center. Municipal rites in honor of the Madonna were repeated daily and demonstrated the devotion of the people towards the Mother of God. In every quarter Marian images manifested a miraculous power and around these images confraternities erected oratories in their honor. In the seventeenth century, the city was consecrated to the Immaculate Virgin. A statue of Our Lady, dressed in sunlight and crowned with twelve stars, stood atop a column that rose heavenwards, and Christian Bologna could appear to early eighteenth-century observers as the Holy City:

> In the course of time Christian piety greatly advanced in Bologna through the work of St. Petronius, the eighth bishop of the city, who needed to multiply churches ... and there are stately churches, beautiful not so much for their architecture as for ornaments of almost all the regular and reformed Orders, even beyond those of the Sacred Virgins ... [A]nd [there are] those still around the City walls, where many oratories can be seen, all dedicated to Mary most Holy, which serve as a rampart to protect the city with no other fortress to defend it from its enemies. [And] the Virgin herself [is] watching over it constantly in the miraculous image painted by St. Lucca on Monte della Guardia.[1]

As mentioned above, it was a literary topos for a city to be described as a heavenly Jerusalem; for Bologna it seemed to reach its concrete realization in the urban design of its walls, enclosed by twelve gates,

---

[1] "In processo di tempo si avanzò tant'oltre la pietà cristiana in Bologna per opera di san Petronio, l'ottavo vescovo della medesima, che bisognò moltiplicare le chiese ... e vi sono chiese grandiose e bellissime non tanto per l'Architettura quanto per gli ornamenti di quasi tutti gli Ordini e Riforme regolari et oltre quelle delle Sacre Vergini ... e quelle ancora intorno alle mura della Città, dove si vedono molti Oratori e tutti dedicati a Maria Santissima, che servono senza verun'altra fortezza, che difenda la Città da' suoi nemici, come di antemurale al riparo della medesima, vegliando di continuo alla di lei custodia la Vergine istessa, nella miracolosa Immagine dipinta da san Lucca sul Monte della Guardia." Francesco Luigi Barelli, *Memorie dell'origine, fondazione, avanzamenti, successi, ed uomini illustri in lettere, e in santità della congregazione de' cherici regolari di s. Paolo* ... (Bologna: Per Costantino Pisarri sotto le Scuole all'Insegna di S. Michele, 1703–1707), 2:154.

emphasized by its twelve Marian oratories and twelve convents. Critics tend, with good reason, to reject the idea of a preconceived plan in pursuit of this aim, which would have had to remain consistent over centuries.[2] And yet, while a deliberate project is absent, we note the persistence of the idea of the city as Paradise and a Holy City throughout different periods of Bologna's history.

2 REVELATION 21:10. *THE HOLY CITY, JERUSALEM, COMING DOWN FROM HEAVEN*

Beginning with the construction of Santo Stefano's *Sancta Jerusalem*, Roman *Bononia* was gradually built as a Holy City. The complex, known popularly as the seven churches, was the topographic reproduction of the Holy Sepulchre (Fig. 1). It came into being over several centuries, though its origins were quite ancient.[3] The first written documents date back to the ninth and tenth centuries, though the archaeological finds and stones are much older. Popular tradition, based on a legendary Latin life written in the twelfth century, ascribes the foundation of the ecclesiastical complex to Saint Petronius, the city's eighth bishop.[4] Born in the fifth century in an unspecified location in Greece, the noble Petronius, brother-in-law of Emperor Theodosius II, was elected bishop of Bologna. Upon arrival at his bishopric, he found the city in ruinous condition from famines and the invasions of the Nordic peoples, and

---

[2] Mario Fanti, "Le chiese sulle mura," in *Le mura perdute: Storia e immagini dell'ultima cerchia fortificata di Bologna*, ed. Giancarlo Roversi (Bologna: Grafis Edizioni, 1985), 97–124.

[3] Cf. Robert G. Ousterhout, "The Church of Santo Stefano: A 'Jerusalem' in Bologna," *Gesta* 20.2 (1981): 311–21; Idem, "Santo Stefano e Gerusalemme," in *Stefaniana: Contributi per la storia del complesso di Santo Stefano in Bologna*, ed. Gina Fasoli (Bologna: Deputazione di St. Patria per le Province di Romagna, 1985), 131–58; *7 colonne & 7 chiese: La vicenda ultramillenaria del Complesso di Santo Stefano* (Bologna: Grafis, 1987); and Beatrice Borghi, *In viaggio verso la Terra Santa: La basilica di Santo Stefano in Bologna* (Argelato: Minerva, 2010).

[4] See the *Vita Sancti Petroni Episcopi et Confessoris* in the lectionary/passionary today conserved as Bologna, Biblioteca Universitaria di Bologna, Ms. 1473 (copied around 1180). Also Lorenzo Paolini, "Un patrono condiviso: La figura di San Petronio: da 'padre e pastore' a simbolo principale della religione civica bolognese (XII–XIV secolo)," in *Petronio e Bologna: Il volto di una storia. Arte storia e culto del Santo Patrono. Catalogo della mostra*, ed. Beatrice Buscaroli and Roberto Sernicola (Ferrara: SATE, 2001), 77–83.

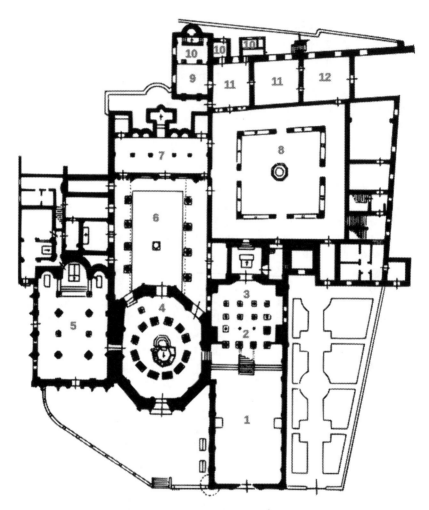

Fig. 1 Basilica di Santo Stefano (Basilica of Saint Stephen). Blueprint of the Basilica: 1–3. Chiesa del Crocifisso (Church of the Crucifix); 4. Crypt; 5. Basilica del Sepolcro (Basilica of the Sepulchre); 6. Basilica dei SS. Vitale e Agricola (Basilica of Saints Vitale and Agricola); 7. Cortile di Pilato (Pilate's Courtyard); 8. Il Chiostro (The Cloister); 9–12. Chiesa della Benda e Museo (Church of Mary's Veil and Museum)

he immediately instituted a building effort to construct the church of Santo Stefano and the entire city. Later, returning from a pilgrimage to Jerusalem laden with relics, he had them placed in the church built in conformity with the Holy Sepulchre.

Thus began the *Sancta Jerusalem* of Bologna, which the saint chose as his burial place. After centuries of neglect, the cult of the Holy Bishop was revived in the twelfth century, after his body was rediscovered by the Benedictines who officiated in the church. From then on the city grew and took shape simultaneously with the consolidation of the cult of Saint Petronius, identified as the city's patron, builder of both the new metropolis and of Bologna's Jerusalem. The church, made rich with indulgences and privileges, became a center of pilgrimage until various untoward events and the decline of the monastery halted the influx of the faithful.

The first half of the fifteenth century brought renewed interest in the Santo Stefano sanctuary. During excavations in the oldest of the seven churches (of the early martyrs, Saints Vitale and Agricola), a Roman tomb was discovered engraved with the name of Simon. Taking advantage of the discovery, the enterprising Legate of Bologna, Baldassarre Cossa, later anti-pope John XXIII, declared that the sarcophagus was the tomb of the Apostle Peter. Curiosity mixed with popular devotion encouraged a large number of pilgrims who came to visit the *Sancta Jerusalem*, which now had become the new Rome. Shortly after, Pope Boniface IX ordered the walling up of the doors of the church of Saints Vitale and Agricola to halt devotion to the false tomb of Peter, and the pilgrimage to the church of Santo Stefano again registered a period of decline.[5]

Other factors must also have contributed to the temporary decline of Bologna's Jerusalem, not least the Basilica of San Petronio whose construction was under way and which was destined to attract the aspirations and devotion of the entire city. Moreover, the robust annuities of the abbey of Santo Stefano became attractive to many. In 1447, for example, Nicholas V granted the monastery *in commendam* and the Benedictine monks were replaced by lay priests.[6] Because of its considerable

---

[5] The episode is narrated by Mariano Guido Uberti in http://www.uberti.eu/destinazioni/italia/emilia-romagna/bologna/cosa-vedere/santo-stefano.html (November 10, 2016) where however Pope Boniface IX is confused with Boniface VIII.

[6] Cfr. Celestino Petracchi, *Della Insigne Abbaziale Basilica di Santo Stefano a Bologna* (Bologna: Nella stamperia di Domenico Guidotti, e Giacomo Mellini sotto il Seminario, 1747), 63–70. Such a grant *in commendam* committed the monastery to a so-called

annuities, but perhaps also because of its importance as symbol and cult, the Abbey of Santo Stefano was later given *in commendam* to high prelates who also filled the positions of legate or bishop of the city.

It was only in the late fifteenth century that the *Sancta Jerusalem* of Bologna regained a significant role in the urban context. To understand this resurgence of devotion we must refer to a historical event of fundamental importance for Christianity: the fall of Constantinople in 1453 and the conquest of the city by the Turks. With the interruption of relations with the East and the Holy Land, the city of Bologna began to take on a special role as guardian of an image attributed to the Apostle Luke which originated in Constantinople.[7] Also, Bologna, as the custodian of one of the oldest topographic reconstructions of the *Sancta Jerusalem*, in the 1450s began plans for reviving the Santo Stefano complex as a place of pilgrimage to a Jerusalem still accessible to the faithful.

The first requisite for resuming worship at Santo Stefano was renovating the sanctuary. Next followed the restitution of the Abbey to the monks through the offices of two illustrious commendatory abbots, Giuliano della Rovere and Giovanni de' Medici, both of whom would become popes. In 1476, the Franciscan Pope Sixtus IV confirmed ample indulgences and privileges for the Bologna abbey, which traced its origins back to the time of Theodosius.[8] Thenceforth the city of Bologna was reintroduced into the circuits of pilgrims who made money for the church from the Jerusalem indulgences through the pilgrims' symbolic visits to holy places.[9] The donations collected from pilgrimages and "pardons" served to launch a series of works and renovations of the sanctuary, which continued during the early sixteenth century, giving the abbey an appearance better suited to the performance of the salient Stations of the Cross.

---

commendatory abbot, who would receive the revenues while taking no part in overseeing the regular life of the monks.

[7] *La Madonna di San Luca in Bologna: Otto secoli di storia, di arte e di fede*, ed. Mario Fanti and Giancarlo Roversi (Cinisello Balsamo: Silvana, 1993).

[8] See Petracchi, *Della Insigne abbaziale basilica di S. Stefano*.

[9] On the other reproductions of Santo Sepolcro in Europe see Franco Cardini, "La devozione al Santo Sepolcro, le sue riproduzioni occidentali e il complesso stefaniano: Alcuni casi italici," in *7 Colonne*, 19–49.

After Sixtus IV confirmed the privileges of Santo Stefano in 1476, there was no concealing the purpose of the entire Franciscan Order to promote the devotion to the Holy Sepulchre through the practice of symbolic journeys and topographic reconstructions of holy places. Shortly after, construction began of the holy mount of Varallo in Lombardy and then of San Vivaldo in Tuscany, both promoted by Franciscan friars.[10] The resumption of the cult in the Abbey of Santo Stefano was thus responding to a very lively religious supply-and-demand in the late fifteenth century.

The Santo Stefano Abbey in Bologna was a symbolic place par excellence, linked to a devotional practice, the Stations of the Cross, as popular as that of the penitential pilgrimage. In the first half of the sixteenth century, it also played a political role in Bologna during the severe crisis that resulted in the expulsion of the Bentivoglios and the reannexation of the city by the Papal State.[11] As a commendatory holding of the legates, the abbey was seen as siding with the papal church, and so was sacked by the Bentivoglio faction.[12] After the defeat of the Bentivoglio supporters and the consolidation of the papal government, the Santo Stefano complex regained a central religious role in Bologna. With the acquisition of the Abbey by the Celestines and its restitution to the monks, spelling the end of its cession *in commendam* to papal legates, the cult was definitively reactivated and the *Sancta Jerusalem* again became an expression of the city's rebirth (as desired by its patron saint) and a privileged place for identifying Bologna as the Holy City descended from heaven.

---

[10] On which see Jonathan Bober, "Storia e storiografia del sacro monte di Varallo: Osservazioni sulla 'prima pietra' del Santo Sepolcro," *Novarien* 14 (1984): 3–98; *La "Gerusalemme" di San Vivaldo e i sacri monti in Europa*, ed. Sergio Gensini (Comune di Montaione: Pacini Editore, 1989).

[11] For a further study of the topic discussed here see Zarri, "I Medici e la 'Gerusalemme bolognese,'" in *Una 'Gerusalemme' toscana sullo sfondo di due giubilei: 1500–1525. Proceedings of the Study Conference. San Vivaldo, Montaione October 4–6, 2000*, ed. Sergio Ginsini (Florence: SISMEL-Edizioni del Galluzzo, 2004), 57–67.

[12] Carla Penuti, "Diario bolognese," in *L'Estasi di Santa Cecilia di Raffaello da Urbino nella Pinacoteca Nazionale di Bologna. Catalogo della mostra*, ed. Carla Bernardini, Gabriella Zarri, and Andrea Emiliani (Bologna: Alfa, 1983), 39–47.

Fig. 2 Joan Blaeu's Map of Bologna (1640)

3 REVELATION. 21:12 *THE CITY IS GIRDED BY A LARGE, HIGH WALL WITH TWELVE GATES*

Today the city of Bologna, like the "BONONIA DOCET" portrayed by Jean Blaeu in 1704 (Fig. 2), has twelve gates, three in each cardinal point, as dictated by the book of Revelation. If it is true, as pointed out by Mario Fanti, that the gates rest on twelve roads whose layout preceded the writing of the prophetic book that for centuries inspired the model of the ideal city,[13] nothing prevented the factual reality of the Middle Ages and the early modern age from being interpreted symbolically and considered as a sign of divine election. The fact is that the

---

[13] See Mario Fanti, *Le chiese sulle mura*, 97.

number of gates of the city of Bologna has varied over time and it must be assumed that for diverse natural or socioeconomic reasons the road network and urban fabric had to submit to innovations or rearrangements that could consequently require opening new entrances or closing old gates.

If we are to believe Antonio di Paolo Masini, who with his *Bologna perlustrata* gives us the most documented guide to the city's churches, devotions, and remarkable occurrences, Bologna was built by Saint Petronius with seventeen gates, six of which were still standing in 1666 and took the name of *torresotti*.[14] Masini goes on to say: "As the expanding city engulfed the villages contiguous with its walls, another circle was formed, as can presently be seen, with its 250 streets and lanes and thirteen gates."[15] The information Masini provides, while being decidedly inaccurate since he purports to describe the Bologna Petronius built in the fifth century based on the state of the city in the twelfth century, nevertheless attests to the connection between the number of gates and the city's development regardless of any reference to religious symbolism. Masini's words do not alter the attribution of the city's construction to its patron saint, which as such was owed to divine intervention.

To better understand Masini's statements we may briefly recall an amply documented aspect of its urban history: the square-shaped Roman *Bononia* substantially shrank during the severe economic crisis of late antiquity, when the populace was concentrated in the urban core closer to the public and religious buildings while the abandoned residential area fell slowly and inexorably into ruin.[16] The "retracted city," as the quadrangular fifth-century urban core was designated, was protected by a high wall of selenite (a gypsum stone typical of the Bolognese Appenines) in which four gates were placed, subsequently increased to seven. In the corners of the circle were four crosses, erected on ancient columns that two different traditions claim to derive from a provision of St. Ambrose or St. Petronius. Even the dedication of the crosses to the Saints, the Virgins, the Apostles, and the Evangelists clearly indicates that

---

[14] Antonio di Paolo Masini, *Bologna perlustrata*, 3rd ed. (Bologna: Per l'erede di V. Benacci, 1666).

[15] "Crescendo la città con i borghi addossati alle mura si fece un altro cerchio come al presente si vede e sono 250 tra strade e vicoli e 13 porte." Ibid., 102.

[16] Francesca Bocchi, *Bologna nei secoli 4.–14.: Mille anni di storia urbanistica di una metropoli medievale* (Bologna: Bononia University Press, 2008).

the protection of the city was entrusted equally to the sturdy stone walls and the celestial city.[17] According to recent studies, at the time the walls were constructed, the Byzantines divided the town into twelve areas, called *horae*, because at different times of day and night the inhabitants of each sector were assigned to keep watch over the city.[18] This new theory connects the number twelve with the allocation of time and day and, while not assigning a symbolic meaning to the figure itself, transfers the numerical context to the register of protection of the urban environment. In short, the city that descends from heaven found support and protection in both the celestial and the terrestrial militia.

The economic and cultural recovery of the eleventh and twelfth centuries favored an enlargement of the city center, "*torresotti*," to recall the particular shape of the gates, surmounted by a defensive tower-like structure. The extension of the urban area expanded from nineteen hectares of selenite walls to 113 hectares of the second circle of *torresotti*. The city wall was opened by eighteen gates also called menageries or posterns.[19] It is certainly this second circle that Masini refers to when he speaks of the city rebuilt by St. Petronius. While the patron saint had lived in the Bologna enclosed within the selenite walls with its four gates protected by four crosses, the saint's hagiographic legend was compiled in the twelfth century at the time of the second wall, which had several gates more than the one to which Masini refers.

Another last extension of the city occurred a century later, with the tracing of the third *circla*, a 7.6 km long perimeter erected in masonry at around 1300. The *circla* had an embankment on the city side and twelve gates with drawbridges to pass over the outer moat. This wall, to which at different times a varying number of posterns were added, substantially retained its size and structure throughout the period of the *ancien régime* (Fig. 3). It withstood unscathed the urban upheaval following the Napoleonic provisions and yet succumbed definitively to nineteenth-century "progress": in the early years of the twentieth century, the city

---

[17] For the history of the town, *Breve storia di Bologna*, Centro "Gina Fasoli," http://www.centrofasoli.unibo.it/cgi-bin/etruschi/carica_scheda.cgi?sezione=b&indice=01.03.01 (accessed November 10, 2016).

[18] Francesca Cerioli and Ilaria Cornia, *Bologna di Selenite* (Bologna: Costa Editore, 2002).

[19] http://www.centrofasoli.unibo.it/cgi-bin/etruschi/carica_scheda.cgi?sezione=b&indice=12.04.02 (accessed November 16, 2016).

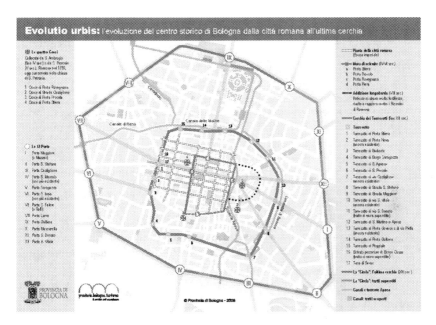

Fig. 3 Bologna's City Wall: the three circles (https://www.cittametropolitana.bo.it/turismo/Home_Page/Per_turisti/Guide_e_mappe/Bologna_mappa_e_itinerari_turistici)

decreed the demolition of the walls and the abolition of customs houses connected to the doors. The population of Bologna, with very few discordant voices, unconditionally approved this irredeemable historic impoverishment. With progressive secularization over the centuries, the celestial court was no longer in a position to protect those walls that had for centuries been the protagonists of a spiritual theater.

4 REVELATION 21:16 *THE CITY IS FOURSQUARE*

As we have seen, the city of Bologna only had a square shape during the Roman period, a form linked to military traditions and not biblical images. But in Christian Bologna, the symbol of the square was applied to women's convents and referred to the holy city and paradise. Once again it was Antonio di Paolo Masini who recalled the persistence of religious significance attributed to the figure of the Apocalypse, and introduced us into the convent of the Poor Clares of Corpus Christi:

> This convent of Holiness and Poverty is considered, in terms of its number, circumference and structure, among the first of Italy, as it measures a third of a mile around, is a perfect square, numbers many blessed women, possesses nothing, and numbers about 250. [It was] founded by the Blessed Caterina Vigri from Bologna on the 13th day of November, 1456.[20]

From its very foundation, this convent was considered in Bologna an example of Franciscan observance, and as late as the mid-seventeenth century enjoyed a reputation for holiness by virtue of its founder, already beatified and in the process of being declared a saint. It was therefore an institution to which, more than any other, could be applied the image of the Holy City of Heaven; nevertheless, the convents of the city had long since acquired a religious significance. The above-cited Francesco Luigi Barelli himself refers to this, counting the convents among Bologna's gems.

In other studies I have investigated the distribution of the convents in the town, wondering if the location of the female monastic institutions might initially have had or have developed a religious meaning.[21] My survey revealed a tendency of the nuns to settle near the walls or at least in areas away from the city center. In the thirteenth and fourteenth centuries, while the third *circla* was being traced and the first mendicant communities were being founded, several female monastic communities settled near the walls. The causes of this choice could have been practical, since the land cost less and the city guards that garrisoned the walls were a guarantee for the sisters. But religious motivations were not lacking: the distance from the commercial and mercantile activities of the city center made possible an isolation that approximated a hermit's solitude

---

[20] Masini, *Bologna perlustrata*, 118: "Questo monastero di Santità, di Povertà, di numero, di circuito e di fabrica è tenuto de' primi d'Italia, imperoché circonda un terzo di miglio; è quadrato perfetto; numera molte beate; non possiede cosa alcuna, e di numero saranno circa 250, fondato dalla Beata Caterina Vigri da Bologna a dì 13 novembre 1456."

[21] Gabriella Zarri, "Recinti sacri: Sito e forma dei monasteri femminili a Bologna tra '500 e '600," in *Luoghi sacri e spazi della santità*, ed. Sofia Boesch Gajano and Lucetta Scaraffia (Turin: Rosenberg & Sellier, 1990), 381–96.

that until a few decades earlier would have been sought in the mountains or in locations far from the town.

Beyond that, the proximity of the convents to the walls gave the convents a sacred character by investing those institutes of consecrated virgins with the role of protecting the city itself. It is common in many cultures for gates to acquire a magical and sacred meaning. Their function is ambiguous—allowing or denying passage to an inhabited place—and therefore they become the subject of attention and vigilance. For example, the popular preachers of the fifteenth century, such as Bernardino da Siena, presented the city gates as a place of contention that stirred up battles between angels and devils.[22] In some villages, sacred images were painted or carved on the doors for apotropaic purposes, and monasteries took on a similar function of being assigned by the city to protect the community through prayer.[23]

It is worth noting that at the end of the seventeenth century in the city of Bologna there were as many as twenty-five cloistered monasteries and convents, twelve of which were located close to or near the city walls.[24] This is clearly illustrated by a map of the Bolognese monasteries and their extension, compiled at the end of the eighteenth century by Napoleonic officials in charge of suppressing the monastic establishments.[25] On the basis of the original document, I have highlighted the locations and layouts of the convents in particular (Fig. 4). Similar to city ramparts, the convents progressively expanded. In addition, after the Council of Trent prescribed strict seclusion, they increased the inner spaces devoted to gardens and orchards where nuns could walk and breathe fresh air and also take part in processional ceremonies at oratories and chapels erected in cloisters and courtyards. Thus monasteries were transformed into Edenic images, as noted

---

[22] Carlo Delcorno, "La città nella predicazione francescana del Quattrocento," in *Alle origini dei Monti di Pietà: I francescani tra etica ed economia nel società del tardo Medioevo* (Bologna: Banca del Monte, 1984), 29–39.

[23] Franco Barbieri and Renato Cevese, *Vicenza, ritratto di una città, guida storico-artistica* (Costabissara: Angelo Colla, 2005), 31–32.

[24] The location of the convents and their settlement in the urban area is described in: Gabriella Zarri, "I monasteri femminili a Bologna tra il XII e il XVII secolo," *Atti e memorie della Deputazione di storia patria per le province di Romagna* n.s., 24 (1973): 133–224.

[25] Bologna, Biblioteca Comunale dell'Archiginnasio Bologna, Ms. B 1015.

Fig. 4   Location and extent of Bologna's convents at the end of the eighteenth century

by the seventeenth-century historian of the Bolognese church Celso Faleoni, who designated the recently founded Capuchin monastery "a paradise."[26]

This image of the monastery as New Jerusalem was also present in the culture and consciousness of religious persons of the *ancién regime*. A *Descrittione della fonzione avutasi nella Chiesa di Santa Cristina della Fondazza* ("Description of the Ceremony that took place in the Church of Santa Cristina della Fondazza") in 1711 at the consecration of eight

---

[26] Celso Faleoni, *Memorie historiche della chiesa bolognese e suoi pastori: All'eminentiss. e reuerendiss. signor card. Nicolo Ludouisio...* (Bologna: Giacomo Monti, 1649), 685.

Camaldolese nuns, for example, presented their church and the decorations in it as a New Jerusalem:

> It proves itself a new Jerusalem, as John in the Apocalypse saw when he wrote: *Vidi civitatem Sanctam Jerusalem discendentem de Coelo a deo paratam, sicut sponsam ornatam viro suo* (Rev 21:12).[27]

5 REVELATION 12:1 *A WOMAN CLOTHED WITH THE SUN, WITH THE MOON BENEATH HER FEET, AND ON HER HEAD A CROWN OF TWELVE STARS*[28]

In 1636 the Friars Minor Conventual requested and obtained the right to erect in the Seliciata and Prato di San Francesco, today Piazza Malpighi, a column with an image of the Immaculate Conception. The statue, in gilded copper, was executed in 1637 after a drawing by Guido Reni. The plaque on the pedestal commemorates the munificence of Cardinal Benedetto Monaldi, then city legate.[29] At the time of its execution, Archbishop Alfonso Paleotti was long dead, and his person could in no way be connected with the project undertaken by the Franciscans, and yet the erection of the column appeared as the last act of a story that had personally involved the mystic archbishop, cousin of Cardinal Gabriele Paleotti.

Alfonso Paleotti (1531–1610), doctor of civil and canon law and theology, taught for several years at the University of Bologna and then went to Rome.[30] There he began to frequent the Oratorio di San Filippo Neri, where he met a visionary mystic named Giovanni Francesco Parenti da Bolsena (whom he called *il Vidente*), on whose advice he decided to take holy orders. He became a priest in his forties, in 1571, and his

---

[27] Bologna, Biblioteca Comunale dell'Archiginnasio Bologna, Ms. Gozzadini 184, fol. 125v.

[28] For further discussion of Marian devotion intertwined with apocalyptic symbolism, see the chapter by Boon in this volume.

[29] Giuseppe Guidicini, "Seliciata e prato di San Francesco," in *Cose Notabili...*, ed. Luigi Breventani. No date or publisher information given in the version available at http://www.originebologna.com/home/seliciata-di-san-francesco-1 (accessed November 10, 2016).

[30] Umberto Mazzone, "Paleotti Alfonso," in *Dizionario biografico degli italiani* 80 (2015), http://www.treccani.it/enciclopedia/alfonso-paleotti_(Dizionario-Biografico) (accessed November 10, 2016).

cousin Gabriele gave him a Canonicate in the Cathedral of Bologna. He then filled other positions until he was made titular archbishop of Corinth and Coadjutor of the Archbishop of Bologna. In 1597 he succeeded his cousin Paleotti and ruled the diocese until his death. He wrote a treatise on the Holy Shroud, after having visited Turin with his cousin and Carlo Borromeo.[31] The first edition of 1598 was censored by the Holy Office and reprinted the following year with amendments. He also wrote an autobiography that was not printed. For many years he was assisted by *il Vidente*, who contributed to Alfonso's mystical tendencies.

It was *il Vidente* who revealed to the Archbishop that the Virgin Mary had chosen him to prepare her triumph, which was supposed to culminate with the proclamation of the dogma of the Immaculate Conception in the city of Bologna.[32] The prophecy never came about, but it is significant that the creator of the column of the Immaculate Conception was Guido Reni, the artist who was most sensitive to the cultural context of visionary mysticism that involved painters and patrons in the last quarter of the sixteenth century and in the first decades of the seventeenth. It is also possible that the young Reni had known *il Vidente*, since it seems that he participated in the competition to design the fresco for the chapel of the Confraternity of Santa Maria dell'Orazione, founded by Parenti himself.

The column of the Immaculate Conception, built by the Franciscans perhaps in response to the column of the Virgin raised in Piazza San Domenico a few years before, was the culmination of centuries of Marian devotion which during the Counter-Reformation pervaded Bologna neighborhood by neighborhood and which found particular extension along the city walls. These walls proved to be a privileged place for the erection of oratories dedicated to Our Lady. Of course, it cannot be ignored that many cities practiced a particular worship of the Virgin, such as Siena, which in the age of the communes called itself "Città della Vergine" and even minted a coin with the inscription "Sena

---

[31] Mario Fanti, "Genesi e vicende del libro di Alfonso Paleotti sulla sindone," in *La Sindone: scienza e fede: Atti del 2. convegno nazionale di sindonologia. Bologna, November 27–29, 1981*, ed. Lamberto Coppini and Francesco Cavazzuti (Bologna: CLUEB, 1983), 369–79.

[32] Mario Fanti, "Voglia di paradiso: mistici, pittori e committenti a Bologna fra Cinquecento e Seicento," in *Dall'avanguardia dei Carracci al secolo barocco: Bologna 1580–1600*, ed. Andrea Emiliani (Bologna: Nuova Alfa Editoriale, 1988), 83–94, esp. 86.

Vetus Civitas Virginis." And yet I suggest that in Bologna the Madonna cult took on special features and was noteworthy for its continuity over time. Bologna's Marian calling was visually documented by the detailed list of sacred images painted or sculpted that decorated the city center and neighboring districts in the late sixteenth century, just in time for Alfonso Paleotti's episcopate.

Among the artists who distinguished themselves in the wave of devotion and mysticism detailed above, we should highlight Francesco Cavazzoni (1559–after 1616), an artist and art critic of lesser stature than the best-known painters of the Bolognese school, such the Carraccis and Guido Reni, and yet significant historically and culturally. Cavazzoni produced a limited number of paintings, though he left a precious manuscript in which he gathered the results of his investigation of the Marian cult in Bologna: the *Corona di gratie*.[33] As its long title on the frontispiece indicates, the work proposes to present the graces, favors and miracles in Bologna made by the Virgin Mary by way of the many "miraculous" images placed in the city's churches or at other locations, images Cavazzoni copied "on the spot" into his manuscript. The work is made up of a pictorial part and a narrative part, and is completed by a series of indices. The Madonnas he found and reproduced in his drawings number fifty, and each image is accompanied by a brief history of its origin, information on its location, and any miracles it was reputed to have worked.[34]

I will not go into a detailed account of the manuscript, to which I have devoted a forthcoming study,[35] but will just mention that it contains a remarkable number of images that were to receive daily public devotion by order of the Senate that governed Bologna. Also remarkable is the peculiar tradition that indicates the depth of the love for the Virgin by the citizens of Bologna: Saturday evenings all the faithful would light candles in their homes before their images of the Madonna, and

---

[33] Francesco Cavazzoni, *Corona di Gratie e Gratie Favori et Miracoli della Gloriosa Vergine Maria fatti in Bologna*. Bologna, Biblioteca Comunale dell'Archiginnasio Bologna, Ms. B 298.

[34] Ranieri Varese, *Francesco Cavazzoni, critico e pittore* (Florence: Marchi & Bertolli, 1969).

[35] Gabriella Zarri, "Bologna, Marian City in the Drawings of Francesco Cavazzoni (1559–1616)," in *Innovation in the Italian Counter-Reformation*, ed. Sarah Shannon McHugh and Anna Wainwright (Newark, DE: University of Delaware Press, forthcoming).

the lights, reverberating in the night, would light up the whole town, thereby transforming a private devotional worship into a collective adoration. Francesco Cavazzoni describes the Bolognese rite with these words:

> And in all places, sacred and profane, you can spy the Holy Image of our intercessor … to whom every Saturday evening every devout person lights candles and lamps that light up the dark night so that it seems midday, which makes a great festivity of devotion for all who pass by.[36]

From Cavazzoni's manuscript, we also learn the story of the prodigious events related to paintings or statues of the Virgin Mary that manifested miraculous powers in the city in the late sixteenth century, particularly in relation to the various city districts. Around these images there soon gathered confraternities that sought to preserve the icons and that encouraged reverence by arranging first to raise money for the construction of an oratory. It was precisely the Counter-Reformation era that gave rise to the shrines of Santa Maria della Libertà, Santa Maria delle Vergini, Santa Maria della Natività, and Santa Maria della Grada, which were added to Santa Maria del Baraccano, the Madonna del Piombo, the blessed Vergine del Soccorso and still others, to eventually twelve oratories all built on the city walls.[37]

In 1704 Bologna displayed itself to the gaze of so careful an observer as the cited Luigi Francesco Barelli, in the form of a city fortified by the oratories devoted to Maria Santissima "that serve with no other fortress to defend the city from its enemies, as a rampart to protect it."[38] But to protect Bologna and qualify it as a Marian city, it was not enough to have the sanctuary of San Luca erected on the hill like a sentinel to sight the enemy, or the twelve oratories that leaned against the wall like the

---

[36] "Et non è luoco così sacro come profano che ivi si vede la Santa Imagine di questa nostra avvocata… che ogni sabbato sera ciascun devoto vi si accende lampade et lumini che per oscura notte risplendono che par da meggio giorno (mezzogiorno), che rendono un gran decoro di devotione a tutti (quelli) che passano." Cavazzoni, *Corona di Gratie*, 2.

[37] Besides Mario Fanti, *Le chiese sulle mura*, see A. Ranaldi, "Frammenti delle mura di Bologna. Chiese e oratori," in *I confini perduti. Le cinte murarie cittadine europee tra storia e conservazione*, ed. Angelo Varni (Bologna: Compositori, 2005), 206–25; Annalisa Sabattini, "Chiese e oratori lungo le mura di Bologna," http://www.emiliaromagna.beniculturali.it/index.php?it/108/ricerca-itinerari/7/0 (accessed November 10, 2016).

[38] "Che servono senza verun'altra fortezza, che difenda la Città da' suoi nemici, come di antemurale al riparo della medesima." Barelli, *Memorie dell'origine* 2:154.

twelve stars of Our Lady of Heaven. It also needed the collaboration of the many prayers that rose each day in honor of Mary from the entire populace of Bologna.

One extraordinary document shows us where a devotee of the Virgin could go day by day to pray before a sacred image. The *Diario Mariale per l'Anno MDCCXXIII* was printed in Bologna by Giovan Battista Bianchi alla Rosa and consisted of a large printed sheet similar to a calendar where, on six columns, it lists, month by month and day by day, the Marian feast days and the churches where the faithful had to go to pray and honor the Madonna.[39] Addressed "To the Devotees of the Virgin Mary," the list is preceded by several notes which make it clear that, for certain liturgical feasts or those of particular saints, the appropriate church in which to worship the image of the Madonna has not been indicated, but in all other cases the *Diario Mariale* was a trustworthy guide for rendering homage to the Mother of God. It is helpful to read it alongside Antonio di Paolo Masini's *Bologna perlustrata*. It advises that the "images of the principal Confraternities of the Rosary, of the Belt… and also some others" often recur, "in view of the fact that our blessed GOD has conceded signal and miraculous graces to the city of Bologna upon the intercession of MARY, as she has been invoked through the worship of the aforementioned Holy Images, and through diverse pious reflections—as is clear to you, my fellow devout citizens, and also to those foreigners who have spent time here."[40] A final word of advice is then directed to those who must work and cannot visit the churches indicated everyday. On Sunday—the author of the diary suggests—they may consecrate to the Virgin "a journey on which they visit the HOLY IMAGES that they previously neglected while working, through this

---

[39] Bologna, Biblioteca Comunale dell'Archiginnasio Bologna, Cartella Gozzadini. On the print shop of Giovan Battista Bianchi alla Rosa, which dealt in ecclesiastical and devotional material, see Alberto Beltramo and Maria Gioia Tavoni, *I mestieri del libro nella Bologna del Settecento* (Sala Bolognese: Forni, 2013), 96.

[40] "Le immagini delle Confraternite principali del Rosario, della Cintura, ecc. ed anche alcune altre, attesocché Grazie segnalate e miracolose ha concedute DIO benedetto ad intercession di MARIA, invocata nel culto delle accennate Sante Immagini, alla Città di Bologna, e per diversi pii riflessi, chiari a voi divoti Concittadini, ed a qualunque, benché Forestiere, da qualche tempo qui dimorante." Ibid.

effort compensating for the difficulties that interrupted their pious exercises."[41]

Just to give an idea of the Marian calendar's structure, I cite the first days of the month of January:

JANUARY

1. Fri. Circumcision of our Lord. To Jesus and Maria Monache.
2. Sat S. Maria della Protezione in S. Michele in Strada Magg.
3. Sun. [S. Maria] del Rosario in S. Domenico.
4. Mon. [S. Maria] della Vita.
5. Tues. De' Tre Magi and degli Angeli. Confraternity at Strada Castiglione.
6. Wed. Epiphany of Our Lord at San Domenico.[42]

From this original document, we certainly cannot conclude that all or many citizens of Bologna paid their devotions on a daily basis, but there is no doubt that it can be inferred that the printed work had its market and that many people bought that pithy guide.

Over the centuries the city of Bologna has kept up its aspiration to present and construct itself as a holy city by recalling the memory of the Lord's Passion with the penitential pilgrimage to the *Sancta Jerusalem*, a reproduction of the earthly Jerusalem and a prefiguration of the heavenly Jerusalem. Side by side with this primitive and important representation of the holy city was the city's image as described by the Apocalypse with high walls closed by twelve gates guarded by twelve convents. Marian devotion added to the preceding figure the twelve stars of the Virgin's crown made up of the twelve sanctuaries located on the walls. The representation of the city devoted to Mary was completed by the four columns that held up an image of the Virgin and that rose skyward in the squares in front of the major mendicant religious orders: two in the churchyard and in the piazza of San Domenico, one in the *seliciata* of San Francesco, and the last in the square of San Martino.[43]

---

[41] "...il viaggio nel visitar le omesse SANTE IMMAGINI ne' precedenti di lavoro, supplendo con questa industria alle frapposte difficoltà in esercizio cotanto pio." Ibid.

[42] Ibid.

[43] Bologna, Biblioteca Comunale dell'Archiginnasio Bologna, Cartella Gozzadini 3, 41-96-01, Figs. 3–82. View of the five columns (the column of the Senato in Piazza del Mercato has no religious character), Pisarri print, 1757.

From the era of the communes till the end of the *ancien régime* the urban development of Bologna seemed to satisfy the desire of every believer to live in an ideal city where peace and prosperity were guaranteed by pious conduct and heavenly protection. Although there was no preordained plan that guided its urban development, there was no denying the centuries-long persistence of a symbolic representation of the heavenly city, which, in connection with its cultural development, juxtaposed to the primitive foursquare city a twelve-starred crown.

PART II

Apocalyptic Theology and Exegesis

CHAPTER 5

Risen to Judgment: What Augustine Saw

Francine Cardman

In his *Sermones ad populum*, Augustine often has recourse to the prospect of future judgment while instructing, encouraging, and admonishing his congregation.[1] Over the course of his ministry, he developed

[1] Preaching both as presbyter and bishop, Augustine delivered, mostly at Hippo and Carthage, approximately 559 sermons that have come down to us as *sermones ad populum*. They are only a small fraction of the estimated 8000 sermons he preached over the course of his ministry from 391 until his death in 430. See Hubertus R. Drobner, "The Transmission of Augustine's Sermons: A Critical Assessment," in *Tractatio Scripturarum: Philological, Exegetical, Rhetorical and Theological Studies on Augustine's Sermons: Ministerium Sermonis II*, ed. Anthony Dupont, Gert Partoens, and Mathijs Lamberigts (Turnhout: Brepols, 2012), 97–116, at 98, citing Pierre-Patrick Verbraken, "Saint Augustine's Sermons: Why and How to Read Them Today," *Augustinian Heritage* 33 (1987): 105–16, at 106.

This essay reflects and is meant to honor a nexus of interests in Ann Matter's scholarship on apocalypse, exegesis, and Augustine, and is indebted to decades of our conversations on ancient and medieval Christianity. From early on I imbibed from her an appreciation for the history of biblical exegesis and what it teaches us not only about the development of theology but, importantly, about the practice of quotidian Christianity in late antiquity.

F. Cardman (✉)
Boston College, Chestnut Hill, MA, USA

© The Author(s) 2019
E. Knibbs et al. (eds.), *The End of the World in Medieval Thought and Spirituality*, The New Middle Ages,
https://doi.org/10.1007/978-3-030-14965-9_5

two approaches to preaching on judgment in relation to poverty and charity, rich and poor, each with its characteristic clusters of scriptural texts and exempla. The two types are not mutually exclusive and may appear together in the same sermon; occasionally Augustine preaches on each theme singly. Use of ancillary texts from the Gospels and wisdom literature give either approach a different inflection. The first approach takes its basic orientation from two passages in 1 Tim. 6 about riches, their temptations, and their ends. The second, by contrast, takes its orientation from the parable of the sheep and the goats in Matt. 25:31-46, the last judgment.

Augustine preached from both perspectives throughout his ministry. His development of the two paradigms of judgment unfolds thematically and contextually rather than progressing along a strictly chronological course. The majority of the sermons considered here were preached between 410 and 417, but a small number of sermons from the last decade or so of his life are significant in his treatment of the two themes.[2] Contextual factors of place, audience, pastoral preoccupations, and theological controversies, along with external events, recent or held in collective memory, all had a bearing on Augustine's treatment of poverty, charity, and judgment in these sermons. The texts he preached on and the use he made of them depended as well on the developing North African lectionary, the annual commemorations of saints and martyrs, and the seasonal cycle of the liturgical year.[3] Attention to set scripture readings was augmented from the vast storehouse of Augustine's memory that led him from scriptural text to scriptural text, as he preached spontaneously, often making the freest of associations. Within the interaction of all these variables it is, nevertheless, possible to discern traces of a trend in what Augustine saw in these two visions of judgment at the day of the Lord's coming.

---

[2] When possible, reliable or likely dates for individual sermons will be footnoted. See Table of Sermon Dates for dating from scholarly studies and indices. Bibliographical references for those works are found there.

[3] See G. G. Willis, *St. Augustine's Lectionary* (London: S.P.C.K., 1962), and Michele Pellegrino's general introduction in *Works of St. Augustine: A Translation for the 21st Century. Part III: Sermons*, trans. Edmund Hill, ed. John E. Rotelle (Brooklyn, NY: New City Press, 1990), 1: 32–36, "Criterion on the Choice of Readings." Also see Martijn Schrama, "*Prima Lectio Quae Recitata Est*: The Liturgical Pericope in Light of Augustine's Sermons," *Augustiniana* 45 (1995): 141–75.

This essay, then, examines Augustine's preaching from these two orientations on poverty, charity, and judgment in the *sermones ad populum*. The first section, "Two Visions of Judgment," describes the characteristic features of each scriptural focus and its related texts, some of which are common to both. The two following sections analyze sermons oriented to each vision of judgment and its related texts: 1 Tim. 6 in "Banking on the Future" and Matt. 25 in "Beggars and Beatitudes." Next, "A World in Ruins" examines sermons on the sacking of Rome in 410 and the heightened eschatological sensibility with which Augustine recontextualizes the evils of the times in light of the future judgment and the present needs of the poor. Augustine's instruction for his congregation on how to live in preparation for that day is the focus of section "Coming on the Clouds." The essay concludes with "Mercy at the End," Augustine's preaching of Matthew's final judgment scene during the final years of his own life.

1 Two Visions of Judgment

Augustine's preaching on poverty, charity, and judgment coalesces around two sets of scriptural texts with distinctive rhetorics and perspectives. One set is centered on banking metaphors of investment and profit (interest) as typified by 1 Tim. 6:17–19, which instructs those who are rich to put their hopes on God, not the uncertainty of riches, do good works, and share generously, "thus storing up for themselves the treasure of a good foundation for the future, so they may take hold of life that really is life." Two kinds of ancillary texts support preaching from 1 Timothy and are frequently found with it in Augustine's sermons. The first are texts from the Gospel of Matthew that are drawn by the resonance of "treasure" in 1 Tim. 6:19 and amplify its meanings. Matthew 6:19–21 warns against storing up treasure on earth, where it can suffer corruption or be stolen by thieves, admonishing the hearer or reader instead to "store up for yourselves treasures in heaven." Similarly, Jesus' advice to the rich young man to sell all he had and give the money to poor also promises "treasure in heaven" (Matt. 19:21). Texts from Proverbs and Psalms coalesce around the metaphors of banking transactions and further nuance their meaning: Prov. 13:7–8, wealth as ransom (redemption) for the soul; Prov. 22:2, "rich and poor have met on the road"; Ps. 39.6, "he stores up and does not know for whom he is collecting." Additionally, exhortations to the rich earlier in 1 Tim. 6:6–10 seek to redirect the desire for riches and its attendant temptations ("the love of money is the root of all evil," v. 10) toward contentment and godliness (v. 6). In Augustine's preaching, the two sections from 1 Tim. 6, though separated by six intervening verses, form a coherent whole.

The second set of scriptural texts centers on the culmination of encountering Christ in the poor, the final judgment scene as represented in Matt. 25:31–46, the separation of the sheep and the goats, when "the Son of Man comes in his glory" (v. 31). On that day he will separate those gathered before him from all nations, some to his right, some to his left, beckoning the one to eternal blessedness in the kingdom, sending the other away to the pains of eternal fire. Augustine refers to this text often in his preaching, making use of short, descriptive phrases, direct quotation, allusions, and coded reminders of what is to come. He also focuses more extensively on Matthew's final judgment scene in several sermons from late in his life that are notable for their tone and intensity. That scenario is so familiar to hearers and readers of scripture, then and now, that it is important to keep in mind that it is part of a longer apocalyptic discourse in Matthew's Gospel that extends from Matt. 24:1–26:1. Ancillary texts related to preaching on Matt. 25:31–46 are mostly from the Gospels: Matt. 5:7, the blessing on the merciful; Matt. 10:40–42, giving a cup of cold water "to one of these little ones"; Matt. 19:16–22, the rich young man; and Matt. 19:23, the camel and the eye of the needle. Two texts from Luke are also important: Lazarus and the rich man in Luke 16:19–31 and the rich fool in Luke 12:18–21, who tore down his barns in order to store even more grain and goods for his future, unaware that his life would be demanded of him that very night. Prov. 22:2, the meeting of rich and poor on the way, is also used in some Matt. 25-oriented sermons, sometimes in conjunction with other ancillary texts and cameo appearances from Job that crossover from 1 Tim. 6-oriented sermons. Even with these shared elements, sermons making prominent use of Matt. 25 and its heightened eschatology belong to a different world than those focused through the lens of 1 Tim. 6.

Two texts from Matthew's Gospel are deployed in both perspectives, with different colorations. They expand upon the notion of storing up treasure, and Augustine uses them often. The first is from the Sermon on the Mount: "Store up for yourselves treasures in heaven, where neither moth nor rust consumes and where thieves do not break in and steal" (Matt. 6:19). The other is from the story of the rich young man: "If you would be perfect, go, sell your possessions, give to the poor, and you will have treasure in heaven; then come, follow me" (Matt. 19:21). When used in conjunction with 1 Tim. 6:19 and Prov. 13:8, these Matthean texts lend the authority of a saying of the Lord to the "treasure of a good foundation" that 1 Tim. 6:19 advises believers to store up in heaven, allowing Augustine wide range for exploiting banking metaphors. When these texts appear in sermons focused on the final judgment in Matt. 25 they lean toward the final verse of Jesus' saying about storing up treasures in heaven: "For where your treasure is, there your heart will also be" (Matt. 6:21). It is noteworthy that Jesus' saying about a camel passing through the eye of a needle more easily than a rich person entering the kingdom (Matt. 19:24) appears only twice in the sermons considered in this essay.[4]

2 Banking on the Future

First Timothy 6:3–10 has in view rich believers who consider faith ("godliness") a means of monetary gain, reminding them instead that "we brought nothing into the world so that we can take nothing out of it" (v. 7), and urging them to be content with having food and clothing (v. 8). Augustine makes frequent use of these verses and of the command in 1 Tim. 6:17 to those rich in the world not to be haughty. He warns rich and poor alike to avoid pride as well as discontent with their lots. A poor person has no reason to put on airs, he says, hence should not be praised for being humble: "Who could endure a person both needy and proud?"[5] They should not pridefully presume that, simply because they

[4] S. 114 B, one of the earliest sermons, uses the camel imagery, as does s. 85.2, which is one of the latest. See the section "Mercy at the End," for analysis of these two sermons and references to their dating. English translations of sermons 1–400 and of newly discovered sermons are found in *The Works of Saint Augustine, A Translation for the 21st Century, Part III: Sermons*, trans. Edmund Hill (11 volumes), the English counterpart of the original Italian project, *Nuova Biblioteca Agostiniana* (Roma: Città Nuova Editrice, 1979–1989). Hill's translation is available in an electronic edition: *The Works of Saint Augustine (4th Release): Part III, vols. 1–11*, ed. Boniface Ramsey (Charlottesville, VA: InteLex Corporation, 2014). Here and throughout this essay I have depended on the *Corpus Augustinianum Gissense*, ed. Cornelius Mayer (Basel: Schwab, 1995), available in an electronic edition, *Saint Augustine: Opera Omnia CAG*, 4th ed. (Charlottesville, VA: InteLex Corporation, 2000).

[5] S. 14.2. Trans. Hill, *Works* 3.1: 317; ed. Cyrille Lambot, *Augustinus: Sermones de Vetere Testamento (1-50)*, Corpus Christianorum Series Latina 41 (Turnhout: Brepols, 1961), 186, ll. 32–33. Cf. s. 36.7, "If a proud rich person is hard to put up with, who can

are poor like Lazarus, they are owed the kingdom. The desire for riches is a form of avarice, a slippery slope to evils of every sort. Affirming that the rich must avoid haughty pride, Augustine also asserts that there are rich people who are not prideful, who are content with their riches and not seeking more.[6] As he maintains in another sermon, "There's a great deal of difference, after all, between being rich and wanting to be rich. It's a very just distinction, it cannot be denied: in the first, means, in the second, greed."[7] Elsewhere he observes that there are those who are rich in the world who are also rich in faith.[8] Almsgiving and its lasting rewards provide the second focal point of Augustine's preaching on 1 Tim. 6. Although concerned for the poor, Augustine empathizes with the anxieties of the rich over acquiring, safeguarding, and increasing their riches, and describes them far more knowingly than he describes the condition of the poor. It is, however, a rhetorical necessity that he reach the rich and those of more modest but sufficient means if the poor are to receive material assistance. Accordingly, he shows them a way through their anxieties, a path toward heaven through good works and generosity, by which they also store up for themselves "the treasure of a good foundation for the future" (1 Tim. 6: 19).

Sermon 36 is a good example of how Augustine employs some of these texts to diagnose the spiritual states of the rich and the poor and recommend virtues and actions that would benefit each in this life and at the gateway to the next. He links the haughty rich of 1 Tim. 6:17 with their mirror opposites in Prov. 13:7, "those who affect to be rich though they have nothing" and "those who humble themselves though they are rich." He plays on the poverty Christ took on for the sake of humankind without losing his riches (quoting Paul, 2 Cor. 8:9: "he became poor

bear a proud poor person?" Trans. Hill, *Works* 3.2: 189; ed. Lambot, *Sermones de Vetere Testamento*, 439, ll. 149–51.

[6] S. 14.3, Lazarus; 14.4, humble rich person. The sermon is extravagant in its array of ancillary texts and exempla. A likely date is 418; one scholar proposes the end of his ministry.

[7] S. 177.5. Trans. Hill, *Works* 3.5: 182; ed. Cyrille Lambot, *Sancti Aurelii Augustini Hipponensis Episcopi Sermones Selecti Duodeviginti*, Stromata Patristica et Mediaevalia 1 (Utrecht: In aedibus Spectrum, 1950), 67, ll. 34–36. Cf. s. 61.10: "The worm in riches is pride." Trans. Hill, *Works* 3.5: 282; ed. PL 38: 413, l. 1. S. 177 is likely from 412; s. 61 from 412–416/21.

[8] S. 36.5.

for us, though he was rich, that you might be enriched by his poverty"), and notes that "what Christ's poverty contributed to us was not money but justness." Throughout the sermon, Augustine employs a paradoxical dialectic of oppositions and reversals regarding the moral valence of riches and poverty, inner and outward riches, who is really rich and who really poor. He shows how it is possible for the materially rich to become inwardly rich through giving to the poor—and do so without loss by storing up treasures in heaven (Matt. 6:20): "I am not telling you to do away with your wealth, but to *transfer* it." He holds up the rich man who took no notice of Lazarus at his door and the rich fool who tore down his barns to build bigger ones, whose fates his hearers can avoid by recalling that "the redemption of a man's soul is his riches" (Prov. 13:8). Invoking Matt. 25:42—"I was hungry and you did not give me to eat"— Augustine observes that the man who razed his barns to build bigger ones "didn't realize that the bellies of the poor were much safer storerooms than his barns."[9] Here the single verse from Matt. 25 interacts with Prov. 13:8 by naming an act of almsgiving with the potential to redeem sin, thus recalling the exhortation to store up treasure in I Tim. 6:17, while also alluding to the judgment that awaits those who do not give from their resources. At the end of the sermon he deploys the parable of the tax collector and the Pharisee praying in the temple (Luke 18:10–14) as a final warning to the mistaken, haughty rich and the spiritually deluded of either station.

Missing in s. 36 is any mention of how the treasure of the rich is to be transferred to heaven. That is supplied, albeit with scant explanation, in s. 60. There Augustine cites Ps. 39.6 (38.6) to describe the futility of storing up riches on earth: "Although man walks in the image yet he is disturbed in vain. He stores up, and does not know for whom he may be collecting them."[10] Their efforts are vain because they will die, and their

---

[9] S. 36.3. Trans. Hill, *Works* 3.2: 175; ed. Lambot, *Sermones de Vetere Testamento*, 435, ll. 46–47: "Puto quia paupertas Christi non nobis attulit pecuniam, sed iustitia." 36.5. Trans. Hill, 177; ed. Lambot, 437, l. 111: "Non dico uobis ut perdatis, sed ut migretis." 36.9. Trans. Hill, 180; ed. Lambot, 441, ll. 224–25: "Nesciebat pauperum uentres apothecis suis esse tutiores." Dating for s. 36 ranges from before 410 to 413. Prov. 13:8 is quoted twice in Sect. 7 and again in Sect. 9.

[10] S. 60.2. Trans. Hill, *Works* 3.3: 133; ed. Cyrille Lambot, "Les sermons LX et CCCLXXXIX de Saint Augustin sur l'aumône," *Revue bénédictine* 58 (1948): 36–42, at 37, ll. 27–28, 32–33; and 38, l. 34 (Augustine breaks up the quotation to comment on each phrase): "quamquam in imagine ambulet homo; tamen uane conturbatur; thesaurizat et nescit cui congreget ea." Ps. 39:6 in the Hebrew Bible is translated in this sermon from

heirs in turn will die, in a vicious cycle—that is, if thieves do not first bear it all away, or the world itself collapse. "Why not listen," Augustine asks, "to him [the maker of the world] and move it all to heaven?" By giving to "Christ's poor" they will find that "the calamities of this world have provided you with plenty of porters."[11] Porters as transfer agents for the rich, depositing their treasure in heaven, are recurring figures in sermons characterized by the perspective of 1 Tim. 6 and Prov. 13.8. In one noteworthy instance, Augustine supplies God's response to worries about how to move treasure to heaven: "seeing that I made you rich...I have made the poor your porters."[12]

3 BEGGARS AND BEATITUDES

Over the course of his ministry, Augustine preached numerous sermons on Matthew's Gospel, most likely following the North African lectionary cycle. Among them are sermons oriented toward the parable of the last judgment in Matt. 25:31–46, some that make ad hoc use of its general point or press isolated verses into service of a wide range of texts and themes, and yet others in which a significant focus on the judgment scenario stands more or less side by side with texts and exposition oriented to storing up treasure. S. 389 is among the latter, juxtaposing the two visions of judgment and their respective texts, yet presenting a strong reading of poverty, charity, and judgment through the lens of encountering Christ in the poor. References to destruction of property and

---

Augustine's Old Latin version of the psalm (Ps. 38.7). Pierre-Marie Hombert, *Nouvelles recherches de chronologie augustinienne* (Paris: Institut d'études augustiniennes), 262, cogently proposes 412 as the date for s. 60, rather than an earlier consensus for 397, because of its close relationship to s. 81 (soon after Rome's sacking in August 410) and its strong resemblance to *De civitate Dei* 1.10 about those who were tormented by the loss of their goods, because of their excessive attachment to them, and those who were not, because they had put them to good use (giving to the poor) and stored their treasure in heaven.

[11] S. 60.6. Trans. Hill, *Works* 3.3: 136; ed. Lambot, "Les sermons," 42, ll. 142–43. Ibid., 42.152–153: "Multos tibi laturarios fecit calamitas mundi." See below for the textual complications of s. 60 and s. 389.

[12] S. 38.9. Trans. Hill, *Works* 3.2: 214; ed. Lambot, *Sermones de Vetere Testamento*, 484, ll. 214–15: "qui te diuitem feci...laturarios tibi pauperes feci." S. 38 is undated. See also s. 25A.4; s. 38.9; s. 53A.6; s. 389.4. Porters receive further attention in the following section of this essay.

loss of monetary treasure during an enemy incursion in which houses were burned, captives taken, and fortunes stolen suggest a context after the Sack of Rome in 410, or perhaps earlier sorties and captive taking; although consonant with the concerns of s. 38, these remarks may suggest a plausible but not firm date for the sermon.[13]

At the start of the sermon, Augustine scants the Gospel reading from John on the bread of heaven (John 6:35–51) in order to speak at length about generosity to the poor, almsgiving to redeem sins, and sending treasure to heaven via the poor. In the last part of the sermon, he focuses intensely on the parable of the last judgment in Matt. 31–46. The seemingly disparate parts of the sermon are held together loosely by the thread of seeking and asking, giving and receiving that runs through them, along with a recurring emphasis on acts of charity. Augustine crystalizes these connections when he advises his hearers to "Ask by praying, seek by knocking, knock by giving alms (*erogando*). Do not let your hand be still."[14] Instead of citing Prov. 13:8, he appeals to Daniel's advice to king Nebuchadnezzar: "Take my advice, O king, and redeem your sins with almsdeeds" (Dan. 4:27), and later quotes Sir. 3:30 and 29.10 along with the verse from Daniel.[15] Augustine urges saving one's treasure by transferring it to heaven with the poor as porters, citing Matt. 19.21 (cf. Mark 10:21) and Matt. 6:21 on storing up treasure. Unlike sermons focused on banking metaphors from 1 Tim. 6: 17–19 and Prov. 13:8, when he refers to Matt. 6:19–21 here, he does not rest his gaze on the stored-up treasure, but looks beyond it, to the heart: "Where your treasure is there will your heart be also" (v. 21). "Lift your heart to heaven," Augustine says,

---

[13] S. 389.4. Before Lambot's 1948 editions of s. 389 and s. 60 (Lambot, "Les sermons"), each sermon had the same text in its concluding section, due to accidents of manuscript deterioration and later copying. Lambot argues that the "shared" sections originally belonged to s. 389 and that s. 60 ends naturally (and typically for Augustine) without it. Hill's translations of these two sermons generally follow Lambot's texts, but at times he makes editorial emendations to each.

[14] S. 389.2, my translation; ed. Lambot, "Les sermons," 45, ll. 35–37: "petite et dabitur uobis, quaerite et inuenietis, pulsate et aperietur uobis. omnia dicta sunt: pete, quaere, pulsa. petis orando, quaeris pulsando, pulsas erogando. non ergo quiescat manus." Hill (*Works* 3.10: 405) follows the Maurist text here: "ask by praying, seek by *discussing*, knock by giving a helping hand. So don't let the hand be idle." My emphasis. Not to help the poor is not to knock at all on the Lord's door, because knocking requires using one's hands to give.

[15] S. 389.3. Trans. Hill, 3.10: 405, Dan. 4:27; ed. Lambot, "Les sermons," 45, ll. 41–42: "consilium meum accipe, rex, et peccata tua elemosinis redime."

speaking for God, "lest it rot in the earth." That sensitivity to the spiritual state of the well-off giver is not reflected in his demeaning reference to the poor who receive: "What are the poor people to whom you give if not our porters, through whom we make transfers from earth to heaven."[16] Immediately afterward, however, he quotes Matt. 25:40: "When you did it for the least of mine, you did it for me."

What is striking about the sermon is not the juxtaposition of texts and perspectives, but the sustained attention Augustine gives to Matt. 25, its commanding place in the long final section, and his compelling interpretation of the parable. He asks for the same kind of attention from his audience: "I'm asking you to think hard about what our Lord Jesus Christ himself will say at the end of the world when he comes to judgment."[17] He confesses that he has often pondered this text and wants to meet their request for an explanation. He probes the reason and meaning of its stark decrees and the dispatching of some to eternal life in the kingdom, others to eternal fire. He asks why the entire judgment comes down to "I was hungry," and why "the Lord kept quiet about all the rest and only mentioned this." When that day comes, Augustine concludes, the Lord "is going to impute nothing but their acts of charity" to those who will be crowned at the judgment. It is not for the overall goodness or badness of their lives that they will be welcomed or barred from the kingdom, but for their generosity to the poor, without which their good lives would be meaningless. The obverse is true for those sent into eternal fire: their sins and crimes could have been redeemed by acts of charity; they are condemned because "I was hungry and you never gave me anything to eat." Two scripture verses quoted at the end of the section underscore the revelatory power of the judgment scene: "Blessed are the merciful, because mercy will be shown them" (Matt. 5:7); "Judgment without mercy upon one who has shown no mercy" (Jas 2:13). It is worth noting that

---

[16] S. 389.4, my translation. Ed. Lambot, "Les sermons," 48, ll. 129–30 and 152–53: "leva, inquit, cor in caelum, ne purescat in terra"; and "quid sunt pauperes, nisi laturarii nostro, per quos in caelum de terra migremus?"

[17] S. 389.5. Trans. Hill, *Works* 3.10: 409; ed. Lambot, "Les sermons," 49, ll. 165–66, 186–87. Also ibid.: Trans. Hill, *Works* 3.10: 410; ed. Lambot, "Les sermons," 50.201: "illis quos coronaturus est solas ipsas elemosinas imputabit."

either Augustine's Old Latin text or his memory omitted the final clause of the verse from James: "mercy triumphs over judgment."[18]

Additional sermons on Matthean texts supply Augustine with the means of constructing an interpretive lens that brings social relationships into greater relief and changes both the semantic and visual field of judgment. There are several significant aspects to sermons focused on Matt. 25 and the cluster of texts that both relate these sermons to and differentiate them from those oriented to 1 Tim. 6. Ancillary texts that are used in both sermon types are reinterpreted in these sermons, which also make more explicit and relational use of Prov. 22:2. They stress the multivalent identity of beggars, and they appeal to the poor Christ. They make more substantive use of Matt. 25 on the final judgment than do sermons focused on 1 Tim. 6, even when the latter may quote isolated verses from the parable.

Sermon 61 exemplifies Augustine's more complex analysis of rich and poor and the vision of judgment that it entails.[19] He gives more attention to the relational implications of Prov. 22:2, in which rich and poor meet on the way, rendering the common humanity of rich and poor more visible and substantial. He urges his hearers to *see*, to take notice of the poor: "those who are doing the asking are exactly like those being asked." In a second step, he reminds the congregation that they, too, are beggars, dependent on God: "We are God's beggars, remember... for him to take notice of his beggars, we in our turn must take notice of ours." He acknowledges that the rich may give from their surplus and count on making a profit from the funds they transfer to heaven, but

---

[18] "Superexaltat misericordia iudicio" in many *Vetus Latina* citations; "superexultat autem misericordia iudicio" in the Vulgate. See the *Vetus Latina Database* by Brepols (http://apps.brepolis.net/vld/). The clause is included in *Enarrationes in Psalmos* 147.13: "Merciless judgment will be passed on anyone who has not shown mercy, but mercy reigns supreme over judgment." Trans. Maria Boulding, *Works of St. Augustine Part III: Expositions of the Psalms* (Brooklyn, NY: New City Press, 2004), vol. 20, 453. Ed. E. Dekkers and J. Fraipont, *Enarrationes in Psalmos*, Corpus Christianorum Series Latina 39 (Turnhout: Brepols, 1956), 2: 2148, ll. 9–10: "iudicium enim sine misericordia illi qui non fecit misericordiam: superexaltat autem, inquit, misericordia iudicio."

[19] Many scholars propose 412–416 as a range of dates for s. 61. In addition to Table, see Luc De Coninck, et al., who propose between 412–421: "À propos de la datation des *sermones ad populum*: s. 51-70A," in *Ministerium Sermonis: Philological, Historical, and Theological Studies on Sermones ad Populum*, ed. Gert Partoens, Anthony Dupont, and Mathijs Lamberigts (Turnhout: Brepols, 2009), 49–67, at 61 and 67.

they must *give* to those in need of succor.[20] The appeal to self-interest remains, as does the financial language, but there is a change in tone and outlook with the more equalizing appeal to common humanity. At the end of the sermon, Augustine reveals how difficult he finds it to move his hearers to give to the poor, and how both he and they fail in meeting the requirements of justice and goodness.

> So give to the poor; I'm begging you, I'm warning you, I'm commanding you, I'm ordering you. Give to the poor whatever you like. You see, I won't conceal from your graces why I thought it necessary to preach this sermon to you. Ever since I got back here, every time I come to the church and go back again, the poor plead with me and tell me to tell you, that they need something from you. They have urged me to speak to you: and when they see they are not getting anything from you, they come to the conclusion that I am labouring among you to no purpose.[21]

These are sharper and sadder words from Augustine than found in sermons oriented to 1 Tim. 6. Interactions between audience and preacher were common in the ancient church, and those present for this sermon applauded him and called out their approval ("You have heard, you have applauded...you have given back words"). He thanks God they have heard him and received the seed he has sown, even though he finds their applause burdensome and dangerous to himself, presumably as a temptation to pride. He leaves them with a challenge: their praise for the sermon is "no more than the leaves of trees; what we are looking for is fruit," that is to say, the good works of giving to the poor.[22] Two sermons on the Beatitudes, s. 53 and s. 53A, are roughly contemporary with s. 61 and share some of its key features.[23] In s. 53A Augustine holds together seemingly divergent sentiments and texts: doing good works and storing up treasure, recommending the poor as porters to transfer their benefactors'

---

[20] S. 61.8. Trans. Hill, *Works* 3.3: 145 (both quotations).

[21] S. 61.13. Trans. Hill, *Works* 3.3: 147; ed. PL 38: 414, ll. 26–35.

[22] Trans. Hill, *Works* 3.3: 149; ed. PL 38: 414, ll. 39–40, 41: "audistis, laudastis... accepistis, uerba reddidistis"; 414, ll. 43–44: "istae laudes uestrae folia sunt arborum: fructus quaeritur."

[23] S. 53 can be reliably dated to 413. See Table and De Coninck, et al., "À propos de la datation," 63–64, 67. S. 53A cannot be dated by any fixed referents, but recent scholarship suggests between 412–416 (Frede), as also De Coninck, et al., 64, 67. S. 53A is useful for its treatment of passages from 1 Tim. 6 in comparison with s. 53.

riches to heaven and commanding the rich to "look at the hungry, look at the naked, look at the needy, look at the immigrants, look at the captives" who will take up the task of transferring their treasures. Yet at the same time, it emphasizes that rich and poor have met (Prov. 22:2) and are walking as companions on the same road. Quoting Matt. 25:40—"What you have done for the least of mine, you have done for me"—Augustine urges, "Let the member of Christ give to the member of Christ, let the one who has give to the one who lacks."[24] Explicating how rich and poor have met, he appeals to 1 Tim. 6:7 to stress their common nakedness in birth and death, entering and leaving the world with nothing. They meet on the road and are meant to encounter each other: the rich help the poor, the poor test the rich. Their interaction is not simply utilitarian, but revelatory: Augustine quotes the beatitude on the poor in spirit (Matt. 5:4) and announces, "They may possess wealth, they may not possess wealth; let them only be poor, and theirs is the kingdom of heaven."[25]

In both sermons, he insists on the necessity of bringing forth fruit, the good works that are the evidence of faith working through love.[26] In both, he also comments briefly on the individual Beatitudes, but from different perspectives in each sermon. In s. 53 he gives particular attention to the beatitude on the pure in heart and what it means to see God. He begins s. 53A with an exhortation to his hearers to put God's word into practice through the way they live and he focuses on the poor in spirit, moving with agility between spiritual and material poverty and stressing the necessity of good works through which rich and poor meet on the way.[27]

By their very nature, the Beatitudes embrace eschatology and earth, deeds and their recompense. When considering the beatitude on mercy and the merciful in these sermons, Augustine reminds the rich that they, too, are beggars whom God will treat in the same manner as they treat those who beg mercy from them.[28] In s. 53A he puts these actions and outcomes in terms of living in a way that is consistent with God's word, thus bearing good fruit and transferring the riches of these good works

---

[24] S. 53A.6, 11. Trans. Hill, *Works* 3.3: 80 ("Look at the hungry..."), 82 ("Let the member of Christ..."). Ed. *Miscellanea Agostiniana* 1 (Rome: Tipografia poliglotta vaticana, 1930), 630, ll. 13–15, 27–28. S. 53A is also indexed as Morin 11.

[25] S. 53A. Trans. Hill, *Works* 3.3: 81; ed. *Miscellanea Agostiniana* 1: 631, ll. 12–13.

[26] S. 53A.1, 4, 5, 15; s. 53.11; see Gal 5:6.

[27] S. 53.6, 7, 9, 10, 12–13; s. 53A.1, 2, 3–4, 5–6.

[28] S. 53.5; s. 53A.10; cf. s. 61.8.

to heaven.[29] He is more direct about work and reward in s. 53: what we look for comes later; now we have to do what we are told is needed to attain it. He observes that anyone acting mercifully toward the poor hopes for mercy in return. Or, as he puts it earlier in the sermon: "Do it, and it will be done; do it with others, that it may be done with you."[30] Two undated sermons reflect a similar mingling of motivations and acts of mercy in conjunction with lending to God and identifying the destitute Christ in the interaction of the rich benefactor and the destitute poor person who have met on the way.[31]

Augustine's more prominent appeals to the poor Christ—whether as the poor beggar who asks, the rich beggar who gives, or the risen beggar who receives what is given—begins to transform his discourse on poverty, charity, and judgment. Preaching more substantively on Matthew's scenario of the last judgment brings out the virtue of mercy implicit in these sermons, begins to draw Augustine's attention beyond the more mundane metaphorical realm of storing treasure and lending at interest, and into the realm of apocalyptic speech and vision where the final judgment is revealed. For Augustine and his hearers, that vantage point is unavoidably caught up in the travail of the times.

4 THE WORLD IN RUINS

The geopolitical event of Rome's fall to Alaric and his Visigothic army on August 24, 410 rapidly made itself felt in North Africa, as Augustine's sermons and other writings attest. Crosscurrents of religious and political allegiances and accusations clashed in a chaotic sea of anxieties and uncertainty. If Rome could fall, what of the empire? What of the world? Whose god(s) had failed? Why were these things happening in

---

[29] S. 53A.1; 53A.5.

[30] S. 53.1; s. 53.8; s. 53.5. Trans. Hill, *Works* 3.3: 67–68; ed. Pierre-Patrick Verbraken, "Le Sermon 53 de saint Augustine sur les Béatitudes selon saint Matthieu," *Revue bénédictine* 104 (1994): 21–33, at 23 l. 55: "fac, et fiet; fac cum altero, ut fiat tecum."

[31] S. 38.8, quoting Matt. 25:40; s. 39.6, quoting Prov. 22:2. Mention of the end of the world at the beginning of 38.11 might be an oblique reference to the sacking of Rome in 410 or simply a general expression of Augustine's eschatological outlook. Regardless of when he preached them, the sermons suggest that he had found a useful way to associate the two visions of judgment.

"Christian times"?[32] Was the end at hand? Was judgment coming, or had it already begun? Augustine's storied response to this event and its cultural disturbances was *The City of God*, written over the course of that decade and into the next. His sermonic responses were more timely, beginning as early as that September and continuing into the new year and beyond. They overlap chronologically with datable sermons on poverty, charity, and judgment which tend to draw on texts associated with 1 Tim. 6 alongside texts oriented to Matt. 25. Just as preaching on the Beatitudes when they are assigned in the lectionary may influence the way in which Augustine narrates either or both of his dual visions of judgment, so too does preaching in the context of Rome's fall and its aftermath.

Soon after news of Rome's fall had reached North Africa, Augustine preached on the suffering and damage the event entailed and the questions of meaning it evoked.[33] Sermon 397, commonly referred to as *De excidio urbis Romae*, is the only sermon entirely given over to the event; but Augustine speaks of the city's fall, sometimes obliquely, in many later sermons, as the readings of the day prompt him. Common themes appear among these post-410 sermons, linking them to the sermons on poverty and charity discussed here and to Augustine's developing view of final judgment. In s. 397 Augustine interprets Rome's fall and consequent suffering through scriptural texts and cultural practices, comparing it to the lashing a devoted father gives his son in order to keep him from further misdoing—a form of chastisement and discipline meant to fend off harsher judgment by reforming the child. "People are surprised...when when God takes the human race to task, and stirs them up with the rod of fatherly correction, disciplining them before passing judgment."[34] He makes

---

[32] The phrase reflects the recriminations of pagans directed at Christians for their abandonment of the gods, as well as Christians' own fears that God's providence had abandoned them. See s. 25.3; s. 113A.11, 13; s. 87.8; s. 105.8, 12; s. 296.1–9.

[33] For analysis of these sermons, see Theodore S. De Bruyn, "Ambivalence Within a 'Totalizing Discourse': Augustine's Sermon on the Sack of Rome," *Journal of Early Christian Studies* 1.4 (1993): 405–21; Jean-Claude Fredouille, "Les Sermons d'Augustin sur la chute de Rome," in *Augustin Prédicateur (395–411): Actes de Colloque International de Chantilly (5 septembre 1996)*, ed. Goulven Madec (Paris: Institut d'études augustiniennes, 1998), 439–48.

[34] S. 397, the *Sermo de excidio urbis Romae*, trans. Hill, *Works* 3.10: 436; ed. M. V. O'Reilly, Corpus Christianorum Series Latina 46 (Turnhout: Brepols, 1969), 250, ll. 36–39: "Et mirantur homines...quando corripit Deus genus humanum et flagellis piae castigationis exagitat, excercens ante iudicium disciplinam...." Augustine's reference to common practice is also an allusion to Prov. 3:12; see also s. 15A.3. Prov. 3:12 (LXX): "If the Lord loves someone he

a similar comparison in s. 296, in which he regards the world as a servant "who knows his lord's will and does not behave properly [and] will be beaten with many lashes" (Luke 12:47), since the Lord's will is known now that the gospel is preached openly throughout the world.[35] The scriptural examples of corrective discipline that Augustine cites in s. 397 coincide with texts that appear repeatedly in sermons on poverty, charity, and judgment, particularly the rich man and Lazarus and the humility of Job in his suffering.[36] Relatedly, he observes in another sermon that "the world is devastated, the press is trodden," but these troubles can serve as "training exercises" for Christians if they are not deceived by the lovers of this world. "Trouble comes; it will be whichever you wish, your education or your condemnation."[37]

Anxiety over a world grown old and falling into ruins pervades sermons preached around 410/11 and soon after, in which Augustine reflects on the tenor of public discourse in Hippo, Carthage and other towns. He frequently refers to complaints about the evils of the times and critiques (from pagans) or the confoundment (of Christians) that Rome's ruin and the world's decline, if not its perishing, should happen in "Christian times."[38] He addresses these anxieties by putting them into a larger framework of God's providential correction and the *telos* of human existence, while also deflecting pagan assertions of Christian responsibility for Rome's fall—anticipating arguments he developed further in the *City of God*. For the purposes of this essay, what is most

---

corrects him; he lashes every son whom he receives" (also quoted in Heb.12:6), is an important scriptural warrant for Augustine cites often in regard to correcting sin and error.

[35] S. 296.11. Trans. Hill, *Works* 3.8: 210.

[36] S. 397.4. See the example of Lazarus in other sermons on Rome's fall: s. 15A.2; s. 33A.4; s. 113A.3; and Job, s. 15A.5–7.

[37] S. 81.7. Trans. Hill, *Works* 3.3: 363; ed. PL 38: 503, ll. 42–43: "uastatur mundus, calcatur torcular"; and 503, ll. 51–52: "iusti estote, et exercitationes erunt. tribulatio uenit: quod uolueris erit, aut exercitatio, aut damnatio." Cf. 379.9. See also s. 105.13, "being schooled in tribulation" (trans. Hill, *Works* 3.4: 96; ed. PL 38: 625, ll. 13–14); s. 113A.11, "we know you as a Father when you make promises, we know you as a Father when you wield the rod; train us well, and give us the inheritance you have promised at the end" (trans. Hill, *Works* 3.4: 179; ed. *Miscellanea Agostiniana* 1: 151, ll. 22–24: "te nouimus patrem promittentem, te nouimus patrem flagellantem.").

[38] S. 25.3, evil days; s. 113A.11, 13; s. 81.7, 8, 9; s. 105.8, 12, Christ has ruined Rome; s. 296.9.

significant about these sermons, in addition to their thematic overlap with the sermons on poverty, charity, and judgment, is their effort to calm apocalyptic fears while maintaining the tension generated by the prospect of future judgment.

Augustine argues for eschatological hope, rejecting hope "in things that are slipping by and passing away," whether personal riches or Rome's empire in the West. He reminds his hearers that, although earthly kingdoms must end, they should remember that they have been promised a heavenly kingdom that has no end. He suggests that these tribulations may not be the end time: "If this is the end now, God can see. Perhaps, after all, it is not yet the end...but does that mean the end will never come? Fix your hopes on God, long for eternal things, look forward to heavenly realities." He acknowledges the temporal losses suffered by that part of the "wandering pilgrim city of Jerusalem" resident in Rome and notes that they have not lost eternal goods.[39] To those discomfited by Christian suffering in the city's fall he asks tartly: "Has it escaped your notice that it is the prerogative of Christians to suffer temporal evils, and hope for everlasting goods?"[40]

As Augustine negotiates the nexus of the temporal and the eternal in his preaching on Rome's fall, he turns his attention to the final judgment, urging believers to live in ways conducive to eternal life, reminding them of the consequences otherwise. He frames s. 113A, preached on September 25 in 410,[41] by proclaiming Christian faith in a life after this world, the resurrection of the dead, the end of the world, and the final judgment. The story of Lazarus and the rich man from the pericope serves as a warning, and the martyr commemorated that day as an example of keeping a faithful eye on the future. That warning is reinforced by Augustine's reference to the coming of Christ "with due payments for both believers and unbelievers," when he will sit in judgment separating the sheep from the goats. Quoting Matt. 25:34, 41, on the respective destinations of each group, he drives home his point. At the end of the sermon, he returns to judgment in relation to the evils of the times and

---

[39] S. 105.7. Trans. Hill, *Works* 3.4: 91; ed. PL 38: 621, ll. 21–22, slipping by; 105.11 (trans. Hill, *Works* 3.4: 94; ed. PL 38: 623, ll. 24–29), end times; 105.12 (trans. Hill, *Works* 3.4: 95; ed. PL 38, 624, ll. 11–12), "portio peregrinantis Ierusalem ciuitatis non ibi magna degit?"

[40] S. 296.10. Trans. Hill, *Works* 3.8: 209; ed. *Miscellanea Agostiniana* 1: 407, ll. 28–29.

[41] Only a month after the event.

God's patience with humankind, urging his hearers to patient acceptance of God's chastisements as a means of avoiding eternal death. His advice has a threatening edge: "So, brothers and sisters, don't let God's chastisements get you down, or he may leave you alone so that you perish forever."[42]

The poor are especially visible in s. 81, in which Augustine prescribes meekness as the way to avoid being scandalized by the evils the world is undergoing. There he urges his congregation to do Christ's work: "I beg you, I beseech you, I exhort you all to be meek, to show compassion to those who are suffering, to take care of the weak; and at this time of many refugees from abroad, to be generous in your hospitality, generous in your good works."[43] In the winter of 411, Augustine preached on what it means to be blessed by the Lord (Ps. 94:12) in evil times, admonishing his congregation not to be angry at the divine judgment and instructing them to "think about the poor, how Christ in his nakedness is to be clothed," imploring them to "listen to the judgment" Christ will pass on what they have done for his least ones.[44] More than half of s. 296 is occupied with Rome's fall and its aftermath. Yet, when Augustine urges his hearers to feed God's sheep, he has in mind bringing schismatic Donatists into the church, not the material needs of the poor; when he speaks of storing up treasure in heaven (Matt. 6:20) the poor are not named or noted. Appealing to those afraid of losing their riches to the barbarians, he directs them to give their treasures to Christ: "What Christ is guarding for you, can the Goth take away from you?"[45] The poor remain in the shadowy background, necessary but only implied, the porters with whom the rich might send their treasures to Christ, in exchange for having given them alms.

---

[42] S. 113A.4. Trans. Hill, *Works* 3.4: 173; ed. *Miscellanea Agostiniana* 1: 144, ll. 26–28, "ueniet cum retributionibus fidelium et infidelium: fidelibus praemia daturus, infideles in ignem aeternum missurus uos, et in aeternum pereatissee." S. 113A.14 (trans. Hill, *Works* 3.4: 181; ed. *Miscellanea Agostiniana* 1: 154, ll. 4–5), chastisements.

[43] S. 81.9. Trans. Hill, *Works* 3.3: 366; ed. PL 38: 506, ll. 9–13.

[44] S. 25.8, referring to Matt. 25:40. Trans. Hill, *Works* 3.2: 86; ed. Lambot, *Sermones de Vetere Testamento*, 339, ll. 149–50 and 161–62.

[45] S. 296.13, feeding sheep. 296.11. Trans. Hill, *Works* 3.8: 210; ed. *Miscellanea Agostiniana* 1: 409, l. 7, "quod custodit Christus, numquid tollit Gothus."

5 COMING ON THE CLOUDS

Reminders of coming judgment appear frequently in Augustine's sermons in the years after Rome's fall. Sermon 265 on the Ascension, preached in 412, is typical. Augustine follows the reading from Acts in pairing Jesus' ascension (Acts 1:6–9) with his coming again, "this Jesus who has been taken up from you into heaven will come in the same way you saw him go into heaven" (Acts 1:11). Turning the apostles' question about when Jesus will return into the question of his audience, Augustine says he does not know, but that when he comes, the Lord will be visible to all, not just his own, and will judge all, welcoming those on the right into the kingdom, dispatching those on the left into eternal fire (Matt. 25:34, 41).[46] In other sermons, he cites John's account of the last day (John 5:24–29), when all in the tombs will hear the Son's voice and come forth, some to the resurrection of life, some to the resurrection of judgment.[47] All will rise in the body, both good and bad, but *not* all will be changed.[48] That day will be like the days of Noah (Luke 17:26), about which the Lord had also given advance notice.[49]

As Augustine preaches resurrection and judgment, he draws repeatedly on metaphors of sorting and separating that refer to kinds of beings and kinds of matter, as well as to the method or means of separation. Hence, we hear of separating sheep from goats, winnowing or threshing wheat from chaff, rooting up weeds, pressing oil from olives and leaving behind the dregs.[50] These images give the strong impression that not many will be saved (see Luke 13:23, "Lord, will only a few be saved?").

---

[46] S. 265.3. See also s. 277.16 (in 413), both the just and the wicked will see him in his real body; s. 127.10, the Lord coming as judge in the same form of his humanity.

[47] S. 277.16; 362.9 (in 411).

[48] S. 362.19, 23, 26. Augustine's text of 1 Cor. 15:51, "we will not all be changed," is from the Vetus Latina and is a variant of the Greek text, which reads "we will *all* be changed" (my emphasis). Trans. Hill, *Works* 3.10: 255; ed. PL 39: 1624, ll. 28–29: "omnes resurgemus, non tamen omnes immutabimur."

[49] S. 361.19 (in 411). See also s. 114B.1–2 (a sermon given in the winter of 403–404) and *En. Ps.* 147.1 (trans. Boulding, *Works* 3.20: 441) for comparison of the Son of Man's coming with "the cataclysm in Noah's day."

[50] Sheep and goats run through the sermons discussed here, as do images of threshing and threshing floors, wheat and chaff, e.g., s. 111.3; s. 113A.11; s. 223.2 (at the Easter vigil!). Related images include grains, good grains, s. 2.25.4; s. 111.2; s. 361.10; weeds, s. 47.6; oil and dregs, s. 113A.11.

Despite the tribulations they have endured and the threats to their possessions, Augustine struggles to wean his congregation from loving the world and what they possess in it. He reminds them it is God who commands him to speak; he is just warning them, as God also warns and terrifies him. "The time to be interrogated is coming," he says, when God will interrogate the just and the wicked, saving and rewarding the former, casting the latter into hell.[51] No wonder that, in another sermon, he asks those assembled, "Do you want this judge to come?"[52]

Concerned to stir up the complacent, console those suffering from the evils of the times, and shepherd his flock toward the life that lasts forever, Augustine cajoles, corrects, commands, and, less frequently, comforts them in sermons on judgment. Sermon 47, "on the sheep," has in view the less-than-zealous flock to whom Augustine preaches, as well as the schismatic Donatists (see below). To his own people, he speaks words of warning and encouragement about the great separation that is to come. He encourages them to "please the Lord in the region of the living, because it is difficult to please him in the region of the dead." He suggests many ways to please God now: asking for mercy, abstaining from sins as much as possible, confessing and weeping for them; showing mercy; forgiving others, as the Lord's prayer asks; giving good example; doing good deeds through which others might glorify God; and bearing good fruit.[53] In another sermon, he encourages them to "fast from the world," which he describes as an "exercise of justice," letting go of love for the world in order to love God with open hands.[54] In another he points out that Christ the judge is doing them a favor by letting them know the final sentence ahead of time, warning them of future punishment so they might avoid it: "Anyone who says, 'Watch out' doesn't

---

[51] S. 125.7–8, quotation at 8. Trans. Hill, *Works* 3.4: 259; ed. PL 38: 695, l. 23. Hombert (*Nouvelles recherches*, 52) argues for 400–405, during the Donatist controversy; other scholars propose 416/17, during the Pelagian controversy.

[52] S. 299.4. Trans. Hill, *Works* 3.8: 231; ed. PL 38, 1370, ll. 4–5.

[53] S. 47.1. Trans. Hill, *Works* 3.2: 298; ed. Lambot, *Sermones de Vetere Testamento*, 572, ll. 19–20; also 47.6, 7, 11, 13, 25.

[54] S. 125.7. Trans. Hill, *Works* 3.4: 258; ed. PL 38: 694, ll. 13–15, "ipsa est exercitatiom iustitiae, ferre tempus hoc, et ab hoc saeculo quodam modo ieiunare." In the same passage Augustine suggests they "think of human love, think of it as the hand of the soul. If it's holding one thing, it can't hold another." Ed. PL 38: 694, ll. 20–21: "intendite amorem hominis: sic putate quasi manum animae. si aliquid tenet, tenere aliud non potest."

want to find anybody to strike."[55] Accepting God's chastisements patiently, also noted in previous sermons, is another way through which Christians might hope to find themselves sitting on the right when the Lord comes as a judge on the final day.

Warnings of judgment and metaphors of sorting and separation were at the tip of Augustine's tongue due to their frequent deployment in his ongoing efforts to end the Donatist schism that had originated in Carthage in 305 during the last great persecution (303–311). When Augustine became the bishop of Hippo, the city was almost evenly divided between his "catholic" congregation and the Donatists. He would be engaged with them for most of the first half of his ministry, roughly from 393 to 413. The key issue for the Donatists was the moral purity of the church, defined by standards of resistance expected from pastors and people in response to imperial edicts prohibiting worship, confiscating church property, and requiring participation in the cult of the emperor. For Augustine a century later, the issue in its most basic terms was twofold: the problem of schism itself and the nature of the church as a mixed body of sinners and saved, their identities unknown until the final winnowing on the last day. In regard to these latter, he held that the Donatists were arrogant and mistaken in their premature judgments of matters known only to God. Regarding the schism itself, Augustine adamantly maintained that the Donatists were sinning against charity by their self-willed separation. Lacking charity, therefore, their seemingly good deeds were not acts of charity at all, because their hearts, their intentions, were wrong. Given that Donatists nevertheless performed outward acts of apparent charity, it became all the more important to Augustine that catholic Christians engage in works of charity and mercy. It was therefore incumbent on him to teach, correct, and persuade them to do so.[56]

[55] S. 113A.4. Trans. Hill, *Works* 3.2: 173; ed. *Miscellanea Agostiniana* 1: 145, ll. 3–4. Augustine makes a similar point at the beginning of his sermon on Ps. 147: God warns about judgment and the last day out of desire to help us, "he does not want to condemn us when he comes to judge." Trans. Boulding, *Works* 3.20: 441; ed. Dekkers and Fraipont, *Enarratio* 147, 2138, ll. 6–8.

[56] For a study of Augustine's preaching during the Donatist controversy, see Anthony Dupont, *Preacher of Grace: A Critical Reappraisal of Augustine's Doctrine of Grace in His Sermones ad Populum on Liturgical Feasts and During the Donatist Controversy* (Leiden: Brill, 2014), 160–98. For Donatism in general, W. H. C. Frend's classic study is foundational: *The Donatist Church: A Movement of Protest in Roman North Africa* (Oxford: Clarendon Press, 1971). Among more recent studies see *The Donatist Schism: Controversy and Contexts*, ed. Richard Miles (Liverpool: Liverpool University Press, 2016); *The Uniquely*

Augustine's expressions of pastoral care for the poor, the rich who can transfer their treasure to heaven, and others who can give alms seem, at times, to suggest a quid pro quo of good works and guarantees of salvation. This is evident in sermons oriented to either of the two visions of judgment identified in this essay, although more prevalent in those oriented to 1 Tim. 6 and its metaphorical field of transactions and actors. Grace is not absent in Augustine's counsel to perform charitable work, but neither is it prominent in most of these sermons. He speaks indirectly about grace, without naming it as such, in terms of God offering opportunities for repentance, giving warnings, and chastising or punishing in order to correct. He often recalls God's gracious love for humankind in creating women and men in God's image; in desiring eternal life for them; and in acting mercifully toward them. There are few explicit references in these sermons on judgment to the controversy over sin, grace, and free will that Augustine pursued with Pelagius and his followers until the last years of his life (411–430).[57] Where Pelagius argued for free will and good works, Augustine stood firm for grace and predestination. Occasionally he qualifies his advice about gaining eternal life through charity to the poor with the proviso that one also needs to be among those whom God has predestined. Yet he does not expand on such assertions, and they do not sit well with his efforts to change the reluctant rich into almsgivers by appealing to the security of storing riches in heaven. In s. 47, on the sheep, he reminds his congregation that only God knows the sheep from the goats by virtue of predestination and foreknowledge. "For the present, because all are under the sign of Christ, and all have access to the grace of God, you consider yourself a sheep, while perhaps God knows you for a goat." Yet, in the meantime, he advises, "you should listen

---

African Controversy: Studies on Donatist Christianity, ed. Anthony Dupont, Matthew Alan Gaumer, and M. Lamberigts (Leuven: Peeters, 2015); and Maureen Tilley, *The Bible in Christian North Africa: The Donatist World* (Minneapolis: Fortress Press, 1997).

[57] For grace and free will in the Pelagian controversy see Lenka Karfíková, *Grace and the Will According to Augustine*, trans. Markéta Janebová, Supplements to *Vigiliae Christianae* 115 (Leiden: Brill, 2012); Gerald Bonner, *Freedom and Necessity: St. Augustine's Teaching on Divine Power and Human Freedom* (Washington, DC: Catholic University of America Press, 2007). For a contextual study of Augustine's theology, see Carol Harrison, *Augustine: Christian Truth and Fractured Humanity* (Oxford: Oxford University Press, 2000); for his theology of grace, see J. Patout Burns, *The Development of Augustine's Doctrine of Operative Grace* (Paris: Institut d'études augustiniennes, 1980).

as a sheep" to what is being preached.[58] Referring to grain and the threshing floor in another sermon, Augustine prefaces his advice with an awkward conditional: "*If* I am speaking to the good grain, *if* those predestined to eternal life recognize the truth of what I have been saying, let them speak with deeds, not voices."[59] In later sermons that focus on Matthew's vision of the last judgment, he does not offer similar qualifications.

The absence of references to theological issues of sin, grace, and free will in these sermons may be a reflection of another aspect of the Pelagian controversy that relates directly to Augustine's preaching on almsgiving and care of the poor. Peter Brown has called attention to Pelagius' critique of wealth and a treatise *On Riches* by one of his followers that calls for the divestment of wealth in order for all to have enough. That proposal ran directly contrary to Augustine's program of care for the poor, which depended upon a steady practice of almsgiving in which small donations to the poor served as penance for the daily sins for which Christians daily sought forgiveness when saying the Lord's prayer. As Brown puts it: "This meant, in effect, that perpetual giving was the counterpart of perpetual sin."[60] So conceived, almsgiving and the ransom of the soul were a practical expression of the clash between Augustine's view of humankind's propensity for sin and Pelagius' view of human freedom and the possibility of human sinlessness.

Even so, the eschatological edge of Augustine's preaching about judgment and its relationship to charity toward the poor sharpens as he

---

[58] S. 47.15. Trans. Hill, *Works* 3.2: 30; ed. Lambot, *Sermones de Vetere Testamento*, 585, ll. 398–400. Cf. s. 81.6, "If you are Sons of God, if redeemed by the grace of the Savior, if bought by his precious blood, if born again by water and the Spirit, *if predestined to the heavenly inheritance*, then of course you are sons of God." Trans. Hill, *Works* 3.3: 363 (my emphasis); ed. PL 38: 503, ll. 25–28. S. 47 is most likely from 407–408 or 410–411; s. 81 from c. 410.

[59] S. 111.4. Trans. Hill, *Works* 3.4: 144 (my emphasis); ed. Cyrille Lambot, "Le sermon CXI de saint Augustin," *Revue bénédictine* 57 (1947), 112–16 at 116, ll. 107–108. See also 111.1, where Augustine refers to Eph. 1:4, 5, being chosen and predestined in Christ. The sermon may be from c. 417.

[60] Peter Brown, *The Ransom of the Soul: Afterlife and Wealth in Early Western Christianity* (Cambridge: Harvard University Press, 2015), 96. For the larger context of this argument and the *sermones*, see his massive work, *Through the Eye of a Needle: Wealth, the Fall of Rome, and the Making of Christianity in the West, 350–550 AD* (Princeton: Princeton University Press, 2012), Part III, An Age of Crisis, particularly Chapters 21–23, on the sermons, Pelagianism, and wealth.

focuses on the Matthean apocalypse of the last judgment. That scene becomes increasingly significant in extant sermons from the final decade of Augustine's life.

6 Mercy at the End

In an undated fragment, s. 358A, Augustine gives a definition of mercy in terms far removed from financial transactions and treasures. Drawing on its etymological roots, he describes *misericordia*, sorrow of heart, as nothing other than being touched by the *miseria* of another.[61] Every good work is related to this heart sadness in face of another's sorrow and need. Echoing Matt. 25, he invokes the feeling of compassion that ought to accompany every work of mercy: feel sorry for the one who is hungry, thirsty, unclothed, in need of hospitality, ill, or has died, and for those whose dispute you have helped resolve. Now is the time, he stresses, to sow the works of mercy—with kindness and tears—as there will be no need for works of mercy in heaven. Sorrow of heart and sowing seeds of kindheartedness have their harvest, their reward. Sowing in tears in the cold of winter is a different and more vulnerable act than packing off treasure to heaven, carried by porters who are recipients of one's alms.[62] The fragment of s. 358A, whatever its date, is akin to the vision of judgment that becomes more evident in the last decade or so of Augustine's ministry.

Another short, undated sermon on almsgiving, laden with the language of financial transactions, is also suggestive of the approach that Augustine takes to these metaphors in sermons from his last years. In the authentic, second part of s. 390, Augustine breaks through the frame of mercantile banking at a high rate of interest by reversing the roles of lender and debtor through his deft use of Matt. 25:37–40, "When you did [it] for one of the least of mine, you did it for me." Here Augustine speaks for Christ: "I it was, I'm telling you, who received it whenever poor people received it; it was in them that I was hungry, in them that I was satisfied." What his hearers lend at interest to God is ultimately transmuted into eternal life. "There is no other remedy to deliver us from death but

---

[61] S. 358A.1. Trans. Hill, *Works* 3.10: 196. Although its brevity makes dating the fragment impossible, scholars consider it authentic.

[62] S. 358A.2. Trans. Hill, *Works* 3.10: 196.

acts of charity."[63] Sermon 42 has a sense of urgency that, along with Augustine's observations about his own feebleness, may suggest a late date.[64] Here, too, he employs financial metaphors, though more sparingly, except for an injunction to "lend at usurious rates" to God."[65] The readings for the day (Isa. 1:11–12, God does not want sacrifices; Luke 6:37–38, "Forgive and you will be forgiven, give and it will be given to you") point to God's leniency toward sins: alms for the poor are the Christians' sacrifice, which in turn cleanses them of sins. The turning point in the sermon is Augustine's evocation of Matt. 25:35–40. By giving to Christ in the poor, they will be delivered from themselves—the "wicked man" of the day's psalm (Ps 140:1)—and can wait with assurance for the Lord's coming. Augustine looks to that day at the sermon's end: "Please be my crop, my harvest so that I may be with you, and all of us together may be the harvest of God."[66]

Among Augustine's latest sermons are three with substantive treatments of poverty, charity, and final judgment. They are similar in length to his typical Sunday sermons and exhibit the mix of banking texts with the last judgment scene from Matthew that is found in the three short sermons just discussed. They evoke the urgency of the times and stress the necessity of giving to the poor. The immediate context of the world's distress in these sermons is not now the Sack of Rome by the Visigoths, but the movement of Vandals and other groups across the coast of North Africa. At the time of Augustine's death in August 430, they were besieging the refugee-filled city of Hippo.[67]

[63] S. 390.2. Trans. Hill, *Works* 3.10: 424; ed. PL 90: 1706, ll. 19–20, 34–35. Recent scholarship (see the concluding table) considers the second part of this sermon to be authentic.

[64] S. 42.1: "ego, fratres, uires paruas habeo, sed uerbum dei magnas habet. ualeat in cordibus uestris. ergo et quod lente dicimus ualde auditis, si obedieritis." Ed. Lambot, *Sermones de Vetere Testamento*, 504, ll. 5–6. Also 42.3, ed. Lambot, 506, ll. 81–82). Hubertus R. Drobner, *Augustinus von Hippo: Predigten su den Alttestamentlichen Propheten (Sermones 42–50), Einleitung, Text, Übersetzung und Amerkungen* (Frankfurt am Main: Peter Lang, 2013), 46–47, allows that the sermon may be from the end of Augustine's life because of his references to himself as weak or frail.

[65] S. 42.2. Trans. Hill, *Works* 3.2: 235; ed. Lambot, *Sermones de Vetere Testamento*, 505, ll. 39–40: "inuenimus quem feneremus. demus in usuram, sed deo, non homini."

[66] S. 42.3. Trans. Hill, *Works* 3.2: 236; ed. Lambot, *Sermones de Vetere Testamento*, 506, ll. 84–85.

[67] See Andy Merrills, "Kingdoms of North Africa," in *The Cambridge Companion to the Age of Attila*, ed. Michael Maas (Cambridge: Cambridge University Press, 2014), 265–74 for the Vandals and related groups crossing into Mauretania Tingitania from

Jesus' advice to the rich young man in Matt. 19:21—"Go, sell all you have and give to the poor, then you will have treasure in heaven; then come, follow me"—is the text for s. 86, likely preached near the end of his ministry.[68] It is no surprise, then, that Augustine employs the language of banking and transferring assets. What is surprising, however, is the immediacy with which he launches into the question of whether storing treasure in heaven means losing riches on earth. Reflecting the urgency of the times, he observes that "our earthly home is falling into ruin" and encourages his congregation to transfer their assets to heaven, their eternal home. Only then does he address the scriptural text itself, on giving to the poor. He suggests that the rich young man in the Gospel story might have been willing to give all to Christ, but drew back when told to give it to the poor. Asserting that "Nobody should be afraid of spending money on the poor," he quotes the Lord's words three verses from Matthew's judgment scene (Matt. 25:35, 37, 40) and does so three more times in the next two sections.[69] He interprets these statements in terms of lending to God and being repaid, but reverses the earthly roles of creditor and lender: God the borrower seeks after the lender rather than the creditor who pursues the debtor; God pays back far more than promised, unlike the creditor who attempts to extort a higher rate of interest.

The theme of reversal gives some coherence to a large block of disparate and seemingly rambling arguments that constitute about half the sermon. Augustine prods his congregation to free themselves from slavery to the competing and contradictory "mistresses," avarice and extravagance. Avarice hoards for the future, extravagance spends while it can; neither truly cares for the self.[70] Both work against the acts of merciful

---

Spain in 422 and later making their way eastward, eventually reaching into Roman Africa. Carthage would be taken in 439.

[68] S. 86 is not dated, except for Christine Mohrmann's reasonable assessment, based on its content, that it is from the end of his ministry; Othmar Perler identifies the season as winter.

[69] S. 86.1. Trans. Hill, *Works* 3.3: 396; ed. PL 38: 524, 19–20: "domus terrena ruinosa est: domus caelestis aeterna est." 86.3 (trans. Hill, *Works* 3.3: 397; ed. PL 38: 524, l. 52, fear of giving to the poor. Matt. 25:34–37, 40 are cited again in 86.4 and Matt. 25:35 in 86.5.

[70] In 86.6 (trans. Hill, *Works* 3.3: 399; ed. PL 38: 526, ll. 14–16), Augustine introduces two "mistresses" (hoard/spend). They recur in several variations throughout the block, from sections 6 through 14.

giving at the heart of the Matthean judgment scenario that appears so often in this sermon. He urges his hearers instead to acknowledge their redeemer, who frees them to become the slaves of God, the slaves of justice. "Be his slaves"—the one who can say the same things that avarice and extravagance say ("save," "spend"), but without contradiction. Augustine's aim is to reverse, redirect, and reconcile the meaning of taking thought for one's future and treating oneself well in this world as he explicates a "holier kind" of avarice.[71] He cautions against the avarice of the rich and cajoles them to give at least one son's portion worth of their wealth to Christ, thus benefitting both their heirs and themselves. Warning them with reminders of the rich fool who tore down his barns to build bigger ones (Luke 12:16–20) and the rich man who gave nothing to Lazarus (Luke 16:22–31), Augustine praises extravagance as a perverse teacher who urges them to "give alms, buy future rest for your soul" and "don't spare your treasure, give as much as you can." As he wryly observes: "This used to be the voice of extravagance; it has become the voice of the Lord."[72]

Crass as these opportunistic arguments may seem, they do not lose sight of the poor Christ or the poor person in need, hungry, thirsty, and homeless. The arguments distract (even detract) from the larger, communal dimension of judgment so evident in Matthew's sermonic vision. But they do not finally depart from it, as Augustine's directives in the opening and closing paragraphs of the sermon demonstrate. In a time of economic and political uncertainty, he instructs his people to "live with Christ in their hearts," for he has gone before them. "Just as his members are going to go where Christ has gone before, so all of us... are going to go where our hearts will now have gone on before."[73] The Christ who goes on before is a new turn for Augustine's preaching on Matt. 25 and meeting Christ in the poor. So, too, is his more explicit emphasis on the heart, which recalls Matt. 6:21, "Where your treasure is,

---

[71] S. 86.7 (trans. Hill, *Works* 3.3: 399), be his slaves. Ed. PL 38: 525, ll. 35–37, "agnosce redemptorem tuum, manumissorem tuum. illi serui: faciliora iubet contraria non iubet." 86.5 (trans. Hill, *Works* 3.3: 399; ed. PL 38: 526, ll. 5–6), holier avarice: "sic ergo compescatur auaritia nostra, fratres, ut alia quae sancta est, inflammetur."

[72] S. 86.17. Trans. Hill, *Works* 3.3: 404; ed. PL 38: 530, ll. 18–21: "de faciendis ergo eleemosynis, et comparanda animae requie in posterum, ut faciamus bene cum anima nostra, quod peruerse dixit luxuria, dixit et Moyses, dixerunt et prophetae."

[73] S. 86.1. Trans. Hill, *Works* 3.3: 396; ed. PL 38: 524, ll. 13, 15–17.

there will your heart be also." He concludes by challenging his hearers: "In the name of Christ, as I see it, you have had a sermon about giving alms. This sound of your voices raised in applause is only acceptable to the Lord when he sees your hands active in the cause."[74]

Preaching again in these last years on the rich young man (Matt. 19; 17–21), Augustine opens s. 85 with an observation on the first verse of the lesson, "If you wish to come to life, keep the commandments." He proclaims that the reading "calls more for hearers and doers than for an expounder." It is not unusual for him to urge his hearers to action or to comment on his role as preacher, but it is rare in these sermons for Augustine to announce, so bluntly and so early on, that action—hearing and doing—outweighs explication, that the words of Jesus in the Gospel are self-evident, that those present know what they need to do if they want life. "The Gospel is the mouth of Christ," he says, listen to it. But he is impatient with his people's resistance, charging them with unwillingness to keep commandments large or small. "What's the good of my shouting at you to sell your possessions, when I can't even twist your arm to stop you plundering other people's?" They should have mercy on themselves and change their evil ways.[75]

The middle sections of the sermon sound familiar themes from 1 Tim. 6:17–18 (not being proud, not putting one's hope in riches) and 6:7–10 (being content with enough, recognizing that they can take nothing with them in death), as Augustine warns both rich and poor against avarice and implores the rich to give to the poor from their surplus. But several elements differentiate this sermon from any others. Most notable is that, immediately after his opening remarks, he cites Matt. 19:23–25: "How difficult it is for anyone who has riches to enter the kingdom of heaven. Amen I say to you, it is easier for a camel to pass through the eye of a needle than for a rich person to enter into the kingdom of heaven." He uses this text only one other time in these sermons, although he frequently quotes the preceding verses on selling all, giving to the poor, and gaining

---

[74] S. 86.17. Trans. Hill, *Works* 3.3: 402; ed. PL 38: 530, ll. 31–34 (applause): "habetis in nomine Christi, quantum arbitror, sermonem de faciendis eleemosynis uox ista uestra laudantium, tunc accepta est domino, si uideat et manus operantium."

[75] S. 85.1. Trans. Hill, *Works* 3.3: 391; ed. PL 38: 520, ll. 37–38, hearers and doers; 520, l. 51, "os Christi evangelium est"; 521, ll. 5–7, plundering. The sermon was given sometime between 426 and 430. Cf. s. 61.13, chastising his hearers for failing to give to the poor, and begging them to do so.

treasure in heaven.[76] In the same paragraph and at the start of the next he remarks on the economic status of his congregation, something he does only occasionally, when he asks both rich and poor to listen to the Gospel: "Most of you are poor"; "the rich...if there are any here."[77] The body of the sermon, after the introduction, is framed by these verses from Matt. 19:23-25 and by Prov. 22:2: "The rich [person] and the poor [person] have met each other; but the Lord has made them both."

Augustine often cites Prov. 22:2 in conjunction with both 1 Tim. 6 texts and Matthaen texts from the Sermon on the Mount and Matt. 25 in the sermons considered in this essay. Prov. 22:2 functions differently in s. 85 than in earlier sermons centering on 1 Tim. 6 and its related metaphors. Here the potential for personal encounter expands as the eye of the needle widens. The rich can pass through it by the simple act of recognizing their common humanity with those who are poor (the Lord made them both) and giving to meet their need. Rich and poor have met. "On what road," asks Augustine, "if not in this life?" Through hearing and doing, it is possible for both to enter the kingdom: "By the one who has plenty [the Lord] helps the one in dire need; by the one who has nothing [the Lord] tests the one who has plenty."[78]

Augustine preached s. 345, the last to be considered here, for the commemoration of three women martyrs who were believed to have died near Thuburbo in 304, during the persecution of Diocletian.[79]

---

[76] S. 85.2. Hill (*Works* 3.3: 392) notes that the scripture quotation is closer to Mark 10:23—than Matt. 19:23. I quote the whole of it here from Matthew, as that was the text for the day. In s. 114B.10 (=Dolbeau 5), an early sermon (403), Augustine sees the camel as a figure of Christ, who has already passed through the eye of the needle, thus opening the way for others, even a rich person.

[77] S. 85.2. Trans. Hill, *Works* 3.3: 392; ed. PL 38: 521, l. 31, "plures estis pauperes." 85.3 (ed. PL 38: 521.39-40): "audiant diuites, si tamen sunt."

[78] S. 85.7. Trans. Hill, *Works* 3.3: 395; ed. PL 38: 523, l. 38: "in qua uia, nisi in ista uita?" Ed. PL 38: 523, ll. 42-43: Lord helps, tests.

[79] The date of the sermon is somewhat uncertain, although there are good reasons to think it is not before 428. Frangipane, the editor of the PL text in 1819, proposed 428. The July 30 commemoration of the Thuburbo martyrs fell on a Sunday in, among other years, in 411, 416, and 428. Fixing the year depends on identifying the sense of danger described in the sermon: Goths in Rome in 410 or Vandals in North Africa in the late 420s. Adalbert Kunzelmann, "Die Chronologie der *Sermones* des hl. Augustinus," *Miscellanea Agostiniana* 2 (Roma: Tipografia poliglotta Vatican, 1931), 509-10, argues that s. 345 should be read together with s. 344, which is reliably dated to 428 by many scholars. Neither Drobner nor Hombert has yet considered s. 345 in their separate projects of redating the *sermones ad populum*. See Table for specifics. Overall, I find the cumulative

There is little historical evidence of their martyrdom, or even their existence, but in Augustine's time three women—Maxima, Donatilla, and Secunda—were remembered in the calendar of martyrs by both Catholics and Donatists. Each community had its own narrative of their martyrdom. Catholics were more circumspect in regard to the three, but the Donatists claimed them enthusiastically, which may help account for their near absence in Augustine's sermon.[80]

Augustine preached s. 345 for a Sunday commemoration of the martyrs. He announces at the outset that he will speak about "indifference or contempt for the present age, and hope for the age to come," which he correlates with the martyrs' indifference to the world and the reality of the Lord's resurrection.[81] The first reading was 1 Tim. 6:17–19, commanding "the rich of this world" not to put their hope in riches but to be rich in good works and store up a foundation for the future. Augustine quotes these verses, in full, twice in the opening section of the sermon, after which the martyrs do not reappear until its closing paragraphs. The balance of the sermon is devoted to developing the implications of the 1 Tim. 6 reading for his topic of contempt for the world. He uses the language of financial transactions that the text invites, but with significant differences from previous sermons.

Here he situates the familiar scripture passage in a narrative of being taken hostage by enemies and negotiating for one's release. He sounds exasperated and demanding as he attempts to convince his congregation that "riches are sought for the sake of life, not life for the sake of riches." He harries them with multiple variations on the question: if you gave away all you had in order to save your life from an enemy, how much more is eternal life worth? "Give Christ something," he insists, "that you may live happily (*beatus*), if you gave the enemy everything that you might live like a beggar (*mendicus*)." A few days are nothing, they all

---

support for 428 compelling and the treatment of Matt. 25:31–46 in s. 345 consistent with that date.

[80] See Rose Lockwood, "*Potens et Factiosa Femina*: Women, Martyrs, and Schism in Roman North Africa," *Augustinian Studies* 20 (1989): 165–82, at 171–72.

[81] Augustine's opening observations that "today is both a feast of the martyrs and the Lord's day" and "today the Lord rose again" do not clarify whether it is simply Sunday or Easter. If the latter, it would seem odd for him not to mention it explicitly and make overt use of that fact in the sermon.

come to an end. Let Christ, "the one who was taken captive for you... make an agreement with you." Keep your life and your riches, by giving them to him: "Do you love them? Send them to where you will follow them, store up treasure in heaven" (see Matt. 6:20).[82] The way to do that is by giving to Christ on earth. "That is the reason," says Christ, that "I came here, so that you could be rich there." Where Christ is to be found is among his members: "Feed me on earth." Give there, and "you feed Christ."[83] Quoting Matt. 25:35–40, the Lord's response to questions from both the sheep and the goats—"I was hungry and you gave me to eat"—Augustine drives home his point. It is Christ himself they fed "when [they] did it for these least of mine."[84]

Augustine invokes the hungry, poor Christ and Matthew's judgment scene in many of the sermons examined in this essay, particularly those from the latter part of his life. Metaphors of borrowing, lending, and earning interest in heaven that derive from 1 Tim. 6:17–19 form the interpretive context for Matt. 25:31–45 in many sermons; they never disappear entirely in Augustine's preaching. In s. 345, however, these metaphors tend to fade into the background as the language of sending on ahead and following takes a more central place. That language derives from two Matthean texts that reshape the context for hearing and interpreting the parable of the last judgment. One is Matt. 6:21: "For where your treasure is, there will your heart be also." The final line of Jesus' saying is not often quoted along with its frequently cited first two lines, about storing up treasure in heaven (Matt. 6:19–21). In s. 345, however, Augustine's emphasis falls on this last verse. His focus shifts from what to do with treasure to the meaning of treasure as that which draws the heart to itself. Here and at the beginning of s. 86, his emphasis is on the heart as he preaches about the final judgment. In each case focusing on the heart leads him to the second interpretive text, the final clause of Matt. 19:21, Jesus' imperative to the rich young man: "then come, follow me."

---

[82] S. 345.2, my translation; ed. *Miscellanea Agostiniana* 1: 203, ll. 1–2, riches; 203.10–11, give to Christ: "Da Christo aliquid, ut vivas beatus, si totum das hosti, ut vivas mendicus"; 203.33–34, send them. Here I depart from Hill's translation (*Works* 3.10: 59) in which he substitutes a dialogue from the 1689 Maurist text in place of Frangipane's edition.

[83] S. 345.3, my translation; ed. *Miscellanea Agostiniana* 1:204, ll. 26–27, why Christ came; s. 345.4, 205.18, 19: feed Christ on earth.

[84] Cf. s. 389.5, about the significance of good lives in relation to acts of charity, feeding the hungry Christ or not, and leading good or sinful lives (above, 102).

It, too, is seldom quoted with its preceding verses on storing up treasure. In s. 86 Augustine combines the language of depositing treasure with the language of the heart that follows Christ and his members to heaven: "Let Christians be preceded by their hearts." Here, in s. 345, he emphasizes the heart: "Follow them [riches], meanwhile, in your *heart.*"[85]

Both s. 86 and s. 345 refer to the *sursum corda* dialogue that precedes the Eucharistic prayer at liturgy. In s. 86 Augustine uses the interchange to encourage the congregation: "If any of you want to lift up your hearts, then it's up there that you must deposit what you love."[86] In s. 345, however, he scolds those who trust their treasure to the earth and he accuses them of lying to God when they respond to the *sursum corda,* "we have lifted them up to the Lord." He continues in this uncompromising vein, asking an imaginary interlocutor if he has followed the Lord's advice. To the man's positive reply—that he gave all that he had to the poor and now shares whatever else he might have—Augustine asks why he is lying. He has only done half of what the Lord advises. "You have more, you have yourself; you have more, include yourself among your goods." Jesus says, "Come, follow me," yet the giver has not followed, he has not given himself.[87] At this point, the three women martyrs reenter the sermon, recalled by Augustine to shame the reluctant interlocutor—"blush, bearded man"—along with any in the congregation who are afraid or feel unable to follow either Christ or the martyrs. "Women have followed, whose birthday we celebrate

---

[85] S. 86. 1. Trans. Hill, *Works* 3.3: 396; ed. PL 38: 524, ll. 14–15. S. 345.5 (trans. Hill, *Works* 3.10: 62, following Frangipane); ed. *Miscellanea Agostiniana* 1: 205, l. 28, "sequere eas interim corde." In s. 344, which scholars agree is not earlier than 428 (see Footnote 80 above), Augustine treats themes similar to those in s. 345, drawing on a scattering of scriptural texts without reference to particular readings for the day: loving God vs. loving the world; the martyrs' love for God and eternal life; right ordering of loves; the relative worth of temporal life and eternal life, and what a person would give for each; ransoming one's life from barbarians or brigands and Christ's ransom of all through his blood; having justice in one's heart; resurrection to judgment of eternal life or eternal death (citing Matt. 25:41).

[86] S. 86.1. Trans. Hill, *Works* 3.3: 396; ed. PL 38: 524, l. 8, "sursum erit cor." 524, ll. 11–12: "qui ergo vult cor sursum habere."

[87] S. 345.5, my translation; ed. *Miscellanea Agostiniana* 1: 207, ll. 4–5: "Habes plus, te ipsum: te habes plus, tu es de rebus tuis, tu addendus es." See s. 177.5 (412), a sermon on avarice, based on 1 Tim. 6:7–19, in which a similar point is made about lying in response to the *sursum corda.* Cf. s. 105.11, be sure not to hear "lift up your hearts" to no purpose; differently, s. 25.3, lift up your hearts to the Lord, not against him; s. 25.7, how to follow peace into heaven by lifting up one's heart; s. 296.3, lift up hearts that are mourning, rise with Christ.

today," walking the highway Christ has opened to heaven; "they did not send their riches ahead, but rather sent themselves ahead in martyrdom."[88]

In the final section of the sermon, Augustine returns to the perilous state of a world that is fulfilling the Lord's predictions of the end of days. He observes ironically that, "The world was despised by the martyrs when it was flourishing…and now it's loved when it's perishing." His hearers should at least let themselves be frightened by the ruins of the world. In case they wonder why he has talked so much, he sums up the sermon in the simplest terms: "Let us lead good lives, and for our good life let us not set our hopes on the fleeting good things of this earth."[89] Rather, they should look to their faith and reckon its worth, which is more than the earth and the heavens. Only the one who made both, says Augustine, is worth more than that.

Taken together, sermons 85, 86, and 345, along with several others from the last decade of Augustine's preaching, represent a view of the final judgment that is significantly different from that of most sermons oriented to 1 Tim. 6 and related texts with metaphors of banking and treasure. These late sermons also present a more tightly focused view of poverty, charity, judgment, and mercy. As the revelatory power of Matt. 25:34–46 comes to the fore in these sermons, the Matthean vision of judgment recontextualizes rather than rejects the financial metaphors from sermons centered on 1 Tim. 6 and its ancillary texts. References to the heart, so central in other writings of Augustine's[90] but scarce in earlier sermons on poverty, charity, and judgment, suddenly multiply in these late sermons. *Misericordia*, the sadness of heart that leads to acts

---

[88] S. 345.6, my translation; ed. *Miscellanea Agostiniana* 1: 207, ll. 14–15: "erubesce, barbate: feminae secutae sunt, quarum hodie natalicia celebramus"; ll. 26–27: "et non suas diuitias praemiserunt, sed eas potius in martyrio praecesserunt." In his translation of the dialogue section, Hill chose to use the older, and in places significantly different, Maurist text of s. 345. Hence my use of the text first printed by Octavius Frangipani in 1819 (repr. PL 46: 971–80) from the *Miscellanea Agostiniana*, which is also the text presented in the CAG electronic edition of the *Opera Omnia*.

[89] S. 345.7. Trans. Hill, *Works* 3.10: 65 (Hill has returned to the Frangipani text). Ed. *Miscellanea Agostiniana* 1: 208, ll. 5–6; 27.

[90] See Kazuhiko Demura, "The Concept of Heart in Augustine of Hippo: Its Emergence and Development," in *Studia Patristica 70: Papers Presented at the Sixteenth International Conference on Patristic Studies held in Oxford 2011*, ed. Markus Vinzent (Leuven: Peeters, 2013), 3–16; Francine Cardman, "Discerning the Heart: Intention as Moral Norm in Augustine's Homilies on 1 John," *Studia Patristica 70*, ed. Vinzent, 195–202.

Table of dates for Augustine's *Sermones ad populum*

Sermon	Scripture or occasion/theme	De Coninck et al.	Hombert	Drobner	Frede	Verbraken (surveying views of earlier scholars)
14	Ps. 9:14				Likely 418	Sunday soon after 27 May 418; toward end of ministry
25	Ps. 93:12				Winter 410/12	Winter c. 410, 411–413
25A = Morin 12	Ps. 93:12–13				After 396, or better 412/13?	After 396, winter 412–13?
36	Prov. 13:7–8			Undetermined (2004, p. 71)	Before 410, or better 410/3?	Before 410; perhaps between 410–413
38	Eccl. 2: 1–3 Ps. 38 continence, endurance			Undetermined (2004, p. 183)	Undated	Undated
39	Eccl. 5:8–9 Matt. 10:42 oppression of poor			Undetermined (2004, p. 211)	Undated	Undated
42	Ps. 139/140I Isa. 1:10–17 Luke 6:37–38 Forgiveness and gift			Undetermined; maybe near end of life—refers to self as frail (2013, pp. 44, 46–47)	Undated	Undated

(continued)

Table 1 (continued)

Sermon	Scripture or occasion/theme	De Coninck et al.	Hombert	Drobner	Frede	Verbraken (surveying views of earlier scholars)
46	Ezek. 34:1–16 (pastors) Ps. 79 Luke 24:46–49		407–408 scriptural arguments parallel anti-Manichaean, anti-Donatist works, pp. 553–54	Undetermined (2013, pp. 323–24)	Likely 410/11	409–410; mid-410; after June 414; after 400; after 17 June 414; c. 408; very likely 410–411
47	Ezek. 34:17–31 Ps. 94/95 Matt. 5:16?		407–408 (see above)	Undetermined (2013, pp. 173–76)	Likely 410/11	Mid-410; 409–410; after 400; after 17 June 414; after 12 Feb 405; c. 408; 410–411
53	Matt. 5:3–12 (Beatitudes) St. Agnes, 21 January	Carthage, 21 Jan, probably 413 (pp. 63–64)			Carthage, 21 Jan 413 (Agnes)	Soon after 415; 413
53A = Morin 11	Matt. 5:3–10 (Beatitudes)	412–416 probably (p. 64)			405/11	412–416
60 = Lambot 19	Ps. 38:7 (detachment) Matt. 6:19–21 (treasure)		412 after fall of Rome; use of scripture parallels works from 411–412 pp. 243–52		Carthage, between 14–22 May 397	14–22 May 397

(continued)

Table 1 (continued)

Sermon	Scripture or occasion/theme	De Coninck et al.	Hombert	Drobner	Frede	Verbraken (surveying views of earlier scholars)
61	Matt. 7:7–11 (ask, search, knock)	412–421 probably (pp. 9, 65–6)	c. 412 p. 360, n. 8		412/16	412–416
61A=Wilmart 12	Matt. 7:7–8	Not before 415 (p. 61)			Not before 425	Not before 425
81	Matt. 18:7–9 (stumbling blocks, sin)		End of 410 uses in proposed date for s. 60 p. 247		410/411	End of 410; 410; 410-411
85	Matt. 19:17–25				19–24 June 426/30	19–24 June after 425
86	Matt. 19:21 (rich young man)				Undated	end of his ministry
90A = Dolbeau 11			397–398		Undated	
94	Matt. 25:24–30 (servant who hides the talent)				Not before 425	425 or later; soon after 29 June 426–430; not before 425

(continued)

Table 1 (continued)

Sermon	Scripture or occasion/theme	De Coninck et al.	Hombert	Drobner	Frede	Verbraken (surveying views of earlier scholars)
105	Luke 11:5–13 (ask, seek, knock)		412 In Carthage for conference with Donatists; Rome's fall parallels first books of *de civ. Dei* p. 247, n. 7		Carthage 410/411	410; end of 410; 410–411; July–Aug 411
111	Luke 13:21–24 (yeast)				Carthage, 417?	c. 417; 19 Jan; 19 Jan 413; soon after 415; maybe 417
113A = Denis 24	Luke 16:19–31 (rich man and Lazarus)		25 Sept 404–invasion over Alps; Denis 24 p. 246, n. 6; sermon list p. 642		25 Sept 410 (or better 403/4?)	Sunday 25 Sept; in 410, 421, or 427; 410; after 410
114B = Dolbeau 5					Carthage, likely Dec 403	
125	John 5:2–5 (pool of Bethsaida)		400–405 Gal 6:14b cited alone, all pre-410; anti-Manichaean; use of Rev. 17:5		416/17	416–417; Lent, 416–417

(continued)

Table 1 (continued)

Sermon	Scripture or occasion/theme	De Coninck et al.	Hombert	Drobner	Frede	Verbraken (surveying views of earlier scholars)
177	1Tim. 6:7–19 (avoid greed)		412 use of 1 Tim. 6, other scripture parallels dated works pp. 358–64		Carthage between 22 May and 24 June 397	410–412; between May–June 397
265	Ascension		23 May 412 after 411 Conference p. 287, n. 17		Ascension, 412	before 405; 412; Thurs 23 May 413
277	St. Vincent (the spiritual body) 22 Jan				Carthage, 22 Jan 413 (St. Vincent)	413; soon after 413
296	Peter and Paul 29 June				Carthage, 29 June 411 (or 413?)	410; 411; 410–411
299	Peter and Paul 29 June		21 Jun 413 soon after s. 293, s. 294, belongs with them; parallels works of 412–413; in manuscripts of sermon lists, pp. 387–98		29 June 418 Peter and Paul	418
344					Not before 428	Not before 428; 428; c. 428

(continued)

Table 1 (continued)

Sermon	Scripture or occasion/theme	De Coninck et al.	Hombert	Drobner	Frede	Verbraken (surveying views of earlier scholars)
345 = Frangipane 3	Contempt for world; Martyrs of Thuburbo 30 July		30 July 411, p. 364		Carthage, 411, or 416, or 428, Martyrs of Thuburbo	30 July, Sunday; 411; c. 410–411; 411, 416, or 428; not before 428
358A	Mercy				Fragment; undated	Undated; authentic
362	Resurrection of the dead				410/11 winter	Winter 410–411
389	Alms				Undated; authentic	Undated not authentic: Maurists, authentic: many
390	Alms				Undated; 2nd half authentic	Undated; doubtful authenticity: Maurists, Lambot[a]

[a] Cyrille Lambot, "Le sermon sur l'aumône à restituer à saint Augustin," *Revue bénédictine* 66 (1956): 20–38

of charity,[91] moves almsgiving beyond self-interest and toward the compassion of the poor Christ who becomes increasingly visible in the poor themselves. Mercy in these late sermons is not a general amnesty from sin.[92] Rather it is the mercy of the merciful, to whom mercy will be shown at the final judgment.[93] It is the mercy of those who send ahead the poor themselves, not as porters, but as members of Christ. That is why Augustine can say with certainty that "there is no other remedy to deliver us from death but acts of charity."[94]

TABLE REFERENCES

De Coninck, Luc, Bertrand Coppieters t' Wallant, and Roland Demeulnaere. "À propos de la datation des *sermones ad populum*: s. 51-70A." In *Ministerium Sermonis: Philological, Historical, and Theological Studies on Sermones ad Populum*, edited by Gert Partoens, Anthony Dupont, and Mathijs Lamberigts, 49–67. Turnhout: Brepols, 2009.
Drobner, Hubertus R. *Augustinus von Hippo: Sermones ad Populum. Überlieferung und Bestand—Bibilographie—Indices*. Leiden: Brill, 2000.
Drobner, Hubertus R. *Augustinus von Hippo: Predigten zum Buch der Sprüche und Jesus Sirach (Sermones 35–51). Einleitung, Text, Übersetzung und Anmerkungen*. Patrologia: Beitrage zum Studium der Kirchenväter, XIII. Frankfurt: Peter Lang, 2004.
Drobner, Hubertus R. *Augustinus von Hippo: Sermones ad Populum: Supplement 2000–2010*. Frankfurt: Peter Lang, 2010.
Drobner. *Augustinus von Hippo: Predigten zu den alttestamentlichen Propheten (Sermones 42–50). Einleitung, Text, Übersetzung und Anmerkungen*. Patrologia: Beitrage zum Studium der Kirchenväter, XXIX. Frankfurt: Peter Lang, 2013.

---

[91] See s. 358A.1.
[92] See Brown, *Ransom of the Soul*, 111–14, on the analogy with imperial amnesty and Augustine's rejection of the concept. Brown cites *De civitate Dei*, 21.24, for Augustine's rejection of the argument that punishment in eternal fire would or could be remitted through the prayers of the church and the saints, since that would void both God's scriptural word and decree of predestination. The long final chapter, 21.27 should also be noted, in which Augustine rejects the view that only those who neglect worthy works of mercy will suffer eternal fire. He argues also against the notion that one may continue to sin with impunity and rely on works of mercy for forgiveness: ongoing fruits of repentance are also required.
[93] See s. 53.5.
[94] S. 390.2. Trans. Hill, *Works* 3.10: 414; ed. PL 39: 1706, ll. 34–35.

Frede, Hermann Josef. *Kirchenschriftsteller: Verzeichnis und Sigel*, AU s. 1–396, 221–57. Freiburg: Verlag Herder, 1995.

Hombert, Pierre-Marie. *Nouvelles recherches de chronologie augustinienne*. Paris: Institut d'études augustiniennes, 2000.

Verbraken, Pierre-Patrick. *Études critiques sur les sermons authentiques de saint Augustin*. Instrumenta Patristica 12 (Steenburgis: Abbatia S. Petri, 1978). Bibliographical information for authors cited, pp. 43–52; superscripts identify each work.

Two Important Studies on Context and Dating of the Sermons Are Also Helpful:

Kunzelmann, Adelbert. "Die Chronologie der *Sermones* des hl. Augustinus." In *Miscellanea Agostiniana* 2, 417–520. Roma: Tipografia Poliglotta Vaticana, 1931.

Perler, Othmar. *Les Voyages de Saint Augustin*. Paris: Institut d'études augustiniennes, 1969.

CHAPTER 6

Berengaudus on the Apocalypse

Eric Knibbs

In volume 17 of Migne's *Patrologia Latina*, readers encounter a mysterious *Expositio super septem visiones libri Apocalypsis*, or a *Commentary on the Seven Visions of the Apocalypse*.[1] For the most part this *Expositio* reads like an ordinary work of medieval exegesis, providing line-by-line explication of John's Apocalypse with allegorical tendencies well known to students of medieval biblical scholarship. Upon closer examination, however, the *Expositio* turns out to harbor a variety of unusual features. Its author is given to intriguing and textured excurses, among them a lengthy recapitulation of Old Testament history, a disquisition on the pitfalls of fraternal correction, and an extended treatise on mendacity.[2] He demonstrates a persistent and sometimes

[1] PL 17:763–71; Frederick Stegmüller, *Repertorium Biblicum Medii Aevi* (Madrid: Consejo Superior de Investigaciones Científicas, 1950–1980), no. 1711.

[2] On fraternal correction: Berengaudus, *Expositio* 1, PL 17:777, prompted by Apoc. 2:2, "I know your works." On Old Testament history from Noah through Moses: *Expositio* 3, PL 17:813–31, prompted by Apoc. 6:3 and the author's conviction that "the opening of the second seal relates to the construction of the ark and to the just who lived before the law." On mendacity, *Expositio* 6, PL 17:940–45, after Apoc. 21:8, "...all liars...will have their portion in the pool burning with fire and brimstone."

E. Knibbs (✉)
Monumenta Germaniae Historica, Munich, Germany

© The Author(s) 2019
E. Knibbs et al. (eds.), *The End of the World in Medieval Thought and Spirituality*, The New Middle Ages,
https://doi.org/10.1007/978-3-030-14965-9_6

startling originality, cultivating his own approach and sometimes even dismissing the ideas of his predecessors. Even his organizational scheme is curious and without apparent precedent. As the title suggests, he divides his commentary into seven sections, according to his view that the Apocalypse narrates seven visions. The first of these "is that which contains the seven letters sent to the seven churches" (through Apoc. 3), while "the second is that in which [John] sees the throne in heaven, as a representation of the church" (Apoc. 4). The third follows as that in which "the lamb opened the book and its seals" (Apoc. 5:1–8:5), the fourth portrays "seven angels... blowing on trumpets" (Apoc. 8:6–15:4), and the fifth tells of the seven plagues, or as our author has it, "the same seven angels...with seven vials" (Apoc. 8:6–15:4). In the sixth, "the resurrection is described" (Apoc. 20:11–21:8), and "in the seventh the glory of the saints is revealed in the form of the city of Jerusalem coming down from heaven" (Apoc. 21:9–22).[3]

The *Expositio* survives in nearly sixty manuscripts dating from the eleventh through the fifteenth centuries.[4] The statesman, scholar and

---

[3] Berengaudus, *Expositio* 1, PL 17:766–67: "Et si diligenter advertas, totus hic liber in septem visiones distinctus est. Prima est, quae septem epistolas ad septem ecclesias destinatas continet... Secunda est, in qua sedem in figura ecclesiae in coelo positam vidit, et supra sedem Christum sedentem.... In tertia agnus librum et sigilla eius aperuit... in quarta septem angeli sunt visi tubis canentes...in quinta septem iterum angeli visi sunt phialas habentes...in sexta resurrectio describitur...in septima gloria sanctorum in figura civitatis Hierusalem de coelo descendentis demonstratur." While Bede and Haimo propose that the Apocalypse be divided into seven parts, their schemes differ substantially from the *Expositio*. See E. Ann Matter, "The Apocalypse in Early Medieval Exegesis," in *The Apocalypse in the Early Middle Ages*, ed. Richard K. Emmerson and Bernard McGinn (Ithaca: Cornell University Press, 1992), 38–50, at 47 and 49 (with the comparative table at 42) for perspective on early medieval tendencies in this regard.

[4] Burton Van Name Edwards lists fifty-eight manuscripts of the *Expositio* in his provisional "Manuscript Transmission of Carolingian Biblical Commentaries," online at: http://www.tcnj.edu/~chazelle/carindex.htm. Unknown to Edwards because it was in private hands when he compiled this list is New Haven, Beinecke Rare Book and Manuscript Library, MS 1083, an eleventh-century codex that may be the earliest extant manuscript. For a full digital reproduction, see http://brbl-dl.library.yale.edu/vufind/Record/3793606. Compare Derk Visser, *Apocalypse as Utopian Expectation (800–1500): The Apocalypse Commentary of Berengaudus of Ferrières and the Relationship between Exegesis, Liturgy and Iconography* (Leiden: Brill, 1996), 16; Achim Dittrich, "Der rätselhafte Berengaudus," in his *Mater Ecclesiae: Geschichte und Bedeutung eines umstrittenen Marientitels* (Würzburg: Echter, 2009), 90–129, at 92. Both hold that Angers, Bibliothèque municipale, MS 68 (s. XII inc.) is the oldest copy.

bishop of Durham, Cuthbert Tunstall, printed the *editio princeps* in 1554 under the name of Ambrose of Milan. Tunstall found the attribution in the medieval tradition, but he must have known that it was unsustainable. The *Expositio* cites Ambrose himself as an august authority, alongside other patristic luminaries from Augustine to Gregory the Great. Elsewhere its author ponders the fall of the Roman Empire and the rise of the barbarian successor states. Tunstall expunged this internal evidence from his printing, and it was left to the great 1686/1690 Maurist edition of the Ambrosian oeuvre to reveal the pseudopatristic nature of Tunstall's edition. To correct the record, Denis-Nicolas le Nourry and Jacques du Frische composed a preface that remains among the best scholarship on the commentary and its origins to date. For all the reasons listed here, they realized that the *Expositio* could hardly have been penned by Milan's most illustrious bishop. They were unable to establish firm dates for its origins, though they noted that its ecclesiastical concerns resonated with Carolingian-era initiatives to reform the Frankish church. The commentary, they argued, was at any rate clearly medieval.[5]

Le Nourry and du Frische were also the first to print an intriguing epilogue to the *Expositio*, excluded for obvious reasons from Tunstall's fraudulent printing but present across the greater part of the manuscript tradition. In this epilogue our mysterious and otherwise anonymous author addresses his readers directly. His words provide an excellent introduction to both the project of his *Expositio* and his own

---

[5] Cuthbert Tunstall, ed., *Expositio Beati Ambrosii Episcopi super Apocalypsin: Nunc primum in lucem edita* (Paris: Michel de Vascosan, 1554); Denis-Nicolas Le Nourry and Jacques du Frische, eds., *Sancti Ambrosii Mediolanensis Opera*, 2 vols. (Paris: Jean-Baptiste Coignard, 1686–90), 2:499–590, preface at 498 (repr. PL 17:763–64). Though all scholarly indices and authors agree that the *editio princeps* appeared in 1548, no libraries that I know of report copies from that year. The 1554 printing seems to be the first, and the earlier date an error originating with the prefatory discussion of le Nourry and du Frische. A telling moment occurs at *Expositio* 4, PL 17:883, where the author interprets the heads of the beast described in Apoc. 13 as heresies, and proceeds from there to list those fathers whose orthodox doctrine displaced heretical beliefs: "Sed omnipotens Deus defensores ecclesiae orthodoxos patres ex filiis ipsius ecclesiae elegit, quos flumine sapientiae suae replens, per eorum doctrinam omnes haereses ab ecclesia sua *exstirpavit*, ut fuerunt Ambrosius, Hilarius, Hieronymus, Augustinus, Gregorius, et multi alii, *qui etiam* maximam copiam librorum ediderunt, quibus omnes haereses, quae fuerunt, et quae esse poterant, destructae sunt...." In a footnote le Nourry and du Frische remark that Tunstall printed the entire passage with the names omitted, concluding the clause at "exstirpavit" and beginning a new sentence with "Qui etiam" (italicized above).

personality, and to my knowledge they have never been provided in English translation:

> Whoever wishes to know the author's name: Attend to the first letters of the commentary at the beginnings of the seven visions. The sum of the four missing vowels, if you write them in Greek, is 81.

> Behold: I have written this book with what brevity I could. Now I beseech you, to whom God gave knowledge of letters and into whose hands this book has come to be read, that you not reject the language of this book because of its filthy and unlearned rhetoric. Instead, imitate him who washes the gem that he has found in the dung-pit in clear water until it returns to its first splendor, and wash the filth of my ignorance with the water of your wisdom, decorating with your beautiful and well-ordered words the necessary discussion of this book, so that its utility is not cast aside by proud readers because of its rusticity.

> I know indeed that my unpolished diction will be despised and derided by the many who are swollen with knowledge of letters. And they will mock me and ask why an idiot like me, who knows nothing, should have presumed to stamp out a volume of commentary on a book of such obscurity. I answer them that, just as a sprinkling of dung is of more use to the sterile earth than some precious metal, so too is divine scripture, expounded with mediocrity, of more use to unlearned men than if it were explained in philosophical or poetic language. And my critics should remember, too, that our Lord Jesus Christ transmitted the mysteries of his teaching first of all not to philosophers, but to fishermen, that these mysteries might come to philosophers through fishermen. For indeed he who granted the ass reasoned words to correct the prophet's folly (Num. 22:30) deigned to grant me, the most vile and unworthy of all men, partial understanding of this book.

> Then I pondered within myself that proverb of Solomon—"Wisdom that is hid, and treasure that is not seen: what profit is there in them both?" (Sir. 20:32)—and at the same time considered that I would risk grave danger if, in keeping silent, I were to hide the small treasure that almighty God deigned to grant me. I moreover supposed that I was not the ideal person to teach those things that I had understood, because nobody was to be found who, as a disciple, would deign to hear the words of my folly. So I decided that I would set forth this small understanding that divine mercy granted me in whatever style, lest, in hiding my master's talent, I be condemned with that servant who "going his way, dug into the earth and hid his lord's money" (Matt. 25:18).

And because I am not fit to double my maser's wealth, I hand it to the bankers, so that when he returns, he may take back what is his with interest. You, to whom I have been speaking—I call you a banker or a money coiner, because just as a coiner adorns unformed money with his inscriptions to make it suitable for attaining profit, so too are you capable of adorning this, the Lord's money, with your wisdom and your well-ordered words, that it may achieve profit for our Lord Jesus Christ. And know that you will receive the highest mercy from him if this book (which I believe is necessary for God's church) should be stripped of the imperfections of its rhetoric through your learning and industry and, adorned with your fitting words, it should become more useful for the instruction of readers or listeners. But this I do not permit, namely that the meaning of this book should be altered, unless perchance (which heaven forbid) it should be found to contain anything contrary to truth, which I declare should be utterly deleted, or at the least revised for the better.[6]

The puzzle that the author outlines at the beginning of his postscript is easily resolved. The seven visions of the *Expositio* begin, successively, with

[6] Berengaudus, *Expositio* 7, PL 17:969–70: "Quisquis nomen auctoris scire desideras, litteras expositionum in capitibus septem visionum primas attende. Numerus quatuor vocalium quae desunt, si Graecas posueris, est LXXXI. Ecce, quanta potui brevitate, hunc librum consripsi. Obsecro autem te, cui dedit Deus scientiam litterarum, et in cuius manibus hic liber ad legendum devenerit, ut non propter foetidam ac rusticissimam elocutionem sermones huius libri abicias; sed imitare potius illum, qui gemmam in sterquilinio repertam tamdiu aqua nitida abluit, usque dum ad splendorem pristinum perveniret; ita et tu aqua sapientiae tuae ablue imperitiae meae sordes, tuisue pulchris et compositis verbis sermones huius libri necessarios adorna, quatenus non iam a superbis lectoribus utilitas libri causa rusticitatis abiiciatur. Scio enim quod haec mea impolita dictatio a multis scientia literrarum tumidis despuetur atque subsannabitur. Indignabuntur etiam contra me, cur ego idiota, et nihil sciens, praesumpserim super tantae obsuritatis librum volumen expositionis cudere. Quibus respondeo quia sicut terrae sterili amplius proficit aspersio stercoris, quam alicuius metalli pretiosi, ita et indoctis hominibus plus proficit divina scriptura mediocriter prolata, quam si philosophico aut poetico sermone proferatur; sciantque Dominum nostrum Jesum Christum sacramenta doctrinae suae non primo philosophis, sed piscatoribus tradidisse, ut per piscatores veniret ad philosophos. Etenim ille qui dedit asinae sensatos sermones ad corrigendam prophetae insipientiam, ipse mihi indigno et omnium hominum vilissimo intelligentiam libri huius ex parte donare dignatus est. Ego autem tractans apud me illud Salomonis: 'Sapientia abscondita, et thesaurus invisus, quae utilitas in utrisque?' simulque considerans grave mihi periculum imminere, si parvissimum thesaurum, quem mihi omnipotens Deus largiri dignatus est, tacendo absconderem—considerans etiam non me esse idoneum ad docenda ea quae intelligebam, eo quod nullus inveniretur, qui more discipuli dignaretur verba insipientiae meae audire—definivi apud me, ut hanc parvam scientiam, quam mihi divina misericordia contulit, qualicumque stylo prosequerer, ne

the letters B, R, N, G, V, D and S, while the four vowels must be alpha, epsilon, epsilon and omicron (with values of 1, 5, 5 and 70). Combined and transliterated, the result is the Frankish name *Berengaudus*.[7] Alongside formulaic excuses for unlearned prose, this Berengaudus praises his readers for having the necessary learning and rhetorical skill to improve the raw genius of his exposition, even as he draws unfavorable comparisons between such learning and the rusticity of the apostles. This uncertain confidence continues through his remarkable deployment of the *numularii*, or money coiners, as a metaphor for his readers. Those who find the commentary are to improve the unrefined *Expositio*, just as a mint imprints form upon bullion. Berengaudus nevertheless hopes that his readers will leave the meaning of his work intact, unless it happens that he has written anything contrary to truth.[8]

The rhetorical adoption of sermo humilis was a common way for medieval authors to insist upon their piety and religious authority.

talentum Domini mei abscondens, cum illo servo damnarer, qui 'abiens fodit in terrum, et abscondit pecuniam domini sui.' Et quia idoneus non sum ad duplicandam pecuniam Domini mei, trado eam nummulariis, ut ipse veniens recipiat quod suum est cum usura. Te autem, cui loqui coepi, nummularium voco, quia sicut nummularius pecuniam incompositam suis superscriptionibus adornat, ut apta sit ad lucra peragenda: ita et tu hanc pecuniam Domini, quam tibi committo, potens es tua sapientia tuisque compositis verbis adornare, ut apta fiat ad lucra Domini nostri Iesu Christi perficienda; scitoque te mercedem optimam ab ipso esse recepturum, si hic liber, ut puto, ecclesiae Dei necessarius, per industriam tuam atque doctrinam sordes dictionum amiserit, tuisque verbis decentibus exornatus, utilior ad aedificationem legentium sive audentium fuerit effectus. Hoc tamen non permitto, ut sensus huius libri in alios sensus permutentur, nisi forte (quod absit) aliquid in eo quod contrarium sit veritati inveniatur, quod funditus esse delendum decerno, vel certe in melius commutandum."

[7] The author introduces each of his "visions" with a brief preface rather than a bare *lemma*, and is therefore able to plant the necessary letters. The name Berengaudus (or Bernegaudus: both forms are attested and equally possible in light of the cryptogram) was uncommon but not unknown in the early medieval period. For the polyptych evidence, Maria-Therèse Morlet, *Les noms de personne sur le territoire de l'ancienne Gaule du VIe au Xe siècle*, 3 vols. (Paris: Centre National de la Recherche Scientifique, 1968–1985), 1:53.

[8] On the metaphor of the *numularii*, see the brief discussion of Markus Mülke, *Der Autor und sein Text: Die Verfälschung des Originals im Urteil antiker Autoren* (Berlin: Walter de Gruyter, 2008), 91–92 with n. 276 (for Mülke, Berengaudus is "Ps.-Ambrose"). On Berengaudus the exegete, Achim Dittrich, "Der rätselhafte Berengaudus," passim; and also more briefly but entirely along the same lines, Dittrich, "Berengaudus," in *The Biographisch-Bibliographisches Kirchenlexikon* 31 (Nordhausen: Traugott Bautz, 2010), 91–92. The major monograph on Berengaudus is Visser, *Apocalypse as Utopian*

Claiming divine inspiration was not, and yet Berengaudus feels his inspiration so keenly that he fears the consequences of not circulating his insights. The most obvious historical analogue to Berengaudus the divinely inspired exegete is Amalar of Metz, the ninth-century liturgist notorious for his difficult commentaries on the Romano-Frankish liturgy. Amalar too claimed divine inspiration for his insights, and with good reason: He was the first Western author to speculate about the meaning of the liturgy in allegorical terms, and he wrote in the face of pronounced cultural tendencies to reject and brand as heretical intellectual approaches that lacked clear antecedents in the patristic tradition.[9]

Berengaudus's inspiration is not so easily explained, for he faced no such obstacles. Allegorical commentary on the Apocalypse enjoyed deep precedent extending to the earliest centuries of Christianity. At the head of this tradition stands Victorinus of Pettau, who set forth an "essentially chiliastic" interpretation of the last book of the Bible around A.D. 300 that reflects the Diocletianic persecutions of his age.[10] The conversion of Constantine and the subsequent Christianization of the Roman Empire made Victorinus's approach uncomfortable if not heterodox for later readers, and Jerome accordingly recast its millenialism along more palatable allegorical lines. Around the same time, the Donatist theologian Tyconius, best known for his *Liber regularum* on the interpretation of scripture, penned his own commentary on the Apocalypse. Both Victorinus/Jerome and Tyconius found their way to the post-Roman world in part through the synthesis of yet a third author, Primasius, the

---

Expectation: regarded by Dittrich and others as the authoritative statement. Beyond Dittrich and Visser, Berengaudus is familiar to art historians for the illuminations his commentary received in the high-medieval world. See, in this connection, the extended discussion in Barbara Nolan, *The Gothic Visionary Perspective* (Princeton: Princeton University Press, 1977), particularly her second chapter.

[9] On Amalar, most recently Eric Knibbs, trans. *Amalar: On the Liturgy* (Cambridge: Harvard University Press, 2014), 2 vols. Also, more specifically on the problem of Amalar's divine inspiration, Celia Chazelle, "Amalarius's *Liber Officialis*: Spirit and Vision in Carolingian Liturgical Thought," in *Seeing the Invisible in Late Antiquity and the Early Middle Ages*, ed. Giselle de Nie, Frederick Morrison, and Marco Mostert (Turnhout: Brepols, 2005), 327–57. Amalar's originality ended with a conviction for heresy, on which see especially Klaus Zechiel-Eckes, *Florus von Lyon als Kirchenpolitiker und Publizist* (Stuttgart: Thorbecke, 1999), 21–71.

[10] Matter, "Apocalypse in Early Medieval Exegesis," 39.

sixth-century bishop of Justinianopolis (Hadrumetum) in North Africa. Primasius's commentary incorporates ideas from both earlier works, and with them forms the basis of the medieval approach to this most difficult book of the New Testament. Authors from the Venerable Bede to Ambrosius Autpertus reworked, simplified and sometimes expanded Tyconius and Primasius for the needs of new audiences, constructing a corpus of interrelated commentaries that proceeded to inform the *Glossa Ordinaria* in the twelfth century.[11]

It is this abundant tradition, with deep roots in patristic orthodoxy, which Berengaudus appears to set aside in insisting upon the divine inspiration of his *Expositio*. This originality or inspiration is most apparent in the local interpretations of individual verses that Berengaudus offers. In his broader interpretative tendencies, Berengaudus is more typical. E. Ann Matter has written that "Apocalypse commentaries from the Carolingian world...show the continuing assumption of the text as an allegory of the Church." Far from the millenialist approach of Victorinus, "early medieval exegesis presents the Apocalypse as a book

---

[11] For the details of this story, see Matter, "Apocalypse in Early Medieval Exegesis," 39–47. For perspective on early literary, cultural and political contexts, see Mary Rose D'Angelo, "The Sobered Sibyl: Gender, Apocalypse and Hair in Dio Chrysostom's *Discourse 1* and the *Shepherd of Hermas*," and Ross S. Kraemer, "The End of the World as They Knew It? Jews, Christians, Samaritans and Endtime Speculation in the Fifth-Century," both in this volume. For the markedly different approach that Joachim of Fiore adopted in the later twelfth century, namely a "spiritual millenariansim," see Bernard McGinn, "Apocalypticism and Mysticism in Joachim of Fiore's *Expositio in Apocalypsim*," also in this collection. Victorinus of Pettau survives only in sparse late medieval manuscript tradition, edited with Jerome's revision on the facing page by Johann Haussleiter, *Victorini Episcopi Petavionensis Opera*, CSEL 49 (Vienna: F. Tempsky, 1916). Tyconius likewise hardly survived the Middle Ages, though unlike Victorinus he acted directly and in unfiltered fashion upon the early medieval commentary tradition. For a reconstruction of his text, primarily from the eighth-century commentary of Beatus of Liébana (who made extensive use of Tyconius; Roger Gryson, ed., *Beati Liebanensis: Tractatus de Apocalipsin*, CCSL 107B–C [Turnhout: Brepols, 2012]), see Gryson, ed., *Tyconii Afri: Expositio Apcalypseos*, CCSL 107A (Turnhout: Brepols, 2011). Primasius was widely read in the Middle Ages and can be securely edited: A. W. Adams, ed., *Primasius Episcopus Hadrumetinus: Commentarius in Apocalypsin*, CCSL 92 (Turnhout: Brepols, 1985). Bede's effort is also ed. Gryson, *Bedae Presbyteri: Expositio Apocalypseos*, CCSL 121A (Turnhout: Brepols, 2001). Finally, for Ambrosius Autpertus, see Robert Weber, ed., *Ambrosii Autperti: Expositio in Apocalypsin*, CCCM 27–27A (Turnhout: Brepols, 1975).

about the integrity and purity of the Church on earth."[12] Berengaudus reads the Apocalypse in precisely this way. Wilhelm Kamlah therefore remarks that Berengaudus chooses "his own unusual direction" in specific matters, while otherwise receiving and extending the tradition of early medieval exegesis pioneered by Tyconius. More recently, Achim Dittrich has declared the *Expositio* "very Augustinian," observing with many others that Berengaudus aims to read the Apocalypse above all as an allegory for Christ and the church.[13]

Berengaudus therefore constitutes a small paradox. The structure and methodology of his *Expositio* are rooted in exegetical trends that originated in Late Antiquity and characterized Apocalypse exegesis throughout later centuries. At the same time, Berengaudus chooses more often than not to set the specifics of the tradition he inherited aside. In details his *Expositio* charts its own path, neglecting and sometimes flatly disputing customary approaches to individual verses. Despite an abundance of references to the *Expositio* in modern scholarship, our understanding of Berengaudus's place in the medieval tradition of Apocalypse commentary remains rudimentary, while the question of Berengaudus's chronological and political context continues to sustain dispute and controversy. Above all, Berengaudus and his *Expositio* have been widely cited but rarely studied.

***

Berengaudus is very clear that he is a monk writing for the edification of his community.[14] Beyond these basic circumstances, disagreement prevails on almost every aspect of his biography. For many scholars, Berengaudus is an eleventh- or twelfth-century author, perhaps associated with Rupert of Deutz. No known manuscripts of Berengaudus predate the eleventh century, and before the *Glossa Ordinaria* nobody seems to have read or cited his work. Another school of thought sees

---

[12] Matter, "Apocalypse in the Middle Ages," 45.

[13] Wilhelm Kamlah, *Apokalypse und Geschichtstheologie: Die mittelalterliche Auslegung der Apokalypse vor Joachim von Fiore* (Berlin: Emil Emering, 1935), 15; Dittrich, "Der rätselhafte Berengaudus," 113.

[14] See, among many possible examples, Berengaudus, *Expositio* 6, PL 17:944, where the author complains about *conversi* (monks who entered the monastery as adults) who take advantage of the naivité of the *nutriti* (monks who have been in the community since childhood) by telling tall tales of their status and position in the world.

the *Expositio* as a Carolingian-era commentary.[15] Proponents of this view invariably cite the correspondence of Lupus of Ferrières, who in 862 commended a certain Bernegaudus, "a monk as yet unformed," to the care of the monastery at Saint-Germain d'Auxerre. Lupus expressed his hope that Bernegaudus would continue his education within the monastic community and learn by example.[16] If this Bernegaudus can

---

[15] Berengaudus was known to the compilers of the *Glossa Ordinaria*, who cite his commentary under the name of Ambrose. See Dittrich, "Der rätselhafte Berengaudus," 94. The foremost proponents of Berengaudus as a ninth-century author are Dittrich and Visser, *Apocalypse as Utopian Expectation*. None of Visser's claims about Berengaudus's date or context are clearly supported by his analysis or the evidence he adduces, while Dittrich for the most part uncritically accepts Visser's conclusions. The foremost proponent of a later, high-medieval Berengaudus is Guy Lobrichon, "L'Ordre de ce temps et les désordres de la fin: Apocalypse et société du IXe à la fin du XIe siècle," in *The Use and Abuse of Eschatology in the Middle Ages*, ed. Werner Verbeke, Daniel Verhelst, and Andries Welkenhuysen (Leuven: Leuven University Press, 1988), 221–41, at 228; also Lobrichon, *La Bible au Moyen Âge* (Paris: Picard, 2003), 132 with n. 16—in both cases gesturing to unspecified congruencies with the thought of Rupert of Deutz. On this quiet controversy see especially the overview in Dittrich, "Der rätselhafte Berengaudus," 97–99.

[16] Lupus of Ferrières, ep. 116, ed. Ernst Perels, MGH Epp. 6 (Berlin: Weidmann, 1925): 100: "...ausi sumus fratrem Berengaudum, rudem adhuc monachum, roganti vestrae paternitati dirigere, vestrae voluntati obsecuturum et in suo proposito perfectiorem exemplis atque doctrina studiosius confirmandum." These remarks had followed an earlier letter from Lupus to Archbishop Wenilo of Sens, from 859, in which Lupus seems to be negotiating for Bernegaudus's reception at Auxerre. See Lupus, ep. 124, MGH Epp. 6:104: "Tunc etiam referre potero, quid super fratre Berengaudo sancti Germani monachi annuerint...." As noted above (note 7), Berengaudus is not an unattested name in the early medieval period, which is good reason to avoid collapsing the various Berengaudi of our historical sources into one and the same biography. Philippe Lauer, "Le Psautier carolingien du Président Bouhier (Montpellier, Univ. H 409)," in *Mélanges d'histoire du moyen âge offerts à Ferdinand Lot* (Paris: E. Champion, 1925), 359–83, at 381–82, discusses a brief historical note from the second half of the ninth century that reports the death of a Berengaudus at the hands of Vikings, and wonders whether it is our author. Visser, *Apocalypse as Utopian Expectation*, 89–90, seems to suggest that the Berengaudus of our *Expositio* might have been abbot of Echternach in the earlier tenth century, on the strength of Echternach abbatial catalogs that are ed. Georg Waitz, MGH SS XXIII (Hannover: Hahn, 1874), 32, 33. Obviously these must be two distinct Berengaudi. See the bibliographical overview at Dittrich, "Der rätselhafte Berengaudus," 97–99. The great French bibliographers were the first to identify the author of our *Expositio* with "Bernegaudus of Ferrières." See Paul Duport, *Histoire littéraire de la France: V*, 2nd ed. (Paris: Victor Palmé, 1866), 653–54; Remi Ceillier et al., *Histoire générale des auteurs sacrés et ecclésiastiques*, 2nd ed., 14 vols. (Paris: Louis Vivès, 1862), 12:702–3. This view has been received with rather more caution in the twentieth century. Compare, therefore, Heinz Löwe, ed.,

be identified with our author, then the *Expositio* has ties to the monastery of Saint-Germain, and therefore to the "Auxerre school" of biblical commentary practiced within its walls. The foremost representative of this school in the Carolingian age was Haimo, whose works include an influential commentary on the Apocalypse.[17] Derk Visser has argued for a clear relationship between Berengaudus's *Expositio* and Haimo's commentary, writing of Berengaudus's "obvious indebtedness" to Ambrosius Autpertus, Alcuin and Haimo, but insisting above all that the relationship between Berengaudus and Haimo is unique. "Berengaudus" therefore "continuously plays with ideas found in Haimo," and we even read that Berengaudus was likely Haimo's student.[18] Dittrich has endorsed Visser's views on this point, though neither author publishes any source analysis.[19] In consequence there remains much to say about the relationship of our *Expositio* to the early medieval commentary tradition, much of it interesting and unexpected.

Most obviously, Berengaudus and Haimo share an authorial approach that is otherwise rare among early medieval exegetes. Scholars have long prized Haimo for his originality, his readiness to compose his own Latin, and his relatively free use of sources. He tends to paraphrase rather than directly quote from his antecedents, and he blends his own ideas freely with the arguments of others. As such, his methods contrast with the bulk of the commentary tradition from the Carolingian era, particularly the work of Alcuin and Hrabanus Maurus, who assembled passages from

---

Wattenbach-Levison, *Deutschlands Geschichtsquellen im Mittelalter V* (Weimar: Hermann Böhlaus Nachfolger, 1973), 565.

[17] On Haimo and the Auxerre school more broadly, see the essays in *L'École carolingienne d'Auxerre: De Murethach à Remi, 830–908*, ed. Dominique Iogna-Prat, Colette Jeudy, and Guy Lobrichon (Paris: Beauchesne, 1991). For centuries, Haimo of Auxerre's commentaries were ascribed instead to Haimo of Halberstadt; it was not until Eduard Riggenbach, *Die ältesten lateinischen Kommentare zum Hebräerbrief* (Leipzig: Deichert, 1907) that the bibliographical error was corrected and major steps toward understanding Haimo's work were undertaken. Most recently key insights on Haimo and his biography have come from John J. Contreni; see, in particular, "Haimo of Auxerre, Abbot of Sasceium (Cessy-les-Bois), and a New Sermon on 1 John V, 4–10," *Revue bénédictine* 85 (1975): 303–20.

[18] Visser, *Apocalypse as Utopian Expectation*, 51 and 63.

[19] Dittrich, "Der rätselhafte Berengaudus," esp. 98–105—all conclusions condensed from Visser.

patristic authors more or less verbatim, often complete with sigla indicating the origins of various interpretations.[20] Berengaudus, we have seen, joins Haimo in departing from this standard practice. He prefers to present his sources in digested and largely unacknowledged form, and the only direct quotes in his *Expositio* are of the Bible. If Berengaudus and Haimo were associates, as the evidence of Lupus's letters has suggested to some, we would have an easy explanation for the more interesting aspects of Berengaudus's commentary, as well as some clarity about the date and context of his work.

There are also more specific textual ties between Berengaudus and Haimo. At base, Haimo's commentary is a reworking of the eighth-century Apocalypse commentary by Ambrosius Autpertus, which is in turn an expansion of Primasius.[21] My own analysis has failed to reveal any Primasian words, phrases or ideas in Berengaudus that did not also make the journey downstream through Ambrosius Autpertus and ultimately Haimo. There is therefore a good prima facie case that Visser and Dittrich are correct, and that Haimo's commentary was the primary source that Berengaudus tapped to construct his *Expositio*. At the same time, nothing warrants Visser's easy assumption that Berengaudus had access to a large library of biblical scholarship. While Berengaudus cites a range of patristic authorities, he never discusses any other commentaries on the Apocalypse.[22] Furthermore, in one telling passage he remarks on

---

[20] See Johannes Heil, "Theodulf, Haimo, and Jewish Traditions of Biblical Learning: Exploring Carolingian Culture's Lost Spanish Heritage," in *Discovery and Distinction in the Early Middle Ages: Studies in Honor of John J. Contreni*, ed. Cullen J. Chandler and Steven A. Stofferahn (Kalamazoo, MI: Medieval Institute Publications, 2013), 88–115, at 92–93, on what he sees as two Frankish schools of biblical scholarship in conflict with one another, an intriguing view that would pit Haimo and his methods against his more conservative contemporaries.

[21] So Riggenbach, *Die ältesten lateinischen Kommentare*, 83: Autpertus is "Haimos Hauptquelle. ... Neben ihm ist...auch der Apokalypsenkommentar Bedas benützt." E. Ann Matter, "Apocalypse in Early Medieval Exegesis," 48–49, arrives at the same conclusions independently.

[22] Multiple patristic authorities are adduced twice, at Berengaudus, *Expositio* 4, PL 17:883 ("...omnipotens Deus defensores ecclesiae orthodoxos patres...elegit...ut fuerunt Ambrosius, Hilarius, Hieronymus, Augustinus, Gregorius, et multi alii qui etiam maximam copiam librorum ediderunt...") and 956 ("Chrysoprasus lapis viridis aureique coloris esse perhibetur...possumus per eum quosdam doctores ecclesiae intelligere, qui et verbis...multos docuerunt, et multo plures suis scriptis erudierunt et erudiunt quotidie, ut fuerunt Hieronymus, Augustinus, Gregorius et multi alii. ..."). Otherwise, Gregory is Berengaudus's most frequently cited authority, and someone whom Berengaudus has

the abundance of commentaries on the Gospel, drawing an implicit contrast with the Apocalypse, which he seems to think has remained largely unexposited.[23] There is every reason to believe that Berengaudus's library was limited, and that Apocalypse exegesis beyond Haimo was unknown or inaccessible to him.

Particular interest therefore attaches to the relationship between Berengaudus and Haimo. An instructive moment occurs at Apoc. 1:11, where John is ordered to write "to the seven churches that are in Asia, to Ephesus and to Smyrna and to Pergamus and to Thyatira and to Sardis and to Philadelphia and to Laodicea." The traditional reading, transmitted with very little distortion from Primasius through Haimo, argues that each of these churches are metonymic for all of Christendom. Primasius sustains this argument by purporting to define the names of each of these churches, and then finding some indication of universality in each of his definitions. Thus Haimo relates, via Primasius, that "Ephesus means 'will' or 'my counsel,'" and that Ephesus therefore represents the entire church, "in which subsists God's will through faith, hope and charity and other good works," and which follows not its own will, "but the will of God, receiving that verse from Solomon: 'Hear counsel, and receive instruction, that you may be wise in your latter end' (Prov. 19:20)." And Smyrna is said to mean "their song," which ought to indicate "the song...of the elect," which again is emblematic of the entire church. Pergamus in turn means "division of horns," and "horns mean kingdoms...the horns of Christ are therefore understood to be the saints about to enter into his kingdom..."

---

clearly read; see *Expositio* 4, PL 17:856 and 868; and *Expositio* 7, PL 17:955 and 964. Jerome, meanwhile, earns only one citation (*Expositio* 5, PL 17:914). Curiously, and despite the clearly "Augustinian" nature of the *Expositio* (above, p. 143 with note 13), Berengaudus invokes Augustine only as a personality.

[23] Berengaudus, *Expositio* 3, PL 17:838–39, sees the opening of the fifth, sixth and seventh seals (from Apoc. 6:9) as an allegory for "the opening of the New Testament." He continues that "quamvis Novum Testamentum apertio sit Veteris Testamenti, tamen multa in eo obscure ponuntur, quae necesse est ut exponantur. Igitur sigillum quintum, sextum et septimum salvator aperuit, quando ea quae per parabolas ipse locutus est et figuraliter gessit, doctoribus ecclesiae patefecit. *Sed de expositione Novi Testamenti* [here Berengaudus seems to understand the "New Testament" as the Gospels in particular] *non est nobis necesse quidquam dicere, eo quod a sanctis patribus mirabiliter et multipliciter sit expositum.*"

But just as the horns of Christ are his members to whom he will give his everlasting kingdom, so too are the horns of the devil his members who will be damned with him. And so the holy church implements a division among these horns, that is to say it divides the just from the reprobate, and the kingdom of Christ from the kingdom of the devil, for it segregates the good from the evil, and the proud from the humble.... The Psalmist also speaks of these horns: "And I will break all the horns of sinners, but the horns of the just will be exalted" (Ps. 74:11).

From there, we read that Thyatira means "illuminated," which once again recalls the whole church, which "is illuminated by him who enlightens every man that comes into this world" (John 1:9–10). Sardis is then "prince of beauty," or the spouse for whom the church has prepared herself "through the ornament of virtue." Philadelphia means "saving God's inheritance," and the church is said to be an inheritance, indeed God's inheritance, for as Haimo has it: "It is God's field, it is his vineyard, which strives through its preachers to save its very self, that it may please God in faith and works and never depart from his will." Laodicea, finally, means "tribe beloved of the Lord," and "from the orders of tribes that pertained among the Jewish people as among the Romans...so too is the church divided...among priests, soldiers and cultivators...."[24]

---

[24] Haimo, *Expositio in Apocalypsin* 1, PL 117:951–53: "Ephesus interpretatur 'voluntas' sive 'consilium meum.' Quo nomine generaliter omnis ecclesia comprehenditur, in qua est Dei voluntas per fidem, spem et charitatem, caeteraque bona opera. ... Quae etiam bene 'consilium meum' dicitur, quia videlicet non suum, sed Dei sui sequitur consilium, audiens illud Salomonis: 'Audi consilium, et suscipe disciplinam, ut sis sapiens in novissimis tuis...' Smyrna dicitur 'canticum eorum'—quorum canticum nisi electorum? ... Pergamus interpretatur 'divisio cornuum.' Cornua significant regna, ut habes in libro Danielis et in Zacharia; cornua ergo Christi intelliguntur sancti ad regnum illius venturi. Sed sicut Christi cornua eius membra sunt, quibus regnum daturus est perpetuum, ita sunt cornua diaboli eius membra, quae cum eo damnabuntur. Inter haec itaque cornua, id est inter iustos et reprobos, et inter regnum Christi et diaboli, sancta ecclesia facit divisionem, quia segregat bonos a malis, superbos ab humilibus. ... De his cornibus et Psalmista dicit: 'Omnia cornua peccatorum confringam, et exaltabuntur cornua iusti.'... Thyatira dicitur 'illuminata,' quo nomine generaliter ecclesia designatur, quae illuminata est ab eo, qui illuminat omnem hominem venientem in hunc mundum.... Sardis sonat in lingua Latina principi pulchritudinis, apta subauditur et ornata.... Philadelphia dicitur 'salvans haereditatem Dei.' Ipsa est ager Dei, ipsa et vinea, quae per praedicatores suos ita salvare satagit semetipsam, ut fide et opere Deo placeat, et ab illius voluntate nunquam recedat.... Laodicia vertitur in nostra lingua 'tribus amabilis Domino'.... A tribus scilicet ordinibus, qui forsitan erant in populo Iudaeorum sicut fuerunt apud Romanos, in senatoribus scilicet, militibus, et agricolis, ita

Berengaudus adopts the Primasian definitions with sufficient textual parallels to prove that he has them from Haimo rather than Ambrosius Autpertus or Primasius himself. We read at once that "Ephesus means 'will' or 'counsel'; Smyrna, 'their song'; Pergamus, 'division of horns'; Thyatira, 'illuminated'; Sardis, 'prince of beauty'; Philadephia, 'saving God's inheritance'; Laodicea, 'the tribe beloved of the Lord.'"[25] Yet Berengaudus is anxious to move beyond the Primasian scheme:

> Ephesus...because it comes first, signifies the beginning of one's conversion. For it means "will" or "counsel." And what better counsel is there than good will, which persuades man to renounce the devil and follow Christ, to abandon vice and take hold of virtue? And because those who wish to be converted to God should implore the Lord's mercy, that they may be able to accomplish what they desire, Smyrna follows, because it means "their song." For he sings well who beseeches the mercy of his creator with a contrite heart and a humbled spirit. The Apostle speaks of this song, saying: "Singing and making melody in your hearts to the Lord" (Eph. 5:19). And because he who wants to be heard by God must abandon vice and give himself over to the performance of good works, insofar as virtue is at hand, Pergamus comes next, which means "division of horns." Two horns in this passage signify good and evil. We divide horns when we discern between good and evil, reject the evil and embrace the good. And since, for as long as we lie in sins we are in darkness, but when we cast evil off from ourselves and embark upon good work, it is as if we progress from darkness to light, it is not unfitting that Thyatira, which means "illuminated," should follow Pergamus. And because through observing God's commandments the soul grows in beauty, and insofar as one grows greater in observing God's commandments, he confers that much greater beauty upon his soul, it is not out of place that Sardis, which means "beginning

---

et ecclesia eisdem tribus modis partitur, in sacerdotibus, militibus, et agricultoribus, quae 'tribus amabilis' dicitur...." This passage has attracted attention for supposedly attesting to the theory of the three orders, the alleged high-medieval belief that society was divided among those who work, those who pray, and those who fight. See Georges Duby, *The Three Orders: Feudal Society Imagined*, trans. Arthur Goldhammer (Chicago: University of Chicago Press, 1982); Edmond Ortigues, "Haymon d'Auxerre, théoricien des trois ordres," in *L'École carolingienne d'Auxerre*, 181–227.

[25] Berengaudus, *Expositio* 1, PL 17:769: "Ephesus namque 'voluntas' sive 'consilium' interpretatur; Smyrna 'canticum eorum'; Pergamus 'divisio cornuum'; Thyatira 'illuminata'; Sardis 'principium pulchritudinis'; Philadelphia 'salvans haereditatem Dei'; Laodicea 'tribus amabilis Domino.'"

of beauty," should follow Thyatira. It is said to be the beginning of beauty because the beauty of the saints begins in this life, and is fully realized in eternal happiness. Philadelphia follows, which means "saving God's inheritance." And what is God's inheritance, if not the entire multitude of the elect, as the Lord says to the prophet: "But Israel is my inheritance" (Is. 19:25)? And in what does the salvation of the elect consist, if not in the observance of God's commandments? For he who comes to search for and recover what he lost grants the salvation of souls to those who keep his commandments, each according to their own strength. Laodicea comes seventh, because it means "tribe beloved of the Lord." For the tribe beloved of the Lord is the entire multitude of elect, which is the church, which through its rejection of vice and through the observance of virtue comes to the point that it may be called the tribe beloved of the Lord.[26]

---

[26] Berengaudus, *Expositio* 1, PL 17:769–70: "Ephesus igitur, quae prima ponitur, initium conversionis uniuscuiusque demonstrat; interpretatur namque 'voluntas' sive 'consilium.' Quod enim melius consilium, quam voluntas bona, quae homini suadet abrenuntiare diabolo, et sequi Christum, relinquere vitia, et apprehendere virtutes? Et quia qui ad Deum converti volunt, necesse est ut Domini misericordiam implorent, ut perficere possint quod desiderant, Smyrna huic supponitur, quae 'canticum eorum' interpretatur. Ille enim bene cantat, qui misericordiam conditoris sui corde contrito et humiliato spiritu deprecatur: de quo cantu Apostolus loquitur dicens: 'Cantantes et psallentes in cordibus vestris Domino.' Et quia qui a Deo exaudiri vult, necesse est ut vitia derelinquat et ad bona opera agenda, in quantum virtus suppetit semetipsum convertat, Pergamus in ordine sequitur, quae 'divisio cornuum' interpretatur. Duo cornua in hoc loco malum et bonum significant. Cornua dividimus, quando inter bonum et malum discernentes malum a nobis repellimus, et bonum amplectimur. Et quia, quamdiu in peccatis iacemus, in tenebris sumus, cum autem mala a nobis reiicimus et bona operari incipimus, quasi a tenebris ad lucem progredimur, non inconvenienter post Pergamum Thyatira sequitur, quae 'illuminata' interpretatur. Et quia ex operatione mandatorum Dei pulchritudo animae accrescit, et quanto quis in operatione mandatorum Dei plus crescit, tanto ampliorem pulchritudinem animae suae confert, non incongrue post Thyatiram Sardis sequitur, quae 'principium pulchritudinis' interpretatur. 'Principium pulchritudinis' ideo dicitur, quia sanctorum pulchritudo in hac vita inchoatur, et in aeterna beatitudine perficitur. Sequitur Philadelphia, quae 'salvans haereditatem Dei' dicitur. Quid est autem 'haereditas Dei,' nisi omnis multitudo electorum, sicut dicit Dominus ad prophetam: 'Haereditas autem mea Israel'? Et in quo salus electorum consistit, nisi in operatione mandatorum Dei? Nam ille, qui venit quaerere et salvare quod perierat, illis salutem animarum largitur, qui mandata eius singuli secundum propriam virtutem custodiunt. Laodicea septima ponitur, quia 'tribus amabilis Domino' interpretatur. Tribus autem amabilis Domino est omnis multitudo electorum, quae est ecclesia, quae per abrenuntiationem vitiorum et per virtutum operationem ad hoc pervenit, ut tribus amabilis Domino vocetur."

Berengaudus uses Haimo for specific information and formal cues, though he prefers to elaborate a tropological rather than an anagogical analysis of the verse before him. Though his reading is different, he constructs it in precisely the same way, proceeding definition-by-definition just as early medieval exegetes since Primasius had done, and the definitions themselves he lifts wholesale from Haimo. A consequence is that traces of the traditional scheme survive in the *Expositio*; the alleogrical church, for example, appears amid Berengaudus's discussion of Laodicea, though with far different significance.

For Berengaudus the two readings are clearly compatible, and he even nods openly to Haimo's interpretation, acknowledging that "The seven churches signify the one catholic church."[27] There is, then, no question of Berengaudus rejecting the traditional analysis of Apoc. 1:11. Further into his commentary, however, Berengaudus comes to handle Haimo more and more critically. At Apoc. 20:3, for example, where Satan is bound and cast into the abyss, Berengaudus provides three alternative readings. The first, of his own making and according to the letter ("simpliciter," as he puts it), forecasts that Satan will actually be confined to the abyss through God's omnipotence "until some foreordained time." A second interpretation, which he has from Haimo, holds that "through the abyss we can understand the hearts of the impious, such that [the devil] is excluded from the hearts of the elect, and bound within the narrow confines of the hearts of the reprobate." A third alternative, also of Berengaudus's own invention, is that Apoc. 20:3 is an allegory for the manner in which God has constrained the devil from working his deceptions upon the elect.[28] Berengaudus is content to let these possibilities coexist until he comes to Apoc. 20:7, when Satan is released from the

---

[27] Berengaudus, *Expositio* 1, PL 17:766: "Per septem ecclesias una ecclesia catholica designatur," and again at PL 17:769: "Per has septem ecclesias una ecclesia catholica, sicut interpretatio nominum docet, designatur."

[28] Berengaudus, *Expositio* 5, PL 17:929: "Alligationem diaboli tribus modis possimus intelligere. Possumus namque hoc simpliciter intelligere, ut virtute Dei omnipotentis in abysso religatus teneatur usque ad tempus praefinitum. Possumus etiam per abyssum corda impiorum intelligere, ut a cordibus electorum exclusus, intra angustias cordium reproborum constrictus et alligatus teneatur. Possumus et hoc tertio modo intelligere: Diabolus nihil aliud desiderat quam deceptionem hominum, et dum per custodiam Dei omnipotentis, qui electos suos custodire et defendere non desistit, ab eorum deceptione arcetur, quasi quibusdam vinculis eius impiissima voluntas religata tenetur...."

abyss after a thousand years. This development prompts him to wonder about the integrity of the second, Haimonian interpretation:

> ...A question arises: Above, *following the opinion of some people*, I said that the abyss could designate the hearts of the impious. ... But if the abyss designates the hearts of the reprobate, how is it that the devil is said to leave the abyss, or the hearts of the reprobate, whom he never abandons? Is it that he will abandon the reprobate and invade the elect? Not at all. *I think the binding of the devil is to be understood according to the letter*, such that divine power holds him bound in some abyss...until the day of his release....[29]

Berengaudus offers Haimo's analysis alongside other alternatives of his own making until it proves problematic, at which point he discards the approach as the opinion of anonymous others and endorses his own view as the correct one. A similar incident occurs at Apoc. 13:18, the famous verse on the number of the beast: "He that has understanding, let him count the number of the beast. For it is the number of a man, and the number of him is six hundred sixty-six." From Jerome onwards, authors had proposed a variety of names whose Greek letters yielded the sum of 666.[30] Berengaudus flatly rejects their efforts:

> Many people have said many things about this number, and they have provided many names in whose letters this number occurs. Yet they were not able to foresee whether the Antichrist would actually possess one of these names. I dare say nothing about so uncertain a matter. For who knows whether the name that his parents will give him is to yield this number?[31]

---

[29] Berengaudus, *Expositio* 5, PL 17:931–32: "Sed interim quaestio oritur: Superius quippe quorumdam opinionem sequens dixi per abyssum corda impiorum posse designari, in quibus diabolus, a cordibus fidelium expulsus, religatus teneatur.... Si ergo per abyssum corda reproborum designantur, quomodo de abysso, id est de cordibus reproborum, exire dicitur, quos numquam derelinquet? Numquid reprobos derelicturus est et invasurus electos? Nullo modo. Alligationem ergo diaboli secundum litteram intellegendam puto, ut in aliquo abyssi loco virtute divina religatus teneatur, vel certe in inferno usque ad diem absolutionis suae."

[30] On this line of speculation, Matter, "Apocalypse in Early Medieval Exegesis," 40 and 43–44.

[31] Berengaudus, *Expositio* 4, PL 17:887–88: "De hoc numero multi multa dixerunt, pluraque nomina repererunt, in quorum litteris hic numerus invenitur. Tamen si aliquod ex iis nominibus Antichristus possideat, praevidere non potuerunt: sed de re tam incerta nihil audeo definire. Quis enim scit, si nomen quod ei a parentibus imponetur, hunc numerum contineat?" Berengaudus's final objection seems to be that commentators cannot know

Here the same reference to the contrary views of multiple yet unspecified others, coupled with the fact of Berengaudus's limited library, suggests that he is rejecting Haimo in particular.

A more nebulous but potentially much more significant rejection occurs very late in the *Expositio*. The occasion is Apoc. 21:8, which declares that various sinners, including "all liars...will have their portion in the pool burning with fire and brimstone." In response, Berengaudus composes an extended excursus on the varieties of mendacity, at one point deploring "the many scholars of divine letters who, trusting the Jews more than is appropriate, take up some of their empty stories and interweave them in their works."[32] Since the pioneering work of Eduard Riggenbach, scholars have discussed the unique facility that scholars from the Auxerre school, particularly Haimo, had with Jewish exegetical traditions, and the use they made of these traditions in their biblical commentaries.[33] Because this characteristic is less apparent in Haimo's Apocalypse commentary than in his other works, particularly his commentaries on the Pauline epistles, we are invited to suppose that Berengaudus had access to other products from Auxerre and that he took exception to the methods these scholars employed.

Not only the content of Berengaudus's thought, but also his Latin style, suggests a growing impatience with Haimo over the course of the *Expositio*. In addition to his relative originality, Haimo is known for a variety of stylistic tics. These are so pronounced that they have permitted scholars to reclaim misattributed works for the Auxerre master. Haimo, for example, has a tendency to introduce an alternative interpretation of a given scriptural passage with a simple, syntactically unincorporated *Aliter* ("Otherwise"). He frequently elects to cast his commentary as a simple rephrasing of the scriptural text in question, prefaced by stereotypical words and phrases; the three most prominent

---

whether the number of the beast will subsist in the Antichrist's name, or in some other aspect of his person.

[32] Berengaudus, *Expositio* 6, PL 17:941–42: "Sunt etiam multi divinis litteris eruditi, qui Judaeis ultra quam oportet credentes quasdam eorum fabulas vanissimas suscipiunt, et suis traditionibus interserunt."

[33] On this point, Heil, "Theodulf, Haimo, and Jewish Traditions."

are *et est sensus, ac si diceret,* and above all various constructions with *subaudire*.[34] These usages recur in Berengaudus with a curious distribution. In twelve cases, Berengaudus introduces an alternate reading with a bald, Haimonian *Aliter* at its head. Eight of these occur in the first thirty *Patrologia* columns of his commentary, and all but one fall in the first half. Berengaudus has a markedly reduced fondness for *subaudire*; only five times does he use it as Haimo might have, three of them in the first thirty columns and the other two in the first half of the commentary. Likewise, two of three occurrences of *et est sensus* fall in the opening pages of the commentary, and *ac si diceret* has a nearly identical distribution.[35] One has the impression that Berengaudus set out to write his *Expositio* after Haimo's example, and that in the course of his work he came to find his own voice and felt increasingly free to depart from the model of his predecessor.

Even if the Berengaudus of our *Expositio* can be identified with the Bernegaudus of Lupus's correspondence, whether our commentary should be associated with the Auxerre school or considered the product of Haimo's student is highly questionable. In addition to the evidence we have surveyed, there is a chronological problem. By all accounts, Haimo's activity at Saint Germain d'Auxerre drew to a close in 865, just three years after Lupus wrote his letter commending the young Bernegaudus to the monks of the Saint-Germain community.[36] The internal evidence of the *Expositio*, meanwhile, suggests only that Haimo served as a literary model and an intellectual source, and not one that Berengaudus regarded as especially weighty. The specific ideas available in Haimo's commentary sink or swim on their own merits. In the course of his *Expositio*, moreover, Berengaudus increasingly sets Haimo aside, and even rejects the tendencies of the intellectual tradition that Haimo represents. The result is the paradox we noted at the start of this paper:

---

[34] On Haimo's intellectual and stylistic tendencies, Riggenbach, *Die ältesten lateinischen Kommentare*, 45–82, esp. 45–49 and 58. Also, more briefly, Contreni, "Haimo of Auxerre's Commentary on Ezechiel," in *L'école carolingienne d'Auxerre*, 229–42, at 231.

[35] For instances of *Aliter*: Berengaudus, *Expositio* 1, PL 17:768 (twice), 769, 771, 775, 783, 790; *Expositio* 2, cols. 794, 804; *Expositio* 3, cols. 831, 834; *Expositio* 4, col. 867; and *Expositio* 6, col. 936. Constructions with *subaudire*: *Expositio* 1, cols. 776, 780, 789; *Expositio* 3, cols. 842, 862. With *et est sensus*: *Expositio* 1, cols. 778, 784; *Expositio* 7, col. 963. With *ac si diceret*: *Expositio* 1, col. 784; *Expositio* 2, col. 794; *Expositio* 3, cols. 813, 832.

[36] For Haimo's dates, Contreni, "Abbot of Sasceium," 316–17.

Berengaudus is simultaneously in touch with, and at some remove from, the early medieval tradition of biblical scholarship. This must tell us something about Berengaudus's chronology and the broader context of his work.

***

Haimo's approach to scriptural commentary is detached and essentialized. A monk himself, he discusses monasticism only rarely. His view of the clergy is schematic and atemporal. Across hundreds of thousands of words, historical details are extremely rare.[37] On all of these points, Berengaudus strikes a different note. He is eager to discuss his own world, and this lends his *Expositio* an immediacy that is often lacking not only in Haimo, but throughout the broader tradition of early medieval exegesis. In indulging his proclivity for tangential discussions, Berengaudus provides remarkably precise information about his political and ecclesiastical environment, and the date of his *Expositio*.

Heinz Löwe has drawn attention to the views of Haimo and Berengaudus on the legacy of Antiquity. Haimo's was an era in which Carolingian rulers deployed the imperial title and characterized their government as a continuation of the western Roman Empire. Haimo, however, has no interest in the political rhetoric of the Carolingians. For him the Roman Empire is defunct, the Frankish kingdoms wholly new and unprecedented polities.[38] Berengaudus takes the same basic view, but the conclusions he draws are far more radical. His intriguing remarks are prompted by Apoc. 17:12, where John hears the meaning of the seven-headed, ten-horned beast from Apoc. 17:3–4: "The ten horns...are ten kings who have not yet received a kingdom, but will receive power as kings one hour after the beast." Ambrosius Autpertus and Haimo read these words in an eschatological light, emphasizing along with Bede parallels to the Book of Daniel (especially Dan. 7:7). In this sense, the verse

---

[37] Riggenbach, *Die ältesten lateinischen Kommetare*, 70–74, for the idealized and generally untextured picture Haimo provides of Christian life and ecclesiastical institutions.

[38] Against Riggenbach, *Die ältesten lateinischen Kommetare*, 78–80, therefore Heinz Löwe, "Von Theodorich dem Großen zu Karl dem Großen: Das Werden des Abendlandes im Geschichtsbild des frühen Mittelalters," *Deutsches Archiv* 9 (1952): 353–401, at 385 n. 126; also Löwe, *Geschichtsquellen im Mittelalter V*, 564–65.

is prophetic, foretelling in some way the conditions that will prevail in the time of the Antichrist.[39] Berengaudus, however, prefers a historical approach. For him, these heads "signify those kingdoms through which the Roman Empire was destroyed":

> For at first the Saracens took part of Asia for themselves, and later they subjugated the whole of it. The Vandals conquered Africa, the Goths Spain, the Lombards Italy, the Burgundians Gaul, the Franks Germany, the Huns Pannonia, and the Alans and Sueves destroyed many regions that fell to their dominion. These kingdoms, then, had "not yet received" power at the time John experienced his vision. And the kings received power for just "one hour," because the power of each of these nations lasted for a short time. They received their kingdoms "after the beast," because with the destruction of the devil's kingdom through Christ, these nations received an impious power.[40]

The Maurists argued that these words place the *Expositio* after 774, the year when the Lombard king Desiderius surrendered to Charlemagne, for Berengaudus includes the Lombards among those kingdoms that "lasted for a short time."[41] This is by far the weaker conclusion to draw from these remarks. Berengaudus regards the Roman Empire with hostility and suspicion. For him, the beast is a symbol for and a condemnation of this "devil's kingdom." The successor states are tainted by extension and association; the Franks no less than the Lombards have "received power for just 'one hour.'" Neither the barbarian kingdoms

---

[39] Ambrosius Autpertus, *Expositio in Apocalypsin* 7, p. 659; Haimo, *Expositio* 6, PL 117:1147. Both draw on Bede, *Expositio Apocalypseos* 3, p. 471. Compare Primasius, *Commentarius in Apocalypsin* 4, pp. 244–45, who sees in the beast a metaphor for the present world, though he does introduce some eschatalogical aspects, including the Daniel reference, in his discussion of Apoc. 17:3 (*Commentarius* 4, p. 238).

[40] Berengaudus, *Expositio* 5, PL 17:914: "Partem namque Asiae per se primitus abstulerunt, postea vero Saraceni totam subegerunt. Vandali Africam sibi vindicaverunt, Gothi Hispaniam, Longobardi Italiam, Burgundiones Galliam, Franci Germaniam, Hunni Pannoniam, Alani autem et Suevi multa loca depopulati sunt, quae eorum subiacebant ditioni. Haec ergo regna eo tempore, quo visio ista Ioanni demonstrata est, potestatem nondum acceperant, sed una hora tamquam reges potestatem acceperunt, quia singularum istarum gentium potestas pauco tempore permansit. Post bestiam regnum acceperunt, quia destructo regno diaboli per Christum, hae gentes impiam potestatem acceperunt."

[41] Comments repr. at PL 17:763–64, where du Frische and le Nourry aim merely to exclude Ambrose's authorship, not to date the *Expositio*.

that inherited and remade the Roman world, nor the Romanizing Carolingian political and ecclesiastical initiatives that characterized the ninth century, hold sway over Berengaudus and his reading of Apoc. 17:3–4. Berengaudus is the clear product of an age that no longer associates itself with Carolingian political aspirations. He could not have written these words before the deposition of the last Carolingian emperor in 888, or indeed all that soon thereafter. All of this makes it hard to read our *Expositio* as a product of the ninth century. Not only divine inspiration, but also substantial chronological distance from the Carolingian age explain why Berengaudus departs so abruptly from the commentary tradition inspired by the Carolingian Renaissance.

It remains to ask how late Berengaudus could have flourished. Here the best indications come in his discussion of Apoc. 18, where John receives the prophecy that the beast, also known as Babylon, will be defeated. At 18:11, an angel tells John that "the merchants of the earth shall weep and mourn over" Babylon, "for no man shall buy their merchandise any more." Berengaudus suggests various interpretations of these "merchants of the earth," before alighting upon "those who sell ecclesiastical office, which divine scripture utterly condemns." The result is a discussion of remarkable specificity and historical value that deserves a wider reception among historians of the early Middle Ages:

> …Although many bishops appear to be innocent of this crime [that is, simony], their ministers nevertheless are often polluted by it. In whatever respects the disciples fall short, it is a reflection upon their teachers. And there is another very terrible wickedness that is committed by those who are called archdeacons. For they take bribes from adulterous priests, and in keeping silent they consent to the evil, which, through the authority granted them by their bishops, they would otherwise be able to correct. And there are also others of this sort among the priests, who, fearing condemnation for their crimes, are more assiduous than the rest in service to the archdeacons. And if anyone dares to raise a word of criticism, the archdeacons defend them, and pretend not to know what they know. And so they are condemned by the prophetic teaching that goes: "Woe to you that call evil good, and good evil, that put darkness for light, and light for darkness" (Is. 5:20). And so I speak to you, who are such a one: Behold, you have sold the soul of your priest to the devil. For who persuaded the priest to fornicate, if not the devil? He who urged fornication, therefore, also urged the fornicator to bribe you, that he might perpetrate his crime without fear. Through the hand of the priest, therefore, the devil paid to

you the price of his soul's perdition. Behold, you have taken the bribe, and you have handed over the soul of your brother, redeemed by the blood of Christ, to the very same devil from whom he was redeemed. In the law it is written that if anyone has sold a man who is his brother, he should be put to death (Ex. 21:16). If, then, he who has sold one man to another is guilty, how much more guilty are you, who have sold a man redeemed by the blood of Christ not to another man but to the devil, which is much worse? Such merchants as these will cry and wail in the inferno, because nobody will bribe them any longer; and they will lose what they appeared to have, and they will fall into the evil that they neglected to foresee.[42]

Berengaudus's startling second-person address—"I speak to you" (*Ad te loquor*)—occurs in two other passages of the *Expositio*, both of them also sermonic denunciations of contemporary vice. In all three instances we are left with the strong suspicion that Berengaudus has folded some sermons into the text of his commentary. In the other two *Ad te loquor* passages, Berengaudus addresses problems in his own monastic community, including brothers who harass each other under the pretense of fraternal correction, and the tendency of *conversi* to exaggerate their endeavors in the outside world before an easily scandalized and naive

---

[42] Berengaudus, *Expositio* 5, PL 17:919: "Et quamvis multi ex episcopis ab hoc scelere videantur immunes, ministri tamen eorum in hoc saepe polluuntur. Ad magistros respicit, quidquid a discipulis delinquitur. Est et aliud scelus valde pessimum, quod ab iis, qui archidiaconi appellantur, committitur. Nam ab adulteris presbyteris pretium accipiunt, et tacendo in malum consentiunt, quod per auctoritatem, quam ab episcopis acceperunt, emendare possent. Sunt etiam alii ex huiusmodi presbyteris, qui timentes se damnari pro sceleribus suis in servitiis archidiaconorum plus sunt assidui quam caeteri, contra quos si quis aliquod verbum contrarium proferre voluerit, defenduntur ab eis; et fingunt se nescire quod sciunt, condemnanturque illa prophetica sententia, quae dicit: 'Vae, qui dicitis malum bonum et bonum malum, ponentes tenebras lucem et lucem tenebras.' Ad te ergo loquor, qui talis es. Ecce: Animam sacerdotis diabolo vendidisti. Quis enim suasit presbytero ut fornicaretur, nisi diabolus? Qui ergo suasit ut fornicaretur, ipse suasit ut pretium tibi daret, quatenus hoc scelus sine timore perpetrare posset. Per manum ergo presbyteri pretium perditionis animae ipsius tibi diabolus dedit. Ecce: Pretium accepisti, et animam fratris Christi sanguine redemptam eidem diabolo, a quo redempta est, tradidisti. In lege scriptum est quod si quis hominem qui frater eius esset, vendidisset, morte moreretur. Si igitur reus est ille, qui hominem homini vendit, quanto magis tu reus existis, qui hominem Christi sanguine redemptum non homini, sed quod perniciosius est, diabolo vendidisti? Tales ergo negotiatores flebunt et lugebunt in inferno, quoniam mercedes eorum nemo emet amplius; amittent enim, quod tenere videbantur, et incident in malum, quod praevidere neglexerunt."

audience of *nutriti*.[43] Here, however, Berengaudus looks beyond the confines of monastic life to address abuses in diocesan administration. He states that simony is unknown among the episcopate, as opposed to related forms of corruption notorious among archdeacons. He must therefore have written before the rise of eleventh-century church reform, which was devoted above all to rooting out episcopal simony from all corners of Western Christendom. Even the most ardent opponents of reform in the eleventh century could hardly introduce the problem of simony without addressing its episcopal aspect in some way. The substance of Berengaudus's complaint, meanwhile, aligns well with Carolingian-era anxieties, as the Maurists noted. Beginning in the ninth century, the Frankish episcopate experienced a radical growth in political power and prominence, and bishops began to delegate their pastoral duties to deputies. These trends elevated archdeacons, present in our sources from the fourth century, to episcopal vicars after the year 800. From the beginning their corruption was a matter of bitter complaint.[44] In 813, the Council of Chalon-sur-Saône lamented that "in many places, archdeacons exercise a considerable dominance over parish priests and extract payments from them, which tends toward tyranny rather than right order…"

> For if bishops, in accordance with apostolic teaching, should not be lording it over the clergy…how much less should archdeacons act in this way. Let them instead be content with regular discipline, keep to their prerogatives and strive to implement their bishop's orders in their diocese, presuming nothing in a spirit of greed or avarice.[45]

[43] Berengaudus, *Expositio* 1, PL 17:777; and 6, col. 944.

[44] On the early medieval archidiaconate and its development see, in particular, A. Amanieu, art. "Archidiacre," in *Dictionnaire de droit canonique* (Paris: Letouzey et Ané, 1935–1958), 1:948–1004; Alfred Schröder, *Entwicklung des Archidiakonats bis zum elften Jahrhundert* (Augsburg: Kranzfelder, 1890). More recent studies are lacking, beyond Kevin Michael O'Conner, *The Archidiaconate in the Ninth-Century Diocese of Auxerre: Carolingian Exigency in the Education of the Secular Clergy as Key to the Growth of a Medieval Church Office*. Ph.D. Dissertation, St. Louis University, 2000.

[45] Chalon-sur-Saône 813, c. 15, ed. Albert Werminghoff, MGH Conc. 2.1 (Hannover: Hahn, 1906), 277: "Dictum est etiam, quod in plerisque locis archidiaconi super presbyteros parroechianos quandam exercent dominationem et ab eis censum exigunt, quod magis ad tirannidum quam ad rectitudinis ordinem pertinet. Si enim episcopi iuxta apostoli sententiam non debent esse dominantes in clero, sed forma facti gregis ex animo, multo minus isti hoc facere debent, sed contenti sint regularibus disciplinis et teneant propriam mensuram et, quod eis ab episcopis iniungitur, hoc per parroechiam suam exercere studeant, nihil per cupiditatem et avaritiam praesumentes."

Complaints of greed were renewed at the great reform council held at Paris in 829, which again urged bishops to curb the avarice of their archdeacons, for it was on this account that "many are scandalized and the sacerdotal ministry is degraded and priests neglect many things in their churches."[46]

Episcopal capitularies, the internal regulations issued by bishops for the governance of their clergy, provide a clear picture of archidiaconal prerogatives and therefore their opportunities for corruption. One such capitulary, issued by Bishop Walter of Orléans in 867, charges the archdeacons of his diocese with investigating "the life, intelligence and teaching" of cardinal priests. Archdeacons are to determine whether these priests are leading modest lives, avoiding drunkenness, and comporting themselves piously.[47] Of even greater relevance is the so-called Second Capitulary of Theodulf, produced by an unknown Frankish bishop in the first half of the ninth century. This bishop was particularly concerned that his priests not involve themselves in adultery:

---

[46] Thus the *Relatio episcoporum* from 829, c. 7, ed. Alfred Boretius, MGH Cap. 2 (Hannover: Hahn, 1883), 33: "Comperimus quorundam episcoporum ministros, id est chorepiscopos, archipresbiteros et archidiaconos, non solum in presbiteris sed etiam in plebibus parrochiae suae avaritiam potius exercere, quam utilitati ecclesiasticae dignitatis inservire populique saluti consulere; quam neglegentiam, immo execrabile ac dampnabile cupiditatis vitium, omnes in commune deinceps vitandum statuimus.... Nam et in communi consensu statuimus, ut unusquisque episcoporum super archidiaconum suum deinceps vigilantiorem curam adhibeat, quia propter eorum avaritiam et morum inprobitatem multi scandalizantur et ministerium sacerdotale vituperatur et in ecclesiis a sacerdotibus multa propter eos negleguntur." Also the related statement issued at the 829 Council of Paris, c. 25, ed. Werminghoff, MGH Conc. 2.2 (Hannover: Hahn, 1908), 628: "Nam et in communi consensu statuimus, ut unusquisque episcoporum super archidiaconis suis deinceps vigilantiorem curam adhibeat, quoniam propter eorum avaritiam et morum inprobitatem multi sandalizantur et ministerium sacerdotale vituperatur et in ecclesiis a sacerdotibus multa propter eos negleguntur."

[47] Walter of Orléans, c. 2, ed. Peter Brommer, MGH Capit. episc. 1 (Hannover: Hahn, 1984), 188: "Ut per archidiachonos vita, intellectus et doctrina cardinalium presbiterorum investigetur. Vita scilicet modestiae et sobrietatis ac studium religiose conversationis in cunctis eorum actibus." Carl Gerold Fürst, *Cardinalis: Prolegomena zu einer Rechtsgeschichte des römischen Kardinalskollegiums* (Munich: Wilhelm Fink, 1967), 80–81, explains that cardinal priests were those priests stationed at significant proprietary churches near the episcopal see—highly visible clergy, in other words, with especially close ties to the bishop. On episcopal capitularies more broadly, see Rudolf Pokorny with Veronika Lukas, MGH Capit. episc. 4 (Hannover: Hahn, 2005), 1–67.

A priest, should he harbor a male or female adulterer in his home and, what is more horrible, consent to the occurrence of adultery in his home, should know that he is to be deprived of the honor of his rank. And should he uncover this crime among the people entrusted to him and not immediately correct it insofar as he can, but instead keep silent and consent to the adulterers, whether because they are powerful or because he derives some service from them, he should know that he is to be excommunicated as soon as this is uncovered. If, however, he has denounced and warned against this crime insofar as he could and excommunicated the offenders, and could not otherwise avert that evil, he has freed his soul. *Yet he should report this with all eagerness to his archdeacon, and the archdeacon to the bishop.*[48]

Berengaudus's complaint connects the general anxiety of Frankish reformers about archidiaconal avarice and mismanagement to the specific duties allotted to archdeacons by the episcopal capitularies. For failing to act against cases of marital impropriety, or merely harboring adulterers, priests could face deposition or even excommunication, and archdeacons were expected to police the morality of diocesan clergy and bring any violations to the notice of their bishop. The archdeacons of Berengaudus's aside are the clear products of this legislative and administrative environment. Still more, Berengaudus's information is precise enough to add texture to our picture of archdeacons in the Carolingian and post-Carolingian world, and it confirms that the *Expositio* is an early medieval composition. Berengaudus wrote well after the collapse of the Carolingian empire, but while the longer-term consequences of ninth-century ecclesiastical and administrative reforms were still very much in force.

***

---

[48] Theodulf, second capitulary, 2.1, ed. MGH Capit. episc. 1:153: "Presbiter, si in domum suam adulterum vel adulteram retinuerit et, quod nefas est, consenserit adulterium in domo sua fieri, sciat se sui gradus honore privandum. Si vero hoc in plebe sibi commissa reppererit et statim, si vires suppetunt, non emendaverit, sed siluerit et consenserit adulteris aut propter potentiam aut propter illorum beneficium, sciat se, cum depalatum fuerit, excommunicandum. Si vero ille, quantum potuit, et increpavit et ammonuit et excommunicavit, et non potuit illud malum vitare, animam suam liberavit. Verumtamen cum omni studio debet archidiacono suo et archidiaconus episcopo nuntiare." On the date and authorship of this problematic text, Pokorny, MGH Capit. episc. 4:98–99.

E. Ann Matter has called the history of early medieval commentary on the Apocalypse "a complicated story of obscure authors" and "tangled texts."[49] Few authors epitomize our inchoate knowledge of the field as perfectly as Berengaudus and his *Expositio* on the seven visions of John of Patmos. Berengaudus has proved difficult to date and place for the very same reasons that he is interesting. He exists in uneasy tension with the Carolingian legacy, sharing in the basic ninth-century project of reading and interpreting the Apocalypse as an allegory for Christ and the church, while rejecting much of the patristic tradition as transmitted through Haimo of Auxerre and going his own way wherever possible. What we can read of Berengaudus's historical outlook and circumstances paints very much the same picture. His complaints about administrative corruption in the diocese align so well with the concerns of Frankish church reformers that they inform our understanding of abuses associated with the early medieval archidiaconate. At the same time, his political outlook embodies a rejection of the Roman Empire together with ninth-century Frankish political pretensions that can only place him firmly in the post-Carolingian era. Berengaudus wrote too late to participate in the cultural and intellectual revival of the Carolingian Renaissance, and he had to wait for the twelfth century to find an audience. By then he had been completely forgotten. His name survived only in the cryptogram of his epilogue, and a great part of his later readership mistook his words for those of Ambrose.

[49] Matter, "Apocalypse in Early Medieval Exegesis," 38.

CHAPTER 7

Apocalypticism and Mysticism in Joachim of Fiore's *Expositio in Apocalypsim*

Bernard McGinn

Apocalypsis Joannis tot habet sacramenta, quot verba.
("The Apocalypse of John has as many mysteries as it does words")
Jerome, *Epistola* 53.8 (PL 22:548b–549a)

Apocalypticism and mysticism are modern terms that reflect ancient traditions. They are both important aspects of the history of Christianity and have been the subject of considerable research, not least by E. Ann Matter, whose rich career and many contributions are being honored in this volume. Apocalypticism is the belief that God has revealed the imminent end of the present age through some form of crisis or destruction brought on by the forces of evil, but that the destruction will be followed by a time of divine reward for the just. Mysticism signifies the element of religion that deals with a sense of the immediate presence of God as the goal of human life. Both apocalyptic and mystical beliefs were found together in early Christianity, as in the case of the Apostle Paul;

B. McGinn (✉)
University of Chicago, Chicago, IL, USA

© The Author(s) 2019
E. Knibbs et al. (eds.), *The End of the World in Medieval Thought and Spirituality*, The New Middle Ages,
https://doi.org/10.1007/978-3-030-14965-9_7

163

but apocalypticism and mysticism came to be separated in the centuries that followed. Some thinkers, however, sought to bring them together again. The Calabrian abbot Joachim of Fiore (ca. 1135–1202) was one of these, and this essay will try to show how he effected this reunification in his central work, the *Expositio in Apocalypsim*.

1 THE VISIONARY ORIGINS OF THE *EXPOSITIO IN APOCALYPSIM*

On Easter night of the year 1183 in the monastery of Casamari south of Rome a guest at the monastery, an abbot from a small house far to the south in Calabria, received a vision. The abbot Joachim later describes the perplexity he had experienced over the past year as he began to try to write a commentary on the Apocalypse, noting that upon reaching only as far as Chapter 1, verse 10, where John says, "I was in the spirit on the Lord's day" (*Fui in spiritu in dominica die...*), he had been stymied, unable to determine what John meant here, let alone in the rest of this most mysterious book of the Bible. Not an auspicious beginning. He continues:

> After a year, the Feast of Easter came round. Awakened from sleep about midnight, something happened to me as I was meditating on this book, something for which, relying on God's gift, I am made more bold to write....Since some of the mysteries I had grasped, but I was ignorant of the greater ones, there was a kind of struggle going on in my mind.... Then, on the already-mentioned night, something like this happened. About the middle of the night's silence, as I think, the hour when it is thought that Our Lion of the tribe of Judah rose from the dead, as I was meditating, suddenly something of the fullness of this book (*plenitudo huius libri*) and of the entire agreement of the Old and New Testaments (*tota veteris ac novi testamenti concordia*) was perceived by a clarity of understanding in my mind's eye.[1]

[1] *Expositio*, fol. 39ra–va (see next note for reference): "Factum est verso anni circulo diem adesse paschalem, mihique circa horam matutinam excitato a somno aliquid in libro isto meditanti occurrere pro quo confisus de dono dei audacior factus sum ad scribendum.... Et enim cum nonnulla iam capere, maiora adhuc sacramenta nescirem, quasi quedam pugna gerebatur in mente mea.... Cum ergo in suprascripta nocte aliquid contigisset. Circa medium (ut opinor) noctis silentium et horam qua leo noster de tribu iuda resurrexisse extimatur a mortuis, subito mihi meditanti aliquid, quadam mentis oculis intelligentie claritate percepta, de plenitudine huius libri et tota veteris ac novi testamenti concordia revelatio facta est...."

This was not only an unusual vision, but it was also unusually productive, because it led Joachim, later to become abbot of the new monastery of Fiore high in the mountainous Sila of Calabria, to write one of the longest and most influential of all commentaries on the Apocalypse, what he called the *Expositio in Apocalypsim*.[2]

What exactly was Joachim claiming in this vision? In terms of a visionary-prophetic authority, Joachim was presenting himself as a new John.[3] The apostle, theologian, and prophet (medieval people did not distinguish between the John of the Gospel and the John who wrote the Apocalypse) was given his prophetic mission only when, "being in the spirit on the Lord's day," he heard the great voice commanding him to write (Apoc. 1:11), and turned around to be given a vision of the Son of Man (Apoc. 1:12–16). Joachim could not understand what this all meant until he had received his own revelation on "the Lord's day" (i.e., Easter). Jesus's rising from the tomb was the source of the grace that effected the change in Joachim, the blocked exegete. Just as the tomb imprisoned Christ for three days, the dead letter of scripture did not allow Joachim to understand the inner meaning of the Apocalypse for a long time; and just as the divine bursting forth from the bonds of death made the true comprehension of scriptural prophecy available to the apostles,[4] so too the power of the Risen Christ gave Joachim, in an instant of intellectual vision, insight into the meaning of the last book of the Bible.[5] Still exegeting the same verse (Apoc. 1:9), Joachim says that it was only when John was "in the spirit on the Lord's day" that

---

[2] Despite the recent critical editions of many of Joachim's works published by the Centro Internazionale di Studi Gioachimiti at San Giovanni in Fiore, there is still no modern edition of the *Expositio*. We depend on *Expositio in Apocalypsim* (Venice: M. Pasini, 1527. Photographic Reprint, Frankfurt-am-Main: Minerva, 1964).

[3] As pointed out by Gian-Luca Potestà, *Il tempo dell'Apocalisse. Vita di Gioacchino da Fiore* (Bari: Laterza, 2004), 344–47. Strictly speaking, Joachim denied being a prophet, because prophecy is found only in the Old and New Testaments and there is no new scripture. What Joachim had been given was the *donum intellectus*, that is, the gift to interpret the full meaning of prophetic revelation.

[4] Commenting on Apoc. 3:14 (*Expos.*, fol. 95rb), Joachim says that after the Resurrection Christ makes the *spiritualis intelligentia* first available only to chosen witnesses, that is, Mary and the disciples.

[5] Joachim often says that Christ's Resurrection from the tomb of the letter marks the beginning of the spiritual interpretation of scripture; see, e.g., *Expositio*, fols. 3va, 88rb, 95va, 99vab, 110ra, 111vb, 139rb, and 153vab.

he began to understand the letter of the Old Testament in a spiritual way, and "...now in a similar way there are some people in the spirit who understand the letter of the New Testament according to this mode of understanding."[6] The abbot certainly included himself in this group.

Joachim describes the basic content of the revelation he received as constituting "...*aliquid... de plenitudine libri huius et tota veteris ac novi testamenti concordia*...." The key terms *plenitudo* and *concordia* are related, but need to be distinguished. Joachim's exegetical breakthrough rests on *concordia*, that is, discerning the literal match-ups, or agreements, between events of the Old and New Testaments that would enable believers, if not to predict the future, at least to have a good sense of what is to come in the light of God's ultimate sovereignty over time as revealed in the Bible. Joachim did not invent the "concordist mentality," one that had been criticized by Augustine, among others.[7] Nonetheless, the Calabrian had been experimenting with concordism for a number of years before his Casamari illumination. What happened at Casamari was important not only for convincing Joachim that such concordism was, indeed, essential for all exegesis, but also for showing him that it pertained to the *whole* of both the Old and the New Testaments. Equally revealing is the term *de plenitudine libri huius*, which claims that the revelation also gave him the *fullness* of the mysterious Apocalypse. For Joachim, the Apocalypse was not only the last book of the Bible, but also the most essential book in the sense that to understand it rightly was to grasp all the prior books from Genesis on. As he put it, "[The Apocalypse] is the key of things past, the knowledge of things to come; the opening of what is sealed, the uncovering of what is hidden. Great and remarkable is the prerogative of this book, because great is the Spirit of God who openly speaks his message in it."[8]

---

[6] *Expositio*, fol. 40va: "...et nunc simili modo erunt quidam in spiritu qui intelligant iuxta hunc intellectum literam novi testamenti."

[7] On the role of concordism in the history of eschatological thought, Bernard McGinn, "The Concordist Imagination: A Theme in the History of Eschatology," in *Revealed Wisdom: Studies in Apocalyptic in Honour of Christopher Rowland*, ed. John Ashton (Leiden: Brill, 2014), 217–31.

[8] *Expositio*, fol. 3rb: "Est enim clavis veterum, notitia futurorum, signatorum apertio, detectio secretorum. Magna est et singularis huius prerogativa voluminis, quia magnus est dei spiritus qui in eo aperte loquitur voces suas...."

We may wonder exactly what "the fullness of this book" consisted of. Joachim's answer is evident once again from his understanding of the meaning of the Resurrection. Commenting on Apocalypse 4:1a (*Post haec vidi: et ecce ostium apertum in caelo*), he identifies the "open door" with the opening of Christ's tomb and proclaims:

> Door in this passage is to be understood as the coming of the spiritual understanding (*spiritualis intellectus*).... When [it says] Christ arose as the first fruits of those who had died (1 Cor. 15:20),...and the stone was removed from the door of the monument (Jn. 20:1), it is indeed [right], because when the right time came the Holy Spirit was sent to humans, and the spiritual and life-giving understanding arose from the heart of the letter [of scripture].[9]

For a millennium prior to Joachim Christian exegetes had insisted that the purpose of reading the Bible was to uncover its inner, spiritual meaning—"The letter kills, but the Spirit gives life" (2 Cor. 3:6). Nevertheless, Joachim's view of the *intellectus/intelligentia spiritualis* was remarkable in its complexity and universality, especially for its grounding in his doctrine of the Trinity and its ability to uncover the meaning of history.[10]

Joachim distinguished three great ages (*status*) of world history as manifestations of the three Persons of the Trinity. For the Calabrian this Trinitarian structure of history is the essence of the spiritual understanding of the two Testaments. As he says in his *Liber de Concordia*: "Therefore, because there are two divine Persons of whom one is ungenerated [i.e., the Father], the other generated [i.e., the Son], two Testaments have been set up, the first of which...pertains especially to the Father, the second to the Son, because the latter is from the former. In addition, the spiritual understanding, proceeding from both

---

[9] *Expositio*, fol. 99va: "Verumtamen in hoc loco per hostium aditus spiritualis intellectus intelligendus est....Ubi autem resurrexit Christus primiticie dormientium,... et lapis amotus est ab hostio monumenti, nimirum, quia ubi afficit tempus opportunum missus est ad homines Spiritus Sanctus, et ascendit de corde littere spiritalis et vivificus intellectus."

[10] Much has been written on Joachim's notion of *spiritualis intelligentia*. For a fuller account, see Chapter 4, "*Intellectus Spiritualis:* Joachim's Understanding of Scripture," in Bernard McGinn, *The Calabrian Abbot: Joachim of Fiore in the History of Western Thought*, ed. Bernard McGinn (New York: Macmillan, 1985), 123–44.

Testaments, is one that pertains especially to the Holy Spirit."[11] The spiritual understanding "proceeds from the concordance of the two Testaments,"[12] because *concordia* pertains to the literal sense of the Bible as a comparison of the letter of the Old Testament and the letter of the New.[13] In a striking image Joachim compares the spiritual understanding to a voice blowing in a trumpet. Speaking of the seven angels preparing to blow the seven trumpets of Apocalypse 8:6, he says: "They prepare themselves to sound the trumpets since that is how they ought to announce that spiritual understanding that they form in the trumpet of the letter which is like a note (*flatus*) proceeding from a trumpet. Just as a note comes from a trumpet, so the spiritual understanding comes forth from the heart of the letter."[14]

Attaining the *spiritualis intelligentia* revealed through the concords, says Joachim, was rare in the time of the Old Testament, although given occasionally as a reward for those who looked forward to the coming of Christ. Christ's Resurrection was the decisive beginning of spiritual understanding, but not its *plenitudo*, which is the work of the Holy Spirit increasingly active in the second *status* and reaching a culmination in the coming third *status*. Joachim says: "Therefore, even though the Fathers wrote much to explain the New Testament, its perfect exposure is being kept to be made in the third *status* of the world."[15] Little-by-little the spiritual understanding has been growing in the church since the Risen Christ first gave it to the apostles. That growth reached a new stage in

---

[11] This text comes from the second of Joachim's major writings, *Liber de Concordia* II.1.10. I will cite the first four books according to the edition of E. Randolph Daniel, *Abbot Joachim of Fiore: Liber de Concordia Noui ac Veteris Testamenti* (Philadelphia: The American Philosophical Society, 1983). This passage is on 79. Similar passages are found in the *Expositio*, e.g., fols. 5ra, 9rb, and 141ra.

[12] *Liber de Concordia* V.106. This passage from Book V can only be found in the old edition, *Concordia Novi ac Veteris Testamenti* (Venice: S. de Luere, 1519), fol. 125rb.

[13] Joachim makes it quite clear that the concords are comparisons between the letter of the Old Testament and the letter of the New in many places; e.g., *Liber de Concordia* II.2.12 (ed. Daniel, 196).

[14] *Expositio*, fol. 127va: "Parent se autem ut tubis canant cum spiritualem intelligentiam que est similis flatui procedenti ex tuba, qualiter illam pronunciare debeant in tuba littere formant. Sicut enim...flatus ex tuba, ita de corde littere spiritualis progreditur intellectus."

[15] *Liber de Concordia* III.1.9 (ed. Daniel, 232): "Ita, etsi multa scripta sunt a patribus in expositione novi testamenti, perfecta tamen eius apertio in tertio statu seculi facienda servata."

the illumination received by Joachim, so that he now was convinced that the fire of the plenitude of meaning was soon to be ignited by the Holy Spirit. Interpreting John's vision of the angel standing on both the sea and the land who gives the prophet the book to eat (Apoc. 10:9–10), Joachim says: "The revelation was not made public when it was shown to John, nor even when it was begun at the Lord's Resurrection, but rather [it was made public] in the church at the sixth *tempus* whose beginning moments we already grasp...."[16] In one passage he compares this progress to the Prophet Elijah in his conflict with the priests of Baal (1 Kings 1:25–40 Vg). The wood on the earthen altar of sacrifice is the Old Testament upon which the water of the New Testament was poured by Elijah as a concord with Christian exegetes using the New Testament to interpret the Old. Like Elijah, "We should wait for the invisible Spirit from above, who, as from the third heaven (2 Cor. 12:2), will direct his spiritual fire, so that when that which is perfect shall have come, what is imperfect will be done away with (1 Cor. 13:10)."[17] Comparing the Bible with the three heavens of Paul's rapture in Second Corinthians, Joachim identifies the first heaven as the *status* of the Old Testament, the second as that of the New Testament, while "the spiritual understanding pertains to the third." "And so," he continues, "at the end of the second *status* and the beginning of the third, the One the Father sends in the name of Christ [i.e., the Holy Spirit] will open up the letter of the New Testament, and especially of this book [i.e., the Apocalypse]."[18] Once again, the Apocalypse is the key to the whole Bible. In another place Joachim says that the five ecclesiastical offices, or orders, of the second *status* (priests, deacons, bishops, virgins, general clergy) were assigned five books (the four gospels and the Acts of the Apostles), but "This book [i.e., the Apocalypse], filled with spiritual mysteries, is principally given to the spiritual men (*viris spiritualibus*) who say farewell to

---

[16] *Expositio*, fol. 27ra: "Non tunc autem facta est palam revelatio ista, que sancto ioanni ostensa est, nec que inchoata est in resurrectione dominica; sed magis in ecclesia tempore sexto cuius initia iam tenemus...."

[17] *Liber de Concordia* II.1.1 (ed. Daniel, 61): "...inuisibilem autem spiritum expectare desuper qui, ueluti de tertio celo, ignem suum dirigere spiritualem, ut, ueniente eo quod perfectum est, euacuetur quod ex parte est."

[18] *Expositio* fol. 139rb: "...ita in fine secundi status et initio tertii, in littera testamenti novi et maxime huius libri, aperiente eo quem misit pater in nomine Christi...." To be sure, the fullness of the *intelligentia spiritualis* will not be given until later in the third *status* after the defeat of the beast (Apoc. 19:20), as Joachim says in *Expositio*, fol. 211rb.

the cares of the world." Thus, "This perfection of the numbers five and seven can be assigned only to the book of the Apocalypse."[19]

On the basis of his status as the "new John," Joachim spent years writing and revising his long *Expositio*, by far the lengthiest of his writings.[20] In the absence of a critical edition, it is hard to recover the stages in the evolution of the text, which probably developed over at least fifteen years (ca. 1183–1200). Internal signs indicate that Joachim originally planned for the book to have seven parts, but later revised this to eight.[21] In order to understand where the mystical dimension fits into Joachim's reading of the Apocalypse, it is necessary to take a look at the structure and general message of the *Expositio*.[22]

2 Joachim's Engagement with the Apocalypse

Joachim was fascinated with the Apocalypse throughout his life. The Calabrian abbot was first and foremost an exegete, one who commented on most of the Bible over the course of his writings. The Apocalypse was never far from his mind. His early *Genealogia* written about 1176 sets out initial forms of concords and uses materials from the Apocalypse.[23] As noted above, he was working on an abortive commentary from the early 1180s, but had apparently given that up before he received the Easter Revelation. This revelation of the keys to biblical interpretation was also influential on his two other major works begun around the

---

[19] *Expositio*, Liber Introductorius, Cap. 18 (fol. 17rb–vb): "Porro liber iste sacramentis spiritalibus plenus viris spiritalibus et vale dicentibus curis seculi principaliter data est.... Verumtamen perfectio ipsa quinarii et septenarii numeri in solo quoque libro apocalipsis assignari potest...." The seven orders of the third *status* are attained by counting the first five orders of the second *status*, though now in "spiritualized" forms, along with the two new orders of *viri spirituales* to be discussed below.

[20] For comparative purposes, the *Liber de Concordia* takes up 135 folios in the 1519 edition, while the *Expositio* takes up 224 folios in the comparable 1527 edition.

[21] This has been shown by Potestà in the chapter he devotes to the *Expositio*; see Chapter 11, "L'interprete dell'Apocalisse," in *Il tempo dell'Apocalisse*, 286–339. This is the most recent treatment of the work.

[22] For a more complete account, see Chapter 6, "'Take the Book and Eat It': Joachim and the Apocalypse," in *The Calabrian Abbot*, 145–60.

[23] The text has been edited by Gian Luca Potestà, "Die Genealogia. Ein frühes Werk Joachims von Fiore und die Anfänge seines Geschichtsbildes," *Deutsches Archiv für Erforschung des Mittelalters* 56 (2000): 55–101.

same time: the *Liber de Concordia*, an exposition of his theory of concords and their application[24]; and the *Psalterium decem chordarum*, a treatise on the Trinity that also included reflections on the number and meaning of the psalms.[25] Joachim also has a number of shorter works that concern the Apocalypse, either by way of direct commentary, or by their dependence on John's Revelation. For example, the *De prophetia ignota*, a text he wrote on an obscure Sibylline prophecy probably in 1183 at papal command, marks the earliest appearance of what became one of the hallmarks of his thought: the concord between the seven persecutions of the church revealed in the seven seals of the Apocalypse and the seven persecutions of the people of Israel in the Old Testament.[26] A number of other short works were related to his ongoing effort in the great *Expositio*.

The first of these is what has been called the *Praefatio Ioachim abbatis super Apocalypsim*, two sermons on the Apocalypse, produced perhaps between 1188 and 1192, and edited by Kurt-Viktor Selge.[27] These appear to include earlier materials that Joachim was trying to put together for use in his commentary. In the 1190s, as the abbot was beginning to realize how massive his commentary would turn out to be, he seemed to turn his attention to producing an introduction. Recent research has identified two versions of this. The first form, finished perhaps around 1195, now exists as a stand-alone work called the *Enchiridion in Apocalypsim*.[28] Joachim substantially revised this, probably between 1195 and 1199, into what he called the *Liber Introductorius in Apocalypsim* of twenty-seven chapters. He put this at the beginning of the *Expositio* (fols. 2vb–26va), describing it as a *summula* of what he was trying to do.[29] In this final decade of his efforts on his masterwork,

---

[24] The *Liber de Concordia* also includes material on the Apocalypse, specifically in its Treatise on the Seven Seals in Book III, whose two parts are devoted to explaining the seals first in the OT and then the NT (ed. Daniel, 208–311).

[25] See the edition of Kurt-Viktor Selge, *Joachim von Fiore. Psalterium decem cordarum* (Hannover: Hahnsche Buchhandlung, 2009).

[26] Matthias Kaup, '*De prophetia ignota.*' *Eine frühe Schrift Joachims von Fiore* (Hannover: Hahnsche Buchhandlung, 1998).

[27] Kurt-Viktor Selge, ed., *Gioacchino da Fiore. Introduzione all'Apocalisse* (Rome: Viella, 1995). See also the comments in Potestà, *Il tempo dell-Apocalisse*, 287–97.

[28] This work has been edited, though in a not totally satisfactory way, by Edward K. Burger, *Joachim of Fiore: Enchiridion Super Apocalypsim* (Toronto: PIMS, 1986).

[29] On the relation of the two texts, see Potestà, *Il tempo dell'Apocalisse*, 327–31.

however, Joachim wrote two other brief treatises that are off-shoots of his views on the Apocalypse and the meaning of history. The first of these, another stand-alone treatise, the *De septem sigillis*, is concerned with the key motif of the seven seals that he had been pondering for several decades. In the past various datings have been given to the book, but the latest research sees it as a late work (ca. 1195–1200).[30] Finally, there is a short treatise entitled *De ultimis tribulationibus* (possibly 1196–1198), which tries to give a synoptic view of the events of the end as described in Daniel and John.[31] Much study has been devoted to the nuances of the interpretation of history and the last things found in these treatises and what they reveal about the Abbot's changing views. But Joachim seems to have always been changing his mind—though within the same general parameters—and so I shall concentrate on his *Expositio* in what follows.

In the 1527 edition the *Expositio* begins with Joachim's letter of 1200 leaving his works, both those that were complete and those still being worked on, to the judgment of the Holy See. There is then a brief *Prologus* (fol. 2ra–vb) followed by the *Liber Introductorius*. The actual interpretation of the Apocalypse begins with John's *praefatio* (Apoc. 1:1–3, fols. 26va–27vb) and then a reading of his *salutatio* to the seven churches in Asia (Apoc. 1:4–8, fols. 27vb–38vb). This last contains an important discussion of the Trinitarian basis of Joachim's theology of history (fols. 33vb–38va). The explanation of the eight parts of the book proper begins on folio 38vb with Apocalypse 1:9, the verse that Joachim cited in recounting his Easter vision.

These eight parts of the work have multiple functions.[32] The first six parts reveal the six times (*tempora*) of the second *status*, that is, the

---

[30] For an edition and detailed study, Julia Eva Wannenmacher, *Hermeneutik der Heilsgeschichte. "De septem sigillis" und die sieben Siegel im Werk Joachims von Fiore* (Leiden: Brill, 2005).

[31] This has been edited by Kurt-Viktor Selge, "Eine Traktat Joachims von Fiore über die Drangsale der Endzeit: 'De ultimis tribulationibus'," *Florensia* 7 (1993): 7–35. See also the comments of Potestà, *Il tempo dell'Apocalisse*, 334–39.

[32] Joachim outlines the eight-part division in Chapter 16 of the *Liber Introductorius* (fol. 16ra). The first four parts are dependent on the Apocalypse commentary of Bede: (1) Apoc. 1:9–3:22; (2) Apoc. 4:1–8:1; (3) Apoc. 8:2–11:18; and (4) Apoc. 11:19–14:20. The last four divisions are Joachim's own: (5) Apoc. 15:1–16:16, which Joachim divides into six *distinctiones*; (6) Apoc. 16:18–19:21, with three *distinctiones*; (75) Apoc. 20:1–10; and (8) Apoc. 20:11–22:21.

history of the church, which is identical with the sixth age (*aetas*) of world history. The seventh part concerns the coming third *status*, which is also the seventh age (*aetas*) of history; and the eighth part treats the final eighth age (*aetas*) of the Heavenly Jerusalem. Joachim's structuring of the treatise is remarkably architectonic, obviously the product of considerable thought. The abbot divides the whole *Expositio* into three *incisiones*, or large "Sections." The bulk of the book (fols. 38vb–213rb) is concerned with earthly history and has many complex subdivisions. Throughout his writings Joachim saw the times of the Old Testament and the New as containing forty-two generations each, and the *Expositio* repeats this basic pattern by subdividing each of the six parts, or *tempora*, of the current life of the church (the second *status*) into seven generations, thus attaining the desired number of forty-two.[33] Hence, the *Expositio* correlates the *incisiones*, an abstract division, with his favorite historical categories: *status, aetas, tempus*, and *generatio*. The first *incisio* (fols. 38vb–209vb) deals with the whole second *status*, the time of the church, which is also the sixth *aetas* of the seven that constitute the total duration of the world, the "World-Week" schema, as it is called, because it correlates the progression of history with the seven days of creation. This large sixth *aetas* takes up the first six parts (*partes*) of the Apocalypse that reveal the six times (*tempora*) of the story of the church. We need not imagine, however, that the first *status*, the time of the Old Testament, is neglected in the *Expositio*, because the use of *concordia* means that the New Testament is always being interpreted in the light of the Old, and vice versa. This is fundamental to Joachim's exegesis. The second *incisio* is much briefer (fols. 209vb–213rb), treating of the seventh part of the Apocalypse (usually described as an *aetas*, and rarely as a *tempus*). This deals with the earthly Sabbath Age, which is identified with the third *status* of history, the time of the Holy Spirit. Finally, the third *incisio* (fols. 213rb–224rb) concerns the eighth age (*aetas*), the eternal rest of the Heavenly Jerusalem.

Joachim broke with most previous commentators on the Apocalypse by seeing the book as a continuous prophecy of the history of the church from apostolic days down to the end. Each of the six parts deals with

---

[33] On the first six parts comprising forty-two generations, see *Expositio*, fol. 9v. In the *Liber de Concordia* II.1.20 (ed. Daniel, 99–100), Joachim says that although the forty-two generations of the Old Testament varied in length, the forty-two of the New Testament are exactly thirty years each.

a particular period and frequently historicizes the images and protagonists of the Apocalypse, that is, interprets them as predicting historical persons and events of the periods in question. The dominant Tyconian-Augustinian line of interpretation of the Apocalypse had resisted such historicizing, preferring to read the images of the book as indicating moral conflict both in the life of the individual and generically in the church in every period. Joachim's reading, however, is far more complex than a simple chronological account, due to the way he mixed in two other hermeneutical strategies—recapitulation and concordance. Chapter 15 of the *Liber Introductorius* stresses the importance of recapitulation: "Indeed, this book in relation to its six parts extends and maintains its tracks within the limits of the second *status*, so that from the beginning of the Lord's Resurrection it reaches its end and again and again returns to its beginning. In each of the [first] five parts there is recapitulation, and its course is directed in each of the parts down to the end of the second *status*."[34] This is perhaps clearest in Part I, the long section dealing with John's letters to the seven churches (Apoc. 1:9–3:22, in fols. 38vb–99rb). This primarily signifies the first *tempus* of church history, the time of the order of the prelates and the struggle against the Jews, but each of the seven churches also signifies one of the other general orders characteristic of the following six *tempora* and thus this first part is a recapitulation of the entire story of the church.[35] The Apocalypse's repeating sequences of sevens (seven churches, seven seals, seven trumpets, seven bowls), which had first given rise to the technique of recapitulation with the third-century exegete Victorinus of Poetevia, made this form of interpretation welcome to Joachim.[36] Along with this recapitulative dimension, we must not forget the concordist aspect pointed out above. Again, Joachim makes this clear in the *Liber Introductorius* when he says: "Now we are ready to speak of

---

[34] *Expositio*, Liber Introductorius, Cap. 15 (fol. 15vb): "Sane liber iste quantum ad sex partes suas infra limitem secundi status extendit et retinet passus suos, ita ut incipiens a resurrectione domini perveniat usque ad finem eius et iterum atque iterum redeat ad principium sui. In singulis denique partium recapitulatio est, et usque ad finem secundi status dirigitur in singulis cursus eius."

[35] Joachim summarizes this in *Expositio*, fol. 99rb–va.

[36] On the role of Victorinus in the history of Apocalypse commentary, Bernard McGinn, "Turning Points in Early Christian Apocalypse Exegesis," in *Apocalyptic Thought in Early Christianity*, ed. Robert J. Daly (Grand Rapids: Baker Academic, 2009), 81–105.

the concordances of the Testaments, and the concordance of the three works which began to be evident in the three *status* of the world one after the other, so that in examining the relation between similar things we may be able to come closer to the intention of the author the more we grasp that things new agree with those old and that they accord in their reality."[37]

Joachim's interacting modes of exegesis give rise to a theology of history based on the Apocalypse that is multi-dimensional. The most significant aspects are: (1) the Trinitarian dimension, namely, that the meaning of history is the revelation of the relations and actions of the three divine Persons; (2) the world-historical dimension, which is evident in the structure outlined above; (3) the "ordinal" aspect, in the sense that the Apocalypse reveals the roles of the diverse forms of religion (*ordines*) in the story of the church; (4) the apocalyptic dimension, because Joachim argues that the end of the second *status* is near; and finally; and (5) the contemplative-mystical dimension, because the dawning millennium, the seventh age predicted in Apocalypse 20, will be a time of collective contemplation, peace, and worship. Each of these five dimensions could be the subject of a long essay, and they all interact. What I have called the "ordinal dimension" is certainly very important,[38] because Joachim was a monk who lived in the midst of intense debates about the best form of religious life (*ordo*), both in the present and in the future. Hence, it should not be a surprise that his view of salvation stressed the role of the *ordines* established by the divine plan, not only the three general *ordines* of married, clerics, and monks that correspond to the three *status* of history, but also the special *ordines* related to the six *tempora* of the second *status*.

Given the fact that history is always a confrontation between good and evil, each of the divinely-appointed *ordines* of the *tempora* of the

---

[37] *Expositio*, Liber Introductorius, Cap. 4 (fol. 5ra): "Nunc in promptu est dicere de duorum concordia testamentorum, seu etiam de concordia trium operum que in tribus statibus mundi alia post alia clarere ceperunt, ut dum similia queque similibus suis respondere perpendimus, eo magis intentione auctore indagare possimus; quo magis convenire nova veteribus, et veluti ex eisdem subsistentia consonare sentimus."

[38] The importance of what I am calling the "ordinal" dimension of the *Expositio* has been emphasized by Potestà, *Il tempo dell'Apocalisse*, 296: "L'analsi del testo ci ha mostrato che le questione per lui prioritaria non era quella dei tre *status*, bensì quella dei tre *ordines* e delle loro relazioni." It seems to me, however, that the two dimensions are so interdependent that it is difficult to say one is more important than the other.

second *status* has an eschatological opponent figured in the animals from Old and New Testament apocalyptic texts. These symbolic confrontations are given historicizing readings by Joachim, that is, he interprets them as providing insight into the history of the church's conflicts over the ages. Thus, the prelates of the first *tempus* (the lion of the four beasts, or Tetramorph, of Apoc. 4:7) combat the synagogue of the Jews (the lioness of Dan. 7:4), while the martyrs of the second time (the cow of Apoc. 4:7) confront the persecuting pagans, the bear of Daniel 7 and Apocalypse 13. In the third time, the doctors of the church (the man figure of Apoc. 4:7) struggle against the heretics figured in the leopard of Daniel. The fourth time sees the confrontation between the order of monks and virgins symbolized by the eagle of the Tetramorph and the Persian and Moslem attacks on Christians (the *bestia quarta* of Daniel). In the fifth time Joachim's identification of the protagonists becomes somewhat more flexible and tentative as he approaches his own days. The basic opposition is between the Roman Church (*universalis ordo dei*) figured in the image of the "Throne of God" (Apoc. 7:15, et al.) and Babylon, the *sedes bestiae* (Apoc. 16:10), which the Abbot conceives of in various ways in the *Expositio* and related works. In Joachim's own sixth time the contrast becomes more difficult to identify. On the good side, the Roman Church has not lost its authority, but it has been compromised by internal decay, so that the presence, at least in an initial way, of the new orders of "spiritual men" (*viri spirituales*—see below) have a central role in the eschatological crisis of the transition between the sixth and the seventh periods.[39] The opposition to the Roman Church and to the hidden "spiritual men" involves both external political threats (sometimes German rulers opposed to the papacy, Saladin, other Moslem rulers, etc.), as well as insidious internal enemies, especially evil clerics and heretics.

---

[39] The interpretation of the sixth *tempus* is complicated, not least because Joachim says that the seventh period (*aetas*, sometimes *tempus*) begins along with it, just as the Apostle John, who represents the *viri spirituales*/septima aetas, was called at the same time as Peter who signifies the sixth time. See, for example, fol. 215va.

3 THE MYSTICAL DIMENSION OF THE *EXPOSITIO*

The first four dimensions of Joachim's complex interpretation of the Apocalypse have been explored by a number of commentators, but the contemplative-mystical dimension has been somewhat neglected,[40] despite the fact that, as Gian Luca Potestà has said, "As far as the seventh age is concerned, what counts is the permanence of an eremitical-contemplative model as the supporting structure of the time that remains."[41]

The mystical dimension is fundamentally millennial or chiliastic, in the sense that it reaches its culmination in the thousand-year reign of Christ and the saints predicted in Apocalypse 20:1-10.[42] Joachim's reading of this famous passage (fols. 209vb-215rb) was unusual, even daring, given the strong suspicion of millenarianism at least since the time of Augustine. He begins by noting that many people are confused about this part of the Apocalypse. As usual, he admits several kinds of readings. Recapitulatively, the thousand years can be referred to the total time of the church, as Augustine and others had argued,[43] but taking it as a reference to the coming earthly Sabbath is not an error, or heresy, but is a *rationabilis opinio*. He goes further. Augustine was correct to dispute a *literal* reading of the thousand years and its carnal implications, but belief in a coming better seventh *aetas* on earth of a spiritual nature and undetermined length is not just an *opinio* that can be held without error, but is "the clearest understanding (*serenissimus intellectus*)."[44] Joachim,

---

[40] I have touched on the mystical dimensions of Joachim's thought briefly in Bernard McGinn, *The Growth of Mysticism: Gregory the Great Through the Twelfth Century* (New York: Crossroad, 1994), 337–41. See also Kevin L. Hughes, "Eschatological Union: The Mystical Dimension of History in Joachim of Fiore, Bonaventure, and Peter Olivi," *Collectanea Franciscana* 72 (2002): 105–43.

[41] Potestà, *Il tempo dell'Apocalisse*, 317: "Per quanto riguarda la settima età, ciò che conta è il permanere di un modello eremitico-contemplativo come architrave del tempo che resta."

[42] On Joachim's form of millenarianism, see Robert E. Lerner, "Joachim of Fiore's Breakthrough to Chiliasm," *Cristianesimo nella storia* 6 (1985): 489–512. In *The Calabrian Abbot*, 153–55, I used the terms millennial, chiliastic, and utopian (in the sense of an ideal society) for the seventh *aetas*.

[43] Augustine, *De civitate dei* 20.9.

[44] *Expositio*, fol. 211ra. See the whole discussion on fols. 210va–212ra.

then, is a spiritual millenarian, but why refer to his millenarianism as mystical in nature?[45]

It was the merit of the great Italian Joachim scholar, Ernesto Buonaiuti (1880–1946) to have first pointed out the mystical aspect of the thought of the Calabrian abbot.[46] In an article first published in 1929 Buonaiuti distinguished between what he called "solitary mysticism" and "associative mysticism" (*misticismo associato*, perhaps better "corporate mysticism"), which attains God not in a purely individual way but by group participation in revealed mysteries. All Christian mysticism, we may suggest, has a corporate dimension, but Buonaiuti was correct in seeing that Joachim's hope in the seventh *aetas*, the coming Sabbath, was essentially corporate, that is, the abbot always emphasized that the perfection of contemplation will be realized in the whole church, though it might be a saved remnant after the persecutions and battles of the transition from the sixth to the seventh age.[47] Thus the mysticism of the abbot can be called a form of "social or corporate apocalyptic mysticism."[48]

I have argued elsewhere that among Joachim's many contributions was his reuniting two essential aspects of Christianity that were born together but came to be separated in the early centuries of the

---

[45] A number of issues regarding Joachim's understanding of the millennium of Apocalypse 20 will not be taken up here, as not germane to my topic. Among the most important of these is its duration. A number of texts suggest that the millennium will be short (e.g., *Liber de Concordia* V.20 and 22 [ed. Venice, fols. 70rab, 71ra]), but others insist that the time is known only to God (e.g., *Expositio*, fol. 210vb). Also important is the return of the Jews in the last age, something that Joachim discussed fairly often and that is mentioned in the *Expositio* (e.g., fol. 220r). See Robert E. Lerner, *The Feast of Saint Abraham: Medieval Millenarians and the Jews* (Philadelphia: University of Pennsylvania, 2001), at Chapter 2.

[46] On Buonaiuti as an interpreter of Joachim, Bernard McGinn, "Joachim of Fiore in the History of Religions: Ernesto Buonaiuti and Mircea Eliade on the Calabrian Abbot," in *Gioacchino da Fiore nella cultura contemporanea*, ed. Gian Luca Potestà (Rome: Viella, 2005), 111–26.

[47] Ernesto Buonaiuti, "Il misticismo di Gioacchino da Fiore," *Ricerche religiose* 5 (1929): 392–411, at 410. This notion is closely tied to a key concept of Buonaiuti's, *la vita associata*, on which see William Murphy, *Vita Associata and Religious Experience in the Writings of Ernesto Buonaiuti* (Rome: Gregorian University, Ph.D., 1974).

[48] McGinn, *The Growth of Mysticism*, 341; Hughes, "Eschatological Union," 105.

church—the apocalyptic element and the mystical.[49] Paul and John (at least the John of the medieval exegetes) were prime examples of how early Christians, or at least many of them, were both apocalyptic visionaries of the end times and mystical contemplatives. Paul certainly lived and preached the expectation that the return of Jesus was near (e.g., 1 Thess. 4:13–18; 1 Cor. 15:20–28, 50–56).[50] But Paul was also looked upon as a mystic, and, indeed, his mysticism is inseparable from his apocalypticism. Paul's account of his rapture to the third heaven in 2 Corinthians 12:3–4 is an apocalyptic ascent, one presented for the first time in the author's own name. The ascent ends in ineffable contact with God. Paul also claimed to have received visions of Christ (e.g., 1 Cor. 9:1, with a parallel in Acts. 9:3–9). Similarly, John's Gospel points to the special contemplative status of the Beloved Disciple, especially due to the divine mystery of the Logos he proclaimed in the Prologue. Christian tradition also ascribed the apocalyptic visions of the last book of the New Testament to same disciple in his old age.[51] The separation of apocalypticism and mysticism between the second and fourth centuries C.E. was the result of many factors, not least the rejection of the literal reading of the Apocalypse, especially the prediction of the millennium of Chapter 20. Other factors at work were the emphasis on the authority of bishops over prophets and the suspicion of esoteric forms of mysticism connected with Gnosticism. Still, the birth-connection of these separated twins allowed for re-combinations, especially when hopes for a better church to come also involved the realization of a deeper consciousness of God on the part of the whole body of believers. When Joachim's Easter vision gave him a sense of authority as a "new John," the stage was set for the emergence of his distinctive apocalyptic mysticism.

The *Expositio in Apocalypsim* reveals the contours of Joachim's corporate apocalyptic mysticism perhaps better than any of his other works. His mysticism is *ecclesial-communal*; it is therefore

---

[49] Bernard McGinn, "Apocalypticism and Mysticism: Aspects of the History of Their Interaction," *Zeitsprünge. Forschungen zur Frühen Neuzeit* 3 (1999): 292–315.

[50] M. C. de Boer, "Paul and Apocalyptic Eschatology," in *The Encyclopedia of Apocalypticism, Vol. 1: The Origins of Apocalypticism in Judaism and Christianity*, ed. John J. Collins (New York: Continuum, 1998), 345–83.

[51] On the relation of John's Apocalypse to the wider world of late Jewish and early Christian apocalyptic traditions, see the survey of Adela Yarbro Collins, "The Book of Revelation," in *The Encyclopedia of Apocalypticism, Vol. 1*, 384–414.

contemplative-affective, as well as *biblical* and *liturgical*. He gave these themes concrete exemplifications in the events and persons of scripture, either those directly mentioned in the Apocalypse, or present in it by way of concord. Among these figures, especially important for the communal, biblical, and contemplative dimensions, is John himself, particularly when Joachim discusses John as signifying the contemplative life in tandem with Peter, who is identified with the active life. There are at least seventeen such discussions in the *Expositio*.[52]

There were other biblical duos that were interpreted as referring to the active and contemplative lives, such as Martha and Mary from Luke 10, and Leah and Rachel from Genesis 29.[53] However, Peter and John, especially as portrayed in John 20:3–10, where both race to the empty tomb and John wins the race but Peter enters first, especially intrigued exegetes.[54] John's precedence in the race, despite Peter's position as the leader of the apostles, prompted many interpreters to read Peter as the active life and John as the contemplative life that finds God more readily.[55] The basic point, as Joachim repeats often in the *Expositio*, is that John, who represents the orders of the monastic "spiritual men" (*viri spirituales*), begins his vocation in the sixth time and therefore co-exists with the order of prelates represented by Peter. But, in the coming seventh *tempus/*aetas, John will outstrip Peter's progeny and will be in charge of the *ecclesia contemplantium* of the third *status*. Joachim announces this supercession in the *Liber Introductorius* where Chapter 19 is entitled "The Active Life Designated in Peter and the

---

[52] My list of these discussions is as follows: *Expositio*, fols. 17vb, 21rb–22ra, 22rb–23va, 38vb–39ra, 47ra–va, 49vab, 50ra–vb, 52vb–53ra, 62rb–va, 67ra–va, 77rab, 78rb, 110va (mostly on John), 137rb, 143ra–vb, 204rb–va, and 211rab. Both the frequency and the length of some of these discussions show that this is a major theme in the *Expositio*. Its importance is recognized by Potestà, *Il tempo dell'Apocalisse*, 299–304, 330–31.

[53] In the *Expositio*, Joachim also uses Martha and Mary (e.g., fol. 215rb–vb) and Leah and Rachel (e.g., fol. 50rab, fol. 93rb) as types of the active and contemplative lives.

[54] The importance of one of these passages (*Expositio*, fol. 143rv) is discussed by Marcia L. Colish in her essay in this volume, "End Time at Hand: Innocent III, Joachim of Fiore, and the Fourth Crusade," 254–55.

[55] This exegesis of John 20 goes as far back as Origen and is found in many authors, some of whom could have been known to Joachim. For a survey, Aimé Solignac, "Vie active, vie contemplative, vie mixte," *Dictionnaire de spiritualité* 16: 592–623.

Contemplative Life Designated in John" (fols. 17vb–19rb).[56] The chapter is a good example of the richness of Joachim's concordist mentality, as well as of his number symbolism in which the perfection of the number twelve is attained by adding a prior imperfect stage of five to a later more perfect stage of seven. Thus, Peter not only represents the active life, but also the five early patriarchal churches (Jerusalem, Antioch, Rome, Alexandria, Constantinople), the five senses, and the first five sons of Jacob. John as the contemplative life represents the seven churches of Asia to whom the Apocalypse was written, the seven virtues that perfect the senses, and Jacob's last seven sons. Peter also signifies the five general orders in the church: prelates, martyrs, doctors, virgins, and the whole church as *sedes dei*, including both the celibate and the laity (fol. 18rb). These five are counted again along with the two coming orders of *viri spirituales* to attain the perfection of the seven orders represented by John. After a number of other concordances with Old Testament figures, Joachim introduces his well-known Trinitarian pattern of *ordines* (fol. 18vb): the *ordo conjugatorum* that characterizes the first *status* "in the image of the Father," and which will continue to exist in both later *status*; the *ordo clericorum* of the second *status* "in the image of the Son;" and finally the *ordo monachorum* of the third *status* "in the likeness of the Holy Spirit." Joachim then returns to Peter and John. The *ordo monachorum*, he says, pertains to John in a double way, because the monks exist in both the second *status* and the third, while the *ordo clericorum* figured in Peter pertains only to the second *status*. "The signification of John is to be taken according to the second *status* in such a way that it much more worthily redounds to the third *status*."[57]

Chapter 24 of the *Liber Introductorius* (fols. 22rb–23va) returns to Peter and John, who are frequently mentioned together in the New Testament. Once again, both Peter and John, the active and contemplative lives, belong to the second *status*, but in this period Peter is the main actor and John stands by (fol. 22va). This is because the second *status* belongs to both the Son and the Holy Spirit, although more properly to the Son (fol. 22vb). Liturgically, Peter represents the season of Lent, while John is the Paschal season. Just as John outlives Peter in the

---

[56] Chapter 22 (fols. 21ra–22rb) illustrates another pattern, "That Peter, Paul, and John Represent the Mystery of the Trinity."

[57] *Expositio*, fol. 19ra: "Significatum vero ioanis sic accipiendum est in secundo statu ut multo tamen dignius refundat ad tertium."

Gospel (Jn. 21:21–23), so too the contemplative monastic life will come into its own better life in the third *status*, when the active life will no longer be needed (fol. 23rb). In the course of this discussion Joachim introduces an important hermeneutical principle: "Wherever in divine scripture there is mention of two men or women, these designate these two lives which God's saints frequently talk about so that we may rightly recognize that the second *status* pertains to both, that is, both to Peter and to John, but that only one figure pertains to the third *status*, that which belongs to John."[58]

The discussions of Peter and John found in the body of the *Expositio* fill out some of the details of general theory laid down in these chapters of the *Liber Introductorius*. For example, a treatment of Apocalypse 1:18b (the keys of death and hell) fastens on Christ's words to Peter (Jn. 21:22) about John remaining until he returns to say that these words mean that John, "or rather that order which is signified by him," will last until the end of the third *status*. This is why John was privileged beyond the other apostles by being commissioned to write about things of both the second and the third *status*, and even the heavenly world beyond them. "This is a great mystery," says Joachim, "to be examined very frequently with careful attention."[59] In another place Joachim says that John's lot is happier than that of Peter, because the Lord loved him more, although Peter too was loved because he loved the Lord (fol. 50ra). Hence, Peter could envy John (i.e., the order figured in John), because of John's priority in love and the sweetness of contemplation, but John could not envy Peter's power as head of the apostles, because the contemplative life is always higher than the active and not concerned with it (fol. 52vb). No wonder, Joachim says, that prelates have more worries than monks in the second *status*. Commenting on Apocalypse 10:11, where the angels tell John that he will prophesy to the peoples and kings, Joachim applies this to the order signified by John, who at the beginning of the third *status* will need to undertake the task of preaching (fol. 142rb). In his brief discussion of the millennium of the seventh

---

[58] *Expositio*, fol. 23rb: "Ubicumque ergo in divina scriptura de duobus viris aut mulieribus sermo est, ad designandas duas vitas istas quas sepe commemorant sancti dei, ita recte a nobis intelligi debet, ut fateamur secundum statum pertinere ad utrunque ac si ad petrum pariter et ioannem, ad tertium vero unam tamen que pertinet ad ioannem."

[59] *Expositio*, fol. 47ra: "Magnum est hoc misterium et diligenti sepe sepius scrutatione pensandum."

aetas, Joachim returns once more to Peter and John. Although the seventh *aetas* begins together with the sixth (i.e., the age of the present church) in the recapitulative understanding of the Great Sabbath, nevertheless, "...it will not be consumed equally with it, just as John who was called together with Peter, nonetheless did not die at the same time, but remained in life a long time after Peter's death."[60]

John signifies the *ordo monachorum* in general, the order born in the sixth *aetas*, but continuing on in plenitude in the seventh. More specifically, Joachim links John with the new kind of monks (either imminent or already present) he calls the "spiritual men" (*viri spirituales*). The spiritual men appear throughout the abbot's writings in a variety of formulations.[61] What does the *Expositio* have to say about these harbingers of the future? The abbot's discussions of the *viri spirituales*, like most of his treatments of what is to come in the Sabbath age, maintain a certain ambiguity and variation. Joachim knew *that* the Holy Spirit was going to act in the third *status*, but neither he nor anyone else could know precisely *how* the Spirit would act. Sometimes the term *viri spirituales* appears as a general description (what we may call the "large sense," comprising all the different orders of the church in the seventh age); at other times, Joachim distinguishes two special orders of spiritual men, although his accounts are not always in complete agreement.[62] One of the most important passages on the special dual orders of spiritual men is found in the exegesis of the eschatological harvest of Apocalypse 14:14–20 (fols. 175rb–177rb). Joachim begins his exegesis on a rare personal note, saying, "I do not want to be seen for what I am not, making up anything from my own arrogance. I do not think anyone should demand something from me, because 'I am a rustic from my youth' (Zach. 13:5), and it is not permitted to demand something even from the prophets themselves before their time." Citing Paul, the abbot says that now we

---

[60] *Expositio*, fol. 211rb: "...maxime propter magnum illud sabbati mysterium quo diximus septimam etatem inchoatam esse pariter cum sexta, nec tamen pariter consumanda, sicut Joannes qui cum Petro simul vocatus est a Christo nec tamen cum eo pariter mortis debitum solvit, sed multo tempore post obitum Petri in hac vita permansit."

[61] On the *viri spirituales*, both in Joachim and his successors, Marjorie E. Reeves, *The Influence of Prophecy: A Study in Joachimism*, 2nd ed. (Notre Dame: University of Notre Dame, 1993), part two.

[62] This is analogous to Joachim's two understandings of the *dies iudicii*, based on Augustine, the *largo modo* pertaining to all the events of the last days, and the *stricte modo* of the actual Judgment Day itself (e.g., *Expositio*, fols. 120ra, 139vb).

can only see in part through a dark mirror (1 Cor. 13:12). He uses the comparison of seeing a city from afar, seeing it from its gates, and finally seeing it from within. "Therefore, we who are at the gates," he goes on, "are able to say a good deal about things that at one time were partly or totally hidden, but [we are not able to speak] like those who will be within the city and will see eye to eye...."[63]

Joachim admits that there is no "sure explanation" (*expositio certa*) of the two angels with sickles who reap the harvest of grain and wine after the defeat of the Beast, because this pertains to the coming seventh age. He does, however, say: "We think that in the person who sits on the white cloud and is similar to the Son of Man (Apoc. 14:14) is signified a certain order of just men to whom it is given to imitate perfectly the life of the Son of Man, as we elsewhere have written about St. John the Evangelist."[64] This order will have a "tongue trained to preach the gospel of the kingdom," and will gather the final harvest of believers. The angel who summons this angel to the harvest (Apoc. 14:15) is identified with Christ himself. Joachim goes on to describe the figure of the angel on the cloud in some detail, specifying that the white cloud indicates this order's dedication to contemplation. Then he turns to the second duo, "the other angel who went forth from the temple in heaven having a sharp sickle" (Apoc. 14:17) and the angel who summons him. A complex series of concords leads Joachim to identify the summoning angel with the Holy Spirit, while "...in the angel who went forth from the temple in heaven is seen an order of hermits imitating the life of the angels" (fol. 175vb). This order is described as burning with zeal to extinguish the evil life of the wicked (fol. 176ra). Hence, there are two orders of *viri spirituales*: the mild order of the monks who gather the elect in the spirit of Moses at the end of the sixth time; and the fierce order of the hermits, who will make a harvest of the reprobate in the spirit of Elijah (fol. 176rb). Joachim ends on a note of caution:

---

[63] *Expositio*, fol. 175rb: "Nolo videri quod non sum, fingens aliquid ex presumptione mea. Nolo extimet aliquis exigere a me, qui sum homo agricola a iuventute mea quod ab ipsis quoque prophetis exigi ante sua tempora non licebat,.... Nos igitur qui ad ianuam sumus multa quidem loqui possumus, que aliquando ex toto vel ex parte latebant, sed non sicut hi qui erunt intus et oculo ad oculum videbunt...."

[64] *Expositio*, fol. 175va: "Arbitrarmur tamen in eo qui visus est sedere supra nubem candidam et esse similis filio hominis significari quondam ordinem iustorum, cui datum sit perfecte imitari vitam filii hominis (sicut alibi scripsimus sancti Joannes evangeliste)."

"I say this not as asserting [its truth], but by way of an opinion, even if perhaps there would be someone who would dare to affirm it."[65] Other passages on the two orders in the *Expositio* reflect this caution, but the details cannot delay us here.[66]

The *viri spirituales*, who are both the new monastics of the time of transition from the second to the third *status*, and, it appears, the dominant group shaping the church in the earthly Sabbath, fulfill all the roles characteristic of the monks of the second *status* as contemplatives, biblical interpreters, and liturgical worshippers, but on a higher level and a more perfect way that constitutes the corporate mysticism of what Joachim called the *ecclesia contemplantium*, or *ecclesia spiritualis*, of the final age.[67] The *Expositio in Apocalypsim* has something to say about all these aspects of their lives. The coming church of the contemplatives is certainly a monastic church, because the third general *ordo*, the *ordo monachorum*, or *coenobia monachorum* (fol. 214vb), now constitutes the essence of the ecclesiastic body, the *sedes Dei*. This does not mean, however, that the *ordo laicorum* and the *ordo clericorum* cease to exist, any more than that the Father and the Son will not be active in the *tertius status*. A number of texts in the *Expositio* make it evident that the orders of both laity and clergy continue into the third *status*, but it is not exactly clear how. It does seem that the lower orders will be transformed and live, in their own ways, the kind of monastic-contemplative life that will characterize the spiritual church of the last age. In the *Expositio* Joachim does not spell out how this will happen or what it will look like.

The text that does this in some detail is the noted *Figura* XII from the abbot's *Liber Figurarum*, which seems to represent his views, but as edited and possibly expanded by his first followers. *Figura* XII

---

[65] *Expositio*, fol. 176rb: "Dico autem hoc non asserendo sed opinando, etsi non desit forsitan qui audeat affirmare."

[66] For more on the *viri spirituales* and their two orders (with the more important passages italicized), see *Expositio*, fols. 17rb, 22ra, 64ra, 74ra, *75rab*, 92vb–93rb, *119vb–120ra*, and *146va–147va* (on the two orders figured first in John, or Moses, and second in Elijah), 156ra, 184vab, 185ra, and *186rb–186vb* (on pouring out of the seven bowls as the zeal of the *viri spirituales* in the seven times), 194ra, 195vb–196ra, 198vab, *209rab*, 217vab, 221ra, and 222rb.

[67] Joachim speaks of the *ecclesia contemplantium designata in ioanne evangelista* in *Expos.*, fols. 24vb and 110va; in fol. 83vb he also says that the *ecclesia contemplantium* is designated in Mary, the Mother of God. For the expression *ecclesia spiritualis*, see, e.g., fols. 137ra and 156ra.

is captioned "The Arrangement of the New People of God after the Model of the Heavenly New Jerusalem" (*Dispositio novi ordinis pertinens ad tertium statum ad instar superne Hierusalem*). It sets out a picture of the "Heavenly New Jerusalem" of the third *status* in which seven oratories (the number of the perfect age) are organized in the form of an altar cross, consisting of five monastic oratories clustered around the center of the cross, and, on the lower shaft, an oratory for the clerics, and at the base one for the laity, containing "the married with their sons and daughters living a common life." Not a few debates accompany this *figura*.[68] Given our attention to the *Expositio*, these cannot be taken up here; but I would argue that the diagram represents Joachim's developed thoughts on the church of the third *status* as a contemplative community in which laity, clerics, and monastics live in harmony under the leadership of a spiritual master, the *pater spiritualis*, who looks much like the Apostle John now ruling in Peter's place. Nonetheless, it seems too much to say that the Petrine church and office fade away completely in the *tertius status*, if only because a number of texts in the *Expositio* and elsewhere testify to some role for the transformed papacy in the age to come.[69] For example, commenting on the Heavenly Jerusalem (Apoc. 21:22), Joachim says that the Trinity will replace the temple in heaven, but on earth some temple must always remain. Solomon built the temple in Jerusalem in the time of the Old Testament. "Much worthier" is that "ecclesiastical dignity (*capitulum*)" that was established at Rome to replace the old temple.

---

[68] On *Figura* XII, see the facsimile in Leone Tondelli, Marjorie Reeves, and Beatrice Hirsch-Reich, eds., *Il Libro delle Figure dell'Abate Gioachino da Fiore* (Turin: SEI, 1953), Vol. II, Tavola XII. For a translation and comment on the *figura*, Bernard McGinn, *Apocalyptic Spirituality* (New York: Paulist Press, 1979), 142–48. There is an extensive literature. The most recent discussion is Marco Rainini, *Disegni dei tempi. Il "Liber Figurarum" e la teologia figurativa di Gioacchino da Fiore* (Rome: Viella, 2006), 182–93.

[69] The extent to which Peter's role does or does not survive into the *tertius status* is a contentious issue in Joachim studies, largely because the abbot's views seem to have changed and are hard to pin down. Against some interpreters, I argue that Joachim never thought that Peter's office, i.e., the papacy, would totally wither away, but it would certainly be transformed into something new. For more on this debate, see Bernard McGinn, "Joachim of Fiore and the Twelfth-Century Papacy," in *Joachim of Fiore and the Influence of Inspiration: Essays in Memory of Marjorie E. Reeves (1905–2003)*, ed. Julia Eva Wannenmacher (Burlington, VT: Ashgate, 2013), 15–34, at 31–34.

In it, according to the abbot, "...the Supreme Pontiff bears Christ's place on earth until he comes who is himself *the* Supreme Pontiff."[70]

4 Contemplative Life in the *Tertius Status*

As is evident from the many treatments of the contemplative John in the dawning seventh *aetas*-third *status*, Joachim felt he was on the cusp of a new stage in the history of salvation—the age marked by the triumph of the monastic way of life dedicated to contemplation. But how did the Calabrian abbot understand the contemplative life? Unlike many monastic authors, Joachim did not write treatises about the nature of contemplation and its various stages. For him, the contemplative life *was* the monastic life, that is, a life given over to single-hearted attention to God's presence in line with the understanding of Gregory the Great, the "master of monastic contemplation" and one of Joachim's favorite authors. If our modern category of mysticism often involves detailed analyses of the progress of levels of contemplation, we will not find much of this in Joachim; nor will we find speculation on the forms of union with God. That does not mean, however, that Joachim was any less of a "mystic," or "contemplative," to use medieval terminology. The *Expositio in Apocalypsim* does contain some texts where the Calabrian tells us more about the nature of contemplation and its centrality in God's plan for history.

One of the most striking sections in the Apocalypse is Chapter 12, which describes the struggle between the Woman in Heaven and the Great Red Dragon with Seven Heads. For Joachim this part of the Apocalypse (11:19–14:20) denotes the fourth *tempus*, the time of the conflict between the order of hermits and virgins and the forces of Islam. He devotes considerable space to the exegesis of Chapter 12 (fols. 154ra–164ra). The Woman is interpreted *generaliter* as *mater ecclesia* and *specialiter* as the church of the hermits and virgins. Much of the detail of Joachim's reading concerns events of this period in church history and the concords that illuminate that particular struggle. The flight of the Woman into the wilderness, however, contains general reflections on contemplation. "The Woman was given two wings of the great eagle in order to fly into the desert to her place...(Apoc. 12:14)."

---

[70] *Expositio*, fol. 220vb: "...in quo et qui presidet summus Pontifex vicem Christi geret in terris donec veniat ipse qui est Summus Pontifex...."

Joachim explains: "Whether here with the wings of the eagle, or in the Psalms with the wings of the dove (Ps. 54:7), the grace of contemplation is designated." There are two wings to elevate the Woman on high and enable her to flee the Dragon, because "...there are two virtues necessary beyond all others for those desiring to know the truth." The abbot explains the two wings:

> These are the wisdom that comes from above and the love of God. One of these, that is, wisdom, by a particular property of the mystery is ascribed to Christ, whom the Apostle calls the "wisdom and power of God" (1 Cor. 1:24). The other, that is, love, is ascribed to the Holy Spirit, of whom the Apostle John says, "God is love" (1 Jn. 4:16). Without these two virtues there can undoubtedly be no perfection of contemplation because just as the light and heat of the sun make the free cultivation of the earth well possible, so too these two gifts are needed for the contemplative.[71]

Therefore, the contemplative life depends on both the action of the Son and the Holy Spirit and is manifested in wisdom and love. As the perfection of the contemplative life, the third *status* will see the highest form of wisdom, which certainly involves profound *intelligentia spiritualis* of the biblical text, and the most burning form of love, both the love of God and the *fraterna caritas* of the monastic life.

For Joachim of Fiore the history of salvation is one with the history of exegesis. The structure and meaning of history can only be seen through the proper understanding of the letter of the Old and the New Testaments by way of *intelligentia spiritualis*, as we have noted. Spiritual understanding was made possible by the Resurrection and it has been slowly growing throughout the second *status*. The revelation that enabled the Calabrian abbot to grasp the meaning of the Apocalypse marks a decisive new stage in this growth, one that can be seen as a harbinger of

---

[71] *Expositio*, fol. 161ra: "Sive hic alis aquile, sive in psalmis pennis columbe contemplationis gratia designator.... Due sunt autem ale iste que date sunt mulieri quibus posit et ipsa elevari in altum et fugere a conspectu draconis, quia due sunt precipue super omnes alias necessarie virtutes scire cupientibus veritatem, sapientia scilicet que desursum est et charitas dei. Harum una, id est, sapientia, proprietate quadam mysterii ascribitur Christo quem nominat apostolus 'dei virtutem et dei sapientiam.' Alia, id est, charitas, Spiritui Sancto, de quo dicit apostolus, 'Deus charitas est.' Absque his duabus virtutibus nulla potest esse contemplationis perfectio nimirum, quia ut splendor solis et calor ad bene operandum faciunt liberum terre cultorem, ita duo ista dona contemplatori necessaria sunt."

fullness to come in the emerging third *status*. Within the context of the account of his Easter vision, Joachim says that the opening of the Old Testament began with Christ's Rising, but that the fact that the Risen Christ did not appear to the two disciples at Emmaus until evening (Lk. 24:29) signifies that the "hidden meaning" (*mysticum intellectum*) of the New Testament will only begin to be fully understood in the sixth *tempus*. "What does this 'until evening' mean save 'until the sixth time'? Therefore, two openings are treated together.... In the first understanding it signifies that the opening of the Old Testament was delayed until Christ. But the opening of the New Testament is not so, but by it is signified at the same time the opening put forth by the spiritual men."[72]

The *viri spirituales* are spiritual exegetes *par excellence* (e.g., fols. 137rb, 138ra). Wisdom is proper to contemplatives (e.g., fol. 111vb), and a-fortiori the wisdom that unlocks the scriptures. That wisdom is acquired laboriously in this time of transition between the second and the third *status*, but Joachim says the monastic *doctores* in the third *status* will come by it easily (e.g., fols. 86rb, 221ra). Eventually, of course, at the end of time and the commencement of the eighth *aetas* in the Heavenly Jerusalem all need for expounding the scriptures will cease (fol. 123rb). Until that time, however, the course of salvation history depends upon the mediation of *intelligentia spiritualis* to the people of God, the *novus ordo pertinens ad tertium statum*.

The *ordo monasticus* both in the present second *status* and its fulfillment in the third is characterized not only by its commitment to Bible study, but also by liturgical worship. Hence, Joachim's corporate mystical church will also continue to be a body of worshippers. Throughout the *Expositio*, as well as in his other works, the abbot gave much attention to the concords between the scriptures and the course of the church's liturgical year.[73] Thus, the *intelligentia spiritualis* of scripture is also a spiritual understanding of the prayer of the church. Joachim's *Tractatus in Expositionem Vite et Regule Beati Benedicti* (ca. 1186–1189) not only contains a commentary on Gregory's *Life of Benedict*, but also provides a spiritual reading of the Benedictine liturgy that ties it to contemporary

---

[72] *Expositio*, fol. 40rab: "Quid est autem 'usque ad vesperum' nisi usque ad tempus sextum? Ergo si de duabus apertionibus simul agitur, ... Significat autem in intellectu primo apertionem veteris testamenti delatam esse usque ad Christum. Apertionem vero novi non sic, sed ab ipso eodem tempore viris spiritualibus propalatam...."

[73] As noted by Potestà, *Il tempo dell'Apocalisse*, e.g., 179, 270, 328, etc.

events and the dawning third *status*.⁷⁴ *Figura* XIX of the *Liber Figurarum*, entitled "The Mystery of the Church" (*Mysterium Ecclesiae*), is a commentary on the liturgical year in circular form. Two concentric circles tie the liturgical season to events of the first and second *status*. There is no spiral for the coming third *status*, but the seven weeks of the Paschal season represent the seventh *aetas* during which presumably the full spiritual understanding of the Old and New Testament readings in the lectionary will emerge. The concord of the three *status* and the liturgical year is clearly set out in a passage from the *Liber de Concordia*: "The first *status* is signified in the three weeks that precede the Lenten fast [i.e., Septuagesima, Sexagesima, Quinquagesima]; the second *status* in Lent itself; the third in the solemn time called Paschal."⁷⁵ The *Expositio* has a number of texts showing the concord between liturgical feasts and the course of history, something already laid out in summary form in Chapter 15 of the *Liber Introductorius*, where Joachim says the fasting of Lent represents the trials of the second *status*, while the feasting of the Easter season is the third *status* (fol. 15va).⁷⁶

As a monk, Joachim chanted the psalms everyday, and the treatise *Psalterium decem cordarum* has much to say about the world-historical meaning of the Psalms, including the fact that the 150 Psalms represent the whole tally of the generations of the three *status*, and therefore the monks recapitulate history by their praying the Psalter.⁷⁷ In the *Expositio* Joachim highlights the importance of the singing of the Psalms revealed

---

⁷⁴For an edition, Alexander Patschovsky, *Ioachim Abbas Florensis. Tractatus in Expositionem Vite et Regule Beati Benedicti* (Rome: Istituto Storico Italiano per il Medio Evo, 2008). For a study of the differing views of the work, Eugène Honée, "Joachim of Fiore: *Tractatus in Expositionem Vitae et Doctrinae Benedicti*. The Question of its Structure and Genesis," *Annali di scienze religiose* 5 (2012): 67–104. On the significance of Joachim's spiritualizing liturgical commentary, Luigi Mantuano, "*Mystica significatio* nei commentari del XII secolo sulla liturgia," in *In principio erat verbum. Mélanges offerts en hommage à Paul Tombeur par des étudiants à l'occasion de son éméritat*, ed. B.-M. Tock (Turnhout: Brepols, 2005), 145–240, at 214–27.

⁷⁵ *Liber de Concordia* V.84 (ed. Venice, fol. 112va): "Et primus quidem status significatus est in tribus illis hebdomadibus que precedent ieiunium quadragesimale; 2o in ipsa quadragesima; 3o in tempore solemni quod vocatur paschale."

⁷⁶For another concord between the three *status* and the liturgical year, see *Expositio*, fol. 215rb–vb.

⁷⁷On the 150 Psalms as signifying the 150 generations of history, see *Psalterium decem cordarum* II [V.2] (ed. Selge, 339).

in "the key of David" (Apoc. 3:7b), claiming that "...it is the hidden and free jubilation of the Psalms that pertains to the Holy Spirit" (fol. 84vb).[78] Since "jubilation belongs to the Holy Spirit," and only "the person who loves can sing psalms and praise" (fol. 85ra), Joachim can say, "Hence, the Psalmist to whom this key belongs, wishing to show that the perfection of teaching can be obtained through psalmody, confesses and says: 'I always hope and will add to all your praise'...." (Ps. 70:14).[79] Singing the Psalms joyfully is the key to obtaining love. Later in the same comment on the key of David, Joachim proclaims:

> If you want to have the love of God, before all and above all, love psalmody....The person who sings Psalms in this way is more blessed than the one who reads, because he finds everything in this one thing... Not in vain does John, who signifies the elect of the third *status*, preach love so greatly, when he says to those to whom he is writing, whom he also names sons, "It is not necessary for you to have someone teach you, but his anointing teaches you all things." (1 Jn. 2:27)[80]

The importance of singing the Psalms is brought out equally forcefully in a text from the *Psalterium decem cordarum*, where the abbot says: "Someone who prays and sings Psalms in this way, praising and invoking his God, knows that his voice reaches the ears of the Most High.... He surpasses the human, climbs above the angelic, he rests in God. There he beholds marvelous mysteries 'which eye has not seen nor ear heard'...." (1 Cor. 2:9).[81] Therefore, liturgy, especially liturgical singing of the

---

[78] This is explained in *Expositio*, fol. 85ra: "Licet ergo tria ista, tribus pariter communia: videtur secundum aliquid opus pertinere ad patrem, lectio ad filium, gaudium spiritus sancti iubilationis tripudium." On the key of David as *spiritualis psalmodia*, see also fol. 87ra.

[79] *Expositio*, fol. 85ra: "Unde et psalmista cuius est ista clavis, volens ostendere perfectionem doctrine obtinere posse per psalmodiam confitetur et dicit, 'Ego autem semper sperabo et adicijam super omnem laudem tuam'...."

[80] *Expositio*, fol. 86va: "Si autem habere cupis charitatem dei ante omnia et super omnia dilige psalmodiam, ... Beatior est ergo qui sic psallit quam qui legit. Iste totum reperit in hoc uno.... Non ergo frustra Joannes qui electos tertii status significat tantopere predicat caritatem dicens eis quibus scribebat, quos et filios nominat, 'Non necesse habetis ut aliquis doceat vos, sed sicut unctio eius docet vos de omnibus'."

[81] *Psalterium decem cordarum* I. Dist. VII (ed. Selge, 111): "Qui sic orat et psallit laudans et invocans Deum suum, noverit vocem suam ad aures Altissimi pervenire, ... Excedit hominem, supergreditur angelum, requiescat in Deo. Ibi respicit mira misteria, ibi *quod oculus non vidit nec auris audivit*...." See also the short Book III (ed. Selge, 345–55),

Psalms, is both intimately connected with *caritas*, the essence of true *contemplatio*, and forms the pathway to seeing God.

5 CONCLUSION

The constant teaching of Christian mystics has been that the essence of deeper consciousness of the presence of God does not consist in visions, locutions, and paranormal experiences, but in deeper growth of the evangelical command of love of God and love of neighbor. This is what Joachim echoes when he says that the two necessary wings for true contemplation, and therefore for a fully-contemplative church, are wisdom and the love of God and neighbor that is *caritas*. Although the Abbot of Fiore has not been much studied in this regard, his writings display, at least from time to time, a deep affective love for Christ and an insistence on the *fraterna caritas* that will be the bond of the monastic church of the *tertius status*. *Caritas fraterna*, as Joachim affirms, is the greatest of all divine gifts. Speaking of the "great exchange" (*magnum commercium*) between the Word and human nature effected in the Incarnation (fol. 32rb), Joachim says that Christ took on our mortal body and the blood that vivifies it. What did he exchange for our blood, asks Joachim? His answer: "Great was the gift which he gave to us in place of his blood—that is, fraternal love, without which no one can be saved."[82] In other words, love of neighbor is the very life-blood of believers, both in the second and the third *status*.

Fraternal love, which has a distinctive flavor in monastic communities and especially in the monastic church of the *tertius status*, must be grounded in love for Jesus Christ. Joachim so often overwhelms the reader with his intricate concords that it is easy to miss the passages where he expresses affective devotion to Christ, something he felt was sure to grow among the *viri spirituales* of the third *status*. Let us remember that Christ is not absent from the *tertius status*, despite its being ascribed to the Holy Spirit. The Spirit is always the "Spirit of Christ," sent by both the Father and the Son who are always co-present and

---

entitled *De institutione psallentium*, where Joachim discusses how monks, clerics, and literate laity all should sing the Psalms: "Debet ergo omnis Christianus diligere psalmodiam."

[82] *Expositio*, fol. 32va: "Magnum est donum quod nobis vice sanguinis dedit, fraternam scilicet charitatem, sine cuius participatione salvus aliquis esse non potest."

co-acting with the Spirit.[83] The Holy Spirit comes only to complete the work begun by Christ (e.g., fols. 69vb–70ra), and therefore Christ can be said to reign in the *viri spirituales*.[84]

Three passages will suffice to show the deep love of Christ, sometimes expressed in nuptial terms, found in the *Expositio*. The first comes in the midst of the long exegesis of the message to the Angel of Philadelphia (Apoc. 3:7–13, in fols. 82vb–92rb), of whom Joachim says, "This angel and his church belong to the third *status* more than the second" (fol. 86vb). Because the seventh *aetas* begins together with the sixth *tempus*, the Angel of Philadelphia has multiple significations, including that of the coming *ordo spiritualis* (e.g., fols. 87rb–va, 89va, 92ra). The figure calls forth many concords from Joachim's fertile mind. For example, Elizabeth's conception of John the Baptist in old age is taken as a concord with the birth of the spiritual order (i.e., this Angel) in the sixth time, whose origins will be hidden until it will be greatly increased in the third *status* (fols. 83va–84rb). The *clavis David* given to the Angel, as we have seen, is the *spiritualis psalmodia* characteristic of the final era. The abbot says that we are very near in time to the coming of the Angel of Philadelphia, and although we cannot pretend to have his powers, we must be ready to resist the "false Christs" and "false prophets" who will soon arise (fol. 87vb).

In verse 12bc of Chapter 3 Christ promises the Angel that he will write his own name and the name of his city, the New Jerusalem, on the Angel. This prompts Joachim to describe the love bond between Christ and the Angel, who represents both the church of the last days and also its individual members. This comment (fols. 90ra–92rb) is too long to be fully analyzed here, but it is notable for the way in which it uses spousal language, including from the Song of Songs, to describe Christ's love for us and the love we should have for him. The inscription of the names signifies that the earthly church is born from the union of the Heavenly Jerusalem and its Celestial Spouse, Christ (fol. 90vb); but this union is meant to flow down to us as children of God and coheirs with Christ (fol. 91va). Joachim issues a call to believers to realize their destiny by

---

[83] Many texts in the *Expositio* treat the relation of the Son and the Holy Spirit; e.g., fols. 32vab, 55ra–va, 56rb, 63vb, 93rb, 111rb–va, 125rb–vb, 126vab, 157vb, 176rb, etc.

[84] This is implicit throughout the *Expositio*, and clearly expressed in a text in *Liber de Concordia* V.67 (ed. Venice, fol. 96rb).

turning away from false love of the world to the true nuptials promised in scripture:

> O delicate virgin, why are you bound tight by such great solicitude for the one who corrupted your flesh? .... Ignoring the sweetness of the love of Christ, you thus do not heed the true nuptials promised you by the friends of the Spouse [i.e., biblical authors], nor do you think them as delightful as those the love of the flesh suggests. O miserable one, you are mistaken; you are mistaken by not knowing the scripture, or God's power, or the abundant delights of Christ. He is the fountain of honey and the source of sweetness; he, I say, is the Spouse promised you, whose nuptials you value lightly because you are ignorant of sweetness....[85]

Later, Joachim turns to the language of the Song of Songs, noting that the church is like "...the sleeping turtledove, who when the winter cold is over, as if awakened from the sleep of death, is aroused and vigilant" (fol. 92ra, see Sg. of Sgs. 2:11–12). But this message is for all the members of the church. "All who are called to the supper of the nuptials of the Lamb (Apoc. 19:9) should diligently acknowledge how great is the dignity of those who have put on Christ (Rom. 13:14), so that they may know what God has given them, and, knowing this, they may joyfully hasten to their promised inheritance, still enlivened by the promise of the Lord in the Gospel saying, 'He who confesses me before men, I will also confess him before my Father'" (Mt. 10:32).[86]

A second passage is the hymn to Christ found in the comment on Apocalypse 19:8, where the great multitude proclaims the marriage of the Lamb and says that his bride has been clothed with "...clean fine linen, the linen that is the justifications of the saints" (fol. 205ra–vb). To marry the Lamb is "...to see him as he is and in this vision to rejoice

---

[85] *Expositio*, fol. 91va: "O virgo delicata, que pro carnis tue corruptore tanta sollicitudine coarctaris? .... Nec ita veras extimas nuptias quas tibi amici sponsi promittunt, nec ita delectabiles ut eas quas amor suggerit carnis, ignorata dulcedine amoris Christi. Erras misera, erras nesciens scripturam, neque virtutem dei, nesciens abundantiam delitiarum Christi. Ipse est enim fons mellis et origo dulcedinis, ipse inquam sponsus qui promittitur tibi cuius ideo parvipendis nuptias, quia dulcedinem nescis...."

[86] *Expositio*, fol. 92rb: "...ut quanta sit dignitas hominum induentium Christum omnes qui vocandi erant ad cenam nuptiarum agni diligenter agnoscent, ut scirent que a deo donata sunt illis, et scientes currerent leti ad hereditanda promissa, et nihilominus animati sponsione domini loquentis in evangelio et dicentis: 'Qui me confessus fuerit coram hominibus, confitebor et ego eum coram Patre meo'."

beyond what can be said or thought" (fol. 205r). Jesus Christ is both the Spouse of the church and our justification, as the Apostle says (Rom. 5:18). Joachim hails the Spouse with a string of noble epithets, exclaiming, "How good it is for us to be here (Mt. 17:4). Shake the soul from its dust; consider all these things and contemplate them" (fol. 205rb). There follows a lengthy purple passage about the love between Christ and the bride based on the Song of Songs and other scriptural passages. Again, both the church and the individual soul are addressed:

> Hear these things, faithful soul; hear, blessed church, who is the bride of Christ, and delight in the Lord your God. You are all these things to him and much more. You are the bride, you are the sister, you are the daughter, you are the lover.... Your chosen one is to you and you are to him (Sg. of Sgs. 6:2). He is everything to you, and you to him, but everything you are is from him, and he is totally from the Father.... Rouse up all your lamps from slumber (Mt. 25:1-10), rise up and be adorned with jewels (Is. 61:10) that you may enter into the marriage rites.[87]

Passages such as these reveal a dimension of the thought of Joachim of Fiore that has perhaps not been sufficiently appreciated. The Calabrian abbot was a major theologian of the Trinity and of salvation history. His complex, often convoluted, scriptural exegesis had as its main purpose to awaken the church to the dangers of the time and to encourage persistence in the faith to await the coming of the age of the Holy Spirit. But Joachim was also a monk who lived a life of contemplation, prayer, and loving dedication to Christ. His conception of the *tertius status* was not so much institutional, as contemplative, even mystical. Although this final *status* was one that would manifest the role of the Holy Spirit in a special way, it was no less the time when the love of Christ would attain its ultimate state, as Joachim says clearly at the end of the *Expositio in Apocalypsim* in explanation of the last words of John's great revelation, *Amen. Veni, Domine Jesu* (Apoc. 22:20):

---

[87] *Expositio*, fol. 205vb: "Audi hec fidelis anima, audi felix ecclesia que es sponsa Christi et delectare in Domino Deo tuo. Tu enim hec omnia illi es, et alia multa. Tu sponsa, tu soror, tu filia, tu amica.... Ipse tibi totum, et tu illi, totum tamen ab ipso quod tu es, ipse vero totum a Patre.... Omnia lampades tuas excitare de somno, exurge et ornare e monilibus ut ingrediaris ad nuptias."

He is the goal of the book, he is the fruit of hope and the reward of our work, he who will come to judge the living and the dead and the world through fire. All these things will cease after he shall have come to judgment, because he will not be what is sought, but what is loved to those who see him as he is and in him know all truth.[88]

---

[88] *Expositio*, fol. 223vb: "Ipse est enim finis libri, ipse fructus spei et premium operis nostri, qui venturus est iudicare vivos et mortuos et seculum per ignem. Cessabunt enim omnia hec postquam ipse venerit ad iudicium, quia iam non erit quod queratur, sed potius quod ametur, videntibus nobis eum sicuti est et scientibus in eo omnem veritatem."

CHAPTER 8

Juan de Horozco y Covarrubias's *Tratado dela verdadera y falsa prophecia* (1588) and the Influence of Medieval Apocalyptic Traditions in Post-Tridentine Spain

James F. Melvin

This essay examines the influence of medieval apocalyptic traditions in Juan de Horozco y Covarrubias's 1588 *Tratado dela verdadera y falsa prophecia* ("Treatise Concerning True and False Prophecy," hereafter *Tratado*).[1] Horozco belonged to a prominent Castilian family and authored a

[1] Juan de Horozco y Covarrubias, *Tratado dela verdadera y falsa prophecia* (Segovia: Juan de la Cuesta, 1588). When quoting from the *Tratado*, I have respected the original orthography and punctuation, except that I have expanded those words that were originally abbreviated. Unless otherwise noted, all translations from the Spanish are mine.

I am grateful to E. Ann Matter and Jodi Bilinkoff for their comments on earlier versions of this paper, and Jes Boon, whose comments have greatly improved the paper's present state.

J. F. Melvin (✉)
Independent Scholar, Toledo, OH, USA

© The Author(s) 2019
E. Knibbs et al. (eds.), *The End of the World in Medieval Thought and Spirituality*, The New Middle Ages,
https://doi.org/10.1007/978-3-030-14965-9_8

197

well-known emblem book, the *Emblemas morales*, first published in 1589.[2] He was an archdeacon in the diocese of Segovia at the time he published the *Tratado*, and was later appointed a bishop by Philip II. During his tenure as bishop of Agrigento in Sicily and then Guadix in southern Spain, Horozco implemented a series of reforms that evoke the Tridentine ethos of Milan's Carlo Borromeo. Horozco's *Tratado* was an influential manual that sought to help confessors discern spirits in their penitents while providing his clerical readers with a systematic explanation and detailed history of prophecy and divination. Discernment manuals such as the *Tratado* have offered historians of early modern Spain much insight into the clergy's construction, maintenance, and negotiation of ecclesiastical authority in a period when Spain experienced a flourishing of interest in mental prayer and a seeming explosion of visionary holy women and charismatic street prophets.[3] Horozco and the authors of similar texts viewed this spiritual

[2] Juan de Horozco y Covarrubias, *Emblemas morales de Don Iuan de Horozco y Couarruuias* (Segovia: Juan de la Cuesta, 1589). Horozco's *Emblemas morales* is well known to scholars of emblem books. Bradley J. Nelson devoted a chapter to Horozco's *Emblemas morales* in *The Persistence of Presence: Emblem and Ritual in Baroque Spain* (University of Toronto Press, 2010), 55–74. See also Christian Bouzy, "Neoestoicismo y senequismo en los *Emblemas Morales* de Juan de Horozco," in *Emblemata Aurea: La Emblemática en el Arte y La Literatura del Siglo de Oro*, ed. Rafael Zafra and José Javier Azanza (Madrid: Akal Ediciones, 2000), 69–78; Julián Gállego, "Los *Emblemas morales* de don Juan de Horozco," *Cuadernos de Arte e Iconografía* 1.2 (1989): 129–42; Jesús M. González de Zárate, "La herencia simbólica de los hieroglyphica en los *Emblemas Morales* de Juan de Horozco," *Boletín del Museo e Instituto Camón Aznar* 38 (1989): 55–72; Juan de Dios Hernández Miñano, "Los *Emblemas morales* de Juan de Horozco," *Norba-arte (Cáceres)* 8 (1988): 97–112; and Bradley J. Nelson, "Emblematic Representation and Guided Culture in Baroque Spain: Juan de Horozco y Covarrubias," in *Culture and the State in Spain: 1550–1850*, ed. Tom Lewis and Francisco J. Sánchez (New York: Garland, 1999), 157–95.

[3] For recent scholarship on priests' manuals in Spain, see especially Andrew Keitt, *Inventing the Sacred: Imposture, Inquisition, and the Boundaries of the Supernatural in Golden Age Spain* (Boston: Brill, 2005); Patrick J. O'Banion, *The Sacrament of Penance and Religious Life in Golden Age Spain* (University Park: The Pennsylvania State University Press, 2012). On anti-superstition campaigns in sixteenth-century Spain, see Fabián Alejandro Campagne, *Homo catholicus, homo superstitiosus: El discurso antisupersticioso en la España de los siglos XV a XVIII* (Madrid: Miño y Dávila Editores, 2002); Lu Ann Homza, "To Annihilate Sorcery and Amend the Church: A New Interpretation of Pedro Ciruelo's *Reprobación de las supersticiones y hechicerías*," in *Religion, Body, and Gender in Early Modern Spain*, ed. Alain Saint-Saens (San Francisco: Mellen Research University Press, 1991), 46–64. On feigned sanctity in early modern Europe and its relationship with prophecy, see Stephen Haliczer, *Between Exaltation and Infamy: Female Mystics in the Golden Age of Spain* (New York: Oxford University Press, 2002); Anne Jacobsen Schutte, *Aspiring Saints: The Pretense of Holiness, Inquisition, and Gender in the Republic of Venice, 1618–1750* (Baltimore: Johns Hopkins University Press, 2001).

foment with unease, especially as they observed the Protestant reformations unfold outside Spain's borders.

Horozco's *Tratado* provides a Spanish example that intersects with at least three of the areas where E. Ann Matter has enriched our understanding of Christian thought and practice—visionary culture, female prophecy, and the subtle manifestations of apocalypticism through the centuries.[4] Historians have long valued Horozco's *Tratado* for its systematic treatment of heterodoxy and its chronicle of heterodox movements in sixteenth-century Spain.[5] It has received particular attention from hispanists for its discussion of female visionary experiences and how their male spiritual directors should interpret and regulate them.[6] In this essay, however, I call attention to another noteworthy aspect of the *Tratado* that may escape readers who have not had the privilege of directly collaborating or studying with Matter: Horozco's own betrayal of an apocalyptic outlook and his embrace of various medieval apocalyptic traditions, even as he attempts to regulate visionary culture.[7] In particular, Horozco points to the circulation of false Joachite prophecies in

---

[4] E. Ann Matter has synthesized all three perspectives in her "Apparitions of the Virgin Mary in the Late Twentieth Century: Apocalyptic, Representation, Politics," *Religion* 31 (2001): 125–53.

[5] Vicente Beltrán de Heredia, "Un grupo de visionarios y pseudoprofetas que actúa durante los últimos años de Felipe II," *Revista Española de Teología* 7 (1947): 373–97; Campagne, *Homo catholicus, homo superstitiosus*; and Julio Caro Baroja, *Las formas complejas de la vida religiosa: Religión, sociedad y carácter en la España de los siglos XVI y XVII* (Madrid: Sarpe, 1985).

[6] Jodi Bilinkoff, "Establishing Authority: A Peasant Visionary and Her Audience in Early Sixteenth-Century Spain," *Studia Mystica* 18 (1997): 36–59; William A. Christian, Jr., *Apparitions in Late Medieval and Renaissance Spain* (Princeton: Princeton University Press, 1981); Haliczer, *Between Exaltation and Infamy*; and Richard L. Kagan, *Lucrecia's Dreams: Politics and Prophecy in Sixteenth-Century Spain* (Berkeley: University of California Press, 1990). In her contribution to this volume, Mary Rose D'Angelo provides references to some of Ann's best-known work on this area in "The Sobered Sibyl: Gender, Apocalypse and Virtue in the *Shepherd of Hermas* and Dio's First Discourse," in this collection, 17–40, at 17–18, notes 1–2.

[7] Throughout this essay I employ Bernard McGinn's understanding of apocalypticism as "a particular form of eschatology, a species of broader genus that covers any type of belief that looks forward to the end of history as that which gives structure and meaning to the whole." *Apocalyptic Spirituality: Treatises and Letters of Lactantius, Adso of Montier-en-Der, Joachim of Fiore, The Franciscan Spirituals, Savonarola*. The Classics of Western Spirituality (Mahwah, NJ: Paulist Press, 1979), 5.

his own time while noting that Joachim of Fiore was a "true" Catholic prophet; he echoes the imperial apocalyptic tradition to express hope in the exaltation of the Catholic faith and Spain's might; he interprets the presence of Spain's unassimilated *morisco* population through prophecies attributed to Hippolytus on the end times; and he closes the *Tratado* with a Spanish translation of the Erythraean Sibyl's acrostic poem on the Last Judgment. Most scholarly attention to prophecy and apocalyptic thought in the late-medieval and early modern period tends to focus on the popular and rebellious expressions of such religiosity and employs a model that usually depicts such thought as the target of church reformers and the enforcers of orthodoxy after the mid-sixteenth century.[8] Horozco's *Tratado* challenges this narrative. Horozco's apocalyptic tone adds a sense of urgency to his campaign against Protestants, superstition, false prophecy, moral laxity, and toleration of Spain's *moriscos*. When considered within the context of Horozco's social position and his career as a highly placed churchman and Tridentine reformer, this aspect of the *Tratado* recalls Bernard McGinn's argument that apocalypticism was primarily an elite phenomenon throughout the long Middle Ages.[9]

---

[8] Most scholars seem to be in agreement that this model is incorrect, yet its force remains as recent studies of such movements continue to place their emphasis on either popular or dissenting movements. For example, the excellent work of Richard Kagan and Sara Nalle has shed much light on the prophetic culture of post-Tridentine Spain, yet we remain without studies of such activity within clerical culture. Kagan, *Lucrecia's Dreams*; Kagan, "Politics, Prophecy, and the Inquisition in Late Sixteenth-Century Spain," in *Cultural Encounters: The Impact of the Inquisition in Spain and the New World*, ed. Mary Elizabeth Perry and Anne J. Cruz (Berkeley: University of California Press, 1991), 105–24; Sara Tilghman Nalle, *Mad for God: Bartolomé Sánchez, the Secret Messiah of Cardenete* (Charlottesville: University Press of Virginia, 2001); Nalle, "The Millennial Moment: Revolution and Radical Religion in Sixteenth-Century Spain," in *Toward the Millennium: Messianic Expectations from the Bible to Waco*, ed. Peter Shäfer and Mark Cohen (Leiden: Brill, 1998), 153–73; and Nalle, "Revisiting El Encubierto," in *Werewolves, Witches, and Wandering Spirits: Traditional Belief and Folklore in Early Modern Europe*, ed. Kathryn A. Edwards (Kirksville, MO: Truman State University Press, 2002), 77–92. Likewise, models persist that portray the Church after the early sixteenth century as being intolerant of apocalyptic or prophetic activity. See especially Robin Barnes, "Images of Hope and Despair: Western Apocalypticism: ca. 1500–1800," in *The Encyclopedia of Apocalypticism*, ed. Bernard McGinn, John Joseph Collins, and Stephen J. Stein (New York: Continuum, 1998), 143–84; Ottavia Niccoli, *Prophecy and People in Renaissance Italy* (Princeton: Princeton University Press, 1990).

[9] Bernard McGinn, *Visions of the End: Apocalyptic Traditions in the Middle Ages* (New York: Columbia University Press, 1998), 32.

Juan de Horozco y Covarrubias belonged to one of the most influential and well-connected families of sixteenth-century Toledo.[10] His father, Sebastian de Horozco, belonged to an illustrious Toledo family, was a prominent jurist and literary figure, and was considered by some to have been the anonymous author of the popular picaresque novel *Lazarillo de Tormes*.[11] Juan's mother was the sister of the influential Antonio and Diego de Covarrubias y Leiva, famous for their contributions at the Council of Trent and immortalized in El Greco's famous painting, *The Burial of Count Orgaz*.[12] Of particular note, Diego de Covarrubias was a professor of canon law at Salamanca and later entrusted with writing the well-known *reformatione* decrees at the Council of Trent; he also held the episcopacies of Santo Domingo, Ciudad Rodrigo, and Segovia. While Diego was the Archbishop of Segovia, Phillip II appointed him to the powerful Council of Castile; he later served as the president of the Council.[13] Antonio de Covarrubias y Leiva also served on the Council of Castile and was a dignitary in Segovia's cathedral chapter.[14]

Juan's older brother Sebastian de Covarrubias Horozco served as a chaplain to Philip II, and later held a canonry in the diocese of Cuenca and a position in the Inquisition. In spite of his distinguished church

---

[10] For Horozco's biography I am indebted to Jack Weiner, whose work on Juan's father Sebastián has produced valuable information about Juan's ecclesiastical career. See especially Jack Weiner, "Genealogía del liçençiado Juan Horozco de Covarrubias (1573)," in *El Cancionero, Sebastian de Horozco. Introducción, edición crítica, notas, bibliografía y genealogía de Juan de Horozco por Jack Weiner*, ed. Jack Weiner (Bern: H. Lang, 1975), 325–45; Weiner, "El camino de Juan de Horozco al obispado de Agrigento," in *En Busca de la Justicia Social* (Potomac, MD: Scripta Humanistica, 1984), 134–48. More recently, Rafael Zafra Molina provides a biography of Horozco, with close attention to his literary production as both author and printer in "Nuevos datos sobre la obra de Juan de Horozco y Covarrubias," *IMAGO: Revista de Emblemática y Cultural Visual* 3 (2011): 107–26.

[11] Hernández Miñano, "Los *Emblemas morales* de Juan de Horozco," 98.

[12] Weiner, "El camino de Juan de Horozco al obispado de Agrigento," 134. For more information on Antonio and Diego de Covarrubias, see Francisco Vicente Gómez and Constancio Gutiérrez, *Españoles en Trento* (Valladolid: Consejo Superior de Investigaciones Científicas Instituto "Jerónimo Zurita" Sección de Historia Moderna "Simancas", 1951), 128–35, 238–45.

[13] Diego was later appointed archbishop of Cuenca, but died before taking his see. Hernández Miñano, "Los *Emblemas morales* de Juan de Horozco," 99.

[14] Horozco lists Antonio de Covarrubias's offices in a letter he writes to his uncle in the opening apparatus of the *Tratado*, s/f.

career, Sebastian is best known for his literary accomplishments, having written an emblem book, and most significantly, the *Tesoro de la lengua castellana*, a dictionary still consulted today by scholars of Golden Age Spanish literature.[15] Despite their family connections, Juan and his brother Sebastian may have faced some obstacles in their careers as a result of Jewish ancestry introduced in the family through their paternal grandmother. Jack Weiner has investigated the family's lineage and suggests that Juan's *converso* status may have barred him from entering the prestigious *colegio mayor* of San Salvador at the University of Salamanca; Juan therefore received his degree from the University of Sigüenza.[16] Weiner's research further indicates that Juan may have been denied a post in the Inquisition because of the same purity of blood (*limpieza de sangre*) statutes.[17]

Juan de Horozco's ecclesiastical career appears to have benefited from his family connections, but his activities as a bishop and his ties to the Discalced Carmelite order suggest that he embraced the spirit of Catholic reform and renewal.[18] From the biography of Horozco in the golden age

[15] Hernández Miñano, "Los *Emblemas morales* de Juan de Horozco," 99, 101. For more information on Juan's brother Sebastián de Covarrubias, see the rich documentation found in Cuenca's archives in Ángel González Palencia, "Datos biográficos del licenciado Sebastián de Covarrubias y Horozco," *Boletín de la Real Academia Española* 12 (1925): 39–72, 217–45, 376–96, 498–514. See also Narciso Alonso Cortés, "*Acervo biográfico*: Don Sebastián de Covarrubias y Horozco," *Boletín de la Real Academia Española* 30 (1950): 11–13. Gonzalez Palencia includes a transcription of Sebastián's testament, which reveals a high standard of living from various ecclesiastical incomes and indicates he employed numerous servants.

[16] Weiner, "El camino de Juan de Horozco al obispado de Agrigento," 135. Although Gonzalez Palencia assumes that Sebastián was educated at Salamanca because of his uncle Diego's position there, he concedes that there is no proof, as Sebastián left a documentary trail only after to his appointment to the cathedral chapter in Cuenca. Gonzalez Palencia, "Datos biográficos del licenciado Sebastián de Covarrubias y Horozco," 40–41. Nelson reiterates Weiner's argument in *The Persistence of Presence*, 65–66, 72.

[17] Weiner, "El camino de Juan de Horozco al obispado de Agrigento," 134. Weiner provides a transcript of the Inquisition's investigation into Juan's *converso* status, in "Genealogía del liçençiado Juan Horozco de Covarrubias (1573)."

[18] Horozco's support of Teresa of Avila's Discalced Carmelites provides a particularly interesting example of the possible connection between his *converso* status and support for Catholic reform, as Teresa herself is thought to have come from a *converso* background. On connections between the Carmelite reforms and *conversos*, see Jodi Bilinkoff, *The Avila of Saint Teresa: Religious Reform in a Sixteenth-Century City* (Ithaca: Cornell University Press, 1989), 146–47.

humanist and cleric Nicolás Antonio's *Bibliotheca hispana nova*, first published in 1672, we know that Horozco obtained a doctorate in theology and held a canonry and archdeaconry in Segovia's cathedral chapter while his uncle Diego de Covarrubias was its Archbishop and his uncle Antonio de Covarrubias was a dignitary in its cathedral chapter.[19] In his *Emblemas morales*, Horozco mentions that he served as a chaplain to his uncle Diego.[20] Before he became the Archdeacon of Cuellar, Horozco served as a chaplain to the Discalced Carmelite nuns in Segovia.[21] The influence of both the Discalced Carmelites and the reforming ethos of Diego de Covarrubias became evident during Horozco's tenure as the Archdeacon of Cuellar. True to the spirit of the Council of Trent, Horozco conducted regular visitations of the parishes in the deanery.[22] He likewise supported the foundation of various Discalced Carmelite convents.[23] Horozco also began his literary career in Segovia, where he published the *Tratado*, another apologetic work in 1592 entitled *Paradoxas christianos contra las falsas opiniones del mundo* ("Christian Paradoxes Against the False Opinions of the World"), and his better known *Emblemas morales*, first printed in 1589 and printed on three further occasions.[24]

In 1594, the Spanish crown employed its right of ecclesiastical patronage (*patronato real*) and appointed Horozco to be the bishop of Agrigento, in Sicily.[25] His tenure there was marked by a devotion to

[19] Nicolás Antonio, *Biblioteca hispana nueva, o, De los escritores españoles que brillaron desde el año MD hasta el de MDCLXXXIV* (Madrid: Fundación Universitaria Española, 1999), 757.

[20] *Emblemas morales de don Iuan de Horozco y Covaruvias arcediano de Cuellar en la santa Yglesia de Segovia: Dedicadas a la buena memoria del presidente don Diego de Covarruvias y Leyua su tio* (Segovia: Juan de la Cuesta, 1591), 3v, 4r.

[21] Horozco indicates this in a letter to Madre Isabel de Santo Domingo, the Prioress of Segovia's Discalced Carmelite Convent. The letter is found in the introductory apparatus of Horozco's *Consuelo de afligidos* (Agrigento, 1601), s/f.

[22] Weiner, "El camino de Juan de Horozco al obispado de Agrigento," 142–43.

[23] Ibid.

[24] Juan de Horozco y Covarrubias, *Paradoxas Christianas contra las falsas opiniones del mundo* (Segovia: Marcos de Ortega, 1592). After its 1589 printing in Segovia, the *Emblemas morales* was printed in Segovia in 1591 and in Zaragoza in 1603 and 1604.

[25] Weiner, "El camino de Juan de Horozco al obispado de Agrigento," 135–36. On the Spanish crown's right to appoint bishops under the *patronato real*, see Ignasi Fernández Terricabras, *Felipe II y el clero secular* (Madrid, 2000); Helen E. Rawlings, "The Secularisation of Castilian Episcopal Office under the Habsburgs, c. 1516–1700," *Journal of Ecclesiastical History* 38 (1987): 53–79.

the Tridentine model of episcopacy, as he not only made regular parish visitations, but also convoked a diocesan synod, opened a diocesan seminary to train priests, invited the Jesuits to establish a college, established confraternities, and encouraged religious processions to venerate Saint Gerlando, an eleventh-century bishop who established the diocese of Agrigento following the Christian reconquest of Sicily.[26] While in Agrigento, Horozco also founded a printing house, where he published the *Consuelo de afligidos* ("Counsel of the Afflicted") and the *Symbola sacra* ("Sacred Symbols"), both in 1601.[27] Like many reforming bishops, Horozco also found himself embroiled in disputes with Agrigento's cathedral canons over episcopal rents, a battle he lost when the papal court sided with the cathedral canons.[28] In 1605, Philip III nominated Horozco to be the bishop of Guadix, in Andalusia, a small diocese that would have been an important post in the campaign to "Christianize" the still recently reconquered Kingdom of Granada.[29] In 1605 Horozco also published a treatise on the formation of early modern Catholic rulers, the *Doctrina de principes enseñada por el santo Job* ("Doctrine of Princes Taught by Job"), which he dedicated to Philip III.[30] After four years governing the diocese of Guadix, Horozco died in 1610.[31]

For a well educated and ambitious cleric committed to church reform, writing a treatise on the discernment of spirits placed Juan de Horozco y Covarrubias in a lineage of ecclesiastical authors that dated back to Jean

---

[26] Weiner, "El camino de Juan de Horozco al obispado de Agrigento," 146–48.

[27] *Symbola sacra* (Agrigento 1601) and *Consuelo de afligidos*.

[28] Weiner, "El camino de Juan de Horozco al obispado de Agrigento," 147. Gonzalez Palencia's research uncovered a royal document recommending Horozco for the see of Guadix that alleges that several of his canons made an attempt on his life in retaliation for his reforming actions. "Datos biográficos del licenciado Sebastián de Covarrubias y Horozco," 71–72.

[29] On the campaign to "Christianize" Andalusia, see especially David Coleman, *Creating Christian Granada: Society & Religious Culture in an Old-World Frontier City, 1492–1600* (Ithaca: Cornell University Press, 2003).

[30] Juan de Horozco y Covarrubias de Leyva, *Doctrina de principes enseñada por el santo Job* (Valladolid: Juan de Herrera, 1605). Note that Horozco had begun to adopt his uncles' additional surname of Leyva.

[31] Pedro Suárez chronicled Horozco's tenure in Guadix in his history of the diocese, originally published in 1696, *Historia del obispado de Guadix y Baza* (Madrid: Artes Gráficas Arges, 1948), 238.

Gerson.[32] The genre of anti-superstition and discernment of spirits treatises had become quite popular by Horozco's time. Andrew Keitt has observed that during the sixteenth and seventeenth centuries, Spanish churchmen "produced a flood of confessors' guides and handbooks for discerning true and false revelations."[33] With regard to confessors' manuals alone, Patrick O'Banion notes that over one hundred were printed in Spain between 1550 and 1700.[34] Keitt argues convincingly that rather than viewing this outpouring of manuals that sought to help priests confess penitents, discern spirits, and fight superstition only as part of a social disciplining campaign, we should understand these texts as an epistemological effort to "isolate causal principals" within religious experience and differentiate the genuinely miraculous from both natural processes and demonic activity.[35]

Turning to the category of anti-superstition and discernment of spirits treatises, among the most popular titles were Pedro Ciruelo's *Reprouacion de las supersticiones y hechizerias*—first published in 1528 and reprinted more than ten times in the sixteenth and seventeenth centuries, and Antonio Arbiol's *Desengaños místicos*—first published in 1706 and reprinted at least eleven times in the eighteenth century alone. At the time Horozco published his *Tratado*, the Jesuit Diego Pérez de Valdivia's *Aviso de gente recogida* (1585) had five printings in its first century, and the Franciscan Juan de los Ángeles's *Dialogo del conquisto del reyno de Dios* (1595) was published four times in its first two decades. By contrast, the *Tratado* was printed only once, by the printing press of Juan de la Cuesta in Segovia. Indeed, anti-superstition treatises and guides for the discernment of spirits published after Horozco gave him little to no attention, despite making frequent reference to Jean Gerson's seminal fifteenth-century treatise on the discernment of spirits.[36] My own analysis of book ownership among a group of 50 priests

---

[32] English translations of Gerson's treatises can be found in Paschal Boland, *The Concept of Discretio spirituum in John Gerson's "De probatione spirituum" and "De distinctione verarum visionum a falsis"* (Washington, DC: Catholic University of America Press, 1959).

[33] Keitt, *Inventing the Sacred*, 76.

[34] O'Banion, *The Sacrament of Penance and Religious Life in Golden Age Spain*, 26.

[35] Keitt, *Inventing the Sacred*, 9.

[36] For example, Juan de los Angeles, despite writing only seven years after Horozco, relies heavily on Gerson but makes no mention of Horozco's *Tratado*. Fray Juan de los Angeles, *Dialogos de la conquista del espiritual y secreto Reyno de Dios* (Madrid: Viuda de P. Madrigal, 1595).

in sixteenth- and seventeenth-century Avila found only one copy of Horozco's *Tratado*—which belonged to Dr. Miguel González Vaquero, the chaplain of the Discalced Carmelite Convent of San José, founded by Teresa of Avila.[37] Nevertheless, we know that Horozco's contemporaries considered the *Tratado* to be sound. When Horozco was being examined for his appointment to the bishopric of Agrigento, one of his personal references made note of Horozco's zeal for propagating the Catholic faith and highlighted the *Tratado*'s importance, attesting: "He has printed very Christian and learned books, especially one entitled *Concerning True and False Prophecy*, in which he demonstrated well that he desires for all faithful Christians to profit from it, and many other Catholic books, and of much learning and doctrine."[38]

Horozco writes in the *Tratado*'s prologue to the reader that he was motivated to write the treatise because "the time has given occasion for this discourse, with so many prophecies—having been published by so many authors—that have risen up at one time."[39] For this reason, Horozco explains that such a treatise was needed to warn his readers of the critical need to understand the difference between true and false prophecy.[40] The text appears to have been directed at a clerical audience rather than lay readers seeking spiritual edification, as Horozco writes: "although everything said [here] is true, it is not for all, because it is not discovered easily…only the very learned and those who are very

---

[37] James F. Melvin, *Fathers as Brothers in Early Modern Catholicism: Priestly Life in Avila, 1560–1636*. Ph.D. Dissertation, University of Pennsylvania, 2009, 219. Vaquero's library was recorded in Avila, Archivo Histórico Provincial, Protocolos 612, fols. 1040r–1043v. Vaquero was also the spiritual director and biographer of a visionary nun who attracted followers in seventeenth-century Avila, Maria Vela. On Vaquero's relationship to Vela, see Jodi Bilinkoff, "Confessors, Penitents, and the Construction of Identities in Early Modern Avila," in *Culture and Identity in Early Modern Europe (1500–1800)*, ed. Barbara B. Diefendorf and Carla Hesse (Ann Arbor: University of Michigan Press, 1993), 83–100.

[38] "…ha compuesto libros de mucha erudición y christiandad en especial un libro yntitulado *De verdadera y falsa prophecía*, en que mostró bien el deseo que tiene de aprouechar a todos los fieles christianos y otros muchos libros cathólicos y de mucha erudición y doctrina,…" Testimony quoted in Weiner, "El camino de Juan de Horozco al obispado de Agrigento," 143–44.

[39] "El tiempo ha dado lugar a esta platica por auerse publicado tantas prophecias de diferentes autores, que a vn tiempo en diuersas partes se han leuantado…" *Tratado*, 1v.

[40] Ibid.

advanced in their profession will come to understand it."[41] This intention is reflected in his quotations from the Bible, which were always in Latin, and his dedication of an entire chapter to the role of the confessor, who must "consider the obligation that they have to attend closely to this business, for it is grave, and they must consider the caution needed, for there is danger within."[42] The *Tratado*'s systematic organization, with a detailed table of contents as well as an index for the topics covered and scriptural references, allowed it to serve as a handbook for consultation when confessors faced challenges ranging from superstition to penitents' claims of receiving visions or prophecies.

Horozco divides the *Tratado* into two separate books. The first leads readers through a well-organized discussion of prophecy and its various forms and grades, followed by a historical outline of prophecy's pre-Christian origins and the role that prophecy continues to play within the Catholic Church.[43] Horozco explains the distinction between true and false prophecy, and discusses the important role of confessors and spiritual directors. He treats at length the dangers of false prophecy and feigned sanctity, and how they enable the Devil to work in the world. Book Two offers an equally systematic, historical analysis of magic and various divinatory arts, with much attention to their pre-Christian origins and manifestation. Horozco ends the *Tratado* with Latin and Spanish translations of Pope Sixtus V's 1586 condemnation of judicial astrology and other occult forms of divination, *Caeli et terrae creator Deus*.[44] Again reflecting the priestly state of the *Tratado*'s intended audience, Horozco reminds his readers that *Caeli et terrae creator Deus* should be read in parishes, in the vernacular, at least once annually.[45]

The *Tratado* also reflects Horozco's humanist background, drawing upon a formidable array of sources from classical antiquity, patristic

---

[41] "...aunque es verdad que todo està dicho, no es para todos, porque no se halla facilmente...y que solo vienen a entenderlo los muy estudiosos, y que estàn muy adelante en su profession." Ibid., 1r.

[42] "...deuen considerar la obligacion que tienen de atender mucho a aquel negocio por ser graue, y de cuydado, por el peligro que ay en el...". Ibid., 56v.

[43] Caro Baroja provides an outline of the *Tratado*'s contents in *Las formas complejas de la vida religiosa*, 55–59.

[44] Although he does not focus on judicial astrology, Richard Kagan describes the popularity of various occult arts within Spanish society, especially among high-ranking churchmen in *Lucrecia's Dreams*.

[45] *Tratado*, 154v.

and scholastic theologians, ecclesiastical history, and conciliar decrees. Indeed, Julio Caro Baroja has observed that Horozco's second book of the *Tratado* reflects the "criteria of an erudite aficionado of antiquities."[46] Horozco likewise demonstrates his knowledge of Greek by providing the Greek etymology of various critical terms and referring to the numeric value of their original Greek letters.[47] Moreover, his interest in examples of both false prophecy and divination in the ancient world, which he sources from classical authors such as Cicero, Virgil, and Pliny, makes Horozco a forebear of the eighteenth- and nineteenth-century anthropologists who gave rise to the study of comparative religions.

Horozco defines prophecy as the ability to tell the events of the future, understand the events of the past, and discern the hidden meaning of the present time.[48] In the third chapter of book one, Horozco provides a survey of the many definitions of prophecy among patristic figures such as Jerome, John Chrysostom, and Augustine, scholastics such as Albertus Magnus and Thomas Aquinas, classical authors such as Plato, even the Renaissance figure Francesco Pico della Mirandola. In chapters fifteen through nineteen Horozco provides confessors with seven criteria to determine whether a prophecy or vision had divine or demonic origins:

(1) the prophecy must harmonize with the Catholic faith[49]; (2) the prophecy must come true[50]; (3) it must be evident that the prophet is not motivated by greed, vanity, or desires for honor and esteem[51]; (4) the prophecy should be of service to God and should not deal with matters contradicting Catholic doctrine and good customs[52]; (5) true prophets should not talk of things they do not understand—which Horozco

---

[46] "...domina en el un criterio de erudito, aficionado a las antiguedades, aunque no deje de contener alusiones a hechos modernos." *Las formas complejas de la vida religiosa*, 56. Note that Caro Baroja's quote refers specifically to Book Two of the *Tratado*.

[47] For example, Horozco explains the Erythraean Sibyl's acrostic poem: "el original fue Griego, pues en otra lengua no podia venir la cuenta que pone del nombre de IESVS, conforme al valor que tienen las letras Griegas en razon de significar los numeros." *Tratado*, 152r.

[48] Ibid., 8r.

[49] Ibid., 43v–44v.

[50] Ibid., 44v.

[51] Ibid., 46r.

[52] Ibid., 46v.

contrasts with feigned prophets who "try to answer everything in order to avoid losing credit and esteem"[53]; (6) true prophets demonstrate the virtue of humility and appear tranquil and recollected[54]; (7) authorities should consider how prophets live and how they treat others.[55] To this last criterion, Horozco adds an observation that prophets who do not belong to a religious order should be viewed with suspicion because true prophets have always worn a religious habit.[56] Throughout the seven criteria, Horozco avoids referencing an earlier discernment manual or authority such as Gerson. Aside from supporting his points with passages from the Bible, his only other references are Gregory the Great's homilies on the prophet Ezekiel, Origen's commentary on the Gospel of John, and the thirteenth-century Byzantine historian Nicetas.

Following these seven criteria, book one's twentieth chapter contains additional considerations from Horozco. For the first consideration, Horozco asserts that prophets should be viewed with suspicion if they are esteemed by the "uneducated public (*el vulgo*)."[57] This consideration was likely a reference to the widespread popularity of visionaries in late sixteenth-century Spain.[58] Horozco's next consideration adds the interesting observation that the direction that a prophet falls when in ecstasy—forward or backward—can indicate the presence of humility and the authenticity of the prophecy: "[A]s a sign of humility and subjection to God, it has been seen that true prophets fall forward on their face...and the evil prophets are those who fall backward, into what they do not see."[59] While he draws upon Scriptural examples to support this

---

[53] "...procuran responder a todo por no perder el credito, y la estima que pretenden." Ibid.

[54] Ibid., 47r.

[55] Ibid., 47v.

[56] Ibid.

[57] "...y lo primero es, que la acepcion del vulgo, y ser estimado entre los suyos, pone sospecha en el que se dize propheta." Ibid., 49v.

[58] Alison Weber discusses the popularity of visionaries and their surrounding controversy in Horozco's time by examining the work of Diego Pérez de Valdivia's *Aviso de gente recogida* (1585) in "Between Ecstasy and Exorcism: Religious Negotiation in Sixteenth Century Spain," *Journal of Medieval and Renaissance Studies* 23 (1993): 221–34. Andrew Keitt provides a monograph length examination of this phenomenon and the role of discernment manuals in *Inventing the Sacred*.

[59] "...por señal de humildad, y de sujecion a Dios, se ha visto en los prophetas verdaderos caer sobre su rostro...Y por esto los malos que caen en lo que no veen, se dize caer atrás..."

observation, Horozco also takes a scientific turn by noting the role that humors or infirmities of the brain can cause individuals to lose their equilibrium and fall backwards.[60] Horozco echoes this concern in chapter twenty-four when he counsels confessors to rule out biological causes for their penitents' prophecies or visions by reminding his readers that melancholy can cause one to imagine things.[61] Horozco closes his chapter of additional considerations for the discernment of spirits to note Jean Gerson's three modes for discernment: through doctrine, experience, and grace.[62]

For Horozco and other Catholic apologists of the sixteenth century, both true and false prophecy were phenomena that had endured from the apostolic era into their own age. Ultimately for Horozco, the purpose of prophecy is to confirm the Catholic faith.[63] For this reason, Horozco devotes the eighth chapter of book one to assert "how the gift of prophecy has continued in the Catholic church."[64] Horozco provides a list of "true" Christian prophets that begins with figures in the New Testament and continues down to the sixteenth century: Simeon, Anna, Elizabeth, John the Evangelist, Agabus, the four daughters of Philip referenced in the book of Acts, the Apostle Paul, Benedict of Nursia, Paulinus, Hildegard of Bingen, Baudolino—an eighth-century prophet mentioned in Paul the Deacon's *History of the Lombards*, Hedwig of Silesia, Brigit of Sweden, Catherine of Siena, and Spain's own Teresa of Avila.[65] While Horozco lists the other prophets in summary form, he devotes more than a page to praise Teresa's accomplishments as a founder of the Discalced Carmelites and the merit of the revelations she received from God. In a 1609 letter to provide testimony in support of Teresa's canonization, Horozco claimed to have written

---

Tratado, 50r–50v. Horozco draws on Origen and Gregory the Great for examples of true prophets, such as St. Paul, who fell forward.

[60] Ibid., 50v–51r. Horozco's acknowledgement of the biological origins of false visionary experiences supports Keitt's arguments in *Inventing the Sacred*.

[61] *Tratado*, 57r.

[62] Ibid., 51r–51v.

[63] Ibid., 20r.

[64] "CAP.VIII. En que se trata que el don de la prophecia se ha continuado en la Yglesia Catolica." Ibid., 21v.

[65] Ibid., 22v–23v.

about Teresa's gift of prophecy in the *Tratado* because his firsthand experience with Teresa had made him certain of her gift.[66] Most interesting for the student of medieval apocalyptic traditions, Horozco's list of approved prophets includes the controversial Joachim of Fiore, a twelfth-century abbot whose exegesis on John's Apocalypse is examined by both Bernard McGinn and Marcia Colish elsewhere in this volume.[67] Concerning Joachim of Fiore's prophecies, Horozco refers his readers to Vincent of Beauvais's *Speculum Historiale* and to "Platina"— possibly a reference to the fifteenth-century Bartolomeo Platina's *Vitae Pontificium*.[68] Unfortunately, Horozco was too cautious to elaborate on which of Joachim's prophecies he considered valuable. However, Horozco makes an observation suggesting that Joachite prophecies continued to find a receptive audience in sixteenth-century Spain. He notes that a number of false prophecies were attributed to the Calabrian abbot—some of which he claims to have seen circulated in manuscript form, yet he urges his readers not to allow them to detract from the veracity of Joachim's actual prophecies.[69] Interest in Joachite prophecy was not a marginal phenomenon or a medieval atavism in Horozco's day. The medievalist Marjorie Reeves has discovered that within the Society of Jesus, often viewed as an embodiment of the "modern" Counter-Reformation Catholic Church, many preachers and Biblical commentators viewed their order as the *viri spirituales* whom Joachim of Fiore

---

[66] Zafra Molina, "Nuevos datos sobre la obra de Juan de Horozco y Covarrubias," 123. Zafra Molina reproduces the letter in full, which provides additional details about Horozco's chaplaincy at the Discalced Carmelite convent in Segovia and recounts his encounters with Teresa.

[67] Bernard McGinn, "Apocalypticism and Mysticism in Joachim of Fiore's *Expositio in Apocalypsim*," in this collection, 163–196; Marcia L. Colish, "End Time at Hand: Innocent III, Joachim of Fiore, and the Fourth Crusade," also in this collection, 251–279.

[68] *Tratado*, 23r.

[69] "Del Abad Ioachin se escriue que tuuo don de prophecia, y en sus escritos ay algunas cosas sin otras sueltas que andan de mano y yo he tenido, mas no he hecho mucho caso dellas, porque debaxo deste nombre se han entre algunos por curiosidad vana guardado algunas prophecias de diferentes autores, sin auer bastante razon, para hazer caso dellas, por ser fingidas, o sacadas de otras verdaderas, y no entendidas bien. Y aunque es verdad que ha de auer gran recato en semejantes cosas, no se ha de cerrar la puerta a todo, porque quando Dios es seruido embia en general a muchos, o en particular a alguno quien auise de lo que ha de suceder...". Ibid., 23r–23v.

believed would evangelize the world.[70] Similarly, one of Philip II's agents at the Council of Trent, Damián Hortolá, interpreted the challenges facing the Catholic Church through a Joachite apocalyptic schema in his commentary on the Song of Songs.[71]

In addition to the false Joachite prophecies, Horozco's list of false prophets includes sixteenth-century Protestants such as Martin Luther, Miguel Servetus, Thomas Muntzer, and David Joris (who he refers to as David George), as well as Jewish Kabbalists and Islam at-large. As Julio Caro Baroja has observed, Horozco's text also provides a chronicle of the false prophets who found adherents within sixteenth-century Spain.[72] Of note, Horozco names Magdalena de la Cruz, a popular visionary and stigmatic from Cordoba tried by the Inquisition for feigned sanctity in 1546.[73] He refers to other cases anonymously, such as a bishop of his own time who was tricked by a peasant girl with fake stigmata, a group of false prophets who claimed to be the successors of the twelve apostles, and the supporters of the apocalyptic street preacher Miguel de Piedrola and Lucrecia de Leon, who prophesied both the Armada's impending defeat in 1588 and the coming of a messianic ruler who would defeat Philip II and lead Spain into a new age.[74]

---

[70] Reeves notes that among the Jesuit adherents of this view was the Spanish commentator, Blasius Viegus, *Joachim of Fiore & The Prophetic Future* (Phoenix Mill, UK: Sutton Publishing, 1999), 116–18. Viegus was well known for a commentary on the book of Revelation, first published in Evora in 1601 and later in Venice (1602), Lyon (1602, 1605, 1606), Cologne (1603), Paris (1615), and Turin (1614).

[71] Ibid., 125.

[72] *Las formas complejas de la vida religiosa*, 56–57.

[73] Ibid., 61r. The case of Magdalena de la Cruz is discussed briefly in Kagan, *Lucrecia's Dreams*, 11, 115; Bilinkoff, *The Avila of St. Teresa*, 118. For a detailed account, see María del Mar Graña Cid, "La santa/bruja Magdalena de la Cruz: Identidades religiosas y poder femenino en la Andalucía pretridentina," in *La mujer (II): Actas del III Congreso de Historia de Andalucía* (Cordoba: Publicaciones Obra Social y Cultural Cajasur, 2002), 103–20.

[74] Piedrola and Lucrecia de Leon are the focus of Kagan, *Lucrecia's Dreams*. Vicente Beltrán de Heredia asserts that Horozco was referring to Piedrola and Lucrecia de Leon's followers when, on folios 42r–42v, he mentions people who, "en estos días...se han creído de algunas personas cuerdas de manera que pone espanto...y se vía en algunos sueños, como es amenazar con grandes mortandades y destruiciones y que se habian de salvar los escogidos en cuevas..." Quoted in Beltrán de Heredia, "Un grupo de visionarios y pseudoprofetas que actúa durante los últimos años de Felipe II," 393, Footnote 26.

At several points in the *Tratado* Horozco discusses the end times. Although he reiterates the decrees of the Fifth Lateran Council that preachers should not announce the time when evils that must occur will arrive, the coming of the Antichrist, or the date of the Last Judgment, nevertheless, Horozco betrays a heightened awareness of approaching events that will alter human history—particularly the Last Judgment itself—and thus suggests an outlook that is more apocalyptic than merely eschatological.[75] Moreover, Horozco reveals sympathies toward the imperial apocalyptic tradition—discussed in Jes Boon's contribution to this volume, which had no representatives on his list of false prophets.[76] Horozco closes his prologue to the reader by observing that the devastation of the "city of the world" is approaching, and he admits:

> I have a great hope that it has to be fulfilled in honor of Spain...that there must be seen within it a great marvel that will frighten and astonish the world, with the exaltation of the empire once more...for the greater honor and exaltation of [the] holy Catholic faith.[77]

---

[75] *Tratado*, 52r. Here I employ McGinn's distinction between eschatology and its subspecies, apocalyptic, which differ in the latter's intensity and its conviction that the end is near. *Visions of the End*, 3–4. Note that this does not require the apocalyptic thinker to predict when the end will actually occur.

[76] Marjorie Reeves notes that within Spain and the Habsburg empire in the early sixteenth century there were some who viewed Charles V as the long awaited Last World Emperor. *Joachim of Fiore & The Prophetic Future*, 110–14. Ronald Cueto Ruíz challenges the older historiographical silence regarding the culture of prophecy among early modern Habsburg monarchs in Spain. He found that in the late sixteenth century, the Franciscan Antonio Ruvio wrote an anti-Erasmian polemic that included an apocalyptic image with Luther and Erasmus comprising the tale of the dragon from John's Apocalypse and Philip II as the new Constantine. "La tradición profética en la monarquía católica en los siglos 15, 16, y 17," *Arquivos do Centro Cultural Portugues* 17 (1982): 411–44, at 419. Boon's contribution to this volume surveys the literature by hispanists concerning the imperial apocalyptic tradition in Spain during the first half of the sixteenth century, and rightly observes that hispanists' focus on apocalypticism's political ramifications has been too restrictive. "The Marian Apocalyptic of a Visionary Preacher: The *Conorte* of Juana de la Cruz, 1481–1534," in this collection, 41–67, at 44–46.

[77] "...tengo gran esperança se ha de cumplir en honra de España...lo que en general està dicho deste tiempo, que se ha de ver en el vna marauilla grande que ha de espantar el mundo, con el ensalçamiento de nueuo Imperio; que todo sea y lo encamine Dios para gloria suya, y para mayor honra y ensalçamiento de su santa Fê Catolica." *Tratado*, 4r.

Caro Baroja suggests that Horozco likely referred here to the Armada's anticipated success and notes that Horozco's own belief in an unfulfilled, even failed prophecy, was a problematic way to begin a manual for the discernment of true and false prophecy.[78]

In other parts of the *Tratado* Horozco shifts from voicing prophecies of imperial might to those of impending doom. In a style similar to the subjects of E. Ann Matter's study of twentieth-century Marian apparitional culture, Horozco provides scathing critiques of his own society and predicts that moral laxity will result in divine punishment.[79] Horozco connects "abominations that in these times are seen in Spain" to signs of the end predicted on a book about the end of the world, pseudonymously attributed to Hipploytus.[80] While cautious of the warnings in Matthew 24 about false prophets who will preach on the end of days, Horozco notes:

> we could bring here some considerations...with which we have the obligation to live with more care, and...if we understand that the day, which we hold through faith must be the end, continually approaches, and since this is from one of the most ancient saints, I will put here one of the signs that the judgment is approaching....[81]

---

[78] Caro Baroja writes: "El problema es que el arcediano, en 1588, creía en lo que indica al final del prologo al lector....1588...Parece que la profecía no se cumplió." *Las formas complejas de la vida religiosa*, 56.

[79] Matter, "Apparitions of the Virgin Mary in the Late Twentieth Century."

[80] "...la abominacion que en estos tiempos se vee en España..." *Tratado*, 32v. For more information on this understudied work by Pseudo-Hippolytus, see Alice Whealey, "*De Consummatione Mundi* of Pseudo-Hippolytus: Another Byzantine Apocalypse from the Early Islamic Period," *Byzantion* 66.2 (1996): 461–69. Horozco would have had access to this text in Marguerin de La Bigne, *Sacra bibliotheca sanctorum patrum supra ducentos qua continentur, illorum de rebus diuinis opera omnia et fragmenta...* (Paris: Michaelem Sonnium, 1575).

[81] "...pudieramos traer algunas consideraciones para ayudar a este proposito con que tenemos obligacion a biuir con mas cuydado, y mas despedidos de las memorias vanas del mundo, si entendemos que se va acercando el dia que por Fê tenemos ha de ser el final, y por ser de vn santo de los mas antiguos, pondre aqui vna de las señales que pone de acercarse el juyzio..." *Tratado*, 32r–32v.

Horozco interprets this "particular revelation" of Pseudo-Hippolytus to refer to his own day, and emphasizes his point with a marginal note stating: "Revelation of a saint about things of this time."[82]

Horozco lists the signs from Pseudo-Hippolytus as being the destruction of churches, disregard for the Scriptures, and that the "singers of [the enemy] will sing wherever the enemy wants."[83] According to Horozco, the persecutions committed by heretics show that the first two signs have already taken place, yet the third has just begun.[84] Horozco interprets Pseudo-Hippolytus's "songs of the enemy" to refer to the immorality he observed in late sixteenth-century Spain:

> these are the songs of the Devil, it is well seen that they are sung wherever he would like, having introduced the abomination of a song accompanied by dances that in reality are understood to have been an invention of the devil among the *Indios*, and it is nothing less than dishonesty as much as lewdness.[85]

While the first two signs of the end borrowed from Pseudo-Hipploytus are obvious references when read through the lens of sixteenth-century Catholic–Protestant polemic, the third is more obscure. Vicente Beltrán de Heredia has argued that Horozco was likely referring to the sarabande (*zarabanda*), a popular and controversial dance that may have come to Spain from the Americas in the sixteenth century and preoccupied moralists.[86] Horozco writes that he fears a great punishment from God

---

[82] "Reuelacion de vn santo en cosas deste tiempo." Ibid., 32v.

[83] "...los cantares del enemigo nuestro, se cantaràn donde quiera." Ibid.

[84] Ibid.

[85] "...lo postrero que son los cantares del demonio, bien se veen que donde quiera se cantan, auiendose introduzido la abominacion de vn cantar acompañado de bayles que en realidad se entiende fueron inuencion del demonio entre los Indios, y no podia ser menos siendo quando siendo quanto es posible deshonestos en todo genero de torpezas..." Ibid., 32v–33r.

[86] "Un grupo de visionarios y pseudoprofetas que actúa durante los últimos años de Felipe II," 383–84. On the sarabande's translation to Spain, see J. Peter Burkholder, "Music of the Americas and Historical Narratives," *American Music* 27 (2009): 399–23, at 411–13. On the controversies surrounding the sarabande's popularity in Spain, see Louise K. Stein, "Eros, Erato, Terpsichore and the Hearing of Music in Early Modern Spain," *The Musical Quarterly* 82 (1998): 654–77, at 660–63. Although he does not discuss the sarabande, Max Harris provides a brief historical sketch of the importation of Native American dance to sixteenth-century Spain in *Aztecs, Moors, and Christians: Festivals of Reconquest in Mexico and Spain* (Austin: University of Texas Press, 2000), 227–34.

because of this laxity, and points to the death of several individuals while dancing as evidence that the punishment has already begun.[87]

Horozco warns that a greater punishment remains, reminding his readers that "there are threats of holy men who have said that Spain was once lost through lewdness, apathy, and dishonesty, and that it has to be lost again because of them."[88] This presumably refers to the Muslim conquest of Iberia in the eighth century. Two chapters later, Horozco expresses his concern about the danger he perceived from the *moriscos*, in the light of their 1568 uprising in Alpujarras, near Granada. He highlights his concern with a marginal note that warns: "Great danger in the *moriscos* that remain to be dispersed and in those that have been dispersed."[89] According to Horozco, the fourteenth-century Francesc Eiximenis's *De natura angelica* foretold the 1568 uprising.[90]

Most significant for Horozco's implied anxiety that he is living near the end of the current age in history, he ends the *Tratado* with a discussion of the Erythraean Sibyl and its acrostic poem concerning the final judgment.[91] Horozco writes: "Because it is now time to put an end to our book, it will come to be very appropriate that we end with the verses of this Erythraean Sibyl, which deal with the end of the world."[92] The Erythraean Sibyl to which Horozco refers was the most popular out of

---

[87] *Tratado*, 33r.

[88] "Tambien ay amenaças de varones santos que han dicho se perdio una vez España, por torpeças, y deshonestidades, y se auia de perder otra vez por ellas, y harta perdiciones la desorden, y lo que sucede en casos particulares que jamas se han visto, mas dexemos esto que serà Dios seruido se remedie." Ibid.

[89] "Peligro grande en los moriscos que quedan por repartir y en los que se han repartido." Ibid., 39v.

[90] Ibid., 39r. Note that Horozco was also writing at the same time of the discovery of the *plomos de Granada*—a series of forged documents that invented a syncretistic Christian history of Granada that incorporated Arab culture, which was determined to be a hoax in the seventeenth century. On the *plomos de Granada*, see especially Coleman, *Creating Christian Granada*, 177–201; A. Katie Harris, *From Muslim to Christian Granada: Inventing a City's Past in Early Modern Spain* (Baltimore: Johns Hopkins University Press, 2007).

[91] The antiquarian Mariana Monteiro noted Horozco's positive view of the Erythraean Sibyl in *As David and the Sibyls Say: A Sketch of the Sibyls and the Sibylline Oracles. Initiated and Projected by the Late Very Reverend Alfred Canon White* (Edinburg, UK: Sands & Co., 1905), 88.

[92] "Y porque ya es tiempo de dar fin a nuestro libro vendra muy a proposito le acabemos con los versos desta Sibyla Erythrea, que tratan del fin del mundo." *Tratado*, 152v.

a collection of fourteen oracles from the ancient world whose prophecies were among some of the most popular apocalyptic writings in medieval Christendom because of the remarkable adaptability of their opaque prophecies to the events of the day.[93] Dating back to the patristic era, when Lactantius used the Sibyls to make Christianity more appealing to his pagan audiences, the Sibyls were considered to provide an objective validation for Christianity's claims.[94] Sometime around the reign of Marcus Aurelius, the eighth of the Sibylline Oracles—popularly known as the Erythraean Sibyl—was adapted from a Jewish Sibylline world history to include prophecies about the birth of the Christian Messiah and an acrostic poem about the Last Judgment.[95] During the Middle Ages, the Erythraean Sibyl usually circulated in fragmentary form or through the writings of Lactantius and Augustine.[96] The Sibyls—particularly the Erythraean—circulated widely within Joachite circles and were employed to prophesy both impending catastrophe and coming glory. Bernard McGinn asserts that by the sixteenth century, "[a]cquaintance with the inherited Sibyl, the prophetess of Christ, was so widespread that in the later Middle Ages it would be impossible to cite all the witnesses."[97]

---

[93] With his use of the Erythraean Sibyl to cap his guide for the priestly discernment of (often female) prophecy, we could view Horozco as a successor to the second-century men who wrote about the Sibylline oracles examined by Mary Rose D'Angelo in her contribution to this volume. "The Sobered Sibyl," 178. For a thorough history of the Sibylline oracles from their origins through the late Middle Ages is in Bernard McGinn, "*Teste David cum Sibylla*: The Significance of the Sibylline Tradition in the Middle Ages," in *Women of the Medieval World: Essays in Honor of John H. Mundy*, ed. Julius Kirshner and Suzanne F. Wemple (New York: Basil Blackwell, Inc., 1985), 7–35. McGinn also includes sections of the Sibyls in his two anthologies of apocalyptic writing, McGinn, *Apocalyptic Spirituality*, and McGinn, *Visions of the End*.

[94] See Bard Thompson, "Patristic Use of the Sibylline Oracles," *Review of Religion* 16 (1952): 115–36.

[95] McGinn, "*Teste David cum Sibylla*," 12.

[96] Ibid., 17. For studies of the complex manuscript tradition of the Erythraean Sibyl in Medieval Europe, see Paul J. Alexander, "The Diffusion of Byzantine Apocalypses in the Medieval West and the Beginnings of Joachimism," in *Prophecy and Millennarianism: Essays in Honour of Marjorie Reeves* (Harlow, UK: Longman, 1980), 55–106; Marjorie Reeves, *The Influence of Prophecy in the Later Middle Ages: A Study in Joachimism* (Notre Dame: University of Notre Dame Press, 1993).

[97] McGinn, "*Teste David cum Sibylla*," 19.

The Sibyls only found their end with the emergence of historical source criticism in the eighteenth century.[98]

Horozco begins his chapter on the Sibyls with a discussion of the oracles of Apollo. He transitions to the Sibylline oracles by noting that Sibyl was a general name for oracles that derived from the Aeolic Greek root words for God (*Sios*) and counsel (*Byli*).[99] Horozco explains that this general application of the name allowed the name Sibyl to be applied to many "prophetesses of the demon."[100] However, he notes that Christian saints and other ancient authors had demonstrated that some of those referred to as Sibyls professed the truth.[101] Horozco concentrates on the Erythraean Sibyl, noting that tradition considered her to be the most important and cites the hymn *Dies Irae* from the requiem liturgy to observe that "the Church sings this about one of them, who told great prophecies of Christ and about the end of the world."[102] Horozco's final chapter in the *Tratado* offers his contemporaries a thorough account of the varying traditions surrounding the Erythraean Sibyl's biography and her history, drawing in particular from the *Bibliotheca Sanctorum Patrum*, Augustine's *City of God*, and the *Oration of the Emperor Constatine* attributed to Eusebius.

Perhaps the best-known prophecy from the Erythraean Sibyl's textual tradition is an acrostic poem, which in its original Greek composition spells "JESUS CHRIST SON OF GOD SAVIOR CROSS" with the first letters of each line. The verses vividly depict Christ's Second Coming and Last Judgment, in which the righteous will be rewarded, the unrighteous damned, and the earth consumed by fire. Horozco notes that the acrostic poem is mentioned in Cicero's *De divinatione*, Augustine's *Oratione contra Iudeos* and *City of God*, and the *Oration of Constantine*.[103] Horozco indicates that the poem was well known in his day, observing: "currently [the Acrostics] circulate in many places in Greek and Latin."[104] Horozco then offers a Spanish translation of the

---

[98] Ibid., 35.

[99] *Tratado*, 149v.

[100] "Y conforme a esta generalidad se puede dezir de las Sibylas auer sido prophetisas del demonio." Ibid., 149v.

[101] Ibid.

[102] "...y la Yglesia lo canta de la vna dellas, que dixeron grandes prophecias de Christo, y de la fin del mundo...". Ibid., 150r.

[103] Ibid., 152v.

[104] "Y ya andan en muchas partes en Griego, y en Latin." Ibid., 152v–153r.

poem, noting that he followed the Latin text available in the *Bibliotheca Sanctorum Patrum*.[105] Horozco's translation of the acrostic spells: "JESUS CHRIST. SON OF GOD. SAVIOR (IESVS CHRISTO. HIJO DE DIOS. SALVADOR)," and proclaims:

> Earth and heaven announced their Judgment
> In their signs, when the eternal King,
> Over the clouds will call to universal judgment
> Where by the evil and the good
> He will be seen surrounded by the Saints
> With royal majesty judging all.
> All the world a burning furnace,
> Rivers and springs will pour out flames,
> Fire and water have been joined, and with such force
> That the sea will raise up waves of fire.
> All will burn, sea, land, and sky.
> Oh blessed are the good, who from such a time
> Have been made participants in the glory.
> They will go in body and soul to enjoy it.
> They will never be able to lose glory, but the evil,
> Oh unfortunate fate, to the eternal fire,
> Of the sad, dark, and fearful abyss,
> They will go in body and soul accompanied
> By the demons, and to the eternal punishment,
> They will go with excess rage and dishonor.
> Oh shameful battle, their evils
> Will be manifest for all the world,
> Their lies and most secret dealings
> There will be understood by all,
> The vanity of the world, its empty pleasures,
> And its flattering gratifications
> There they will be shown that which they served.
> Undeceived too late about their evils
> They will happen to see what remains for them.
> It remains for them that they must die eternally.[106]

---

[105] "...segui la traslacion de los que estan referidos en la bibliotheca de los Santos padres...". Ibid., 153r.

[106] Iuyzio anunciaron la tierra y cielo
En sus señales, quando el Rey eterno
Sobre las nuues llamará al juicio
Universal, a dó del malo y bueno

The Erythraean Sibyl would have been well known to Horozco's contemporary readers.[107] Within the Spain of Horozco's time, various locales such as his native Toledo incorporated the Erythraean Sibyl's prophecy of the nativity of the Messiah into Christmas and Holy Week

> Será visto de Santos rodeado
> Con majestad Real juzgando a todos.
> Horno encendido sera todo el mundo,
> Rios y fuentes yran vertiendo llamas,
> Iuntarse han fuego y agua, y de tal suerte
> Será, que el mar levante olas de fuego,
> Todo tendrá un calor mar, tierra, y cielo.
> O dichosos los buenos, que a tal tiempo
> Hechos particioneros de la gloria
> Iran en cuerpo y alma a gozar della.
> Iamas podran perderla, mas los malos
> O desdichada suerte al fuego eterno,
> Del triste obscuro y temeroso abysmo,
> En cuerpo y alma yran acompañados
> De los demonios, y a la eterna pena
> Iran con rabia de pesar y afrenta.
> O vergonçoso trance, sus maldades
> Seran a todo el mundo manifiestas,
> Sus enredos y tratos mas secretos
> Alli seran de todos entendidos;
> La vanidad del mundo, sus plazeres
> Vanos, y sus deleytes lisonjeros
> Alli se mostraron de que sirvieron
> Desengeñados tarde de sus males
> Ocurrían a ver lo que les queda,
> Restarles ha morir eternamente. Ibid., 153r–154r. Note that the phrase "Todo tendra un color mar, tierra, cielo" should read "Todo tendra un calor" according to contemporary translations of the acrostic in Luis de Granada and Alonso de Villegas, which both read "abrasará un fuego las tierras, la mar, el cielo." Fray Luis de Granada, "Introducción del Símbolo de la Fe IV," in *Obras completas*, ed. Alvaro Huerga (Madrid: Fundación Universitaria Española, 1994), 192; Alonso de Villegas, *Flos sanctorum segunda parte: Y historia general en que se escriue la vida de la Virgen Sacratissima madre de Dios, y Señora nuestra, y las de los sanctos antiguos, que fueron antes dela venida de nuestro Saluador al mundo* (Barcelona: En casa de Hubert Gotard: A costa de Francisco Simon, 1587), 152r.

[107] A sketch of the diffusion and reception of the Sibyls in sixteenth-century Spain, which includes the *Tratado* in a list of golden age Spanish authors who discussed the Sibyls, can be found in José Enrique Laplana Gil's critical notes to Ambrosio Bondía, *Cítara de Apolo y Parnaso en Aragón. Edición, introducción y notas de José Enrique Laplana Gil* (Zaragoza: Instituto de Estudios Altoaragoneses, 2000), 1: clxvii–clxxxi. LaPlana Gil observes that Horozco's *Tratado* showed the Sibyls "excessive praise (*elogio excesivo*)" compared to the other authors who wrote about them (1: clxvii, Footnote 230).

liturgies.[108] With the liturgical reforms prompted by the Council of Trent, the use of the Sibyl in local church rituals became increasingly frowned upon over the course of the sixteenth century because of their presumed pagan authorship, but Henry Kamen's research has found that attempts to remove the Sibyl from para-liturgical use often met with resistance from cathedral chapters.[109] Despite the hesitation among some Catholic reformers to use the Sibyl in the Church's rituals, they continued to be esteemed as an apologetic tool. Indeed, the Spanish literature scholar José Enrique LaPlana Gil suggests that the Sibyls were actually employed as an apologetic tool of the Counter-Reformation offensive.[110]

Beginning with the 1465 publication of Lactantius's *Institutes*, followed by the 1545 publication of the complete set of Sibylline oracles by Sixtus Betuleius in Basil, the Sibyls were diffused throughout Renaissance society in such a way that they have been labeled "one of the characteristics of Humanism."[111] In addition to the chapter in the *Bibliotheca Sanctorum Patrum* that appears to have been his primary source material, the Sibyls could also be found in texts by popular spiritual writers of the sixteenth and early seventeenth centuries. The well-known preacher and reformer Juan de Avila made reference to the oracle in one of his Advent sermons.[112] Biographies of the Sibyls could be found in the best-selling Luis de Granada's *Introduction to the Symbol of Faith*, first published in 1583, and the second installment of Alonso de Villegas's widely read collection of saints' lives, the *Flos Sanctorum*.[113] Only a decade before Horozco printed the *Tratado*, the Jesuit reformer Peter Canisius used the Erythraean Sibyl to defend Catholic teachings about

[108] Kamen, *The Phoenix and the Flame*, 100.
[109] Ibid., 100–1.
[110] LaPlana Gil, in Bondía, *Cítara de Apolo y Parnaso en Aragón*, 1: clxxi.
[111] LaPlana Gil mentions the influence of these two publications, and cites Santiago Sebastián López's remark about the Erythraean Sibyl as "una de las caractéristicas del Humanismo" in Bondía, 1: clxix–clxx. LaPlana Gil refers to Sixtus Betulius, *Sibyllinorum oracvlorvm libri octo* (Basel: Ioannis Oporini, 1545); Lactantius, *De divinis institutionibus* (Subiaco: Sweynheym and Pannartz, 1465).
[112] Juan de Avila, "Sermones de tiempo: '¡Grande es el día del Señor, y muy terrible!' Domingo I de Adviento," in *Obras Completas del Santo Maestro Juan de Avila, Edición Crítica*, ed. Luis Sala Balust and Francisco Martín Hernández (Madrid: Biblioteca de Autores Cristianos, 1970), 19.
[113] Granada, "Introducción del símbolo de la fe IV," Chapter 21; Villegas, *Flos sanctorum segunda parte*, 152r–152v.

the Virgin Mary.[114] One of Horozco's successors in the campaign against false prophecy and feigned sanctity, Gerónimo Planes, included the Sibyls among a list of true prophets in his 1634 *Tratado del examen de las revelaciones verdaderas y falsas*.[115] Perhaps the crowning moment for the Sibyls in post-Tridentine Spain was the 1621 publication of the Sibylline oracles in Spanish by Baltasar Porreño's *Oráculos de las doce Sibilas, profetisas de Cristo nuestro Señor*. Indeed, Porreño references Horozco's "most learned book concerning true and false prophecy" to note the existence of false prophecies that circulated under the Sibylline label, in contrast to authentic Sibylline prophecies such as the Erythraean.[116]

Conclusion

A careful reading of Juan de Horozco y Covarrubias's *Tratado* illustrates the role that apocalyptic traditions continued to play for ecclesiastical reformers and social elites in post-Tridentine Spain. Horozco—who belonged to a well-connected family and enjoyed a rather privileged ecclesiastical career under the patronage of his powerful uncles Antonio and Diego de Covarrubias y Leyva—provides a counter-example to the marginal position of the popular and heterodox prophets and visionaries he chronicles and denounces in the *Tratado*. For Horozco, prophetic and apocalyptic traditions—when in line with church teaching—were not atavisms to eradicate or voices of protest to silence. To the contrary, in the *Tratado* he shows his sympathy toward certain apocalyptic prophecies. Although he never goes as far as stating the date of the Last Judgment, Horozco betrays a pronounced apocalyptic sense of his own.[117] Moreover, he marshals certain apocalyptic

---

[114] Baltasar Porreño made reference to Canisius's *De Maria Virgine incomparabile et Dei genitrice Sacrosancta libri quinque* (Ingolstadt: David Sartorius, 1577) in his own *Oráculos de las doce Sibilas, profetisas de Cristo nuestro Señor* (Cuenca: Domingo de la Iglesia, 1621), 5v.

[115] *Tratado del examen de las revelaciones verdaderas y falsas, y de los raptos*, 86r. Unlike Horozco, Planes does not seem to employ the Sibyls for his own commentary on the age.

[116] *Oráculos de las doce Sibilas, profetisas de Cristo nuestro Señor*, 4r.

[117] Indeed, thirteen years after the *Tratado*'s publication, Horozco's *Consuelo de los afligidos* placed great emphasis on God's mercy toward those who persevere through tribulations. In the topical index of this text one finds under the heading for the letter F: "Fin del mundo esta cerca", that is, the end of the world is near. The section indicated by the index, however, makes no concrete predictions about the end, and instead exhorts those who have persevered through the tumultuous religious climate of the sixteenth century to maintain hope. *Consuelo de los afligidos*, 188.

traditions, particularly the Pseudo-Hippolytus and the Erythraean Sibyl, to support his own positions as an apologist for the Catholic faith, a supporter of the Spanish monarchy, and a proponent for the expulsion of the *moriscos* from Spain. These traditions colored Horozco's attempt to explain the challenges facing church and state in post-Tridentine Spain, and allowed him to express hope that both the Catholic faith and the Spanish crown would enjoy future vindication. Horozco's *Tratado* provided a useful tool for his fellow priests to discern spirits and root out superstitious practices among the faithful while giving meaning to the various challenges facing the Church in Spain. As McGinn has argued, apocalypticism is "as often designed to maintain the political, social, and economic order as to overthrow it."[118] Horozco attempts just that with his *Tratado* by labeling the various threats to Catholic orthodoxy and Spanish imperial might as abominable "signs" of an approaching end.[119]

---

[118] McGinn, *Visions of the End*, 30.

[119] Bradley Nelson's study of Horozco's emblem books similarly contends that the author employed a "socially and ethically conservative mnemonic strategy" as part of an ideological campaign in support of the Spanish crown. Nelson, "Emblematic Representation and Guided Culture in Baroque Spain," 160.

PART III

The Eschaton in Political, Liturgical, and Literary Contexts

CHAPTER 9

The End of the World as They Knew It? Jews, Christians, Samaritans and End-Time Speculation in the Fifth Century

Ross S. Kraemer

1   Introduction[1]

Historians of religions have long observed that some moments are rife with end-time speculation and anticipation, while others are not. In the late fourth and fifth centuries, extensive military conflicts (not the least of which was the sack of Rome in 410), together with natural calamities such as earthquakes and outbreaks of plague provided ample reasons to think that the end was near.[2] For Christians, prophecies such as those

---

[1] This essay draws heavily on aspects of my forthcoming study, *The Mediterranean Diaspora in Late Antiquity: What Christianity Cost the Jews?* (New York and Oxford: Oxford University Press, 2019).

[2] All this, of course, has been the subject of extensive scholarly treatment. For a useful introduction, if now somewhat outdated, see Scott L. Bradbury, *Severus of Minorca, Letter on the Conversion of the Jews* (New York: Oxford University Press, 1996), 47–53. Particularly noteworthy is his mention of predictions of the demise of Christianity, 48–49.

R. S. Kraemer (✉)
Brown University, Providence, RI, USA

© The Author(s) 2019
E. Knibbs et al. (eds.), *The End of the World in Medieval Thought and Spirituality*, The New Middle Ages,
https://doi.org/10.1007/978-3-030-14965-9_9

227

in Matthew 24:6–8 might well have seemed on the verge of fulfillment, despite the fact that such events were regular occurrences in the ancient Mediterranean: "You will hear of wars and rumors of wars…nation (*ethnos*) will rise against nation, and kingdom against kingdom, and there will be famines and earthquakes[3] in various places: all this is but the beginning of the birth pangs."

By these decades, Christians, Jews and Samaritans had fairly distinctive ideas about God's plan for humanity, in which, unsurprisingly, their own group played a privileged central role. The resources on which Jews, Samaritans and Christians drew for the shape of these expectations differed and authorized diverse and somewhat competing scenarios, which nevertheless generally fell into two categories, a total termination (or radical transformation) of this current world and the restoration of an idealized but still earthly prior world. As they had in prior centuries, Jewish and Samaritan end-time scenarios often envisioned the defeat of the present ruling powers, the restoration of an autonomous kingdom, and the re-establishment of a central cult site for the worship of Israel's God (whether in Jerusalem or on Mt. Gerizim). Relatively few passages in Jewish and Samaritan scripture[4] provided explicit blueprints for such events, although various biblical texts could be marshaled in support of expectations for the restoration of the Davidic kingdom, and Genesis 1–3, Deuteronomy 18:18 (the divine promise to send a prophet like Moses) and perhaps a few others constituted resources for other future expectations. Christian expectations relied on schematics from diverse writings, particularly those of the New Testament, from the apocalyptic predictions in Matthew 24 and in Mark 13, to the eschatological scenarios of 1 Thessalonians 4:13–5:11 and Romans 9–11 in the letters of Paul,[5] and most of all the complex and cryptic drama of a new heaven, a new earth and a new Jerusalem in Revelation (itself a much contested book well into the fourth century).[6]

---

[3] Some manuscripts also read "and pestilences [*loimoi*]."

[4] The question of precisely which books Samaritans and Jews accepted as of ultimate authority is beyond the consideration of this essay, as is the question of whether Jews themselves differed on their acceptance of particular books, notably those included in the Septuagint. At a minimum, though, Jews and Samaritans both revered the Pentateuch, although their exact texts differed somewhat.

[5] 1 Corinthians 15:51–52 might be adduced here as well.

[6] For these exact phrases, see Revelation 21:1–2.

Yet contingent historical situations mattered. Christian end-time speculation invariably involved the ultimate return of Christ, but such speculation was much less likely to envision an assault on a divinely sanctioned Christian political order. Certainly, orthodox Christian Roman emperors seem to have envisioned the subjugation of the entire world to an orthodox empire as part of the divine plan. While the orthodox prevailed, Donatists, Montanists, Arians and others might well have envisioned their fall from power as part of a divine eschatological plan, just as, under Arian emperors, the orthodox might have fantasized about the restoration of orthodoxy. As I shall shortly consider, some Jews may have anticipated the overthrow of the now-Christian empire and the restoration of the Davidic kingdom in Jerusalem, while others may have envisioned a different, other-worldly redemption. Samaritan expectations, too, may have been shaped by particular historical events.

Further, as we shall see, in the fifth century, Jewish and Christian end-time expectations were inextricably linked. Grounded especially in Romans 11:25–26 (within the larger discourse of Romans 9–11), in which at least some Jews must resist Christ until all[7] Gentiles have accepted him, Christians expected the end to entail the conversion of the Jews, their inclusion/incorporation into the church body, and thus their disappearance as a distinct people. Jews in the Roman orbit, on the other hand, envisioned the restoration of the temple and of a political theocracy that would overthrow, or at least mitigate the power of, the now Christianized Roman empire.[8] Whether they were more likely to do so when orthodox emperors reigned is difficult to determine, but it may be relevant that Jews and Arians seem at least occasionally to have made common cause against the Orthodox, and Jews seemed to have fared better under Arian emperors.[9]

Samaritans, like Jews, seem similarly to have envisioned the restoration of political and cultic autonomy in their homeland. Whether these expectations entailed a competition with Jews seems quite

---

[7] Whether this is precisely what Paul envisioned by the phrase *to pleroma ton ethnon* (Rom. 11:25) is immaterial for how later Christians would read it [tōn ethnōn].

[8] The situation in the more multi-cultural Persian orbit is beyond the scope of this article.

[9] The details are beyond the purview of this piece. For further discussion, see Kraemer, *Mediterranean Diaspora*.

plausible, if again difficult to determine. While Samaritan eschatology necessarily entailed release from an oppressive Christian empire, if not also the destruction of that empire, it's less clear what place Samaritans held in Christian eschatological expectations. New Testament scenarios offered no explicit blueprints for the conversion of Samaritans, although the prophecy of Jesus in John 4 concerning the Samaritan worship on Mt. Gerizim plays a starring role in one of the episodes explored in this article. Samaritans play no role in the death of Jesus in Christian accounts, but in the fifth century, Samaritans are regularly pressured to convert to Christianity and targeted by same tactics deployed against Jews, traditionalists and dissident Christians.[10]

In this tribute to my friend and colleague of forty years, I attend not so much to discourse(s) about end-times,[11] but to four instances in which end-time expectations and scenarios may have played some significant role. I hope to demonstrate that they constitute part of the extensive contestation between Jews, Christians and Samaritans in the fifth century, in the wake of intensifying orthodox Christian pressures to conform the entire empire to that orthodoxy. I look first at the end-time framework for Severus of Minorca's *Letter on the Conversion of the Jews* set in 418 C.E. Then I consider an event on Crete in the 430s, perhaps narrated by Socrates of Constantinople, which he claims led to the mass conversion of Jews there. Third, I examine an account in the Syriac *Life of Barsauma* concerning a roughly contemporaneous possible messianic uprising in Jerusalem. Last, I consider accounts of a Samaritan revolt in the late fifth century.

[10] On which see again Kraemer, *Mediterranean Diaspora*.

[11] For some recent treatments of these, see Nicholas de Lange, "Jewish and Christian Messianic Hopes in Pre-Islamic Byzantium," in *Redemption and Resistance: The Messianic Hopes of Jews and Christians in Antiquity*, ed. M. Bockmuehl and J. Carleton Paget (London: T&T Clark, 2007), 274–84. Despite its title, the article looks almost entirely at Jewish sources such as rabbinic writings and *piyyutim*, a serious limitation given that we have no writings in Greek or Latin demonstrably authored by Jews from this period. Another essay in this volume surveys Christian writers on "messianism" in the Latin West and North Africa, but, like de Lange, not actual instances of end-time activities: Wolfram Kinzig, "The West and North Africa," 198–214. A search of the volume itself returns virtually no hits for any of the incidents discussed in the present article.

2 Severus of Minorca: Christian End-Time Speculation and the Conversion of Jews

In the early fifth century, a priest named Paul Orosios traveled across the Mediterranean, transporting relics of the protomartyr, Stephen, whose remains were said to have been exhumed in the Holy Land only a few years earlier.[12] The arrival of the relics prompted Christians on the island of Minorca to pressure Minorcan Jews to convert, under the aegis of the recently appointed bishop, Severus. On Saturday, February 2, 418, after a day of tense verbal confrontations, the synagogue in the eastern port of Magona burned. By the end of that week, sometimes in response to pressure, sometimes in response to numerous small miracles, all 540 Jews accepted Christ, and began construction on a new Christian basilica, probably on the site of the old synagogue. Minorcan Christians rejoiced.

Much of our evidence for events on Minorca comes from the so-called *Letter on the Conversion of the Jews*, which explicitly claims to be written by Severus himself.[13] Of particular interest is the closing of the *Letter*, which its author represents as an encyclical whose readers he now exhorts to "take up Christ's zeal against the Jews, but do so for the sake of their eternal salvation."[14] The conversion of the Jews of Minorca, he writes, may portend the fulfillment of Paul's end-time expectations: "Perhaps

---

[12] *Revelatio Sancti Stephani* (PL 41:807–81, as the *Epistula Luciani*); Evodius, *De miraculis sancta Stephani protomartyris* (PL 41:833–54); *The Passion of St. Stephen*, trans. M. van Esbroeck, "Jean II de Jérusalem et les cultes de S. Étienne, de la Sainte-Sion et de la Croix," *Analecta Bollandiana* 102 (1984): 1–2, 101–5.

[13] Critical edition, lengthy introduction, translation and brief notes Bradbury, *Severus of Minorca, Letter*; also J. Amengual i Batle, *Orígens del cristianisme a les Balears i el seu desenvolupament fins a l'època musulmana* (Palma de Mallorca: Universitat de les Illes Balears, Facultat de Filosofia i Lletres, 1991). Additional reference to these events may be found in correspondence between Consentius and Augustine, whose account Severus may have utilized, particularly Letter *12. Latin text ed. Johannes Divjak, *Sancti Aureli Augustini Opera: Epistolae ex Duobus Codicibus nuper in lucem Prolatae*, Corpus Scriptorum Ecclesiasticorum Latinorum 88 (Vienna: Hölder-Pichler-Tempsky, 1981); English translation in Robert B. Eno, trans., *Augustine, Letters* 6: 1*–29*, Fathers of the Church 81 (Washington, DC: Catholic University Press), 1989; S. J. Roland Teske, trans., *The Works of Saint Augustine: A Translation for the 21st Century*, Letters 211–270, 1*–29*, Hyde Park: NY: New City Press, 2005, 279–86.

[14] *Letter* 31.2.

that time predicted by the Apostle has indeed now come when the fullness of the Gentiles will have come and all Israel shall be saved."[15]

Numerous New Testament passages authorized ancient Christian desires to convert the entire inhabited world. In Matthew 28:19, for instance, the resurrected Jesus instructs his disciples to "go now and make disciples of all nations."[16] But it is particularly Paul's letter, Romans 9–11, that links the conversion of the Jews to the fulfillment of the divine plan for salvation, and on which the *Letter* of Severus explicitly relies as justification for its thinly veiled call for Christians elsewhere to employ the tactics that were apparently so successful on Minorca, of intimidation and arson. "And perhaps the Lord wished to kindle this spark from the ends of the earth, so that the whole breadth of the earth might be ablaze with the flame of love in order to burn down the forest of unbelief."[17]

As Bradbury points out in his 1996 edition and translation that brought the *Letter* to the attention of scholars of Late Antiquity, in so doing, Severus takes a position at odds with such major figures as Augustine. The bishop of Hippo, he notes, wrote a particularly extensive denunciation of end-time speculation in precisely the same year that events on Minorca transpired, 418.[18] But as he also points out, beyond the calamities that had afflicted the entire region, Spain in particular had been subjected to extensive turmoil with the Germanic invasions, which all but severed it from control by the court at Ravenna, and which may have contributed to heightened end-time speculation in the region. While acknowledging that millennial ideas are absent from Severus' narrative as a whole, Bradbury thinks that they "provided an intellectual framework in which the deliberate provocation of communal violence could be understood and in some sense justified."[19] In this instance, at least, end-time speculation provided a rationale, if not necessarily the impetus, for concerted efforts to coerce the conversion of Jews, through

---

[15] *Letter* 31.3. Severus' Latin, "plenitudine gentium," conforms to the Vulgate for *to plerōma ton ethnōn* (Rom 11:25).

[16] In contrast to his earlier instructions in Matt 10:5 to go "nowhere among the Gentiles, and enter no town of the Samaritans, but go rather to the lost sheep of the house of Israel."

[17] *Letter* 31.4.

[18] Augustine, *Letters*, 197–99: Bradbury, *Severus of Minorca, Letter*, 52, 129.

[19] Bradbury, *Severus of Minorca, Letter*, 51–52.

a complex combination of arson, intimidation, and some violence on the one hand, and offers of affection and economic advantage on the other.[20]

3 SOCRATES OF CONSTANTINOPLE: A MOSAIC PRETENDER AND THE CONVERSION OF JEWS ON CRETE

Ancient accounts of mass Jewish conversions like that of the *Letter* of Severus are actually quite rare.[21] Socrates of Constantinople's *History of the Church*, written in the latter part of the fifth century, contains a brief account of Jewish mass conversion that occurred on another island, Crete, sometime soon after 431.[22] Unlike Severus' account of the events on Minorca about fourteen years earlier, there's not even a hint that Christians in any way instigated or orchestrated these events, let alone engaged in violence or coercion. They were not precipitated by Christian millennial fervor. Rather, the prior year, a Jewish man appeared on Crete, claiming to be Moses, sent again from heaven to lead the Jews safely through the sea to the land of promise (*tēn gēn tēs epaggelias*). For an entire year, he traveled to several cities on the island, urging Jews to believe him. He exhorted them to relinquish their money and property, which many did, abandoning their businesses and giving away their resources.

On an appointed day, he then led a substantial number of Jews (women, children and men) to a promontory overlooking the sea and ordered them to throw themselves off. Those who did so died when they hit the rocks,

---

[20] For further discussion, see Ross S. Kraemer, "Jewish Women's Resistance to Christianity in the Early Fifth Century: The Account of Severus, Bishop of Minorca," *Journal of Early Christian Studies* 17 (2009): 4: 635–65; also as "Artemisia of Minorca: Gender and the Conversion of the Jews in the Fifth Century," in Ross Shepard Kraemer, *Unreliable Witnesses: Religion, Gender and History in the Greco-Roman Mediterranean* (New York and Oxford, Oxford University Press, 2011), 153–78; Kraemer, *Mediterranean Diaspora*. The appeal to Romans 9–11 might be a rhetorical strategy rather than a genuine reflection of such beliefs. There's no way to know, although one might wonder why the author needed that particular tactic.

[21] One of the only other comparable narratives is that of Gregory of Tours, *History of the Franks*, 5.11, on the Jews of Clermont: Kraemer, *Mediterranean Diaspora*.

[22] On the date, see Pieter van der Horst, "The Jews of Ancient Crete," *Journal of Jewish Studies* 39 (1988): 1: 183–200, here 191, reprinted in *Jews and Christians in Their Graeco-Roman Context* (Tübingen: Mohr Siebeck, 2006), 12–27. All citations are from the initial publication.

or drowned in the sea. Providentially, Socrates claims, some Christian fishermen and merchants happened to be there. They rescued some Jews from drowning, and warned those who had not yet leapt of the fate of those who had. In the aftermath, the Jews came to their senses, and sought to find the false Moses and kill him. When they could not find him, they speculated that he was in reality a malevolent being who had assumed human form in order to destroy them. But where this might then have prompted the resumption of their lives and relief that he had not succeeded in destroying them, the story ends with the conversion of many Jews, who "as a result of this experience...bid farewell to Judaism (*Ioudaismos*) and attached themselves to belief in Christianity (*Christianismos*)."[23]

It's difficult to assess the historicity of any aspect of this account. As the *Letter* of Severus is the only literary account of Jews on Minorca, so Socrates' account is the only literary evidence for Jews on Crete in the later Roman period.[24] There is very little archaeological data: currently, only three inscriptions from late antique Crete can be classified with certainty as Jewish, and their dates are contested.[25] Interestingly, they come from different parts of the island, consonant with Socrates' claim that the false Moses sought followers in its several cities.

Scholars who have written on this episode have often argued for some historical kernel. Just as Bradbury connects early fifth-century Christian millennial expectations with historical and ecological events so, too, van der Horst adduces these as possible triggers for the Jewish episode[26] on Crete, together with even more proximate events such as the arrival of Vandals

---

[23] On the possible valences of these terms, see Steve Mason, "Jews, Judeans, Judaizing, Judaism: Problems of Categorization in Ancient History," *Journal for the Study of Judaism* 38 (2007): 457–512.

[24] Van der Horst, "Ancient Crete."

[25] David Noy, Alexander Panayatov and Hanswulf Bloedhorn, eds., *Inscriptiones Judaicae Orientis* (hereafter *IJO*), vol. 1: *Eastern Europe*, Texts and Studies in Ancient Judaism 101 (Tübingen: Mohr Siebeck, 2004), Cre1-3. For additional discussion of inscriptions now excluded from *IJO*, see van der Horst, "Ancient Crete," who was unaware of *IJO* 1, Cre2, published in 1990, a Greek epitaph, perhaps imperial period, for a husband and wife whose names, Josephos and Berenike, suggest that they are Jews. Van der Horst rightly points out (concurring with my own earlier position) that many inscriptions by Jews may well not be recognizable as such, a larger problem with ancient inscriptions.

[26] Van der Horst terms this a "messianic movement," "Ancient Crete," 191, but I have deliberately chosen to redescribe it without utilizing the term "messiah" for the false Moses, or the term "movement" for the participants.

in North Africa in 430. The various harsh restrictions imposed on Jews by Christian emperors might have increased Jewish suffering and heightened Jewish interest in millennial offerings.[27] Van der Horst hypothesizes that the timing of the Crete episode, precisely 300 years after the messianic bar Kokhba revolt, might reflect renewed messianic hopes in the early-mid 430s.[28] Christians were not the only ones engaged in end-time calculations: van der Horst notes that several passages from the Babylonian Talmud calculate the messiah's appearance to be due somewhere between 365 and 400 years after the fall of Jerusalem in 70,[29] including a saying ascribed to R. Ashi that one should not expect the messiah before the eighty-fifth jubilee, i.e., 440–490 C.E.[30] Although I am in general deeply wary of using rabbinic sources as evidence for the thought and practice of Greek and Latin-speaking Jews in the Mediterranean diaspora, it seems plausible that Jews outside the rabbinic orbit might also have engaged in similar calculations and speculation.

---

[27] Among the various laws restricting Jews issued by Christian emperors in the late fourth and early fifth centuries are an edict by Honorius in March 418, excluding Jews from the public offices of Executive Agents and Palatini, permitting those currently in office to serve out their terms, and dismissing Jews from the military (*Codex Theodosianus* 16.8.24, in Amnon Linder, *The Jews in Roman Imperial Legislation* (Detroit: Wayne State, 1987), no. 45 (hereafter *JRIL*) and a law of Theodosios II in 423 (*CTh* 16.8.25; *JRIL*, no. 47), prohibiting the construction of new synagogues (while also prohibiting attacks on synagogues and permitting their repair). In addition to *JRIL*, see also Linder, "The Legal Status of Jews in the Byzantine Empire," in *Jews in Byzantium: Dialectics of Minority and Majority Cultures*, ed., R. Bonfil et al., Jerusalem Studies in Religion and Culture 14 (Boston and Leiden: Brill, 2012), 149–217. For the Theodosian Code itself, the Sources Chretiennes edition is particularly helpful: Jean Rougé, trans., *Les Lois Religieuses des Empereurs Romains de Constantin à Théodose II (312–438)*, vol. 1: *Code Théodosien Livre XVI*, Introduction et notes, Roland Delmaire, SC 497 (Paris: Éditions du Cerf, 2005); Jean Rougé and R. Delmaire, trans., *Les Lois Religieuses des Empereurs Romains de Constantin à Théodose II (312–438)*, vol. 2: *Code Théodosien Livre I-XV, Code Justinien, Constitutions Sirmondiennes*, Introduction et notes, Roland Delmaire, SC 531 (Paris: Éditions du Cerf, 2009). A full treatment of imperial restrictions on Jews (as well as on all non-orthodox persons) is far beyond the scope of this article: for extensive discussion, see Kraemer, *Mediterranean Diaspora*.

[28] Van der Horst, "Ancient Crete," 191.

[29] *b. Avodah Zarah* 9a-b, *b. Sanhedrin* 97a-b and 99a; on which see van der Horst, "Ancient Crete," 198.

[30] *b. Sanhed* 97b. Afterwards one may expect him (*b. Sanhed* 97b). Ashi appears to have sought to tamp down messianic speculation, rather than to support it: he is thought to have worked in the 5th century.

Intriguingly, Socrates' story lacks many of the stereotypical elements found in Severus' account, and in other Christian conversion narratives: no Jewish resistance to Christ, no conflict or scriptural contestations with Christians, no coercion (subtly masked or otherwise), no references to the guiding hand of Christ, no miraculous occurrences of any kind. Stripped of its opening and closing frames, nothing in the story points to a denouement in which Jews convert to Christianity, solely as a result of their disillusionment with the false Moses and the kindness of their Christian neighbors. At the same time, this episode bears considerable resemblance to episodes in many other contexts which are often categorized as millenarian.[31] A person appears in a community we perceive to be under duress (although Socrates does not acknowledge this aspect), claiming to have divine authorization, and promising to deliver followers into a better realm. He offers not a pragmatic solution to their situation,[32] but an otherworldly one, drawing on a highly valued culturally specific paradigm, in this case a re-enactment of the liberation from Egypt. Members of the community are urged to divest themselves of their earthly possessions, perhaps as the Israelites in Egypt were thought to have done, in preparation for their coming salvation (which we might envision to have taken place on Pesach, although Socrates gives no indication of when "the appointed day" was). It is particularly interesting that the person whom Socrates claims instigated these events is said to have represented himself as a new Moses, rather than a claimant to the Davidic throne.[33] Traditions about a prophet like Moses (Deut. 18:18) had particular salience for Samaritans, but Socrates is quite clear that this episode involved Jews, for whom such instances are not

---

[31] I have in mind here a paradigm analyzed by Kenelm Burridge, *New Heaven, New Earth: A Study of Millenarian Activities* (New York: Schocken, 1969). See more recently Catherine Wessinger, ed. *The Oxford Handbook of Millennialism* (New York and Oxford: Oxford University Press, 2011), with extensive bibliographies. Despite the volume's many contributions on historical instances, the chapter by James Tabor, "Early Jewish and Christian Millennialism," 252–66 considers no instances after 200 C.E. and a search of the entire volume for "Samaritans" produces no results.

[32] For instance, actual overthrow of the current government, or emigration to a less-pressured locale, although I recognize that neither of these is likely to have feasible, if for different reasons.

[33] These expectations might, hypothetically at least, be seen to coalesce in a single person, but this is not the case in the Crete episode, where the pseudo-Moses seems to make no claims to royalty or political transformation.

without historical precedent. Centuries earlier, Josephus wrote of an "impostor" named Theudas, who "persuaded a majority of the masses to take up their possessions" and follow him to the Jordan River, which he would then part. This seeming symbolic reenactment of a reverse Exodus evoked the figure of Moses, and perhaps also Deut 18:18, that God would ultimately send the Israelites a "prophet like Moses."[34] Nevertheless, this paradigm is far less well attested among Jews than that of persons aspiring to reinstitute the theocratic monarchy.

In the end, though, the expectations of Jews on Crete are proven false, at a cruelly high price, and those who survive are forced to address the resulting cognitive dissonance.[35] Thus it seems worth considering that Socrates here does present us with evidence for a failed Jewish millenarian episode on Crete in the mid-fifth century, whether or not it then led some of those Jews to leave their ancestral practices and take up those of the Christians said to have so kindly rescued them.

4 The *Life of the Monk Barsauma*: Another Jewish End-Time Moment in Fifth-Century Jerusalem?

A different account of a Jewish restoration episode just a few years after that on Crete comes from the Syriac *Life of Barsauma*, a Christian monk who is valorized for his repeated violence against both Jews and practitioners of traditional religions in the region of Syria-Palestine in the first half of the fifth century.[36] When the Empress Eudocia, wife of

---

[34] *Judean Antiquities* 20.5.1. The several similarities here are mildly provocative, and might be more so if we thought Socrates (or someone else) had knowledge of the account in Josephus.

[35] The classic work here is Leon Festinger, Henry W. Riecken, and Stanley Schacter, *When Prophecy Fails* (Minneapolis: University of Minnesota Press, 1956). For some application of these analyses to earliest Christianity, see John G. Gager, *Kingdom and Community: The Social World of Early Christianity* (Englewood Cliffs, NJ: Prentice-Hall, 1975). Other particularly salient historical instances include the seventeenth-century movement around Shabbatai Zvi and more recently the messianic candidacy of the Lubavitcher rebbe Menachem Schneerson, on which see, inter alia, Simon Dein, *Lubavitcher Messianism: What Really Happens When Prophecy Fails?* (New York: Continuum, 2011).

[36] A new Syriac edition of the text is forthcoming, together with an English translation by Andrew Palmer, *The Life of Barsawmo of the Northern Mountain*, in *Die syrische Vita Barsauma: Edition, Übersetzung und Analyse*, ed. J. Hahn and V. Menze (forthcoming). Especially helpful for the historiography of the *Life* is the somewhat apologetic but still

Theodosios II, was in Palestine, the Jews of the Galilee and surrounding areas told her that Constantine had forbidden them from living in the environs of Jerusalem and asked her for permission to pray at the ruins of the temple built by Solomon, which she granted. In this account, a seemingly minor permission to pray at the temple mount morphs into something very different. The Jews sent letters "to all the Jews of Persia and the great cities of the Roman empire," announcing that the end of the dispersion and the day of reunion of the Jewish people had arrived. They urged their fellow Jews to hasten to Jerusalem for Sukkoth, as the Roman kings have decreed that Jerusalem is to be returned, and the Jewish kingdom re-established there.[37] The account in the *Life* indicts these false expectations.

On the first day of Sukkoth, a crowd of 103,000 Jewish men and women assembled at the site of the ruined temple. That they are dressed in black and weeping may undercut the claim that they have come to witness the restoration of Jerusalem. Suddenly, heavenly troops stone many of the Jews, who, ignorant of their true attackers, instead accuse the disciples of Barsauma, who had come to see what would transpire on that day. (Conveniently, the *Life* claims that the monk himself was not present in Jerusalem at the time). Since harming the Jews had been forbidden by the Empress, Barsauma's disciples were then arrested and beaten. A group of Romans, Christian clerics and Jews then appear before the empress at her palace at Bethlehem, charging that many monks had come from Mesopotamia and attacked Jerusalem, murdering many people and leaving their bodies littered in public places, including courtyards and cisterns. The disciples are exonerated when the bodies of the dead Jews turn out not to have stab wounds as the Jews have alleged, and the chief of the Jews realizes that heaven itself was responsible for the attacks. Eudocia comes under threats for her apparent support of the Jews—having granted their request to pray on the site of the Temple,

---

valuable article by Palmer, "The West-Syrian Monastic Founder Barsawmo: A Historical Review of the Scholarly Literature," in *Orientalia Christiana: Festschrift für Hubert Kaufhold zum 70. Geburtstag*, ed. Peter Bruns and Heinz Otto Luthe (Wiesbaden: Harrassowitz Verlag, 2013), 399–414. The works of Barsauma are divided into "signs and wonders," that seem to evoke the language of Deut 6:22 for the things which God did against the Egyptians, both in Hebrew and Syriac (as well as other biblical passages). The specific section here is the 50th "wonder." I thank Robert Doran for his assistance with the Syriac here.

[37] The *Life* claims to quote the letter in full.

and trusted their mistaken accusations against the innocent disciples. Ultimately, a series of miracles vindicates Barsauma and his monks, and verifies that heaven had stoned the Jews, presumably for their impiety and presumption that their kingdom was about to be restored.

Here, too, what may actually have transpired in Jerusalem is extremely difficult to discern through the thicket of Christian interests. The precise date is debated. Many scholars connect this episode with a lengthy law of Theodosios, of January 438, six sections of which consolidate and reiterate restrictions on the participation of Jews and Samaritans in public life.[38] (A substantial portion of the law similarly targets dissident Christians and traditionalists.) They thus date it to the following fall, but there are good reasons to think that a date after 443 is more likely, when Eudocia moved permanently to the palace at Bethlehem.[39] Numerous elements in the story may be challenged for their obvious Christian interests, including the exoneration of Barsauma and his associates from any charges of violence, and the identification of members of a heavenly army as the true perpetrators, implementing divine judgment against the presumptuous Jews. Yet the story seems to concede the death of some significant number of Jews assembled at the temple site. At the very least, an outbreak of violence by Christian monks against Jewish pilgrims seems plausible, given the prevalence of such occurrences throughout the late antique Mediterranean.[40]

The question remains whether such violence was related to Jewish expectations of restoration, perhaps triggered by some action of the empress. Evidence for the first rests primarily on the language of the alleged letter announcing the restoration of the Jewish kingdom. Such a

---

[38] *Novella* 3, *JRIL*, no. 54.

[39] This argument seems to go back to François Nau, who published substantial sections of the Syriac text, with French translation in the early twentieth century: François Nau, *Revue de l'Orient Chretien* 18 (1913): 170–76; 379–89; 19 (1914): 113–34; 278–89. It seems to have been accepted by numerous scholars, but the issues here are beyond the scope of this article, on which see Kraemer, *Mediterranean Diaspora*. If a date in the early 440s is more likely, the connections with the law of 438 become more tenuous.

[40] The desire to exonerate Barsauma seems to continue in Palmer, who writes (without supporting references): "Scholars state blandly that the *Vita* boasts of a massacre of Jewish pilgrims in the time of the empress Eudocia....[hearing a story about stones falling out of the sky] the author perhaps embroidered his own fantasy that the stones struck the Jews, who in his view ought not to have hoped for the restoration of the Temple" ("Bar Sawmo," 410).

letter might easily be a convenient fabrication by the author of the *Vita* (or someone else), designed to demonstrate the audacity and error of Jewish expectation. One might wonder, certainly, just how the author of the life of a pugilistic Christian monk knew its precise wording. And the disjunction between what Eudocia does (grant a request to pray at a prohibited site) and what the "letter" says (hasten to Jerusalem, the day of redemption is hand), certainly invites skepticism. Yet we might also imagine that some Jews did, in fact, anticipate the restoration of the kingdom on the site of the Temple, during Sukkoth, and did attempt to garner support from Jews outside the immediate region.

If so, what role did Eudocia play? Scholars routinely accept that Jews did petition her to pray on the site of the temple at Sukkoth, and that her consent stemmed from a general sympathy to Jews tracing back to her youth.[41] She was the daughter of a traditionalist teacher of rhetoric, educated in traditional philosophy and religion. Only a month after her marriage to Theodosios II in January, 423, her uncle, Asklepiodotes, was appointed Praetorian Prefect. During Asklepiodotes's short tenure, the emperor promulgated several laws protecting synagogues and the rights of Jews, which scholars have seen as indications of the Jewish sympathies of both the Prefect and his niece, but the evidence is ambiguous at best. As a young woman, Eudocia may have had little sympathy for Christians yet some sympathy for Jews and Samaritans who, like traditionalists, were the targets of Christian antagonism. But even if that was initially the case, there are other indications that by this point in her life, Eudocia was not necessarily so kindly disposed toward Jews. On her first visit to Jerusalem, she engaged in numerous public performances demonstrating her orthodox piety. She attended the consecration of a church to St. Stephen,[42] whose strong associations with anti-Judaism were considerably heightened in the fifth century. In the *Life of Barsauma*, she seeks

---

[41] This argument, rarely subject to critical assessment, was made especially by Nau in two articles pertaining to these events: "Deux épisodes de l'histoire juive sous Théodose II (423 and 438), d'après la vie de Barsauma le Syrienm," *Revue des Études Juives* 83 (1927): 184–206 and "Sur la synagogue de Rabbat Moab (422), et un mouvement sioniste favorisé par l'impératrice Eudocie (438), d'après la Vie de Barsauma le Syrien," *Journal Asiatique* 210 (1927): 189–91.

[42] For details, see Kenneth G. Holum, *Theodosian Empresses: Women and Imperial Dominion in Late Antiquity* (Berkeley: University of California Press, 1982), 187.

the favor and blessing of the monk, whose virulent attacks on Jews his biographer praises.

In his insightful study, Kenneth Holum argues that Eudocia's public performances in the Holy Land may have been designed to assert Eudocia's own piety in the face of the intense piety long claimed by her sister-in-law Pulcheria, including devotion to Stephen, and currying favor with stringently ascetic monks. Holum also thinks that Pulcheria was deeply antagonistic to Jews, and either orchestrated or supported numerous Theodosian edicts restricting Jewish rights, including the law of January 438. If Eudocia did grant a petition from Jews to assemble and pray at the temple mount, it might have been less out of support for Jews and more part of her on-going contestations with Pulcheria, who, as the emperor's elder sister, also held the position of empress (Augusta). For Holum, Jews may well have been a proxy for the complex power struggles between the two empresses, struggles which were partly responsible for Eudocia's presence in the Holy Land in the first place. Whether or not this is true, Eudocia may have, deliberately or otherwise, nourished the hopes of Jews for the alleviation of their oppression.

The Jewish letter in the *Life of Barsauma* contains no mention of a messianic candidate, or the person who will be crowned when the kingdom is restored. We might imagine many reasons for this. The letter might be a patent fiction, by an author who failed to notice this crucial omission. Alternatively, the author might have been aware of a real candidate, but deliberately suppressed this, in order not to enable such speculation. Or perhaps there was no royal candidate at that moment, but Jews simply assumed that God would supply one at the opportune time. With the data we have, there is no way to tell.

If this episode does, in fact, reflect an instance of Jewish expectation for the restoration of Israel, is there any relationship between this and the tradition ascribed to R. Ashi in the Babylonian Talmud? The timing is tantalizing, but by no means dispositive. Claiming that the messiah would not come before the 85th Jubilee (that is, not before 440 C.E.), might refute a messianic moment in 438, but would, on the contrary, lend support for one only a few years later (corresponding to later proposed dates for the Sukkoth contestation may well be). Yet again, it is difficult to say, if intriguing to consider.

5 A SAMARITAN EPISODE IN THE LATE FIFTH CENTURY?

One last episode for the fifth century makes clear that end-time expectations characterized not only Jewish and Christian contestations, but those with Samaritans as well. Two sixth-century writers, Procopius of Caesarea and John Malalas, each provide accounts of Samaritan attacks against Christians during the reign of the Constantinopolitan emperor Zeno (474–91).[43] (Scholars regularly date these events to 484, but on the strength of only one later source, the *Chronichon Pascale*.[44]) Writing about Neapolis in Palestine, Procopius narrates how, precisely, the prophecy of Jesus came at this time to be fulfilled, that "thereafter, the Samaritans would not worship (*proskynēsousin*) on this mountain, but that the true worshippers, the Christians, would worship [God] there." (This is clearly a reference to Jesus's conversation with a Samaritan woman in the Gospel of John, although, as will become more relevant later, in that passage, Jesus does not, in fact, predict that "true worshippers" or anyone else will worship on Mt Gerizim.[45]) Samaritans had been accustomed to going up on the mountain to pray, "not because they had ever built any temple (*neōn*) there, but because they worshipped

---

[43] Procopius, *Buildings* 5.7.1–17; Malalas, *Chronicle* Bk. 15:8 [382–83]. Texts and translations in, inter alia, Reinhard Pummer, *Early Christian Authors on Samaritans and Samaritanism: Texts, Translations and Commentary*, Texts and Studies in Ancient Judaism 92 (Tübingen: J.C.B. Mohr [Paul Siebeck], 2002), with discussion of the events under Zeno on 256–59 (on Malalas); 288–94 (on Procopius). The Greek text in Hans Thurn, *John Malalas, Chronographia* (Berlin: Walter de Gruyter, 2000), was not available for the 1986 English translation of Malalas, which should be used with caution: Elizabeth Jeffreys, Michael Jeffreys, and Roger Scott, et al., *The Chronicle of John Malalas: A Translation*, Byzantina Australiensia 4 (Melbourne: Australian Association for Byzantine Studies, 1986). See also Leah Di Segni, "*Early Christian Authors on Samaritans and Samaritanism*: A Review Article," *Journal for the Study of Judaism* 37 (2006): 241–259; eadem, "The Samaritans in Roman-Byzantine Palestine: Some Misapprehensions," in *Religious and Ethnic Communities in Later Roman Palestine*, ed. H. Lapin (College Park, MD: University Press of Maryland, 1998), 51–66.

[44] Pummer, *Early Christian Authors*, 256.

[45] Somewhat to the contrary, in Jn 4:21, Jesus says, "Believe me, woman, the hour is coming when neither on this mountain nor in Jerusalem will you will worship the father." In 4:23, he says "But the hour is coming, and is now, when the true worshippers will worship the Father in spirit and truth." Pummer apparently takes this as evidence of Procopius' own deviousness, but di Segni ("Review," 254) sees it as a deliberate misquotation by Terebinthius to persuade Zeno to avenge the Christians.

the summit itself with the greatest reverence."[46] Procopius then relates a series of contestations between Samaritans and Christians over the site. In the first, which occurred while Zeno was emperor, Samaritans "suddenly banded together" and attacked Christians in Neapolis (the Samaritan home city at the base of Mt. Gerizim), who were celebrating Pentecost, killing many. In particular, they assaulted the bishop Terebinthius while he was offering the Eucharist, slicing off his fingers. The bishop then went to Zeno to seek retribution, reminding the emperor of the divine prophecy that opens Procopius' account. Zeno responded immediately. The Samaritans were forced off the mountain, which was turned over, as predicted, to Christians. Zeno then built a church on the summit dedicated to the Theotokos, protecting it with a stone wall. Soldiers were garrisoned in the city below, with a small number at the fortified church. The Samaritans remained aggrieved but did nothing further until some years later, in the reign of Anastasius (491–518), when they mounted a brief unsuccessful attack on the site.[47]

Malalas' account of Samaritan contestation during the reign of Zeno differs substantially from that of Procopius. As Malalas tells it, Samaritans rebelled and crowned a man named Justasas, here denigrated as a "robber-chief" (*lēstarchos*). Subsequently, while Porphyry was the governor of First Palestine, Justasas went into Caesarea (not Neapolis), where

---

[46] *oudena anientes kairon ouk hoti veōn tina entautha ōkodomēsato pōpote, alla tēn akrōreian autēn sebomenoi etethēpesam pantōn malista.* This is a somewhat surprising claim. According to Josephus, *Judean Antiquities* 13.275–276 [cf. *Judean War* 1.64–65] there had been a Samaritan temple on a Mt. Gerizim, destroyed by John Hyrcanus in the second century BCE, although whether Procopius knew that cannot be determined. Pummer thinks there was one, but he concedes that the matter is complicated, and that archaeological excavations have not yet (as of 2000 or so) found unequivocal proof for it: *Christian Authors*, 289. Di Segni ("Review") notes that Samaritan tradition to this day denies that there was a temple on Mt. Gerizim. And certainly, in John 4, there is no mention of Samaritans worshipping at a temple, but only "on" the mountain itself (although by the first century, there would not have been one in many years).

[47] The Samaritans went up a steep but unguarded rear path to the church, killed the few guards there, and shouted for Samaritan compatriots from the city below. These, however, were afraid of the soldiers in the city and failed to come to the support of the attackers. Procopius attributes the Samaritan assault to the suggestion of an unidentified woman, which invites analysis as a rhetorical move grounded on widespread ancient characterizations of men who act badly at the behest of women. Not long after, Procopius of Edessa, governor of the area, arrested and executed the perpetrators.

he watched (*etheōrēsen*) chariot races, and slaughtered many people.[48] Justasas also burnt the *Hagion Prokopion* while Timothy was bishop of Caesarea. The *dux* of Palestine, Asklepiades, then went after him, together with Rheges, called, perhaps too conveniently, *lēstodiōktēs* (robber-police),[49] and other forces. Justasas was caught and decapitated. His severed head, complete with its crown, was sent to Zeno. Immediately, the emperor then made the Samaritan synagogue, which was on Mt. Gerizim, into a chapel to the holy Theotokos Mary, and restored the *Prokopion*. Finally, he issued an edict prohibiting Samaritans from military service[50] and confiscated the property of the wealthy among them. Malalas concludes with the observation that there was "fear and peace."

Both accounts result in the building of a shrine or church to the Theotokos on Mt. Gerizim. Other than this, they have little in common, as numerous scholars have noted, and many substantial differences. They take place in different locations, whether Neapolis in Procopius or Caesarea in Malalas. They identify different Christian targets of Samaritan aggression—the church in Neapolis in Procopius, or the *Prokopion* in Malalas. Apart from Zeno himself, the cast of characters is almost entirely different. Justasas appears only in Malalas; in Procopius, no Samaritan leader is even mentioned, let alone captured and decapitated. Each account specifies a different Christian bishop, namely Terebinthius of Neapolis in Procopius and Timothy of Caesarea in Malalas. In Procopius' account, other than the emperor himself, no imperial officials or forces play any role. It is Zeno who inflicts punishment on the offenders, drives the Samaritans from the mountain, builds and dedicates the church and establishes the garrison. In Malalas, by contrast, Justasas is pursued by the *dux*, the *lēstodiōktēs*, and other official forces. Procopius' account begins with a denial that the Samaritans ever had a cult building on

[48] Jeffries et al. read "many Christians," but the more recent edition of Thurn (305) considers this erroneous.

[49] The only occurrence cited in G. W. H. Lampe, *A Patristic Greek Lexicon* (Oxford: Clarendon, 1961), 801, is this reference in Malalas, and the later account in the *Chronicon Paschale*, almost certainly following Malalas.

[50] *mē strateuesthai*. Jeffries et al., translate this as "public *service*" (emphasis mine), an interpretation followed by others, including Pummer, but its ordinary meaning is as I have translated it here (e.g. Lampe, s.v.), and such a translation makes the edict more consistent with the Samaritan transgression. Linder takes the Latin militia in *Sirmondian Constitutions* 6 (*JRIL* 51) in 425 to prohibit Jews from lower administrative echelons, but Delmaire argues (SC 531, 495, no. 1) that the term included both military service and various bureaucratic positions.

Gerizim, while Malalas insists they had a synagogue there, which Zeno "immediately" made into a shrine to the Theotokos. His language fosters the impression that the synagogue was quickly consecrated as a shrine with minimal alteration. Procopius makes no mention of any legal actions against the Samaritans that figure in Malalas' account. Where Malalas concludes with the statement that "there was fear [*phobos*] and peace,"[51] Procopius claims that the Samaritans continued to be angry and resentful, serving as a segue into further accounts of Samaritan resistance under Anastasius and then Justinian.

While differing substantially from Procopius', Malalas' account here has some striking similarities to his portrayal of a subsequent far more substantial Samaritan revolt under Justinian, almost a half century later. Both accounts claim, in identical language, that the Samaritans "rebelled and crowned a bandit-chief named" either Justasas (in the first instance) or Julian (in the second).[52] Even the similarity of their names is intriguing. Justasas is said to burn the *Prokopion* and kill many people: Julian's rebel forces burn churches and estates and kill many Christians. Justasas enters Caesarea and watches (*etheōrēsen*) chariot races. Julian enters Neapolis, watches chariot races (*etheōrēsen*), and has the victorious charioteer beheaded when he learns that the conveniently named Nikeas is a Christian. Justasas is pursued by the *dux* of Palestine, the *lestodioktes*, and various forces; Julian is pursued by the *dux* and the *phylarchon* of Palestine. Both were apprehended and executed, and their decapitated heads, with their crowns, sent to the emperor.

Malalas' account of the revolt under Justinian differs from his own account of that under Zeno particularly in its framing and its conclusion. It begins with Samaritan outbreaks against both Christians[53] and Jews, causing Justinian to depose the governor. In response, the Samaritans then crown Julian. After Julian's death, 20,000 Samaritan men die at the hands of Justinian's forces, while others flee to Gerizim and Trachon. Another 20,000 Samaritan boys and girls (*paidōn kai korasiōn*) are sold into slavery in Persia/India. Justinian dismisses the *dux* for failure to put down the revolt earlier, and slaughters many of the remaining Samaritans

---

[51] Alternatively, "fear, yet peace."

[52] The name is plausible enough, at least for a Samaritan: it is, in any case, evocative of the "apostate" emperor Julian.

[53] An elaboration on these attacks on Christians occurs in Constantine Porphyrogenitus, *De excerpta insidiis*: in Thurn, *Malalas*.

holed up in the mountains. Many issues concerning a Samaritan revolt under Justinian lie beyond the (somewhat artificial) scope of this brief contribution, not the least of which is a third major account by another sixth-century author, Cyril of Scythopolis.[54] But at the very least, these similarities and differences justify skepticism about Malalas' account of a Samaritan revolt under Zeno.[55]

Is it possible that during the reign of Zeno, end-time expectations were implicated in Samaritan violence? It's important to note here that Samaritan sources envision a future restoration quite distinct from those of Jews, often centered on the appearance of the Taheb, the prophet like Moses promised in Deut. 18:15, 18, rather than a royal figure with Davidic lineage.[56] However we may discount its historical value, Malalas' account reads as an instance of yet another outbreak of anti-imperial hostility and violence, without any acknowledgment of the particular religious claims that Justasas or his followers might have made. Unquestionably, there are elements of religious contestation: Justasas burns a church (not, say, a public bath), and Zeno retaliates both by rebuilding that church, and transforming a Samaritan synagogue on the summit of the mountain into a chapel to the Theotokos. Zeno's two

---

[54] Cyril of Scythopolis, *Life of (Saint) Saba*, in Pummer, *Christian Authors*, no. 140. Pummer has a lengthy discussion of the revolt: *Christian Authors*, 259–69 and passim; di Segni, "Review."

[55] Di Segni also points out that the archaeological data favors Procopius here: excavations of the remains of a church to the Theotokos on Mt. Gerizim above Neapolis indicate that it was built de novo, not on the ruins of an earlier building, synagogue or otherwise. While these questions are beyond the scope of this article, see most recently Reinhard Pummer, "Was There an Altar or a Temple in the Sacred Precinct on Mt. Gerizim?" *Journal for the Study of Judaism* 47 (2016): 1–21. Pummer, *Christian Authors*, 256, no. 30, is dismissive of di Segni's position (in her "Metropolis and Provincia in Byzantine Palestine," in *Caesarea Maritima: A Retrospective After Two Millennia*, ed. A. Rabban and K. G. Holum, Documental et Monumenta Orientis Antiqui, 21 [Leiden: Brill, 1996], 586, no. 64) that the two accounts in Malalas are duplicative, but this seems eminently reasonable to me.

[56] On the Taheb, see F. Dexinger, *Der Taheb: Ein "messianicher" Heilsbringer Samaritaner*. Kairos. Religionswissenschaftliche Studien 3 (Salzburg: Otto Müller, 1986). Pummer notes that the earliest Christian testimony to this comes in Eulogius, in the sixth century, but he does not include this in his anthology: *Christian Authors*, 9.

edicts lack overtly religious dimensions: Samaritans are prohibited from military service and the property of wealthy Samaritans is confiscated.[57]

But whether religious contestation invariably entails end-time expectations, messianic or otherwise, and whether such expectations may be implied here is by no means clear. Two small details in the account of Justasas hint at these: his crowning and his "watching" of chariot races, both of which might be associated with claims to kingship.[58] His crowning is far more obvious, especially when his severed head is sent to Zeno still wearing its presumptuous diadem. The reference to "watching" chariot races may seem more of a stretch, until we parse Malalas' second account, where Julian does not simply attend the races, but presides over them even if his actions parody that of a rightful ruler. And if we may read Justasas as a royal pretender, it is not too far a stretch to think that a Samaritan pretender to kingship was also asserting a messianic claim, or at least that Samaritans might construe it as such.

Interestingly then, in Procopius' account of the occurrences under Zeno, precisely the elements that might construct Justasas as a messianic pretender are conspicuously absent.[59] First and perhaps foremost, the Samaritans in Procopius have no leader at all: no one to crown, no one to play the role of ruler at chariot races, no one whose decapitated head can be sent to Constantinople. Further, in Procopius, the language of rebellion that permeates both of Malalas' accounts is strikingly absent here. Without Malalas' counter-narrative, we might have no reason to wonder whether Procopius has here stripped an account of a Samaritan revolt of

---

[57] Pummer comments that no edict against Samaritans in public service is known to have promulgated by Zeno, but he allows that Zeno might have re-issued *Novella* 3 of Theodosios, from 438 (*Christian Authors*, 257). He doesn't seem to have noticed that these laws actually look like the anti-Samaritan edicts of Justinian, e.g. *Codex Justinianus* 1.15.17, which calls for the destruction of existing Samaritan synagogues; prohibits new ones; and requires that Samaritans can only have orthodox heirs. The law is described at length but not quoted in Alfred Rabello, "The Samaritans in Justinian's Corpus Iuris Civilis," *Israel Law Review* 31 (1997): 724–43, reprinted with original pagination in his *The Jews in the Roman Empire: Legal Problems, From Herod to Justinian*, (Ashgate: Variorum, 2000). The relationship of these laws to the revolt of 529 is unclear. In Procopius, they are issued before the revolt, and thus potentially part of its cause, but in Cyril of Scythopolis account they are its consequence.

[58] Pummer, *Christian Authors*, 257, takes the crowning this way.

[59] In the interests of space, I will not pursue further what Procopius says about the revolt under Justinian.

precisely the elements that index its religious framing. (This being said, one might observe that all revolt in the fifth-century empire necessarily contained religious implications, given the presumption that political authority was inextricably linked with divine favor and authorization).

But if this is what Procopius did, he was not the only one to do so. While we lack external attestation of the other events considered in this article, we do have a relevant Samaritan account of persecution under Zeno that similarly lacks any messianic components, or any representation of revolt. In it, Zeno came to Nablus[60] and tried to force the Samaritans to convert. Those who refused were killed. He took a synagogue built by a priest named'Aqbūn, "and put a throne in it and made in front of it a place of sacrilege." The synagogue was not on the mountain, but at its foot. In one account, Zeno is said to have built a church inside the Temple precinct; another claims he built a convent or a monastery there.[61] One explanation for the differences between this account and that of Malalas is that Samaritans themselves have sanitized the narrative, denying any culpability for revolt, messianic or otherwise.[62]

Whatever Procopius was doing with the sources he had, he provides elements of intra-religious contestation. The violence begins when Samaritans attack Christians in church as they are celebrating the Eucharist. Even the timing is suggestive: they attack not on some random day of the week, or even some random Sunday, but during Pentecost, whose association, if not coincidence, with Shavuot might have seemed an auspicious moment for a Samaritan messianic revolt.[63] But it is critical to recall that Procopius

---

[60] I am indebted here to the account and discussion in Pummer, *Christian Authors*, 258, where he relies on the *Chronicle Adler* (E. N. Adler and M. Séligsohn, "Une novelle chronique samaritaine," *Revue des études juives* 45 [1902]: 235–37); and the Kitāb al-Tarīkh (ed. Paul Stenhouse, *The Kitāb al-Tarīkh of Abu l-Fat*, Translated into English with Notes. Studies in Judaica 1, Sydney, Mandelbaum Trust, 1985), 182–84. Pummer observes that Zeno did not, in fact, ever go to Nablus. One might couch this more cautiously that there is no evidence (other than this account, of course) that Zeno did so.

[61] The *Kitab* and *Chronicle Adler*, respectively.

[62] It seems to me far less likely that Malalas, or the material on which he drew, cast the revolt in such theologically charged terms, but this may require further consideration.

[63] A spring agricultural festival, Shavuoth also celebrates the giving of the Torah, for both Jews and Samaritans. Pummer notes but ultimately disagrees with Katherine Adshead's argument that Procopius was a crypto-Samaritan (converted to Christianity but retaining Samaritan identification): "Procopius and the Samaritans," *Byzantina Australiensia* 10 (1996): 35–41 (cited in Pummer, *Christian Authors*, 292).

explicitly frames these events as the divine fulfillment of a very particular version of Jesus's prophecy in John 4, in which Samaritans both cease to worship on the mountain and are replaced by Christians, who now worship at the newly erected shrine to the Theotokos. Pummer thinks that there really was a Samaritan attack on both the church and the person of Terebinthius, and that the bishop then offered a conveniently altered version of John 4 to Zeno in support of his quest for imperial vengeance. This presumes, of course, either that Zeno did not know his gospels well enough, or was willing to overlook the textual refashioning. It may suggest the same of Procopius. Alternatively, of course, the whole story is a fifth-century "origins" myth for the shrine to the Theotokos on the summit of Mt. Gerizim, whose only verifiable historicity is that it was actually built (on virgin soil, as it were) around this time.

Still. The seventh-century account of the revolt under Justinian in John of Nikiu contains material that makes the royal element explicit, even as his account lacks details such as the name of the royal candidate or the name of the Christian charioteer.[64] "And there was a Samaritan brigand chief who assembled all the Samaritans, and raised a great war, and assumed the royal crown in the city of Nablus and said, 'I am king.' And he seduced many of his people by his lying statement when he declared 'God hath sent me to re-establish the Samaritan kingdom'; just as (Je)roboam the son of Nebat who, reigning after the wise Solomon son of David, seduced the people of Israel and made them serve idols." It's by no means apparent, of course, that John's version of these accounts has any historical merit, let alone that it points to a messianic component in whatever transpired in the erection of a shrine to the Theotokos on Mt. Gerizim. Conversely, however, one might argue that the very erection of such a shrine could be construed as a Christian refutation of Samaritan royal claims, but clearly, Christians regularly erected shrines on contested sites without thereby combating messianic pretensions. And whether, in the fifth century, Samaritans put forth contenders who sought both to contest Christian sovereignty and challenge rival Jewish claims, they unquestionably had done so earlier, and would do so again, marshaling both textual argument and armed resistance against Roman Christian oppression and domination.[65]

---

[64] *Chronicle* 93.4–9 (Ethiopic), cited here from Pummer, *Christian Authors*, 380.

[65] Others include the well-known revolt under Baba Rabbah, whose date is somewhat disputed; the revolt during the reign of Justinian (often dated to 529) and another in 556.

6 CONCLUSION

As is usually the case with sources such as those I have considered here, scrutinizing these episodes yields much skepticism and minimal certainty. Nevertheless, they suggest that Christian, Jewish and Samaritan imaginings of end-times were closely interwoven, and intimately related to Christian efforts—orthodox and otherwise—to transform the inhabited world into a homogeneity. The *Letter* of Severus of Minorca illuminates how Christians might position coercion, intimidation and arson as evidence of the fulfillment of Pauline prophecies about the conversion of Jews and the implementation of a divine plan. Intensifying Christian pressure in the fifth century provided fertile ground for Jewish and Samaritan experimentation with end-time speculation and participation in diverse actions they hoped would bring about the end of Christian oppression and domination. Socrates offers us a portrait of Jews duped by a Mosaic pretender who sought otherworldly relief from the difficulties of their lives by flinging themselves into the sea, expecting not death, but transformation. Only the kindness of their Christian neighbors rescued them, in recognition of which they conveniently then embraced precisely the position from which they may have been fleeing. The *Life of Barsauma* gestures toward an alternative expectation of actual earthly restoration of the Israelite monarchy, one that would be brought about, more or less miraculously, by God directly, perhaps in response to a massive demonstration of Jewish penitence.

The accounts of Jews evidence no active resistance, while narratives of Samaritan behavior under Zeno come much closer to an instance of active revolt. This is even more the case for a revolt under Justinian in 559 that lies largely outside the purview of this brief foray. Specific historical contingencies may account for much of this. At the very least, it is worth noting that in the fifth century, while there was unquestionably a Samaritan diaspora, many Samaritans were still living on their ancestral lands, while the vast majority of Jews lived far from theirs, and had been banned at least from Jerusalem for centuries. All four instances, and perhaps many others, may be understood as a product of the complex contestations of the fifth century, amplified by other calamities that we now categorize as natural and human, although ancient persons might well have construed them otherwise.

CHAPTER 10

End Time at Hand: Innocent III, Joachim of Fiore, and the Fourth Crusade

Marcia L. Colish

In October 1204 Pope Innocent III received a letter from Baldwin of Flanders. Rehearsing the history of the Fourth Crusade since 1203, he announced the conquest of Constantinople on 12 April 1204 and his coronation as its first Latin Emperor on 16 May. A canny propagandist, he ascribed the victory to God and omitted the horrors of the city's sack on 13–15 April. Innocent was not Baldwin's sole addressee. For he sent a circular including most of this text to prelates and rulers throughout Europe, reporting the news and requesting recruits for his new regime's defense. The runaway Fourth Crusade had once more ignored Innocent's commands and prohibitions. Innocent was once more presented with a *fait accompli*. Responding to Baldwin on 7 November 1204, the pope wrote as if he himself were actually guiding these events. Seconding Baldwin's joy at this manifestation of God's power, he then turned to power on earth. He placed the Latin Empire under papal protection and adjured Baldwin to reunite the Greek and Latin churches. For Baldwin, papal protection was inconsequential and other concerns more pressing. So, on 13 November 1204, Innocent wrote to the Latin

M. L. Colish (✉)
Department of History, Yale University, New Haven, CT, USA

© The Author(s) 2019
E. Knibbs et al. (eds.), *The End of the World in Medieval Thought and Spirituality*, The New Middle Ages,
https://doi.org/10.1007/978-3-030-14965-9_10

251

clergy in Constantinople, urging them to step up to the plate. Offering an elaborate argument as a vehicle for bringing the Greeks to Rome, Innocent cites Joachim of Fiore's *Expositio in Apocalypsim*. Innocent also alludes to the End Time elsewhere in his crusade-related *oeuvre*. But it is his verbatim quotation of Joachim in his 13 November 1204 letter that has drawn scholarly attention. Some commentators read this text as proof that Innocent was committed to Joachim's vision of the future and, putting his papal stamp of approval on it, he ratified Joachim's thought as thoroughly mainstream. The goal of this paper is to reassess this claim.

First, Joachim. Joachim wrote the *Expositio*, along with two shorter works later incorporated into its introduction, as abbot of Corazzo and resident at the Cistercian monastery of Casamari (1182/3–1185). He gained permission from Pope Lucius III (1184) and Pope Urban III (1186) to leave Corazzo and his duties as abbot in order to write, producing several of his major works in this period. In 1188 Pope Clement III urged him to finish the *Expositio*, which he did in 1200. Meanwhile, having lobbied for the incorporation of Corazzo into the Cistercian order since 1177, he won its acceptance in 1188. Yet, in 1189, Joachim reproached the Cistercians for failing to uphold the monastic ideal and left to found his own community of contemplatives at S. Giovanni in Fiore. The Cistercian response to this rebuff was to expel Joachim as a *fugitivus*, or renegade, at their general chapter meeting in 1192. Pope Celestine III formally approved the Florensian order in 1196.[1]

Joachim's jumping-off point for the passage of the *Expositio* that concerns us is Rev. 12:1–3: "And a great portent appeared in the heavens,

[1] Joachim of Fiore, *Enchiridion Super Apocalypsim*, ed. Edward Kilian Burger (Toronto: PIMS, 1986), 1–3; Joachim of Fiore, *Introduzione all'Apocalisse*, ed. Kurt-Victor Selge, trans. Gian Luca Potestà (Rome: Viella, 1995), 9–14; Joachim of Fiore, *Expositio in Apocalypsim* (Venice, 1527, repr. Frankfurt: Minerva GMBH, 1964). The best recent treatments of Joachim's career are Giorgio Picasso, "Gioacchino e i cistercensi," in *Gioacchino da Fiore tra Bernardo di Clairvaux e Innocenzo III*, Atti del 5° congresso internazionale di studi gioacchimiti, San Giovanni in Fiore, 16–21 settembre 1999, ed. Roberto Rusconi (Rome: Viella, 2001), 93–101; Bernard McGinn, "Joachim of Fiore and the Twelfth-Century Papacy," in *Joachim of Fiore and the Influence of Inspiration: Essays in Memory of Marjorie E. Reeves (1905–2003)*, ed. Julia Eva Wannenmacher (Farnham: Ashgate, 2013), 15–34 at 19–21. For a reading of Joachim on Apocalypse with a different thematic focus and emphasis see McGinn, "Apocalypticism and Mysticism in Joachim of Fiore's Expositio in Apocalypsim," at 163–196 in the present volume. Here and elsewhere in this paper, biblical quotations in English are drawn from the RSV.

a woman clothed in the sun, and with the moon under her feet, and on her head a crown of twelve stars; she was with child and she cried out in her pangs of birth, with anguish for delivery." There are two main points that Joachim extracts from, and adds to, this text. The woman represents the suffering church. In particular, she represents the hermits and male virgins who will groan and travail as they give birth to those destined to be saved. These are the famous *viri spirituali* who are to play a starring role in the third *status* of Joachim's Trinitarian theology of history. Unpolluted by contact with women, they will replace the doctors in engendering true knowledge and understanding. The woman of Rev. 12:1–3 also stands for the universal church as the bride of Christ, or at least those Christians who convert fully to Christ, who replace carnal with spiritual love, and who excel in contemplation; they will head the list of those who enjoy eternal life.[2] Joachim brings forward Mary Magdalene to support this claim. It is because she chose the better part, as a contemplative, that she was the first witness of Christ's Resurrection; she thus models and undergirds the calling of Joachim's male virgins and hermits.[3]

In his further commentary on Rev. 12:1–3, Joachim assigns to the Magdalene a second role. To be sure, biblical intertextuality was the common coin of medieval exegesis. But Joachim's application of it to this text is unusual. He folds John 20:1–18 into his exegesis of Rev. 12:1–3, selectively and not always accurately. It will be recalled that, in contrast with the other evangelists (Matt. 28:1–10, Mark 16:1–8, Luke 24:1–11), John's Magdalene goes to the empty tomb alone, and does so twice. Finding Christ's body gone, she runs to notify Peter and John. Arriving at the tomb, John gets there first but pauses at the entrance; Peter enters first (John 20:4–8). Seeing the abandoned funeral cloths, they both believe (John 20:8). What they believe at this point is not clear, the Evangelist says, "for as yet they did not know the scripture, that he must rise from the dead" (John 20:9). So the disciples depart (John 20:10). But Mary returns to the tomb. She now finds two angels who ask why she weeps and whom she seeks. Before they can respond to her reply, she discovers a figure first taken to be a gardener whom she recognizes and worships as the risen Lord. As he bids, she refrains from

---

[2] Joachim of Fiore, *Expositio*, 154rb–154vb.

[3] *Expositio*, 154vb: "Inde est quod dei filius in die resurrectionis sue primo apparuit Marie Magdalene."

touching him and reports to the disciples that she has seen him and that he will appear to them later that day.

Joachim abbreviates, alters, and enlarges this account. He omits the Magdalene's second visit to the tomb and conversation with the angels. Oddly, given his praise of her as the first witness of the Resurrection, he also omits her encounter and conversation with the risen Christ. What Joachim adds is an elaborate theological and polemical gloss. The Magdalene stands for the Synagogue, that is, those Jews of Christ's day and later who interpret the Old Testament prophesies correctly, recognizing their fulfillment in Christ. It is thus appropriate for her to bring the Good News to Peter and John. Departing from the Evangelist's account, Joachim's John enters the tomb first. He represents the bringing of the gospel to the Greeks, the first Gentiles to receive it. Joachim's Peter, who follows John into the tomb, represents the transmission of the gospel to the Latins. Joachim presents all three of these biblical persons as initially getting it right. But this happy state did not continue. Most of the Jews have rejected the Magdalene's faith, misjudging the doctrine of the Trinity as incompatible with monotheism. And, despite their initial advantage, the Greeks have fallen into Trinitarian error by denying the *filioque*. Joachim has a good deal to say in defense of the *filioque*, not all of it relevant. The successors of Peter alone have preserved the true Trinitarian faith. And, as the Book of Revelation foretells, this true faith, and the Petrine primacy, will be recognized in the third and final *status* of history, thanks to the male virgins and hermits, when the Jews and the Greeks, renouncing their errors, will be brought into communion with Rome.[4]

How mainstream is this passage of Joachim's *Expositio*? There was no lack of prior and current discussion of the Book of Revelation, or of visual illustration of its themes.[5] In exculpating him from the heterodoxies professed by some of his followers, many Joachim scholars insist that

---

[4] *Expositio*, 143rb–145vb. Cf. Joachim, *Enchiridion*, 22, 29, 50–51, 54, 67, 89 on the early acceptance of the Christian message by (some) Jews and by the Greeks, who both now err. Neither in this text nor in his *Introduzione* does he refer to the Magdalene-Peter-John account.

[5] See, in general, Richard Marsden, "Introduction," in *The New Cambridge History of the Bible*, ed. Richard Marsden and E. Ann Matter (Cambridge: Cambridge University Press, 2012), 2:1–16 at 9–10; Nigel Morgan, "Latin and Vernacular Apocalypses," in ibid., 2:404–26; and James T. Palmer, *The Apocalypse in the Early Middle Ages* (Cambridge: Cambridge University Press, 2014).

he was a standard monastic writer of his time, basically recycling traditional ideas and methods.[6] A more drastic way of "normalizing" Joachim is to claim that he was not really a millenarian but rather an Augustinian-style proponent of church reform.[7] Some scholars have recognized Joachim's exegetical innovations. Unlike other commentators who compare the readings of past authorities and who focus on Revelation's moral message in the light of a "realized eschatology," Joachim prophesies a future End Time and relies on the authority of his own inspiration.[8] While situated in an apocalyptic tradition, his own Trinitarian theology of history pushes it in a utopian direction, off the standard track, as does his stress on the *viri spirituali*.[9] Joachim's departures from

---

[6] For a useful summary of her seminal contribution to this position, see Marjorie Reeves, "The Originality and Influence of Joachim of Fiore," *Traditio* 36 (1980): 269–316 at 269–88. More recently, treating Joachim's exegesis as completely traditional, coupled with a review of scholarship on this point and an appeal for his canonization on the eighth centenary of his death, see Fabio Troncarelli, *Gioacchino da Fiore: La vita, il pensiero, le opere* (Rome: Viella, 2002), 37–42.

[7] E. Randolph Daniel, "Abbot Joachim of Fiore, a Reformist Apocalyptic," in *Fearful Hope: Approaching the New Millennium*, ed. Christopher Kleinhenz and Fannie J. LeMoine (Madison: University of Wisconsin Press, 1999), 207–10; idem, "A New Understanding of Joachim: The Concords, the Exile, and the Exodus," in *Gioacchino da Fiore tra Bernardo di Clairvaux e Innocenzo III*, Atti del 5° congresso internazionale di studi gioacchimiti, San Giovanni in Fiore, 16–21 settembre 1999, ed. Roberto Rusconi (Rome: Viella, 2001), 209–22. This position would appear to modify Daniel's earlier view that Joachim's apocalypticism was "truly innovative," as in idem, "Joachim of Fiore: Patterns of History in the Apocalypse," in *The Apocalypse in the Middle Ages*, ed. Richard K. Emmerson and Bernard McGinn (Ithaca: Cornell University Press, 1992), 72–88; quotation at 83.

[8] For Joachim's immediate predecessors, see Guy Lobrichon, "Stalking the Signs: The Apocalypse Commentaries," in *The Apocalyptic Year 1000: Religious Expectation and Social Change, 950–1050*, ed. Richard Landes, Andrew Gow, and David C. Van Meter (Oxford: Oxford University Press, 2003), 67–79; idem, "Les commentaires sur l'Apocalypse du prétendu 'siècle obscur' jusque vers 1100," in *Tot sacramenta quot verba: Zur Kommentierung der Apokalypse des Johannes von den Anfängen bis ins 12. Jahrhundert*, ed. Konrad Huber, Rainer Klotz, and Christoph Winterer (Münster: Aschendorff, 2014), 195–213.

[9] Bernard McGinn, *The Calabrian Abbot: Joachim of Fiore in the History of Western Thought* (New York: Macmillan, 1985), 51–97; idem, *Visions of the End: Apocalyptic Traditions in the Middle Ages*, rev. ed. (New York: Columbia University Press, 1998), 126–41; idem, "*Ratio* and *visio*: Reflections on Joachim of Fiore's Place in Twelfth-Century Theology," in *Gioacchino da Fiore tra Bernardo di Clairvaux e Innocenzo III*, Atti del 5° congresso internazionale di studi gioacchimiti, San Giovanni in Fiore, 16–21 settembre 1999, ed. Roberto Rusconi (Rome: Viella, 2001), 27–39; and John Van Engen, "Medieval Monks on Labor and Leisure," in *Faithful Narratives: Historians, Religion, and the Challenge of Objectivity*, ed. Andrea Sterk and Nina Caputo (Ithaca: Cornell University Press, 2014), 47–62 at 59–61.

eschatological and exegetical tradition were noticed and found unacceptable by contemporary Premonstratensians and not just by aggrieved Cistercian ex-*confrères* such as Geoffrey of Auxerre.[10] Joachim's yoking of the conversion of the Jews to the return of the Greeks to Rome has been flagged as "unprecedented," as has his off-beat application of John 20:1–18 to the exegesis of Rev. 12:1–3.[11]

These debates on Joachim's exegetical traditionalism all relate him to his monastic predecessors and contemporaries. Another perspective on this topic emerges when we compare Joachim on Rev. 12:1–3 with the *Glossa ordinaria*. Here, his unconventionality is even more noticeable. Nowhere does the glossator on Revelation mention hermits or virginal contemplatives; the Magdalene, Peter, and John at the empty tomb; or the Greeks' doctrinal divergences from Rome. He certainly upholds the

---

[10] Ferruccio Gastaldelli, "Goffredo di Auxerre e Gioacchino da Fiore: Testi e personaggi a confronto," in *Studi su San Bernardo e Goffredo di Auxerre* (Florence: SISMEL Edizioni di Galluzzo, 2001), 375–422; Picasso, "Gioacchino e i cistercensi," 97–98; see also Kurt-Viktor Selge, "L'origine delle opere di Gioacchino da Fiore," in *L'attesa della fine dei tempi nel medioevo*, ed. Ovidio Capitani and Jürgen Miethke (Bologna: Il Mulino, 1990), 87–131 at 107–8, 123–24, all of whom focus on the critique of Geoffrey of Auxerre. Cf. Julia Eva Wannenmacher, "Ein Wandel in der Auslegung der Apokalypse durch Joachim von Fiore?" in *Tot sacramenta quot verba: Zur Kommentierung der Apokalypse des Johannes von den Anfängen bis ins 12. Jahrhundert*, ed. Konrad Huber, Rainer Klotz, and Christoph Winterer (Münster: Aschendorff, 2014), 289–310, who roots Joachim's exegetical innovations in his reappropriation of Tyconius, with his own eschatological twist, seen as prophetic in his own day by both supporters and detractors. For the Premonstratensians, see Carol Neel, "Man's Restoration: Robert of Auxerre and the Writing of History in the Early Thirteenth Century," *Traditio* 44 (1988): 253–74 at 271–74; Robert (†1211) was "dubious about Joachim's chiliasm," at 273.

[11] Brett Edward Whalen, *Dominion of God: Christendom and Apocalypse in the Middle Ages* (Cambridge, MA: Harvard University Press, 2009), at 9–41 for the pre-Joachim background, at 100–24 for Joachim, his use of the Fourth Gospel, and his treatment of Judaism; quotation at 102. For other insights on Joachim and the Jews, see Beatrice Hirsch-Reich, "Joachim von Fiore und das Judentum," in *Judentum im Mittelalter: Beiträge zum christlich-jüdischen Gespräch*, ed. Paul Wilpert (Berlin: Walter De Gruyter, 1966), 228–63, who focuses on Geoffrey of Auxerre's canard that Joachim was a Judaizer or of Jewish extraction owing to his emphasis on the continuities between the Old and New Testaments; and Anna Sapir Abulafia, "The Bible in Jewish-Christian Dialogue," in *The New Cambridge History of the Bible*, ed. Richard Marsden and E. Ann Matter (Cambridge: Cambridge University Press, 2012), 2:616–37 at 626–27, who notes that, while Joachim thought that the finding of common ground between Christian and Jewish understandings of the Old Testament would hasten the arrival of the End Time and the conversion of the Jews, he offered no specific strategy for achieving it.

sanctity and authority of the papacy, founded on the rock of Peter. But, as the challenge to it, he highlights heretics who criticize the church or reject its sacraments (at Rev. 6, 9, and 13). Jews and Gentiles get some attention. Those who persist in unbelief will be damned, along with bad Christians (at Rev. 6 and 21). Those who accept the Trinity will be saved; the "eternal gospel" is simply the Good News that brings them, and the rest of the faithful, to eternal life (at Rev. 14). Throughout, the glossator stresses that those adhering to the Petrine church can rest secure in its possession of the true faith, which will arm them with the patience to endure whatever travails await them.[12] If we take the *Glossa ordinaria* to be the norm in twelfth-century Revelations exegesis, Joachim's departures from it are striking.

But exegetical texts are not our only access into contemporary Christian thought about the apocalypse, or about the Magdalene, Peter, and John whom Joachim associates with it. These biblical worthies also found expression in manuscript illuminations and liturgical drama. Among the charismatic roles assigned to the Magdalene in popular devotion, she was perhaps best known to medieval Christians as "the apostle to the apostles" through the genre of the *Quem quaeritis* plays introduced into the Easter liturgy starting in the tenth century.[13] The earliest of these plays feature "the three Marys" and not the Magdalene alone. The playwrights freely convert the Salome of Mark 16:1 and the Joanna

---

[12] *Biblia Latina cum glossa ordinaria*, ed. Karlfried Froelich and Margaret T. Gibson, 4 vols. (Turnhout: Brepols, 1992 [repr. of Strasbourg: Adolph Rusch, 1480–81]), 4:547–78. See Wilhelm Kamlah, *Apokalypse und Geschichtstheologie: Die mittelalterliche Auslegung der Apokalypse vor Joachim von Fiore* (Berlin: Emil Ebering, 1935), 7–38; Guy Lobrichon, "Un nouveauté: Les gloses de la Bible," in *Le moyen âge et la Bible*, ed. Pierre Riché and Guy Lobrichon (Paris: Beauchesne, 1984), 95–114; both accent features of the *Glossa ordinaria* that differentiate it from Joachim on Revelation. For another approach to that contrast, cf. Robert E. Lerner, "The Medieval Return to the Thousand-Year Sabbath," in *The Apocalypse in the Middle Ages*, ed. Richard K. Emmerson and Bernard McGinn (Ithaca: Cornell University Press, 1992), 51–71.

[13] On the range of saintly and patronal functions ascribed to Mary Magdalene in the Middle Ages, see Jacobus de Voragine, *The Golden Legend*, trans. William Granger Ryan, 2 vols. (Princeton: Princeton University Press, 1993), 1:379–83 (no. 96); Katherine Ludwig Jansen, *The Making of the Magdalene: Preaching and Popular Devotion in the Middle Ages* (Princeton: Princeton University Press, 2000); for the Cistercians' promotion of her cult and specific "take" on her, see Alcuin Scarcez, "The Proto-Cistercian Office for Mary Magdalene and Its Changes in the Course of the Twelfth Century," in *Mary Magdalene in Medieval Culture: Conflicted Roles*, ed. Peter V. Loewen and Robin Waugh (New York:

of Luke 24:1 into a Mary who accompanies Mary Magdalene and Mary, mother of James. This trio finds a single angel on a single visit to the empty tomb. Neither their encounter with the risen Christ in Matt. 28:9 nor the Magdalene's in John 20:14–17 is staged in the early versions of the play. Instructed by the angel, all three Marys bring the news to all eleven disciples. Starting in the thirteenth century some texts single out the Magdalene as the only messenger, and send her to Peter and John, leaving directors with the problem of what to do with the other two Marys, already on stage.[14] In many *Quem quaeritis* plays the Magdalene and whichever disciples she meets are given a standardized dialogue. The disciples ask, "Tell us Mary, what you saw on the way" (*Dic nobis Maria quid vidisti in via*). She replies, "I saw the tomb of the living Christ and the glory of his Resurrection" (*Sepulchrum Christi viventis et gloriam vidi resurgentis*).[15] In these versions the accent is on the Magdalene as the sole first witness of the Resurrection, and as the apostle to the apostles.

There also exist two deluxe twelfth-century illuminated manuscripts that depict these events. Art historians who have studied them have been hard pressed to find their sources, describing them as "most unusually illustrated," "rare in western art," and "a rarefied iconographical choice."[16] These illuminations are found in the St. Albans Psalter (second quarter of the twelfth century) and the Gospels of Henry the Lion and Matilda (1173–88), made by Herman of Helmarshausen. The

---

Routledge, 2014), 51–74. On the *Quem quaeritis* plays, the most exhaustive resource remains Karl Young, *The Drama of the Medieval Church*, 2 vols. (Oxford: Clarendon Press, 1933), 1:201–410; see also Ronald W. Vinge, *A Companion to the Medieval Theatre* (New York: Greenwood Press, 1989), xiv, 26, 40–41, 65, 66, 118, 172, 209–10, 294; he notes that "the Easter *Quem quaeritis* trope gave rise to the largest body of extant liturgical plays," at 210; Peter Martin, ed., "Latin Liturgical Drama," in *The Medieval Stage, 500–1500*, ed. William Tydeman (Cambridge: Cambridge University Press, 2001), 53–98 at 81–98, 133–34.

[14] Noted by Young, *Drama*, 1:278, 280–81, 283–84, 295–97, 317–68, 385; Martin, "Latin Liturgical Drama," 82.

[15] Examples with this identical wording are cited by Young, *Drama*, 1:278, 280–81, 283–84, 295–97, 317–68, 385; E. K. Chambers, *The Medieval Stage*, 2 vols. (Oxford: Oxford University Press, 1903), 2:317 first flagged the use of these formulae in a fourteenth-century Dublin version.

[16] Thus, ignoring Émile Mâle, *Religious Art from the Twelfth to the Eighteenth Century* (New York: Noonday Press, 1958), 26–27, who suggests liturgical drama as a source for iconography, Jane Geddes, *The St. Albans Psalter: A Book for Christina of Markyate*

Psalter has two illuminations of interest here. The first shows the three Marys at the tomb conversing with the angel. The second shows Mary Magdalene alone, bringing the news to the full complement of eleven disciples.[17] The Henry and Matilda Gospels depict Mary Magdalene seven times in multiple roles drawn from all four Gospels: as the penitent washing Christ's feet, with Martha at the raising of Lazarus in Bethany, as witness of the Passion, at the empty tomb, as witness of the Resurrection, and as sole reporter of the Resurrection to a group of seven disciples—not the eleven, and not just Peter and John. In the latter image both she and the disciples hold banderoles with inscriptions containing the dialogue standardized in many *Quem quaeritis* plays quoted

(London: British Library, 2005), 20 and 55; Kristin Collins, Peter Kidd, and Nancy K. Turner, *The St. Albans Psalter: Painting and Prayer in Medieval England* (Los Angeles: The J. Paul Getty Museum, 2013), 29. At 36 n. 61 Collins and her associates note only three possible models in western art for the images in their MS, a Romanesque cloister capital from Pamplona now in the Museo de Navarra, the Casket of Paschal I (817–24) now in the Vatican Museum, and the Uta Codex (ca. 1025), now Munich Staatsbibliothek Clm. 13601 at fol. 41. Diane Apostolos-Cappadona, "From *Apostola Apostolorum* to Provençal Evangelist: On the Evolution of a Medieval Motif for Mary Magdalene," in *Mary Magdalene in Medieval Culture: Conflicted Roles*, ed. Peter V. Loewen and Robin Waugh (New York: Routledge, 2014), 160–80 at 168–79 notes that visual representations of the tomb scene, in the earliest Christian art, are all Byzantine and always depict the Magdalene as part of a group of women, never alone. Also regarded as iconographically innovative, with the St. Albans Psalter as its only hypothetical model, is the German MS here discussed, on which see Elizabeth Monroe, "Mary Magdalene as a Model of Devotion, Penitence, and Authority in the *Gospels of Henry the Lion and Matilda*," in ibid., 99–115. While Henry II of England made two grants to St. Albans in person and could have seen the Psalter, there is no evidence that Matilda visited St. Albans before her marriage in 1168 or that she and the Henry the Lion did so during their stay at Henry II's court between 1182 and 1185. On these travels see Nicholas Vincent, "The Pilgrimages of the Angevin Kings of England, 1154–1272," in *Pilgrimage: The English Experience from Becket to Bunyan*, ed. Colin Morris and Peter Roberts (Cambridge: Cambridge University Press, 2002), 12–45 at 20; Colette Bowie, *The Daughters of Henry II and Eleanor of Aquitaine* (Turnhout: Brepols, 2014), 35–39, 52, 53, 103–5. The possible connection between St. Albans and Helmarshausen is speculative. Henry the Lion and Matilda donated the Gospels to the church of St. Blaise, Brunswick, in 1188. Since Thomas Becket is depicted in its illuminations, they were likely designed after 1173, when he was canonized. For alternate datings, given by some scholars as 1185–88 after Henry and Matilda returned to Germany, see Richard Gameson, "The Early Imagery of Thomas Becket," in *Pilgrimages* (as above), 46–89 at 52; Bowie, *Daughters*, 157.

[17] Geddes, *St. Albans Psalter*, 54–55, plates 41 and 42, reproducing Hildesheim Dombibliothek MS. St. Godehard 1, fols. 50 and 51.

above.[18] The art historians would do well to consider liturgical drama as a visual no less than a textual and auditory source for the images in these manuscripts. While the artists, like the dramatists, feel free to select what they want from the Bible and to add their own changes and improvisations, it has to be said that Joachim's *Expositio* takes a line on the Magdalene, Peter, and John as independent of contemporary drama and art as it is of contemporary exegetical traditions.

There is one other contemporary context within which we can assess the conventionality of Joachim's exegesis of Revelation, the apocalypticism connected with the Crusades. There was a notable apocalyptic element in the understanding of this movement, found in upper-crust participants, papal propagandists, Crusade preachers, and Crusade chroniclers, and not just the downtrodden or neurotic.[19] For some, the key figure was a charismatic military leader who would defeat the infidels and bring about the consummation of human history. For others, the key figure was an inspired pope leading a morally rearmed expedition to that same end. Where did Joachim stand on this issue? As a number of scholars have noted, Joachim met with Richard I of England in Messina in 1191 as the king awaited transport to the Holy Land. Reported by the chronicler Roger of Howden, who accompanied Richard's crusade, Joachim prophesied that Richard was destined to defeat Saladin and

---

[18] Monroe, "Mary Magdalene," 101, 102–5, 106, 108, and plate 99, reproducing Wolfenbüttl Herzog August Bibliothek Cod. Guelf. Noviss. 2°, fol. 74v for the three Marys at the tomb and fol. 171r for the Magdalene's encounter with the risen Christ and report to the disciples. At 109, Monroe argues for the St. Albans Psalter as a possible source despite the differences between the Magdalene's images in these two MSS which she herself notes. She does not address the problem of access to the Psalter by the Gospel's artist or patrons; cf. the literature cited in n. 16 above.

[19] From a large bibliography on this subject see, for example, André Vauchez, "Les composantes eschatologiques de l'idée de croisade," in *Le concile de Clermont de 1095 et l'appel à la croisade*, Actes du colloque universitaire international de Clermont-Ferrand (23–25 juin 1995) organisé et publié avec le concours du Conseil Régionale d'Auvergne (Rome: École Française de Rome, 1997), 233–43; Jean Flori, *L'Islam et la fin des temps: L'intérprétation prophétique des invasions musulmans* (Paris: Seuil, 2007), 234–95, 410–11; idem, *Prêcher la croisade, XIe-XIIIe siècle: Communication et propagande* (Paris: Perrin, 2012); idem, "Jerusalem terrestre, céleste et spirituelle: Trois facteurs de sacralisation de la première croisade," in *Jerusalem the Golden: The Origins and Impact of the First Crusade*, ed. Susan B. Edgington and Luis García-Guijario (Turnhout: Brepols, 2014), 25–50; and Jay Rubenstein, *Armies of Heaven: The First Crusade and the Quest for Apocalypse* (New York: Basic Books, 2011). Whalen, *Dominion of God*, 42–49 stresses more heavily than other scholars the link between this issue and the centralizing efforts of the papacy.

explained how that victory would expedite the arrival of the End Time as he envisioned it. Some of the churchmen in Richard's suite found these ideas ludicrous. In any case, the Third Crusade's failure to recover Jerusalem soon soured Joachim on warfare as a means of converting the infidel and hastening the arrival of the Last Day.[20]

While Joachim stuck to his chiliastic itinerary and his *viri spirituali* after this bump on the road, Innocent could certainly avail himself of the coupling of expeditions to the Holy Land and apocalypticism already in the crusading and papal *imaginaire* without the need for Joachim's input. In explaining why he chose to cite Joachim in his letter of 13 November 1204, some scholars argue for the mediation of Rainer of Ponza.[21] In his youth Rainer had been an associate of Joachim and, like him, an ex-Cistercian expelled from the order in 1192. Nothing is known of his status or whereabouts after that date until he surfaced as a member of Innocent's curia, entrusted with important assignments and legatine missions. The idea that Rainer was Innocent's confessor

---

[20] E. Randolph Daniel, "Apocalyptic Conversion: The Joachite Alternative to the Crusades," *Traditio* 25 (1969): 127–54; repr. in idem, *Abbot Joachim of Fiore and Joachism* (Farnham: Ashgate, 2011), 11; Flori, *L'Islam*, 308–12, although he calls Joachim's message to Richard "très classique," at 310. Less classic was Joachim's detailed knowledge of Islam and the politics of the Near East noted by Alexander Patschovsky, "Semantics of Mohammed and Islam in Joachim of Fiore," in *Conflict and Religious Conversation in Latin Christendom: Essays in Honour of Ora Limor*, ed. Israel Jacob Yuval and Ram Ben-Shalom (Turnhout: Brepols, 2014), 115–31. Whalen, *Dominion of God*, 116–18, 123 notes Joachim's ambivalence on crusading; Penny J. Cole, *Preaching the Crusade to the Holy Land, 1095–1220* (Cambridge, MA: Medieval Academy of America, 1991), 86–87 notes the objections of Richard's advisors to Joachim's ideas.

[21] On Rainer's biography, writings, connections with Joachim, career in Innocent's curia, and presumed influence on him, see Bruno Griesser, "Rainer von Fossanova und sein Brief an Abt Arnald von Cîteaux," *Cistercienser Chronik* 60 (1953): 151–67, with the text of the letter at 163–66; Herbert Grundmann, "Per la biographia di Gioacchino da Fiore e Raniero da Ponza," in *Gioacchino da Fiore: Vita e opere*, ed. Gian Luca Potestà, trans. Sergio Sorrentino (Rome: Viella, 1997 [first pub. 1950]), 107–20; Fiona Robb, "Joachimist Exegesis in the Theology of Innocent III and Rainier of Ponza," *Florensia* 11 (1997): 137–52 at 139–44; Christoph Egger, "Joachim von Fiore, Rainer von Ponza und die römische Kurie," in *Gioacchino da Fiore tra Bernardo di Clairvaux e Innocenzo III*, Atti del 5° congresso internazionale di studi gioacchimiti, San Giovanni in Fiore, 16–21 settembre 1999, ed. Roberto Rusconi (Rome: Viella, 2001), 129–62 at 136–37; Troncarelli, *Gioacchino*, 32–33; Marco Rainini, *Disegni dei tempi: Il "Liber Figurarum" e la teologia figurativa di Gioacchino da Fiore* (Rome: Viella, 2006), 162–63, 202–4, 233; idem, *Il profeta del papa: Vita e memoria di Raniero da Ponza, eremita di curia*

has been taken seriously in some quarters. Aside from the shaky evidence for this assumption, his frequent absences from Rome on papal business make it unlikely. Rainer's only extant work is a letter to Abbot Arnold of Cîteaux in 1202; it reflects his knowledge of and sympathy with Joachim's Trinitarian theology of history. The purported Joachim–Rainer–Innocent connection has distracted its advocates from the objections Herbert Grundmann leveled against it some time ago.[22] In support of Grundmann it is now known that, before his death in 1202, Joachim made a point of depositing final versions of his major works in the papal library.[23] Innocent thus had unmediated access to these works, including the *Expositio*. So, does his citation of that work in his 13 November 1204 letter make Innocent a robust supporter of Joachim's "take" on Rev 12:1–3?[24]

In proposing our own answer to this question, we will address three issues. First, we will consider Innocent's self-projection as leader and theorist of the Fourth Crusade before, during, and after 13 November 1204. Second, we will analyze what he actually says, and does not say,

(Milan: Vita e Pensiero, 2016), 13–57, 60–75, 121–23, which also prints the letter to Arnold of Cîteaux at 131–37. Those rejecting the claim that Rainer was Innocent's confessor include Griesser, "Rainer von Fossanova," 157; Grundmann, "Per la biografia," 112; Robb, "Joachimist Exegesis," 139–40, reversing the position taken in eadem, "Who Hath Taken the Better Part? (Luke 10,42): Pope Innocent III and Joachim of Fiore on the Diverse Forms of the Religious Life," in *Monastic Studies*, ed. Judith Loades, 2 vols. (Bangor, UK: Headstart Victory, 1991), 2:157–70 at 160–61, 165–68. Cf. Brenda Bolton, "Innocent III's Providential Path," in *Innocenzo III: Urbs et orbis*, Atti del congresso internazionale, Roma, 9–15 settembre 1998, ed. Andrea Sommerlechner, 2 vols., Miscellanea della Società Romana di Storia Patri 44 (Rome: Presso la Società alla Biblioteca Vallicelliana, 2003), 1:21–55; at 43–44 Bolton seems to be alone in arguing that it was Bernard of Clairvaux, not Joachim, whose ideas Rainer mediated to Innocent.

[22] Grundmann, "Per la biografia," 120.

[23] Joachim of Fiore, *Psalterium decem chordarum*, ed. Kurt-Victor Selge, MGH, Quellen zur Geistesgeschichte des Mittelalters 20 (Hannover: Hahnsche Buchhandlung, 2009), xxiii–xxiv.

[24] Among the strongest proponents of this view are Alfred J. Andrea, ed. and trans., *Contemporary Sources for the Fourth Crusade* (Leiden: Brill, 2000), 116, 131; idem, "Innocent III, the Fourth Crusade, and the Coming Apocalypse," in *The Medieval Crusade*, ed. Susan Ridyard (Woodbridge, UK: Boydell Press, 2004), 97–106; Troncarelli, *Gioacchino*, 32; John C. Moore, *Innocent III (1160/61–1216): To Root up and to Plant* (Leiden: Brill, 2003), 133–39, 254; Flori, *L'Islam*, 314–28; idem, *Prêcher la croisade*, 203–4; Whalen, *Dominion of God*, 100–48, where he proposes that Joachim derived his ideas from papal apocalypticism, not vice versa; idem, *The Medieval Papacy* (New York: Palgrave Macmillan, 2014), 138; McGinn, "Joachim of Fiore and the Twelfth-Century Papacy," 21–22.

in this letter, and its influence, or lack of influence, on the rhetoric and policy of his later crusade-related writings. Finally, we will examine how Innocent addresses themes developed in the 13 November 1204 letter in documents and activities not related to crusading.

The first and most fundamental fact to be kept in mind in understanding the letter of 13 November 1204 is one obvious to historians of the Fourth Crusade: Innocent lost his vaunted control of the expedition from the get-go.[25] And, the terms in which he conceptualized the crusade changed over time. Apocalypticism was not a part of the initial package. In his crusade encyclical of 15 August 1198, Innocent adds to the standard motifs of pilgrimage and spiritual reward the idea that Christians have a moral obligation to avenge the insult done by the infidels to Christ by retaking Jerusalem. He issues the call to nobles and townsmen. He stresses the importance of self-funding, or the surrogate funding, of competent warriors. He proclaims the Holy Land indulgence and the protection of crusaders' property. He sends two cardinals, the crusade legates-to-be Peter of Capua and Soffredo, along with a Templar and a Hospitaller, to coordinate crusade preaching. Pointedly ruled out, or omitted from the list of those urged to take the cross, are two groups: the unfit, and kings. Innocent does not want his expedition sullied by the demagogues, pogrom leaders, or rag-tag and bobtail who had disgraced some earlier crusades. Omitting kings was a sore point. True, royal conduct of the Second and Third Crusades made

---

[25]Without trying to exhaust the extensive bibliography on the Fourth Crusade, particularly helpful recent accounts accenting Innocent's abortive efforts to proclaim and assert papal control over it include Cole, *Preaching the Crusades*, 80–84; Werner Maleczek, *Pietro Capuano: Patrizio amalfitano, cardinale, legata alla quarta crociera, teologo (†1214)*, trans. Fulvio Delle Donne (Amalfi: Centro di Cultura e Storia Amalfitana, 1997), 9, 74–89, 103–220; Donald E. Queller and Thomas F. Madden, *The Fourth Crusade: The Conquest of Constantinople*, 2nd ed. (Philadelphia: University of Pennsylvania Press, 1997), 1, 2–4, 8, 48, 49, 52, 101, 103, 174, 207, 233, although they do not take the story beyond the coronation of Baldwin; Jonathan Phillips, *The Fourth Crusade and the Sack of Constantinople* (London: Jonathan Cape, 2004), passim with a good summary at 298–303, although he thinks that Innocent did not really want to rule out the participation of kings; Andrea, *Contemporary Sources*, 5–176 in comments on documents largely taken from Innocent's Registers; Alfred J. Andrea and John C. Moore, "A Question of Character: Two Views on Innocent III and the Fourth Crusade," in *Innocenzo III: Urbs et orbis*, Atti del congresso internazionale, Roma, 9–15 settembre 1998, ed. Andrea Sommerlechner, 2 vols., Miscellanea della Società Romana di Storia Patri 44 (Rome: Presso la Società alla Biblioteca Vallicelliana, 2003), 1:525–85, with useful historiography.

their leadership a cautionary tale. True, current kings had more pressing preoccupations. Also true, confining the host to sub-royal participants would heighten the pope's profile and restore the papal leadership of crusading in abeyance since 1095. But there was a downside to this policy. Kings had largely financed the Second and Third Crusades, and not just out of their own deep pockets. They had the authority to impose crusade taxes on their subjects, to collect them, and to penalize tax delinquencies with secular sanctions, an authority the pope conspicuously lacked. Hence, to compensate for the loss of royal funding, Innocent placed a new and heavy emphasis on the participants' self-funding, supplemented, in 1199, by his levy of an unprecedented crusade tax on the clergy.

In the event, neither these careful preparations nor the developments that ensued squared with Innocent's plans. The preacher who actually rallied support was not one of his appointees but the self-starter Fulk of Neuilly. Innocent co-opted Fulk but he could not monitor his message and audience. When Peter of Capua reached Venice in 1202, he found that the unfit—poor, sick, and female crusaders—had already arrived and had to send them home. The clerical tax remained mostly unpaid. The financial insufficiency of the host that assembled in Venice, unable to meet their contractual responsibility for the fleet they had commissioned, occasioned their notorious diversion of the crusade to Zara and then to Constantinople. Innocent's injunctions and threats made no difference. The Franks excommunicated for the attack on Zara were forgiven in 1203 without fulfilling their agreed-on obligations. The Venetians ignored their own excommunication. Although Innocent warned crusaders to steer clear of Byzantine imperial succession disputes, whatever the claimants' merits, they committed themselves to install the son of the deposed Isaac II as Alexius IV. In exchange, Alexius agreed to two terms: He would grant the crusaders supplies, funds, and troops. And he would bring the Greek church back to Roman obedience. Both before and during his brief reign (crowned 1 August 1203, deposed 27 July 1204, assassinated 8/9 August 1204), Alexius simply lacked the power to meet these terms.

None the less, Innocent grasped at the second of these straws. Starting in the spring of 1203, his letters return again and again to a new crusade theme, the return of the Greek church to Rome. Writing to Alexius in February 1204, Innocent reminds him of his pledge to effect it. Implausibly, as well, he asserts that Alexius will be able to overcome his domestic enemies only through papal support.[26] But neither the pope nor anyone else could prevent the *coup d'état* that replaced Alexius IV with an Alexius V who had no engagements to the crusaders or to Innocent.

Nor, when he was crowned on 16 May 1204, did Baldwin of Flanders pick up the baton dropped by Alexius IV. This brings us back to his letter to Innocent of October 1204, the preemptive maneuver with which this paper began.[27] It now requires a closer look. Opening with a *pro forma* statement of obedience to the pope, Baldwin describes the host's brilliantly coordinated amphibious attack on Constantinople as a divinely granted victory. It justly punished the perfidious tyrant Alexius V, who "thoroughly rejected obedience to the Roman Church and the aid for the Holy Land, which Alexius [IV] had promised by oath and imperial writ."[28]

Baldwin's letter elides a number of important facts. He observes that rich booty was taken by the victors, in line with standard military practice, but omits the sack of Constantinople which ravaged the city for three full days, complete with looting, arson, the rape and slaughter of noncombatants, and the spoliation of churches. Nor does he mention the fact that, in March 1204, the victors had divided the spoils and the lands conquered, set up the constitution of the Latin Empire, and chosen him as its first ruler, with no reference to the pope. Moreover, they had installed as Latin patriarch Tommaso Morosini, elected by his fellow Venetians—still laboring under excommunication—without papal notification or approval. Innocent was later outraged when he learned that these events were a done deal and that he had been excluded from the decision-making. But not yet.

---

[26] Innocent III to Alexius IV, February 1204, in *Die Register Innocenz' III*, ed. Othmar Hageneder et al., 13 vols. to date (Vienna: Österreichischen Akademie der Wissenschaften, 1974–2015), 6:228. Subsequent references to Innocent's letters will cite them by volume and item numbers, with pagination given in the case of quotations.

[27] Andrea, *Contemporary Sources*, 99 gives a rhetorical analysis of the letter, for which see *Reg.* 7:152.

[28] *Reg.* 7:152, 257: "Obedientiam autem Romanae ecclesie et subventionem Terre sancte, quam iuramento et scripto imperiali firmarat Alexius, adeo refutavit, ut vitam amittere preeligeret Greciamque subverti, quam quod Latinis pontificibus orientalis ecclesia subderetur." Trans. Andrea, *Contemporary Sources*, 104–5. This translation of passages quoted from Innocent's letters will be cited unless otherwise noted.

While the pope had been treated as essentially irrelevant in the regime change, Baldwin gives galling proof that other eminent persons had validated it in a pointed description of his coronation: "Residents of the Holy Land, clerics and soldiers, were on hand. In comparison with everyone else, their joy was incalculable and unrestrained, and they were more thankful in declaring manifest homage to God, just as if the Holy City had been restored to Christian worship."[29] Constantinople, Baldwin suggests, is now on a par with Jerusalem as a crusade destination, and is recognized as such by these delegates from the crusader states themselves.

That foundation laid, Baldwin raises two other issues. If there is going to be a payoff for the Roman church in Constantinople, his own rule must be stabilized. Thus, he asks that new recruits be sent, "nobles and commoners of every sort of class and of each sex, ... with an Apostolic indulgence offered to all who come to us and will faithfully serve our empire either for a while or for life."[30] These arrivals, some of whom do not meet Innocent's original fitness requirements, are clearly those needed for the long-term settlement of the Latin Empire, whatever lip service Baldwin may pay to a Holy Land expedition. As to how the Greek church can best be brought to Roman obedience, Baldwin offers a plan with a sting in its tail. Innocent should organize and preside over an ecumenical council in Constantinople—an idea which, as Baldwin is aware, Innocent had aired but dropped early in his pontificate—so that he can receive the submission of the Greeks in person. The ecclesiastical ball, he concludes, is in Innocent's court.

Responding to this extremely slick performance put Innocent to the test. His first sally is his letter to Baldwin of 7 November 1204. After rejoicing *pro forma* at the divine favor shown to the host, he gets down to business. He places the Latin Empire under papal protection. This is a grant less illusory than the one offered to Alexius IV. For Innocent instructs the clergy to support all recruits who come to Baldwin's aid,

---

[29] *Reg.* 7:152, 259: "Aderant incole Terre sancte, ecclesiastice militaresque persone, quorum pre omnibus inestimabilis erat et gratulabunda letitia, exhibitumque Deo gratius obsequium asserebant, quam si civitas sancta Christanis esset cultibus restituta ..." Trans. Andrea, 108.

[30] *Reg.* 7:152, 260: "nobiles et ignobiles cuiuslibet conditionis aut sexus eisdem desiderii accentos ... proposita venientes omnibus apostolica indulgentia nobis et imperio nostro aut temporaliter aut perpetuo fideliter servituris." Trans. Andrea, 110.

"in defending and holding onto the empire of Constantinople"; these arrivals are not to be excommunicated or their lands interdicted, or the clergy involved will forfeit their own crusade indulgence.[31] Innocent stops well short of granting these new recruits the crusade indulgence requested. Nor does he mention the church council idea. Rather, he adjures Baldwin to take the ecclesiastical initiative himself, "to preserve in obedience to the Apostolic See the Greek Church and the Empire of Constantinople, which Divine Grace subjected to you at the Apostolic See's behest."[32] And so, tossing the ball right back into Baldwin's court, Innocent concludes that he should enforce an obedience not yet rendered in a peroration that also takes papal credit for mediating the host's divinely accorded victory.

This epistolary exchange, with its would-be shifting of responsibilities, its disingenuous claims, and its strategic omissions on both sides, left the issue of the Greek church at an impasse. This is what led Innocent to try a new approach, that of his letter to the Latin clergy of 13 November 1204. His earlier injunctions and fulminations having yielded no crop, he now hitched Joachim to the plow. A closer look at this document will clarify how Innocent actually uses the passages he quotes and the techniques he borrows from Joachim's *Expositio* on Rev. 12:1–3.

The first noticeable feature of this letter is its sloppiness. In contrast with the clear, elegant, and well-organized documents issued by Innocent, supported as needed with apposite biblical, theological, or canonical references, his letter of 13 November 1204 is rambling, repetitive, and weakened by internal contradictions, some derived from Joachim and some self-inflicted. Innocent was certainly too busy to compose all his letters personally, although he discussed matters with his staff and subjected correspondence drafted in his name to his own scrutiny and approval.[33] The authenticity of this letter is not in dispute.

---

[31] *Reg.* 7:153, 263: "ut ad defendendum et retinendum Constantinopolitanum imperium ..." Trans. Andrea, 114.

[32] *Reg.* 7:153, 263: "quatinus Grecorum ecclesiam in Constantinopolitanum imperium, quod ad invocationem apostolice sedis gratia tibi divina subiecit, in ipsius obedientia studeas conservare ..." Trans. Andrea, 115.

[33] On this issue, see Christoph Egger, "Papst Innocenz III als Theologe," *Archivum Historiae Pontificae* 30 (1992): 55–123 at 113–17; Atria A. Larson, *Master of Penance: Gratian and the Development of Penitential Thought and Law in the Twelfth Century* (Washington, DC: Catholic University of America Press, 2014), 455–60, 468, with a review of the literature at 455 n. 39.

What can be challenged is the thesis that Innocent's sudden interest in Joachim represents a significant and enduring change in his mind-set, rather than a temporary and ad hoc effort to motivate the Latin clergy in Constantinople while circumventing Baldwin's ploy with a lateral one of his own.[34]

Innocent dances away from Joachim even as he invokes him selectively, as can be seen from the letter's outset. He opens with an allusion to the successive kingdoms prophesied by Daniel (Daniel 2:36–45). But, rather than expatiating on Joachim's baroque Trinitarian elaboration of this theme, all it means, says Innocent, is that times change. Kingdoms rise and fall. We are now witnessing one such event: God "has transferred the empire of Constantinople from the proud to the humble, from the disobedient to the obedient, from schismatics to Catholics, namely from the Greeks to the Latins."[35] This *translatio imperii* recalls an earlier and more basic one, the Donation of Constantine that buttresses papal authority.

That point established, Innocent now moves to Joachim's—and his own—account of John 20:1–18. His letter makes no reference to Rev. 12:1–3. Mary Magdalene, he agrees, stands for the Synagogue, that is, for the true Israel whose members recognize the fulfillment of the Old Testament prophesies in Christ, for salvation comes from the Jews (John 4:22). Likewise, John represents the Greeks and Peter the Latins. Before continuing with his own discussion of the tomb scene, Innocent makes the point that "Peter built one church, clearly the head of all the churches.... John, however, established many churches in Asia, like many members of a single head."[36] This observation implies that centralized structure, characterizing the Petrine church from its inception, has always been preferable to the Greeks' multiform arrangements.

---

[34] For alternative assessments of Innocent's attitude, cf. Andrea, *Contemporary Documents*, 115, opting for an enthusiastic conversion marked by the letter's "exuberant style" and Nikolaus G. Chrissis, *Crusading in Frankish Greece: A Study of Relations and Attitudes, 1204–1282* (Turnhout: Brepols, 2012), 2–15, 45–51, 95, who reads it as devious self-promoting rhetoric.

[35] *Reg.* 7:154, 264–70, quotation at 264: "Constantinopolitanum imperium a superbis ad humiles, ab inobedientibus ad devotos, a scismaticis ad catholicos, a Grecis videlicet transtulit ad Latinos." Trans. Andrea, 116–17.

[36] *Reg.* 7:154, 265: "Petrus unam construxit ecclesiam, videlicet ecclesiarum omnium unum caput. ... Ioh(anne)s autem in Asia plures ecclesias stabilivit tamquam unius capitis multa membra." Trans. Andrea, 119.

Arrived at the tomb, Innocent's disciples follow the text of the Fourth Gospel from which Joachim departs. John gets there first. But, stopping at the entrance, he does not see all the funeral cloths. This means that, while the Greeks received the gospel first, John did not acquire or communicate a complete and accurate message. Hence the problem: "Thus far and not even now, the Greek doctors, except for maybe a few, have not fully grasped the Old Testament and fathomed the profound mysteries of the deity."[37] Innocent agrees with Joachim that the Greeks are at fault for rejecting the *filioque*. But, unlike Joachim, he sees this error as derived from an original lapse on John's part. At the same time, the two passages from the *Expositio* he quotes, which deal only with the *filioque*, do not always support or even coincide with that opinion. Innocent includes Joachim's irrelevant and problematic digressions, such as the apocryphal tale of Peter's encounter with Christ en route to Rome and the point that, while John is a "type" of the Spirit, it is precisely the authentic doctrine of the Holy Spirit that the Greeks did not receive from him. Innocent makes no effort to deal with the gap between his own treatment of John's defective faith at the tomb and Joachim's argument that John was initially correct and that the *filioque* problem emerged later.[38] Whenever this error arose, Innocent's Peter, entering the tomb without stopping and seeing all the funeral cloths, demonstrates that "the Latins have plumbed the deeper and more inward mysteries of the Old Testament."[39] Without addressing the anomalies appropriated from Joachim or those he introduces himself, Innocent reroutes this version of the tomb scene back to the Roman primacy: "Thus, the first shall be last and the last first. For he [John] will see what Peter has seen and will believe what the Latin church believes; so may they walk together in concord in the house of the Lord from now on."[40]

---

[37] *Reg.* 7:154, 266: "doctores Grecorum ad plenam intelligentiam Veteris Testamento et profunda misteria deitatis nec hactenus nec nunc etiam pervenerunt nisi forte perpauci." My trans.

[38] *Reg.* 7:154, 267–68 for the passages quoted from Joachim. Andrea, *Contemporary Documents*, 121–22, 123, conveniently prints these passages in Italics in his translation. For Joachim's own text, see *Expositio*, 143vb–144va.

[39] *Reg.* 7:154, 266: "quia Latinus populus usque ad interiora et profundiora Veteris Testamenti misteria penetravit ..." My trans.

[40] *Reg.* 7:154, 268: "et sic facti sunt primi novissimi et novissimi primi. Videbit enim quod Petrus viderat, et credet quod credit ecclesia Latinorum, ut ammodo simul ambulant in domo Domini cum consensu." My trans.

This irenic outcome is one that can start now. Innocent does not project it as a future End Time event but as an item on the current ecclesiastical agenda.

Innocent has a second polemic to level against the Greeks, which he ties to an interpretation of Mary Magdalene not found in Joachim. In this version of her story, Innocent's Magdalene returns to the empty tomb, converses with the angels, and recognizes the risen Christ. What needs explaining here is not her role as apostle to the apostles but the meaning of Christ's *Noli me tangere* command (John 20:17). According to Innocent, Christ chastises her: "Although you believe in me as the Messiah promised by the Law and all the prophets, nevertheless you do not believe me to be the equal of God the Father."[41] No longer the sign of the true Israel, the Magdalene here stands for the imperfect faith of Christians who deny the consubstantiality of the Father and Son. This Christological heresy is one with which Innocent now taxes the Greeks along with their denial of the *filioque*. Despite his peroration concerning one flock and one shepherd (John 10:16) and the salvation of all Israel when the full number of Gentiles are brought in (Rom. 11:25–26),[42] what Innocent really speaks to in this letter is not the End Time conversion of non-Christians but the energizing of the Latin clergy's current ministry to the Greeks.

It is perhaps not surprising that this far from lucid argument, with its bipolar Magdalene and confusing treatment of John, did not have a long shelf life. The Latin clergy did not swallow the pep-pill Innocent prescribed. So, less than three months later, he replaced it. Writing to the Latin clergy on 25 January 1205, he drops the Christological and *filioque* polemics, hammers home the Donation of Constantine theme, and frames it in a different biblical event, the miraculous draft of fishes at which Christ tells his disciples that they will now become fishers of men (Luke 5:1–10). As Innocent explains, "The boat of Simon is, therefore, the Church of Peter, ... which Christ entrusted to Peter's rule so that unity excludes division. Moreover, Jesus steps up, in effect, into the boat of Simon whenever He causes the Church of Peter to step up, which has been manifestly evident since the time of

---

[41] *Reg.* 7:154, 269: "quasi diceret: Licet Messiam esse me credas a lege ac prophetis omnibus repromissum, tamen Deo Patri me non credis equalem." Trans. Andrea, 125.

[42] *Reg.* 7:154, 269: "Deus hoc misterium per vestrum ministerium operatur ... ut, cum plenitudo gentium ad fidem intraverit, tunc etiam Isr(ae)l salvus fiat."

Constantine."[43] The Latin clergy must man their nets and haul in the Greeks. For the conversion of the Gentiles and all Israel will occur only "after all Christians have been entirely been brought back to obedience to the Apostolic See."[44] The Greek church remains the immediate priority.

At the point when Innocent wrote this letter of 25 January 1205, times had changed, and continued to do so dramatically during the following months. Perforce, Innocent's tone shifted from the triumphant to the irritated to the concessive. In the same letter just mentioned and in one sent on the same date to Baldwin, while he expresses his aggravation at the non-canonical election of Morosini, Innocent confirms his status as patriarch, now cast as a papal appointee. On ca. 29 January 1205 he lifted the Venetians' excommunication.[45] Taking advantage of the regime change, the Bulgarians attacked and inflicted a devastating defeat on the Latin Empire, capturing Baldwin at Adrianople on 14 April 1205. This Bulgarian victory was so conclusive that their king, having no need of Baldwin as a hostage, put him to death. In March 1205 Peter of Capua had returned to a beleaguered Constantinople from a fact-finding trip to the Holy Land and had concluded, correctly, that the time was not propitious for an expedition to the crusader states. At the end of March, he released the crusaders from their Holy Land vow. Innocent complains about this decision in a letter to Philip II of France dated 10/15 July 1205 and on 12 July he wrote to Peter himself. By now Innocent had learned of the sack of Constantinople and

---

[43] *Reg.* 7:203, 354: "Navis ergo Simonis est ecclesia Petri, … quam Christus commisit Petro regendam, ut unitas divisionem excludat. Ascendit autem Iesus per effectum in navem Symonis, cum ecclesiam Petri fecit ascendere, quod a tempore Constantini apparuit evidenter …" Trans. Andrea, 132. See also Barbara Bombi, "Innocent III and the Baltic Crusades," in *Crusading on the Edge: Ideas and Practice of Crusading in Iberia and the Baltic Region, 1100–1500*, ed. Torben Kjersgaard Nielsen and Iben Fonnesberg-Schmidt (Turnhout: Brepols, 2016), 117–33, who notes this shift in Innocent's rhetoric, relating it to the politics informing his support of Waldemar II of Denmark's Baltic expedition.

[44] *Reg.* 7:203: 356: "Sed postquam ad obedientiam apostolice sedis omnes omnino reversi fuerint Christiani, tunc multitudo gentium intrabit ad fidem, et sic omnis Isr(ae)l salvus fiet." Trans. Andrea, 135–36.

[45] *Reg.* 7:203 for the letter to the clergy; *Reg.* 7:204 for the letter to Baldwin; *Reg.* 8:19, written 30 March 1205 to Morosini himself, confirms his plenipotentiary authority as patriarch. See *Reg.* 7:206 to Doge Enrico Dandolo for Innocent's lifting of the Venetians' excommunication.

was bitterly aware that it roadblocked the path to Rome. Unfairly, he castigates Peter for all that had gone wrong during his legateship, of which the pope relieves him. But he does not countermand Peter's action.[46]

Even before he learned of the crusaders' release from their Holy Land vows, Innocent worried that many of them would go home. And so, finally granting what he had withheld from Baldwin in 1204, on 25 April 1205 he declared to the entire host that their original Holy Land indulgence now applied to the defense of Constantinople.[47] On 15 August/15 September 1205 he confirmed the same in a letter to Boniface of Montferrato, the generalissimo of the host's ground forces.[48] Moreover, in an encyclical dated 16 August 1205, he extended the crusade indulgence to any and all recruits who would come to Constantinople's aid.[49]

In the same months in which Innocent bit the bullet in these ways, he also tried to marshal other kinds of support for the Latin Empire. On 25 May 1205 he wrote to a number of addressees including the king of France, the French archbishops, the University of Paris, the cathedral chapter of Soissons, and religious orders, asking for what they could provide: funding, supplies, liturgical books, schoolbooks, monastic or scholastic personnel. Some religious orders did establish abbeys in the Latin Empire. The Paris masters declined to set up a satellite university in Constantinople. The fate of the other requests is unknown. The only one of these letters offering a theological rationale is the one sent to Archbishop Guy of Reims, with copies to his fellow prelates in Bordeaux, Bourges, Lyon, Rouen, Sens, Tours, and Vienne. Here Innocent presents his latest argument to date for church union as the goal of the Fourth Crusade. Returning to the *translatio imperii*, to whose possibilities he adds the transfer "of the superstitious to the

---

[46] *Reg.* 8:126 for the letter to Philip; *Reg.* 8:127 for the letter to Peter of Capua. An excellent summary of the conditions in the Holy Land which made Peter's decision a rational response to the logic of immediate circumstances there is provided by Maleczek, *Pietro Capuano*, 201–3.

[47] *Reg.* 8:64.

[48] *Reg.* 8:134.

[49] *Reg.* 8:131. On Innocent's recognitions and concessions at this juncture, see Andrea, *Contemporary Sources*, 172; Phillips, *Fourth Crusade*, 306.

religious,"[50] the pope now omits the imperfect beliefs of John and Mary Magdalene. The problem, as he presents it, is administrative. In contrast with the Roman church, whose centralization guarantees its orthodoxy, the Greeks' division into the seven churches of Asia is why they went off the rails. Once that organizational issue has been solved, the Greeks can be brought to believe that "the Holy Spirit, since he is the connection of unity and equality, proceeds from the Son in the same way that he proceeds from the Father." This *unitas-equalitas-conexio* formula offers a fresh defense of the *filioque* that is remote from both Joachim on Rev. 12:1–3 and from Innocent's own earlier argument in November 1204. It had a venerable genealogy from Augustine to Thierry of Chartres to Clarenbald of Arras to Peter Lombard and beyond.[51] At length accepting Constantinople as a valid crusade destination, Innocent has concluded, by May 1205, that the best way to inspire Christians to move goods and services there in aid of church union is to signpost for them a well-mapped route, in place of the off-putting itinerary which he had so recently proposed.

But this is not all there is to say about Innocent, crusading, and the idea of the coming End Time. Indeed, the single most apocalyptic statement made in his entire crusade-related dossier is in Innocent's encyclical *Quia maior*, issued 19/29 April 1213. On the heels of the disastrous Children's Crusade of 1212, he decided to launch a new, and suitable, expedition to the Holy Land. This document offers the same rationale for crusading as in 1198, with a few refinements. Innocent now waives the fitness requirement; he includes kings in the call; he condemns pirates who interfere with Mediterranean transport; and he excommunicates those who sell the Muslims war *matériel*. While planning is clearly important, Innocent's appeal goes beyond logistics. We must put our trust in the Lord, "who has already given us a sign that good is to come,

---

[50] *Reg.* 8:70, 127: "a superbis ad humilis, a superstitiosis ad religiosis, a scismaticis ad catholicos, ab inobedientes transferens ad devotos." My trans. The other letters in this group are *Reg.* 8:71 to the same French archbishops requesting liturgical books and monks; *Reg.* 8:72 to the University of Paris requesting school books and scholars; *Reg.* 8:73 to the cathedral chapter of Soissons and Philip II of France requesting funds and supplies; *Reg.* 8:74 to religious orders dragging their feet on the clerical tax assessed in 1199.

[51] *Reg.* 8:70, 127: "quod Spiritus sanctus, qui est unitatis equalitatisque conexio, procedat a Filio, sicut a Patre procedit." My trans. For discussion, literature, and reference to figures who cite this formula, see Marcia L. Colish, *Peter Lombard*, 2 vols. (Leiden: Brill, 1994), 1:104–5, 238–30.

that the beast is approaching, whose number, according to St. John, will be completed in 666 years, of which already 600 have passed."[52] This papal projection of an End Time to begin in ca. 1279 is ironic indeed, given the condemnation of Joachim's later followers for heralding the arrival of his third *status* in 1260.

Innocent did not live to mount the crusade announced in *Quia maior* and he omitted the beast of Revelation when he gave crusading his last hurrah at the final session of Lateran IV on 30 November 1215. As with the approach—inflected by Joachim or not—that he took on 13 November 1204, followed by the swiftly shifting rhetorical strategies adopted in his later Fourth Crusade letters, so too in 1213 and 1215 Innocent felt free to invoke new arguments, and to drop them, as needed. In each case he was guided by his estimate of his audience and situation, rather than by a durable commitment to any one position. The main theme which his Fourth Crusade letters stress consistently from 1203 onward is the ingathering of the Greeks. He does not propose the evangelization of the Jews, whose legally protected status he reinforced; the Gentiles to be converted were those targeted in the Baltic Crusade under the rubric of *compelle intrare*.[53] We can gain a more realistic sense of the circumstantial, and expendable, nature of Innocent's appeals to apocalypticism, and to Joachim, by considering how he handled the themes borrowed from Joachim's *Expositio* in works and policies undertaken when he was not in crisis mode and not writing in connection with crusading.

One such theme was the contemplative versus the active life. Joachim's stress on contemplative *viri spirituali* as agents in his Trinitarian theology of history was not one Innocent shared. Innocent

---

[52] Innocent III, *Reg.* 15:218, in *Opera omnia* 3, PL 216: 817A–822A; quotation at 818B: "qui jam fecit nobiscum signum in bonum, quod finis huius bestiae approprinquat, cuius numerus secundum Apocalypsin Joannis intra sexcenta sexaginta sex clauditur, ex quibus jam pene sexcenti sunt anni completi." Trans. Jonathan and Louise Riley-Smith, eds., in *The Crusades: Idea and Reality, 1095–1274* (London: Edward Arnold, 1981), 120; noted also by Cole, *Preaching the Crusades*, 103–8, 117–26, 140–41; Flori, *L'Islam*, 335–36; idem, *Prêcher la croisade*, 231–39.

[53] On Innocent's policy toward the Jews, see *Reg.* 3:276, issued 15 September 1199 to addressee(s) unspecified; on the Baltic Crusade, see *Reg.* 12:103 of 31 October 1209 to King Waldemar II of Denmark. For discussion and literature on these letters, see Marcia L. Colish, *Faith, Fiction, and Force in Medieval Baptismal Debates* (Washington, DC: Catholic University of America Press, 2014), 275–76, 285–86; on the letter to Waldemar see Bombi, "Innocent III," 122–33.

was on the wavelength of the twelfth-century revaluation of Martha, which put her on the same plane as Mary, or even ahead of her.[54] A nice sense of this reappraisal can be seen even in a heavyweight monastic figure such as Geoffrey of Auxerre. In a sermon preached to his Cistercian *confrères* on Gregory the Great, Geoffrey advances Bernard of Clairvaux as their true guide: Bernard did not succumb to selfish absorption in the joys of contemplation but applied the illumination gained therein to the active service of others.[55] Innocent also hailed Bernard, not least for his promotion of crusading and support of papal authority. He cites Bernard, and Martha, in writing to abbots who resisted appointment as bishops, to bishops who sought to retire to monastic life, and to papal legates, including his own Rainer of Ponza, who wanted to opt out.[56] In his non-crusade writings, Innocent treats Mary Magdalene neither as a contemplative nor as an emblem of incorrect Christology but as a species of Martha herself. She exemplifies two concerns dear to Innocent that inspired his early support for

---

[54] Giles Constable, "The Interpretation of Mary and Martha," in *Three Studies in Medieval Religious and Social Thought* (Cambridge: Cambridge University Press, 1995), 1–141, at 14–43 for the period before the twelfth century, at 44–92 for that century, and at 13, 93–96 on Joachim on contemplation as the *unum necessarium*.

[55] Ferruccio Gastaldelli, "Spiritualità e missione del vescovo in una sermone inedito di Goffredo di Auxerre su San Gregorio," in *Studi su San Bernardo e Goffredo di Auxerre* (Florence: SISMEL Edizione del Galluzzo, 2001), 587–606, at 601–6 for the sermon text.

[56] Constable, "Mary and Martha," 97–99; Kenneth Pennington, *Pope and Bishops: The Papal Monarchy in the Twelfth and Thirteenth Century* (Philadelphia: University of Pennsylvania Press, 1984), 108–12; Egger, "Papst Innocenz III," 65–67; Robb, "Who Has Chosen the Better Part?" 157–60; eadem, "Joachimist Exegesis," 141; Moore, *Pope Innocent III*, 162. On Innocent's devotion to Bernard and support of his liturgy, see Egger, "Papst Innocenz III," 64. On Bernard as a major source for Innocent's view of papal primacy, which he went well beyond, see Pennington, *Pope and Bishops*, 39, 42–58, 78–100, 154–95; Klaus Schatz, *Papal Primacy: From Its Origins to the Present*, trans. John A. Otto and Linda M. Mahoney (Collegeville, MN: Liturgical Press, 1996), 81–93; Francis Oakley, *The Mortgage of the Past: Reshaping the Ancient Political Inheritance, 1050–1300* (New Haven: Yale University Press, 2012), 174–84, with an excellent review of the literature on this subject at 180–81. Scholars emphasizing the influence of previous popes, scholastics, and canonists over that of Bernard include Colin Morris, *The Papal Monarchy: The Western Church from 1050 to 1250* (Oxford: Oxford University Press, 1989), 418, 421–33, 450; Robert L. Benson, *Law, Rulership, and Rhetoric: Selected Essays*, ed. Loren J. White, Giles Constable, and Richard H. Rouse (Notre Dame: University of Notre Dame Press, 2014), nos. 20–36, 204–45; James M. Powell, "Two Popes Before and After the Fourth Lateran Council," in idem, *The Papacy, Frederick II, and Communal Devotion in*

the mendicants who took her as their patron. The Magdalene whom Innocent preaches is the penitent who openly acknowledges her sin and receives absolution, and the apostle to the apostle who brings the Good News to the disciples and whose post-biblical career as an evangelist is a model for the pastoral ministry.[57] Also, in Innocent's preaching on John 20, his Mary Magdalene, who is first at the tomb and who returns to it after Peter and John depart, surpasses both disciples in her constancy and fidelity.[58]

While the mendicants were not formally approved until after Innocent's reign, he licensed two new religious orders. His choices are telling. Both orders had a strongly activist calling and one had an innovative organization. In 1184 Pope Lucius III had condemned as heretics the Humiliati, a group of pious Lombard clerics and lay people. Innocent thought they merited another look. After receiving the report of the committee, he empaneled to provide it, he overruled Lucius and approved the Humiliati as a religious order in 1201. The Humiliati included priests, laypeople living in community, and laypeople—married or single—living at home. This last subdivision looked ahead to the lay confraternities to come and to the tertiaries associated with the mendicants. The Humiliati engaged in manual labor, notably in the cloth industries of their native towns, and some held positions in urban government, in addition to engaging in poor relief

Medieval Italy, ed. Edward Peters (Farnham: Ashgate, 2014), no. 6 at 3, 8, 12. For Bernard himself on the papacy, see Alice Chapman, *Sacred and Temporal Power in the Writings of Bernard of Clairvaux* (Turnhout: Brepols, 2013), 6, 123–45, 159–61, 168–69; at 194 she agrees that Innocent went beyond him.

[57] Jansen, *Making of the Magdalene*, 50–92, at 100–4 for Innocent, the early mendicants, and the Magdalene; for another of Innocent's sermons on the Magdalene, see eadem, "Innocent III and the Literature of Confession," in *Innocenzo III: Urbs et orbis*, Atti del congresso internazionale, Roma, 9–15 settembre 1998, ed. Andrea Sommerlechner, 2 vols., Miscellanea della Società Romana di Storia Patri 44 (Rome: Presso la Società alla Biblioteca Vallicelliana, 2003), 1:369–82. It is also worth noting that, while the mendicant orders were not officially constituted until after Innocent's pontificate, the best known image of this pope is Giotto's portrayal of him in the upper church at Assisi dreaming of St. Francis, who props up the Lateran basilica just before Lateran IV; on this image, see Michael Goodich, "Biography, 1000–1250," in *Historiography in the Middle Ages*, ed. Deborah Mauskopf Deliyannis (Leiden: Brill, 2003), 353–85 at 369.

[58] Jansen, *Making of the Magdalene*, 63–64, 89, 100–1.

and hospital care.[59] The second new order, licensed by Innocent in 1198, was the Trinitarians, founded by the former Paris scholar John of Matha. This group, with its more traditional organization as a monastic order, had a strikingly novel mission. The Trinitarians ransomed Christians captured by the Muslims and provided hospices for the rehabilitation of those redeemed, a service they also extended to others who might need housing or healing. As has been observed, "For the Trinitarians, religious life was seen not as a flight from the world but rather as the most effective way to generate works of charity."[60] Both of these new religious orders well reflect Innocent's priorities.

These priorities also gain high-profile visibility in three individuals whom Innocent canonized during his pontificate. None of them was a contemplative. One was Gilbert of Sempringham (†1189), declared a saint in 1202. Learned and modest, he remained a parish priest and took vows in the monastic order he had founded only on retiring from its administration in extreme old age. The Gilbertine order included nuns, the canon-priests who ministered to them, and lay brothers and sisters. Members were not required to give up their personal wealth and they joined it with that of the order in sponsoring hospitals, leprosaria, hostels, and almshouses. Beyond these humanitarian services, Innocent may well have appreciated the Gilbertines' activism, sheltering Thomas Becket from the wrath of Henry II in 1164 and spiriting him safely to France in

---

[59] On the Humiliati, see Brenda Bolton, "Tradition and Temerity: Papal Attitudes toward Deviants, 1159-1216;" "Poverty as Protest: Some Inspirational Groups at the Turn of the Twelfth Century;" "The Poverty of the Humiliati," all in eadem, *Innocent III: Studies in Papal Authority and Pastoral Care* (Aldershot: Ashgate, 1995), nos. 12, 13, and 14; and most fully in Frances Andrews, *The Early Humiliati* (Cambridge: Cambridge University Press, 1999), 12, 39-44, 48, 57, 59, 62-98, 136-37, 254-58. Cf. Robb, "Who Hath Chosen the Better Part?" 168-70, who sees Innocent's support of the Humiliati as consonant with the desiderata of Joachim, as mediated by Rainer of Ponza.

[60] Giulio Cipollone, *Trinità e liberazione tra cristianità e islam* (Assisi: Citadella, 2000), quotation at 210: "La vita religiosa trinitaria non è una *fuga mundi*, ma il mezzo ritenuto più efficace per produrre opera di carità," with the Trinitarian *Rule* given in Latin, at 72-79 and in Italian, at 79-87. My trans. For a less effusive discussion, see James M. Powell, "Innocent III, the Trinitarians, and the Renewal of the Church, 1198-1200," in *La liberazione dei "captivi" tra cristianità e islam: Oltre la crociata e il gihad. Tolleranza e servizio umanitario*, Atti del congresso interdisciplinare di studi storici (Roma, 16-19 settembre 1998) organizzato per l'VIII centenario dell'approvazione della regola dei Trinitari da parte del Papa Innocenzo III il 17 dicembre 1198, ed. Giulio Cipollone (Vatican City: Archivio Segreto Vaticano, 2000), 245-54.

the garb of one of their *conversi*. Another English cleric he canonized, in 1203, was Wulfstan of Worcester (†1095). One of the few Anglo-Saxon prelates to survive the Norman Conquest, Wulfstan seamlessly joined his role as a monastic superior with that of a bishop. A fearless and energetic pastor, preacher, and politician, he was a social as well as an ecclesiastical reformer, enforcing clerical celibacy in his diocese and banning the slave trade between England and Ireland.[61] Even more significant is Innocent's canonization of Omnobono of Cremona (†1197) in 1199. A layman, husband and father, and merchant by profession, he was "the first non-royal lay person ever to be officially canonized," celebrated by Innocent for devoting his free time and disposable income to the needy no less than for his orthodoxy and piety.[62] As with the religious orders he licensed, the figures Innocent held up as saints for his times display his fundamental values. Above all they reflect the importance he attached to the ministry to the corporal and not just the spiritual needs of fellow Christians.

---

[61] Brian Golding, *Gilbert of Sempringham and the Gilbertine Order, c. 1130–c. 1300* (Oxford: Clarendon Press, 1995), 7–60, 85, 109, 236–39 on Gilbert's life and the foundation, structure, history, and calling of his order; 61–66 on his canonization; on Wulfstan see David Hugh Farmer, *Oxford Dictionary of Saints*, 4th ed. (Oxford: Oxford University Press, 1997), 518–19. For Wulfstan as a reformer of the slave trade and promoter of clerical celibacy see David Wyatt, *Slaves and Warriors in England and Ireland, 800–1200* (Leiden: Brill, 2009), 150, 219, 292, 299; for Wulfstan's political career see David Bates, *William the Conquerer* (New Haven: Yale University Press, 2016), 215, 250, 275, 343–44, 376, 381, 432–33, 458. As is noted by Emma Mason, *St. Wulfstan of Worcester, c. 1008–1095* (Oxford: Blackwell, 1990), 113–14, during the dispute over the election of Stephen Langton King John chose Wulfstan as his patron saint, in light of his reputed loyalty to the crown; one wonders what Innocent thought of this calculated act of devotional provocation.

[62] Jansen, *Making of the Magdalene*, 104–5; beyond this quotation she notes the connection between this innovative canonization and Innocent's concern for ministries of all kinds to and by the laity. For more on Omnobono, see André Vauchez, *The Laity in the Middle Ages: Religious Beliefs and Devotional Practices*, ed. Daniel E. Bornstein, trans. Margery J. Schneider (Notre Dame: University of Notre Dame Press, 1993), Chapter 6; idem, *Omnobono di Cremona (†1197), laico e santo: Profilo storico* (Cremona: Nuova Editrice Cremonese, 2001); idem, "Innocent III, Sicard de Crémone, et la canonization de Saint Homobon (†1197)," in *Innocenzo III: Urbs et orbis*, Atti del congresso internazionale, Roma, 9–15 settembre 1998, ed. Andrea Sommerlechner, 2 vols., Miscellanea della Società Romana di Storia Patri 44 (Rome: Presso la Società alla Biblioteca Vallicelliana, 2003), 1:435–53; Donald S. Prudlo, *Certain Sainthood: Canonization and the Origins of Papal Infallibility in the Medieval Church* (Ithaca: Cornell University Press, 2015), 63–66, 116–17.

This snapshot of Innocent's wider ideas and preferences, coupled with a fuller appreciation of the highly concrete conditions in which he produced his crusade-related writings, should make it clear that apocalypticism, whether in general or apocalypticism as professed by Joachim of Fiore, was neither a deeply engrained feature of Innocent's mentality nor a position which he officially endorsed. Rather, as with his other crusade-related arguments, it was but one arrow in his quiver, to be used or abandoned as the political situation required. When Innocent did appeal to the End Time, he could draw on a mainstream far wider and deeper than the waters from which Joachim drank. Innocent was never in danger of confusing the earthly with the heavenly Jerusalem. In his fabled letter of 13 November 1204, Innocent makes no reference to Joachim's Trinitarian theology of history; he ignores the *viri spirituali* and their role in Joachim's scenario; and the parturient woman of Rev. 12:1–3 makes no appearance. What he takes from Joachim is his rather garbled defense of the *filioque* and the idea of yoking John 20:1–18 to anti-Greek polemic. This move also departs from Joachim by imputing Trinitarian error to John from the start and by assigning the Magdalene the double role of true Israel and Christological heretic. While Innocent reveals his own rhetorical opportunism in this letter, and across all his crusade-related writings, his use of Joachim, not to mention Joachim himself, emerge as less conventional than many of Joachim's scholarly defenders argue, especially in the light of the varied genres and disciplines that informed contemporary attitudes on the themes, theories, and personages Innocent discussed. In the end, what Innocent envisioned in the crusade movement was not Joachim's End Time at hand, to be ushered in by contemplatives, but a vision of the church unified and reformed by the ministry of the clergy and laity under the leadership of the Roman pontiff, acting in the here and now.

CHAPTER 11

The End of a Single World: The Sacrament of Extreme Unction in Scholastic Thought

Lesley Smith

Far removed from the drama of the Apocalypse and End of the World comes the end of a single life. This essay eschews the grand scale of this volume's theme and brings it to a much narrower focus, to consider the development of the sacrament of extreme unction—the anointing of the sick—from the mid-twelfth century to the mid-thirteenth, a key period in the history of both sacramental theology and pastoral care in the Middle Ages. We shall approach the question by looking at some of the milestones of writing about unction as it was examined and debated in the schools and early university of Paris, the European centre of biblical and theological research, and from these try to draw out links to the broader history of the period. Unction is an example in miniature of how sacramental theory as a whole was changing; but it gives us glimpses, too, of other contemporary preoccupations, such as the idea of purgatory and the theory of sin. I hope to show how this intimate action,

---

I offer this essay to Ann Matter in gratitude for our many years of friendship, and in admiration for her leadership in the community of the medieval Bible.

L. Smith (✉)
Harris Manchester College, University of Oxford, Oxford, UK

© The Author(s) 2019
E. Knibbs et al. (eds.), *The End of the World in Medieval Thought and Spirituality*, The New Middle Ages,
https://doi.org/10.1007/978-3-030-14965-9_11

which many Christians might never experience, was related to some of the biggest debates of the time. In doing so, however, I do not want to lose track of the particularity of unction and the problems it posed for theologians. Anointing had a long history, and Eastern and Western Churches had evolved diverse rites for it. In addition to the varieties of liturgy, there were different views about precisely what the practice was thought to achieve.[1] The Bible was not much help: there were only two recognized New Testament texts which mentioned this sort of unction and, if anything, they made things more confusing.[2] Moreover, once unction had been accepted as a sacrament, scholars were left trying to fit an array of customs and traditional beliefs into a concept of sacrament that, over the century that we shall examine, was very much in flux. What a sacrament was and what it did were still the subject of debate.

Although unction was a minor sacrament in comparison to baptism or the eucharist, with a much smaller place in the overall discussions, nonetheless it posed difficult problems. Indeed, its position as something of an outlier in various ways raised questions that were not always easy to fit into the solutions offered by broader sacramental theory. We might even think that unction remained, in a phrase used about the modern understanding of confirmation, "a sacrament in search of a theology." What I shall chart here, then, is not smooth sailing to a clear destination, but a voyage through rather choppier waters. The voyage ends in the harbour designed by Albert the Great and Thomas Aquinas; but when we reach it, we might yet wonder if we would not have preferred a different destination. While their solution accords with the wider context of the Last Things, it loses sight of the importance that the ritual action of unction might assume in the life of an individual believer.

Let us begin, then, with a lightning tour of unction up to the middle of the twelfth century, and its entry into the sacramental discussions of the Paris schools. Unction—from the Latin noun *unguens* (oil), and verb *unguere*—was a relatively common biblical practice. Along with corn and wine, oil—specifically, olive oil—was a sign of God's

---

[1] Placid Murray, "The Liturgical History of Extreme Unction," in *Studies in Pastoral Liturgy* 2, ed. Vincent Ryan (Dublin: The Furrow Trust, 1963), 18–38; see also three linked articles on the origin and development of rites for anointing by H. B. Porter in *Journal of Theological Studies* n.s. 7 (1956): 211–25 and 10 (1959): 43–62, 299–307. The greatest developments in liturgy occur in the Carolingian period.

[2] Mark 6:13; James 5:14–15.

blessing, and anointing in a religious context was a sign of consecration, at first of priests such as Aaron, and sacred objects, and then, from the time of Saul, of kings.[3] But oil was also used medicinally and in quasi-medicinal situations, such as in the purification rite after leprosy.[4] In the New Testament, two passages note the anointing of the sick with oil. In Mark 6:13, the twelve disciples are sent to "cast out many demons, and anoint...with oil many that were sick, and heal...them"; and the Letter of James, 5:14–15, notes: "Is anyone sick among you? Let him bring in the priests of the church; and let them pray over him, anointing him with oil in the name of the Lord. And the prayer of faith shall save the sick man."[5] These verses of James were to prove the key text for the establishment of anointing the sick as a practice of the Church, even before its recognition as a sacrament. Bede (d. 735) supplies the first commentary on the Epistle, and his text tells us (whether or not this was true in practice) that anointing the sick with oil was well-established: "And we read that the Apostles have done this in the Gospel, and now the custom of the Church holds that the sick be anointed with consecrated oil by priests and made well with accompanying prayers."[6] Bede is our first milestone: before him, evidence of anointing and its purpose in the Early Church is limited; scholars writing after him, such as Rabanus Maurus and Paschasius Radbertus, all followed his lead.[7] It was not clear, however, what unction was thought to achieve, although Bede does say that for it to be effective,

---

[3] Anointing of Aaron and objects: Exodus 29:7, 36; 40:9–10, 13, 15; Leviticus 8; Psalm 132 [133]: 2. Anointing of kings: 1 Kings 10; 16:13; 3 Kings 1:34, 39, for example.

[4] Leviticus 14.

[5] "Infirmatur quis in vobis? Inducat presbyteros Ecclesiae, et orent super eum, ungentes eum oleo in nomine Domini: et oratio fidei salvabit infirmum..." (Vulgate; my translation).

[6] Bede, *In epistolas VII catholicas*, ed. M. L. W. Laistner, Corpus Christianorum Series Latina 121 (Turnhout: Brepols, 1983), 221, on James 5:14–15.

[7] For overviews of the history of unction see L. Godefroy, "Extrême Onction," in *Dictionnaire de Théologie Catholique*, 5, ed. A. Vacant and E. Mangenot (Paris: Letouzey et Ané, 1912), cols. 1897–2022; Heinrich Weisweiler, "Das Sakrament der Letzen Ölung in den systematischen Werken der ersten Frühscholastik," *Scholastik* 7 (1932): 321–53, 524–60; linked articles on extreme unction by A. Verhamme, in *Collationes Brugenses* 45 (1949): 39–47, 114–19, 119–22, 199–205, 280–86, 364–71; 46 (1950): 15–23, 100–7, 186–94, 267–75, 339–44, 457–60, 460–63; 47 (1951): 65–69, 69–72; Henry S. Kryger, *The Doctrine of the Effects of Extreme Unction in Its Historical Development: A Dissertation* (Washington, DC: Catholic University of America Press, 1949); and Bernhard Poschmann, trans. and rev. Francis Courtney, *Penance and the Anointing of the Sick* (Freiburg: Herder/Burns and Oates, 1964).

it can only be administered after penance. It is only from around the ninth century that unction was discussed in relation to sacraments, along with the development of a variety of rites for anointing; the term "extreme unction" appears from around the tenth century.[8]

The question was not whether the Church could and should anoint the sick, but the status of the action when it did so. Should it be counted as a sacrament—a guaranteed occasion of grace—or as merely sacramental—something which aided the reception of or prepared for grace, but did not in itself confer it? Sacrament as a concept had been recognized by the Church Fathers, with Augustine supplying the well-known definitions of a "visible form of invisible grace," and "a sign of a sacred thing."[9] But these apparently simple formulations left some basic questions unanswered, such as what the list of sacraments included; Augustine, for example, counted the Lord's Prayer and the Apostles' Creed within his tally. And were sacraments purely a part of the New Covenant, or had they existed in some form in the Old Law? Of the possible contenders, only circumcision was commonly regarded as an Old Testament "sacrament," in this case of initiation or entrance into religion, and as a sort of precursor of the Christian collection—so much so that Alan of Lille (d. 1203) describes each New Law sacrament as a form of spiritual application of circumcision. In his formulation, confirmation was the circumcision of weakness from the soul, the eucharist was the circumcision of venial sin, and marriage was the circumcision of sexual incontinence, and so on.[10] In Alan's schema, extreme unction was the circumcision of an imminent corporeal or spiritual infirmity—his longest definition, and one full of hidden assumptions, as we shall see.

Although sacraments were discussed by earlier theologians, it is not until the middle of the twelfth century that the theory of sacrament received concentrated attention. Our next milestone is the

---

[8] Poschmann, *Penance*, 246. Verhamme notes that, prior to Peter Lombard, in ecclesiastical documents the common terms for the action are *unctio infirmorum*, *unctio sancti olei*, *sacra unctio*, and *unctio olei sanctificati*: *Collationes Brugenses* 45: 40.

[9] See for instance, Augustine, *De civitate Dei*, 10.5; *Quaestiones in Heptateuchum*, 3.84: D. Van den Eynde, "Les définitions des sacrements pendant la première période de la théologie scolastique," *Antonianum* 24 (1949): 183–228; 25 (1950): 3–78.

[10] Alan of Lille, *Postquam consummati sunt dies octo*, in MS Paris, BnF, lat. 3818, fol. 18v, quoted in Jean Longère, *Oeuvres Oratoires de maîtres parisiens au XIIe siècle*, 2 vols. (Paris: Études augustiniennes, 1975), 1:275.

comprehensive treatise *On the Sacraments of the Christian Faith* (*De sacramentis christianae fidei*), by Hugh, the influential head of the school at the Augustinian abbey of St. Victor, in Paris.[11] Hugh (d. 1142) shared Augustine's expansive vision of what the concept of sacrament might include. He characterises three types: the principal type, which included baptism and the eucharist, and which were necessary for salvation; the second type, such as aspersion, the reception of ashes and making the sign of the cross, which were not essential but were of benefit because they increased devotion; and the third sort which was preparatory to the others, such as holy orders or consecration.[12] Hugh considers the anointing of the sick in comparison to the greater unctions of baptism and confirmation. "It is a sort of special medicine for the body and soul.... For oil heals ailing members. Thus oil is of benefit in curing both."[13]

In spite of his reputation, and the common-sense persuasiveness of his arguments, Hugh did not have the discussion to himself. Almost contemporary with him, Peter Lombard (d. 1160) was Master of the cathedral school of Notre Dame in Paris, and for a short time the city's bishop. Although he had been resident at St. Victor, and a proponent of many of Augustine's ideas, Peter nevertheless pursued a different line on sacraments to Hugh, and it is he who is credited with settling their number, scope, and order in subsequent debate. Peter's discussion of sacraments comes in distinction 23 of the fourth book of his best-selling text, *Four Books of Sentences*.[14] Collections of sentences (*sententiae*) had become popular from the early twelfth century. They provided material for (and were notes of) classroom discussions of tricky theological problems—issues that derived from biblical commentary but which were lifted out of direct scriptural exegesis into thematic debates about

---

[11] Hugh of St. Victor, *Hugonis de Sancto Victore: De sacramentis christianae fidei*, Corpus Victorinum. Textus historici 1, ed. Rainer Berndt (Aschendorff: Corpus Victorinum, 2008); *De sacramentis christianae fidei*, ed. and trans. Roy J. Deferrari (Cambridge, MA: Mediaeval Academy, 1951), whose translation is quoted here.

[12] *De sacramentis*, 1.9.7 (Deferrari, 164).

[13] *De sacramentis*, 2.15.3 (Deferrari, 432).

[14] *Magistri Petri Lombardi ...Sententiae in IV Libris Distinctae*, 3 vols., ed. I. C. Brady (Grottaferrata: Coll. S. Bonaventura, 1971); trans. Giulio Silano, *The Sentences*, 4 vols. (Toronto: Pontifical Institute of Medieval Studies, 2007–2010).

particular issues.[15] Peter's was by no means the first such collection, but it came at the right time and in the right place, and with his reputation behind it, the *Sentences* became a runaway success. By the 1220s, Peter's text had become an indispensable starting point for teaching, and for several centuries thereafter, doctoral students in theology could not graduate without having lectured on at least part of it.

Peter's four books covered the whole of the Christian life, from God and angels in book one, to the sacraments and the four last things ("the doctrine of signs") in book four. He followed Augustine in his definitions of sacrament and sign, but chose to draw on recent discussions to propound a list of seven New Law sacraments, in the order: baptism, confirmation, the eucharist ("the bread of blessing"), penance, extreme unction, holy orders, and marriage. Seven was a biblically significant number, representing completion and fulfilment, from the number of days of Creation in Genesis to the seven seals on the Book of Life in Revelation; and seven was a perfect number, made up of two other perfect numbers, three and four. This was not simply a matter of playing with arithmetic: God had woven number into the fabric of the universe, and the number of any particular thing was a clue to its essence. There were seven gifts of the Holy Spirit, as well as the seven planets, days of the week, pillars of the Temple, original churches, petitions of the Lord's Prayer, last words on the Cross, joys and sorrows of Mary, and journeys of Christ.[16] Since the sacraments were undoubtedly linked to the completion of Christ's sacrifice by the grace of the Holy Spirit at Pentecost, it is not surprising that they, too, should number seven.

Peter may have taken his material from a septenary list of sacraments (the first we know of) by the anonymous author of the *Sententiae divinitatis* (c. 1147–48), who included unction (referred to as *unctio solemnis infirmorum*) in the tally.[17] From that point, all scholars who

---

[15] Many of these often-fragmentary collections are edited and printed by Odo Lottin in *Psychologie et morale aux XIIe et XIIIe siècles*, vol. 5: *L'École d'Anselme de Laon et de Guillaume de Champeaux* (Gembloux: J. Duculot, 1959). See also, Cédric Giraud, '*Per verba magistri': Anselme de Laon et son école au XIIe siècle* (Turnhout: Brepols, 2010).

[16] V. F. Hopper, *Medieval Number Symbolism: Its Sources, Meaning and Influence on Thought and Expression* (New York: Cooper Square, 1938); Nigel Hiscock, *The Symbol at Your Door: Number and Geometry in Religious Architecture of the Greek and Latin Middle Ages* (Aldershot: Ashgate, 2007).

[17] Godefroy, "Extrême Onction," col. 1988; Poschmann, *Penance*, 249.

argued for a definitive list of seven sacraments included unction among their number, although a few still disputed the total. Peter's contemporary, master Gilbert of Poitiers (d. 1154), was amongst a minority that regarded the anointing of the sick as sacramental, in the same category as the washing of feet on Maundy Thursday, but not a sacrament.[18] It was not an unreasonable view: unlike other sacraments, unction had not been modelled by Jesus in the Gospels, and given that it obviously did not always produce bodily healing, it was unclear how it could have been instituted and what exactly it achieved. However, the influence of the Lombard's *Sentences* was such that the inclusion of unction as a full sacrament became the common view. In addition, Peter's use of the term "extreme unction" took over from the various other possibilities to become the common name.[19]

Peter devotes four chapters to extreme unction, beginning by defining it as the anointing of the sick which is done in extremis with oil consecrated by a bishop. Giulio Silano, the *Sentences*' modern translator, renders in extremis as "at the end of life," but as we shall see, when exactly the sacrament should be administered was a matter for debate. So it is better, I think, to leave the Latin phrase untranslated, retaining its common English connotation of "serious danger," rather than specifying the last action before death, since it is important for most of those who discuss unction in the twelfth century that the sick person might yet recover. Having defined his terms, Peter moves on to their elaboration, first discussing the types of unction used in other sacraments, then asking about the institution of the sacrament, and finally considering the question of repeatability—whether you could receive the sacrament more than once. His treatment formed the cornerstone of all subsequent discussions.

Peter begins by noting that there are three different types of unction to be found within the list of seven sacraments. Christians are anointed in baptism, in confirmation, and in extreme unction; and in addition, kings and bishops are anointed when they take office. All except extreme

---

[18] Nikolaus M. Häring, ed. "Die *Sententiae Magistri Gisleberti Pictavensis episcopi* I," *Archives d'Histoire Doctrinale et Littéraire au Moyen Age* 45 (1978): 83–180 at 154–55, n. 61.

[19] Verhamme, *Collationes Brugenses*, 45: 40 n. 6, notes a seventh-century bishop of Reims using the term extreme unction (see PL 80: 444), although a more recent edition places the text in the ninth century: MGH Capit. episc. 3:375ff.

unction use a mixture of olive oil and balsam, which was generally known by its Greek name, chrism. The mixture is interpreted spiritually, with oil representing good conscience and balsam good reputation. Both good conscience and a good reputation are needed for all anointings except extreme unction, since for those facing sickness, reputation becomes trivial; only a clear conscience—that is, oil alone—is necessary.[20]

Peter next asks about the institution of the sacrament, which he credits to the Apostle James, as can be seen from the Epistle (5:14–15). More importantly for Peter, the biblical text shows that the sacrament was instituted for a double cause—for spiritual sickness, i.e., the remission of sins, and for physical sickness. "And so it is established that anyone who receives this anointing with faith and devotion is relieved in body and soul, so long as it is expedient that he should be relieved in both. But if perhaps it is not expedient that he should have bodily health, he acquires in this sacrament that health which pertains to the soul."[21] Peter uses Augustinian language to distinguish between the sacrament in its outer form—the anointing—and the *res* or "thing" of the sacrament, which is "the inner anointing...brought about by the remission of sins and the increase of the virtues."[22] Finally, he notes that if the sacrament is omitted because of negligence or contempt, then the consequences may be "dangerous and damnable."

As ever in the *Sentences*, in a short space, Peter has covered a lot of ground. He does this in part by presenting only solutions to problems, rather than explaining the problems themselves or giving more than one possible response to the issue. As expressed by Peter, one would not know that there were differences of opinion about many of these questions. Here, for instance, Peter does not mention an important problem with the institution of extreme unction, which is whether or not sacraments could be instituted by anyone except Christ: since sacraments rely on the rightness of their institution to be efficacious, all must derive from him. Peter simply states that the sacrament was instituted by James and leaves aside the other questions this solution raises. He spends more time on that age-old problem of religious healing: why it does not always work. Peter's explanation is that unction has two main purposes and only

---

[20] Lombard, *Sententiae*, IV, d. 23, c. 3; Hugh, *De sacramentis*, 2.15.1 (trans. Deferrari, 430–31).
[21] Lombard, *Sententiae*, IV, d. 23, c. 3 (trans. Silano, *Sentences*, 4:137).
[22] Ibid.

one of these—the remission of spiritual sickness—will *always* be successful. In comparison to this spiritual relief, bodily healing is relatively unimportant. He also glosses over the issue behind his statement about the *res* of the sacrament, which was part of what distinguished the sacraments from one another—that is, what constituted the unique purpose of each sacrament and made it necessary. And his final, almost throwaway point, that neglecting to take or administer this sacrament had serious consequences, was in part an attempt to cement the sacrament within the list of seven, and to habituate clergy and laity to it: as we shall see, under some understandings of extreme unction, it should not be administered until it was certain the invalid would not survive. In addition, unlike baptism, extreme unction was never regarded as necessary for salvation, but this did not mean that those who could receive it should neglect to do so.

The last of Peter's four chapters on extreme unction concerns its repeatability. Here Peter does give some idea of the reason for the question, and the history of its discussion. Iteration was important because it seemed to be possible for some sacraments but not others. The picture was clouded by the response of Augustine to the Donatist Parmenian, over the issue of whether those moving from belief in one of the various interpretations of Christianity (which would now be defined as orthodox and heterodox) to another should be re-baptized. Augustine's answer was unequivocal: no injury should be done to a sacrament, he says, which means no repetition.[23] This declaration of non-iterability, which appeared to encompass all sacraments, was a complication for later theologians: how could the eucharist and penance fit into this schema?[24] Peter's understanding of Augustine's meaning is briskly practical: Augustine was not referring to all sacraments; in context, he was speaking only of baptism and orders. So Peter allows that baptism, confirmation, and orders may only be administered once, but the eucharist, penance, and marriage are repeatable.

Into which group does extreme unction fit? Here, Peter for the first time makes reference to differences of opinion. Some argue that anointing can be repeated, for just as medicine is renewed when illness returns, so the patient should be anointed again. After all, prayer for the sick

---

[23] Lombard, *Sententiae*, IV, d. 23, c. 4 (trans. Silano, *Sentences*, 4:137), quoting Augustine, *Contra epistolam Parmeniani*, 2.13.28.

[24] Nikolaus M. Häring, "The Augustinian Axiom: *Nulli Sacramento Iniuria Facienda Est*," *Mediaeval Studies* 16 (1954): 87–117.

person is repeated, and since the Apostle mentions prayer and anointing together in the Epistle, it makes sense that unction should be repeatable too. But others have different views. They solve the iterability question by making a fine distinction about what it is in a sacrament that is repeated. Since one does not, for instance, receive a second host blessed at the same eucharist, but a host from a new mass, then the sacrament is not, in this sense, repeated; and so the sacrament can be received many times. To those who object that this same argument could be extended to baptism, as long as one was not baptized in the same water, the response is that the water in baptism does not have the same sacramental importance as the elements of the eucharist or the oil of unction, for someone can, in necessity, be baptized in unblessed water, because the water is not part of the power of the sacrament, and it is blessed only "pro reverentia et decore"; but the eucharist and unction need the bread and wine and oil to be blessed in order to have effect—the materials are part of the *virtue* of the sacrament. Having given both sides, Peter does not come to a conclusion; instead, he attempts to sum up the positions. If you think the sacrament should not be repeated, your reasoning must refer to the blessing of the material through which the sacrament is effected, and your argument must include all sacraments. If, however, you think that some sacraments may be received more than once, it appears that your argument is based on tradition rather than specific reasoning, for "it is true of some that they are not repeated by a frequent reception, but not of others, because they are received frequently, like this sacrament of anointing, which is often repeated in almost every Church."[25] Earlier in the *Sentences*, Peter had discussed the same issue of repeatability with regard to baptism and confirmation, referring each time to Augustine, but he does not come to a universal conclusion that holds for the sacraments as a whole; rather, he decides the question for each sacrament individually, apparently on the grounds of custom.

This then is Peter's short and practical guide to extreme unction. And as is often the case when reading him, one needs to know the portion of the iceberg under the surface of the water. His sources are a mixture of the anonymous *Summa sententiarum* and Hugh of St. Victor's *De sacramentis*, and he follows the structure of Hugh's discussion.[26]

---

[25] Lombard, *Sententiae*, IV, d. 23, c. 4 (trans. Silano, *Sentences*, 4:138).
[26] *Summa sententiarum*, tr. 6, c. 15 (PL 176: 153B–54C); Hugh, *De sacramentis*, 2.15.

Peter's counter-arguments are drawn from contemporary scholars: Master Simon, Master Rolandus (Bandinelli, later Alexander III) and the canonist Omnebene, all of whom deny the repeatability of the sacrament.[27] His aim was not to be original, but rather to tread a path between the authorities of the day and plot out landmarks for subsequent scholars. In this, he succeeded almost too well. Peter makes his discussion of unction short, neat and almost uncontentious, skimming over most of the problems its inclusion as a sacrament raised: Christ had neither received it nor done it himself; it was commonly administered by a single priest, rather than the "priests" ordered in the Epistle of James, which appeared to speak of the healing power of an accompanying prayer, rather than the unction itself; it used oil which had to be pre-consecrated by a bishop rather than the water or wine confected as part of the sacrament by baptism and the eucharist; it often did not heal the sick, so it was not clear what effect ensued; it was not clear when and to whom the sacrament should be given, and at whose request; and opinions differed as to whether or not it could be received more than once. These were only the most obvious points that required consideration, but one would not realize it from reading the *Sentences*.

We find a more discursive response to the anointing of the sick in the work of Peter the Chanter (d. 1197). The Chanter, like the Lombard before him, was head of the cathedral school in Paris and a master renowned for his interest in the application of theology to everyday life. His wide-ranging questions on sacraments and moral guidance were gathered together from his mostly oral teaching to produce the *Summa de sacramentis et anime consiliis*.[28] Four sacraments—baptism, confirmation, extreme unction and the eucharist—make up the first part of the *Summa*, followed by a long second section on penance. The Chanter poses questions on unction under eleven broad headings. The order in which he deals with his issues is a little random (which probably reflects

---

[27] Heinrich Weisweiler, *Maître Simon et son groupe De sacramentis* (Louvain: Spicilegium sacrum Lovaniense, 1937). For Rolandus and Omnebene see Weisweiler, "Das Sakrament," 527-31. In denying repeatability they are following contemporary Bolognese legal teaching.

[28] *Petrus Cantor: Summa de sacramentis et animae consiliis*, ed. Jean-Albert Dugauquier, Analecta Mediaevalia Namurcensia 4 (Louvain: Nauwelaerts, 1954), part 1, §§41-51; and John W. Baldwin, *Masters, Princes and Merchants: The Social Views of Peter the Chanter and His Circle*, 2 vols. (Princeton: Princeton University Press, 1970), 1:13-14.

the *reportatio* process by which the *Summa* was recorded, and its manuscript tradition), but the discussion conveys the sense of a live issue, as opposed to the more static treatment in the *Sentences*, and of an intelligent and sympathetic man. We begin with a question that arises directly from the biblical text: whether the sacrament can be administered by a single priest or whether more than one is needed.[29] This comes from the text of the Epistle, which reads "call for priests" ("presbyteros"). The Chanter answers that only one priest is needed, and his reason for apparently contradicting Scripture is that this dispensation was revealed by divine inspiration. What Peter does not say here is that the question of how many priests are needed is secondary to the fact that priests alone could administer this sacrament, unlike the more important sacrament of baptism which could nevertheless be administered by anyone, in extremis. After this somewhat pragmatic start, Peter asks the more pressing question of when a sick person should request anointing: should one do so as soon as one becomes ill, or should one wait until death is imminent? This was an important point, as it touched both on the repeatability of the sacrament and also on the effect it was thought to have. Peter is sure that one should call for the sacrament immediately ("statim"), so that it might still be possible to affect the body as well as the soul. This is the precautionary principle at work: act now, so that whatever happens, one is protected against a bad outcome. But if it is right to call for extreme unction, should one not even more call immediately for the eucharist? Peter thinks not. The eucharist is a much greater sacrament than unction (an interesting example of the ranking of sacraments), and one needs to be prepared in order to receive it to one's benefit. A sick person might well not be able to make those preparations. Some scholars, Peter notes, say that anointing is the conclusion and sum of all other sacraments, and so should be delayed until the very end of life.[30] But he takes a very different view: the sacrament should be administered as soon as there are signs of distress, whether life-threatening or not—and he is careful to note that canon law gives no definite ruling on this question. Throughout his treatment of extreme unction, Peter's model is the medical remedy. Just as one would not delay sending for a doctor until the

---

[29] *Summa*, §41.
[30] *Summa*, §42.

patient was beyond cure, so one should not delay sending for the priest. He is convinced that the sacrament has the power of physical healing.

Did the invalid himself have to request the sacrament and be aware of what was happening? Peter takes his answer from the example of the Apostles, who anointed the possessed, the raving mad, people who did not and could not ask for unction to be administered, and even those who did not want to be anointed. This seems to him to be the model to follow, since even "in our own day" we have seen "lunatics and others struck by strange phenomena" healed by this sacrament.[31] He raises the question of the blessed Genevieve, a laywoman who carried holy oil so that she could anoint those who needed it. Genevieve's example was to become a commonplace in later discussions of extreme unction, causing problems because she was not a priest. The Monte Sainte Geneviève was a landmark in Paris and the site of a number of thriving schools which taught the liberal arts, without which no student could go on to study theology. Genevieve's story must have raised classroom questions that the Chanter could not ignore; and so he addresses issues such as how she got hold of the oil, whether a woman could anoint, and whether the anointing had validity if it did not include a blessing, which only a cleric could give. Peter does not directly answer any of these points, and it is tempting to think that he sidesteps them because he does not necessarily agree with the tradition of unction as a clerical preserve. Although he does not say so, it was generally agreed that the oil used in extreme unction had to be the olive oil blessed by a bishop on Maundy Thursday; only clerics were allowed to anoint, even in extremis; and the anointing had to be accompanied by a blessing. But since Peter's model for extreme unction is the medical analogy to a physical remedy, then these customary restrictions on its use would not suit him. He notes, too, that modern custom was not to anoint unless the sick person had himself requested it—another development which Peter preferred not to endorse.

Next comes the question of iterability.[32] Peter distinguishes between a sick person receiving the sacrament more than once during the same illness and one given the sacrament anew when another illness strikes. He quotes Cistercian practice, that there has to be an interval of a year between administrations of extreme unction, although the eucharist

---

[31] *Summa*, §43.
[32] *Summa*, §44.

can be repeated each week.[33] Why the difference? "I don't see why" ("*non video*"), he says, before suggesting, without any arguments, that it might be because the eucharist is a much more useful sacrament and a greater one, and "a different sort of medicine." Certainly, he thinks there is no reason *not* to repeat extreme unction when a year has passed.

Peter links the question of whether lunatics and the possessed could be anointed to the issue of whether or not children should be anointed.[34] The fundamental concern here was their ability to understand and prepare for the sacrament. In line with his generally inclusive stance, the Chanter thinks that they can—especially since the greater sacraments of baptism and confirmation are administered to them. Again, he turns to the words of Scripture for an argument against, noting that the phrase in the Epistle is "let him call for priests" ("vocet presbyteros"), but that the action of this verb, *vocare*, is an adult action, that children cannot do.[35] Peter is sceptical: if you say that children cannot be anointed then you must apply the same logic to baptism. A more common objection, he reports, is that the liturgy of anointing refers to the sick person having sinned, when this language is not appropriate to children, who are unable to sin (their original sin having been washed away in baptism). But Peter refuses to think that the particular form of words in the rite supplies the substance of the sacrament: all that is needed is a blessing of some sort.

In what circumstances should the sacrament be given? We can be sure, from his general approach and from his earlier points, that Peter does not believe that one need wait until death is inevitable; but he wonders whether or not it is possible to be proactive in anointing.[36] Should those

---

[33] This casual note that the eucharist can be received every week puts in perspective canon 21 of the Fourth Lateran Council of 1215, which mandated the reception of the eucharist once a year, for all those who were to be considered Christians. Peter's aside, and a similar remark by his pupil Robert Courçon, who refers to daily eucharist and weekly penance, show that the Lateran decree was an absolute minimum, and that much more frequent reception was not at all uncommon. *Decrees of the Ecumenical Councils*, ed. Norman P. Tanner, 2 vols. (London and Washington, DC: Sheed and Ward/Georgetown University Press, 1990), 1:245. Cf. V. L. Kennedy, "The Handbook of Master Peter Chancellor of Chartres," *Mediaeval Studies* 5 (1943): 1–38, at 19, n. 103, cols. 1–2.

[34] *Summa*, §45.

[35] Note that Peter is not quoting the usual Vulgate text, where the verb is "inducat," but a variation of the Vetus Latina text.

[36] *Summa*, §46.

who know they are going into dangerous situations ("with foul air or other cause of sudden death") request it before they go? It is not clear here if Peter thinks that unction can be preventative or whether it is more a question of dying without receiving the sacrament. Peter reckons this proactive position has merit; indeed, he wonders whether not asking for unction in this situation might not be said to hold it in contempt. Ultimately, however, he worries that it might be a slippery slope: if we allow it in these cases, then where do we stop? Anyone about to go on a sea voyage, for instance, might justly worry about danger. But somehow this is a step too far: "this we dare not concede." Nevertheless, he is not entirely convinced that the Church is wrong to deny the sacrament to those who reasonably believe they are about to go into danger: "if it were to be conceded in the previous case," he comments, "it would not be absurd." Indeed, the circumstances need not be so unusual: what about elderly people with chronic illnesses who are in danger of sudden choking or inability to breathe? "Perhaps," he says, "that's not so silly."

It is one of the Chanter's characteristics that he can shift in a single bound from the microscopic to the bigger picture, and indeed he turns next to the interesting question of why there is such a diversity of sacraments.[37] Given there are so many, why, on his deathbed, is the believer not baptized, confirmed, shriven, given the eucharist—the whole armoury—rather than just extreme unction? Could a priest be said to sin by not administering all possible sacraments to the dying person? Peter's answer is somewhat unsatisfactory—it is, after all, a very good question—but he thinks perhaps it might be useful to distinguish between the sacrament of prime necessity (baptism, presumably) and the others.

Must extreme unction only be administered by a priest, as seems mandated by James?[38] The Chanter is unusual in declaring that, just as baptism and the eucharist can be given by a layperson, in necessity, then so can unction. In fact, it does not seem to matter who it is that administers, "just as an unbelieving Jewish servant can baptize, if need be, if ordered to do so by his master." Yet Peter knows that this is a little controversial, and so, "because this is doubtful, experts think that, if the sick person recovers or relapses, then the sacrament should be completed ("implere") by a priest." How, though, can he disregard the words of

[37] *Summa*, §47.
[38] *Summa*, §48.

the Epistle? He makes an analogy with the eucharist, where it matters who says the words of the Mass, but not who hands it out; similarly, it is important that the oil used in anointing should be that blessed by a bishop, but who actually employs it is not so significant.

Must the oil, in fact, always be blessed by a bishop?[39] This is Peter's next questioning of shibboleths: "after all," he says, "it's not the blessing of the oil that makes the sacrament, but its application." In this way, unction differs from the eucharist, say, where the bread and wine are the sacrament; here, the oil is only a part of the action of anointing and blessing, which together make the sacrament. In that case, surely if the anointings are done properly with their proper accompanying words, then the blessing of the original oil would seem to be a very minor issue. Such is the Chanter's reasoning, but he cannot follow it perhaps as far as he would like to: "let us not dare to presume more than Church usage; for it seems in Church usage that sanctified oil is the substance ('substantia') of the sacrament." It is hard to know, from the format in which the Chanter's teaching has come down to us, what his classroom tone would have been at this point. Was he serious about respecting the Church's position, or did he deliver the line with a conspiratorial smile?

Whatever his opinion, Peter next moves to consider the two blessings—the first to consecrate the oil and the second used during the anointing: is one more worthy than the other?[40] One might imagine that the first is the worthier blessing, since it can only be done by a bishop, in the same way that confirmation is said to be worthier sacrament than baptism or the eucharist, because it requires a bishop to administer it. But the contrary view might also hold, that the second blessing has more merit because it is that which effects the sacrament per se. "Perhaps there's no simple answer." The Chanter draws analogies between extreme unction, with its two blessings (of the oil and of the sick person) separated in time; and baptism, with two blessings (of the water and the baptisand) given at the same time; and the eucharist, with a single blessing of the bread and wine. A "curious questioner" ("curiosus inquisitor")—a phrase which takes us right into the classroom and now surely said with amusement—might ask why the baptismal water is not blessed in advance, as the oil of unction must be; or why the eucharist does not need more blessings. The questions end with something of

[39] *Summa*, §49.
[40] *Summa*, §50.

an oddity, asking whether a bishop can make chrism (using the term to encompass only oil, as well as the oil and balsam mixture) at times other than Maundy Thursday, or is the solemnity of Maundy Thursday necessary for the blessing to take effect.[41] Peter leaves this point deliberately unanswered, which again makes us wonder whether he would not have preferred to say yes.

Peter the Chanter has taken us further than Peter Lombard, but he is a milestone on a rather different path. Reading the *Summa* is always a vivid experience, for we are never far from the two-way conversation of the classroom, with Peter fielding student questions, or pre-empting them by the points he raises. And his answers to those questions, and the arguments he employs, illustrate his approach to dogmatic theology, which is always one which favours a pastoral response over the demands of theory for its own sake. In addition to Peter Lombard's questions, the Chanter looks at who may be given extreme unction, under what circumstances, and whether or not they themselves must ask for the sacrament. He questions who might administer the sacrament, and how this should be done. Despite his attempts to achieve some form of consistency in sacramental practice, he is really more interested in unction as an opportunity for the Church to minister to the world. Peter's answers show the difficulty of trying to encompass the variety of sacraments in one coherent schema. Believing that extreme unction can effect bodily as well as spiritual healing, he is concerned to make sure that as many people as possible benefit from it and that the Church uses the occasion to mediate grace. He is, of course, aware of current debates, and of the history of these questions, but sacramental theory was still in the process of formation and Peter is not afraid to state his own views, whether or not they conform to the more conservative opinions apparent in the Lombard. His student, Robert Courçon, reflects many of the Chanter's uncertainties, and his concern for the Church's role in the community; in particular, Robert repeatedly highlights the silence of the Bible and canon law on many of these questions, which leaves theologians in a delicate position: because these things are not defined in Scripture, he says, we do not wish to define or assert anything about them rashly.[42]

---

[41] *Summa*, §51.

[42] Robert Courçon, *Summa*: section on extreme unction transcribed from Bruges, Stadsbibliotheek, Ms. 247 in Kennedy, "The Handbook of Master Peter," 18 n. 103, col. 1, among several other similar remarks.

The Chanter was not the only Churchman concerned with unction in its pastoral setting. The sacrament received a fillip at the Fourth Lateran Council of 1215 which ordered the sick person to call for a priest before a doctor, highlighting the role of the clergy and strengthening the importance of sacraments for the laity.[43] Writing at exactly the time of the Lateran canons, Thomas of Chobham (d. 1233/36) produced a manual for priests and laity which became known as the *Summa confessorum*. Article 4 of the *Summa* dealt with penance, and within *distinctio* 2 ("What priests ought to know"), Thomas considered extreme unction.[44] He defines it as having effect for both bodily and spiritual disease, but although it will "often" alleviate the pain of physical suffering, it will always act for the remission of sins to the penitent. Nevertheless, Thomas wants to stress the possibility of physical improvement—"many are cured", he says—and to urge the invalid to call for extreme unction. He is responding to an "error of the laity" who say that they do not wish to receive unction unless they are actually dying. On the contrary, Thomas says, it is much better to be anointed at the beginning of an illness. It is not called *extreme* unction because it must be done at the end of life, so that nothing can follow it, but simply because it is often given to those at the limits of suffering ("laboranti in extremis").

Thomas wishes to refute the apparently common lay belief that once a sick man had been anointed, he could no longer have sex with his wife. Clearly, extreme unction was being seen as something of an orthodox form of the Cathar *consolamentum*, the sacramental act which turned a believer into a *perfectus*, and after which he had to foreswear all corporeal pleasures, which included not eating meat or food that was the result of sexual acts, and not having sex himself. This was bearable for those really on their deathbed, but rather off-putting if you thought you might recover. Thomas strongly opposes these beliefs: although anyone who recovers after being anointed should take better care of themselves in future and abstain from "filthy" ("sordes") behaviour, this is no reason not to receive extreme unction in the first place. The Lateran IV canon which orders all faithful people to take communion and go to confession

---

[43] Fourth Lateran Council, c. 22 (ed. Tanner, *Decrees*, 245–46). Indeed, the canon instructs the doctor to tell the patient to summon a priest before the doctor can act, so that the presence of a priest will become normal, and not cause the invalid to despair of his life.

[44] *Thomae de Chobham Summa confessorum*, ed. F. Broomfield, Analecta Mediaevalia Namurcensia 25 (Louvain; Paris: Nauwelaerts, 1968), art. 4, d. 2, q. 9a.

once a year is also recalled in Thomas's note that the benefits of unction last for a year, "just as the penance for common sins" runs out after a year. Unction, then, is repeatable on an annual basis. His explanation for why it should not be repeated before a year is up makes it sound rather like vaccination—the protection a single anointing affords lasts the whole year long. This is why the blessing of oil (he says "chrism") is renewed by the bishop each year, not because the old oil has lost its virtue, but because new oil is held in more reverence by the laity than the old—and so that all the old oil can be used in a year. Finally, Thomas notes that, although the Bible does mention "priests" anointing, one is sufficient: the text speaks in the plural simply because the prayers of many are worth more than the prayers of one. Matter of fact and commonsensical, Thomas is not concerned with the niceties of sacramental theory so much as to promote the practical use of extreme unction for its beneficial effects.

This period around and just after Lateran IV was rich in theological discussion. Scholars found themselves pulled in more than one direction: on the one hand, the Church was attempting to speak more directly to its lay members—in modern language, to become more relevant—and it needed materials to help do that; on the other, the emergence of a single University of Paris from the multiplicity of twelfth-century schools required a settled syllabus and curriculum—securing the position of the *Sentences* as its textbook—and provided a forum for experiments in speculative theology, challenged by the (re-)introduction of Aristotelian ideas.

Reading Paris-trained scholars of this period, such as William of Auxerre (d. 1231) and Guy of Orchelles (d. not after 1233) we can trace developments in the form of university teaching and academic debate, as well as in sacramental theory.[45] Guy's *Tractatus* (or *Summa*) *de sacramentis* and William's *Summa aurea* were both written probably in the 1220s. Both are notably systematic in their discussions of extreme unction, presenting arguments for and against each question before setting out their conclusions. Guy, for instance, begins by explaining that he will divide his treatment of extreme unction into six questions: What is it? Why is it called "extreme"? By whom was it instituted? What effect does it have? By whom should it be administered? To whom and

---

[45] *Guidonis de Orchellis, Tractatus de sacramentis*, ed. D. Van den Eynde and O. Van den Eynde (St. Bonaventure, NY: Franciscan Institute, 1953), c. 7, §§170–180. William of Auxerre: *Magistri Guillelmi Altissiodorensis. Summa Aurea*, ed. Jean Ribaillier, Spicilegium Bonaventurianum 19 (Grottaferrata; Paris: Coll. S. Bonaventura; CNRS, 1985), bk 4, tr. 15.

when should it be administered? We have seen most of these questions addressed (at least in part) already, but not with such comprehensive organization—a trait of university training. Both discuss unction as it functions as a sacrament, raising questions and using terminology that derive from the Aristotelian language of causation, and from an approach that deemed it necessary to explain biblical and pastoral acts in Greek philosophical terms. For example, William starts by asking what the *materia* and the *essentia* of the sacrament consist in—questions close to those addressed by Peter the Chanter, but posed in a new formal language and reflecting a very different underlying thought-world.

The *materia* (material or matter) of the sacrament is commonly understood to be the olive oil used in the anointing; but what is its essence? In particular, is its essence the imparting of a new character to the anointed person?[46] Although unction is one of the triptych of sacraments that mark the beginning (baptism), coming-of-age (confirmation) and end of the Christian life cycle, it does not imprint a new character on the believer as they do. William and Guy illustrate the three stages with examples ("figurae") from the life of David. In 1 Kings 16:12–13, David is anointed as he enters into his father's house, a sign of his future kingdom (baptism); in 2 Kings 2:1–4, he is anointed king in Hebron and fights many wars (confirmation); and in 2 Kings 5, he is once again anointed in Hebron, this time as king over the whole of Israel, after which he reigns in peace—just as, after the final anointing, believers will reign in peace with Christ, as universal kings. The linkage does not hold, however, because whereas baptism and confirmation need not and cannot be repeated, since a single reception of each permanently alters character, extreme unction can, by tradition and custom, be administered more than once. Either it is unrepeatable, or else its essence is not the same as in the other two.[47] The argument here is circular (if the sacrament were not repeatable then it would imprint character; but since it is repeatable then it cannot do so; but it is repeatable because it does not imprint character) and William is clearly not happy with the reasoning. If the sacrament of entering this life imparts character, then how much more should this be true of the sacrament at the end of life—which needs to identify the recipient for his entry into the next world. Guy tries

---

[46] *Summa aurea*, bk 4, tr. 15, c. 1, q. 2. *Guidonis de Orchellis*, §§171–173.
[47] *Summa aurea*, bk 4, tr. 15, c. 1, q. 2.

two other approaches. The principal *res* of baptism is an infusion of grace which imparts a new character to the baptized person; it is signified by the immersion in the water which can wash him clean. Unction is not like this. The exterior anointing imparts a new sheen—a quality ("qualitas")—to the body, which signifies the interior anointing which imparts a new quality to the soul.[48] In addition, he says, we should look at the purposes for which unction was instituted—the alleviation of sickness and the remission of sin. Since both sickness and sin are likely to return, so the sacrament itself must be repeatable. And because it is iterable, it cannot imprint character.[49]

The unction itself is not a single event, but consists of a number of anointings at various points on the body—in particular, at those sense organs which can be the cause of sin. At what point does the sacrament come into effect during these multiple blessings, and is it rightly thought of as a single sacrament, or a series? William tries to tease out an answer by considering the specific effect of the sacrament: the anointing is done to forgive those sins which are not forgiven in the sacrament of penance. "Unction was instituted for the completion of penance, so that what was not forgiven in penance can be forgiven in extreme unction."[50] This is a notable point because it gives some idea of what spiritual sickness unction might be being thought to heal. William agrees that the sacrament can effect bodily healing, but clearly this is not always the case, and so it cannot be its main effect: many who receive the sacrament worthily still die, he says. Guy puts the sentiment in more formal language: the *res* of the sacrament cannot be bodily healing, this can only be an effect.[51] The question is not so much the worthiness of the recipient as the utility for God of their being healed. If God does not think that bodily healing is expedient to his aims, then he will not effect it. Spiritual healing, however, will always occur. Once again, however, William struggles with the inconsistencies of sacramental theory and practice. Extreme unction should not be given to healthy people, because its "principal and proper" purpose is bodily healing—even though the worthier effect is

---

[48] *Guidonis de Orchellis*, §171.

[49] *Guidonis de Orchellis*, §173.

[50] *Summa aurea*, bk 4, tr. 15, c. 1, q. 3. The link of unction with penance is shown in the need for a priest to anoint, since only a priest has the power to forgive sins.

[51] *Guidonis de Orchellis*, §176.

the remission of sins. Extreme unction is instituted as the completion of penance, and all the blessings constitute one sacrament because they all signify the same thing: the remission of sins. And this means that, since penance does not imprint character, extreme unction cannot do so either, since both are fundamentally connected. It is for this reason that children do not need extreme unction, since they do not need remission of sins. Their original sin is washed away by baptism, and they cannot sin further until they reach adulthood.

These considerations are important because they bring into focus the delicate relationship between sin and illness—that is, between spiritual and bodily infirmity. In the Gospel passage associated with unction, Mark 6:13, the Apostles first cast out demons before anointing the sick with oil and healing them. The order of these actions suggested to medieval scholars that spiritual health was prior to bodily health, both in time and causation. Bede had already made the connection: "On account of sins in the soul, many are punished by bodily infirmity or even death."[52] Until your sins are forgiven, your body cannot be healed. But if the proper purpose of extreme unction is the remission of sins, how does it differ from penance? Why is another sacrament needed, if penance can remit the sin which causes illness? New ways of thinking about sacraments had made William and Guy aware of new issues that must be addressed, but they were not really in a position to answer them all convincingly. They stand with one foot in the past and one in the future. Although the world of direct pastoral care is no longer as obviously important to the discussion, their treatment of extreme unction has not fully mastered the language and mindset of sacramental theology in the new-Aristotelian world. For that development, we must move on to our final milestone, the work of the mendicant masters of the mid-thirteenth century.

As examples of these scholars, I have chosen two pairs of master and pupil, one Franciscan, Alexander of Hales (d. 1245) and Bonaventure (d. 1274), and the other Dominican, Albert the Great (d. 1280) and Thomas Aquinas (d. 1274).[53] All taught in Paris, and all would have

---

[52]Bede, *In epistolas VII catholicas*, on James 5:15: "Et si in peccatis sit" (ed. Laistner, 221).

[53]Alexander: *Glossa in IV Libros Sententiarum Petri Lombardi*, Bibliotheca Franciscana Scholastica Medii Aevii 15 (Quaracchi: Coll. S. Bonaventura, 1957); Bonaventure: *Commentarius in IV Libros Sententiarum*, in *Opera omnia* 4 (Quaracchi: Coll. S. Bonaventura, 1889); Albert: *Commentarius in Librum IV Sententiarum*, in *Opera omnia* 30 (Paris: Vivès, 1894); Thomas: *In quattuor libros sententiarum*, in *Opera Omnia* 1 (Stuttgart/Bad Connstatt: Frommann-Holzboog, 1980), all at bk IV, d. 23. In addition:

known one another to some degree. The similarity of their training and the argumentative method they all employ allow us to discuss their treatment of the sacrament as a single whole, though each has a distinctive voice. Alexander, the earliest, seems less constrained by the bounds of the scholastic method of proceeding, but because the textual transmission of his work is less straightforward than for the others, we cannot be sure that the way it appears is original. But it is evident that he is always pressing into new areas of discussion, even if the result is now not always coherent. In contrast, his pupil Bonaventure exudes a clarity of expression and organization that mark out all he writes. He is rarely someone who takes on poor opponents, even if he is making their arguments for them; he always takes them seriously. In fact, the arguments are sometimes so good that his subsequent responses do not fully convince: at times he finds himself an apologist for Church teaching and practice that do not always cohere logically. Albert and Thomas share many qualities of systematic comprehensiveness, which is also manifest in a characteristic thirteenth-century expansion in the length of most of these discussions. Dealing with unction, Albert reveals himself in a lively practicality, while Thomas impresses with a completeness of coverage that leaves no stone unturned. Although all are working within a particular tradition, they do so with individuality.

The four masters cover all the points raised by previous discussions, but their treatment develops the material in particular ways, many of which concern the way the sacrament works: what is it precisely that extreme unction does, and how does it do it? Two of our scholars attempt precise definitions, and they allow us to see where each places the emphasis of understanding: Alexander's

---

Alexander, *Quaestiones disputatae "Antequam esset frater,"* Bibliotheca Franciscana Medii Aevi 20–21 (Quaracchi: Coll. S. Bonaventura, 1960), q. 48 and Appendix 3, q. 2 (1–49); Thomas, *Supplement*, qq. 29–33, in *Summa theologica 3ª pars et Supplementum*, in *Opera Omnia* 12 (Rome: Sac. Coll. de Propaganda Fide, 1906): the supplement was put together by confrères from the earlier "*Scriptum*," *Sentences* Commentary; trans. (s.n.), *The "Summa Theologica" of St Thomas Aquinas, Third Part*, Second Revised Edition (London: Burns Oates & Washbourne, 1928).

sacrament administered through oil to a sick person, by a priest whose office it is, with the intention of effecting what the Church does in the prayer of faith[54];

contrasts with Albert's

sacrament of anointing by touch with consecrated oil, conferring on the sick a remedy for remaining sin and, if it is expedient, alleviating bodily infirmity.[55]

The specific nature of Albert's definition takes us a long way from the biblical root of the sacrament in James. The priority Albert gives to spiritual healing is reinforced when he adds that certain physical infirmities come from the mind, but the opposite is not the case, except very occasionally; so healing the soul heals the body. Bonaventure has a similar conclusion, but in the context of asking why extreme unction was instituted.[56] Unction, he states, was instituted for the healing of bodily and spiritual sickness, and principally, for spiritual weakness, that is, to deal with venial sin. "Per accidens"—that is, as a secondary benefit—it also deals with corporeal weakness. But Bonaventure, like his teacher Alexander, suggests that this illness is a result or a bi-product or in some other way joined to this spiritual sin. Indeed, although Alexander nods to the fact that unction can alleviate bodily infirmity (with the usual caveat that this happens only if it is expedient to God), he is more interested in its spiritual effects in taking away sin, not least because he is not sure what sins there are that would still need taking away, if the sick person has been baptized, and confessed his sins in penance. It is an excellent question: if bodily healing is not the main purpose of the sacrament, and if it is still possible to receive the sacrament of penance, what remains for extreme unction to do?

To answer, Alexander distinguishes between three sorts of sin: original sin, which is washed away by baptism, actual sins (even mortal sins), which are forgiven in the sacrament of penance, if the penitent is suitably contrite, and then the remaining or venial sins, which are remitted by extreme unction. The sacrament both remits the venial sins and, by

---

[54] Alexander, *Glossa*, IV, d. 23, no. 1; cf. *Quaestiones*, App. 3, q. 2, no. 8.
[55] Albert, *Commentarius*, IV, d. 23, art. 2.
[56] Bonaventure, *Commentarius*, IV, d. 23, art. 1, q. 1.

repairing the effects of sin in the soul, signifies the full grace which will come after death, when the believer has made satisfaction in purgatory. In this world, the sacrament of unction mitigates the sickness of venial sin; in the next, the believer will be anointed like a king, with the unction of glory.[57] It is true that baptism, penance and the eucharist are all capable of removing venial sin during one's lifetime, but only extreme unction has been instituted for this purpose at the end of life, because it signifies the full anointing that will come with the resurrection. It is inevitable, Alexander says, that every adult carries a weight of venial sin: there is not a man living on the earth who does not sin [Ecclesiastes 7: 21]. And this sin can manifest itself in a sickness of the soul, but also in a sickness of the body. Heal the sin, then, and both body and soul can be healed. And so, he says, extreme unction both decreases or vitiates the punishments of purgatory by the remission of venial sin, and cures bodily sickness, "if it comes from the inside" ("si sit ordinabilis ad interiorem"). In this key phrase, Alexander is not so much explaining the apparent failure of the sacrament when the body is not healed, as he is making a distinction between those illnesses which are a response to sin and those which are not—what today we might think of loosely as psychosomatic. Like Alexander, modern medicine increasingly realizes the mental element involved in a great deal of disease—"si sit ordinabilis ad interiorem." And although Alexander employs the language of venial sin to explain how this might come about, rather than modern psychology, the exterior manifestation of the interior disorder is the same, whichever explanatory theory is deployed.

This use of venial sin to explain the purpose of extreme unction is continued by Bonaventure. He agrees that venial sin, which is an inevitable companion on the journey through life, does not need its own sacrament (since it is forgiven by the eucharist and penance); but when it is time to leave this world, there is a new and particular need to clear up all such leftover sin, and extreme unction acts as a kind of last chance saloon for just this purpose. The sacrament thus has a *res*, which is the cure of venial sin; it has a *signum*, which is the exterior anointing; and together, the *res* and *signum* stimulate devotion in the believer, which creates an interior spiritual anointing to remit venial sin. When the soul is cured, so too, often, the body is healed; and so a consequence of the remission of venial sin is bodily healing.

---

[57] Alexander, *Quaestiones*, q. 48.

The approach taken by Alexander and Bonaventure was adopted by other Franciscan scholars. The Dominicans, however, pursued a slightly different line. Both Albert and Thomas begin their discussions with the question of whether or not unction really is a sacrament. There are a number of objections to its inclusion in the list: anointing with oil in other rites, such as baptism, is not a considered a sacrament; unction has no precursor in the Old Law; unction appears to offer corporeal, not spiritual, healing, so any grace in evidence must come from the accompanying prayer, rather than the anointing; and finally, unction has no specific "disease of sin" proper to it: baptism deals with original sin, and penitence and confirmation with actual sins, so there is nothing left for unction to do. Despite these problems, both masters conclude that unction certainly is a sacrament, but their reasons for doing so are worth noting. Unction does indeed heal the disease of sin, and the sin proper to it is the venial sin that remains at the end of life. Remitting this sin is not an action proper to any of the other sacraments, because unction alone is the sacrament of leaving this world ("exeuntium"). And although anointing on its own is only sacramental, extreme unction combines anointing with prayer, and together they comprise the operation of the sacrament. For Albert and Thomas, however, this explanation is not quite enough. They attempt to define more closely what sort of sin the sacrament washes away. It cannot be original or mortal sin, and neither does it seem reasonable for it to be venial sin, because penance remits this well enough. Rather, following penance, unction must be a remedy for the defects that are left as a kind of stain in the soul as a consequence of sin, which leave human beings spiritually weakened and less able to draw down the grace which will take them to glory. The sacrament gives enough grace for the recipient to be able to resist sin with contrition, and to remit the guilt of sins remaining in the soul. Bodily healing may be effected as a secondary effect, but only insofar as this promotes the principal effect, which is spiritual cleansing.[58] This is why extreme unction should not be administered to those still healthy in the body, even if they might need to be healed in the mind, because the interior spiritual healing the sacrament effects is signified by the exterior bodily illness.[59]

---

[58] Thomas, *Supplement*, q. 30, arts 1–2; Albert, *Commentarius*, IV, d. 23, art. 14.
[59] Thomas, *Supplement*, q. 32, art. 1; Albert, *Commentarius*, IV, d. 23, art. 9.

Despite their differences, for both Franciscans and Dominicans, the result of their emphasis on the excision of the remnants of venial sin as its primary purpose is to conclude that extreme unction should only be given to those on the very edge of death, because it is their last chance at remission. According to Thomas, the very name extreme unction makes it clear that the invalid must be at the extremity of his life. It is "the last remedy the Church can give, since it is the immediate preparation for glory."[60] The discussion is linked to others about who might be given the sacrament, with all four masters considering the cases of children, the raving mad ("furiosi") and those lacking understanding ("moriones").[61] Does it not make sense for any faithful person to be able to receive this sacrament, in the same way that any faithful person may be baptized, since unction is medicine for sin? For Alexander, the key issue is whether or not you have the use of reason: the recipient must desire the sacrament, and this requires both reason and will. This allows him to distinguish between those who lack understanding because of extremes of age (old or young) or nature, who can never receive the sacrament because their soul is not rational, and those who are now raving but who have been lucid in the past and who may yet have lucid moments. If, in those rational intervals, they call for extreme unction, then it should be administered to them. But take care, for *furiosi* and *moriones* are liable to dishonour the sacrament by their behaviour; and since it is only a sacrament of utility and not one of necessity, it can be reasonably withheld, even though it may do some good. Not receiving this sacrament will do no-one lasting harm.

The mendicants' emphasis on venial sins takes us from sacramental theory to another contemporary extension of speculative theology, the so-called birth of purgatory.[62] Although the idea of purgation after death had a long history, purgatory as a particular place where venial sins—that is, precisely those sins which were by definition forgivable between death and Judgement—could be expunged by penitence and punishment, is

---

[60] Thomas, *Supplement*, q. 32, art. 2.

[61] See, for instance, Alexander, *Glossa*, IV, d. 23, no. 6; *Quaestiones*, App. 3, q. 2, nos. 31–38; Bonaventure, *Commentarius*, IV, d. 23, art. 2, q. 2; Albert, *Commentarius*, IV, d. 23, arts. 9–12, Thomas, *Supplement*, q. 32, arts. 3–4.

[62] Jacques Le Goff, *The Birth of Purgatory*, trans. Arthur Goldhammer (London: Scolar, 1984).

a creation of the late twelfth century. According to Le Goff, Peter the Chanter was the first scholar to integrate a place of purgation into his theological teaching and to consider what actions, such as prayers or almsgiving, might lessen the time spent there.[63] Given Peter's thought about the purpose of unction, it is not surprising that it does not appear in this list: his discussion is focussed on its effects in the here and now, not what it might do for those in the world to come. The same is not the case, however, for Alexander of Hales. He considers purgatory in his *Sentences* commentary, immediately prior to extreme unction, and like unction, it is tied to the virtue of hope.[64] He links the two explicitly in the *Quaestiones*, where he distinguishes between the guilt of venial sins, which is remitted by unction, and the penalty to be paid for them, which happens in purgatory. The other mendicant scholars are equally concerned to situate the remission of sin with the work of purgation. For Alexander and the others, rather than being the last act of this world, unction becomes the first act of the next. So the correct sacramental definition of extreme unction and its effects is significant to our mendicants not only for its own sake, but because it must fit into their wider theory of purgation.

Given this view, the form of the sacrament—how the anointing should be done—becomes especially important: which parts should be anointed, and what words should be said? Bonaventure spells out in detail where on the body the oil should be placed.[65] He considers various possibilities: if the sacrament relates to spiritual infirmity, perhaps the oil should go everywhere, since the spirit is not confined to a particular organ; if, as Matthew's Gospel states (15:19), sin begins in the heart, then perhaps only the heart should be anointed; if the sick person has missing or mutilated limbs, does the priest simply omit the anointing meant for those places? His answers illuminate his idea of "good practice." Since the sacrament is intended to remit venial sin, the places which should be anointed are those which generate such sin: the sense organs, the sex organs, and the "motive" organs, by which he means the feet. Mutilated limbs should be anointed, but he allows practicality to trump theory by forbidding the anointing of genitalia—it would just be too shaming (for both priest and

---

[63] Le Goff, *Birth*, 165–66; Peter, *Summa* (ed. Dugaquier), pt 2, 103–4, 125–26.
[64] Alexander, *Glossa*, IV, dist. 18, 20, 21; Le Goff, *Birth*, 247–48.
[65] Bonaventure, *Commentarius*, IV, d. 23, art. 2, q. 3.

recipient), he says, even to think about it; the loins (*lumbi*) can stand in, as being close enough. This gives him a total of seven parts of the body for anointing: eyes, ears, nostrils, mouth, hands, loins and feet. However, Bonaventure's was not the only list; other scholars kept to the sense organs, although Albert discusses the forehead, crown of head, chest and shoulders, all of which were anointed in other rites.[66] Only a priest can do the anointing, by reason of material (only consecrated hands must touch the consecrated oil), by reason of form (since the words used must be that of a prayer, which is a priest's particular domain), and by reason of authority (because the Epistle specifies priests).[67]

The several anointings nevertheless form one single sacrament, and if any is missed (as long as the recipient still has all the requisite organs and parts) then the sacrament is not complete.[68] Thomas explains that "oneness" can encompass three things: something indivisible; something continuous, which might be divided but is not; and something in several parts, only complete when they are all together. In the sacrament of baptism, whether the baptisand is immersed in the blessed water once or (better) three times, the action of the sacrament still takes place. But with the eucharist or extreme unction, the sacrament is not complete unless all the parts are carried through. The effect of unction does not occur until all the anointings are finished, even if this means another priest taking over part-way through, if the first is indisposed: "the unity of the smith's work is not destroyed by his using several hammers."[69]

From the Letter of James, it would seem that the anointing must be accompanied by words—"the prayer of faith"; but since no canonical form for unction is given by Christ or the Apostles, and a variety of rites existed in different parts of the Church, Thomas asks whether it is possible to say the sacrament has any form at all. Given that the oil is pre-consecrated, perhaps the form of the sacrament in simply the anointing, with no words needed; the example of St. Genevieve, who merely touched the sick with oil, suggested that nothing more was necessary.[70]

---

[66] Albert, *Commentarius*, IV, d. 23, art. 16.
[67] Bonaventure, *Commentarius*, IV, d. 23, art. 2, q. 1.
[68] Alexander, *Quaestiones*, App. 3, q. 2, nos. 8–9, 16.
[69] Thomas, *Supplement*, q. 29, art. 2.
[70] Albert, *Commentarius*, IV, d. 23, art. 4.

But Thomas thinks that scholars who say that the words are unimportant are wrong, for the oil by itself is nothing unless what is intended by its use is spelled out in words. What form those words should take thus becomes a key question. Since the effect of the sacrament is guaranteed—that is the nature of sacrament, after all—it seems right that the words should be declamatory or assertive, as in those rites which use a form such as: "I anoint you with consecrated oil in the name of the Father..." ("Unguo te oleo sanctificato in nomine Patris..."), a formulation which conveys the certainty of the sacrament to the recipient. But the contrary opinion is that the words must be in the form of a prayer or petition: "Through this holy unction, and his most tender mercy, may the Lord pardon whatever sins you have committed (by sight/hearing, etc.)."[71] All the scholars we have discussed here prefer this formulation. Albert's explanation for why this is so is particularly convincing. The form of the sacrament is twofold, he says: the first part expresses the action of the sacrament, and that is in the indicative mood—we can be certain of it; but the second part is the committal of the dying person to the hands of God, and this must take the form of a petition, asking God to receive them. For although the efficacy of the prayer of the Church as a whole is assured, individual prayers are not. This means that the action of the sacrament can be relied upon, but because the effect of the sacrament is to rid the dying person of all residual sin, then not only the sacrament, but the intervention of God's mercy is required—and it must be called for in a prayer.[72] Thomas is slightly less sure. Unlike other sacraments, the effect of extreme unction "is not such that it always results from the minister's prayer, even when all essentials have been duly observed." Indeed, he adds:

> This sacrament...considered in itself, is sure of its effect; yet this effect can be hindered though the insincerity of the recipient (though by his intention he submit to the sacrament), so that he receives no effect at all. Hence there is no parity between this sacrament, and the others wherein some effect always ensues.[73]

---

[71] "Per istam suavissimam unctionem et suam piissimam misericordiam remittat tibi Dominus quidquid peccasti [per visum/auditum, etc.]".
[72] Albert, *Commentarius*, IV, d. 23, art. 4.
[73] Thomas, *Supplement*, q. 29, art. 8.

Alexander of Hales is equivocal on the status and form of the accompanying words: "I do not decide," he says, whether the prayer is sacramental or part of the sacrament itself; but it is at least sacramental, so should not be omitted.[74] The version used depends on Church tradition in different places, and is valid as long as the Trinity is invoked. The important words are not these, but the earlier prayer with which the bishop consecrated the oil to make the *materia* of the sacrament. Alexander's answer shows the influence of Aristotelian categories on sacramental thought: the material cause of the sacrament is the anointing, but the efficient cause is the prayer.[75]

Aristotle, it seems, has helped Christian scholars achieve precision about the nature and operation of their sacraments: Aquinas' theory of the working of extreme unction is undoubtedly neater and logically more convincing than the explanations of scholars before him. He could not have reached it without employing the habits of thought and language of a pagan Greek, but his mastery of this different world provided Christian theologians with a philosophical foundation for their faith that they had not had before, expressed with a clear and comprehensive persuasiveness. Yet with these gains came also losses. Aristotle had helped solve these problems—but he had also created them, to a large extent; entering into his thought-world, Christian scholars discovered difficulties they never knew they had. It may be a matter of personal taste whether one finds scholastic theologians' attempts at an inclusive theory of sacrament heroic or misguided. Do they resemble Galileo's elegant celestial mechanics or the Ptolemaic system of orbits and epicycles designed to accommodate the errant movement of the planets seen from the standpoint of the earth rather than the sun?

Caught up in the challenges of the new philosophy, university-based theologians of the thirteenth century—even the mystical Bonaventure—focus more on the consistency of sacramental theory and less on its reception by the Church at large. In extreme unction, we can see this grappling for position played out in miniature. The Bible provided little help in answering their questions, and the varieties of customary practice were, if anything, positively contradictory. We can see two definite lines

---

[74] Alexander, *Glossa*, IV, d. 23, no. 1.
[75] Alexander, *Quaestiones*, Appendix 3, q. 2, nos. 16–21, here 20.

of approach. Old-school masters such as Peter the Chanter or Thomas Chobham placed their emphasis on the Church's response to individuals as members of the body of Christ, and on the use of sacraments to make the most of everyday occasions for pastoral care. The more modern mendicant theologians, however, worked in a world that required consistency and coherence; a world where the vagueness of so many answers to questions about God could no longer be tolerated. Peter the Chanter was less concerned with precisely how the sacrament worked because, for him, the more important answer was that it worked because Christ had promised it would. For Aquinas and Albert, faced with challenges from many sides—heretics, other faiths, philosophers, and doubters—such a response no longer seemed sufficient. They had to play Aristotle at his own game, and win. And so, whereas Peter is open-handed, Bonaventure must restrict extreme unction to a single reception for those at the very point of death, because anything else is in contradiction to his theory of sin.

So much depended on what anointing actually did. Over the century of discussion we have followed, optimism about the possibility of physical healing appears to decrease as sacramental theory grows more sophisticated. This was very much a Western phenomenon: in the Greek Church, the main purpose of the sacrament was, and remains, physical recovery—a position perhaps linked to their relatively sceptical position on purgatory. Moreover, the growth of academic medicine in the West, encouraged by translations of Greek and Arabic medical texts contemporary with the translations of Aristotle, perhaps forced theologians to re-consider their stance on bodily healing, even at Paris, where the medical faculty was never as strong as at Salerno or Montpellier. As medicine and theology each sought to assert the scope of their discipline in the University, the doctors of the soul adjusted the nature of their claims over the body. Leaving the "lower," corporeal realm to the physicians released the theologians from some difficult explanations. Bodily healing is rarely granted, says Bonaventure, because it would detract from the spiritual effect of the sacrament.[76] Nevertheless, their recognition of the place of the mind in some bodily illness is impressive; the best of their theology is accompanied by insightful and sympathetic psychology. Yet here too we must acknowledge that the tradition holds a double-edged sword. For along with an agreement on the mental

---

[76] Bonaventure, *Commentarius*, IV, d. 23, art. 1, q. 1.

and spiritual foundation of some physical conditions—whether through stress, guilt, sadness or life's many other burdens—is a strand which reads illness as a *result* of sin and blames the invalid for his own condition, and which has had tragic consequences for many sick people.

During the thirteenth century, the purpose of extreme unction was increasingly bound up with the concept of venial sin and its place in the complex economy of sinfulness. Within this economy we can chart the so-called birth of purgatory and the notion that penalties for some sorts of sinning may be remitted, either in a place of purgation before the Final Judgement, or by penance during one's lifetime. For many scholars, extreme unction was the last chance of washing away venial sins before death, or of cleansing the soul to make it ready for grace. Aquinas' attempt to place extreme unction into a coherent theory of sacrament is conceptual theology of an elegance beyond the dreams of twelfth-century schoolmen. But its very complexity took unction away from its roots as a pastoral tool, and lost sight of the need to explain its purpose in ways that made sense to lay believers. In the messy and inconsistent formulation of Peter the Chanter, extreme unction was an occasion for the Church to offer healing, an opportunity to step into the lives of the faithful and provide comfort. In the tidier explanation of Aquinas, unction instead developed a role in the war against the hierarchy of sins. Thomas's brilliance allowed him to square away the Chanter's logical inconsistencies; but in so doing, he and the other scholastic masters came worryingly close to making Christianity look like a commercial exchange, in which sin might be bought off in instalments, either in this world or the next, and with unction as an advance payment on the Last Judgement. It is only ironic that it was scholars from the mendicant orders, founded on poverty and dedicated to pastoral care, who were at the forefront of this new theology.

CHAPTER 12

Religious and Amorous "Apocalypses" in John Donne's Metaphysical Imagination

Angela Locatelli

1 A SHORT PREMISE

This essay examines the poetry of John Donne in the light of its "apocalyptic" dimension, which will be here understood as a philosophical, literary, cultural, and experiential category. In a wider perspective, it also aims at proposing a method for discerning the apocalyptic as a tone or theme in authors who are not usually classed in the genre. My discussion of "the apocalyptic" will be literary, rather than strictly theological; however, detailed reference to one of Donne's sermons (on Apoc. 7:2–3) will confirm the unity of his mindset in approaching both the secular notion and the religious understanding of this subject. I wish to show that "the apocalyptic," in terms of religious eschatology within an established theological tradition, figures prominently in Donne's extraordinary mental and experiential landscape. However, his highly original and often surprising elaboration of biblical images and motifs stems from a very personal and refreshing conceptualization

---

A. Locatelli (✉)
University of Bergamo, Bergamo, Italy

© The Author(s) 2019
E. Knibbs et al. (eds.), *The End of the World in Medieval Thought and Spirituality*, The New Middle Ages,
https://doi.org/10.1007/978-3-030-14965-9_12

315

of traditional views, in which the emotional, imaginative, and poetic dimensions play a significant and synergic role.

I propose to consider "the apocalyptic" as a cultural motif which is closely related to time-specific frames, and can therefore be properly assessed primarily in terms of the history of ideas, rather than as an ahistorical concept. "The apocalyptic," once it is seen in a constructivist perspective rather than in essentialist terms, can be understood as a time-specific cultural category, which necessarily reflects the more or less complex epistemology of any age.

In such a perspective, one can appreciate how the apocalyptic motif in Donne's poems becomes the purveyor of the layered, conflicting, and shifting discourses in theology, religion, politics, and science that make the late sixteenth and the seventeenth centuries a unique moment in English and European culture.[1] For Donne, "the apocalyptic" has cognitive, emotional, cultural, and political implications. His imagination is imbued with apocalyptic fears, *vis à vis* the deep uncertainties that were questioning traditional hierarchies while driving the contemporary exploration of new worlds and new forms of knowledge in a largely uncertain cognitive horizon.

Another approach to "the apocalyptic" involves its perception and definition in phenomenological and experiential terms; in this case, a subjective articulation of the concept as a personal, emotional, and/or intellectual configuration allows for a plurality of phenomena that are felt to be "apocalyptic" according to the various forms that the sense of "endtimes" can take in the vicissitudes of individual lives.

It is indeed on the ground of Donne's lifelong understanding of his personal experiences, emotions, and cogitations in terms of cosmic and metaphysical realities (the power of analogy in his habit of thought cannot be underestimated) that one may plausibly read his oeuvre in a perspective that connects individual experiences of crisis to the biblical idea of endtimes. This idea is present in Donne's original and very personal

---

[1] E. M. W. Tillyard, *The Elizabethan World Picture* (London: Chatto & Windus, 1943); Arthur A. Lovejoy, *The Great Chain of Being* (Cambridge, MA: Harvard University Press, 1936); Basil Willey, *The Seventeenth Century Background: Studies in the Thought of the Age in Relation to Poetry and Religion* (London: Chatto & Windus, 1967); and Debora Kuller Shuger, *Habits of Thought in the English Renaissance* (Berkeley: University of California Press, 1990).

take on "the apocalyptic" as a pervasive sense of vulnerability, implicit in the various phases and passages of life. The experiences of a new beginning and of an incumbent end, i.e. of the rise and fall of both love and faith, specifically the experience of falling in love and of a moment of religious fervor followed by loss of love or of religious enthusiasm, cast a metaphorically "apocalyptic" light on Donne's love poems, as well as on his religious poems and sermons. "The apocalyptic" is in fact associated with the mutability of the subject and the world and with images of the incessant metamorphosis of decaying worlds and new worlds which transpose the biblical images of endtime into an intense emotional narrative.

2 A Note on Figuring "the Apocalyptic" in Both a Narratological and a Historical Perspective

In his opening paragraph of *The Apocalyptic Imagination: An Introduction to Jewish Apocalyptic Literature*, John J. Collins warns his readers that the term "apocalyptic" is loaded with meaning, and even outright suspect in the context of recent Religious Studies.[2] Moreover, Collins abandons the dominant emphasis on the eschatological and utopian sense of the term in order to invite a narratological approach to it. He therefore speaks of "the apocalyptic" as a literary genre or as a literary motif, obviously grounded in a specific *doxa*:

> More recent scholarship has abandoned the use of "apocalyptic" as a noun and distinguished between apocalypse as a literary genre, apocalypticism as social ideology, and apocalyptic eschatology as a set of ideas and motifs that may also be found in other literary genres and social settings.[3]

---

[2] John J. Collins, *The Apocalyptic Imagination: An Introduction to Jewish Apocalyptic Literature* (New York: Crossroad, 1984), 1: "The word 'apocalyptic' is popularly associated with fanatical millenarian expectation, and indeed the canonical apocalypses of Daniel and especially of John have very often been used by millenarian groups. Theologians of a more rational bent are often reluctant to admit that such material played a formative role in early Christianity. There is consequently a prejudice against the apocalyptic literature which is deeply ingrained in biblical scholarship. The great authorities of the nineteenth century, Julius Wellhausen and Emil Schürer, slighted its value."

[3] Collins, *Apocalyptic Imagination*, 2.

According to this "genre approach," an apocalypse can be defined as:

> a genre of revelatory literature with a narrative framework, in which a revelation is mediated by an otherworldly being to a human recipient, disclosing a transcendent reality which is both temporal, insofar as it envisages eschatological salvation, and spatial insofar as it involves another, supernatural world.[4]

I will try to show that this definition can productively be applied to the study of Donne's poems and sermons. Collins is undoubtedly a relevant reference in my discourse on the concept of "the apocalyptic," as well as E. Ann Matter's "The Pseudo-Alcuinian 'De Septem Sigillis': An Early Latin Apocalypse Exegesis" and "The Apocalypse in Early Medieval Exegesis."[5] These essays trace, with rare scholarly competence and insight, the developments, interfaces, and independent lines of apocalyptic literature in both exegetical and liturgical terms, from the early tradition of Victorinus, Jerome, Tyconius, up to the Carolingians (Alcuin and Haimo) and into the *Glossa Ordinaria* (c. 1100). Matter also discusses the most representative authors on the subject in the sixth century (Primasius, Caesarius, Apringius, Cassiodorus), and those of the eighth century (the Venerable Bede, Ambrose Autpert, and the Beatus of Liébana). Her historical perspective sheds light on the interpretative vicissitudes of the term "apocalyptic" and its diverse contextual relevance. This approach to the exegesis of Revelation proves valuable to my discussion of "the apocalyptic" in Donne's works, by inviting, as it does, an accurate perception of his writings in his historical context. Furthermore, by elaborating on Collins and Matter's contributions, I will introduce a meta-discursive perspective on Donne's religious and secular texts, and extend the prevalent concept of "the apocalyptic"

---

[4] Collins, *Apocalyptic Imagination*, 5, where he goes on to argue that "This definition is sufficiently broad and yet remains usefully specific," and that it can be shown to apply to "various sections of 1 Enoch, Daniel, 4 Ezra, 2 Baruch, Apocalypse of Abraham, 3 Baruch, 2 Enoch, Testament of Levi 2-5, the fragmentary Apocalypse of Zephaniah, and with some qualification to Jubilees and The Testament of Abraham (both of which also have strong affinities with other genres). It also applies to a wide body of Christian and Gnostic literature and to some Persian and Greco-Roman material."

[5] E. Ann Matter, "The Pseudo-Alcuinian 'De Septem Sigillis': An Early Latin Apocalypse Exegesis," *Traditio* 36 (1980): 111–37. See also Matter, "The Apocalypse in Early Medieval Exegesis," in *The Apocalypse in the Middle Ages*, ed. Richard K. Emmerson and Bernard McGinn (Ithaca: Cornell University Press, 1992), 38–50.

to encompass a literary and experiential, but not exclusively religious, dimension.

3 Donne's Sermon XLIII on Apoc. 7:2–3: An Allegorical and Poetic Exegesis[6]

Given Donne's demonstrable knowledge of patristic and medieval literature, it is tempting to speculate which of the authors mentioned in Matter's articles would have been known (and how well they would have been known) to him, either as firsthand sources or through subsequent comments. Augustine, Jerome, and Ambrose are, as we know, among his most cited references; not surprisingly, they are also mentioned in his sermon on Apoc. 7:2–3. Patristic influence on Donne has been highlighted,[7] particularly in the work he carried out in the period 1602–1615 before his ecclesiastical ordination and, after that, in the writing of his sermons. The metaphysical poets who held ecclesiastical roles were certainly familiar with the church fathers, whose widespread cultural and theological influence in English Christian Humanism has convincingly been discussed, among others, by E. Harris Harbison in *The Christian Scholar in the Age of the Reformation*.[8]

A reference to Alcuin in Donne's *Biathanatos*[9] suggests that Donne knew some of Alcuin's writings, but it is difficult to ascertain if he knew the pseudo-Alcuin exegetical text discussed in Matter's seminal article. The knowledge of this pseudo-Alcuin on the part of Donne remains, I believe, a very remote possibility. As Matter suggests: "From the perspective of dissemination and influence, this is not a very important text"[10]

---

[6] On the issue of exegesis, besides the above mentioned contributions of E. Ann Matter on medieval biblical interpretations, the following references seem valuable: Winfried Schleiner, *The Imagery of John Donne's Sermons* (Providence: Brown University Press, 1970); Stanley E. Fish, *Self-Consuming Artifacts* (Berkeley: University of California Press, 1972), in particular the section "Donne: The Word as All," 43–77.

[7] Katrin Ettenhuber, *Donne's Augustine* (Oxford: Oxford University Press, 2011). See also Mark Vessey, "John Donne (1572–1631) in the Company of Augustine: Patristic Culture and Literary Profession in the English Renaissance," *Revue des Etudes Augustiniennes* 39 (1993): 173–201.

[8] E. Harris Harbison, *The Christian Scholar in the Age of the Reformation* (New York: Charles Scribner's Sons, 1956).

[9] Vessey, *John Donne*, 188.

[10] Matter, "The Pseudo-Alcuinian 'De Septem Sigillis'," 1.

and its relevance lies mostly in the presentation of "early medieval exegetical commonplaces" and in specific liturgical contexts (Mozarabic liturgies). In Donne's "Apocalypse Sermon" XLIII there is no explicit reference to some important "medieval commonplaces," for example, to the "seven seals" as allegories of events in the life of Christ or as representations of the seven gifts of the Holy Spirit, which, on the contrary, prominently figure in the pseudo-Alcuin text. Donne's omission is probably understandable since such allegorical correspondences are missing in Jerome, one of Donne's familiar references. His distance from the tradition of Visigothic lectionaries and Mozarabic liturgies is also visible in his choice to preach on the Book of Revelation on All-Saints Day, rather than in the season from Easter to Pentecost.[11] There is, however, a Christological interpretation of "The Angel ascending from the East," as we shall now see.[12]

Sermon XLIII on Apoc. 7:2–3 is based on the following quotation:

> And I saw another Angel ascending from the East, which had the seale of the living God, and he cryed with a loud voyce to the foure Angels, to whom power was given to hurt the earth, and the sea, saying, hurt yee not the earth, neither the sea, neither the trees, till we have sealed the servants of our God in their foreheads.[13]

The occasion of the sermon was, as I have pointed out, the liturgical celebration of All-Saints Day on 1st November of presumably 1623. Its focus is the doctrine of "the Communion of the Saints," i.e. the unity of the "Church Triumphant" of the saints in heaven and the "Church Militant"[14] of the believers on earth, but the slant of the argument also implies a strong defense of the Anglican Church against its enemies, identified respectively as the "Atheists," "Papists" (Roman Catholics), "Sectaries" (anxiety about the growing role of Puritans was clearly

---

[11] Donne did, however, also preach on Apoc. 4:8 upon Trinity Sunday at St. Dunstan's: sermon XLII. See: Henry Alford, ed., *The Works of John Donne*, vol. 2 (London: John W. Parker, 1839), 247–70.

[12] Donne writes: "This Angel which does so much for Gods Saints is, not inconveniently, by many Expositors, taken to be our Saviour Christ himselfe," sermon XLIII. Alford, ed., *Works*, 2: 278.

[13] Ibid., 271.

[14] Ibid., 272.

widespread in Anglican circles), and the "Carnal indifferent men, who all would hinder the blowing of this wind, the effect of this Gospel."[15]

This partly links Donne to the contemporary political readings of the Book of Revelation, and to the widespread assumption that current events were literally "apocalyptical." Political interpretations of Revelation in (pre) revolutionary England are not the specific concern of this essay. I wish, however, to point out that apocalyptic expectations and apocalyptic interpretations of contemporary events were already circulating in Donne's times and society, and gained impetus in 1688–1689. The works of Warren Johnston and others[16] must be mentioned as relevant contributions to the understanding of Donne's cultural context, even if Donne's preoccupations were not primarily political (except insofar as the defense of the Anglican Church was itself an intrinsically political act). Donne's interest is mostly philosophical and psychological, so that the political dimension is not emphasized, and there is no proper actualization of the Apocalypse in contemporary history in his sermon, despite the fact that this perspective was well known to the divines of his age, several of whom subscribed to it.

Returning to the sermon, Donne's preference for an allegorical, rather than a historical and literal, approach to the Book of Revelation is made clear within the very text: "... all the parts, and the style and the phrase of this Book is figurative and Metaphoricall...."[17] His reading explicitly discards a literal interpretation, as he suggests that the literal meaning is

---

[15] Ibid., 292.

[16] Warren Johnston, *Revelation Restored. The Apocalypse in Later Seventeenth-Century England* (Woodbridge: The Boydell Press, 2011). Earlier studies have convincingly suggested that political interpretations of the Book of Revelation were widespread and highly influential in Sixteenth and Seventeenth century England: C.A. Patrides and Joseph Wittreich, *The Apocalypse in English Renaissance Thought and Literature: Patterns, Antecedents and Repercussions* (Manchester: Manchester University Press, 1984); Christopher Hill, *The World Turned Upside Down: Radical Ideas During the English Revolution* (London: Maurice Temple Smith, 1972); Robert Ashton, *The English Civil War: Conservatism and Revolution, 1603–1649* (London: Weidenfeld and Nicholson, 1989); Patrick Collinson, *The Birthpangs of Protestant England: Religious and Cultural Change in the Sixteenth and Seventeenth Centuries* (Basingstoke: Macmillan, 1988); Jonathan Goldberg, *James I and the Politics of Literature: Jonson, Shakespeare, Donne, and their Contemporaries* (Baltimore: Johns Hopkins University Press, 1983); and Arthur F. Marotti, *John Donne, Coterie Poet* (Madison: University of Wisconsin Press, 1986).

[17] Alford, ed., *Works*, 2: 291.

hic et nunc beyond human comprehension, until "the prophecies of this book be accomplished"[18]; he thereby distances himself from the Puritan apocalyptic readings of the historical moment. Donne emphasizes the necessity of his own allegorical exegesis, and while he provides a very close, phrase-by-phrase, and even word-by-word, reading of the short biblical text he has chosen (a widespread exegetical practice among cultivated preachers), he identifies a number of specific elements to which he confers special symbolic meaning. Among the most prominent are: "The Angel ascending from the East,"[19] the four Angels who are given the power to destroy the earth, the four corners of the earth (i.e. East, South, West, and North),[20] the Seal of the living God,[21] and the (same) Seal on the forehead of God's servants.[22] "Seal" becomes a pivotal term in his interpretation, and he uses a quotation from Ambrose to interpret the seal as "signaculum Christi in corde, ut diligamus, in fronte, ut confiteamur, in brachio ut operamus; God seales us in the heart, that we might love him, and in the fore head, that we might professe it, and in the hand[23] that we might declare and practice it."[24] The seal for Donne is a symbol endowed with multiple, disparate (from different exegetic origins), and even fanciful connotations. He multiplies these elements when he proposes not one, but two seals for the faithful: the first is Baptism, and the second is participation in the Ministry of the Church.[25]

After an Old Testament reference to Moses and Aaron being guided by Angels, he also speaks of the seals as the "Sacraments of the New Testament" and the "Absolution of sinnes."[26] He introduces the element of "wind,"[27] not included in his quotation, but of vital importance in traditional exegesis as a symbol of "The Spirit." Donne sometimes corroborates his views with references to previous "Expositors." However,

[18] Ibid., 273.
[19] Ibid., 271, 274, 283, 284.
[20] Both ibid., 288 and 289.
[21] Ibid., 274, 284, 285, 286, 292.
[22] Ibid., 271, 272, 273, 274, 294, 295.
[23] The Latin "brachio" is, of course, literally "arm," but "hand" is Donne's own translation in the sermon.
[24] Donne, s. XLIII, Alford, ed., *Works*, 2: 296.
[25] Ibid., 294.
[26] Ibid., 286.
[27] Ibid., 291 and 292.

he fails to provide the specific names of the authors or of the commentaries to which he alludes, but it is significant that the ones he mentions are among the Church Fathers, i.e. "S. Hierome (who indeed in that followed Origen),"[28] Ambrose, and Augustine.

Angels are another prominent element in the chosen passage.[29] Readers who are familiar with Donne immediately recall that angels are often present in his poetry from the *Holy Sonnets* and *The Anniversaries* to the amorous *Air and Angels* ("So in a voice, so in a shapeless flame/*Angells* affect us oft, and worship'd bee," ll. 3–4) and *The Dreame* ("Yet I thought thee / For thou lovest truth/ an Angel, at first sight," ll. 13–14).[30] The theme of physical love and theology is intertwined in this poem, and angels are related to the philosophy of Plotinus and to the theology of Thomas Aquinas. The controversial theological issue of how angels can manifest themselves to humans is wittily elaborated into the argument that even the purest love must be expressed in the body, and that the soul itself needs a body "else could nothing doe" (l. 8). In Donne's "Apocalypse Sermon," angels are center stage. He explains that, like men, they have a "common best thing," i.e. "reason, understanding, knowledge, discourse, consideration," and that they also have "grace," which is "above reason," and does not intrinsically belong to the human or angelic nature but is infused by God. Angels are "seduli animae pedissequae," i.e. "faithfull and diligent attendants upon all our steps."[31]

For Donne angels are significant presences in the mediation between earthly realities and the supernatural world; in this sense they are strictly apocalyptic figures (*sensu* Collins). The four angels in Revelation are said, as we have seen, to correspond to the four corners of the earth, an idea which forcefully returns in Sonnet VII, entitled "At the round earth's imagined corners," and they are said to represent the geographical directions of East, South, West, and North, which in the sermon receive an

---

[28] The very brief (and vague) quotation is ibid., 288.

[29] Recent studies on angels include the following interesting contributions: *Angels in the Early Modern World*, ed. Peter Marshall and Alexandra Walsham (Cambridge: Cambridge University Press, 2006); David Keck, *Angels and Angelology in the Middle Ages* (New York: Oxford University Press, 1998); Meredith J. Gill, *Angels and the Order of Heaven in Medieval and Renaissance Italy* (Cambridge: Cambridge University Press, 2014).

[30] Unless otherwise noted, poetry quoted from A. J. Smith, ed. *John Donne: The Complete English Poems* (Harmondsworth: Penguin, 1996).

[31] Alford, ed., *Works*, 275, 276.

elaborate and indeed surprising anthropomorphic interpretation. Donne's fancy typically anthropomorphizes "the four corners" and connects them to human situations (thereby confirming the pervasive analogy of micro- and macrocosm in his writings).[32] He suggests that the South indicates "the contemplation of thine owne honour, thine offices, thy favour, thy riches, thy health," for the South is "the sunshine of world prosperity." The West is "the ignorance of God's providence," the North is to "blow away and scatter [human] sadness with false, illusory, and sinful comfort," while the East is the fountainhead of goodness. Our Angel comes from the East (a denotation of splendor and an illustration of understanding and conscience), and there is more: he comes Ascending (I saw an Angel ascending from the East) that is "still growing more cleare and more powerfull upon us."[33] This figure is interpreted as Jesus Christ, in connection with his Ascension. Donne writes: "This Angel which does so much for Gods Saints is, not inconveniently, by many Expositors, taken to be our Saviour Christ himselfe."[34]

Donne's religious sermon on Apoc. 7:2–3 is remarkably close to Holy Sonnet VII, which is also a meditation on the Day of the Last Judgment. But the Sonnet is an intense poetical and existential meditation, which differs in this respect from the theological take on the theme proper to the sermon. The poet contemplates the many causes of death that have spawned "the numberless multitude" of Revelation. They were destroyed by war, disease, desperation (suicide), legal punishment (ll. 5–7), and at the sound of the angels' trumpets (angels remain the unquestioned protagonists of the endtimes) the souls of the deceased will be united to their former bodies (l. 4), in order to appear before God. On the one hand, the poet invites angels to sound the trumpet that will call the final judgment but, on the other hand, he implores God to let the angels "sleep" (l. 9), and thus delay the end, so that he may repent and be himself included among those "whose eyes/ Shall behold God and never taste death's woe" (ll. 7–8). He feels that his sins abound, and he

---

[32] In sermon XLIII, the four angels of Revelation 7 are also taken anthropomorphically as equivalents of the human activities of "worldly profession," "bodily refection," "honest recreation," and "religious service of God" (ed. Alford, *Works*, 2: 289). Donne also suggests (ibid.) that there is an angel of temptation at every corner to whom "power was given to hurt," *ex potestate data*.

[33] Ibid., 282–83.

[34] Ibid., 278.

will not be able to ask for forgiveness, once deceased. Donne's religious doctrine on the endtimes is orthodox in this poem, and yet orthodoxy is reinterpreted into a very personal narrative. The biblical narrative is turned into a subjective "Apocalypse," and the theological awareness of the former is transmuted into an excruciating existential vision.

4 The Apocalyptic Sensibility in the Poems: Destruction and Redemption in Sacred and Secular Terms

Before discussing some poetic texts in detail, I wish to recall that Donne's creativity was powerfully nourished by a vast erudition in the Bible, in patristic literature, in civil and ecclesiastical law, in alchemy, geography, astronomy, and the "New Philosophy;" it was also shaped by his military and political experience and by his ecclesiastical profession. What forbids a reading of his oeuvre simply and crudely in terms of these biographical dimensions is the fact that his art reached beyond all of his scholarly and professional knowledge and transformed it into a unique vision and poetic achievement. Donne's "apocalyptic sensibility" is evident throughout his oeuvre, not exclusively in the religious texts. His complex poetic voice makes room for the most disparate moods, from cynicism to devotion, from physical desire to the uplifting of fervent belief, from the bitter disillusion of erotic love to the self-reproach of a repentant sinner.

Very often religious imagery is used to sustain secular emotions, for example, in the explicitly erotic "Epithalamion made at Lincolnes Inne" (presumably composed in 1595), in which the virgin's amorous "rites" are daringly juxtaposed to the sacrifice of the Lamb, and the bed is compared to an altar.[35] In the well-known poems "The Canonization" (composed 1603–1615) and "The Exstasie" (composed before 1609), passion is "sanctified" and lovers cast themselves in the role of saints who set an example for others to imitate; on the other hand, secular and even sexual emotions are found in Donne's unquestionably religious poetry. An exemplary case is Sonnet XIV, which reads: "But I am betroth'd unto your enemie,/ Divorce mee, untie, or break that knot againe,/

---

[35] In other poems the bed is associated with the grave, and the image is supported by the current early-modern meaning of "to die" as a synonym of "experiencing orgasm."

Take mee to you, imprison mee, for I/ Except you enthrall mee, never shall be free,/ Nor ever chast, except you ravish me" (ll. 10–14). Sacred and secular become complementary dimensions, and cease to be mere opposites, in Donne's passionate love and equally passionate devotion.[36] A conceptual and aesthetic homogeneity orchestrates both kinds of texts, which are therefore mutually illuminating in their rich figurality. In other words, Donne's "unified sensibility" (sensu T.S. Eliot[37]) juxtaposes religious and erotic themes; his style is often similar, and unmistakably recognizable in both the religious and secular poetry for its daring imagination and exuberance of language, for the pervasive use of metaphors, *topoi*, neologisms, and strange turns of phrase.

More importantly, I hope that the discussion that follows will show in greater detail that "the apocalyptic" is one of the most visible ciphers of Donne's imaginative and poetic unity.

A deeply ingrained and culturally mainstream perception of the analogy between self and cosmos, between the vicissitudes of the human microcosm and the ultimate meaning of the universe, allows Donne to project the sense of cosmic endtime onto his life experiences, particularly onto the ones that spell conceptual and emotional beginnings and ends (as we have seen, for example in sermon XLIII on Apoc. 7:2–3 and in Sonnet VII). Donne's amorous poetry repeatedly proposes a view of

---

[36] The dichotomy that several of Donne's interpreters have wished to outline, between a young, libertine, immoral Donne versus a mature, repentant, and finely theological persona fails, in my opinion, to acknowledge the richly contradictory elements of his personality, the wit of his poetic voice and the depth of his theological knowledge, as well as his ability to simultaneously experience (and successfully convey in extraordinary poems) faith and doubt, sexual desire and yearning for divine grace. The often proposed contrast between the "wanton" youth and the "latter-day Augustine" of his biographers (starting with Izaac Walton's 1640 'agiography' of Donne), has, reductively in my opinion, also been applied to the amorous and the religious poetry, thereby emphasizing a questionable determinism between his art and biography, and thus establishing a clear-cut separation between the love poems and the devotional poems. Among Donne's biographies I recall: Izaak Walton, *The Lives of John Donne, Sir Henry Wotton, Richard Hooker, George Herbert, and Robert Sanderson* (London: Oxford University Press, 1927); R. C. Bald, *John Donne: A Life* (Oxford: Clarendon Press, 1970); John Carey, *John Donne: Life, Mind, Art* (London: Faber & Faber, 1981); and David Edwards, *John Donne: Man of Flesh and Spirit* (London: Continuum, 2001).

[37] T. S. Eliot, "The Metaphysical Poets" (from 1952), in *Selected Essays* (London: Faber & Faber, 1964), 281–91.

"the apocalyptic" in metaphysical and subjective terms at the same time. Donne provides abundant, eloquent examples of lovers who reciprocally establish and consolidate an entire universe between them. This universe (an individual microcosm) is the equivalent of the macrocosm, but it belongs to them in a unique form of reciprocity and it follows that crisis between the lovers is then configured as a private apocalypse. The topos of the lovers' universe is present in the following poems: "The Sunne Rising," "A Fever," "The Anniversarie," "A Valediction: Of The Booke," "A Valediction: Of Weeping," and "The Good Morrow," which is perhaps the most paradigmatic in the elaboration of this motif: "Let sea-discoverers to new worlds have gone,/ Let maps to others, worlds on worlds have showne,/ Let us possess one world, each hath one, and is one" (ll. 12–14).

The image of the micro/macro cosmos is applied to the poet himself in his "Holy Sonnets" and in the sermons, in close relation to his treatment of apocalyptic motives. "Sonnet V," in particular, is explicit: "I am a little world made cunningly / of elements..." (ll. 1–2). The fact that the micro/macro cosmos analogy was mainstream among thinkers, poets, and divines of his age does not diminish Donne's very original reinterpretation of it, his unique and compelling writing and re-writing of this parallelism. The analogy allows, as I have mentioned above, a special articulation of "the apocalyptic," whereby Donne links the theological to the personal. The anthropomorphic equivalence between the world (or a kingdom) and the beloved is central to all amorous poetry by Donne; lovers create and dwell in a universe in which the music of the spheres and the light of knowledge exist in harmony. In fact, in "A Valediction: Of the Booke," we read: "...in this our Universe/Schooles might learne Sciences, Spheares Music, Angels Verse" (ll. 26–27).

The intensity of human passion, the cult of an Augustinian "dilectio ordinata" (lawful love), and the sublimation of Neoplatonic love find different expressions in the amorous poems, where the "dilectio" (the force that orients the choice of a lover according to virtue and beauty) is often tinged with noble hues in the celebration of an aristocratic, immortal, and even ineffable kind of love. A few lines must be quoted as examples of Donne's complex philosophy of love, even if the extraordinary poems to which they belong cannot be here discussed at length:

Dull sublunary lovers's love
(Whose soule is sense) cannot admit
Absence, because it doth remove
Those things which elemented it.

But we, by a love so much refin'd
That our selves know not what it is
Inter-assured of the mind,
Care lesse, eyes, lips, hands to misse.
("A Valediction: Forbidding Mourning", ll. 13–20)

Call us what you will, wee are made such by love;
Call her one, mee another flye,
We're tapers too, and at our owne cost die,
And wee in us finde the Eagle and the Dove.
The Phoenix riddle hath more wit
By us; we two being one, are it.
("The Canonization", ll. 19–24)

And by these hymnes, all shall approve
Us canoniz'd for Love.
("The Canonization", ll. 35–36)

When love, with one another so
Interanimates two soules,
That abler soule, which thence doth flow,
Defects of loneliness controules.

Wee then, who are this new soule, know
Of what we are compos'd, and made,
For th'Atomies of which we grow,
Are soules, whom no change can invade.
("The Extasie", ll. 45–48)

I have proposed that the literary topos of the lovers as a cosmos paves the way to the articulation of several "apocalyptic" experiences within Donne's love poetry. Their world is, in fact, always under threat of dissolution, and the Apocalypse is not caused by absence, as it would be in the case of the "sublunary lovers whose soul is sense." Instead, it is caused by lack of a shared supernatural vision, or when reciprocity fails (if the lovers are not "inter-assured of the mind").

4.1 Death and Judgment: The Novissimi[38] in Sonnet VII: "At the Round Earth's Imagined Corners," and the Second Anniversary

In his religious poetry the apocalyptic theme is predictably more closely connected to the biblical text, and yet Donne's re-elaborations are original. In Sonnet VII, preoccupation with endtimes is combined with the poet's sense of unworthiness and fear of the Last Judgment, but in the longer poem *The Second Anniversary* he is also prepared to play the part of angels in the context of the *Novissimi*. A very interesting view of poetry is part of Donne's interpretation of the last days, since an almost sacramental function or redeeming power is attributed to his verse. To show this I will quote Sonnet VII in full, and the longer poem briefly:

> At the round earth's imagined corners, blow
> Your trumpets, angels, and arise, arise
> From death, you numberless infinities
> Of souls, and to your scattered bodies go,
> All whom the flood did, and fire shall, o'erthrow,
> All whom war, dearth, age, agues, tyrannies,
> Despair, law, chance, hath slain, and you whose eyes,
> Shall behold God, and never taste death's woe.
> But let them sleep, Lord, and me mourn a space;
> For, if above all these, my sins abound,
> 'Tis late to ask abundance of thy grace,
> When we are there. Here on this lowly ground,
> Teach me how to repent; for that's as good
> As if thou' hadst seal'd my pardon with thy blood.

A strictly religious perspective is held in this holy sonnet. The angels at the four corners of the earth correspond to the figures dominating Donne's Apocalypse sermon, already discussed. The specific image of the "four corners" may indicate, as some have suggested, a still presumably traditional view of a flat earth in cosmic space, but, given Donne's awareness of the new astronomical and geographical discoveries,[39] it is

---

[38] Helen Gardner has traced the four *Novissimi* (Death, Judgment, Heaven and Hell) in Donne's Sonnets. See Helen Gardner, ed., *The Divine Poems* (Oxford: Clarendon Press, 1978); Helen Gardner, ed., *John Donne: A Collection of Critical Essays* (Englewood Cliffs, NJ: Prentice Hall, 1962).

[39] In his *Ignatius His Conclave* (1610–1611), Donne mentions Galileo and the new views of the moon and the planets disclosed by his "glasse." Astronomical imagery is abundant in the love poems and in the *Anniversaries*.

more likely to represent a map, a sketch of the newly discovered spaces. The sonnet is typically direct and "dialogical," as opposed to "descriptive" (this is a typical feature of Donne's poems that makes them compelling), since the angels and God become the poet's immediate interlocutors and they are called to witness the shifts and turns in his meditative mood. In a hyperbolic and idiosyncratic gesture, the poet asks God to delay the summoning angels and to postpone the Day of Judgment for the multitudes, so that he may repent and be sealed with Christ's redeeming seal. The image of angels blowing their trumpets to summon mankind alludes, of course, to a widespread exegetic tradition of apocalyptic literature, but Donne's very personal treatment of this *topos* deserves closer attention. One should, in fact, remember that in the final lines of "The Second Anniversarie" the poet casts himself in the implicitly angelical role of player of the apocalyptic trumpet:

> Since His will is, that to posterity/ Thou should'st for life and death a pattern be,/ And that the world should notice have of this,/ The purpose and th' authority is His./ Thou art the proclamation; and *I am/ The trumpet, at whose voice the people came*. (ll. 529–530, emphasis mine)

Poetry per se is thus ennobled, by being associated with angelic sound, and the poet puts himself among the angelic host. Since the chosen moral function of his own art consists in waking the dead and insensitive souls of "carnal indifferent men," Donne attributes to his own work the same redeeming power of the little girl he has idealized and celebrated in both the *First* and *Second Anniversary*.

Holy Sonnet VII, which I have briefly discussed above in relation to Revelation, shows a great concern for the manifold factors of human weakness. "War, death, age, agues, tyrannies, despair, law, chance" are all enlisted as the mortal agents of the destruction of the human microcosm, regardless of the fact that some causes of the Apocalypse for the "numberless multitude" are accidental and others procured by human action. In the famous Sonnet X, "Death be not proud," the fatal dangers are similarly outlined as chance, royal death sentences, Fate, despair leading to suicide, poison, war, and sickness. The forceful image of death with its manifold insidious ways of penetrating mankind's frail condition stems from Donne's recurrent and original meditative mood on the theme. His *Devotions upon Emergent Occasions* (1624)[40] clearly illustrates and develops, according to the fine rhetorical art of *copia*,[41] Donne's obsession, in terms of a long and elaborate working of the theme of human weakness in which "the ague" is given a prominent role. A similar imagery is evident in the love poem "A Feaver," where the beloved's illness becomes itself an apocalyptic omen: "To leave this world behind is death,/ But when thou from this world wilt go/ The whole world vapors with thy breath" (ll. 7–8). The rapid shift of meaning, and the witty double meaning of "this world," which, in succession, refers to "the earth" and to "the beloved's body," is the key to Donne's very private and emotional, not just philosophical, interpretation, and appropriation of the Apocalypse motif.

The theme of the end of the world is explicitly and further addressed a few lines later in "A Feaver," with reference to the philosophical and theological debates on how the world would end: "O wrangling schools,[42] that search what fire/ Shall burn this world, had none the wit/Unto this knowledge to aspire,/ That this her fever might be it?" (ll. 13–16). The anthropomorphic and strictly personal reading of the end of the world is given again in the *Anniversaries*, in connection with the death of the young Elizabeth Drury. The bereavement of the beloved, just like the departing of the virtuous young girl (who is depicted as a spiritual presence akin to the apocalyptic figures mediating human salvation, *sensu* Collins[43]) are felt as nothing less than the annihilation of love and holiness. The ensuing destruction of what gives energy and meaning to the

---

[40] J. Sparrow, ed., *John Donne: Devotions Upon Emergent Occasions* (Cambridge: Cambridge University Press, 1923).

[41] *Copia* was a dominant strategy of rhetorical elaboration, essentially consisting in the ability to express an idea in a number of different forms, usually by enriching the bare sentence conveying the essential message. This art was taught in most grammar schools throughout the humanist period and the Renaissance. One of the most famous textbooks was Erasmus' *De Copia*, a text which was very popular at Cambridge, where John Colet, a friend of Erasmus recommended it to his pupils. Angela Locatelli, "The Land of Plenty: Erasmus' *De Copia* and English Renaissance Rhetoric," in *Silenos: Erasmus in Elizabethan Literature*, ed. Claudia Corti (Pisa: Pacini, 1998), 41–57.

[42] "Wrangling schools" may of course refer to the schoolmen, but also to the Stoics and to the second letter of St. Peter indicating that the world would end in fire. The concept was a commonplace in biblical readings that maintained that God had promised to spare humankind from a second universal flood.

[43] Collins, *Apocalyptic Imagination*, 5.

world will last until such meaning is restored in the accomplishment of "the progress of the soul" in a sort of personal eschatology from destruction to redemption.

4.2 "The Apocalyptic" as Loss of Epistemic Coordinates: The Anniversaries and "A Nocturnall upon S. Lucies Day, Being the Shortest Day"

What the poet aims at in both *An Anatomy of the World: The First Anniversary* and in *An Anatomy of the World: Of the Progress of the Soul. The Second Anniversary* is to awaken in his contemporaries an ethical stance against corruption. The following well-known lines of *The First Anniversary* articulate the apocalyptic sense of the loss of epistemic coordinates, and the concomitant bewildered perception of a world turned upside down:

> And new philosophy calls all in doubt;
> The element of fire is quite put out;
> The sun is lost, and th' earth, and no man's wit
> Can well direct him where to look for it.
> And freely men confess that this world's spent,
> When in the planets, and the firmament
> They seek so many new; they see that this
> Is crumbled out again to his atomies.
> 'Tis all in pieces, all coherence gone,
> All just supply, and all relation.
> Prince, subject, father, son, are things forgot... (ll. 205–215) [44]

"The Apocalyptic" is here clearly connoted as a cognitive, cultural, and political position. Donne's imagination is fueled by apocalyptic fears, concerning the deep uncertainties that were driving the modern quest for new worlds, producing new empirical (as opposed to metaphysical) forms of knowledge, and challenging traditional power configurations in both kingdom and family. Crisis is an attitude which Hamlet epitomizes in his radical doubt, Giordano Bruno in his subversive (meta)physics, and which the "new (natural) philosophers" address in unprecedented

---

[44] Here quoted from T. W. Craik and J. R. Craik, eds. *John Donne: Selected Poetry and Prose* (London: Methuen, 1986), 131–44.

scientific terms, by abandoning the old school investigation of "second causes" and circumscribing the field of knowledge purely to the phenomena that can undergo empirical verification.[45] This radically anti-metaphysical gesture spells a symbolic and cultural Apocalypse for Donne whose fear is grounded in a profound diffidence toward the "new philosophy," and causes a deep psychological, philosophical, and poetic restlessness in him.

In their edition of Donne's poetry, T.W. and J.R. Craik have suggested that "In An Anatomy (that is, a dissection) of the World, Donne points out, in ingenious detail, how the world has been declining ever since the Fall of Man and may now be considered dead."[46] The following verses in *The First Anniversary* confirm this reading:

> This great consumption to a fever turn'd
> And so the world had fits; it joy'd, it mourn'd.
> And as men thinke that Agues physicke are,
> And th' Ague being spent, give over care,
> So thou, sicke world, mistak'st thy selfe to bee
> Well, when alas, thou'rt in a Lethargee. (ll. 19–24)
> [...]
> Thou know'st how poor a trifling thing man is,
> And learn'st thus much by our Anatomy,
> The heart being perish'd, no part can be free,
> And that except thou feed, not banquet, on
> The supernatural food, religion,
> Thy better growth grows withered and scant;
> Be more than man, or thou'rt less than an ant.
> Then as mankind, so is the world's whole frame,
> Quite out of joint, almost created lame;
> For before God had made up all the rest,
> Corruption enter'd and depraved the best... (ll. 184–194)

The gloom is reinforced in *The Second Anniversary*, starting from the surprising images and counterintuitive similes (of the ship sailing against

---

[45] Amos Funkenstein, *Theology and the Scientific Imagination: From the Middle Ages to the Seventeenth Century* (Princeton, NJ: Princeton University Press, 1986); Angela Locatelli, "'This Phantasie May Be Resembled to a Glasse': Collisions and Collusions in Early-Modern Literary and Scientific Discourse," in *La conoscenza della letteratura/The Knowledge of Literature*, vol. VII, ed. Angela Locatelli (Bergamo: Bergamo University Press, Sestante, 2008), 157–72.

[46] Craik and Craik, *John Donne*, 272.

the wind, the beheaded man's frantic motion, and the sound of the damp lute) that inaugurate the mournful threnody.

The apocalyptic crisis extensively dealt with in *The Anniversaries* finds a rich and intense poetic expression in "A Nocturnall Upon S.Lucies Day, being the shortest day,"[47] in which a rich symbolism unites the feast of the saint to the end of the year and the endtimes.

> 'Tis the yeares midnight, and it is the dayes,
> *Lucies*, who scarce seaven houres herself unmaskses;
> The Sunne is spent, and now his flasks
> Send forth light squibs, no constant rayes;
> The world's whole sap is sunke;
> The generall balme th' hydroptique earth hath drunk,
> Whither, as to the beds-feet, life is shrunke,
> Dead and interr'd; yet all these seeme to laugh,
> Compar'd with mee, who am their Epitaph. (ll. 1–9)

The apocalyptic is clearly stated in the image of the dying world: "the Sunne is spent" and the earth is sick ("hydroptique earth"). The endtimes are interpreted as a fatal malady of the macrocosm and associated with the climax of darkness ("the yeares midnight"). Time and space are here questioned in their ordinary dimension and are reframed as cosmic categories at risk of dissolution. The poet associates himself with this scenario in the by now familiar gesture of analogy between universal and personal eschatological vicissitudes.

> Study me then, you who shall lovers bee
> At the next world, that is, at the next Spring:
> For I am every dead thing,
> In whom love wrought new Alchimie.
> For his art did expresse
> A quintessence even from nothingnesse,
> From dull privations, and lean emptinesse:
> He ruin'd mee, and I am re-begot
> Of absence, darknesse, death; things which are not. (ll. 10–18)
> [...]

---

[47]The quotations from "A Nocturnall" are taken from Alessandro Serpieri and Silvia Bigliazzi, eds., *John Donne: Poesie* (Milan: BUR, 2007), 312–19.

If I an ordinary nothing were,
As shadow, a light and body must be here.
But I am None; nor will my Sunne renew.
You lovers, for whose sake the lesser Sunne
At this time to the Goat is runne
To fetch new lust, and give it you,
Enjoy your summer all:
Since shee enjoyes her long nights festivall,
Let mee prepare towards her, and let mee call
This hour her Vigil, and her eve, since this
Both the yeares, and the dayes deep midnight is. (ll. 35–45)

Several parallelisms with the eulogies for Elizabeth Drury can be traced here, but this text has a superior poetical quality over *The Anniversaries* and has a special conceptual density which is worth exploring more closely. "The Nocturnall" possesses the aesthetic and philosophical complexity of great poetry, and it is a conceptual *tour de force*, a special feature which poses a renewed challenge to interpreters through the ages. This poem is, of course, "apocalyptic" in both a commonsensical and a philosophical acceptation of the term.

In terms of genre, a "Nocturnal" is a night rhapsody or a night meditation; it is also a prayer service of the church on the eve of some important celebration; in this case it is the feast of the martyr Saint Lucy, whose name is etymologically linked to "light." St. Lucy's day in the popular imagination is the shortest day of the year and its night the longest, it is associated to the Winter Solstice, and, of course its midnight is deemed the darkest moment in absolute terms. The occasion drives Donne's imagination toward a meditation on the ideas of light and darkness and their multiple symbolic meanings, extending to the concepts of being and "nothingnesse." Again, this is a poem about the "apocalyptic" epistemological crisis of the seventeenth century, where "light," in the sense of a sound and sure understanding, cannot be found, and no unequivocal explanation of physical or metaphysical phenomena can be given. The image of Lucy's "mask" visually conveys the impossibility of positive knowledge. The mask covers the Saint's face, her intrinsic light, and obscures her splendor of beauty, intelligence, and grace.

Countless lexical elements speak about this dimming of light into darkness as a doomsday. "The Sunne is spent," its energy exhausted: it does not send off rays but just "squibs" (fitful sparks). Likewise, the terrestrial world is heavy (it is made of water and earth, elements that cannot be lifted, i.e. the opposites of air and fire, the most volatile, noble, and light elements), nor can the lymph ("sap") ascend to vivify plants. The earth is dropsical, sick with a fatal disease, and the scenario becomes that of a funeral: the whole world is eventually "interred." The reiterated rhyme of "sunke," "drunk," "shrunke" reinforces the meaning of the fall into utter decadence and echoes the leaden sound of funeral bells. It is worth noticing that this Apocalypse, even if not caused by a flood, is an unusual death by water, not fire. With a typically idiosyncratic gesture, Donne refers the universal state of doom to himself, through the two metaphors of "the epitaph" and of "the book" in which death is written. This dissolution for the poet is the "ruin" brought about by love, which has been associated with the death of the beloved, resulting in an apocalypse (like in "A Feaver," as I have suggested above). The bereaved lover is thus himself "a dead thing." The invitation to "Study me then, you who shall lovers be/ at the next world, that is, at the next Spring," is a call to look at him as a paragon of dissolution, as the sign of universal death, and as the example of his readers' future mortal fate. On the other hand, the allusion to "the next world," and the temporal rebirth implicit in "the next Spring," does not allow Death to have the last word (one easily recalls the last line in Sonnet X: "Death thou shalt die").

The poet's argument in "The Nocturnall" is far from simple. It hinges on the paradox of life coming out of an original "nothingnesse" (this term is Donne's original neologism[48] to indicate a lack and a subtraction, visually conveyed in "lean emptinesse" and "dull privations") through love's distillation. Individual immortality seems to be denied ("nor will my sun renew") once the lover is bereft of his love object, and yet mortality is reversed to be both the birth of a new immortal self and the perpetual regeneration of new lovers. Love is seen as the cosmic *vis vitalis* that will renew the earth into a new eschatology because it perennially transforms and traverses the micro and macrocosms. The whole process is metaphorically articulated in alchemical terms. The poet knowingly explains the process; because he has experienced it, he is both the

---

[48] The word "nothingnesse" is Donne's own creation and gift to the English language, just like the neologisms "interanimates" (l. 42) in "The Exstasie" and "inter-assured of the mind" (l. 19) in "A Valediction: Forbidding Mourning."

subject and object in the experiment of love's alchemy and is reborn from "dull privations, and lean emptinesse," from "absence, darknesse, death." In this process, love "expresses"[49] (in the alchemical sense of "press out," "squeeze out," and "distil") a quintessence, an immortal substance. This substance was traditionally equated with light, the fifth element (with fire, air, water, and earth), i.e. literally the "the fifth essence."[50] Donne connects it symbolically, poetically, and philosophically to love. Love is the light, love is the powerful element that metamorphoses "nothingnesse" into the alchemy of the new life. This daring meditation on "nothingnesse" turns the poem into a cosmic theological meditation: in this sense love is associated with the idea of God in the Gospel of John (i.e. God as love and light). The poem is a witty and profound meditation on the end and regeneration of the universe and of the individual. The last stanza returns to the devout celebration of St. Lucy's day: the "deep midnight" coincides with the beginning of a new light, and is thus paradoxically turned into the climax of a feast vigil.

5 Conclusion

I hope to have shown that the variations on the emotional and poetic spectrum which are evident in Donne's treatment of "the apocalyptic" spell a consistent continuity, and confirm a psychological and even theological unity in the midst of plurality, contradiction, and paradox. The new scientific perspective and the traditional religious world picture are the elements that jointly fuel Donne's imagination; his vision and style oscillate between these two major poles, regardless of whether his discourse be religious, erotic, or both at the same time. We clearly perceive that the apocalyptic themes of death and rebirth, the motive of supernatural figures mediating human salvation, the belief in ultimate realities beyond (but not entirely severed from) the present world of earthly and human phenomena are crucial components of his "apocalyptic" vision.

---

[49] Angela Locatelli, "The Common desire of Representation: or How to 'Express' in Literature and Science," in *La conoscenza della letteratura/The Knowledge of Literature*, vol. VI (Bergamo: Bergamo University Press/Sestante, 2007), 7–22.

[50] Angela Locatelli, "Discursive Intersections on the Subject of 'Light' in English Renaissance Literature," in *Representing Light across Arts and Sciences: Theories and Practices*, ed. Elena Agazzi, Enrico Giannetto, and Franco Giudice (Göttingen: V&R Unipress, 2010), 69–87.

These are all elements that John J. Collins has defined as proper to "the apocalyptic genre," and that E. Ann Matter has traced in the exegesis of the Apocalypse through the centuries. Donne's appropriation of them offers an original theological, philosophical, but also subjective and phenomenological approach to this Biblical motif, which he uniquely re-interprets in late early-modern culture.

BIBLIOGRAPHY

Primary

Abu l-Fat. *Kitāb al-Tarīkh.* Ed. Paul Stenhouse. Studies in Judaica 1. Sydney: Mandelbaum Trust, 1985.
Albert the Great. *Commentarius in Librum IV Sententiarum.* In *Opera omnia* 30. Paris: Vivès, 1894.
Alberto Aflieri. *Ogdoas.* Ed. and trans. E. Ann Matter and Carla P. Weinberg. *Education, Civic Virtue, and Colonialism in Fifteenth-Century Italy: The Ogdoas of Alberto Alfieri.* Tempe, AZ: Arizona Board of Regents, 2011.
Alcuin. *De fide sanctae Trinitatis et de Incarnatione Christi.* Ed. Eric Knibbs and E. Ann Matter, Corpus Christianorum: Continuatio Mediaevalis 249. Turnhout: Brepols, 2012.
Alexander of Hales. *Glossa in IV Libros Sententiarum Petri Lombardi.* Bibliotheca Franciscana Scholastica Medii Aevii 15. Quaracchi: Coll. S. Bonaventura, 1957.
———. *Quaestiones disputatae "Antequam esset frater."* Bibliotheca Franciscana Medii Aevi 20–21. Quaracchi: Coll. S. Bonaventura, 1960.
Amalar. *De ecclesiastico officio/On the Liturgy.* Ed. and trans. Eric Knibbs. Dumbarton Oaks Medieval Library, vols. 35–36. Cambridge: Harvard University Press, 2014.
Ambrose of Milan. *Opera.* Ed. Denis-Nicolas le Nourry and Jacques du Frische. *Sancti Ambrosii Mediolanensis: Opera,* 2 vols. Paris: Jean-Baptiste Coignard, 1686–90.

Ambrosius Autpertus. *Expositio in Apocalypsin.* Ed. Robert Weber. Corpus Christianorum: Continuatio Medievalis, vols. 27–27A. Turnhout: Brepols, 1975.

Andrea, Albert J., ed. and trans. *Contemporary Sources for the Fourth Crusade.* Leiden: Brill, 2000.

"Arte de bien morir." In *Arte de bien morir y Breve confesionario (Zaragoza, Pablo Hurus: c. 1479–1484).* Ed. Francisco Gago Jover, 81–119. Barcelona: Medio Maravedí, 1999.

Augustine, letter 12*. Ed. Johannes Divjak, *Sancti Aureli Augustini Opera: Epistolae ex duobus codicibus nuper in lucem prolatae.* Corpus Scriptorum Ecclesiasticorum Latinorum 88. Vienna: Hölder-Pichler-Tempsky, 1981. Trans. Roland Teske. *The Works of Saint Augustine: A Translation for the 21st Century,* 279–86. Hyde Park: NY: New City Press, 2005.

Augustine. *Enarrationes in Psalmos.* Trans. Maria Boulding. *Works of Saint Augustine: A Translation for the 21st Century. Part III: Expositions of the Psalms,* 6 vols. Brooklyn, NY: New City Press, 2000–2004.

Augustine. *Sermones ad Populum.* Trans. Edmund Hill and ed. John E. Rotelle. *Works of Saint Augustine: A Translation for the 21st Century. Part III: Sermons,* 11 vols. Brooklyn, NY: New City Press, 1990–1997.

Augustine. *Sermones de Vetere Testamento (1-50).* Ed. Cyrille Lambot. Corpus Christianorum Series Ltaina 41. Turnhout: Brepols, 1961.

Avila, Juan de. "Sermones de tiempo: '¡Grande es el día del Señor, y muy terrible!' Domingo I de Adviento." In *Obras Completas del Santo Maestro Juan de Avila: Edición Crítica.* Ed. Luis Sala Balust and Francisco Martín Hernández. Madrid: Biblioteca de Autores Cristianos, 1970.

Barelli, Francesco Luigi. *Memorie dell'origine, fondazione, avanzamenti, successi, ed uomini illustri in lettere, e in santità della congregazione de' cherici regolari di s. Paolo ... ,* vol. 2. Bologna: Per Costantino Pisarri sotto le Scuole all'Insegna di S. Michele, 1703–1707.

Beatus of Liébana. *Tractatus de Apocalipsin.* Ed. Roger Gryson. Corpus Christianorum: Series Latina, vols. 107B–C. Turnhout: Brepols, 2012.

Bede. *In epistolas VII catholicas.* Ed. M. L. W. Laistner. Corpus Christianorum: Series Latina 121. Turnhout: Brepols, 1983.

———. *Expositio Apocalypseos.* Ed. Roger Gryson. Corpus Christianorum: Series Latina 121A. Turnhout: Brepols, 2001.

Berengaudus. *Expositio super Septem Visiones Libri Apocalypsis.* Ed. Jacques-Paul Migne, *Patrologia latina cursus completus,* vol. 17, 763–970. Paris, 1845.

Betulius, Sixtus. *Sibyllinorum oracvlorvm libri octo.* Basel: Ioannis Oporini, 1545.

Biblia Latina cum glossa ordinaria. Strasbourg: Adolph Rusch, 1480–81. Reprint. Karlfried Froelich and Margaret T. Gibson, 4 vols. Turnhout: Brepols, 1992.

Bigne, Marguerin de La. *Sacra bibliotheca sanctorum patrum supra ducentos qua continentur, illorum de rebus diuinis opera omnia et fragmenta ...* Paris: Michaelem Sonnium, 1575.

Bonaventure. *Commentarius in IV Libros Sententiarum*. In *Opera omnia* 4. Quaracchi: Coll. S. Bonaventura, 1889.
Brocadelli, Lucia. "Seven Revelations." Trans. E. Ann Matter in *Dominican Penitent Women*. Ed. Maiju Lehmijoki-Gardner, 212–43. New York: Paulist Press, 2005.
Craik, T.W., and J.R. Craik. *John Donne: Selected Poetry and Prose*. London and New York: Methuen, 1986.
Crosby, H.L., ed. *Dio Chrysostom: Vol. 5*, Loeb Classical Library 385. Cambridge: Harvard University Press, 1946.
Dante Alighieri. *La traduccio[n] del Dante de lengua toscana en verso castellano*. Trans. Pedro Fernandez del Villegas. Burgos: Fadrique Aleman de Basilea, 1515.
Deledda, Grazia. *La chiesa della solitudine*. Milan: Treves, 1936. Trans. E. Ann Matter. *The Church of Solitude*. Albany NY: State University of New York Press, 2002.
Descrittione della fonzione avutasi nella Chiesa di Santa Cristina della Fondazza. Bologna, Biblioteca Comunale dell'Archiginnasio Bologna, Ms. Gozzadini 184.
Diario Mariale per l'Anno MDCCXXIII. Bologna, Biblioteca Comunale dell'Archiginnasio Bologna, Cartella Gozzadini.
Donne, John. *Devotions Upon Emergent Occasions*. Ed. John Sparrow. Reprint. Cambridge: Cambridge University Press, 1923.
———. Sermons XLII and XLIII. In *The Works of John Donne, D.D., with a Memoir of His Life*. Ed. Henry Alford M.A, vol. 2, 247–94. London: John W. Parker, 1839.
Evodius. *De miraculis sancta Stephani protomartyris*. Ed. Jacques-Paul Migne, *Patrologia latina cursus completus*, vol. 41, 833–54. Paris, 1864.
Faleoni, Celso. *Memorie historiche della chiesa bolognese e suoi pastori: All'eminentiss. e reuerendiss. signor card. Nicolo Ludouisio ...* Bologna: Giacomo Monti, 1649.
Gardner, Helen, ed. *John Donne: The Divine Poems*. Oxford: Clarendon, 1978.
Gilbert of Poitiers, *Sententiae*. Ed. Nikolaus M. Häring. "Die *Sententiae Magistri Gisleberti Pictavensis episcopi* I," *Archives d'Histoire Doctrinale et Littéraire au Moyen Age* 45 (1978): 83–180.
Granada, Fray Luis de. "Introducción del Símbolo de la Fe IV." In *Obras Completes*. Ed. Alvaro Huerga. Madrid: Fundación Universitaria Española, 1994.
Gregory of Tours, *History of the Franks*. Trans. Lewis Thorpe. London: Penguin, 1974.
Guy of Orchelles. *Tractatus de sacramentis*. Ed. D. Van den Eynde and O. Van den Eynde. Bonaventure, NY: Franciscan Institute, 1953.
Haimo of Auxerre, erroneously Haimo of Halberstadt. *Expositio in Apocalypsin*. Ed. Jacques-Paul Migne, *Patrologia latina cursus completus*, vol. 117, 937–1220. Paris, 1852.
Horozco y Covarrubias, Juan de. *Tratado dela verdadera y falsa prophecia*. Segovia: Juan de la Cuesta, 1588.

———. *Emblemas morales de Don Iuan de Horozco y Couarruuias*. Segovia: Juan de la Cuesta, 1589.

———. *Emblemas morales de don Iuan de Horozco y Covaruvias arcediano de Cuellar en la santa Yglesia de Segovia: Dedicadas a la buena memoria del presidente don Diego de Covarruvias y Leyua su tio*. Segovia: Juan de la Cuesta, 1591.

———. *Paradoxas Christianas contra las falsas opiniones del mundo*. Segovia: Marcos de Ortega, 1592.

———. *Consuelo de afligidos*. Agrigento, 1601.

———. *Symbola sacra*. Agrigento, 1601.

———. *Doctrina de principes enseñada por el santo Job*. Valladolid: Juan de Herrera, 1605.

Hugh of St. Victor. *De sacramentis christianae fidei*. Ed. and trans. Roy J. Deferrari. Cambridge, MA: Mediaeval Academy, 1951.

———. *Hugonis de Sancto Victore: De sacramentis christianae fidei*. Ed. Rainer Berndt. Corpus Victorinum: Textus historici 1. Aschendorff: Corpus Victorinum, 2008.

Innocent III. *Opera omnia III*. Ed. Jacques-Paul Migne, *Patrologia latina cursus completus*, vol. 216. Paris, 1855.

———. *Die Register Innocenz' III*. Ed. Othmar Hageneder et al., 13 vols. to date. Vienna: Österreichischen Akademie der Wissenschaften, 1974–2015.

Jacobus de Voragine. *The Golden Legend*. Trans. William Granger Ryan, 2 vols. Princeton: Princeton University Press, 1993.

Joachim of Fiore. *Concordia Novi ac Veteris Testamenti*. Venice: S. de Luere, 1519. Also ed. Randolph Daniel, *Abbot Joachim of Fiore: Liber de Concordia Noui ac Veteris Testamenti*. Philadelphia: The American Philosophical Society, 1983.

———. *De prophetia ignota*. Ed. Matthias Kaup, "'*De prophetia ignota*': Eine frühe Schrift Joachims von Fiore*. Monumenta Germaniae Historica, Studien und Texte 19. Hannover: Hahnsche Buchhandlung, 1998.

———. *De ultimis tribulationibus*. Ed. Kurt-Viktor Selge, "Eine Traktat Joachims von Fiore über die Drangsale der Endzeit: 'De ultimis tribulationibus'," *Florensia* 7 (1993): 7–35.

———. *Enchiridion super Apocalypsim*. Ed. Edward Kilian Burger. Toronto: Pontifical Institute of Mediaeval Studies, 1986.

———. *Expositio in Apocalypsim*. Venice: M. Pasini, 1527. Photographic reprint Frankfurt: Minerva, 1964.

———. *Introduzione all'Apocalisse*. Ed. Kurt-Victor Selge, trans. Gian Luca Potestà. Rome: Viella, 1995.

———. *Liber figurarum*. Ed. Leone Tondelli, Marjorie Reeves, and Beatrice Hirsch-Reich, *Il Libro delle Figure dell'Abate Gioachino da Fiore*. Turin: SEI, 1953.

———. *Psalterium decem chordarum*. Ed. Kurt-Victor Selge. Monumenta Germaniae Historica, Quellen zur Geistesgeschichte des Mittelalters 20. Hannover: Hansche Buchhandlung, 2009.

———. *Tractatus in Expositionem Vite et Regule Beati Benedicti.* Ed. Alexander Patschovsky. Rome: Istituto Storico Italiano per il Medio Evo, 2008.

John Malalas. *Chronicle.* Trans. Elizabeth Jeffreys, Michael Jeffreys, Roger Scott, et al. *The Chronicle of John Malalas: A Translation,* Byzantina Australiensia 4. Melbourne: Australian Association for Byzantine Studies, 1986.

Juan de los Angeles. *Dialogos de la conquista del espiritual y secreto Reyno de Dios.* Madrid: Viuda de P. Madrigal, 1595.

Juana de la Cruz. *El Conhorte: Sermones de una mujer. La Santa Juana (1481–1534).* Ed. Inocente García de Andrés, 2 vols. Madrid: Fundación Universitaria Española, 1999.

———. *Mother Juana de la Cruz, 1481–1534: Visionary Sermons.* Trans. Ronald E. Surtz and Nora Weinerth, ed. Jessica A. Boon and Ronald E. Surtz. Toronto; Tempe, AZ: Iter Academic Press; Arizona Center for Medieval and Renaissance Studies, 2016.

Lactantius, *De divinis institutionibus.* Subiaco: Sweynheym and Pannartz, 1465.

Lake, Kirsopp, ed. *Apostolic Fathers: Vol. 2,* Loeb Classical Library 25. Cambridge: Harvard University Press, 1913.

Life of Barsauma. Ed. François Nau, *Revue de l'Orient Chretien* 18 (1913): 170–76, 379–89; 19 (1914): 113–34; 278–89, 399–414. Also Andrew Palmer, ed. and trans. "The Life of Barsawmo of the Northern Mountain." In *Die syrische Vita Barsauma: Edition, Übersetzung und Analyse,* ed. J. Hahn and V. Menze, forthcoming.

Lucan, *De bello civili.* Ed. J.D. Duff, *Lucan: The Civil War,* Loeb Classical Library 220. Cambridge: Harvard University Press, 1928.

Martín Martínez Dampiés. *Libro del Antichristo.* Ed. Patricia Claire, "A Critical Edition of Martín Martínez Dampiés's *Libro del Antichristo,* Zaragoza, 1496." Ph.D. dissertation, Boston University, 2001.

Masini, Antonio di Paolo. *Bologna perlustrata,* 3rd ed. Bologna: Per l'erede di V. Benacci, 1666.

Montesino, Ambrosio de. *Epistolas y euangelios por todo el año: Con sus doctrinas y reformas.* Toledo: Juan de Ayala, 1535.

Noy, David, Alexander Panayatov, and Hanswulf Bloedhorn, eds. *Inscriptiones Judaicae Orientis Vol. 1: Eastern Europe.* Texts and Studies in Ancient Judaism 101. Tübingen: Mohr Siebeck, 2004.

Paschasius Radbertus. *De Partu Virginis.* Ed. E. Ann Matter, Corpus Christianorum Continuatio Mediaevalis 56C, 3–96. Turnhout: Brepols, 1985.

Passion of St. Stephen. Trans. M. van Esbroeck, "Jean II de Jérusalem et les cultes de S. Étienne, de la Sainte-Sion et de la Croix," *Analecta Bollandiana* 102 (1984): 1–2, 101–5.

Peter the Chanter. *Summa de sacramentis et animae consiliis.* Ed. Jean-Albert Dugaquier, Analecta mediaevalia Namurcensia 4. Louvain: Nauwelaerts, 1954.

Peter Lombard. *Sententiae.* Ed. I. C. Brady. Grottaferrata: Coll. S. Bonaventura, 1971. Trans. Giulio Silano. *Peter Lombard: The Sentences,* 4 vols. Toronto: PIMS, 2007–2010.

Planes, Gerónimo. *Tratado del examen de las revelaciones verdaderas y falsas, y de los raptos.* Valencia: Viuda de Juan Chrysostomo Gárriz, 1634.

Porreño, Baltasar. *Oráculos de las doce Sibilas, profetisas de Cristo nuestro Señor.* Cuenca: Domingo de la Iglesia, 1621.

Primasius. *Commentarius in Apocalypsin.* Ed. A.W. Adams, Corpus Christianorum Series Latina 92. Turnhout: Brepols, 1985.

Pummer, Reinhard. *Early Christian Authors on Samaritans and Samaritanism: Texts, Translations and Commentary.* Texts and Studies in Ancient Judaism 92. Tübingen: J.C.B. Mohr, 2002.

La reuelacion de sant Pablo. Seville: Meynardo Ungut, Stanislau Polono, 1494.

Revelatio Sancti Stephani. Ed. (as the *Epistula Luciani*) Jacques-Paul Migne. *Patrologia latina cursus completus,* vol. 41, 807–81. Paris, 1864.

Riley-Smith, Jonathan and Louise, ed. and trans. *The Crusades: Idea and Reality, 1095–1274.* London: Edward Arnold, 1981.

Rougé, Jean, and Roland Delmaire, trans. *Les Lois Religieuses des Empereurs Romains de Constantin à Théodose II (312–438). Vol 1: Code Théodosien Livre XVI.* Sources chrétiennes 497. Paris: Éditions du Cerf, 2005.

———. trans. *Les Lois Religieuses des Empereurs Romains de Constantin à Théodose II (312–438). Vol 2: Code Théodosien Livre I-XV, Code Justinien, Constitutions Sirmondiennes.* Sources chrétiennes 531. Paris: Éditions du Cerf, 2009.

Savonarola, Girolamo. "The Compendium of Revelations." In *Apocalyptic Spirituality: Treatises and Letters of Lactantius, Adso of Montier-en-Der, Joachim of Fiore, The Franciscan Spirituals, Savonarola.* Ed. Bernard McGinn, 192–275. New York: Paulist Press, 1979.

Serpieri, Alessandro and Silvia Bigliazzi, eds. *John Donne. Poesie.* Milano: BUR, 2007.

Severus of Minorca. *Letter on the Conversion of the Jews.* Ed. and trans. Scott L. Bradbury. New York: Oxford University Press, 1996.

Smith, A.J., ed. *John Donne: The Complete English Poems.* Harmondsworth: Penguin, 1971, 1976, 1996.

Tanner, Norman P., ed. *Decrees of the Ecumenical Councils.* London: Sheed and Ward, 1990.

Thomas Aquinas. *Summa theologica 3ª pars et Supplementum.* In *Opera Omnia* 12. Rome: Sac. Coll. de Propaganda Fide, 1906. Trans. Fathers of the English Dominican province. *The "Summa Theologica" of St. Thomas Aquinas, Third Part,* 2nd rev. ed. London: Burns Oates & Washbourne, 1928.

———. *In quattuor libros sententiarum.* In *Opera Omnia* 1. Stuttgart: Frommann-Holzboog, 1980.

Thomas of Chobham. *Summa confessorum.* Ed. F. Broomfield, Analecta Mediaevalia Namurcensia 25. Nauwelaerts: Louvain, Paris, 1968.

Tunstall, Cuthbert, ed. *Expositio Beati Ambrosii Episcopi super Apocalypsin: Nunc primum in lucem edita.* Paris: Michel de Vascosan, 1554.
Tyconius Afer. *Expositio Apcalyseos.* Ed. Roger Gryson, Corpus Christianorum Series Latina 107A. Turnhout: Brepols, 2011.
Victorinus of Pettau. *Commentarii in Apocalypsin.* Ed Johann Haussleiter, Corpus Scriptorum Ecclesiasticorum Latinorum 49. Vienna: F. Tempsky, 1916.
Villegas, Alonso de. *Flos sanctorum segunda parte: Y historia general en que se escriue la vida de la Virgen Sacratissima madre de Dios, y Señora nuestra, y las de los sanctos antiguos, que fueron antes dela venida de nuestro Saluador al mundo.* Barcelona: En casa de Hubert Gotard, a costa de Francisco Simon, 1587.
Walton, Izaak. *The Lives of John Donne, Sir Henry Wotton, Richard Hooker, George Herbert, and Robert Sanderson.* London, 1640. Reprint. London: Oxford University Press, 1927.
William of Auxerre. *Summa Aurea.* Ed. Jean Ribaillier, Spicilegium Bonaventurianum 19. Paris: Coll. S. Bonaventura, Grottaferrata and CNRS, 1985.

Secondary

7 colonne & 7 chiese: La vicenda ultramillenaria del Complesso di Santo Stefano. Bologna: Grafis, 1987.
Abulafia, Anna Sapir. "The Bible in Jewish-Christian Dialogue." In *The New Cambridge History of the Bible.* Ed. Richard Marsden and E. Ann Matter, vol. 2, 616–37. Cambridge: Cambridge University Press, 2012.
Adeva Martín, Ildefonso. "Los 'artes de bien morir' en España antes del maestro Venegas." *Scripta Theologica* 16.1–2 (1984): 405–15.
Adshead, Katherine. "Procopius and the Samaritans." *Byzantina Australiensia* 10 (1996): 35–41.
Alexander, Paul J. "The Diffusion of Byzantine Apocalypses in the Medieval West and the Beginnings of Joachimism." In *Prophecy and Millenarianism: Essays in Honour of Marjorie Reeves.* Ed. Ann Williams, 55–106. Harlow: Longman, 1980.
Almond, Philip C. *The Devil: A New Biography.* Ithaca, NY: Cornell University Press, 2014.
Alonso Cortés, Narciso. "*Acervo biográfico*: Don Sebastián de Covarrubias y Horozco." *Boletín de la Real Academia Española* 30 (1950): 11–13.
Amanieu, A. "Archidiacre." In *Dictionnaire de droit canonique*, vol. 1, 948–1004. Paris: Letouzey et Ané, 1935–58.
Amengual i Batle, J. *Orígens del cristianisme a les Balears i el seu desenvolupament fins a l'època musulmana.* Palma de Mallorca: Universitat de les Illes Balears, Facultat de Filosofia i Lletres, 1991.

Andrea, Albert J. "Innocent III, the Fourth Crusade, and the Coming Apocalypse." In *The Medieval Crusade*. Ed. Susan Ridyard, 97–106. Woodbridge, UK: Boydell Press, 2004.

Andrea, Albert J., and John C. Moore. "A Question of Character: Two Views on Innocent III and the Fourth Crusade." In *Urbs et orbis*. Ed. Sommerlechner, 1, 525–85. Rome: Presso la Società alla Biblioteca Vallicelliana, 2003.

Andrés Martin, Melquiades. "Desde el ideal de la conquista de Jerusalén al de la cristianización de América." *Mar Oceana: Revista del Humanismo Español e Iberoamericano* 9 (2001): 125–38.

Andrews, Frances. *The Early Humiliati*. Cambridge: Cambridge University Press, 1999.

Antonio, Nicolás. *Biblioteca hispana nueva, o, De los escritores españoles que brillaron desde el año MD hasta el de MDCLXXXIV*. Madrid: Fundación Universitaria Española, 1999.

Apostolos-Cappadona, Diane. "From *Apostola Apostolorum* to Provençal Evangelist: On the Evolution of a Medieval Motif for Mary Magdalene." In *Mary Magdalene in Medieval Culture: Conflicted Roles*. Ed. Peter V. Loewen and Robin Waugh, 160–80. New York: Routledge, 2014.

Ashton, Robert. *The English Civil War: Conservatism and Revolution, 1603–1649*. London: Weidenfeld and Nicholson, 1989.

Attridge, Harold W. "Greek and Latin Apocalypses." *Semeia* 14 (1979): 162–67.

Bald, R.C. *John Donne: A Life*. Oxford: Clarendon Press, 1970.

Baldwin, John W. *Masters, Princes and Merchants: The Social Views of Peter the Chanter and His Circle*. Princeton: Princeton University Press, 1970.

Bargetto-Andrés, Teresa M., ed. *Dante's* Divina Comedia: *Linguistic Study and Critical Edition of a Fifteenth-Century Translation Attributed to Enrique de Villena*. Newark: Juan de la Cuesta, 2010.

Barnes, Robin. "Images of Hope and Despair: Western Apocalypticism: ca. 1500–1800." In *The Encyclopedia of Apocalypticism, Vol. 2*. Ed. McGinn, 143–84. New York: Continuum, 2000.

Barral, Paulino Rodríguez. *La justicia del más allá: Iconografía en la Corona de Aragón en la baja Edad Media*. Valencia: Universitat de València, 2007.

Barral, Paulino Rodríguez. "Los lugares penales del más allá. Infierno y purgatorio en el arte medieval hispano." *Studium Medievale. Revista de Cultura Visual - Cultura Escrita* 3 (2010): 1–34.

Bartel, Renana. *Gender, Piety, and Production in Fourteenth-Century English Apocalypse Manuscripts*. London: Routledge, 2016.

Bates, David. *William the Conquerer*. New Haven: Yale University Press, 2016.

Beltramo, Alberto, and Maria Gioia Tavoni. *I mestieri del libro nella Bologna del Settecento*. Sala Bolognese: Forni, 2013.

Beltrán de Heredia, Vicente. "Un grupo de visionarios y pseudoprofetas que actúa durante los últimos años de Felipe II." *Revista Española de Teología* 7 (1947): 373–97.

Bennett, Julian. *Trajan: Optimus Princeps*, 2nd ed. Bloomington, IN: Indiana University Press, 2001.
Benson, Robert L. *Law, Rulership, and Rhetoric: Selected Essays*. Ed. Loren J. White, Giles Constable, and Richard H. Rouse. Notre Dame: University of Notre Dame Press, 2014.
Berceo, Gonzalo de. "Poema de Santa Oria." In *Vida de Santo Domingo de Silos; Poema de Santa Oria*. Ed. Aldo Ruffinatto, 179–216. Madrid: Espasa Calpe, 1992.
Bilinkoff, Jodi. *The Avila of Saint Teresa: Religious Reform in a Sixteenth-Century City*. Ithaca, NY: Cornell University Press, 1989.
Bilinkoff, Jodi. "A Spanish Prophetess and Her Patrons: The Case of María de Santo Domingo." *Sixteenth Century Journal* 23.1 (1992): 21–34.
Bilinkoff, Jodi. "Confessors, Penitents, and the Construction of Identities in Early Modern Avila." In *Culture and Identity in Early Modern Europe (1500–1800)*. Ed. Barbara B. Diefendorf and Carla Hesse, 83–100. Ann Arbor, MI: University of Michigan Press, 1993.
Bilinkoff, Jodi. "Establishing Authority: A Peasant Visionary and Her Audience in Early Sixteenth-Century Spain." *Studia Mystica* 18 (1997): 36–59.
Boatwright, Mary Taliaferro. "Plancia Magna of Perge: Women's Roles and Status in Roman Asia Minor." In *Women's History and Ancient History*. Ed. Sarah B. Pomeroy, 242–78. Chapel Hill, NC: University of North Carolina Press, 1991.
Bober, Jonathan. "Storia e storiografia del sacro monte di Varallo: Osservazioni sulla 'prima pietra' del Santo Sepolcro." *Novarien* 14 (1984): 3–98.
Bocchi, Francesca. *Bologna nei secoli 4.–14.: Mille anni di storia urbanistica di una metropoli medievale*. Bologna: Bononia University Press, 2008.
Bockmuehl, M., and Carleton Paget. *Redemption and Resistance: The Messianic Hopes of Jews and Christians in Antiquity*. London: T&T Clark, 2007.
Boer, M.C. de. "Paul and Apocalyptic Eschatology." In *The Encyclopedia of Apocalypticism, Vol. 1: The Origins of Apocalypticism in Judaism and Christianity*. Ed. John J. Collins, 345–83. New York: Continuum, 1998.
Boland, Paschal. *The Concept of Discretio spirituum in John Gerson's "De probatione spirituum" and "De distinctione verarum visionum a falsis."* Washington, DC: Catholic University of America Press, 1959.
Bolton, Brenda. "Innocent III's Providential Path." In *Urbs et orbis*. Ed. Sommerlechner, 1, 21–55. Rome: Presso la Società alla Biblioteca Vallicelliana, 2003.
———. "Poverty as Protest: Some Inspirational Groups at the Turn of the Twelfth Century." In *Innocent III: Studies in Papal Authority and Pastoral Care*, no. 13. Aldershot: Ashgate, 1995.
———. "The Poverty of the Humiliati." In *Innocent III: Studies in Papal Authority and Pastoral Care*, no. 14. Aldershot: Ashgate, 1995.

———. "Tradition and Temerity: Papal Attitudes Toward Deviants, 1159–1216." In *Innocent III: Studies in Papal Authority and Pastoral Care*, no. 12. Aldershot: Ashgate, 1995.

Bondía, Ambrosio. *Cítara de Apolo y Parnaso en Aragón. Edición, introducción y notas de José Enrique Laplana Gil.* Zaragoza: Instituto de Estudios Altoaragoneses, 2000.

Boon, Jessica A. "The Agony of the Virgin: The Swoons and Crucifixion of Mary in Sixteenth Century Castilian Passion Treatises." *Sixteenth Century Journal* 38 (2007): 3–26.

———. "Introduction." In *Mother Juana de la Cruz, 1481–1534: Visionary Sermons*. Ed. Jessica A. Boon and Ronald E. Surtz, 1–33. Toronto, Tempe: Iter Academic Press, Arizona Center for Medieval and Renaissance Studies, 2016.

———. "Mother Juana de la Cruz: Marian Visions and Female Preaching." In *A New Companion to Hispanic Mysticism*. Ed. Hilaire Kallendorf, 127–48. Leiden: Brill, 2010.

Bombi, Barbara. "Innocent III and the Baltic Crusades." In *Ideas and Practice of Crusading in Iberia and the Baltic Region, 1100–1500*. Ed. Torben Kjersgaard Nielsen and Iben Fonnesberg-Schmidt, 117–33. Turnhout: Brepols, 2016.

Bonner, Gerald Bonner. *Freedom and Necessity: St. Augustine's Teaching on Divine Power and Human Freedom*. Washington, DC: Catholic University of America Press, 2007.

Borghi, Beatrice. *In viaggio verso la Terra Santa: La basilica di Santo Stefano in Bologna*. Argelato: Minerva, 2010.

Bouzy, Christian. "Neoestoicismo y senequismo en los *Emblemas Morales* de Juan de Horozco." In *Emblemata Aurea: La Emblemática en el Arte y La Literatura del Siglo de Oro*. Ed. Rafael Zafra and José Javier Azanza, 69–78. Madrid: Akal Ediciones, 2000.

Bowie, Colette. *The Daughters of Henry II and Eleanor of Aquitaine*. Turnhout: Brepols, 2014.

Boyarin, Jonathan. *The Unconverted Self: Jews, Indians, and the Identity of Christian Europe*. Chicago: University of Chicago Press, 2009.

Brasher, Brenda E., and Lee Quinby, eds. *Gender and Apocalyptic Desire*. New York: Routledge, 2014.

Brown, Judith C. "Lesbian Sexuality in Renaissance Italy: The Case of Sister Benedetta Carlini." *Signs* 9.4 (1984): 751–58.

———. *Immodest Acts: The Life of a Lesbian Nun in Renaissance Italy*. New York: Oxford University Press, 1986.

Brown, Peter. *The Ransom of the Soul: Afterlife and Wealth in Early Western Christianity*. Cambridge: Harvard University Press, 2015.

———. *Through the Eye of a Needle: Wealth, the Fall of Rome, and the Making of Christianity in the West, 350–550 AD.* Princeton: Princeton University Press, 2012.
Buonaiuti, Ernesto. "Il misticismo di Gioacchino da Fiore." *Ricerche religiose* 5 (1929): 392–411.
Burkert, Walter. *Ancient Mystery Religions.* Cambridge: Harvard University Press, 1987.
Burkholder, J. Peter. "Music of the Americas and Historical Narratives." *American Music* 27 (2009): 399–423.
Burns, J. Patout. *The Development of Augustine's Doctrine of Operative Grace.* Paris: Études augustiniennes, 1980.
Burridge, Kenelm. *New Heaven, New Earth: A Study of Millenarian Activities.* New York: Schocken, 1969.
Bynum, Caroline Walker, and Paul Freedman, eds. *Last Things: Death and the Apocalypse in the Middle Ages.* Philadelphia: University of Pennsylvania Press, 2000.
Callahan, Meghan. "Suor Domenica da Paradiso as *alter Christus*: Portraits of a Renaissance Mystic." *Sixteenth Century Journal* 43.2 (2012): 323–50.
Camille, Michael. "Visionary Perception and Images of the Apocalypse in the Later Middle Ages." In *The Apocalypse in the Middle Ages.* Ed. Emmerson and McGinn, 276–89. Ithaca: Cornell University Press, 1992.
Campagne, Fabián Alejandro. *Homo catholicus, homo superstitiosus: El discurso antisuperstisioso en la España de los siglos XV a XVIII.* Madrid: Miño y Dávila Editores, 2002.
Cardini, Franco. "La devozione al Santo Sepolcro, le sue riproduzioni occidentali e il complesso stefaniano: Alcuni casi italici." In *7 colonne & 7 chiese*, 19–49. Bologna: Grafis, 1987.
Cardman, Francine. "Discerning the Heart: Intention as Moral Norm in Augustine's Homilies on 1 John." In *Studia Patristica* 70. Ed. Vinzent, 195–202. Leuven: Peeters, 2013.
Carey, John. *John Donne: Life, Mind, Art.* London: Faber and Faber, 1981.
Caro Baroja, Julio. *Las formas complejas de la vida religiosa: Religión, sociedad y carácter en la España de los siglos XVI y XVII.* Madrid: Sarpe, 1985.
Cátedra, Pedro M. *Poesía de pasión en la Edad Media: El Cancionero de Pero Gómez de Ferrol.* Salamanca: Seminario de Estudios Medievales y Renacentistas, 2001.
———. *Sermón, sociedad y literatura en la Edad Media: San Vicente Ferrer en Castilla (1411–1412).* Valladolid: Consejería de Cultura y Turismo, 1994.
Cavazzoni, Francesco. *Corona di Gratie e Gratie Favori et Miracoli della Gloriosa Vergine Maria fatti in Bologna.* Bologna, Biblioteca Comunale dell'Archiginnasio Bologna, Ms. B 298.
Cerioli, Francesca and Ilaria Cornia. *Bologna di Selenite.* Bologna: Costa Editore, 2002.

Chambers, E.K. *The Medieval Stage*, 2 vols. Oxford: Oxford University Press, 1903.
Chapman, Alice. *Sacred and Temporal Power in the Writings of Bernard of Clairvaux.* Turnhout: Brepols, 2013.
Chazelle, Celia. "Amalarius's *Liber Officialis*: Spirit and Vision in Carolingian Liturgical Thought." In *Seeing the Invisible in Late Antiquity and the Early Middle Ages.* Ed. Giselle de Nie, Frederick Morrison, and Marco Mostert, 327–57. Turnhout: Brepols, 2005.
Chrissis, Nikolaus G. *Crusading in Frankish Greece: A Study of Relations and Attitudes, 1204–1282.* Turnhout: Brepols, 2012.
Christian, William A., Jr. *Apparitions in Late Medieval and Renaissance Spain.* Princeton, NJ: Princeton University Press, 1981.
Cipollone, Guido. *Trinità e liberazione tra cristianità e islam.* Assisi: Citadella, 2000.
Cole, Penny J. *Preaching the Crusade to the Holy Land, 1095–1220.* Cambridge, MA: Medieval Academy of America, 1991.
Coleman, David. *Creating Christian Granada: Society and Religious Culture in an Old-World Frontier City, 1492–1600.* Ithaca, NY: Cornell University Press, 2003.
Colish, Marcia L. *Faith, Fiction, and Force in Medieval Baptismal Debates.* Washington, DC: Catholic University of America Press, 2014.
———. *Peter Lombard*, 2 vols. Leiden: Brill, 1994.
Collins, Adela Yarbro. "The Early Christian Apocalypses." *Semeia* 14 (1979): 61–121.
———. "Introduction: Early Christian Apocalypticism." *Semeia* 36 (1986): 1–11.
———. "The Book of Revelation." In *The Encyclopedia of Apocalypticism, Vol. 1.* Ed. Collins, 384–414. New York: Continuum, 1998.
Collins, John J., ed. *The Encyclopedia of Apocalypticism, Vol. 1: The Origins of Apocalypticism in Judaism and Christianity.* New York: Continuum, 1998.
Collins, John J. *The Apocalyptic Imagination: An Introduction to Jewish Apocalyptic Literature.* New York: Crossroad, 1984.
———. *The Oxford Handbook of Apocalyptic Literature.* Oxford: Oxford University Press, 2014.
Collins, Kristin, Peter Kidd, and Nancy K. Turner. *The St. Albans Psalter: Painting and Prayer in Medieval England.* Los Angeles: The J. Paul Getty Museum, 2013.
Collinson, Patrick. *The Birthpangs of Protestant England: Religious and Cultural Change in the Sixteenth and Seventeenth Centuries.* Basingstoke: Macmillan, 1988.
Comstock, Gary David, and Susan E. Henking, eds. *Que(e)rying Religion: A Critical Anthology.* New York: Continuum, 1997.

Constable, Giles. "The Interpretation of Mary and Martha." In *Three Studies in Medieval Religious and Social Thought*, 1–141. Cambridge: Cambridge University Press, 1995.
Contreni, John J. "Haimo of Auxerre, Abbot of Sasceium (Cessy-les-Bois), and a New Sermon on 1 John V, 4–10." *Revue bénédictine* 85 (1975): 303–20.
———. "Haimo of Auxerre's Commentary on Ezechiel." In *L'École carolingienne d'Auxerre: De Murethach à Remi, 830–908*. Ed. Dominique Iogna-Prat, Dolette Jeudy, and Guy Lobirchon, 229–42. Paris: Beauchesne, 1991.
Courtney, Francis. *Penance and the Anointing of the Sick*. Trans. and rev. Bernhard Poschmann. Freiburg and London: Herder/Burns and Oates, 1964.
Cueto Ruíz, Ronald. "La tradición profética en la monarquía católica en los siglos 15, 16, y 17." *Arquivos do Centro Cultural Portugues* 17 (1982): 411–44.
D'Angelo, Mary R. "Veils, Virgins and the Tongues of Men and Angels: Women's Heads as Sexual Members in Ancient Christianity." In *Off with Her Head! The Denial of Women's Identity in Myth, Religion, and Culture*. Ed. Howard Eilberg-Schwarz and Wendy Doniger, 131–64. Berkeley CA: University of California Press, 1995.
Daniel, E. Randolph. "Abbot Joachim of Fiore, a Reformist Apocalyptic." In *Fearful Hope: Approaching the New Millennium*. Ed. Christopher Kleinhenz and Fannie J. LeMoine, 207–10. Madison: University of Wisconsin Press, 1999.
———. "Apocalyptic Conversion: The Joachite Alternative to the Crusades." *Traditio* 25 (1969): 127–54.
———. "Joachim of Fiore: Patterns of History in the Apocalypse." In *The Apocalypse in the Middle Ages*. Ed. Emmerson and McGinn, 72–88. Ithaca: Cornell University Press, 1992.
———. "A New Understanding of Joachim: The Concords, the Exile, and the Exodus." In *Gioacchino da Fiore tra Bernardo di Clairvaux e Innocenzo III*. Ed. Roberto Rusconi, 209–22. Rome: Viella, 2001.
De Bruyn, Theodore S. "Ambivalence Within a 'Totalizing Discourse': Augustine's Sermon on the Sack of Rome." *Journal of Early Christian Studies* 1.4 (1993): 405–21.
De Coninck, Luc, Bertrand Coppieters 't Wallant, and Roland Demeulnaere. "À propos de la datation des *sermons ad populum*: s. 51-70A." In *Ministerium Sermonis: Philological, Historical, and Theological Studies on Sermones ad Populum*. Ed. Gert Partoens, Anthony Dupont, and Mathijs Lamberigts, 49–67. Turnhout: Brepols, 2009.
Dein, Simon. *Lubavitcher Messianism: What Really Happens When Prophecy Fails?* New York: Continuum, 2011.
Delcorno, Carlo. "La città nella predicazione francescana del Quattrocento." In *Alle origini dei Monti di Pietà: I francescani tra etica ed economia nel società del tardo Medioevo*, 29–39. Bologna: Banca del Monte, 1984.
Demura, Kazuhiko. "The Concept of Heart in Augustine of Hippo: Its Emergence and Development." In *Studia Patristica 70*. Ed. Vinzent, 3–16. Leuven: Peeters, 2013.

Dexinger, F. *Der Taheb: Ein "messianicher" Heilsbringer Samaritaner.* Salzburg: Otto Müller, 1986.
DeVun, Leah. *Prophecy, Alchemy, and the End of Time: John of Rupescissa in the Late Middle Ages.* New York: Columbia University Press, 2009.
Díaz Tena, María Eugenia. "El *Otro mundo* en un milagro mariano del siglo XV." *Peninsula: Revista de Estudios Ibéricos* 2 (2005): 25–43.
di Segni, Leah. "Metropolis and Provincia in Byzantine Palestine." In *Caesarea Maritima: A Retrospective After Two Millennia.* Ed. A. Rabban and K.G. Holum, 575–92. Leiden: Brill, 1996.
———. "The Samaritans in Roman-Byzantine Palestine: Some Misapprehensions." In *Religious and Ethnic Communities in Later Roman Palestine.* Ed. H. Lapin, 51–66. College Park, MD: University Press of Maryland, 1998.
———. "Early Christian Authors on Samaritans and Samaritanism: A Review Article." *Journal for the Study of Judaism* 37 (2006): 241–59.
Dittrich, Achim. "Berengaudus." In *Biographisch-Bibliographisches Kirchenlexikon* 31, 91–92. Nordhausen: Traugott Bautz, 2010.
———. *Mater Ecclesiae: Geschichte und Bedeutung eines umstrittenen Marientitels.* Würzburg: Echter, 2009.
Drobner, Hubertus R. *Augustinus von Hippo: Sermones ad Populum, Überlieferung und Bestand, Bibilographie—Indices.* Leiden: Brill, 2000.
———. *Augustinus von Hippo: Sermones ad Populum: Supplement 2000–2010.* Frankfurt: Peter Lang, 2010.
———. "The Transmission of Augustine's Sermons: A Critical Assessment." In *Tractatio Scripturarum: Philological, Exegetical, Rhetorical and Theological Studies on Augustine's Sermons: Ministerium Sermonis II.* Ed. Anthony Dupont, Gert Partoens, and Mathijs Lamberigts, 97–116. Turnhout: Brepols, 2012.
———. *Augustinus von Hippo: Predigten zu den Alttestamentlichen Propheten (Sermones 42–50). Einleitung, Text, Übersetzung und Anmerkungen.* Frankfurt am Main: Peter Lang, 2013.
Dupont, Anthony. *Preacher of Grace: A Critical Reappraisal of Augustine's Doctrine of Grace in His Sermones ad Populum on Liturgical Feasts and During the Donatist Controversy.* Leiden: Brill, 2014.
Dupont, Anthony, Matthew Alan Gaumer and M. Lambergits, eds. *The Uniquely African Controversy: Studies on Donatist Christianity.* Leuven: Peeters, 2015.
Edwards, Burton Van Name. "Manuscript Transmission of Carolingian Biblical Commentaries." Online at http://www.tcnj.edu/~chazelle/carindex.htm.
Edwards, David. *John Donne: Man of Flesh and Spirit.* London: Continuum, 2001.
Edwards, John. "Elijah and the Inquisition: Messianic Prophecy Among Conversos in Spain, c. 1500." *Nottingham Medieval Studies* 28.1 (1984): 79–94.
Egger, Christoph. "Joachim von Fiore, Rainer von Ponza und die römische Kurie." In *Gioacchino da Fiore tra Bernardo di Clairvaux e Innocenzo III.* Ed. Roberto Rusconi, 129–62. Rome: Viella, 2001.

———. "Papst Innocenz III als Theologe." *Archivum Historiae Pontificae* 30 (1992): 55–123.
Eire, Carlos. *From Madrid to Purgatory: The Art and Craft of Dying in Sixteenth-Century Spain.* Cambridge: Cambridge University Press, 1995.
Eliot, Thomas Stearns. "John Donne." *The Nation and the Athenaeum* 33.10 (1923): 331–32.
———. "The Metaphysical Poets." In *Selected Essays*, 281–91. London: Faber & Faber, 1952.
Emmerson, Richard K., and Bernard McGinn, eds. *The Apocalypse in the Middle Ages.* Ithaca, NY: Cornell University Press, 1992.
Ettenhuber, Katrin. *Donne's Augustine.* Oxford: Oxford University Press, 2011.
Fanti, Mario. "Genesi e vicende del libro di Alfonso Paleotti sulla sindone." In *La Sindone: scienza e fede: Atti del 2. convegno nazionale di sindonologia. Bologna, November 27–29, 1981.* Ed. Lamberto Coppini and Francesco Cavazzuti, 369–79. Bologna: CLUEB, 1983.
———. "Le chiese sulle mura." In *Le mura perdute: Storia e immagini dell'ultima cerchia fortificata di Bologna.* Ed. Giancarlo Roversi, 97–124. Bologna: Grafis Edizioni, 1985.
———. "Voglia di paradiso: mistici, pittori e committenti a Bologna fra Cinquecento e Seicento." In *Dall'avanguardia dei Carracci al secolo barocco: Bologna 1580–1600.* Ed. Andrea Emiliani, 83–94. Bologna: Nuova Alfa Editoriale, 1988.
Fanti, Mario, and Giancarlo Roversi, eds. *La Madonna di San Luca in Bologna: Otto secoli di storia, di arte e di fede.* Cinisello Balsamo: Silvana, 1993.
Farmer, David Hugh. *Oxford Dictionary of Saints*, 4th ed. Oxford: Oxford University Press, 1997.
Fernández Terricabras, Ignasi. *Felipe II y el clero secular.* Madrid: Sociedad Estatal para la Conmemoración de los Centenarios de Felipe II y Carlos V, 2000.
Festinger, Leon, Henry W. Riecken and Stanley Schacter. *When Prophecy Fails.* Minneapolis: University of Minnesota Press, 1956.
Fish, Stanley E. *Self-Consuming Artifacts.* Berkeley: University of California Press, 1972.
Flori, Jean. *L'Islam et la fin des temps: L'intérprétation prophétique des invasions musulmans.* Paris: Seuil, 2007.
———. *Prêcher la croisade, XIe-XIIIe siècle: Communication et propaganda.* Paris: Perrin, 2012.
———. "Jerusalem terrestre, céleste et spirituelle: Trois facteurs de sacralisation de la première croisade." In *Jerusalem the Golden: The Origins and Impact of the First Crusade.* Ed. Susan B. Edgington and Luis García-Guijarro, 25–50. Turnhout: Brepols, 2014.
Frede, Hermann Josef. *Kirchenschriftsteller: Verzeichnis und Sigel*, 4th ed. Freiburg: Herder, 1995.

Fredouille, Jean-Claude. "Les Sermons d'Augustin sur la chute de Rome." In *Augustin Prédicateur (395–411): Actes de Colloque International de Chantilly.* Ed. Goulven Madec, 439–48. Paris: Institut d'etudes augustiniennes, 1998.

Frend, W.H.C. *The Donatist Church: A Movement of Protest in Roman North Africa.* Oxford: Clarendon Press, 1971.

Funkenstein, Amos. *Theology and the Scientific Imagination: From the Middle Ages to the Seventeenth Century.* Princeton, NJ: Princeton University Press, 1986.

Gager, John G. *Kingdom and Community: The Social World of Early Christianity.* Englewood Cliffs, NJ: Prentice-Hall, 1975.

Gállego, Julián. "Los *Emblemas morales* de don Juan de Horozco." *Cuadernos de Arte e Iconografía* 1.2 (1989): 129–42.

Gameson, Richard. "The Early Imagery of Thomas Becket." In *Pilgrimage: The English Experience from Becket to Bunyan.* Ed. Colin Morris and Peter Roberts, 46–89. Cambridge: Cambridge University Press, 2002.

García Mahíques, Rafael García. "Perfiles iconográficos de la mujer del apocalypsis como símbolo mariano (I): *Sicut mulier amicta sole et luna sub pedibus eius.*" *Ars Longa* 6 (1995): 187–97.

Gardner, Helen, ed. *John Donne: A Collection of Critical Essays.* Englewood Cliffs, NJ: Prentice Hall, 1962.

Gastaldelli, Ferruccio. "Goffredo di Auxerre e Gioacchino da Fiore: Testi e personaggi a confronto." In *Studi su San Bernardo e Goffredo di Auxerre,* 375–422. Florence: SISMEL Edizioni di Galluzzo, 2001.

———. "Spiritualità e missione del vescovo in una sermone inedita di Goffredo di Auxerre su San Gregorio." In *Studi su San Bernardo e Goffredo di Auxerre,* 587–606. Florence: SISMEL Edizioni del Galluzzo, 2001.

Geddes, Jane. *The St. Albans Psalter: A Book for Christina of Markyate.* London: British Library, 2005.

Gensini, Sergio, ed. *La "Gerusalemme" di San Vivaldo e i sacri monti in Europa.* Comune di Montatone: Pacini Editore, 1989.

Gill, Meredith J. *Angels and the Order of Heaven in Medieval and Renaissance Italy.* Cambridge: Cambridge University Press, 2014.

Giraud, Cédric. *'Per verba magistri': Anselme de Laon et son école au XIIe siècle.* Turnhout: Brepols, 2010.

Godefroy, L. "Extrême Onction." In *Dictionnaire de Théologie Catholique* 5. Ed. A. Vacant and E. Mangenot, 1897–2022. Paris: Letouzey et Ané, 1912.

Goldberg, Jonathan. *James I and the Politics of Literature: Jonson, Shakespeare, Donne, and Their Contemporaries.* Baltimore: Johns Hopkins University Press, 1983.

Golding, Brian. *Gilbert of Sempringham and the Gilbertine Order, c. 1130-c. 1300.* Oxford: Clarendon Press, 1995.

Gómez Redondo, Fernando. *Historia de la prosa de los reyes católicos: El umbral del Renacimiento,* 2 vols. Madrid: Ediciones Cátedra, 2012.

Gómez, Francisco Vicente and Constancio Gutiérrez. *Españoles en Trento.* Valladolid: Consejo Superior de Investigaciones Científicas/ Instituto "Jerónimo Zurita"/ Sección de Historia Moderna "Simancas," 1951.
González Palencia, Ángel. "Datos biográficos del licenciado Sebastián de Covarrubias y Horozco." *Boletín de la Real Academia Española* 12 (1925): 39–72, 217–45, 376–96, 498–514.
González de Zárate, Jesús M. "La herencia simbólica de los hieroglyphica en los *Emblemas Morales* de Juan de Horozco." *Boletín del Museo e Instituto Camón Aznar* 38 (1989): 55–72.
Goodich, Michael. "Biography." In *Historiography in the Middle Ages.* Ed. Deborah Mauskopf Deliyannis, 353–85. Leiden: Brill, 2003.
Graña Cid, María del Mar. "La santa/bruja Magdalena de la Cruz: Identidades religiosas y poder femenino en la Andalucía pretridentina." In *La mujer (II): Actas del III Congreso de Historia de Andalucía*, 103–20. Cordoba: Publicaciones Obra Social y Cultural Cajasur, 2002.
Griesser, Bruno. "Rainer von Fossanova und sein Brief an Abt Arnald von Cîteaux." *Cistercienser Chronik* 60 (1953): 151–67.
Grundmann, Herbert. "Per la biografia di Gioacchino da Fiore e Rainiero da Ponza." In *Gioacchino da Fiore: Vita e opere.* Ed. Gian Luca Potestà, trans. Sergio Sorrentino, 107–20. Rome: Viella, 1997.
Grypeou, Emmanouela, and Juan Pedro Monferrer-Sala. "'A Tour of the Other World': A Contribution to the Textual and Literary Criticism of the 'Six Books Apocalypse of the Virgin'." *Collectanea Christiana Orientalia* 6 (2009): 115–66.
Guadalajara, José. *El Anticristo en la España medieval.* Madrid: Ediciones del Laberinto, S.L., 2004.
———. "La venida del Anticristo: Terror y moralidad en la Edad Media hispánica." *Culturas Populares. Revista Electrónica* 4 (2007): 1–20.
Haliczer, Stephen. *Between Exaltation and Infamy: Female Mystics in the Golden Age of Spain.* New York: Oxford University Press, 2002.
Häring, Nikolaus M. "The Augustinian Axiom: *Nulli Sacramento Iniuria Facienda Est.*" *Mediaeval Studies* 16 (1954): 87–117.
Harris, A. Katie. *From Muslim to Christian Granada: Inventing a City's Past in Early Modern Spain.* Baltimore: Johns Hopkins University Press, 2007.
Harris Harbison, Elmore. *The Christian Scholar in the Age of the Reformation.* New York: Charles Scribner's Sons, 1956.
Harris, Max. *Aztecs, Moors, and Christians: Festivals of Reconquest in Mexico and Spain.* Austin: University of Texas Press, 2000.
Harrison, Carol. *Augustine: Christian Truth and Fractured Humanity.* Oxford: Oxford University Press, 2000.
Hasbany, Richard L. *Homosexuality and Religion.* New York: Routledge 2013.

Heil, Johannes. "Theodulf, Haimo, and Jewish Traditions of Biblical Learning: Exploring Carolingian Culture's Lost Spanish Heritage." In *Discovery and Distinction in the Early Middle Ages: Studies in Honor of John J. Contreni*. Ed. Cullen J. Chandler and Steven A. Stofferahn, 88–115. Kalamazoo: Medieval Institute Press, 2013.

Hernández Miñano, Juan de Dios. "Los *Emblemas morales* de Juan de Horozco." *Norba-arte (Cáceres)* 8 (1988): 97–112.

Herrera, María Teresa. "Dos cartas apocalípticas en un manuscrito de la Universidad de Salamanca." In *Salamanca y su proyección en el mundo: Estudios históricos en honor de D. Florencio Marcos*. Ed. Florencio Marcos Rodríguez and José Antonio Bonilla Hernández, 637–42. Salamanca: Universidad de Salamanca, 1992.

Herzig, Tamar. *Savonarola's Women: Visions and Reform in Renaissance Italy*. Chicago: University of Chicago Press, 2008.

Hilgers, Joseph. "Sabbatine Privilege." In *The Catholic Encyclopedia*, vol. 13. New York: Robert Appleton Company, 1912.

Hill, Christopher. *The World Turned Upside Down: Radical Ideas During the English Revolution*. London: Maurice Temple Smith, 1972.

Hirsch-Reich, Beatrice. "Joachim von Fiore und das Judentum." In *Judentum im Mittelalter: Beiträge zum christlich-jüdischen Gespräch*. Ed. Paul Wilpert, 228–63. Berlin: Walter De Gruyter, 1966.

Hiscock, Nigel. *The Symbol at Your Door: Number and Geometry in Religious Architecture of the Greek and Latin Middle Ages*. Aldershot: Ashgate, 2007.

Holum, Kenneth G. *Theodosian Empresses: Women and Imperial Dominion in Late Antiquity*. Berkeley: University of California Press, 1982.

Hombert, Pierre-Marie. *Nouvelles recherches de chronologie augustinienne*. Paris: Institut d'Études augustiniennes, 2000.

Homza, Lu Ann. "To Annihilate Sorcery and Amend the Church: A New Interpretation of Pedro Ciruelo's *Reprobación de las supersticiones y hechicerías*." In *Religion, Body, and Gender in Early Modern Spain*. Ed. Alain Saint-Saens, 46–64. San Francisco: Mellen Research University Press, 1991.

Honée, Eugène. "Joachim of Fiore, *Tractatus in Expositionem Vitae et Doctrinae Benedicti*: The Question of its Structure and Genesis." *Annali di scienze religiose* 5 (2012): 67–104.

Hopper, V.F. *Medieval Number Symbolism: Its Sources, Meaning and Influence on Thought and Expression*. New York: Cooper Square, 1938.

Horst, Pieter van der. "The Jews of Ancient Crete." *Journal of Jewish Studies* 39.1 (1988): 183–200.

———. *Jews and Christians in Their Graeco-Roman Context*. Tübingen: Mohr Siebeck, 2006.

Hughes, Kevin L. "Eschatological Union: The Mystical Dimension of History in Joachim of Fiore, Bonaventure, and Peter Olivi." *Collectanea Francescana* 72 (2002): 105–43.

Iogna-Prat, Dominique, Colette Jeudy, and Guy Lobrichon, eds. *L'École carolingienne d'Auxerre: De Murethach à Remi, 830–908*. Paris, 1991.
Jansen, Katherine Ludwig. "Innocent III and the Literature of Confession." In *Urbs et orbis*. Ed. Sommerlechner, 1, 369–82. Rome: Presso la Società alla Biblioteca Vallicelliana, 2003.
———. *The Making of the Magdalene: Preaching and Popular Devotion in the Middle Ages*. Princeton: Princeton University Press, 2000.
Johnston, Warren. *Revelation Restored: The Apocalypse in Later Seventeenth-Century England*. Woodbridge, Suffolk, UK: The Boydell Press, 2011.
Kagan, Richard L. *Lucrecia's Dreams: Politics and Prophecy in Sixteenth-Century Spain*. Berkeley: University of California Press, 1990.
———. "Politics, Prophecy, and the Inquisition in Late Sixteenth-Century Spain." In *Cultural Encounters: The Impact of the Inquisition in Spain and the New World*. Ed. Mary Elizabeth Perry and Anne J. Cruz, 105–24. Berkeley: University of California Press, 1991.
Kamen, Henry. *The Phoenix and the Flame: Catalonia and the Counter Reformation*. New Haven: Yale University Press, 1993.
Kamlah, Wilhelm. *Apokalypse und Geschichtstheologie: Die mittelalterliche Auslegung der Apokalypse vor Joachim von Fiore*. Berlin: Emil Ebering, 1935.
Karfíková, Lenka. *Grace and the Will According to Augustine*. Trans. Markéta Janebová. Leiden: Brill, 2012.
Keck, David. *Angels and Angelology in the Middle Ages*. New York: Oxford University Press, 1998.
Keitt, Andrew. *Inventing the Sacred: Imposture, Inquisition, and the Boundaries of the Supernatural in Golden Age Spain*. Boston: Brill, 2005.
Kennedy, V. L. "The Handbook of Master Peter Chancellor of Chartres." *Mediaeval Studies* 5 (1943): 1–38.
Kinane, Karolyn, and Michael A. Ryan, eds. *End of Days: Essays on the Apocalypse from Antiquity to Modernity*. Jefferson, NC: McFarland & Company, 2009.
Kinzig, Wolfram. "The West and North Africa." In *Redemption and Resistance*. Ed. Markus Bockmuehl and James Carleton Paget, 198–214. New York: Continuum, 2007.
Klibansky, Raymond, Erwin Panowsky, and Franz Saxl. *Saturn and Melancholy: Studies in the History of Natural Philosophy, Religion and Art*. Edinburgh: Nelson, 1964.
Kraemer, Ross Shepard. "Jewish Women's Resistance to Christianity in the Early Fifth Century: The Account of Severus, Bishop of Minorca." *Journal of Early Christian Studies* 17.4 (2009): 635–65.
———. *Unreliable Witnesses: Religion, Gender and History in the Greco-Roman Mediterranean*. New York and Oxford: Oxford University Press, 2011.
———. *Dispersed: Greek and Latin Speaking Jews of the Late Ancient Mediterranean and the Rise of Catholic Hegemony*. New York: Oxford University Press, forthcoming.

Kryger, Henry S. *The Doctrine of the Effects of Extreme Unction in Its Historical Development: A Dissertation.* Washington, DC: Catholic University of America Press, 1949.

Kunzelmann, Adelbert. "Die Chronologie der Sermones des hl. Augustinus." In *Miscellanea Agostiniana* 2, 417–520. Rome: Tipografia Poliglotta Vaticana, 1931.

Lambot, Cyrille. "Le sermon CXI de saint Augustin." *Revue bénédictine* 57 (1947): 112–16.

———. "Les sermons LX et CCCXXXIX de Saint Augustin sur l'aumône." *Revue bénédictine* 48 (1958): 23–35.

Lampe, G.W.H. *A Patristic Greek Lexicon.* Oxford: Clarendon Press, 1961.

Lange, Nicholas de. "Jewish and Christian Messianic Hopes in Pre-Islamic Byzantium." In *Redemption and Resistance.* Ed. Bockmuehl and Paget, 274–84. New York: Continuum, 2007.

Larson, Atria A. *Master of Penance: Gratian and the Development of Penitential Thought and Law in the Twelfth Century.* Washington, DC: Catholic University of America Press, 2014.

Lauer, Philippe. "Le Psautier carolingien du Président Bouhier (Montpellier, Univ. H 409)." In *Mélanges d'histoire du moyen âge offerts à Ferdinand Lot*, 359–85. Paris: E. Champion, 1925.

Le Goff, Jacques. *The Birth of Purgatory.* Trans. Arthur Goldhammer. London: Scolar, 1984.

Lerner, Robert E. "Joachim of Fiore's Breakthrough to Chiliasm." *Cristianesimo nella storia* 6 (1985): 489–512.

———. "The Medieval Return of the Thousand-Year Sabbath." In *The Apocalypse in the Middle Ages.* Ed. Emmerson and McGinn, 51–71. Ithaca and London: Cornell University Press, 1992.

———. *The Feast of Saint Abraham: Medieval Millenarians and the Jews.* Philadelphia: University of Pennsylvania, 2001.

Lévy, Carlos. "Philo's Ethics." In *The Cambridge Companion to Philo.* Ed. Adam Kamesar, 146–74. Cambridge: Cambridge University Press, 2009.

Levy, Ian Christopher. "Wycliffites, Franciscan Poverty, and the Apocalypse." *Franciscan Studies* 73 (2015): 295–316.

Linder, Amnon. *The Jews in Imperial Roman Legislation.* Detroit, MI: Wayne State, 1987.

———. "The Legal Status of Jews in the Byzantine Empire." In *Jews in Byzantium: Dialectics of Minority and Majority Cultures.* Ed. R. Bonfil, Oded Irshai, Guy G. Stroumsa, and Rina Talgam, 149–217. Boston and Leiden: Brill, 2012.

Lobrichon, Guy. "Un nouveauté: Les gloses de la Bible." In *Le Moyen Âge et la Bible.* Ed. Pierre Riché and Guy Lobrichon, 95–114. Paris: Beauchesne, 1984.

———. *La Bible au Moyen Âge.* Paris: Picard, 2003.

———. "Stalking the Signs: The Apocalypse Commentaries." In *The Apocalyptic Year 1000: Religious Expectation and Social Change, 950–1050*. Ed. Richard Landes, Andrew Gow, and David C. Van Meter, 67–79. Oxford: Oxford University Press, 2003.

———. "Les commentaires sur l'Apocalypse du prétendu 'siècle obscur' jusque vers 1100." In *Tot sacramenta quot verba: Zur Kommentierung der Apokalypse des Johannes von den Anfängen bis ins 12. Jahrhundert*. Ed. Konrad Huber, Rainer Klotz, and Christoph Winterer, 195–213. Münster: Aschendorff, 2014.

Locatelli, Angela. "The Land of Plenty: Erasmus, *De Copia* and English Renaissance Rhetoric." In *Silenos: Erasmus in Elizabethan Literature*. Ed. Claudia Corti, 41–57. Pisa: Pacini, 1998.

———. "The Common Desire of Representation, or: How to 'Express' in Literature and Science." In *La conoscenza della letteratura/The Knowledge of Literature*. Ed. Angela Locatelli, vol. 6, 7–22. Bergamo: Bergamo University Press/Sestante, 2007.

———. "This Phantasie May Be Resembled to a Glasse: Collisions and Collusions in Early-Modern Literary and Scientific Discourse." In *La conoscenza della letteratura/The Knowledge of Literature*. Ed. Angela Locatelli, vol. 7, 157–72. Bergamo: Bergamo University Press/Sestante, 2008.

———. "Discursive Intersections on the Subject of 'Light' in English Renaissance Literature." In *Representing Light Across Arts and Sciences: Theories and Practices*. Ed. Elena Agazzi, Enrico Gianetto, and Franco Giudice, 69–87. Goettingen: V&R Unipress, 2010.

Lockwood, Rose. "*Potens et Factiosa Femina*: Women, Martyrs, and Schism in Roman North Africa." *Augustinian Studies* 20 (1989): 165–82.

Longère, Jean. *Oeuvres Oratoires de maîtres parisiens au XIIe siècle*. Paris: Études augustiniennes, 1975.

Lottin, Odo. *Psychologie et morale aux XIIe et XIIIe siècles, Vol. 5: L'École d'Anselme de Laon et de Guillaume de Champeaux*. Gembloux: J. Duculot, 1959.

Lovejoy, Arthur A. *The Great Chain of Being*. Cambridge, MA: Harvard University Press, 1936.

Löwe, Heinz, Wilhelm Wattenbach, and Wilhlelm Levison, eds. *Deutschlands Geschichtsquellen im Mittelalter. V*. Weimar: Hermann Böhlaus Nachfolger, 1973.

Löwe, Heinz. "Von Theodorich dem Großen zu Karl dem Großen: Das Werden des Abendlandes im Geschichtsbild des frühen Mittelalters." *Deutsches Archiv* 9 (1952): 353–401.

Mâle, Émile. *Religious Art from the Twelfth to the Eighteenth Century*. New York: Noonday Press, 1958.

Maleczek, Werner. *Pietro Capuano: Patrizio amalfitano, cardinale, legata alla quarta crociera, teologo (†1214)*. Trans. Fulvio Delle Donne. Amalfi: Centro di Cultura e Storia Amalfitana, 1997.

Mantuano, Luigi. "*Mystica significatio* nei commentari del XII secolo sulla liturgia." In *In principio erat verbum: Mélanges offerts en hommage à Paul Tombeur par des étudiants à l'occasion de son éméritat*. Ed. B.-M. Tock, 145–240. Turnhout: Brepols, 2005.

Marotti, Arthur F. *John Donne, Coterie Poet*. Madison: University of Wisconsin Press, 1986.

Marsden, Richard. "Introduction." In *The New Cambridge History of the Bible*. Ed. Richard Marsden and E. Ann Matter, 2, 1–16. Cambridge: Cambridge University Press, 2012.

Marshall, Peter and Alexandra Walsham, eds. *Angels in the Early Modern World*. Cambridge: Cambridge University Press, 2006.

Martin, Peter. "Latin Liturgical Drama." In *The Medieval Stage: 500–1500*. Ed. William Tydeman, 53–98. Cambridge: Cambridge University Press, 2001.

Mason, Emma. *St. Wulfstan of Worcester, c. 1008–1095*. Oxford: Blackwell, 1990.

Mason, Steve. "Jews, Judeans, Judaizing, Judaism: Problems of Categorization in Ancient History." *Journal for the Study of Judaism* 38 (2007): 457–512.

Matter, E. Ann. "The *De partu Virginis* of Paschasius Radbertus: Critical Edition and Monographic Study." Ph.D. Dissertation, Yale University, 1976.

———. "The Pseudo-Alcuinian 'De Septem Sigillis': An Early Latin Apocalypse Exegesis." *Traditio* 36 (1980): 111–37.

———. "The *Revelatio Esdrae* in Latin and English Traditions." *Revue bénédictine* 92 (1982): 376–92.

———. "My Sister, My Spouse: Woman-Identified Women in Medieval Christianity," *Journal of Feminist Studies in Religion* 2.2 (1986): 81–92.

———. "Discourses of Desire: Sexuality and Christian Women's Visionary Narratives," *Journal of Homosexuality* 18 (1989): 119–32.

———. "Alcuin's Question-and-Answer Texts." *Rivista di storia della filosofia* 4 (1990): 645–56.

———. "The Song of Songs in the *Exercitia spiritualia* of Gertrude the Great of Helfta." *Laurentianum* 31 (1990): 39–49.

———. *The Voice of My Beloved: The Song of Songs in Western Medieval Christianity*. Philadelphia: University of Pennsylvania Press, 1990.

———. "The Apocalypse in Early Medieval Exegesis." In *The Apocalypse in the Middle Ages*. Ed. Richard K. Emmerson and Bernard McGinn, 38–50. Ithaca and London: Cornell University Press, 1992.

———. "The Personal and the Paradigm: The Book of Maria Domitilla Galluzzi." In *The Crannied Wall: Women, Religion, and the Arts in Early Modern Europe*. Ed. Craig A. Monson, 97–103. Ann Arbor, MI: University of Michigan Press, 1992.

———. "The Bible in the Center: The *Glossa ordinaria*." In *The Unbounded Community: Conversations across Times and Disciplines*. Ed. Duncan Fisher, 33–42. Hamden CT: Garland Publishing, 1996.

———. "The Church Fathers and the *Glossa ordinaria*." In *The Reception of the Church Fathers in the West*. Ed. Irena Backus, 1, 83–111. Leiden: Brill, 1997.

———. "Apparitions of the Virgin Mary in the Late Twentieth Century: Apocalyptic, Representation, Politics." *Religion* 31 (2001): 125–53.

———. "Theories of the Passions and the Ecstasies of Late Medieval Religious Women." *Essays in Medieval Studies* 18.1 (2001): 1–17.

———. "Exegesis of the Apocalypse in the Early Middle Ages." In *The Year 1000*. Ed. Michael Frassetto, 29–40. New York: Palgrave, 2002.

———. "Lucia Brocadelli: Seven Revelations Introduced and Translated." In *Dominican Penitent Women*. Ed. Maiju Lehmijoki-Gardner, 212–43. Mahwah, NJ: Paulist Press, 2005.

———. "Alcuin's Theology." In *Alkuin von York und die geistige Grundlegung Europas*. Ed. Ernst Tremp und Karl Schmuki, 91–105. Sankt-Gallen: Verlag am Klosterhof, 2010.

Matter, E. Ann, and John Wayland Coakley, eds. *Creative Women in Medieval and Early Modern Italy: A Religious and Artistic Renaissance*. Philadelphia: University of Pennsylvania Press, 1994.

Matter, E. Ann, Armando Maggi, Maiju Lehmijoki-Gardner, and Gabriella Zarri. "Lucia Brocadelli da Narni: Riscoperta di un manoscritto pavese." *Bollettino della Società pavese di storia patria* (2000): 173–99.

Matthews, Shelly. *First Converts: Rich Pagan Women and the Rhetoric of Mission in Early Christianity and Judaism*. Stanford: Stanford University Press, 2001.

McGinn, Bernard. *Apocalyptic Spirituality: Treatises and Letters of Lactantius, Adso of Montier-en-Der, Joachim of Fiore, the Franciscan Spirituals, Savonarola*. Mahwah, NJ: Paulist Press, 1979.

———. "Savonarola." In *Apocalyptic Spirituality: Treatises and Letters of Lactantius, Adso of Montier-en-Der, Joachim of Fiore, the Franciscan Spirituals, Savonarola*. Ed. Bernard McGinn, 183–91. New York: Paulist Press, 1979.

———. *The Calabrian Abbot: Joachim of Fiore in the History of Western Thought*. New York: Macmillan, 1985.

———. "*Teste David cum Sibylla*: The Significance of the Sibylline Tradition in the Middle Ages." In *Women of the Medieval World: Essays in Honor of John H. Mundy*. Ed. Julius Kirshner and Suzanne F. Wemple, 7–35. New York: Basil Blackwell, 1985.

———. *Antichrist: Two Thousand Years of the Human Fascination with Evil*. San Francisco: Harper San Francisco, 1994.

———. *The Growth of Mysticism: Gregory the Great through the Twelfth Century*. New York: Crossroad, 1994.

———. *The Encyclopedia of Apocalypticism, Vol. 2: Apocalypticism in Western History and Culture*. New York: Continuum Books, 2000.

———. *Visions of the End: Apocalyptic Traditions in the Middle Ages*, rev. ed. New York: Columbia University Press, 1998.

―――. "Apocalypticism and Mysticism: Aspects of the History of their Interaction." *Zeitsprünge: Forschungen zur Frühen Neuzeit* 3 (1999): 292–315.

―――. "*Ratio* and *visio*: Reflections on Joachim of Fiore's Place in Twelfth-Century Theology." In *Gioacchino da Fiore tra Bernardo di Clairvaux e Innocenzo III*. Ed. Roberto Rusconi, 27–39. Rome: Viella, 2001.

―――. "Joachim of Fiore in the History of Religions: Ernesto Buonaiuti and Mircea Eliade on the Calabrian Abbot." In *Gioacchino da Fiore nella cultura contemporanea*. Ed. Gian-Luca Potestà, 111–26. Rome: Viella, 2005.

―――. "Turning Points in Early Christian Apocalypse Exegesis." In *Apocalyptic Thought in Early Christianity*. Ed. Robert J. Daly, 81–105. Grand Rapids, MI: Baker Academic, 2009.

―――. "Joachim of Fiore and the Twelfth-Century Papacy." In *Joachim of Fiore and the Influence of Inspiration: Essays in Memory of Marjorie E. Reeves (1905–2003)*. Ed. Julia Eva Wannenmacher, 15–34. Farnham: Ashgate, 2013.

―――. "The Concordist Imagination: A Theme in the History of Eschatology." In *Revealed Wisdom: Studies in Apocalyptic in Honour of Christopher Rowland*. Ed. John Ashton, 217–31. Leiden: Brill, 2014.

McGinn, Bernard, John J. Collins, and Stephen J. Stein, eds. *The Continuum History of Apocalypticism*. New York: Continuum Books, 2003.

Melvin, James F. "Fathers as Brothers in Early Modern Catholicism: Priestly Life in Avila, 1560–1636." Ph.D. Dissertation, University of Pennsylvania, 2009.

Mensa i Valls, J. "¿Fue Arnau de Vilanova un profeta apocalíptico?" *Bulletin de philosophie médiévale* 38.1 (1996): 129–40.

Merrills, Andy. "Kingdoms of North Africa." In *The Cambridge Companion to the Age of Attila*. Ed. Michael Maas, 265–74. Cambridge: Cambridge University Press, 2014.

Miles, Richard, ed. *The Donatist Schism: Controversy and Contexts*. Liverpool: Liverpool University Press, 2016.

Milhou, Alain. *Colón y su mentalidad mesianica en el ambiente franciscanista español*. Valladolid: Casa-Museo de Colón y Seminario Americanista de la Universidad, 1983.

Monroe, Elizabeth. "Mary Magdalene as a Model of Devotion, Penitence, and Authority in the *Gospels of Henry the Lion and Matilda*." In *Mary Magdalene in Medieval Culture: Conflicted Roles*. Ed. Peter V. Loewen and Robin Waugh, 99–115. New York: Routledge, 2014.

Monteiro, Mariana. *As David and the Sibyls Say: A Sketch of the Sibyls and the Sibylline Oracles. Initiated and Projected by the Late Very Reverend Alfred Canon White*. Edinburgh: Sands & Co., 1905.

Moore, John C. *Innocent III (1160/61–1216): To Root Up and to Plant*. Leiden: Brill, 2003.

Morgan, Nigel. "Latin and Vernacular Apocalypses." In *The New Cambridge History of the Bible*. Ed. Richard Marsden and E. Ann Matter, 2, 404–26. Cambridge: Cambridge University Press, 2012.

Morris, Colin. *The Papal Monarchy: The Western Church from 1050 to 1250.* Oxford: Oxford University Press, 1989.

Mülke, Markus. *Der Autor und sein Text: Die Verfälshung des Originals im Urteil antiker Autoren.* Berlin: Walter de Gruyter, 2008.

Muñoz Fernández, Ángela. *Beatas y santas neocastellanas: Ambivalencia de la religión y políticas correctoras del poder (ss XIV-XVII).* Madrid: Comunidad de Madrid, 1994.

———. "Santidad femenina, controversia judeoconversa y reforma (Sobre las agencias culturales en el reinado de los Reyes Católicos)." In *Modelos culturales y normas sociales al final de la Edad Media.* Ed. Patrick Boucheron and Francisco Ruiz Gómez, 387–428. Cuenca, Spain: Casa de Velázquez, 2009.

———. "'Amonestando, alumbrando, y enseñando': Catolicidad e imaginarios del purgatorio en la Castilla bajomedieval." *La corónica* 41.1 (2012): 181–206.

Murphy, William. "Vita Associata and Religious Experience in the Writings of Ernesto Buonaiuti." Ph.D. Dissertation, Gregorian University, 1974.

Murray, Placid. "The Liturgical History of Extreme Unction." In *Studies in Pastoral Liturgy.* Ed. Vincent Ryan, 2, 18–38. Dublin: The Furrow Trust, 1963.

Nalle, Sara T. "The Millennial Moment: Revolution and Radical Religion in Sixteenth-Century Spain." In *Toward the Millennium: Messianic Expectations from the Bible to Waco.* Ed. Peter Schäfer and Mark Cohen, 151–71. Leiden: Brill, 1998.

———. *Mad for God: Bartolomé Sánchez, the Secret Messiah of Cardenete.* Charlottesville: University Press of Virginia, 2001.

———. "Revisiting El Encubierto." In *Werewolves, Witches, and Wandering Spirits: Traditional Belief and Folklore in Early Modern Europe.* Ed. Kathryn A. Edwards, 77–92. Kirksville, MO: Truman State University Press, 2002.

Nasrallah, Laura. *An Ecstasy of Folly: Prophecy and Authority in Early Christianity.* Cambridge: Harvard University Press, 2003.

Nau, François. "Deux épisodes de l'histoire juive sous Théodose II (423 and 438) d'après la vie de Barsauma le Syrienm." *Revue des Études juives* 83 (1927): 184–206.

———. "Sur la synagogue de Rabbat Moab (422), et un mouvement sioniste favorisé par l'impératrice Eudocie (438), d'après la Vie de Barsauma le Syrien." *Journal Asiatique* 210 (1927): 189–91.

Neel, Carol. "Man's Restoration: Robert of Auxerre and the Writing of History in the Thirteenth Century." *Traditio* 44 (1988): 253–74.

Nelson, Bradley J. "Emblematic Representation and Guided Culture in Baroque Spain: Juan de Horozco y Covarrubias." In *Culture and the State in Spain: 1550–1850.* Ed. Tom Lewis and Francisco J. Sánchez, 157–95. New York: Garland, 1999.

———. *The Persistence of Presence: Emblem and Ritual in Baroque Spain*. Toronto: University of Toronto Press, 2010.

Newman, Barbara. *From Virile Woman to WomanChrist: Studies in Medieval Religion and Literature*. Philadelphia: University of Pennsylvania Press, 1995.

Niccoli, Ottavia. *Prophecy and People in Renaissance Italy*. Princeton: Princeton University Press, 1990.

Nicholson, Marjorie H. *The Breaking of the Circle: Studies in the Effect of the 'New Science' upon Seventeenth-Century Poetry*. New York: Columbia University Press, 1960.

Nieto, José C. "The Franciscan *Alumbrados* and the Prophetic-Apocalyptic Tradition." *Sixteenth Century Journal* 8.3 (1977): 3–16.

Nolan, Barbara. *The Gothic Visionary Perspective*. Princeton: Princeton University Press, 1977.

O'Banion, Patrick J. *The Sacrament of Penance and Religious Life in Golden Age Spain*. University Park: The Pennsylvania State University Press, 2012.

O'Brien, David. "The Cumaean Sibyl as the Revelation-Bearer in the Shepherd of Hermas." *Journal of Early Christian Studies* 5 (1997): 473–96.

O'Conner, Kevin Michael. "The Archidiaconate in the Ninth-Century Diocese of Auxerre: Carolingian Exigency in the Education of the Secular Clergy as Key to the Growth of a Medieval Church Office." Ph.D. Dissertation, St. Louis University, 2000.

Oakley, Francis. *The Mortgage of the Past: Reshaping the Ancient Political Inheritance, 1050–1300*. New Haven: Yale University Press, 2012.

Osiek, Carolyn. "The Genre and Function of the Shepherd of Hermas." *Semeia* 36 (1986): 113–21.

———. *The Shepherd of Hermas: A Commentary*. Minneapolis: Fortress Press, 1999.

Ousterhout, Robert G. "The Church of Santo Stefano: A 'Jerusalem' in Bologna." *Gesta* 20.2 (1981): 311–21.

———. "Santo Stefano e Gerusalemme." In *Stefaniana: Contributi per la storia del complesso di Santo Stefano in Bologna*. Ed. Gina Fasoli, 131–58. Bologna: Deputazione di St. Patria per le Province di Romagna, 1985.

Palmer, Andrew. "The West-Syrian Monastic Founder Barsawmo: A Historical Review of the Scholarly Literature." In *Orientalia Christiana: Festschrift für Hubert Kaufhold zum 70. Geburtstag*. Ed. Peter Bruns and Heinz Otto Luthe, 399–414. Wiesbaden: Harrassowitz Verlag, 2013.

Palmer, James T. *The Apocalypse in the Early Middle Ages*. Cambridge: Cambridge University Press, 2014.

Paolini, Lorenzo. "Un patrono condiviso: La figura di San Petronio: Da 'padre e pastore' a simbolo principale della religione civica bolognese (XII–XIV secolo)." In *Petronio e Bologna: Il volto di una storia. Arte storia e culto del Santo Patrono. Catalogo della mostra*. Ed. Beatrice Buscaroli and Roberto Sernicola, 77–83. Ferrara: SATE, 2001.

Parke, H.W. *Sibyls and Sibylline Prophecy in Classical Antiquity*. Ed. B.C. McGing. London: Routledge, 1988.
Parker, Geoffrey. "Messianic Visions in the Spanish Monarchy, 1516–1598." *Caliope* 8.2 (2002): 5–24.
Patrides C.A. and Joseph Wittreich. *The Apocalypse in English Renaissance Thought and Literature: Patterns, Antecedents and Repercussions*. Manchester: Manchester University Press, 1984.
Patschovsky, Alexander. "Semantics of Mohammed and Islam in Joachim of Fiore." In *Conflict and Religious Conversation in Latin Christendom*. Ed. Israel Jacob Yuval and Ram Ben-Shalom, 115–31. Turnhout: Brepols, 2014.
Pennington, Kenneth. *Pope and Bishops: The Papal Monarchy in the Twelfth and Thirteenth Century*. Philadelphia: University of Pennsylvania Press, 1984.
Penuti, Carla. "Diario bolognese." In *L'Estasi di Santa Cecilia di Raffaello da Urbino nella Pinacoteca Nazionale di Bologna. Catalogo della mostra*. Ed. Carla Bernardini, Gabriella Zarri, and Andrea Emiliani, 39–47. Bologna: Alfa, 1983.
Perler, Othmar. *Les Voyages de Saint Augustin*. Paris: Études augustiniennes, 1969.
Petracchi, Celestino. *Della insigne abbaziale Basilica di S. Stefano di Bologna*. Bologna: Nella stamperia di Domenico Guidotti, e Giacomo Mellini sotto il Seminario, 1747.
Phelan, John Leddy. *The Millennial Kingdom of the Franciscans in the New World*, 2nd rev. ed. Berkeley: University of California Press, 1970.
Phillips, Jonathan. *The Fourth Crusade and the Sack of Constantinople*. London: Jonathan Cape, 2004.
Picasso, Giorgio. "Gioacchino e i cistercensi." In *Gioacchino da Fiore tra Bernardo di Clairvaux e Innocenzo III*. Ed. Roberto Rusconi, 93–101. Rome: Viella, 2001.
Popkin, Richard H. "Jewish Christians and Christian Jews in Spain, 1492 and After." *Judaism* 41.3 (1992): 248–67.
Porter, H. B. "The Origin of the Medieval Rite for Anointing the Sick or Dying." *Journal of Theological Studies* n.s. 7 (1956): 211–25; 10 (1959), 43–62, 299–307.
Potestà, Gian Luca. "Die Genealogia. Ein frühes Werk Joachims von Fiore und die Anfänge seines Geschichtsbildes." *Deutsches Archiv* 56 (2000): 55–101.
———. *Il tempo dell'Apocalisse: Vita di Gioacchino da Fiore*. Bari: Laterza, 2004.
Powell, James M. "Innocent III, the Trinitarians, and the Renewal of the Church, 1198–1200." In *La liberazione dei "captivi" tra cristianità e islam: Oltre la crociata e il gihad. Tolleranza e servizio umanitario*. Ed. Giulio Cipollone, 245–54. Vatican City: Archivio Segreto Vaticano, 2000.
———. "Two Popes Before and After the Fourth Lateran Council." In *The Papacy, Frederick II, and Communal Devotion in Medieval Italy*. Ed. Edward Peters, 6. Farnham: Ashgate, 2014.

Prudlo, Donald S. *Certain Sainthood: Canonization and the Origins of Papal Infallibility in the Medieval Church.* Ithaca, NY: Cornell University Press, 2015.

Pummer, Reinhard. "Was There an Altar or a Temple in the Sacred Precinct on Mt. Gerizim?" *Journal for the Study of Judaism* 47 (2016): 1–21.

Queller, Donald E., and Thomas F. Madden. *The Fourth Crusade and the Conquest of Constantinople*, 2nd ed. Philadelphia: University of Pennsylvania Press, 1997.

Rabello, Alfred. "The Samaritans in Justinian's Corpus Iuris Civilis." *Israel Law Review* 31 (1997): 724–43.

———. *The Jews in the Roman Empire: Legal Problems from Herod to Justinian.* Farnham: Ashgate, 2000.

Ranaldi, A. "Frammenti delle mura di Bologna. Chiese e oratori." In *I confini perduti. Le cinte murarie cittadine europee tra storia e conservazione.* Ed. Angelo Varni, 206–25. Bologna: Compositori, 2005.

Ranieri, Varese. *Francesco Cavazzoni, critico e pittore.* Florence: Marchi & Bertolli, 1969.

Rainini, Marco. *Disegni dei tempi: Il "Liber Figurarum" e la teologia figurativa di Gioacchino da Fiore.* Rome: Viella, 2006.

———. *Il profeta del papa: Vita e memoria di Raniero da Ponza, eremita di curia.* Milan: Vita e Pensiero, 2016.

Rawlings, Helen E. "The Secularisation of Castilian Episcopal Office under the Habsburgs, c. 1516–1700." *Journal of Ecclesiastical History* 38 (1987): 53–79.

Reeves, Marjorie. "The Originality and Influence of Joachim of Fiore." *Traditio* 36 (1980): 269–316.

———. *The Influence of Prophecy in the Later Middle Ages: A Study in Joachimism*, 2nd ed. Notre Dame: University of Notre Dame Press, 1993.

———. *Joachim of Fiore and the Prophetic Future.* Phoenix Mill, UK: Sutton Publishing, 1999.

Remensnyder, Amy G. *La Conquistadora: The Virgin Mary at War and Peace in the Old and New Worlds.* Oxford: Oxford University Press, 2014.

Rich, Adrienne. "Compulsory Heterosexuality and Lesbian Existence." *Signs* 5.4 (1980): 631–60.

Riggenbach, Eduard. *Die ältesten lateinischen Kommentare zum Hebräerbrief.* Leipzig: Deichert, 1907.

Robinson, Cynthia. *Imagining the Passion in a Multiconfessional Castile: The Virgin, Christ, Devotions, and Images in the Fourteenth and Fifteenth Centuries.* University Park: Pennsylvania State Press, 2013.

Robb, Fiona. "Who Hath Taken the Better Part? (Luke 10, 42): Pope Innocent III and Joachim of Fiore on the Diverse Forms of the Religious Life." In *Monastic Studies 2: The Continuity of Tradition.* Ed. Judith Loades, 2, 157–70. Bangor, UK: Headstart Victory, 1991.

———. "Joachimist Exegesis in the Theology of Innocent III and Rainier of Ponza." *Florensia* 11 (1997): 137–52.

Rosenstock, Bruce. *New Men: Conversos, Christian Theology, and Society in Fifteenth-Century Castile.* London: Department of Hispanic Studies, Queen Mary, University of London, 2002.

Rossi, Paolo, ed. *Agrippa, Cardano, Fludd: La magia naturale nel Rinascimento.* Torino: Utet, 1989.

Rubenstein, Jay. *Armies of Heaven: The First Crusade and the Quest for Apocalypse.* New York: Basic Books, 2011.

Ryan, Michael A., ed. *A Companion to the Premodern Apocalypse.* Leiden: Brill, 2016.

Sánchez Domínguez, Lucía. "La Gloria de María entre el Cielo y el Infierno: Revisión de la iconografía de la Puerta de la Majestad de la Colegiata de Toro. Fray Juan Gil de Zamora ¿posible autor del programa?" In *La catedral de León en la Edad Media.* Ed. Joaquín Yarza Luaces, María Victoria Herráez Ortega, and Gerardo Boto Varela, 637–48. León: Universidad de León, 2004.

Scarcez, Alcuin. "The Proto-Cistercian Office for Mary Magdalene and Its Changes in the Course of the Twelfth Century." In *Mary Magdalene in Medieval Culture: Conflicted Roles.* Ed. Peter V. Loewen and Robin Waugh, 51–74. New York: Routledge, 2014.

Schatz, Klaus. *Papal Primacy: From Its Origins to the Present.* Trans. John A. Otto and Linda M. Mahoney. Collegeville, MN: Liturgical Press, 1996.

Schleiner, Winfried. *The Imagery of John Donne's Sermons.* Providence: Brown University Press, 1970.

Schrama, Martijn. "*Prima Lectio Quae Recitata Est*: The Liturgical Pericope in Light of Augustine's Sermons." *Augustiniana* 45 (1995): 141–75.

Schröder, Alfred. *Entwicklung des Archidiakonats bis zum elften Jahrhundert.* Augsburg: Kranzfelder, 1890.

Schutte, Anne Jacobsen. *Aspiring Saints: The Pretense of Holiness, Inquisition, and Gender in the Republic of Venice, 1618–1750.* Baltimore: Johns Hopkins University Press, 2001.

Selge, Kurt-Viktor. "L'origine delle opere di Gioacchino da Fiore." In *L'attesa della fine dei tempi nel medioevo.* Ed. Ovidio Capitani and Jürgen Miethke, 87–131. Bologna: Il Mulino, 1990.

Shuger, Debora K. *Habits of Thought in the English Renaissance.* Berkeley: University of California Press, 1990.

Smoller, Laura Ackerman. *The Saint and the Chopped-Up Baby: The Cult of Vincent Ferrer in Medieval and Early Modern Europe.* Ithaca, NY: Cornell University Press, 2014.

Solignac, Aimé. "Vie active, vie contemplative, vie mixte." In *Dictionnaire de spiritualité*, vol. 16, 592–623. Paris: Beauchesne, 1937–1995.

Sommerlechner, Andrea, ed. *Innocenzo III, Urbs et orbis: Atti del congresso inernazionale, Roma, 9-15 settembre 1998*, 2 vols. Rome: Presso la Società alla Biblioteca Vallicelliana, 2003.
Southern, Pat. *Domitian: Tragic Tyrant*. London: Routledge, 1997.
Stein, Louise K. "Eros, Erato, Terpsichore and the Hearing of Music in Early Modern Spain." *The Musical Quarterly* 82 (1998): 654–77.
Stratton, Suzanne L. *The Immaculate Conception in Spanish Art*. Cambridge: Cambridge University Press, 1994.
Strickland, Debra Higgs. "Antichrist and the Jews in Medieval Art and Protestant Propaganda." *Studies in Iconography* 32 (2011): 1–50.
Suárez, Pedro. *Historia del obispado de Guadix y Baza*. Madrid: Artes Gráficas Arges, 1948.
Surtz, Ronald E. *The Guitar of God: Gender, Power, and Authority in the Visionary World of Mother Juana de la Cruz (1481–1534)*. Philadelphia: University of Pennsylvania Press, 1990.
Sweet, Leonard I. "Christopher Columbus and the Millennial Vision of the New World." *The Catholic Historical Review* 72.3 (1986): 369–82.
Tabor, James. "Early Jewish and Christian Millennialism." In *The Oxford Handbook of Millenialism*, ed. Catherine Wessinger, 252–66. Oxford: Oxford University Press, 2011.
Thompson, Bard. "Patristic Use of the Sibylline Oracles." *Review of Religion* 16 (1952): 115–36.
Tilley, Maureen. *The Bible in Christian North Africa: The Donatist World*. Minneapolis: Fortress Press, 1997.
Tillyard, E.M.W. *The Elizabethan World Picture*. London: Chatto and Windus, 1943.
Toro Pascua, María Isabel. "Imagen y función del Anticristo en algunos textos castellanos del siglo XV." *Via spíritus* 6 (1999): 27–63.
Trens, Manuel. *María: Iconografía de la virgen en el arte español*. Madrid: Editorial Plus-Ultra, 1946.
Troncarelli, Fabio. *Gioacchino da Fiore: La vita, il pensiero, le opere*. Rome: Viella, 2002.
Valero Moreno, Juan Miguel. "La revelación à Lope de Salazar." *Estudios Humanísticos: Filología* 32 (2010): 105–39.
Van den Eynde, D. "Les définitions des sacraments pendant la première période de la thólogie scolastique." *Antonianum* 24 (1949): 183–228; 25 (1950): 3–78.
Van der Meer, Frederick. *Augustine the Bishop: The Life and Work of a Father of the Church*. Trans. Brain Battershaw and G.R. Lamb. London: Sheed and Ward, 1961.
Van Engen, John. "Medieval Monks on Labor and Leisure." In *Faithful Narratives: Historians, Religion, and the Challenge of Objectivity*. Ed. Andrea Sterk and Nina Caputo, 47–62. Ithaca: Cornell University Press, 2014.

Vauchez, André. *The Laity in the Middle Ages: Religious Beliefs and Devotional Practices*. Ed. Daniel E. Bornstein, trans. Margery J. Schneider. Notre Dame: University of Notre Dame Press, 1993.

———. "Les composantes eschatologiques de l'idée de croisade." In *Le concile de Clermont de 1095 et l'appel à la croisade*, 233–43. Rome: École Française de Rome, 1997.

———. *Saints, prophètes, et visionnaires: Pouvoir surnaturel au Moyen Age*. Paris: Albin Michel, 1999.

———. *Omnobono di Cremona (†1197), laico e santo: Profilo storico*. Cremona: Nuova Editrice Cremonese, 2001.

———. "Innocent III, Sicard de Crémone, et la canonization de Saint Homobon (†1197)." In *Urbs et orbis*. Ed. Sommerlechner, 1, 435–53. Rome: Presso la Società alla Biblioteca Vallicelliana, 2003.

Verbraken, Pierre-Patrick. *Études critiques sur les sermons authentiques de saint Augustin*. Steenburgis: In Abbatia S. Petri, 1978.

———. "Saint Augustine's Sermons: Why and How to Read Them Today." *Augustinian Heritage* 33 (1987): 105–116.

———. "Le Sermon 53 de saint Augustine sur les Béatitudes selon saint Matthieu." *Revue bénédictine* 104 (1994): 21–33.

Verhamme, A. Untitled series on unction. *Collationes Brugenses* 45 (1949): 39–47, 114–19, 119–22, 199–205, 280–86, 364–71; 46 (1950): 15–23, 100–107, 186–94, 267–75, 339–44, 457–60, 460–63; 47 (1951): 65–69, 69–72.

Vessey, Mark. "John Donne (1572–1631) in the Company of Augustine: Patristic Culture and Literary Profession in the English Renaissance." *Revue des Études augustiniennes* 39 (1993): 173–201.

Vincent, Nicholas. "The Pilgrimages of the Angevin Kings of England, 1154–1272." In *Pilgrimage: The English Experience from Becket to Bunyan*. Ed. Colin Morris and Peter Roberts, 12–45. Cambridge: Cambridge University Press, 2002.

Vinge, Ronald A. *A Companion to the Medieval Theatre*. New York: Greenwood Press, 1989.

Vinzent, Markus, ed. *Papers Presented at the Sixteenth International Conference on Patristic Studies Held in Oxford 2011: Studia Patristica 70*. Leuven: Peeters, 2013.

Visser, Derk. *Apocalypse as Utopian Expectation (800–1500): The Apocalypse Commentary of Berengaudus of Ferrières and the Relationship Between Exegesis, Liturgy and Iconography*. Leiden: Brill, 1996.

Walls, Jerry L., ed. *The Oxford Handbook of Eschatology*. Oxford: Oxford University Press, 2007.

Wannenmacher, Julia Eva. *Hermeneutik der Heilsgeschichte. "De septem sigillis" und die sieben Siegel im Werk Joachims von Fiore*. Leiden: Brill, 2005.

———. "Ein Wandel in der Auslegung der Apokalypse durch Joachim von Fiore?" In *Tot sacramenta quot verba: Zur Kommentierung der Apokalypse des Johannes von den Anfängen bis ins 12. Jahrhundert*. Ed. Konrad Huber,

Rainer Klotz, and Christoph Winterer, 289–310. Münster: Aschendorff, 2014.

Warr, Cordelia. "Performing the Passion: Strategies for Salvation in the Life of Stefana Quinzani (d. 1530)." *Studies in Church History* 45 (2009): 218–27.

Webster, Jill Rosemary. *Carmel in Medieval Catalonia*. Leiden: Brill, 1999.

Weiner, Jack. "Genealogía del liçençiado Juan Horozco de Covarrubias (1573)." In *El Cancionero, Sebastian de Horozco. Introducción, edición crítica, notas, bibliografía y genealogía de Juan de Horozco por Jack Weiner*. Ed. Jack Weiner, 325–45. Bern: H. Lang, 1975.

———. "El camino de Juan de Horozco al obispado de Agrigento." In *En Busca de la Justicia Social*, 134–48. Potomac, MD: Scripta Humanistica, 1984.

Weisweiler, Heinrich. "Das Sakrament der Letzen Ölung in den systematischen Werken der ersten Frühscholastik." *Scholastik* 7 (1932): 321–53, 524–60.

———. *Maître Simon et son groupe De sacramentis*. Louvain: Spicilegium sacrum Lovaniense, 1937.

Wessinger, Catherine, ed. *The Oxford Handbook of Millennialism*. New York and Oxford: Oxford University Press, 2011.

Whalen, Brett Edward. *Dominion of God: Christendom and Apocalypse in the Middle Ages*. Cambridge, MA: Harvard University Press, 2009.

Whealey, Alice. "*De Consummatione Mundi* of Pseudo-Hippolytus: Another Byzantine Apocalypse from the Early Islamic Period." *Byzantion* 66.2 (1996): 461–69.

Willey, Basil. *The Seventeenth Century Background: Studies in the Thought of the Age in Relation to Poetry and Religion*. London: Chatto and Windus, 1967.

Williams, John. "Introductory Essay." In *Visions of the End in Medieval Spain*. Ed. Therese Martin. Amsterdam: University of Amsterdam Press. Forthcoming.

Willis, G.G. *St. Augustine's Lectionary*. London: S.P.C.K., 1962.

Wire, Antoinette Clark. *Corinthian Women Prophets: A Reconstruction Through Paul's Rhetoric*. Minneapolis: Fortress, 1990.

Woolf, Virginia. "Donne After Three Centuries." In *The Common Reader*, Second Series. London: The Hogarth Press, 1932.

Whalen, Brett Edward. *The Medieval Papacy*. New York: Palgrave Macmillan, 2014.

Wyatt, David. *Slaves and Warriors in England and Ireland, 800–1200*. Leiden: Brill, 2009.

Young, Karl. *The Drama of the Medieval Church*, 2 vols. Oxford: Clarendon Press, 1933.

Young, Stephen. "Being a Man: The Pursuit of Manliness in the Shepherd of Hermas." *Journal of Early Christian Studies* 2 (1994): 237–55.

Zafra Molina, Rafael. "Nuevos datos sobre la obra de Juan de Horozco y Covarrubias." *IMAGO: Revista de Emblemática y Cultural Visual* 3 (2011): 107–26.

Zambrano González, Joaquín. "Animas benditas del Purgatorio. Culto, cofradías y manifestaciones artísticas en la provincia de Granada." In *El mundo de los difuntos: Culto, cofradías, y tradiciones II*. Ed. Francisco Javier Campos y Fernández de Sevilla, 1071–88. El Escorial, Spain: R.C.U. Escorial-Mª Cristina, Servicio de Publicaciones, 2014.

Zarri, Gabriella. "I monasteri femminili a Bologna tra il XII e il XVII secolo." *Atti e memorie della Deputazione di storia patria per le province di Romagna* n.s. 24 (1973): 133–224.

———. "Recinti sacri: Sito e forma dei monasteri femminili a Bologna tra '500 e '600." In *Luoghi sacri e spazi della santità*, ed. Sofia Boesch Gajano and Lucetta Scaraffia, 381–96. Turin: Rosenberg & Sellier, 1990.

———. "Living Saints: A Typology of Female Sanctity in the Early Sixteenth Century." In *Women and Religion in Medieval and Renaissance Italy*. Ed. Daniel Bornstein and Roberto Rusconi, 219–304. Chicago: University of Chicago Press, 1996.

———. "I Medici e la 'Gerusalemme bolognese'." In *Una 'Gerusalemme' toscana sullo sfondo di due giubilei: 1500–1525. Proceedings of the Study Conference. San Vivaldo, Montaione October 4–6, 2000*. Ed. Sergio Ginseni, 57–67. Florence: SISMEL-Edizioni del Galluzzo, 2004.

———. "Bologna, Marian City in the Drawings of Francesco Cavazzoni (1559–1616)." In *Innovation in the Italian Counter-Reformation*. Ed. Sarah Shannon McHugh and Anna Wainwright. Newark, DE: University of Delaware Press, forthcoming.

Zechiel-Eckes, Klaus. *Florus von Lyon als Kirchenpolitiker und Publizist*. Stuttgart: Thorbecke, 1999.

Index

A
Aeneid, 5, 18, 21, 23, 25, 29, 30
Aetas, 173, 176–178, 183, 187, 189, 190, 193
Albert the Great, 12, 282, 302
Alcuin, 7, 8, 145, 318, 319
Alexander of Hales, 12, 302, 308, 311
Alexius IV, 264–266
Aliter, 153
Alms, 101, 110, 114, 116, 117, 119, 120, 131
Ambrose of Milan, 137
Angel, 30, 31, 34, 39, 43, 48–50, 55, 56, 61–65, 67, 81, 157, 168, 169, 182, 184, 193, 253, 254, 258, 259, 270, 286, 322–324, 329, 330
Anointing, 191, 281–285, 287–294, 296, 299–302, 304–306, 308, 309, 311, 312
Antichrist, 44, 46, 48, 51, 54–57, 60, 66, 152, 153, 156, 213
Apocalypse/Apocalyptic, 1–6, 8–14, 19, 21, 29, 30, 35, 41–60, 65–67, 69, 70, 80, 83, 88, 93, 96, 106, 109, 116, 135, 136, 141–143, 145–147, 153, 162–166, 169–181, 187, 188, 197, 199, 200, 211–213, 217, 222, 228, 252, 255, 257, 260, 273, 281, 315–318, 321–323, 325, 327–338
Apocalypticism, 3, 9, 17, 42, 46, 56, 57, 59, 61, 65, 163, 164, 179, 199, 200, 213, 223, 255, 260–263, 274, 279, 317
Apollo, 20–23, 29, 218
Appius, 23, 24
Aquinas, Thomas, 12, 208, 282, 302, 303, 311–313, 323
Arcadia, 31, 33
Archangel Michael, 56, 61, 63
Aristotelian philosophy, 13
Aspersion, 285
Attridge, Harold W., 21
Augustine, 4, 8, 49, 54, 55, 93–126, 132, 137, 147, 166, 177, 183,

374 INDEX

208, 217, 218, 231, 232, 273,
284–286, 289, 290, 319, 323
Augustus, 22, 39
Auxerre school, 145, 153, 154

B
Babylonian Talmud, 235, 241
Bacchant, 22
Baldwin of Flanders, 12, 251, 265
Baptisand, 296, 309
Baptism, 282, 285–287, 289–292,
294–296, 300–302, 304–306,
309, 322
Bar Kokhba, 235
Baroja, Julio Caro, 199, 207, 208,
212, 214
Basileia, 25, 26, 28, 29, 32, 33, 38
Basileus, 25–27
Beast of Revelation, 274
Beatitudes, 100, 104, 105, 107, 127
Beatus, 59, 122
Bentivoglio, 75
Berengaudus, 8, 9, 19, 136, 139–147,
149–159, 161, 162
Bernardino da Siena, 81
Biblical exegesis, 2–5, 7, 13
Blaeu, Jean, 76
Blessed Genevieve, 293
Bologna, 6, 7, 69–71, 73–81, 83–89
Bonaventure, 12, 63, 177, 302–309,
311, 312
Boniface IX, 73
Bononia, 69, 71, 77
Book of Revelation, 1, 49, 51, 54, 59,
76, 254, 320, 321, 330
Bradbury, 232, 234
Brocadelli, Lucia, 5, 40, 50, 61, 69
Brown, Peter, 115, 132
Bruno, Giordano, 332

C
Calabrian abbot, 170, 178, 187, 188,
195, 211
Caritas, 192
Carlini, Benedetta, 40
Carlo Borromeo, 10, 84, 198
Carolingian, 7, 9, 12, 137, 142, 144,
145, 155, 157, 159, 161, 162,
318
Cathar, 298
Catherine of Siena, 18, 61, 210
Cavazzoni, Francesco, 85, 86
Charity, 94, 95, 100–102, 106–109,
113–115, 117, 123, 125, 132,
147, 277
Chiliastic, 177, 261
Christ's poverty, 99
Chrysostom, Dio, 5, 18, 25, 142
Cicero, 27, 208, 218
Circla, 78, 80
The City of God, 107, 108
Cleopatra, 22
Collins, Adela Yarbro, 19, 30
Collins, John J., 3, 13, 21, 179, 200,
317, 338
Communal-ecclesiastical mysticism, 9
Concordia, 166, 168, 173
Concordism/Concordist, 9, 166, 174,
181
Conorte, 6, 42, 45, 52, 57, 59
Conquest of Constantinople, 251
Consolamentum, 298
Convents, 5–7, 42–44, 57–59, 66, 70,
71, 79–81, 88, 203, 211,
248
Cosmic warfare, 19
Council of Chalon-sur-Saône, 159
Council of Trent, 81, 201, 203, 212,
221

INDEX 375

Counter-Reformation, 7, 10, 84, 86, 211, 221

D
d'Ampiés, Martinez, 43, 48, 49, 54
Dante, 46, 47, 50
de la Cruz, Juana (1481-1534), 4, 6, 19, 42, 50, 66, 213
Delphic oracle, 23
De sacramentis, 12, 285, 288, 290
De septem sigillis, 172
Dialogical, 330
Diario Mariale per l'Anno MDCCXXIII, 87
Diocletian, 121, 141
Dionysius of Halicarnassus, 21
Di Paolo Masini, Antonio, 77, 79, 87
Discalced Carmelites, 202, 203, 206, 210, 211
Dittrich, Achim, 136, 140, 143–146
Dominican, 12, 302, 306, 307
Domitian, 24–27, 29, 38, 40
Donatists, 110, 112, 113, 122, 129, 141, 229
Donne, John, 4, 13, 19, 315–333, 335–338
du Frische, Jacques, 137, 156

E
Ekstasis, 36, 37
Elis or Arcadia, 26
Elysian Fields, 22
Enarrationes in Psalmos, 103
Enchiridion in Apocalypsim, 171
End of time, 1, 2, 6, 9–11, 43–49, 52, 54, 56, 61, 64–66, 189, 227–232, 235, 242, 246, 247, 250, 316, 317, 324–326, 329, 334
Ephesus, 147, 149

Erythraean Sibyl, 10, 20, 200, 208, 216–218, 220, 221, 223
Eschatological, 1, 2, 8, 11–14, 19, 35, 95, 106, 109, 115, 121, 155, 166, 176, 183, 213, 228–230, 256, 317, 318, 334
Eucharist, 124, 243, 248, 282, 284–286, 289–296, 305, 309
Eudocia, 11, 237–241
Eurystheus, 27
Eusebius, 218
Expositio, 9, 12, 135–137, 139, 140, 142–147, 151, 153–158, 161, 162, 164–178, 180–196, 252–254, 260, 262, 267, 269, 274
Expositio in Apocalypsim, 9, 19, 142, 164, 165, 179, 185, 187, 195, 211, 252
Expositio super septem visiones libri Apocalypsis, 8, 135

F
Fall of Constantinople, 7, 74
Ferrer, Vincent, 46, 50, 60, 61, 64
Filioque, 254, 269, 270, 273, 279
Final judgment, 8, 10, 95–97, 103, 106, 107, 109, 117, 123, 125, 132, 216, 324
Flos Sanctorum, 221
Four columns, 88
Fourth Crusade, 11, 12, 251, 262, 263, 272, 274
Fourth Lateran Council, 294, 298
Franciscan, 12, 45, 50, 75, 80, 83, 84, 302, 306, 307
Fulk of Neuilly, 264

G
Gates, 70, 76–78, 81, 88, 184
Gender and sexuality, 3, 4

Gentiles, 12, 34, 36, 37, 229, 232, 254, 257, 270, 271, 274
Gerson, Jean, 204, 205, 209, 210
Gilbertine order, 277
Gospels of Henry the Lion and Matilda, 258, 259
Grace, 85, 87, 104, 114, 115, 165, 188, 210, 284, 286, 297, 301, 305, 306, 313, 323, 326, 335
Grundmann, Herbert, 261, 262
Guy of Orchelles, 12, 299

H

Haimo of Auxerre, 9, 145, 162
Hair, 5, 19, 22–24, 32–35, 39
Harrowing of Hell, 61
Heavenly Jerusalem, 5, 69, 70, 88, 173, 186, 189, 193, 279
Hera, 20, 26
Herakleitos, 21
Herakles, 26–29
Hercules Gaditanus, 27
Hermas, 5, 18–21, 24, 25, 30–36, 38, 40
Holum, Kenneth, 240, 241, 246
Holy Sepulchre, 7, 71, 73, 75
Holy Sonnets, 323, 327
Holy Spirit, 9, 31, 51, 54, 64, 167–169, 173, 181, 183, 184, 188, 191–193, 195, 269, 273, 286
Horns of Christ, 147, 148
Horozco y Covarrubias, Juan de, 4, 10, 197, 198, 201, 203, 204, 222
Hugh of St. Victor, 12, 290
Humiliati, 276, 277

I

Il Vidente, 83, 84
Immaculate Conception, 7, 60, 83, 84

In extremis, 287, 292, 293
Innocent III, 11, 251, 261–263, 265, 274
Inquisition, 40, 45, 201, 202, 212
Intelligentia spiritualis, 167, 169, 188, 189
Italy, 5, 21, 22, 42, 47, 49, 50, 61, 80, 156

J

Jerome, 48, 141, 142, 147, 152, 163, 208, 318–320
Jews, 11, 12, 37, 43, 49, 55–57, 153, 174, 176, 228–241, 245, 246, 250, 254, 256, 257, 268, 274
Joachim of Fiore, 4, 9–11, 19, 65, 142, 164, 177, 188, 195, 200, 211, 252, 253, 255, 262, 279
Joachite, 10, 12, 199, 211, 212, 217
John of Rupescissa, 46, 60
John XXIII, 73
Juan de Avila, 221
Justasas, 243–247

L

Lactantius, 217, 221
Last Days, 12, 261
Last Things, 1, 3, 13, 46, 47, 49, 57, 282
Lateran IV, 274, 276, 298, 299
Lazarus, 96, 98, 99, 108, 109, 119, 129, 259
Lectionary cycle, 100
Le Goff, Jacques, 307, 308
Le Nourry, Denis-Nicolas, 137, 156
Liber de Concordia, 167, 170, 171, 190
Liber Figurarum, 185, 186, 190, 261
Liber Introductorius in Apocalypsim, 171

Libro del Antichristo, 43, 48, 49, 54, 56
Life of Barsauma, 11, 230, 237, 240, 241, 250
Limpieza de sangre, 202
Living saint, 6, 42, 69
Livy, 21
Locks, 19, 23, 24, 28, 36
Lombard, Peter, 12, 63, 273, 284, 285, 288–290, 297
Lucan, 23, 24, 36
Lucifer, 57, 63–66

M

Madness, 20, 22–24, 37
Madonna, 70, 85, 87
Malalas, John, 11, 242–248
Mandates, 30
Mania, 19, 20, 22, 23, 28, 29, 34, 37
Mantis/manteuomai, 36
Maria Domitilla Galuzzi, 18, 40
Marian apocalyptic, 5, 6, 44, 57, 60, 61, 66, 67
Marian apparitions, 6, 41, 42, 44, 57, 59, 66
Marian devotion, 5, 7, 57, 58, 83, 84, 88
Marriage of the Lamb, 194
Martyrs, 35, 73, 94, 121, 122, 124, 125, 131, 176, 181
Mary Magdalene, 253, 257–259, 268, 270, 273, 275, 276
Materia, 300, 311
Matter, E. Ann, 3–10, 14, 17, 18, 41, 42, 44, 50, 57, 59, 60, 67, 69, 93, 136, 141–143, 146, 152, 162, 163, 197, 199, 214, 254, 256, 281, 299, 318, 319, 338
Maurists, 101, 123, 125, 131, 137, 156, 159
Maurus, Hrabanus, 145, 283

McGinn, Bernard, 2, 3, 9–11, 44, 46, 47, 55, 56, 59, 65, 136, 142, 166, 167, 174, 177, 178, 186, 199, 200, 211, 213, 217, 223, 252, 255, 257, 262, 318
Messiah, 45, 55, 217, 220, 234, 235, 241, 270
Messianic, 11, 212, 230, 235, 237, 241, 247–249
Metempsychosis, 21
Misericordia, 116, 125
Montanists, 6, 36, 229
Morisco, 200, 216, 223
Moses, 184, 185, 228, 233, 234, 236, 237, 246, 322
Mozarabic liturgies, 320
Mt. Gerizim, 228, 230, 243, 244, 249
Music, 17, 327
Muslims, 43, 44, 49, 57, 273, 277
Muthos, 26
Mysticism, 2, 4, 9, 11, 84, 85, 163, 164, 178, 179, 185, 187

N

Nerva, 26, 38
New Prophets, 5, 36, 39, 40
Nicholas V, 73

O

Olive oil, 282, 288, 293, 300
Oratories, 70, 71, 84
Ordinal dimension, 175
Ordines, 175, 181
Ordo, 175, 185
Ordo clericorum, 181, 185
Ordo laicorum, 185
Ordo monachorum, 181, 183, 185
Original sin, 294, 302, 304, 306
Osiek, Carolyn, 30, 31, 33, 35
Otherworldly journey, 20, 21, 28, 29
Ovid, 21, 23

P

Paleotti, Alfonso, 83, 85
Pannychis, 33
Patristics, 4, 14, 48, 137, 141, 142, 146, 162, 207, 208, 217, 319, 325
Paul, 6, 37–39, 130, 169, 179, 183, 210, 228, 229, 231, 232
Pelagius, 114, 115
Penance, 115, 284, 286, 289, 291, 298, 299, 301, 302, 304–306, 313
Peri Basileia, 25
Personifications, 28, 30, 32–35
Peter, 73, 130, 176, 180–183, 186, 253, 254, 256–260, 263, 264, 268–272, 276, 285–297, 312, 331
Peter the Chanter, 12, 291, 297, 300, 308, 312, 313
Petrine primacy, 254
Phaedrus, 20, 23
Philo, 27, 28, 37
Plato, 23, 26, 208
Pliny, 25, 38, 40, 208
Plotinus, 323
Plutarch, 21
Poor Clares, 80
Praefatio Ioachim abbatis super Apocalypsim, 171
Presbytera, 31
Presbyteros, 159, 283, 292, 294
Primasius, 141, 142, 146, 147, 149, 151, 156, 318
Princeps, 25–27, 137
Procopius of Caesarea, 11, 242
Prodicus, 27
Propertius, 21, 23
Prophecy, 4, 6, 10, 18, 20, 22–24, 27, 29–32, 34–37, 39, 40, 45, 46, 54, 66, 84, 157, 165, 171, 173, 183, 197–200, 206–211, 213, 214, 217, 218, 220, 222, 230, 237, 242, 249
Prophetic authority, 19, 165
Prophets, 5, 10, 17–20, 22, 24, 28, 29, 36–40, 138, 150, 165, 169, 179, 183, 193, 198, 200, 208–214, 222, 228, 236, 237, 246, 270
Psalterium decem cordarum, 171, 190, 191
Pseudo-Hippolytus, 214, 215, 223
Purgatory, 6, 43, 47–49, 51, 52, 57, 58, 61–66, 281, 305, 307, 308, 312, 313
Pythia, 20, 23, 36
Pythic spirit, 36

Q

Quem quaeritis, 257–259

R

Radbertus, 7, 283
Rainer of Ponza, 261, 275, 277
R. Ashi, 235, 241
Raymond of Capua, 18
Reception of ashes, 285
Reni, Guido, 83–85
Res, 288, 289, 301, 305
Resurrection, 109, 111, 122, 124, 131, 136, 165, 167–169, 174, 188, 253, 254, 258, 259, 305
Rome, 12, 17, 20–22, 25, 27, 29–32, 34, 73, 83, 95, 100, 105–111, 115, 121, 127, 129, 164, 171, 178, 181, 186, 190, 252, 254–256, 260–264, 269, 272, 276, 278, 303

INDEX 379

S
Sack of Constantinople, 263, 265, 271
Sack of Rome, 101, 107, 117, 227
Sacraments, 11, 12, 198, 205, 257, 281–298, 300–313, 322
Saint Petronius, 7, 23, 26, 70, 71, 73, 77, 78
Saints Vitale and Agricola, 73
Samaritans, 11, 228–230, 236, 239, 240, 242–250
Sancta Jerusalem, 7, 69, 71, 73–75, 88
San Filippo Neri, 83
Santo Stefano, 7, 69, 71, 73–75
Savonarola, 47, 49, 50, 60
Seal, 136, 171, 172, 174, 286, 320, 322, 329, 330
Second Capitulary of Theodulf, 160
Secular, 5, 13, 264, 315, 318, 325, 326
Sentences, 12, 63, 285–292, 299, 303, 308
Sententiae, 285, 286
Septuagint, 36
Sermones ad populum, 8, 93, 95, 103, 113, 121, 126
Seven gifts of the Holy Spirit, 286, 320
Severus of Minorca, 11, 230, 231, 250
Shavuot, 248
Shepherd, 30, 31, 33–35, 112, 270
Shepherd of Hermas, 5, 18, 30, 32, 142, 199
Sibylline Oracles, 18, 21, 37, 217, 218, 221, 222
Sibylls, 5
The sign of the cross, 58, 285
Signum, 274, 305
Similitudes, 30–33, 39
Simony, 157, 159
Sixtus Betuleius, 221
Sixtus IV, 74, 75
Smyrna, 147–150

Sobriety, 19, 28, 29, 38
Society of Biblical Literature, 19
Socrates, 20, 230, 234, 236, 237, 250
Socrates of Constantinople, 11, 12, 233
Song of Songs, 5, 59, 60, 193–195, 212
Son of Man, 8, 96, 111, 165, 184
Spain, 6, 10, 42, 45–47, 49, 50, 52, 59, 63, 118, 156, 198–200, 205, 209–216, 220, 222, 223, 232
Spiritual millenarian, 178
St. Albans Psalter, 258
Stars, 19, 48, 52, 54
Statius, 24, 26, 29, 38
Status, 9, 167–170, 172–176, 180–183, 185–193, 195, 253, 254, 261, 274
Stephen protomartyr, 11
Summa aurea, 12, 299
Summa confesorum, 12
Summa de sacramentis, 12
Summa de sacramentis et anime consiliis, 12, 291
Suns, 7, 19, 27, 48, 52, 54, 60, 83, 88, 188, 253, 311, 332, 336
Supercession, 180

T
Tempus, 112, 151, 167, 169, 173, 174, 176, 180, 187, 189, 193
Teresa of Avila, 202, 206, 210
Tertius status, 185–187, 192, 195
Tertullian, 36, 39
Theodosios, 239, 247
Theotokos, 243–246, 249
Thomas of Chobham, 12, 298
Three Marys, 257–260
Tibullus, 21, 23
Tractatus in Expositionem Vite et Regule Beati Benedicti, 189, 190
Trajan, 25–29, 38, 40

Tratado, 10, 197–201, 203, 205–208, 210, 211, 213, 214, 216, 218, 220–223
Tratado dela verdadera y falsa prophecia, 10, 197
Tridentine, 10, 198, 200, 204
Trinitarians, 9, 167, 172, 175, 181, 253–255, 262, 268, 274, 277, 279
Tropological, 9, 151
Tunstall, Cuthbert, 137
Turannos, 25
Twelve stars, 70, 83, 87, 88, 253
Tyconian-Augustinian, 174
Tyconius, 141–143, 256, 318
Tyranny, 25, 26, 28, 29, 159

U
Unction, 11–13, 281–313
Unguere, 282
University of Paris, 272, 273, 281, 299

V
Varallo, 75
Venial sin, 284, 304–308, 313
Vergil, 5
Victorinus of Pettau, 141
Virgin, 7, 33, 35, 39, 53, 57–60, 64, 66, 70, 77, 81, 84, 85, 87, 88, 169, 176, 181, 187, 194, 199, 249, 253, 254, 325

Viri spirituales, 170, 176, 180, 181, 183–185, 189, 192, 193, 211
Virtues, 18, 26–29, 32, 33, 38–40, 80, 98, 106, 114, 148–150, 181, 188, 199, 209, 288, 290, 299, 308, 327
Visionaries, 3, 5, 6, 9, 10, 51, 179, 209, 222
Visions, 1, 2, 4, 6, 9, 10, 29–32, 34, 35, 39–41, 43–45, 47, 48, 50, 51, 57–59, 94, 95, 100, 103, 106, 107, 114–116, 119, 125, 136, 138–141, 156, 162, 164, 165, 169, 172, 179, 189, 192, 194, 200, 207, 208, 210, 213, 217, 223, 252, 255, 279, 285, 325, 328, 337
Visser, Derk, 136, 140, 144–146

W
White hair, 30, 34
William of Auxerre, 12, 299
Woman of the Sun, 2, 59, 65

X
Xenophon, 27

Z
Zeno, 11, 242–250